POETRY AND REVOLUTION

AN ANTHOLOGY OF BRITISH AND IRISH VERSE

1625–1660

POETRY AND REVOLUTION

AN ANTHOLOGY OF BRITISH AND IRISH VERSE 1625–1660

Selected, Edited, and with an Introduction by

PETER DAVIDSON

OXFORD
UNIVERSITY PRESS

OXFORD
UNIVERSITY PRESS
Great Clarendon Street, Oxford OX2 6DP
Oxford University Press is a department of the University of Oxford.
It furthers the University's objective of excellence in research, scholarship,
and education by publishing worldwide in
Oxford New York
Athens Auckland Bangkok Bogotá Buenos Aires Cape Town
Chennai Dar es Salaam Delhi Florence Hong Kong Istanbul Karachi
Kolkata Kuala Lumpur Madrid Melbourne Mexico City Mumbai Nairobi
Paris São Paulo Shanghai Singapore Taipei Tokyo Toronto Warsaw
with associated companies in Berlin Ibadan
Oxford is a registered trade mark of Oxford University Press
in the UK and in certain other countries
Published in the United States
by Oxford University Press Inc., New York

First published in 1998
First published in paperback 2001

British Library Cataloguing in Publication Data
Data available
Library of Congress Cataloging in Publication Data
Data available
ISBN 0-19-818441-7(hbk)
ISBN 0-19-924280-1(pbk)
1 3 5 7 9 10 8 6 4 2
Printed in Great Britain
on acid-free paper by
Bookcraft Ltd,
Midsomer Norton, Somerset

for JANEY STEVENSON

beati sunt immaculati in via

CONTENTS

In this list of contents, titles of poems generally follow those in the MS or edition chosen as copy-text, with the exception that, words in upper case are given as lower. No attempt has been made to reproduce the often very complex lineation given to titles in the printed sources. When poems have been given titles from their first lines, the punctuation at the end of the line has been ignored. Titles which have been supplied from first lines, and titles of works from which extracts have been taken are placed within square brackets. Poems of uncertain authorship, and reworkings and parodies of existing material are indicated by placing the most probable authorial name within square brackets, qualified either with a question mark for uncertain attributions or with 'rev.' for appropriations or adaptations of earlier texts.

ABBREVIATIONS

c.	circa
ed.	edited by
edn(s)	edition(s)
f(f).	folio(s)
intro.	introduction by, introduced by
MS(S)	manuscript(s)
no(s).	number(s)
p(p).	page(s)
qv	which see
r	recto
rev.	revised
sig(s).	signatures
v	verso
vol(s).	volume(s)

Where no place of publication is given for works which are cited, it can be assumed to be London.

PREFACE

The poetry of the mid-seventeenth century is unavoidably the product of social, intellectual, and personal crisis and change. Apart from a few unassailable figures who represent a continuing and strengthening poetic tradition, it was until recently one of the least studied phases of poetry written in the British islands, and yet, paradoxically, one which speaks eloquently and in satisfyingly diverse voices to the late twentieth-century reader.

The first part of this preface sets out the kinds of reasons which have determined the selection of texts for this book. It also discusses some of the difficulties of trying to pack some representation of a period of unparalleled richness and diversity into a generous, but finite, anthology. This first section also should serve to welcome and reassure the reader by offering maps for the exploration of the selection of poems. The most important element in this is to stress that the anthology is not attempting to be rebarbative, strange, other: much of the point of its diversity is to enrich the context of the most familiar poems of the time, and to present them freshly in at least an attempted replica of their original settings.

The second part of this preface explores the ways in which the canon of mid-seventeenth-century poetry has been shaped. This is not just a catalogue of the sometimes arbitrary decisions of the publisher and the academic: it involves ideas of history and historiography, for this has long been recognized as the period where literature and events are more *visibly* interwound than at any other time in the history of the British islands. This section will argue that historical fiction itself has played a key part in forming ideas of this period of war and revolution, influencing the choices of anthologists and editors who have made their own 'historical fictions' of the Civil War.

1. THIS ANTHOLOGY: SELECTION, PRESENTATION, ANNOTATION.

This anthology represents something of a fresh start. Editors, however much they think they may be examining a body of past writing afresh and without prejudice, cannot avoid bringing with them the agenda and anxieties of their own times. To pretend otherwise would be to engage in self-deception and in public fraud. But an attempt has been made not only to look over what might be called the old canon of mid-seventeenth-century poetry, but also to look, as if for the first time, at disparate and divergent voices. One of the most important things about the period of transition and upheaval with which this book deals is that those divergent voices become increasingly public and articulate.

Given this scope, the problems of inclusion and exclusion have seemed at times insurmountable. There is an old-fashioned kind of arrogance which assumes that nothing can be worth reading if it has not held its public place consistently. This kind of thinking does not work for a period in which many poets were killed before they could produce a body of work substantial enough to attract posthumous notice. In this respect, the mid-century is comparable to the period of the First World War. Similarly, even for those not so crucially affected by the conflict, there is an observable and parallel phenomenon of burn-out and lassitude to be taken into account. Even a cursory reading of the biographies in Appendix 3 produces a surprising number of writers who survived the war, but who published or circulated little or nothing after the mid-1640s. Sometimes single poems survive, as nos. 53 and 275 have done, and even enjoy a steady degree of critical approval, but they do so under false colours: by being taken for the work of an established and relatively prolific poet, rather than for what they are in both cases, part of the small output of unknown poets whose works are preserved under their own names only in MS. What I am suggesting here is that this period must be treated as a unique case to which conventional methods of selection cannot apply. From 1640 onwards, the machinery of scribal and printed distribution of verse in the British islands was destabilized by emergency, faction, and censorship. It is therefore the duty of the editor to look beyond those poems which chance, as much as merit, has placed in the canon.

There are other arrogances just as dangerous: the delight in the obscure for its own sake is one of them. The unconscious determination to re-make the defenceless past in the image of the present is another. Refusal of the known and the obvious is perhaps the most subtle of all.

In collecting these poems from the years 1625–60, I have been continually frustrated by what I have had to leave out, rather than by any lack of urgent candidates for inclusion. It is perhaps impossible even to gesture towards the ambition of including some representative of the many, crosscutting, diverse modes and genres of writing which were employed in the mid-century. As it is, any editor must be aware of omissions: here the worst that come immediately to mind from a long list are poems of middle length and longer, represented only by Cowley (no. 287), Waller (no. 203), and Denham (no. 215) and confined to this number for simple reasons of space and practicality. There are many other areas: ideally room should have been found for more popular religious writing, for more documentary verse, and for more translations.

A book like this has to try to be at once self-sufficient and practical. Where an important text has been excluded, the final deciding factor has always been its availability elsewhere. However, in many cases, easily available texts have been included where I have felt that they gain a new aspect from their place in this book. It could be argued that Andrew Marvell's 'Upon Appleton House' is the central text of the mid-century, working with, focusing, and re-focusing many of the concerns and images which surface in this book in all levels and genres of writing. But it can be accessed with real ease, and is at time of writing in print in three or four different books. Cowley's 'The Civill Warre' (no. 287), on the other hand, has not yet had time to establish a place and a status for itself, since the full text was only discovered in the 1960s: however, I would argue that this poem displays the most courageous channelling of poetic energy in its week-by-week extension of existing techniques of poetry, as Cowley attempts to write about hitherto-unimaginable events. The crucial factor in my decision to include a substantial part of this text has been that it is only available in university libraries, in the excellent edition by its discoverer.

More will be said about past selections of texts and about the way in which the academy and the book trade have formed the canon of mid-seventeenth-century verse in the second part of this preface. It is important here to emphasize that the inclusiveness of this selection is meant naturally to provoke debate, but it is not intended to bewilder or rebuff the reader. Far from it, this act of attempted re-creation, offering at least some sampling of the vast diversity of verse writing which would have been available to a voracious contemporary reader, is meant to work for and with the late twentieth century in a number of ways. One of the most important is to place in context and illuminate the better-known texts of the period by juxtaposing them with their less familiar contemporaries. This does not only work by setting up oppositions, although by doing so we clearly expand our understanding of a period where much verse is inevitably controversial. It works more frequently by pointing up hitherto-unknown common ground, common sources, common ways of articulating particular experiences. Henry King's lament on the death of his wife is a comparatively well-known text; Katherine Dyer's poem on the death of her husband is printed here in full for the first time. When the poems are read together, they do not only resemble each other in mode, verbal form, and movement, they counterpoint and complete each other: male and female experiences answering each other on the same topic and in a similar form. This kind of illumination can then be taken on and used to deepen our readings of other poems in the anthology. This particular closeness between poems might suggest no more than the 'influence' beloved of the last generation (Katherine Dyer's poem cannot in fact be dated precisely); but, taken creatively, in the way in which I would hope that this book might be used, it can tell us many other things about public expression of private feeling, about perceptions of appropriate discourse and style.

It may seem to be a concession to the obvious to include a poem as well known as Lovelace's 'The Grasse-hopper' (no. 296), which uses winter as a metaphor for adversity. It is a poem which, read in a certain way, can support a comfortable fiction of Cavalier melancholy: Tomkins's broken music in 'A Sad Pavan for these Distracted Times', William Dobson's sunset portraits of the officers of the King's Army, Lovelace's poem about personal survival in the obliterating winter of the Interregnum. When it is read together with other imitations of the eleventh Ode of the first book of Horace (nos. 225, 222, 316) it acquires perspective and context as one of Lovelace's many experiments with extensions of the mode of writing of the 1630s to make it a vehicle for an irredeemably altered experience in the 1640s. If, on the other hand, it is read with other poems which use metaphors of changed seasons to express the changed circumstances of the 1640s, different perspectives emerge. Both Gerrard Winstanley (no. 262) and Morgan Llwyd (no. 297) express royalist defeat by metaphors of spring and release from imprisonment and winter. Another possible way of reading Lovelace's poem is simply as one of his oblique, despairing beast-fables (nos. 293, 295). This making of new patterns, enabling poems to illuminate each other inside and outside the conventional canon, is one of the chief aims of this book.

A final example: a temptation when working on a book like this is to make visible historical relevance an exclusive criterion. I have resisted this to an extent, feeling that the weight and significance of the poem which seems to refuse a response to contemporary events should not be passed over. This sort of refusal can be seen as a response as much as the public voice of a poem which tries to intervene in events. Gertrude Aston, as a Catholic from a royalist and courtier family, wrote no. 31 in 1651, at the time when royalist Catholics had reached the nadir of their fortunes. Yet the poem is a calm, accomplished celebration of her relationship with her husband, completely focused, completely still in the eye of the storm.

The division of this book into sections attempts to serve the reader, rather than to work out any academic agenda. The first part includes much of the most familiar material, such as 'Cavalier' amatory poems of the 1630s and 1640s. It also seeks to extend the definition of love into poems celebrating marriage and friendship, into epitaphs, and into love poems from the Irish and Gaelic traditions which coexisted with more familiar kinds of writing in English.

The second section includes both song-texts and poems about music. The making of public and private music was a daily cement at all levels of society in all the cultures of early-modern Britain. While it may seem perverse to include in this section songs whose subject-matter might have qualified them for a place in the section on love or on the war, the criterion has been that they share the concision of statement and the care in the placing of vowels which is necessary for a successful song-text. This grouping emphasizes that the skill of writing for music is parallel but not identical to that of the writing of lyric. It also emphasizes how central the constraints of writing for music are to forming the developing lyric mode. These texts travelled further and wider than many of the other writings in this book: they had a life in performance, recollection, and adaptation which might last for many years, sometimes decades. When, later in the anthology, many propagandist songs and ballads are encountered, it is helpful to have been reminded of the ubiquity of music in early-modern life.

In the third part, a diversity of religious and prophetic poems are brought together. This section in particular could have been expanded almost infinitely without including inferior matter. As it stands, attempting a kind of summary view of the major strands of seventeenth-century religious experience, it may serve as a vehicle for further explorations. Writings on religion were more strictly censored than any other by the successive regimes of early-modern England. This censorship, this attention, is itself an index of the absolute centrality of religious experience and religious affiliation to the individual and to society in the period. The range is wide: poems of consolation, epitaphs whose focus is on death and afterlife rather than on earthly affection, religious songs, meditation poems for the saints, prophecies. The contrasts of private and public utterance are at their sharpest here. At one extreme stands an enclosed act of mourning, such as no. 166, a poem addressed to the dead child, to the author herself, to no one. At the other, there are the public prophecies of Anna Trapnel, words intended to convey an urgent message to a fallen world, and the carefully poised orator's epigrams of Richard Crashaw (nos. 141–3), words for public speaking, attempting to give a baroque newness to familiar scraps of the Bible.

The fourth part is the loosest, the most compendious, the area of greatest danger for the anthologist who is trying not to be an historical novelist. In retrospect, it is fatally easy to fill a section such as this one, dealing with social life and the diverse human concerns of the Britain of the 1630s, with hints, shadows, and meaningful summer storms. The twentieth-century reader cannot help reading these poems in the knowledge of subsequent historical events, but it is here particularly important to try to read them as a celebration of a continuum, of the diverse creations of ordinary days. Their concerns are as wide as the breadth of human interest: places, landscapes, houses, cities, gardens, social rituals, and recreations. What is legitimate is to read some of the poems in this section as themselves a contributing factor to the divisions which hardened into war: the splendid introversion, the glorious lack of contact with political reality which marks much court verse (nos. 181, 191) plays its own part in fomenting conflict. They are part of the insidious process by which the Court came to believe in, and then act on, its own propaganda.

The fifth section, which traces the progress of division, war, and exile, is naturally the longest in the book. Again it tries to capture something of the sheer range of voices, many of them unnoticed until social upheaval made them audible, which burst on the consciousness of Britain in the 1640s. Rather than itemize here the kinds of poetry to be found, it may be more helpful to give some indication of how the section might be used. Poems are arranged by date of author's birth, as throughout the book, but the large number of anonymous poems present a problem. Where a date is known, or can be inferred from internal evidence, it is invariably recorded in the Notes on the Text. Where a poem cannot be precisely dated, it is placed where it may work hardest with the adjacent poems to illuminate dissensions or differing uses of the same tropes. Cross-referencing directs the reader to poems in controversy with each other, and to parodies and appropriations of other texts. One aspect of this section which perhaps requires notice is the inclusion of a substantial number of Welsh, Irish, and Scots Gaelic poems. Recent historical writing on the Civil War has increasingly taken account of the part played by the Celtic-speaking peoples in the conflict. Hitherto there has been little material available from which to attempt an understanding of their motives for allegiance and action. These poems may begin to fill that gap, giving some idea of the ways in which the war appeared to different social and literary traditions. For the reader whose point of departure is primarily historical, both Appendix 2 and the chronology in Appendix 4 have cross-references to poem numbers, in the first case to poems in which an individual is mentioned, in the second to poems relating particularly to the events of a year.

The selection of Restoration poems in the final section can be only an indication of the kinds of writing which were brought into play for the purpose of hasty celebration. Rachel Jevon's long panegyric (no. 337) gives a real sense of joy and renewal, but other poets have other agenda: while Iain Lom Macdonald delights in the promised downfall of the parliamentarian chieftain of the Campbells, John Ogilby reverts to the tropes of the last court masques before the war. An event which appeared temporarily unitary, the imposition of an authoritarian single voice on the diverse voices of the mid-century, is none the less still celebrated in divergent ways and is being questioned, as the last poem in the book reminds us, even before the new king began to issue acts legally enforcing on his people forgetfulness of the past twenty years.

2. THIS ANTHOLOGY AND THE CANON OF MID-SEVENTEENTH-CENTURY VERSE

About a quarter of the material in this anthology is, broadly speaking, new: to be precise, forty poems are publicly printed here for the first time, and another forty poems are given which, even if they were printed in this century, were printed in books now out of print or otherwise only accessible to specialists. Yet, I would argue, there is nothing included which does not add to our knowledge and appreciation of the poetry of the period. I would argue in addition that every poem in this book is worth reading for its own sake: for enjoyment or for historical illumination, as a specimen of an overlooked genre or as a discovery of a neglected voice.

When we think about how the canon of mid-century verse has been formed, it has to be with an awareness that this period is exceptional in its disturbance of the normal channels of literary circulation, and therefore that it is a period which requires special responses from the anthologist. Some understanding of the way in which the canon has formed goes a long way to explain why an editor working in the last few years of the twentieth century feels justified in attempting, in some respects, a new start.

Who made the canon in the first place? This complex question can receive a misleadingly simple answer, which would ignore all the early-modern factors which might enable or disable a writer from even entering the competition. It would be simplistic to say that the canon was first formed by the book trade and then, after English Literature became a university subject in the later nineteenth century, by the academics. First of all, it has to be remembered that for many élite male writers, it was not considered particularly desirable to commit original verse to print. It is perfectly possible that much poetry has been lost, simply through an initial failure to generate multiple copies. For some groups in early-modern society it was considered inappropriate or immodest to print literary compositions. This would apply to many women and to many working-class writers. For those in the early-modern British isles who did not speak English, other factors apply: the survival of manuscript is less important than the survival of a poem in the human memory. These are some of the initial limitations which may serve to render the survival and distribution of a text problematical.

The next factor depends on the book trade. If a writer is to become canonical (which is to say no more than that the writer's works are generally known to exist and are thought to have some value) they have to be at least to some degree available. If a late seventeenth-century or eighteenth-century publisher wanted to reprint a mid-seventeenth-century text, he would be much more likely to do so if there was a convenient copy-text available. What this means in practice is this: if the work of a mid-seventeenth-century poet was printed in a single author collection in the 1640s or 1650s, there was a potential for an easy reprint, and therefore for inclusion amongst the ranks of known writers of the period. In almost all cases, the poetry now admired as 'Cavalier' went through the following stages of publication: a mid-century printed collection, late seventeenth-century reprint or reprints, eighteenth-century reprints, subsequent inclusion in the series of 'The British Poets' which appeared in the late eighteenth and nineteenth centuries, entry to the canon when English Literature becomes an academic discipline, critical attention, frequent appearance in anthologies thereafter. This pattern holds good in a very substantial number of cases. Because of the uncertainties of the mid-century, it is clear that some even of those authors who published their poems in collections had to publish abroad (Crashaw, Corbet), while others (particularly working-class radicals) were printed in short print runs even by the modest standards of the day: either of these factors would reduce the chance of copies surviving, and thus their chances of making it to a reprint. It is interesting that this was recognized even at the time: some of the most self-aware authors (such as Cowley and the Duchess of Newcastle) took the precaution not only of ensuring that their works were printed as (high-status) large folios rather than small quartos, but also of presenting copies to the libraries of Oxford and Cambridge. Even given these considerations, an author in print in 1650 is not by any means inevitably reprinted after the Restoration: questions of taste and demand influenced reprints as well as availability of text. This question of contemporary print is vital: clearly, authorial manuscripts could survive into the eighteenth century and beyond, but their chance of being admitted into the canon was slim. There are counter-examples of un-canonical texts which were continuously in print until the late nineteenth century: the *Emblems* of Francis Quarles survived in the subculture of non-conformist piety, continuously in print and continuously ignored outside this specific readership. A good example of a writer from the early seventeenth century who 'ought' to belong to the canon is that of Robert Sidney, brother of Philip Sidney. He was, after all, male, aristocratic, conventionally literate, and a member of a well-known, notably intellectual, and well-connected family. In terms of their literary and historical interest his works have considerable claims on the public attention; but their printing history only begins with their discovery and publication in the 1980s. They are not in the teaching anthologies, they are not in the lecture notes of those who studied Renaissance poetry even a decade ago. They are still in a kind of limbo without a canonical status, never having gone through the progress of the canonical author, described above.

The decisions of the book trade, often highly arbitrary for the reasons outlined above, act as a crude filter sifting what material is available to form public taste and perceptions. After the book trade comes the academy (a useful term inclusive of universities, sixth forms, academic publishers, and the specialist media). The reasons for which professional academics have chosen to regard works as canonical or non-canonical are more complex than those of fashion and availability of text, although these factors inevitably play a part. When the histories of literature start to be written, then patterns and movements become visible: once labels such as 'Metaphysical', 'Cavalier', and 'Augustan' are in use, the status of writers who do not fit the categories becomes problematic. In undergraduate courses, until very recently (recent change in this is one of the many benign effects of feminist studies on the modern academy) there has rarely been time to teach the 'minor poets', the exceptions who do not conform to the rules of the literary guides. For academic purposes, those poets of whom I wrote earlier who were killed or silenced by the war before they had time to accumulate a substantial collection of work, present a different problem. Unless studied as a group (as the 'Poets of the First World War' are studied) they are hard to fit into schedules, there is not enough 'evidence' about them for Edwardian biographical study, too small a body of work for 1920s textual study and close-reading, or for the analysis of post-war 'new critics'. Their works tend to be hard of access, simply because they never achieved the first printed collection which might have facilitated subsequent reprints. They become 'rarities'—almost by definition the province of the economically independent amateur of literature.

The whole period covered by this anthology has until very recently been in itself something of an academic misfit. It has received as much scholarly attention outside the academy as within it, it has persisted in failing to fit into the patterns which are seen as the most important literary movements of the seventeenth century. This has led to some very curious things: to Milton and Marvell being studied almost in isolation, to a general impression amongst sixth-form students that the war was sufficiently traumatic somehow to stop people from writing poetry for twenty years. Terminology is a real problem with the first fifty years of the seventeenth century: enough of a problem to have kept the general reader away from much of the poetry in this book, simply because there is no adequate label under which to present it. The rediscovery of Donne coincided with the establishment of the study of English Literature as an academic subject. Donne's prestige has generated a grave imbalance in the way in which the seventeenth century is perceived. If the fixed points are the 'Metaphysicals' at the beginning of the century and the 'Augustans' at its close, the mid-century loses definition, and is categorized as either 'decadent Metaphysical' or 'anticipated Augustan'. Some highly subjective, and widely quoted, pronouncements of Samuel Johnson gave early reinforcement to this view. Johnson saw Cowley, Denham, and Waller, the most neoclassical poets of the mid-century, as forerunners of the unified achievements of eighteenth-century English poetry. He relegated the work of the poets who wrote in a continuation of the style associated with Donne to the status of a sterile experiment, a literary dead-end. This literary topography has stood more or less unchallenged until comparatively recently. The 'Cavalier' poets have engaged the imagination of the historical novelist as much as of the scholar, their works have been seen as part of a literary decadence ending neatly in personal and national catastrophe. This serves to marginalize these poets in several ways: to interpret historical disaster as a literary judgement on their triviality and sensuality, to relegate them to the status of a weakened second generation.

There are two very real problems here: one is a determination to read English literature in isolation from the literatures of contemporary Europe. The other is a reluctance to approach on its own terms a period which is marked by diversity rather than by a central high style. Insularity alone can account for belief in a one-generation 'Metaphysical school': if it were possible to substitute the word 'Baroque' for the word 'Metaphysical' a very different pattern would emerge. The activities and preferred styles of a succession of English poets from Donne to Philip Ayres would look like a parallel movement to the prevailing poetic style of the greater part of seventeenth-century Europe. It is remarkable how strong traditionalist resistance to such a proposal remains: 'Baroque' is still a term of insult in England, rather than a label for a period of verbal and visual art. To categorize English writing as 'Baroque' is to stress the kinship of that writing with the Continent: there is still real resistance to the stress on kinship rather than difference, resistance which has its roots in the fortress mentality of Elizabethan England. Responses to Crashaw are a case in point: they focus barely articulable suspicions of foreignness, of the invasive 'otherness' of Counter-Reformation Catholicism. Academic rejection of Crashaw's 'bad taste', 'hysteria' and 'emotionalism' arose from anxieties which had become, in the course of nineteenth-century religious antagonism, as much sexual as sectarian. In this account, Cavalier arguments are too accommodating, the reader is given too much for too little, the toughness of the 'Metaphysicals' has become decadent sensuality, a poetic which justly died out without an heir. I would suspect that the same fears of sexuality have much to do with the marginalization of the more sensual poets of the 1630s, particularly of Lovelace's freezing, fetishistic poems which celebrate details of gesture or clothing, refusing engagement with the whole body, far less the whole person.

Academic responses to the lack of a dominant style in the mid-century are simpler. It is hard to construct simplifications of a complex period. It is upsetting to come upon a period without a unifying central spine, carrying the torch from what came before to what came after. It is simpler to concentrate on major figures and leave the diversity of their contemporaries to take their chance in anthologies labelled with warnings such as 'Silver Poets of the Seventeenth Century'.

The label 'Cavalier Poetry' (which clearly applies to only a part of the poetry which is collected in this book) at once declares itself as the product of historical retrospect. It identifies a school by allegiance and period, rather than by a distinguishing literary feature. It ignores the question of whether there might be any parliamentarian poets apart from Milton and the (ambiguous) Marvell. I would suggest that the category 'Cavalier' itself, and the kinds of attention which the poets of the mid-century have achieved, are governed by ways of perceiving the period formed by historical fiction, rather than by the examination of the surviving literature.

In a serious sense, it is hard to say when the Civil War ended. In Scotland, the conflict renewed itself through the 'killing time' of the 1670s and 1680s, with the same polarizations and the same catch-words, only reaching stasis with the arrival of William of Orange in 1688. In all parts of the British islands, William's accession prompted the renewal of the conflict, albeit in a sporadic and diluted form. The rallying-cries, the catch-words, and many of the songs of the supporters of Charles I were appropriated by the supporters of the exiled James II. The Whig supporters of William of Orange claimed the moderate parliamentarians as intellectual and political forebears. The Stuart claim to the throne may have ceased to be a political reality after 1745, but the last pretender did not die until the first decade of the nineteenth century. The death of Henry Benedict in Rome had virtually no political implications for the British society of the 1800s, but it had one vital cultural effect: with the Stuart controversy at an end after a century and a half of conflict, it became a safe subject for historical fiction. More precisely, this availability released Walter Scott into the writing of historical fiction, and into the invention of Cavalier Poetry. It is remarkable how completely Scott established a lasting fictional archetype for the Civil War. In his *Old Mortality* (1816), the ageing Cavalier Bothwell not only creates the stereotype of a sensual and drunken aristocrat, redeemed by elements of courtesy and loyalty, he is also the author of a poem (Scott's own pastiche) hovering stylistically somewhere between Suckling and Rochester. Scott is known to have been one of the first collectors of Cavalier books and manuscripts: his later Civil War fictions deploy a considerable quantity of impeccable period detail in the service of a simplified and essentially anachronistic account of the period. Subsequent fictions of the Civil War and of the seventeenth century do not much vary from the patterns set by Scott: even his central plot-device of lovers from opposing parties continues into the present century to be the mainspring of Civil War fictions. The imitations of Civil War poetry written by, for example, Robert Browning do little to challenge the stereotypes: the represented authors are swaggering, gallant, and loyal. Their only ancestor among the real poets of the war might be Alexander Brome, but they conform much more closely to the diction and mode of Scott's pastiches. The succession of these historical fictions could be seen surviving, even down to plot construction, in the 1980s television series *By the Sword Divided*. There are exceptions: Daphne du Maurier's *The King's General* (1946) is more concerned than most with the suffering and disorientation caused by the war; Rose Macaulay's *They Were Defeated* (1932) is more concerned with the literature of the period, with poem no. 275 in this book taking on almost the status of a protagonist.

This unity of perception is shared by the mainstream anthologists down to recent years. George Saintsbury's *The Caroline Poets* (1926–9) is a somewhat different enterprise: it is a series of reprints of the complete collections of Caroline authors whose books are hard of access. The old *Oxford Book of Seventeenth Century Verse* (ed. Grierson and Bullough, 1934) includes few anonymous poems, and gives priority in its selection to lyrics by the writers of the 1630s and 1640s who are seen as the central figures in the Cavalier canon: Herrick, Lovelace, Suckling, and Carew. Most of the anonymous poems are either song lyrics or royalist laments. Robin Skelton's *The Cavalier Poets* (1970) ranges in time well beyond the Restoration: there are brief selections from a much greater number of poets, but the repertory of material is all from printed sources and there is no political or documentary material. An alternative tradition of anthology is represented by Norman Ault's *Seventeenth Century Lyrics* (1928), which makes extensive use of poems from rare printed editions and from manuscript. It is wide-ranging, giving particular attention to poems by poets whose outputs are slender and whose names are little known. The kind of poem which Ault favours, however, does little or nothing to challenge or expand established ideas of seventeenth-century poetry.

It is only comparatively recently that perceptions of the period have altered and opened out: there can be little doubt of the part played by the work of the historian Christopher Hill in bringing the radical and working-class writers of the period into the debate. Since the publication of *The World Turned Upside Down* in 1972, there has been general awareness that there is much more range and diversity in the writing of the period than that represented by the literary anthologies. This opening up is reflected in Alastair Fowler's *New Oxford Book of Seventeenth Century Verse* (1991), which includes a proportion of political writing and anonymous writing together with a meditated selection from the established canon. Another radical change has concerned women's writing: the first substantial collection of early-modern women's poetry, Greer, Hastings, Medoff, and Sansone's *Kissing the Rod* (1988) gave a clear indication of the range and achievement of a corpus of work which had been largely overlooked by the anthologists. It would be impossible to give a full account of the historical studies which have recently emphasized the diversity of voices which became heard publicly from the mid-1640s, but two works of literary history and exploration, Lois Potter's *Secret Rites and Secret Writing* (1990) and Nigel Smith's *Literature and Revolution in England, 1640–1660* (1994) seem to me to make a re-exploration of the verse of the mid-seventeenth century timely and perhaps essential. The student and the general reader need to have access to some of the verse texts which have now been brought into the foreground of literary and historical debate. Perceptions of the Civil War have changed so radically in the last decade that it is perhaps Lovelace and Crashaw who need to be re-introduced to a generation of readers to whom Gerrard Winstanley is a known figure. Leon Rosselson's 'World Turned Upside Down' is widely known and sung in contemporary contexts of political dissent, Winstanley's life has been filmed. Some of the vocabulary of radical dissent from the 1640s is being appropriated by a Britain which can, in many ways, be seen as not unlike the world of 1641 depicted in Richard Brome's *A Jovial Crew*, the last new play before the theatres closed.

I have written above about anthologies shadowing historical fictions: perhaps this is a *Sexing the Cherry* anthology, even a *Draughtsman's Contract* anthology. It will date in time, but it is intended for now to serve the needs of the present in doing what we perceive to be justice to a crucial era of the past.

P.R.K.A.D.

Wormleighton
1998

ACKNOWLEDGEMENTS

The editor is greatly indebted to the following individuals and institutions for permission to include, and help in preparing, poems in their possession: the Library of the University of Aberdeen; the British Library; the Bodleian Library, Oxford; the Cambridge University Library (to all the staff of the Rare Books Room, and most particularly to Brian Jenkins and Thyrsa Costello-Cortes); the National Library of Scotland, particularly the music department and Dr Ruzena Wood; the libraries of St John's College, Cambridge, and its former Librarian, Guy Lee; the Library of Corpus Christi College, Oxford; the Taylorean Institution in Oxford; Houghton Library, Harvard; The James Marshall and Marie-Louise Osborn Collection, Beinecke Library, Yale University, particularly its Curator, Stephen Parks; the library of Trinity College, Cambridge; Derby Central Library; the Royal Library, The Hague; The University Library, Leiden; the Henry E. Huntington Library, San Marino.

I have particular cause to thank those in whose works I first found the Celtic texts included in this volume: the Scottish Gaelic Texts Society, Seán Ó Tuama and Thomas Kinsella and Dolmen Press. It should perhaps be emphasized that exigencies of presentation have compelled the revision of most texts given in this book from all the Celtic languages.

A project of this scope is of its nature beyond what an author working alone can afford: I am therefore particularly grateful to the following bodies for research and grant support. St Edmund's College, Cambridge, provided a secure base from which to undertake the first researches. The following have all made a tangible contribution: the Department of English and Comparative Literature in the University of Warwick, particularly Michael Edwards; Warwick Humanities Research Centre, particularly Peter Mack; the Research and Innovations staff of the University of Warwick, particularly Philip Harvey. I am abidingly grateful for the humane and imaginative backing of the Harold Hyams Wingate Foundation, particularly its secretary, Jane Reid, to whom I am also personally indebted for moral support which has extended far beyond any call of duty.

It is only just to record a debt to the editors of *The Penguin Book of Renaissance Verse*: although this book had almost reached its final form when their work was published (and although this book is very different in its scope and intentions), David Norbrook and H. R. Woudhuysen encouraged it enormously by example: the generosity of their selection and incisiveness of their editing reassured me that I was not being unduly catholic as regards the former or obsessive as regards the latter. I have, as the acute reader will observe, found virtually no point of difference on text or annotation in those areas where our selections overlap, but have, on the other hand, not been unduly inhibited from including a certain number of the same texts, feeling that they speak differently in such a different context, different publisher, different scale. David Norbrook has also done more than can readily be described to foster this book into its final form.

Many less specific debts have accumulated over the decade in which this book has been in preparation: the Sir Thomas Browne Institute and the Vakgroep Engels of the University of Leiden and the Department of English and Comparative Literature in the University of Warwick have both provided so much that it is perhaps invidious to render specific thanks, but I do so, in Leiden to Bart Westerweel, Robin Smith, Martina Noteboom, Adriaan van der Weel, Cecilia and Alastair Hamilton; in Warwick to Michael Edwards, Peter Mack, Martin Wright, Anthea Callan, Georgina Paul, Dominic Montserrat, Bridget Bennett, Sue Wiseman, Paulina Palmer. Jeremy Treglown has made attempts to advance the fortunes of this work. Vicki Burke, currently of Nottingham Trent University, supplied vital information from her own forthcoming work on the text of the Marquis of Montrose.

Pauline Wilson of the University of Warwick has, with extraordinary patience and kindness, undertaken the computer work which has brought the book into its final form.

The Latin translations are my own in consultation with Jane Stevenson, the translations from the Irish are revisions made for this book by Jane Stevenson from texts, taken with thanks and acknowledgement, from Ó Tuama and Kinsella's standard work; the translations from the Welsh are new work specially undertaken (with extraordinary kindness and generosity) by Robin Chapman; Patrick Sims-Williams was generous with initial advice about the Welsh texts; the whole selection, translation, and annotation of the Scots Gaelic poems are Meg Bateman's, working in collaboration with her colleague at Aberdeen, Colm O Baoill.

Carolien Schamhardt made the initial selection of poems by the Duchess of Newcastle, Mary Wroth, and the Tixall Poets and has also helped greatly with the preparation of the book and with suggestions for annotation and presentation. Ann Sinnett, with a rare generosity to which I would very much like to draw attention, entrusted me with her unpublished work on Clement Paman which has provided invaluable information on texts and attributions. At the time of the first gestation of this book, Richard Luckett, Michael Halls, John Adamson, and Bernice Hamilton all contributed suggestions and support. Elsie Duncan-Jones, amongst many other gifts, first set me thinking about exile and suffering as part of the texture of the period. Alex Lindsay has been generous with knowledge and advice. Bernard Capp and Anne Laurence have both made their specialist historical knowledge available with very great generosity. I should stress that any historical inadequacies remaining are all my own. Anthony Milton has read the historical appendices to their great betterment. Jamie Reid-Baxter has kept a benign eye on the Scots. The discussion of the phenomenon of 'othering' in the Introduction came to focus through conversations with Sabina Sharkey, and her sharing of her own work on early-modern Ireland; I should like to draw attention to her vast intellectual generosity.

I have been fortunate in having had the help of two research assistants who have assumed the status of respected and valued collaborators: Carol Morley and Mark

Kilfoyle, both of whom have contributed to the content as much as to the form of the book.

This book was completed in circumstances of ill health and adversity: without the skill and patience of my physician, Peter Christopher, it is doubtful whether it would have been completed at all.

Jason Freeman and Sophie Goldsworthy of Oxford University Press have been as patient as they have been supportive in bringing this work to completion. Jeremy Maule, who emphatically cannot be held responsible for some of my more experimental textual decisions, has freely put his great knowledge of primary texts at my disposal. Nigel Smith has, with baroque generosity, given of his time, his energy and enthusiasm as well as of his unique knowledge of the period. Kate Chedgzoy has constantly shared her wide knowledge of early-modern women's writing, her talents as a reader of seventeenth-century texts, and her clarity as a critic of the prose of the contemporary academy. Sarah Ross gave some timely and much-needed help. Siobhàn Keenan came to the rescue, both technically and personally. David Morley read as a poet, to the betterment of the entire project. Jane Stevenson, as the dedication records, has contributed vastly in every part of this book: it would be impossible to quantify how much it owes to her.

INTRODUCTION

1: PROBLEMS AND DEFINITIONS

> The Cavaleers are foes, stand uppe now, stand uppe now
> The Cavaleers are foes stand uppe now
> The Cavaleers are foes, themselves they do disclose,
> by verses not in prose, To please the singing boyes
> Stand uppe now diggers all.

These lines from no. 262 identify verse exclusively with the royalist side of the conflicts of the mid-century and honest prose with the parliament and the radicals. Thus, on the face of it, they ratify and support the old route-map of conventional literary studies where a few 'Cavalier' poets fill the gap in English verse between 'The Metaphysicals' and 'The Augustans'. Yet the very existence of the lines quoted above questions and subverts the simplistic statement which they make. The making of verse is criticized through the medium of forceful and disturbing verse: verse is speaking from the most radical end of the parliamentarian spectrum (or beyond it). This verse constitutes a direct challenge to the old order represented by the institutions of monarchy, aristocracy, and Church hierarchy. And yet it includes the use of verse as one of the charges drawn up against an enemy, whose poets are the 'Cavalier poets' identified by the conventional literary histories.

This is a fair example of the contradictions which the verse writing of the mid-century offers to the reader. These problems have inevitably worked their way into the very shape of this anthology: there is necessarily a kind of split intrinsic to any collection which tries to give a broad representation of the writing of this complex period. In the conditions of the years of war and revolution, when new voices from the most divergent religious and political backgrounds became audible alongside the canonical (though newly outlawed) lamentations of the royalists, the position is very different. In the 1620s and 1630s it is indeed generally true to say that verse is the more visible literary form of the traditional élite, prose the more visible literary form of those beginning, ever more urgently, to question that élite's policies and assumptions. Thus, it is appropriate that much of the material in Parts I, II, and IV of this anthology are drawn from the published or scribally circulated works of already-canonical writers, from the stock of writing generally labelled as 'Cavalier'. But there is also much other material and there are numerous exceptions to this grand simplification. Much women's writing of this period maintains the persisting modes of sixteenth-century popular verse and thus appears stylistically distinct. A flourishing tradition of English and Scots-language ballad-making persisted, and is represented here. The parallel traditions of Irish, Scots Gaelic, and Welsh poetry are dependent on a different educational tradition, and on a thousand-year-old formal poetic with its own metres and allusions which also forms a part of the overall literary map. In the 1630s, when attitudes and divisions were only in the process of hardening, no effective generalizations can even be made about the literary activities of those élite writers who were later to declare parliamentarian allegiance. However, enough of a 'Cavalier' core remains in these sections of this book for the second part of this Introduction to be devoted to suggestions for the effective reading of the 'Cavalier' canon. In this section I have particularly tried to serve the needs of readers who have little acquaintance with the modes of 'Cavalier' writing, and also those readers who have only encountered them as a marginal element in school or university survey courses.

The third part of this Introduction offers some strategies for reading the other voices, those voices which are only now beginning to find a place in an expanding canon of mid-seventeenth-century verse. The poem quoted above itself suggests that parliamentarians (and those more radical than the parliament) were also publishing and circulating verses from 1640, particularly for purposes of religious and political propaganda. It could equally well be read as suggesting that a tradition of popular verse which had been marginal in the 1630s was gaining increasing visibility both through the adoption of the ballad by both sides as a medium for propaganda and through the proliferation of illegal publications. Part V of this book focuses on the verse directly generated by conditions of national crisis: many divergent styles and shades of religious and political opinion require answeringly diverse strategies from the reader. A poem which is meant to be public, which is meant to influence opinion and action, is clearly going to interact with its intended reader in ways which are very different from those governing poetry whose chief end is introspective.

This is equally true of parts of the third section of the book, which contains a sample of the religious verse of the period. The visibility of religious verse in the seventeenth century is a kind of microcosm of the changing degrees of public attention which other kinds of verse writing receive. In the Note on the Text and Annotation, I draw attention to the rigour with which all early-modern regimes censored dissident religious writing. The spectrum of religious verse represented in this book alone forcefully represents the degree of change in the censoring authorities which allowed successively for very different kinds of public religious expression to use the permitted and exclusive channels of distribution. It also argues for the central importance of such expression in early-modern lives: Anna Trapnel's extended prophecies (nos. 159–61) seem to have been published by an amateur, dissident publishing venture, a group of her co-sectaries who constituted themselves as printers and distributors for her text only. Crashaw's overtly Catholic poems (nos. 140–1) were published abroad (although the conditions of the 1640s had allowed publication in England of earlier versions of these poems already stretching Laudian Anglicanism to breaking-point in the direction of Catholicism.) Other religious poems (nos. 134,166) seem to have been intended barely to circulate at all, to be sufficient to their authors as acts of worship or recollection.

The fourth part of this Introduction focuses on one of the central actions of all controversial writing: definitions of the enemy. In a body of writing where the majority of poems are either propaganda or are meant to have a unifying force within a group already bonded by ideology or allegiance, a vital part of the poetic which it becomes necessary to invent will be concerned with representing the other side. This is the poetry represented in the fifth section of this book. Throughout the controversies of the mid-century, a vital part of self-definition is the definition of the opposition: in simplistic terms, the more clearly the other side can be verbalized as different, aberrant, or vicious, the more the writer can forge an identity and selfhood for those who share their allegiance.

This process of 'othering' is vital not only to this poetry of conflict, but also to the development of the satirical forms and strategies of the later seventeenth century. However much the period of war may have served to hone future, Augustan strategies of verbal attack, the representation of a dehumanized enemy has a long and unhappy tradition behind it. Many of the accusations by which writers of the Civil War period sought to defame and dehumanize their enemies had long been current as articulations of the fears of medieval Europe: accusations of anarchy, sexual deviation, and blasphemy had long been used to strengthen a succession of perceived social centres against what they perceived as threatening marginal groups.

Much of the propaganda effort of the 1640s and 1650s was carried on through visual as well as verbal media: the last part of the Introduction gives some indications of ways in which this worked, focusing on those poems (nos. 311–12 particularly) where a knowledge of contemporary visual communication, as well as of the shared stock of allusion to classical writers, can serve as a key to unlock poems which seem at best mystifying and elusive when treated in isolation. The use of visual referents goes further than propagandist concerns, informing many of the poems about the execution of Charles I in their shared 'iconography'. This section will also try to trace images and allusions once part of a widely comprehensible scheme of communication, which have now become obscure. The more that early-modern history and culture are seen as a unity, the more such considerations come to seem useful if not essential as enhancements of a modern reading. As always, it is my intention that such apparently specialist focus should enhance the use of this book as a starting-point, signing more and more aspects of the diversity and vitality of the mid-seventeenth-century, not only in a wide range of texts, but also in an equally wide range of possible readings of them.

2. READING THE CAVALIERS

We face numerous problems of style and intervening literary history before we can begin to approach or understand the 'Cavalier' literary response to one decade of strained normality and two of disorientation, trauma, and intermittent anarchy.

There are three closely related problems here: one is the categorization of the élite poetry of the mid-century as the superficial production of literary amateurs. The depiction of these literary amateurs in historical fiction offers another vast obstacle to any direct reading or enjoyment of their poetry: there is a pervading sense that certain kinds of critical study on 'Cavalier verse' have rendered these texts and their authors picturesquely unreal.

Another problem is the lingering distaste of conventional literary history for a period which, in significant ways, frustrates the literary historian. It defies assimilation to any narrative account of the progressive evolution of English poetry. This period also fails to offer the historian of style a single 'high style' which can be seen as part of an evolving poetic. These difficulties are the creation of hindsight and historical method. There are many periods when, to a contemporary, diversity rather than unity would have been the most apprehensible feature of poetic activity. This point is important: it is as futile to pass over mid-seventeenth-century élite poetry because it lacks 'cohesion' as it would be to apply the same standard to the poetry being written in the British islands in the 1990s.

This comparison is helpful at least as a shorthand. Like the contemporary British islands, in which poetry is being written in at least six languages other than standard English (Irish, Scots Gaelic, Welsh, Scots, Caribbean English, and Classical Arabic as well as a minority survival of Greek and Latin), the mid-seventeenth century supported verse in a diversity of languages. Early modern élites throughout Europe accorded higher status to writing in Latin than to writing in the vernacular. Traditions of writing in Irish, Welsh, and Scots Gaelic continued to build on a millennium of achievement, despite early colonialist attempts to disrupt them. However, writing in Lowland Scots was temporarily in decline as many Scottish poets turned to Latin and standard English, although the early-modern gap in Scottish literature sometimes alleged by literary histories is a serious misrepresentation of the facts. It would be more true to say that there is a gap in the transmission of Scottish writing at this time: a good example of this would be the poems attributed to James Graham, Marquis of Montrose in this book, many of which only survive in standard English 'translations' of Montrose's Scots (nos. 271, 274) and all of which have an unsatisfactory and complex textual history. Two epigrams by Thomas Urquhart are published here for the first time (nos. 211 and 265).

We have already a picture of comparable linguistic diversity: the comparison holds good for diversity of styles at all levels of literary activity. The late twentieth century has no single 'high style' any more than the mid-seventeenth century had one: there are rather a diversity of possibilities on which poets can draw. The high style of the previous generation is one: the use of the poetic of Eliot and Pound (a style partly formed by international modernism) could be compared to the early-modern use of the style which Donne shared with the poets of the continental baroque. On the other hand late twentieth-century poets can also draw on the consciously English stylistic range defined by Auden and the poets of the thirties, which bears serious comparison with the republican neoclassicism that Ben Jonson contributed to the range of stylistic possibilities. The acts of ventriloquism, the appropriation of past styles practised by a poet such as Geoffrey Hill, have an answering strain in the antiquarians and Spenserians of the seventeenth century. Both the present and the period covered by this book have a visible tradition of radical, urban writing, drawing on the common stock of vernacular ballad and song. Both periods also show a considerable quantity of poetic activity in a continuum with the prevailing lyric styles of contemporary song. Equally, 'amateur' poets of both eras have a tropism towards literary styles established around fifty years in the past. Many other comparisons could be made: the working-class professional poets working in a version of the urban vernacular, the women poets of meditation in deliberate rural retirement, the university-based translators and imitators. Without undue extension of the comparison, I hope that the essential points have been made: both our own era and the mid-seventeenth-century are marked by diversity rather than unity, and that diversity, which offers little difficulty to a modern reader of contemporary poetry, can offer equal opportunities to a modern reader of the poetry of the mid-seventeenth century.

A different problem for modern readers is the sheer distance of the Cavalier mode from those kinds of writing with which they are most at ease. Early-modern writing is poised on an uneasy cusp of distance from us: whereas the writing of the late seventeenth century gives a sometimes-misleading impression of familiarity, and the writing of the British Renaissance registers as unequivocally of the past, the writing of the mid-century can initially appear approachable while concealing aesthetic priorities which are foreign to those of the present. Paradoxically, a radical utterance such as no. 261, or a poem as confessional as no. 162, will present a contemporary reader with far fewer problems of intention or style, than will a poem as central to the Cavalier canon as no. 290, whose sentiments and mode will tend to cause an honest modern reader acute anxiety as to what exactly is going on. On the other hand, the late nineteenth-century admission of Blake to the canon has the effect of making much early-modern radical religious writing look more approachable. Blake might particularly offer the modern reader a key to nos. 146 and 161 in this book.

All this having been said, our difficulty with the seriousness of Cavalier poetry is still acute and problematic. I am not talking here about our evaluation of amatory or fugitive poetry from the earlier part of the reign of Charles I, rather about our difficulties with reading the Cavalier response to defeat and adversity. It must be remembered that the reply of many active poets of the 1630s and early 1640s to the Civil War and its aftermath was simply silence, in itself valid as a literary statement. Those whose response was an attempt to come to terms with events, an attempt to turn what had been a diversity of celebratory poetic modes into consolatory or lamenting ones, present us with the lingering difficulty of reading their intentions and their styles as consonant rather than simply disjunct. I would like to focus first then on the dislocation and trauma of the mid-century and try to understand Cavalier sorrow, Cavalier depression, as an essential element in the writing included in this anthology.

There are official lamentations from the period which offer us some insight into the way in which at least the royalists (and, by extension, the Cavalier poets of the conventional canon) perceived their circumstances. The first is from the *History of the Rebellion* by the Earl of Clarendon. He is making the contrast between the apparent felicity of the first decade of the reign of Charles I and the dislocations which followed:

> The happiness of the times I mentioned was enviously set off by this, that every other kingdom, every other province were engaged, some entangled, and some almost destroyed, by the rage and fury of arms; those which were ambitiously in contention with their neighbours, having the view and apprehensions of the miseries and desolation, which they saw other states suffer by a civil war; whilst the kingdoms we now lament were alone looked upon as the garden of the world . . . But all these blessings could but enable, not compel us to be happy: we wanted that sense, acknowledgment, and value of our own happiness, which all but we had; and took pains to make, when we could not find, ourselves miserable.
>
> In this blessed conjuncture, a small scarce discernible cloud arose in the north, which was shortly after attended with such a storm, that never gave over raging till it had shaken, and even rooted up the greatest and tallest cedars of the three nations; blasted all its beauty and fruitfulness; brought its strength to decay, and its glory to reproach, almost to desolation.

The second official lamentation comes from *A Collection of Prayers and Thanksgivings* printed at Oxford in 1643, at which time the Headquarters of the Royal Army and the Court were both in that city:

> We confesse that we were a wealthy and a carelesse Nation and our land was as the garden of Eden. Peace was within our walls and plenteousnesse within our Pallaces. But when we had eaten and were full, and had waxed fat, we kicked against thee our Maker who hadst done so great things for us. And now o Lord behold the sword is drunk with our blood and we are numbered to the slaughter. The high-wayes are unoccupied and the travellers go through by-paths, our fields are divided, our inheritance is for a spoile and our substance to the robbers . . . The mean man is risen against the honourable, and the fire out of the bramble devoureth the lofty Cedars.

The last lamentation is more indirect, more the expression of a personal desolation. It is the inscription on the church of Staunton Harold in Leicestershire built illegally for the Church of England service after the execution of Charles I.

In the yeare 1653
When all thinges sacred were throughout this nation
Either demollisht or profaned
Sir Robert Shirley Barronett
Founded this church
Whose singular praise it is
to have done the best thinges in the worst times
AND
hoped them in the most callamitous.

These prose extracts (only one of which is from a work intended for 'literature' rather than for present use) speak eloquently to us about defeat and adversity. In all three cases, significantly, the passages turn on an appeal directed outside the troubled Britain of the mid-century: to the nostalgic myth of a Stuart Golden Age; to the intervention of God; to the remembrance and approval of an imagined posterity. We probably have little trouble in accepting such examples as these as documentary, as somehow 'true'; but the poetic response to the Cavalier winter of the late 1640s and 1650s still offers problems of register and communication. A poem such as no. 316 seems at first to offer a lack of response to events. It seems to the post-romantic (far less the post-modern) reader to be simply too indirect, too polished to function as a verse reflection of social marginalization, personal grief, or public insecurity. What would seem to a modern reader the essential point of the poem, the refusal of mourning and the value of friendship in adversity, is obliquely conveyed almost in passing in the last four lines. Yet for a contemporary reader this poem's use of the imagery of winter would have been unsurprising; specifically, it evokes the same Horatian source which Richard Lovelace used to make very similar points about adversity and friendship in his poem 'The Grasse-hopper' (no. 296).

There is an element of encodement here: of a polished and indirect mode of writing being used not for amatory intrigue or for university riddles but as a secret poetic in a time when members of the former élite were turned into exiles and keepers of secrets. The same indirection will be found in Lovelace's curious, obsessive beast-fables (nos. 293, 295) which may initially surprise the reader simply by their placing amongst the poems dealing with the war and its aftermath. Indirection and allusiveness are again the keys: the points of the fables, the comparisons of the animal and human worlds, are made again only at the very ends of the poems. Their concluding lines compel a second reading in which the beast-world becomes a metaphor for the uncertainties and brutalities of the times. Categorization of poets has been unusually destructive here. While readers are conditioned both to expect and enjoy such extremes of indirectness and reticence from Marvell, the 'Cavalier' classification obtrudes itself to deny that Vaughan and Lovelace might be working with an equal degree of obliquity. The cleverness of their earlier amatory verses has somehow been allowed by literary historians to cast their developed poems of loss into question.

Secrecy is not the only possible response of the royalist poet attempting to adapt the poetic modes of the 1630s to new conditions: there are one or two cases where an abandonment of high style seems a deliberate response to the disordering of the nation. Charles Cotton's disoriented, drifting response to the death of the Marquis of Montrose (no. 332) abandons mode and category, as it abandons sequential argument. The adoption of something very like the voice of popular poetry (quite different here from the use of ballad modes for propaganda purposes) is clearly a deliberate aesthetic choice. This poem could be read as denying that any further response is possible after the defeat and death of Montrose (and the consequent damage to royalist hopes). Cotton's poem moves mechanically through statements of despair and alienation, discontinuous from verse to verse, deliberately echoing and juxtaposing clichés of mourning from the ballad and folk-song repertories.

Another indirect response is possible: it is not only historians like Clarendon who invoke the classical past. Many Civil War poets produced translations or imitations of classical poems which gained new meanings in the context of the 1640s and 1650s. This is very much the case with Fanshawe's stoic imitation of Horace's praise of the man who remains true to himself in degraded times (no. 256) and with Denham's formally innovative translation of Homer (no. 282). Denham arrived at this triumph of directed obliquity after experiment with a whole range of possible styles and genres for the poetry of conflict and adversity. His originality is rooted in the very diversity of 1630s poetic possibilities. After experiment with propagandist ballad and with the crudest discourse of 'othering', he composed no. 215, apparently a topographical meditation, a poem about a landscape and its history. 'Cooper's Hill' was revised and adapted as the conflicts of the mid-century progressed: even in its earliest form it is a remarkably troubled work, continually hinting at tensions building up the more the poet considers the past of England in relation to a landscape with specifically royal associations. Much of what is successful in the poem lies in its atmosphere of tension and unease, the feeling that its historical allusions and metaphors may transform themselves at any moment into contemporary commentary. The sense that the past is modified by the present, and that the present is changing so fast that the past is destabilized from moment to moment, is intensified by the deceptive transparency of the poem's topographical intentions. It is valuable to read Anne Kemp's 'A Contemplation on Bassets down-hill', no. 223, in conjunction with Denham's poem. Much the same process is in operation, but she is more reticent still, only hinting that the lamentation of the town for the innocent and irrecoverable country with which the poem closes is also a lamentation for an enforced change in personal circumstances, a lamentation about a happy past and a disturbed present.

Denham's imitation of Homer (no. 282) has acquired a canonical status by merit of its innovatory and, in some ways, prophetic handling of neoclassical versification. It is also important to see it as a Civil War poem, a return to beginnings, a return to the most celebrated ancient statement of what war is and what the motives for fighting are. Its anticipatory Augustan coolness reads disturbingly in a mid-century context. Although Denham and Waller achieved the posthumous approval of Samuel Johnson and almost all subsequent literary historians for the regularity of their versification, the effect of the poem when it is read beside its contemporaries is of a discourse icily remote, a deliberately forensic examination of human motivation. It is as though Denham had removed himself in style and voice from his contemporaries, denying his context and time.

Having looked at the question of Cavalier seriousness, suggesting some strategies for reading and interpreting the Cavalier war poems, the Cavalier style itself requires some consideration. It is unhelpful, however, to talk about a single Cavalier style: as stated above, one of the chief problems which the élite poetry of the 1630s and 1640s presents to those seeking to make classifications and trace developments is its lack of consensus, its employment of diverse modes. Conventional wisdom on the subject attempts a simplification: it categorizes the poetic of the 1630s and 40s as binary. There is the 'School of Jonson' and the 'School of Donne'. While it is true to say that Jonson was one of the very few English poets who consciously formed a following of younger poets around him on a recognizable continental (or Scottish) model, it is more difficult to assert that this school continued to function to any unified purpose after his death. The whole question of whether such a thing as a 'School of Donne' existed at all is intensely subjective. (Carew's superb elegy on Donne looks like the work of a disciple; however, his poem to George Sandys (no. 126) rejects much of Donne's poetic along with its general rejection of profane poetry.) It might be more helpful to say that there are two central strands of method and versification on which élite poets of the mid-century could draw: one concerned with transparent statement and clear diction, one concerned with involutions of discourse and expressive diction. It is helpful to look beyond the figures of Donne and Jonson to their origins and affinities. Beyond Donne is the whole of baroque Europe from Huygens in the Netherlands to Gongora in Spain: he is to a very considerable extent simply writing in a version of the international style of his time. Jonson places himself rather in a direct poetic line stretching back to the poets of Republican Rome. His stated model as a poet is Horace, his style is an invented neo-classicism strongly rooted in the plain poetic speech of northern Europe and in the classicizing experiments of the academies. Conventional literary history has, until very recently, been content to tease these two threads out of the texture of mid-century poetry. The matter of Cavalier style is, however, still more complex and more interesting.

At least two other strains on which the poets of the mid-century drew can usefully be identified. The song tradition is perhaps the most important: because of their nature, successful song lyrics, which universally tend to display a simplicity in their movement and thought and a smoothness of diction which renders them apt for music, are marginalized by those literary standards of judgement which foreground difficulty and argumentation. Like much of Cavalier poetry itself, they tend to become the province of the economically independent literary amateur. This again is far from how the matter would have appeared to a contemporary. Writing words for music remained a high-status literary activity throughout the period covered by this anthology. The first decade of the seventeenth century saw the establishment of a lyric style which survived until musical innovations of the 1670s, which gave music unequivocal prominence over words, rendered it obsolete. Lute-songs, consort-songs, and theatre songs all made up parts of the continuum on which Cavalier poets could draw. The typical song-manuscript of Herbert Aston, who collected nos. 196–9 and 253, (Beinecke Library, Yale University, MS Osborn 1634), is a perfect example of the persistence of the song-repertory of the 1600s into the 1630s and 1640s. The song tradition fed also into the masque tradition which directly nourished the matter as well as the style of Cavalier poetry. Thomas Campion (1566–1620) was not only an admired writer of solo songs (some of which are in Herbert Aston's MS), but also a writer of masques. His *Lord Hay's Masque* (1607), with its combination of visual spectacle and extended lyricism, can be seen as a forerunner of the masque-style which persisted at the court of Charles I in the works of Carew, Townshend, and Davenant. Masque lyrics and solo song lyrics continued to be written in a style strongly rooted in the 1600s for the greater part of the century. Although subject-matter altered and diversified, the achievements of the Jacobean solo-song and masque composers set a standard which was accepted with comparatively little modification.

The influence of the masque overlaps with the influence of the poet and playwright John Fletcher (1579–1625), who is not now perceived as a central figure although his influence on his immediate successors was considerable. On the evidence of citation, imitation, and even of translation into the international Latin of the day, his works enjoyed the highest status with the next generation. His rhymed pastoral *The Faithfull Shepherdess* (1610) employed the smooth, forward-moving, four-stress couplets widely used in the mid-century for a great variety of poetic purposes. Milton's *Comus* (1634) is heavily indebted to Fletcher stylistically, perhaps unsurprisingly in that it is an entertainment very much in the tradition of his masque-like pastoral plays. It is also worth observing how widely Fletcher's influence is diffused: poems as diverse as Henry King's 'Exequy' for his dead wife (no. 14) and Henry Vaughan's winter epistle (no. 316) owe a great deal to Fletcher in their form and versification. It would be no exaggeration to assert that Fletcher's influence can also be seen clearly in the diction and pastoral mode of Marvell's '*The Nymph complaining for the death of her* Faun' (no. 312), however much Marvell's poem is a bitter and complex appropriation of pastoral.

Having suggested that the choices open to an élite poet of the mid-century were far wider than the traditional diagnosis of 'School of Jonson' or 'School of Donne', it remains to survey some of the uses which the poets actually made of these diverse possibilities, and then, to consider those elements of Cavalier thought and diction which are furthest from those kinds of writing with which a late twentieth-century reader feels at ease.

It is unhelpful to think of any of the strands of style and manner discussed above as being mutually exclusive for a seventeenth-century poet. It is also dangerous to take style as an invariable marker of political or religious allegiance. For example, the moderate Protestant Clement Paman's elegy for Edward King (no. 139) is more wildly baroque in its contorted imagery than anything by Crashaw (nos. 140–1) or by the soberly recusant William Habington (no. 132). It is more useful, in general, to think of the varying stylistic strands of the mid-century as being combined and used for different purposes, often by the same poet, rather than as belonging to opposing schools.

Most English people in the early-modern period used two distinct kinds of handwriting: the English 'secretary script' and the formal continental 'italic', very often using combinations of letter forms in a 'mixed hand'. It is much the same with poetic styles: a single poet like Richard Fanshawe wrote in a plain Jonsonian style (significantly used for translations of Horace such as no. 256) as well as an intricate and emotionally charged continental style which he used for his translations from the Spanish and Portuguese. One style would come to hand for a discursive poem (Clement Paman's no. 276, which is complex, abounding in extended metaphors), another for an epigram (no. 275, which is written in a clear development of the epigrammatic style of Jonson). Points where poets such as Cotton and Denham move to the margins of accepted 'high style' have already been discussed above. The existence of a wholly distinct Scottish high style will be discussed briefly below.

Perhaps the aspect of all this which remains most consistently problematic for the modern reader is the application of style to subject-matter, which can, in many cases, seem perverse or disjunctive. This is often the result of reading with hindsight, applying the expectations formed by later poetry to a period with different intentions. The most persistent of such problems is likely to be the lack of simplicity or apprehensible sincerity in Cavalier writing. It is very easy for a modern reader to be moved by a street ballad like no. 243, particularly if it is experienced in conjunction with its haunting tune, and to feel that it is communicating unmediated experience from the past. Much the same might be said of no. 266, the plain production of an amateur poet moved to verbal expression by guilt and fear of the future.

It is much more difficult to give a sympathetic reading to such writings as Herrick's polished and allusive no. 235, a poem written at a time of acute national and personal crisis, and addressed to a king already all but defeated. This poem feels simply inauthentic to a modern reader: its polish and its complicated scheme of literary reference, its adoption of the personae of shepherds in a court entertainment, seem too intricate and too inappropriately decorative to answer the desperate circumstances of its composition. Drummond of Hawthornden's snarling 'plague on both your houses' (no. 231) seems a much more authentic response to his circumstances.

This reaction, however understandable, stems from anachronistic reading: if Herrick's poem is read in its own terms it becomes comprehensible, possibly even moving. Again we have problems of encodement: he is referring to Guarini's pastoral play *Il Pastor Fido* (1589), which had a very wide currency in the England of the 1640s, when it was read as a metaphor for the divided state of the country. (Sir Richard Fanshawe's 1647 translation of it makes the connection wholly explicit.) Herrick is attempting an act of literary sympathetic magic in this poem: if he grafts the present ruined hopes of Charles I as an interpolation into Guarini's text he is also expressing hopes for the miraculous peace and reconciliation with which the play ends. This explanation is troublesome in that it does not offer a strategy for reading, depending as it does on the same kinds of precise knowledge which we need to unlock two of Marvell's most problematic poems, a subject which will be discussed in the fifth part of this Introduction. It is perhaps more helpful to suggest that Herrick had confidence in his own poetic, that he believed the styles and devices of the 1630s were still viable in changed circumstances, that his own refusal to abandon his version of the 'high style' was in itself an action of defiance of social and literary confusion. A strategy for reading might also import to this poem skills developed for reading Shakespeare's romance plays: accepting and celebrating the ways in which early-modern writing can use the remote setting, the remote metaphor for the most pressing human concerns.

These problems of style and intention inevitably affect our readings of Cavalier amatory poetry: there are many cases where it is perhaps necessary for the reader simply to respect the otherness of the past. It is also useful to remember that an apparent 'love poem' can be a literary exercise rather than an attempt to communicate with a single, living person. Richard Crashaw had the honesty to admit as much in the very title of his 'Wishes. To his (supposed) Mistresse' (no. 49). It can be safely assumed that the mistresses addressed in poems by his fellow academics Briggs (no. 53) and Cleveland (nos. 50 and 52) are imaginary or platonic: celibacy was a basic requirement for the holder of a university post, yet academics frequently published love poetry. The fact of publication argues that the love poem was widely understood as a conventional mode of writing in the period rather than as a declaration of feeling or intention. This does not only apply to academics: a number of poets (bourgeois, courtiers, and gentry) write love poetry as a literary exercise rather than as an expression of romantic (or post-Romantic) feeling. To take a well-known example, the palpable intensity of feeling in Andrew Marvell's 'To his coy mistress' appears on reflection to attach itself to considerations of transience and the inevitability of death, as well as to the erotic persuasion which is the ostensible theme of the poem. The same might be said for other poems classified hastily as erotic, which are in fact poems of compliment (nos. 70–1), or are amatory poems as deliberately general and impersonal as those of Waller (nos. 32–4), which might be imagined as poems made to be quoted in circumstances of actual human dialogue, rather than poems urged into being by the desire to communicate with a specific person. This is not a universal rule: there are poems in this collection where personal affection appears unequivocally to be the mainspring of the composition. Several of these are in fact epitaphs (nos. 14, 22, 79), one despite its bizarre imagery is a direct address to a known individual (no. 15), perhaps even a private joke between them. The amatory poems of Richard Lovelace provide us with a further problem: most of them are addressed to the same individual, 'Lucasta', but they are inconsistent in the ways in which they address her. I cited no. 289 as a poem inevitably problematic to the modern reader (the conceit of the poem is that to be worthy of the beloved the poet has to prefer going to war to staying with her) raising as it does immediate problems of who is speaking to whom and about what. Yet elsewhere in Lovelace's work there are poems addressed to the same individual which are palpably, even obsessively, erotic in their focus (nos. 67–8). It could be argued that even these poems look past the ostensible beloved to their real audience in a male literary coterie, but the texts themselves would seem to work strongly against such an interpretation. Not all problems of approach can be answered by simple solutions; but if the reader bears in mind the possibility of the love poem as literary exercise some difficulties are resolved. On the other hand, if the possibility is also borne in mind that what may seem to us over-intricate expression need not necessarily signal lack of personal engagement in the context of the mid-seventeenth century, then the machinery is in place for the kind of flexible approach which honours the difference of the past.

3. READING THE OTHER VOICES

Compared to the strategies of reading which the Cavalier mode can demand, the problems of reading the miscellaneous 'other voices' of the seventeenth century may seem comparatively slight. Most of this material, which has entered the canon comparatively recently, is unlikely to offer modern readers any great problems of interpretation or style. The very presence of these 'other' voices is also unlikely now to cause any surprise after more than two decades of critical and historical attention to the sheer diversity of voices which became audible in the British islands at the time of the Civil War. Furthermore, readers now are much less narrow in their definitions of literature than they were even a decade ago. There is perhaps one chief difficulty which will haunt some readers in reading the poems in this anthology which are not drawn from the 'old' canon of English literature: the problem of 'literary quality' and the subsidiary problem of reading the intention of the poet.

I have already written at some length about the reasons for my inclusion of this material drawn from outside the old canon of 'Cavalier Poetry'. It is unnecessary to air these reasons yet again; what is more relevant here is to try to give the reader some points of orientation for those parallel traditions of writing in the British islands which may be unfamiliar. To this end, I will first sketch some background for the poems in this book which are not written in standard English and will then go on to give some brief consideration to the questions of 'literary quality' and poetic intentions. It will also be essential to sketch the ways in which popular and radical writing has a distinct tradition of its own.

It is essential to begin this process by giving some indication of the status which Latin enjoyed in the early-modern period. As well as being the international language of the Roman Church, it was the language of international diplomacy, the first literary language of Europe, the language of international scientific learning, and the daily language of many schools and most universities. It was the highest-status language for a poet hoping to attract an international readership. Latin prose and poetry played a very real part in the daily political life of the Civil War and Interregnum as the means of communication with foreign states and the medium for international propaganda. The composition of Latin poetry and Latin oratory was an essential part of school and university education. The conditions of distribution of Latin poetry were different from those in the vernacular languages: there is little of the real or feigned modesty about vernacular writing often shown by early-modern élites. Latin poetry tended in general to be published under the author's name and with the author's approbation. In some ways it was so much the literary first language, particularly of the university poets, that it is unsurprising that Milton, for example, turned to Latin as much as to English for the most personal poems of his career. The early elegy given here (no. 207) has an extraordinary freedom and vitality, rarely apparent in his earlier English poems.

Along with this use of Latin as a medium for poetry went an élite obsession with the poets of classical Rome who provided the models for early-modern Latin composition. This point will inevitably recur in the fifth part of this Introduction, in connection with Marvell's lifelong dialogue with the Roman poet Virgil, but it is worth stressing how universally the Roman poets were known and how much of élite poetry is to a greater or lesser extent in dialogue with their familiar works. I have already shown how automatically a poem of Horace's came to the minds of Vaughan and Lovelace as they tried to invent a poetic of adversity, how Fanshawe most naturally turned to Horace to express his own stoicism in defeat. This interpenetration of classical Rome and early-modern England continued throughout the period covered by this anthology. Were there space here to do so, one clear barometer of the development of élite response to contemporary events could be constructed through a survey of seventeenth-century translations of the *Aeneid*, from Fanshawe's 1648 translation of Book IV (addressed as a lesson in governance to the future Charles II) through John Denham's nervous imitation of Book II (describing the fall of Troy) to John Ogilby's post-Restoration version of the whole poem, with its stress on insurrection and civil war.

This complex relationship with the poets of antiquity was also a feature of the Celtic literary cultures which developed in parallel with standard English throughout the mid-century. Poem no. 335 is no isolated phenomenon with its blending of classical mythology and Irish history. It is easy to forget that Celtic culture was Latinate from the very early Middle Ages and that, since the majority of Irish people and Scots highlanders were Catholics and therefore barred from conventional public education, the Latin education offered by the Catholic colleges on the Continent was the only university culture open to them. Foreign soldiering was another possible option, productive of links with the continental vernaculars. In addition to this continental input, very visible in the Irish baroque of poem no. 23, all the Celtic languages had intensely sophisticated native poetic traditions on which to draw. This is hard to grasp today, from the other side of eighteenth- and nineteenth-century attempts to eradicate the Celtic languages and cultures, first by violence and then by attrition. In the early-modern period, however, although the economic and social status of all the Celtic peoples was marginal, it was only in Ireland that they had sustained concerted attempts to fragment and suppress their language and traditions. Thus the poets writing (or composing) in the Celtic languages had, at the time of the Civil War, a learned tradition within which to work and an élite audience for sophisticated poetry. The status of poet was extremely high within all Celtic societies which were managing to function traditionally in the face of attacks from outside. Paradoxically, the Irish nobleman Piaras Feiritéar satisfies all criteria for being considered a Cavalier poet, except that of choice of language.

The Gaelic poems from Scotland included in this anthology represent two forms of the language: Classical Gaelic and Scottish Gaelic. The former was a literary language, not spoken by anyone, but acquired through apprenticeship to the learned professions and association with aristocratic patrons. Classical Gaelic functioned as a shared language for the élites of Scottish and Irish society, despite considerable variation in vernacular dialects. The Gaelic areas of both countries considered themselves as a single cultural unit until the Reformation, and the learned classes, particularly professional poets, would visit both countries when travelling. Classical Gaelic was first formulated around 1200 and, as the language was bound by the strictest rules, remained unchanged for four and a half centuries thereafter. Changes in Gaelic society in the seventeenth century were such that the chiefs no longer either desired or could afford to patronize the professional poets and Classical Gaelic died out with them. Associated with the language of Classical Gaelic were highly ornate metrics based on syllable counts, multiple internal and end rhymes and alliteration. The work of a professional such as Cathal Mac Mhuirich (no. 129) represents the Classical language as used by a poet whose family had produced poets for eighteen generations.

A popular tradition of song-poetry coexisted with the high Classical culture, using vernacular dialects and stressed metres. This tradition is represented here (no. 324) by a song in which an anonymous woman of Clan Campbell laments for the men killed at the battle of Inverlochy in 1645. As the professional poets of the Classical language died out, their place (and much of their rhetoric) was taken over by untrained (although generally aristocratic) poets who continued to produce praise-poems in the vernacular. The poems of Mary McLeod (no. 216) and Iain Lom (nos. 321–3, 340), who both belonged to the ruling families of their clans, fit into this category. A half-way point between the Classical and vernacular traditions is evident in the work of the fourth and fifth chiefs of the MacKenzies of Achilty (nos. 24, 327–8): the language is vernacular Scottish Gaelic, but the metrics are based on Classical syllabic systems.

Clearly a work like this can only give a cursory idea of the poetry of the Celtic languages in the seventeenth century, but, in the light of increasing historical interest in the Scots, Irish, and Welsh involvement in the war, it is useful to have at least some indication of the nature of the culture and tradition which governed their loyalties and actions.

The problems of (Lowland) Scots writing are simpler: there is comparatively little which survives from the period. I have already argued that this probably reflects a failure of transmission and a diversification of literary energies rather than the Calvinist silence of the conventional histories. It is important for the understanding of the few Scots poems given here to stress the separation in the early-modern period of Scots language and culture from the parallel culture of England. Until the departure of the court from Edinburgh in 1603, Scotland had sustained a literary culture of some variety and achievement. The major achievements in translation and original poetry belonged to the sixteenth century, but a tradition survived which moved freely in register (often in the compass of one poem) between an extreme of Latinate formality ('aureation') and the style and diction of the vernacular ballads and songs. Drummond (no. 231) stands at an oblique angle to this tradition: his models were metropolitan and his language is standard English. Lady Lothian (no. 128) is typical of one kind of Scots poetic activity, showing the distinctively Scottish mixture of registers: her poem is essentially in ballad style, but with scriptural references and traces of the 'aureate' high style as in the introduction of the emblem-figure of Fortune. The poems attributed to the Marquis of Montrose are more problematic, since only two (nos. 48 and 272) appear to survive in the author's own language and spelling, the others having become anglicized by the processes of transmission. If it is by Montrose at all, no. 274 still shows traces of its original Scots diction. Perhaps the most distinctively Scottish of Montrose's poems (or of the corpus of poems attributed to him) is the ballad 'My deare and only Love' (no. 268), despite its having lost its original orthography. The ballad style is varied with elements of 'high' diction: the whole works within the tradition of deepened and appropriated folk-song which is one of the most notable achievements of Scottish literature.

Having surveyed some of the poems from the parallel traditions, it is necessary to take up the deferred question of the 'other voices' writing in standard English. It is hard to discuss the women writers represented in this book as a group: to do so would seem to multiply problems rather than to solve them. They wrote in three different languages, and those who wrote in English are as remarkable for their diversity as is the writing of the period considered as a whole. Neither is it helpful to class them with the radical writers by their common exclusion from élite education: although few women in early-modern England had access to anything like the most basic education available to men, there were notable exceptions. Chief amongst them in this book is Rachel Jevon (no. 337), who also published a version of her Restoration address to Charles II in highly accomplished Latin verse. The social group least likely to educate women would seem to have been the Anglican bourgeoisie and élite: it is unlikely to be coincidental that two of the women poets represented here were Catholics (nos. 31, 133–4 and no.163) from a social group who were denied official education regardless of gender; that one is from a radical religious background (nos. 159–61); and that two are central or peripheral members of unconventional élite families with their own literary traditions (nos. 22, 127 and nos. 4–7, 83–4). Rachel Jevon's background was marginal by virtue of national events: although her father was an Anglican clergyman, he remained actively royalist through the Interregnum years, and was deprived of his church position. Katherine Philips, interestingly, appears to have been regarded as canonical for some time: her work appears extensively in Saintsbury's *Caroline Poets* in 1905, and is at least represented (albeit by two poems) in the old *Oxford Book of Seventeenth Century Verse* (1934). There are, however, general considerations which are frequently raised with regard to all non-élite writers, the most contentious of which is that of 'literary quality'.

Having argued at some length for the value of non-élite writing of this period, both for its own eloquence and documentary value and for the important position which it occupied in the years of war and aftermath, it seems perverse to have to argue the question of 'literary quality' at all. Relatively recent changes of historical and literary approach to this period, and the consequent expansion of the canon to a more representative state, leave some readers bewildered as to why the criteria for inclusion in a collection such as this seem, in some degree, to have changed.

Two questions, neither of them particularly hostile, can be offered as answer. We can ask whether it is even possible to evaluate the success of a poem by arbitrary criteria formulated long after the event. Further, we can ask how objective criteria of literary quality can ever be, given that the criteria themselves are vulnerable to the effects of changes in the canon.

To expand the first question: we can only evaluate the merit of a poem by having some preconception as to what that poem should be like. Thus, we are back where we started, vulnerable to the simplifications of old literary history, whereby the diversity of any period is sacrificed to the demands of a narrative, to the wish to see (or to create) a single evolving thread of English poetic style. It is easy to draw this fallacy out to absurd lengths: it would be equally easy to assemble an anthology of unreasonable critical pronouncements which condemn one poem for not being another poem. Samuel Johnson's pronouncements on mid-seventeenth-century poetry are fine and canonical examples of this failure of historical sense. It now seems comically anachronistic for him to condemn nearly all Cavalier poets for not writing in the style of Denham's neoclassical experiments; it seems equally comic to suggest that Donne failed as a poet by failing to observe the rules of eighteenth-century versification. Yet, there are ways in which this is merely an exaggerated version of the criteria which condemn Morgan Llywd for not being Cowley, Vavasour Powell for not being Henry King.

The second question raises some genuinely interesting points: I would argue that, like the canon of literature itself, the notion of 'literary quality' is fluid, subject to constant imperceptible amendments. For example, the adoption of the once-marginal John Donne as a cornerstone of academic English Literature (there was no modern edition of Donne until 1872) similarly almost reversed the consensus on what constituted 'literary quality', bringing the wheel full circle by relegating the prevailing modes of the eighteenth century to an inferior place. This argument could be protracted indefinitely, but the point is clear: 'literary quality' is as shifting as are the boundaries of the canon themselves and should not be applied rashly as a criterion for excluding the 'other voices' of any period, far less of one in which some of those voices occupied, for a brief period, the centre of attention.

It might be more useful to evaluate poetic success in terms of a poet's intentions and the audience to which a poem was originally directed. Thus the calm understatements of Gertrude Aston's poems (nos. 31, 133–4) are appropriate to their intended coterie readership, are appropriate to poems which address an audience who share both religious and social certainties with the poet. There is no need for the public attention-grabbing of the baroque style, the whirling caught breaths and inspirations of Crashaw, where the plain style which persisted as a viable mode of English poetry from the sixteenth century answers perfectly to the purpose of the poems. Similarly, Anne Kemp's lamenting prospect-poem (no. 223) sits comfortably within its undemonstrative couplets, the form of Katherine Philips's retired meditations: form and intention are again in accord.

The range of styles in which the more radical 'other voices' work should offer few difficulties to the modern reader, although it is worth remembering that the radical poets have certain encodements of style and allusion of their own. Their style is often one of a set of possible variants on ballad metre, the vehicle of popular poetry in English and Scots for centuries; these rhythmically flexible rhymed quatrains are very much part of a continuing tradition of popular verse. Encodement comes in where a particular ballad tune has particular connotations: this is clearly a system of signs familiar both to vernacular writers and to élite writers appropriating a popular style. Thus the tune 'Tom a Bedlam' to which Richard Corbet sets his anti-Puritan verses (no. 229) signals immediately to the listener that Corbet has made the simple equation of religious extremism and madness; the 'Weladay' refrain of no. 245 associates with a long-popular ballad on the Passion of Christ, and thus puts its subject, the execution of Charles I, in direct parallel with the death of Christ. The tune which was composed for no. 243 came to have an identity of its own in the mid-century, as a royalist statement. It is not impossible that no. 311, Marvell's 'The Unfortunate Lover', picks up hints of the tune and even runs of words from Parker's ballad as part of its complex tissue of political allusion. The tune of Parker's ballad had also an eighteenth-century afterlife when the Stuart royal family was again in exile and opposition.

Apart from this, the chief allusive source for the radical writers is the Bible, a text known intimately and appropriated as often as classical antiquity was appropriated by the élite poets. Biblical citations are very often given as side-notes or end-notes to the original texts of the poems, claiming the authority of the Book for spontaneous compositions. In Anna Trapnel's prophetic songs, the Apocalypse, the prophecy of the last days which ends the Bible, is omnipresent. It is the degree of mapping of the last days on to the England of the 1650s which is important here. Just as classical Rome and seventeenth-century England were coexistent for the royalist poets, so the Bible was a living guide for prophetic radicals to the present and future of England.

4. REWRITING THE ENEMY

This is not the place for large historical speculations on allegiance and loyalty in the turmoil of the mid-seventeenth century. What is, however, potentially useful is to give brief consideration to the way in which writers of both sides defined and strengthened their own identities by exclusion, by inscribing the otherness, the wrongness and inhumanity of the opposition. It might be possible to argue that many of the conflicts of early-modern England, from the Civil War to the Hanoverian settlement, were fuelled by this very rhetorical process. Early-modern England worked to a notable extent by negative definition: that all groups were quicker to define themselves by what they were not than by what they were. It is very easy for genuine dissension to resolve almost instantly into tribalism, labelling, othering. It is significant that one of the first pieces of legislation of the restored Charles II was an act against exactly this sort of automatically divisive labelling. The 'Act of Oblivion and Indemnity' specifically prohibited the calling of

> any name or names, or other words of reproach tending to revive the memory of the late differences or the occasions thereof

a provision which can be seen as rooted in a pragmatic awareness of the extent to which labelling and generalization can be as powerful in promoting conflict as genuine grievance or meditated ideology.

The history of othering in Europe is long and unhappy. There are stock accusations which have been levelled throughout history against any group, usually a marginal group, by which the centre of society feels threatened. These have been variously applied to religious opponents, heretics, Jews, lepers, Templars, Anabaptists, witches. These charges, revived as each wave of paranoia swept the various centres of society, are what might be expected. They are calculated to dehumanize and diabolize those against whom they are levelled: sexual deviance, child-murder, conspiracy to overthrow all settled social distinctions, conspiracy to overthrow 'true religion'. Aside from such extreme allegations, the essential charge levelled at the 'other' is that they are attempting to subvert the economic and social norms by which the threatened centre conducts its life. Echoes of the rhetoric of othering are still to be heard in Britain at time of writing, most obviously in the degraded vocabulary of racial hatred, but also, more significantly, in the disproportionate fear and hatred directed against the comparatively small contingent of 'new age travellers': the discourse directed against them is remarkably close to the élite perceptions of 1640s beggars recorded in Richard Brome's *A Joviall Crew*. Discourses of othering are also aimed at those who would perceive themselves as unequivocally 'the centre' of contemporary Britain. This operates particularly in local responses to economically privileged settlers from south-eastern England in the more economically vulnerable parts of Wales and Scotland. This is not to say that English settlers are routinely accused of eating their children, rather that the groundswell of objection to them is rooted in the old rhetoric: that they are the agents of the subversion both of the economy and of the moral and social consensus of the host community.

When the propagandists of the mid-seventeenth century began to work on othering their respective enemies, they had an immediate tradition on which to draw: the fortress or *laager* mentality which the ruling élite deliberately fostered in Elizabethan England. There were clear advantages to the élite in so doing: unitary pressure towards conformity was exerted on a diverse society by the threat of the enemy without. Loyalty and religious conformity could be presented as an active necessity in the life of the individual citizen, in the face of the threat from the enemy within. The other for the Elizabethans was the whole of Catholic Europe: the other within England was identified as the English Catholics and their missionary priests. This single strand of othering is visible at all levels of literature and public discourse: it is manifested in the allegories and origin-myths of Spenser's *Faerie Queene*. It surfaces at a popular and local level in scares and rumours of Jesuit plots. It is the enterprise of othering which gives John Webster's plays, set amongst the élites of Catholic Europe, their primary *raison d'être*. The terror inscribed in Shakespeare's *Othello* focuses on the potential relapse of the other brought into society: the fear that any outsider allowed inside the defences which protect society may relapse into barbarism once inside. The fears articulated in *Othello* move in parallel to the fears of Jacobean England directed at those in England who could be seen as having divided, foreign allegiances because of religious difference. This terror was impelled into paranoia by the Gunpowder Plot, which was publicly interpreted as the result of allowing the enemies within sufficient freedom that they could work their way to the constitutional heart of the fortress. The other strand of Elizabethan othering which resurfaces in the mid-seventeenth century is the othering which forms an inevitable part of the colonial process: the denigration of the neighbouring barbarians, presented as so dehumanized that their only possible future lies in the hands of a benign colonial conqueror. Thus the shapes and traditions of Irish society were deliberately perceived as barbarous (the word 'barbarous' itself is a Greek term of othering: those who speak babble and nonsense rather than proper Greek). The allegations refine themselves into what become the standard accusations of the Civil War period: that the marginal Celts, with their alien language and religion (and their tradition of pastoral rather than cereal-based farming), are the foes to 'good husbandry' with all that that phrase implies both for the cultivation of the land and the preservation of the hierarchies of settled patriarchal society. Much is revealed about the priorities of the early-modern mentality, in this connection and juxtaposition of inadequate cultivation of the land with sexual promiscuity and deviance.

The otherings of Civil War propaganda have their roots in this Tudor discourse. The othering of the royalists, their dehumanization in parliamentarian propaganda, essentially picks up on the strategies of denigration which had been applied by the Elizabethans to the English and foreign Catholics. Because of the foreign religion of Henrietta Maria, and because Charles I was widely perceived as moving the English Church towards Catholicism, the extension of discourse was easy. Interestingly, parliamentarian and radical othering of the royalists does not generally present them as conservatives: they are presented as innovators, attempting to force the social harmony originating in an imaginary Tudor golden age in the direction of foreign political and religious absolutism. The term 'cavalier' itself is the foundation of this discourse: 'cavaliero'—the licensed, élite soldiery of absolutism, the unconstitutional executives of arbitrary rule. Much of the Elizabethan *bricolage* of hate survives as well: the anti-Catholic 'black legend', rumours of initial subversion leading to rule by inquisition, of the enslavement of the spiritually and constitutionally free citizen. This is the centre of parliamentarian othering. Dehumanizing allegations are selectively directed against the royalists: allegations of war atrocities, of rape and robbery are not uncommon. The verses by Gerard Winstanley at the head of this Introduction use a discourse which survived into the nineteenth century, hinting at an aesthetically and spiritually dangerous nexus of foreign aestheticism in life, literature, and religion, with buried suggestions of deviant sexuality.

The royalist allegations against the parliament and the radicals essentially turn on an opposed interpretation of conservatism and the past. The royalists saw themselves as the conservative guardians of the traditional social order. To them, the King had a sacred right to governance of Church and State, so much so that his actions, however innovative, were seen as instantly assimilated to the traditional and desirable ordering of society. It is unsurprising, therefore, that royalist othering of the enemy focuses on social subversion, on the centrally frightening image of 'the world turned upside down'. The social, religious, and military actions of the parliament are always presented as pseudo-action, the charades of a mock-élite of low origins, revealing the vices of the petty bourgeoisie the more that they show themselves in positions of power or authority.

Sexual allegations against the parliament focus themselves in the traditional patterns: the most radical theories of marriage are held to apply to all the opposition. Thus they are continually depicted as scheming to overthrow the institution as well as the church sacrament of marriage: a direct attack on the normative 'good husbandry' of early-modern propaganda. The social and financial ambitions of upstarts are also inscribed as an attack on 'good husbandry': parliamentarian fines and sequestrations of royalist goods and estates are seen as a central attack on the ownership of property and land, as an attack on the fruitful body of the British island.

Two metropolitan dramatic works dating from the beginning of the war show these images in operation, and will serve to bring this survey to a close. The use of the imagery of social reversal in Richard Brome's last comedy before the closing of the theatres, *A Joviall Crew* (1641), and the last of the Caroline court masques, *Salmacida Spoilia* (performed 21 January 1640), follows the same lines of royalist othering of the enemy.

In Brome's play, a single metaphor dominates the action, that of social reversal and the breakdown of traditional class distinction. The play juxtaposes two opposed social groups: a provincial rural élite and the beggars. The metaphor of reversal and marginalization operates through a plot that shows the young élite characters trying on the identities of the marginal beggars as a response to the breakdown of social distinction which they perceive in the nation around them. At the end of the play, the beggars perform a kind of masque for the squires and justices: one argument of the masque is that all England is being reduced to the condition of the marginalized beggars.

Salmacida Spoilia is an extraordinary extension of the set forms and genres of the court masque, responding by its inversion of the masque-world of the court to 'the world turned upside down' outside the privileged space of the palace. The usual form of the Stuart court masque is in three parts: introduction, anti-masque, and masque. The anti-masque traditionally presents those opposed to the Stuart court consensus as figures of otherness: witches, enchanters, enemy knights. In the usual form of the masque, these figures are swept away and banished by the disguised courtiers who are the protagonists of the masque proper and the entertainment resolves in the praise of the social order which derives from the monarch. These rules are stretched in Davenant's last masque: where previously the anti-masques, the intrusions of the disorderly other, had been relatively short in proportion to the entertainment as a whole, here they dominate the scene. There are anti-masques of insurgents and hermeticists, of the storm-lit forces of the radical carnival. The introductory part of the masque also includes a curious scene of poised allegory in which 'the Good Genius of Great Britain' is shown in the heavens, hovering over troubled England. (This is a clear parallel with the classical allegory by which Justice, 'Astrea', left the earth at the end of the golden age, the mythical happy past.) The resolution of the masque is edgy and tentative. Charles is depicted as 'Philogenes', 'the lover of his people' bringing conflict to an end and offering his people (and the chief spectator Marie de Médicis) a vision of what the monarchy might have achieved. This ending is far from triumphalist (however inappropriately) in that the texts of the songs question the stage-picture of Stuart absolutism in apotheosis. The words of these songs seem to belong not to the world of court triumphs, but rather to the orchestration of the propagandist iconography of royalist defeat which is the subject of the conclusion of this Introduction.

> O who but he thus could endure
> To live and govern in a sullen age
> When it is harder far to cure
> The people's folly than resist their rage?

5. READING PICTURES

This last section will focus very briefly on some uses of iconography and allusion in Civil War writing. The whole subject of the use of visual images as communication devices and signs in the early-modern period can only be glanced at here. Rather than generalize, I will offer specific examples of how this kind of reading helps one to understand Marvell, to illustrate how a historicist reading, an attempt to decode a poem within the terms of its own time, can sometimes be a highly fruitful strategy for the modern reader. (I have attempted throughout this book to provide the reader with the required specialist knowledge, both in the notes to individual poems and in the Appendices.)

First, then, two examples of the use of allusion, of which the first example is the simplest: it demonstrates how an understood reference to a single line from a classical poet can tip the balance to alter the whole emphasis of an early-modern poem. The criticism of Marvell's '*An* Horatian *Ode upon* Cromwel's *Return from* Ireland' (no. 313) has long focused on the central, and ultimately misdirected, question of whether Marvell is celebrating or denigrating Cromwell. It is, however, agreed that the poem is extremely indirect and allusive, even by

Marvell's own standards of reticence and obliquity. The real problem with poising the final reading of a poem which has maintained a tightrope balance throughout between praise of Cromwell and praise of the dead King, comes in the last two stanzas, which describe Cromwell as a huntsman in chase of the 'Caledonian deer' (the generalized royalist Scot, or possibly the Marquis of Montrose), using a highly technical vocabulary. Marvell appears on a superficial reading to be describing a successful hunt and then going on to urge Cromwell to vigilance on behalf of his people. But, by the rules of early-modern hunting, the hunt goes wrong: the deer is started and the chase moves to the kill. At this point, the poem swerves away, the deer escapes (though the syntax suggests this is only one of various possibilities). The proper end of the hunt is that the huntsman should use his sword to kill the deer—the deer which is last seen lying-up in an already-searched thicket ('tufted brake')—while Cromwell's sword, instead of being used for the 'last effect' of the hunt, turns into the sword of Aeneas. In Book VI of the *Aeneid*, when the hero descends to hell to discover the future of his people, his sword is drawn (l. 294) only to keep the ghosts at bay.

Still keep thy Sword erect:
Besides the force it has to fright
The Spirits of the shady Night.

So Cromwell's sword is diverted into a weapon useful only against the clustering ghosts of those killed in the wars: it is disabled from functioning as it should to give the final blow to the hopes of the royalists. Once the connection with Book VI of the *Aeneid* has been made, other possibilities emerge: the 'shady night' of Marvell's poem derives from Virgil's simile for Aeneas' journey to hell (ll. 268–72), a passage which also writes indirectly about the isolation of the ruler and of the inhuman demands made by leadership.

> They went lonely through the shadows under the night, through the empty halls of Dis and the kingdom of nothingness; like one who travels through a wood by the unfavourable light of an uncertain moon, when Jupiter has hidden the sky with shadows, and black night has stolen the colour away from things.

A reading of the poem, in the light of this, has to remain consciously poised and ambiguous: Cromwell is neither celebrated nor denigrated, the poem remains in suspension on a statement of hard fact:

The same *Arts* that did *gain*
A *Pow'r* must it *maintain*.

They that take the sword shall perish by the sword. A similar illumination from the *Aeneid* helps to form a reading of Marvell's '*The Nymph complaining for the death of her* Faun'. This is a deceptive, elusive poem, continually frustrating the reader by hints of contemporary or religious reference. On the surface it is simply an imagined lamentation spoken by a nymph for a pet faun which has been killed at random by passing soldiers. One illumination from Virgil cannot unriddle the whole poem, it is far too subtle, far too polysemic for that. However, the allusion to the death of a pet faun in the seventh book of the *Aeneid* (ll. 483 onwards) serves to root at least one of the strands of Marvell's poem as a lamentation for the condition of a country desolated by civil war. At this point in Virgil's poem, Aeneas and the refugee Trojans have arrived in the country of their promised empire, Italy, and the indigenous Italians are initially friendly. The implacable gods, however, stir up civil war; and the beginning of this war comes when Aeneas' son shoots the pet stag of the royal herdsman's daughter, Silvia. Suddenly the connections of Marvell's poem are clear at least in one aspect: he is writing a lament, spoken by the Silvia in Virgil's text, he is creating a passage which could have occurred at this point in the *Aeneid*. This interpolation maps the beginning of the most celebrated treatment of civil war in classical literature on to the condition of the British islands in the 1640s. Other elements of the poem attain new explicitness from this emphasis: the description of gardens vulnerable to assault from the wilderness comes into relationship with the trope of royalist lamentation for a spoiled garden used by the historian Clarendon in the passage quoted above. The more the two texts, Marvell's and Virgil's, are read in parallel, the more this directive intertextuality emerges.

The case of Marvell's mysterious poem 'The Unfortunate Lover' (no. 311) is clarified not by reference to a classical poet, but by reference to propaganda images circulating on the continent amongst the exiled royalists. It is perhaps necessary to say at once that I am not claiming this as an unequivocally royalist poem on the strength of these connections. What is clarified by the reference to the iconography of royalist defeat is the subject of the poem, which would appear to be an allegorical painting of the exiled Charles II. However, the way in which the poem develops preserves the ambiguity of Marvell's own response to such a picture.

Marvell's poem focuses on the central image of a wounded and bleeding lover on a rock in a stormy sea. There are two contemporary accounts which suggest that such a picture actually existed and that Charles II and his brother the future James II were both depicted in such an allegorical setting. The allegory develops accepted and widespread early-modern visual symbols of royalty in adversity. The first account relates to an allegorical depiction of James II, seen by Sir Richard Fanshawe in the year 1648 in the course of his continental exile. (Marvell travelled through France in 1648, so the connection seems valid.) Fanshawe first describes the image:

> he is represented as one in peril on a stormy sea, the captain thrown overboard, the ship broken up, thrust upon a rock, but clinging to an anchor, the trident of the ruler of the sea

and then addresses the image in terms which relate very closely to Marvell's poem

> Yet sink down, ye waves, lest he should clothe himself in fury like yours, he in whom rough valour lies hidden under a gentle countenance.

Corroboration that such imagery circulated on the Continent comes from the Dutch polymath Constantijn Huygens, who addressed a poem to a depiction of Charles II in a poem prefixed to a pamphlet published in the year of the Restoration. (The poem is called 'Op de afbeelding van Carel de Tweede, Coning van Groot Britannien', 'On the depiction of Charles II, king of Great Britain' and comes from *De Historie van Karel de Tweede*, published at Dordrecht in 1660.) It again picks up the storm imagery of Marvell's poem:

> geduldigh in den noot
> En tegens allen Storm, en tegens allen Donder

('patient in distress, and against all storms and against all thunder'), providing thereby a triangulation, a mapping which enables us with some confidence to read Marvell's poem as directly concerning itself with a propagandist allegory of Charles II. Marvell's last lines, reread in this light, suddenly come clear to support the reading. ('Story' in early-modern English can mean 'depiction' or 'legendary picture' as often as it carries the modern sense of the word.)

> And he in story only rules,
> In a field sable a lover gules.

No such specialized information, thankfully, is needed for the explication of most of the poems in this collection, but it is a useful closing reflection that our understanding of the ways in which some mid-seventeenth-century poetry works is greatly deepened by reading that poetry as part of a cultural continuum, rather than in the selective isolation of old literary studies whereby 'high' and 'low' poetry of the same period were kept apart and poetry was not read in the context of the cultural milieu which produced it. I hope that some of that cultural contexting has been performed by the inclusiveness of the selection of poems for this book. Readers can deepen that context further for themselves by historical reading, by reading the vigorous and diverse prose of the Civil War period, and by looking at the visual artefacts of the time, which often work in parallel with its verse. There are the vernacular woodcuts of radical and parliamentarian propaganda and journalism to be read in opposition to the mystical, crypto-sacred depictions of Charles I which circulated after his death. Further illumination of Marvell's poems could indeed be drawn from the emblematic stormy sea depicted in the crucial visual image of Charles as martyr, the frontispiece to the *Eikon Basilike* of 1649.

This image is of the King at prayer, his eyes fixed on a heavenly crown, his feet spurning an earthly crown. In the background is a darkened landscape: trees, seashore, storm.

What this is telling the viewer seems clear: the King is a martyr, half-paralleled with the suffering Christ. His qualities have emerged more clearly out of the landscape of earthly suffering: the events of war and defeat, which are represented by the left-hand half of the picture. He looks to the light which streams from the top right, his back is turned to the scene of his trials. The eye scanning the picture, after it has registered the 'King as martyr' image encoded in the figure, is going to begin reading the image again scanning from the left, following thus the King's emblematic history. At the left of the landscape is a weighted palm-tree with its inscription 'crescit sub pondere virtus' ('virtue grows under pressure'). This emblem has a long history, having been used as the image of constancy in adversity by Charles IX of France, as well as by the persecuted French Huguenots. This is the first image to register on the eye, which then moves to the black stormy sea with its rock inscribed 'immota triumphans' ('triumphing unmoved'). This is telling us again about Charles's reaction to adversity. The tranquil rock in the storm is expressive of fixed resolution, reminiscent as it is of the emblem of the battered and unmoved rock found in that most popular of English emblem-books, Geoffrey Whitney's *A Choice of Emblems* (1586), as the symbol of moral constancy. This image also echoes the motto of William the Silent, first ruler of beleaguered Holland, 'saevis tranquillus in undis' ('unmoved amidst the wild waters'): a specific image of royal survival in adversity. From the clouds above the rock, that is, from the part of the picture emblematically representing the centre of the troubled world which the King rejects to fix his eyes and mind on heaven, another beam of light is inscribed 'Clarior e tenebris' ('Brighter because of the shadows'). The continuity with the world in which Marvell's poem moves is clear.

When this kind of image is read in conjunction with other manipulations of the iconography of royalist defeat (perhaps with the nostalgic portraits which William Dobson painted during the last beleaguered years of the court at Oxford) the visual culture and the verbal culture form a whole. The same applies equally to the carnival woodcuts of the years of revolution and to the vigorous street-poetry of the radicals. It is chiefly by such actions of inclusive reading and looking that the modern reader can begin to penetrate the mentality of a crucial period in the past of the British islands.

NOTE ON THE TEXT AND ANNOTATION

If Renaissance texts were circulated and read in a diversity of ways which now appear foreign to the reader conditioned by the idea of an invariable progression from author to printer to public, the problems of diversity of kinds of publication apply even more acutely to the period of the reign of Charles I, the civil war and the interregnum. In the late 1620s and for most of the 1630s the pattern of circulation was very much as it had been at the beginning of the century: print, although on the increase, was far from being the exclusive medium for the circulation of poetry. Poems continued to circulate in manuscript just as much as they had done previously. The poems of a Caroline poet now as canonical as Henry King were not printed as a collection with their author's approval: for all but a handful of his poems the modern editor is still dependent on three scribal manuscripts compiled with care apparently under his direction (see nos. 12–14 in this book). The same might be said to apply to Charles Cotton, who published no collection in his lifetime, and even to Sir Richard Fanshawe, a typically transitional figure whose career spanned the mid-century, who clearly tried careful scribal publication in the 1630s, before committing his poems to deliberate and public print in the late 1640s (see nos. 205, 206). Fanshawe went on to take unusual care in correcting his English poems for the press, causing a revised issue of his Horatian translations to be issued within a few months of the first, imperfect appearance of the book. In this particular case the delay between publication and correction was caused by the imprisonment of the author: a fact which in itself gives some idea of the further random complexities of publication and authorship in a society in turmoil. Fanshawe brings the wheel of possibilities full circle by having made manuscript corrections of printer's errors in the copies of his later books which he gave to his friends. What is true of a poet and translator of the middle rank, is also to a considerable extent true of major figures including Marvell and Milton. Marvell published no collection in his lifetime, although the existence of Marvellian poems such as no. 79 in this book is obviously evidence for the circulation of his works in manuscript. When Marvell's poems eventually reached print, in 1681, the chief reasons for their publication seem to have had, in fact, little or no connection with considerations of literary merit or reputation. For the 'Mary Marvell' who signed the preface, and presumably owned the copy-text, the publication was part of a campaign to assert her married status and her claim on some tenements near what later became the site of the British Library. Even then, two poems on Cromwell (including the far from simply laudatory no. 313) were cancelled from most copies while the edition was going through the press. The circulation of poetry is not only complicated in the period covered by this book by a surviving ambivalence about print or circulated manuscript as the preferred medium: events, censorship and political considerations serve further to complicate the process.

So far there have been hints of the extent to which political circumstances served to complicate the publication of canonical or elite poetry: what also must be remembered is that civil disorder, changing policies, and changed priorities opened the means of the circulation of verse and prose to those who had before had comparatively little access to print other than to that genre of popular writing which is typified by such phrases as 'come all ye young women, take warning by me.'

For both these groups of writers, traditional élite and newly-articulate, the conditions of war, censorship, and civil unrest bred perhaps a genuine committment to print, to circulation of words intended as interventions in developing events. While, on the one hand, this sometimes produced a stronger bond between printer and writer than had been usual before, on the other, it enforced conditions even more productive of random error than the usual pressures of the early-modern printing house. The prophetic verses of Anna Trapnel (nos. 159–161) were taken down, printed and published apparently by a group of her friends and sympathisers: the resultant volume, surviving in an unique copy in the Bodleian Library, is, considering the circumstances of its production, a most meticulous piece of printing. Conversely, the degree of variation between the two texts of Thomas Jordan's satirical litany (no. 228) gives some idea of the conditions attending the publication of a poem which is meant, urgently, to work on public opinion, but a poem which has to be printed, because of that very urgency, in secrecy and in haste. Circumstances could do more than that to a writer: by the time that Richard Crashaw was at liberty to publish the openly Catholic versions of nos. 140 and 141 he was in exile and dependent on a printer ignorant of the language in which the poems were written. I have given Crashaw's texts in all their exiled roughness, feeling that their imperfection is itself eloquent of the realities of the 1650s. For similar reasons, I have (experimentally) preferred a manuscript, circulating text of no. 37 over a normalised printed version, to give some sense of the form in which an accomplished and popular poem appeared to its first generation of readers.

As we move further towards what might conventionally be perceived as the margins of literary activity, randomness of text intensifies. Scribe and printer are no longer neccessarily the intermediaries: time, memory, language and the stonemason may equally be factors affecting the transmission of text. The remarkable epitaphs which constitute the surviving works of Katherine Dyer (nos. 22 and 127) have been transcribed from the original inscriptions: the diffiult reading in line 20 of no. 22 (surely a stonecutter's omission dictated by spacing) enforced an uncomfortably transgressive moment of climbing into the monument between the life-size effigies of the Dyers. The writings of the circle of poets centring on Tixall in Staffordshire survive, for the most part, only in an antiquarian's transcriptions from the Walter Scott period (and in an anthology undertaken, I suspect, at Scott's instigation). A nationalist printer in early eighteenth-century Edinburgh preserved the majority of the poems attributed to the Marquis of Montrose (nos. 46–8, 268–274) at the end of a collection of determinedly Scottish verse produced when, or because, Scotland was sliding towards the cultural dilution of the 1707 Union. When we move outside

English-language poetry, the textual problems radically change their nature: at least one poem (no. 324) is an unmistakable account of a specific event of 1645, but was carried from human memory to human memory for nearly three centuries before reaching writing, far less print. To a greater or lesser extent, many of the Irish, Welsh and Gaelic poems in this book have similarly had a purely oral existence for the first part of their history.

Political dissidence can render an author anonymous or pseudonymous for simple prudential reasons (the child who wrote no. 163 is named in a Recusant manuscript which leaves all other poems unattributed, probably because she is legally too young to answer for her utterance), or can cause diverse and improbable texts to be attributed to a named figure of contemporary significance, as is the case with the chaotic attributions clustering round John Cleveland and the Marquis of Montrose.

The mid-seventeenth century reader (we have perhaps to assume a reader as voracious, as eclectic as the London bookseller George Thomason) would, like the Renaissance reader, be accustomed to very divergent levels of formaliity in the presentation of texts, and would also be puzzled by the idea of a 'correct' text fixed in all its details. They would have been very accustomed to intertextuality: to parody, dittying, allusion, appropriation.

The editorial policies for this edition have been formed by the very diversity which it seeks to represent: texts are in general reproduced from copy-text with all their idiosyncrasies of presentation intact. Rather than trying to identify an earliest or 'most authorial' text in every case, weight has been given to the form in which a poem circulated in the period. This moves in parallel with the inclusion of some texts (no. 257, for example) which clearly originate well before the accession of Charles I, but which gain a new identity as poems which can be seen as referring to contemporary events, and circulate widely as such. In a similar way, some poems are included which were written well after the Restoration but in the mode of the mid-century. This bias towards the form in which a poem worked at the time has, to a great extent, governed such decisions as the choice of copy-text for Waller's 'To the KING, upon his Majesties Happy Return' (no. 336) which is given from the pamphlet of 1660, not from any subsequent, more polished version. A large number of the poems given here only survive in one text; a very few survive in a diversity of texts, apparently remote in time and transmission from any authorial original. In these cases variants have been given in some detail, and the reader is as free as the editor to attempt a recension. Composite texts have been avoided (except in the unavoidable case of nos. 140 and 141, where missing lines have been supplied from an earlier edition). Complete poems have been given where possible: poems of impossible length, containing matter which seemed essential to the shape of the anthology (no. 342) have been given in extract, but the reader must be warned that the shape and the agenda in these cases are the editor's and not the poet's. To summarise: the versions of the poems given here are, wherever possible, versions which were in existence and circulation in the period which the anthology covers. It is now unknowable in most cases whether they represent their author's final intentions, if we can assume that their authors had any such thing. We should, indeed, beware of assuming that even an authorial fair-copy manuscript is in any real sense 'final': the poems by Mary Wroth (nos. 4–7) exist in just such a manuscript, but it is abundantly clear that the author herself looked to the printer to give the texts their final form. Unavoidably, a number of pamphlet and propaganda texts have had to be given from the only versions which survive, many of them dating from after the Restoration.

Many of the texts in this book exist in modern, scholarly editions. A good number, however, are given here for the first time. As well as recording the copy-text from which an edition is taken (and trying to explain the history of that copy-text wherever it is relevant or interesting) the Notes to the Text record the best or most accessible (usually Penguin) modern edition. (I have not recorded rare interim editions, mostly those of nineteenth century antiquarians, which are often as hard to find as their early-modern originals.)

I have used the same guides and works of reference as *The Penguin Book of Renaissance Verse*: A.W. Pollard and G.R. Redgrave, *A Short-Title Catalogue of Books Printed in England, Scotland & Ireland and of English Books Printed Abroad 1475–1640*, 2nd edn, revised and enlarged by W.A. Jackson and F.S. Ferguson, completed by Katherine F. Pantzer, 3 vols., 1976–91; Donald G. Wing, *Short Title Catalogue of Books Printed in England and America 1641–1700*, 2nd edn., 3 vols., New York 1972–88. Supplementary information on printing and publishing can be found in *A Transcript of the Registers of the Stationers' Company* of London: 1554–1640, 5 vols., London and Birmingham, 1875–94, edited by Edward Arber. For certain authors, those who form the central spine of the old canon, the fullest information on MS texts can be found in volume 2 of Peter Beal's *Index of English Literary Manuscripts*,1987—. Margaret Crum's *First-Line Index of English Poetry 1500–1800 in Manuscripts of the Bodleian Library Oxford*, 2 vols.,Oxford 1969, has been invaluable for this book, allowing as it does an instant means of locating different copies of a text, and of browsing around the names of less well-known poets. Maureen Bell, George Parfitt and Simon Shepherd's *A Biographical Dictionary of English Women Writers 1580–1720*, Harvester Wheatsheaf, Hemel Hempstead 1990, is a useful tool for preliminary work. Beyond these guides, for the mid-seventeenth century, there are two vital collections of pamphlet literature: that of George Thomason, a London bookseller, in the British Library and of the Oxford Antiquary Anthony Wood in the Bodleian Library. Nigel Smith's *Literature and Revolution in England, 1640–1660* provides a comprehensive companion to much of the material collected by Thomason and Wood.

This edition has examined almost all texts afresh: the exceptions are the Irish and Welsh texts which have been taken from standard editions, although all translations from the Welsh were undertaken specially for this book and translations from the Irish have been recast and revised; Gaelic texts, based as they frequently are on nineteenth-century transcriptions of pieces preserved by oral tradition, have been re-examined by Meg Bateman and Colm O Baoill. It must be said that it is rare for the English texts given here to diverge in more than the smallest details from the monumental series of recensions published by the Clarendon Press, they are, on the other hand often very divergent from the normalised editions of the early twentieth century. It must be emphasised that the recording of variant readings in the Notes on the Text is highly selective: in most cases, particularly where there is a Clarendon edition of an established author, I have recorded variants sparingly, if at all. An exception is Richard Crashaw; a full collation of variants for two of his religious poems seems to offer information on revisions which it is perhaps rather hard to extract at a glance from the Clarendon edition. I have always given authorial manuscript interpolations in printed or scribal texts where these have been traced. The poems for which most variants are recorded are those whose surviving texts are particularly remote from the author. For those poems which I have, deliberately, given from manuscript in preference to a printed edition, the more important substantive variants are recorded. All variations from copy-text, with the exception of the silent correction of faulty accidentals, are recorded. Thus, readings in Notes to the Text which have no attributed authority may be assumed to be editorial emendations.

References to early-modern printed editions in Notes to the Text, are by the page on which the poem is found. In cases where the page number is in error within the sequence of the copy-text it is given as found, in inverted commas, followed by the 'correct' number in square brackets. Where the copy-text is not paginated, references are to printer's signatures, the numbers and letters at the foot of the page with which the printer kept track of the gatherings in which the book was printed. References to manuscripts are given by folio numbers, or where the manuscript has a consistent system of contemporary pagination, by pages. With signatures and folio numbers, r indicates the recto (right-hand) leaf, and v the verso (left-hand) leaf.

It is to be hoped that old spelling and punctuation will cause less trouble to readers now than they might have done even a decade ago, but there is real alternative, short of actually translating or falsifying the majority of the texts, particularly in a book which addresses itself partly to historians and which aspires in some ways to the condition of the documentary. To impose modern conventions of presentation, even on those manuscript poems whose punctuation and capitalization is minimal, would inevitably result in some degree in pastiche, or in the creation of a hybrid. With the more carefully presented printed texts of the period, where the punctuation is carefully worked out within a convention governed by reading aloud, rather than by the marking of grammatical units, re-punctuation would constitute a serious falsification. In the very few cases where the thinness of the punctuation would be liable to lead a modern reader into confusion in reading the syntax (most conspicuously no. 139) brief paraphrases are supplied in the explanatory footnotes. In the end, to have attempted any kind of modernisation of punctuation or spelling would have resulted in a futile attempt to impose some kind of uniformity on a collection of texts whose point and vitality lies in their very diversity.

There are a few conventions of presentation, gratuitously misleading to the modern reader, which have, however, been emended: following essentially the spelling conventions of Latin, seventeenth century writers treat both upper- and lower-case 'i' and 'j' as the same letter, and treat upper- and lower-case 'u' and 'v' as equally interchangable. (The layout of a printer's type-case still enshrines this convention.) These letters have been given following modern practise throughout. Long 's' has been given as 's' throughout; initial 'ff' has been treated as what it is: a form of upper-case 'f'. Contractions of words, whether indicated originally by superscript or by a tilde placed over the line have been expanded. Raised letters have been lowered. Ampersand for 'and' and various forms of 'etc' have been retained as unlikely to obtrude on, or delay, the modern reader. Purely typographic conventions have been silently brought into line with modern practise: thus, dropped or ornamented initial capitals, and the purely aesthetic custom of printing all or part of the first word or words of a text in upper-case are not preserved. Authors' names at the ends of poems, and such terminations as 'Finis' or 'The End' have also been omitted. Where the stanzas of a poem are numbered in the original, the numbering is preserved: this is particularly important in cases such as no. 36 where the numbers and letters which divide the stanzas also serve to indicate the two speakers in the dialogue. The typography of titles of poems is preserved as regards use of upper case, roman and italic, although lineation and type-size is not represented. (Presentation of titles has been simplified for the Contents and Index.) Where a title is lacking and has been supplied from the title of the work in which the poem appears, the same conventions apply as in the contents and indices of this book. Layout of poems on the page is reproduced throughout as in the copy-text, with no attempt being made to rearrange lineation. In practise, for this period, there is very little (except perhaps the strange, obsessive little prose-poem (no.281) which is itself an odd poem in an early-modern context) in this collection which will give the contemporary reader any difficulty. There is, however, just enough strangeness in the presentation of the texts to remind the reader that they *are* texts from the past, produced by conditions and systems of values foreign to the present.

Where a poem has no authorial title, a heading has been supplied in square brackets, either reproducing the first line, or, usually in the case of verse passages from texts otherwise in prose, from long works and from plays, square bracket and *from* is followed by the title of the pamphlet, book or play.

The ordering of the poems has proved particularly difficult, for all the reasons which might be expected in a book which includes so many anonymous and illegally-circulated texts. The solution which has been found does not claim to be ideal: within each section, poems are arranged by date of birth of author, where a date of birth is known. For poems from a particular literary circle presented together, and in cases where a date of birth is not known, a kind of averageing has been attempted on the assumption that the age of thirty will fall within the period of a writer's literary productivity. This still leaves the problems of doubtfully-attributed and anonymous poems: in the first case every effort has been made to find a convincing place within the sequence, usually taking into account both possible period of the most likely author's literary activity and the context in which the poems first appeared. With the anonymous poems, and they are many, the problem is more acute: to have allowed the sheer number of anonymous poems to impose an arrangement by date of first likely circulation would have created a chaotic sequence of conjectures. To have arranged them, and therefore the rest of the book, by date of first publication would, although it might seem a logical proceeding at first, have produced a strange and indigestible set of clusters. The solution which has been adopted is a compromise: to intersperse the undated and anonymous poems through the main sequence governed by the birthdates of known authors. In the fifth part of the book, the poems reflecting the war and revolution, a little experimental freedom has been attempted in the placing of anonymous texts, governed mostly by an attempt to juxtapose opposed poems, and to group together poems which respond to related events.

Annotation is an even greater problem than sequence, with a book such as this which attempts to address itself as much to students of history as students of literature. To avoid constant and distracting mythological and biographical footnotes, Appendix 1 contains a full list of both mythological and Biblical references. The footnotes to the poems simply refer the reader to the relevant entry. Appendix 2 contains short biographies of the contemporary figures, usually those who are referred to more than once in the texts, and again the footnotes to the poems refer the reader to the relevant entry. For the developing events of the years 1625–1660, readers are referred to Appendix 4, which offers a short chronology of the years covered by the book. One poem which engages in extensive detail with the events of one particular year of the war (no. 287) is provided with full annotation below the text, to make reading easier. Where a contemporary figure only appears once in the texts, the biographical note is to be found at the foot of the relevant page, unless there is more relevant information than can be accomodated, in which case the reader is referred to the relevant appendix.

Annotations of words have attempted to confine themselves to words which have changed their meanings, to the elucidation of puns which are now invisible and to the glossing of rare and obsolete words. At any point where the original spelling might possibly obtrude a wrong or irrelevant word on the ear of a modern reader, there is inevitably a gloss. The poems in Scots are obviously glossed more heavily, but with these, as with most apparent difficulties encountered in reading these texts, reading aloud will always go a long way towards the solution of most problems.

PART ONE

FRIENDSHIP, AFFECTION, AND LOVE

LADY TANFIELD

1 [Tomb of Sir Lawrence Tanfield obiit 30 Ap. 1625 erected by Lady Tanfield 1628.]

Here shadow lie
Whil’st life is sadd,
Still hopes to die
To him she hadd

In bliss is hee,
Whom I lov’d best
Thrise happie shee
With him to rest.

So shall I be
With him I loved
And hee with mee
And both us blessed

Love made me Poet
And this I writt,
My harte did doe yt
And not my witt.

SIR FRANCIS KYNASTON

2 ### To Cynthia.

On concealement of her beauty.

Do not conceale thy radiant eyes,
The starre-light of serenest skies,
Least wanting of their heavenly light,
They turne to *Chaos* endlesse night.

Do not conceale those tresses faire,
The silken snares of thy curl’d haire,
Least finding neither gold, nor Ore,
The curious Silke-worme worke no more.

Do not conceale those brests of thine,
More snowe white, then the Apenine,
Least if there be like cold or frost,
The Lilly be for ever lost.

Do not conceale that fragrant scent,
Thy breath, which to all flowers hath lent
Perfumes, least it being suppresst,
No spices growe in all the East.

Do not conceale thy heavenly voice,
Which makes the hearts of gods rejoyce,
Least Musicke hearing no such thing,
The Nightingale forget to sing.

Do not conceale, nor yet eclipse
Thy pearly teeth with Corrall lips,
Least that the Seas cease to bring forth
Gems, which from thee have all their worth.

Do not conceale no beauty grace,
That's either in thy minde or face,
Least vertue overcome by vice,
Make men beleeve no Paradice.

2 4 *Chaos* see Appendix 1 6 *snares* traps 10 *Apenine* Italian mountains, proverbially snowy 21 *eclipse* cover

3

TO CYNTHIA.

On her changing.

Dear *Cynthia*, though thou bear'st the name
Of the pale Queen of night,
Who changing yet is still the same
Renewing still her light:
Who monethly doth her selfe conceal,
And her bright face doth hide,
That she may to *Endymion* steal,
And kisse him unespide.

Do not thou so, not being sure,
When this thy beautie's gone,
Thou such another canst procure,
And wear it as thine owne,
For the by-sliding silent houres,
Conspiratours with grief,
May crop thy beauties lovely flowres,
Time being a slie thief.

Which with his wings will flie away,
And will returne no more;
As having got so rich a prey,
Nature cannot restore:
Reserve thou then, and do not waste
That beauty which is thine,
Cherish those glories which thou hast,
Let not grief make thee pine.

Thinke that the Lilly we behold,
Or July-flower may
Flourish, although the mother mold,
That bred them be away.
There is no cause, nor yet no sence,
That dainty fruits should rot,
Though the tree die, and wither, whence
The Apricots were got.

3 1 *Cynthia* 7 *Endymion* see Appendix 1 26 *July-flower* gillyflower: wallflower or carnation
27 *mold* earth, soil 30 *dainty* delicate, precious

LADY MARY WROTH

4 [Love leave to urge, thou knowest thou hast the hand]

Love leave to urge, thou knowest thou hast the hand
'Tis Cowardize to strive where none resist,
Pray thee leave off, I yeeld unto thy band,
Doe not thus still in thine owne power persist.

Beehold, I yeeld; let forces be dismist,
I am thy Subject conquer'd bound to stand
Never thy foe, but did thy claime assist,
Seeking thy due of those who did withstand.

But now it seemes thou would'st I should thee love,
I doe confesse, 'twas thy will made mee choose,
And thy faire shewes made mee a Lover prove,
When I my freedome did for paine refuse.

Yett this, Sir god, your Boy-ship I despise,
Your charmes I obey, but love not want of eyes.

4 3 *band* constraint 10 *will* male member 13 *Sir god* Cupid, the god of love, the blind son of Venus, see Appendix 1

5 [Griefe, killing griefe: have nott my torments beene]

Griefe, killing griefe, have nott my torments beene,
Already great and strong enough? but still
Thou dost increase, nay glory in mine il,
And woes new past, afresh new woes begin?

Am I the only purchase thou canst win?
Was I ordain'd to give despaire her fill,
Or fittest I should mount misfortunes hill,
Who in the plaine of joy cannot live in?

If it be so, Griefe come as welcome guest,
Since I must suffer for anothers rest;
Yet this (good griefe) let mee intreat of thee,

Use still thy force, but not from those I love
Let me all paines and lasting torments prove;
Soe I miss these, lay all thy waights on mee.

5 8 *plaine* level ground 13 *prove* experience

6 [An end fond Jelousie, alas I know]

An end fond Jelousie, alas I know
Thy hiddenest, and thy most secret Art,
Thou canst no new invention frame but part,
I have already seene, and felt with woe.

All thy dissemblings, which by faigned showe,
Wonne my beliefe, while truth did rule my heart,
I, with glad mind embrac'd, and deemd my smart
The spring of joy, whose streames with blisse
should flow;

I thought excuses had beene reasons true,
And that noe falshood could of thee ensue,
So soone beliefe in honest mindes is wrought;

Butt now I find thy flattery, and skill,
Which idely made me to observe thy will,
Thus is my learning by my bondage bought.

6 14 *bondage* apprenticeship, servitude

7 [When I beheld the Image of my deare]

When I beheld the Image of my deare,
With greedy lookes mine eies would that way bend,
Feare and Desire, did inwardly contend;
Feare to bee mark'd, Desire to draw still neere.

And in my soule a Spirit would appeare,
Which boldnes waranted, and did pretend
To bee my *Genius*; yet I durst nott lend,
My eyes in trust, where others seem'd so cleare,

Then did I search, from whence this danger rose,
If such unworthynesse in me did rest,

As my starv'd eyes must not with sight be blest;
When jealousie her poyson did disclose.

Yett in my heart unseene of Jealous eye,
The truer Image shall in tryumph lye.

7 7 *Genius* guardian spirit 11 *starv'd* deprived, slain

ROBERT HERRICK

8 *To* Electra

More white then whitest Lillies far,
Or Snow, or whitest Swans you are:
More white then are the whitest Creames,
Or Moone-light tinselling the streames:
More white then *Pearls*, or *Juno's* thigh,
Or *Pelops* Arme of *Yvorie*.
True, I confesse; such Whites as these
May me delight, not fully please:
Till, like *Ixion*'s Cloud you be
White, warme, and soft to lye with me.

8 1 *then* than 5 *Juno* 6 *Pelops* 9 *Ixion* see Appendix 1 10 *lye* have sex with

9 *The frozen Zone: or, Julia disdainfull.*

Whither? Say, whither shall I fly,
To slack these flames wherein I frie?
To the Treasures, shall I goe,
Of the Raine, Frost, Haile, and Snow?
Shall I search the under-ground,
Where all Damps, and Mists are found?
Shall I seek (for speedy ease)
All the floods, and frozen seas?

Or descend into the deep,
Where eternall cold does keep?
These may coole; but there's a Zone
Colder yet then any one:
That's my *Julia*'s breast; where dwels
Such destructive Ysicles;
As that the Congelation will
Me sooner starve, then those can kill.

9 Title *Zone* place 2 *slack* slake, cool with water 3–4 see Job 38: 22 'Hast thou entered into the treasures of the snow? or hast thou seen the treasures of the hail?' 15 *Congelation* freezing 16 *starve* slay

10 *Lovers how they come and part.*

A *Gyges* Ring they beare about them still,
To be, and not seen when and where they will,
They tread on clouds, and though they sometimes fall,
They fall like dew, but make no noise at all.
So silently they one to th'other come,
As colours steale into the Peare or Plum,
And Air-like, leave no pression to be seen
Where e're they met, or parting place has been.

10 1 *Gyges* see Appendix 1 7 *pression* impression, mark

11 *A Dialogue betwixt* Horace *and* Lydia, *Translated* Anno 1627. *and set by Mr.* Ro: Ramsey

Hor. WHILE, *Lydia,* I was lov'd of thee,
Nor any was preferr'd 'fore me
To hug thy whitest neck: Then I,
The Persian King liv'd not more happily.

Lyd. While thou no other didst affect,
Nor *Cloe* was of more respect;

Then *Lydia,* far-famed *Lydia,*
I flourish't more then Roman *Ilia.*

Hor. Now *Thracian Cloe* governs me,
Skilfull i'th' Harpe, and Melodie:
For whose affection, *Lydia,* I
(So Fates spares her) am well content to die.

Lyd. My heart now set on fire is
By *Ornithes* sonne, young *Calais;*
For whose commutuall flames here I
(To save his life) twice am content to die.

Hor. Say our first loves we sho'd revoke,
And sever'd, joyne in brazen yoke:
Admit I *Cloe* put away,
And love againe love-cast-off *Lydia?*

Lyd. Though mine be brighter then the Star;
Thou lighter then the Cork by far:
Rough as th' *Adriatick sea*, yet I
Will live with thee, or else for thee will die.

11 Translation of Horace, *Odes* III. 9 (see nos. 74, 119) 1 *Lydia,* 6 *Cloe*, 8 *Ilia*, 14 *Ornithes*, *Calais* see Appendix 1 3 *Then* than 15 *commutuall* reciprocal 17 *revoke* call back

HENRY REINOLDS

12 *A Blackamore Maid wooing a faire Boy.*

Stay lovely Boy, why flyst Thou mee
That languish in these flames for Thee?
I'me black, tis true: why so is Night
And Love does in darke Shades delight.
The whole world, doe but close thine Eye,
Will seeme to Thee as Black as I,

Or op't, and see what a black shade
Is by thine owne faire Body made,
That followes Thee, where e're Thou goe;
(Oh who allow'd would not doe so)
Let mee for ever dwell so nigh
And Thou shalt need no other shade then I.

12 4 *Love* Cupid, see Appendix 1 7 *op't* open it *shade* shadow

HENRY KING

13 *The Boyes answere to the Blackamore*:

Black Maid, complaine not that I fly
When Fate commands Antipathy.
Prodigious might that Union proove
Where Night and Day together moove,
And the Conjunction of our Lips
Not Kisses make but an Eclipse,
In which the mixed black and white
Portends more Terrour then Delight.
Yet if my shadow Thou wilt bee
Enjoy thy dearest wish. But see
Thou take my Shadowes property
That hast's away, when I come nigh
Else stay till Death hath blinded Mee
And then I will bequeath my selfe to Thee.

13 2 *Antipathy* dislike, opposition 3 *Prodigious* monstrous 5 *Conjunction* joining; also, in astrology, the alignment of planets, here imaged as portending disaster and the eclipse of the sun

14 *An Exequy*:

To his Matchles never to bee forgotten Friend.

Accept Thou Shrine of my dead Saint
In stead of Dirges this Complaint,
And for sweet flowers to crowne thy Hearse
Receive a strew of weeping Verse

From thy griev'd Friend; whom Thou might'st see
Quite melted into teares for Thee.
   Deare Losse, since thy untimely Fate
My taske hath beene to meditate
On Thee, on Thee: Thou art the Booke
The Library whereon I looke
Though almost blind. For Thee (Lov'd Clay)
I Languish out, not Live the Day,
Using no other Exercise
But what I practise with mine Eyes.
By which wett glasses I find out
How lazily Tyme creepes about;
To one that mournes, This, only this
My exercise and Bus'nes is:
   So I compute the weary houres
With sighes dissolved into Showres.
Nor wonder if my Tyme goe thus
Backward, and most praeposterous;
Thou hast benighted mee. Thy Sett
This Eve of Blacknes did begett,
Who was't my Day (Though over cast
Before Thou hadst Thy Noone-tyde past)
And I remember must in Teares
Thou scarce hads't seene so many yeares
As Day tells houres. By thy cleare Sun
My Life and Fortune first did runne;
But thou wilt never more appeare
Folded within my Hemispheare,
Since both Thy Light and Motion
Like a fled Starre is fall'n and gone,
And twixt mee, and my Soules deare wish
An Earth now interposed is,
Which such a strange Eclipse doth make
As ne're was read in Almanack.
   I could allow Thee for a tyme
To darken Mee, and my sad Clyme,
Were it a Moneth, a Yeare, or Ten,
I would Thy Exile live till then,
And all that Space my mirth adjourne
So Thou would'st promise to returne,

And putting off Thy ashy Shrowd
At length disperse this Sorrowes Cloud.
   But woe is mee! The longest date
Too narrow is to Calculate
These empty hopes. Never shall I
Be so much blest as to descry
A Glimpse of Thee, till that Day come
Which shall the Earth to Cinders doome,
And a fierce Feaver must calcine
The Body of this World like Thine,
(My little World) That Fitt of Fire
Once off, our Bodyes shall aspire
To our Soules Blisse: Then wee shall rise
And view our Selves with clearer eyes
In that calme Region where no Night
Can hide us from each others sight.
   Meane tyme Thou hast Her Earth: Much good
May my harme doe thee. Since it stood
With Heavn's will, I might not call
Her longer Mine; I give thee all
My short liv'd right and Interest
In Her, whom living I lov'd best.
With a most free and bounteous Griefe
I give Thee what I could not keepe.
Bee kind to Her, and prethee looke
Thou wryte into thy Doomesday Booke,
Each parcell of this Rarity
Which in thy Caskett shrin'd doth lye:
See that thou make thy reck'ning streight,
And yield Her back againe by weight,
For thou must Auditt on thy trust
Each graine and Atome of this Dust
As thou wilt answer Him that lent
Not gave the my deare Monument.
   So close the ground, and 'bout Her shade
Black Curtaines draw, My Bride is laid.
   Sleepe on my Love in thy cold Bed
Never to bee Disquietted:
My last Good-night! Thou wilt not wake
Till I Thy Fate shall overtake:

Till Age or Griefe or Sicknes must
Marry my Body to that Dust
It so much loves; and fill the roome
My Heart keepes empty in thy Tombe.
Stay for mee there: I will not faile
To meet Thee in that hollow Vale.
And thinke not much of my delay
I am already on the way,
And follow Thee with all the Speed
Desires can make, or Sorrowes breed.
Each Minute is a short Degree
And ev'ry Houre a stepp towards Thee.
At Night when I betake to rest
Next Morne I rise nearer my West
Of Life, almost by eight Houres saile
Then when Sleep breath'd his drowsy gale.
   Thus from the Sun my Bottome steares,
And my Dayes Compasse downeward beares.
Nor Labour I to stemme the Tyde
Through which to Thee I swiftly glide.
   'Tis true, with Shame and Griefe I yield
Thou, like the Vanne, first took'st the Field,
And gotten hast the Victory
In thus adventuring to Dye,
Before mee; whose more yeares might crave
A just precedence in the Grave.
But harke! My Pulse like a soft Drum
Beates my Approach, Tells Thee I come;
And slow how-e're my Marches bee
I shall at last sitt downe by Thee.
The thought of which bids mee goe on
And wayt my Dissolution
With Hope and Comfort; Deare (forgive
The Cryme) I am content to live
Divided, with but halfe a Heart
Till wee shall Meet and Never part.

14 See no. 22 2 *Dirges* laments, more precisely Catholic services for the dead *Complaint* lament; King is playing in these opening lines with ideas of various rituals (some Catholic, some Protestant) which serve to articulate death and is asserting the adequacy of his verses to supplement or replace them 4 *strew* scattering 15 *glasses* his tears are imaged as the sands in the hourglass 22 *praeposterous* unnatural 23 *Sett* death 29 *tells* counts 40 *Clyme* region 41 *Moneth* month 53 *calcine* 'reduce to ashes',also 'purify by burning' 71 *Doomesday Booke* when the bodies of the dead are resurrected on the day of Judgement, the earth must give an exact account of those committed to its keeping 75 *Auditt* account 101 *Bottome* keel of ship 106 *Vanne* vanguard, advance party 116 *Dissolution* death

WILLIAM CAVENDISH, DUKE OF NEWCASTLE

15 *Loves Transmigration.*

If livinge can not meete, then lett us trie
If after death wee can, Oh let us die!
By Transmigration, bodys still doe raigne
In thousand things in one another chainge.
In Roses you for finer Poseys fitt
I winding silke, your tender stalkes to knitt
And so Imbrace you, or you heavens due
Fallinge on me, a dead leafe may renue
With hony'd kisses, you lillies newly gott
And putt in me turn'd now a Purslaine pott
Or sweeter Grapes, whose squees'd Juce is divine
Mingling our selfes makinge but one pewr Wine.
Or wholsom Salletts mingl'd to our wishe
Thus may be Joynd both, in one Sallett dishe
Our Norrishment turn'd to the quintessence
Of what makes man, and is his first Essence
Aptly dispos'd by Hymen wee may then
Bee gott, brought forth, two twinnes, be us againe
In spight of fate, death, Grave, still joyned thus
Wise Nature still will make us both, both us.

15 Title *Transmigration* the movement of souls at death to new bodies (not necessarily human) 5 *Poseys* bouquets 10 *Purslaine* porcelain 12 *pewr* pure 13 *Salletts* salads 15 *quintessence* most refined essence (alchemical term for substance purified through five stages of refinement) 17 *Hymen* see Appendix 1

THOMAS CAREW

16 *To my Mistris sitting by a River's side.*

AN EDDY.

Marke how yond Eddy steales away,
From the rude streame into the Bay,
There lockt up safe, she doth divorce
Her waters from the chanels course,
And scornes the Torrent, that did bring
Her headlong from her native spring.
Now doth she with her new love play,
Whilst he runs murmuring away.
Marke how she courts the bankes, whilst they
As amorously their armes display,
T'embrace; and clip her silver waves:
See how she strokes their sides, and craves
An entrance there, which they deny;
Whereat she frownes, threatning to flye
Home to her streame, and 'gins to swim
Backward, but from the chanels brim,
Smiling, returnes into the creeke,
With thousand dimples on her cheeke.
  Be thou this Eddy, and I'le make
My breast thy shore, where thou shalt take
Secure repose, and never dreame
Of the quite forsaken streame:
Let him to the wide Ocean hast,
There lose his colour, name, and tast;
Thou shalt save all, and safe from him,
Within these armes for ever swim.

16 Title *Eddy* a small whirlpool 2 *rude* rough 11 *clip* hug

17 *A Looking-Glasse.*

That flattring Glasse, whose smooth face weares
Your shadow, which a Sunne appeares,
Was once a river of my teares.

About your cold heart, they did make
A circle, where the brinie lake
Congeal'd, into a crystall cake.

Gaze no more on that killing eye,
For feare the native crueltie
Doome you, as it doth all, to dye.

For feare lest the faire object move,
Your froward heart to fall in love,
Then you your selfe my rivall prove.

Looke rather on my pale cheekes pin'de,
There view your beauties, there you'le finde
A faire face, but a cruell minde.

Be not for ever frozen, coy;
One beame of love, will soone destroy,
And melt that yce, to flouds of joy.

17 2 *shadow* reflection 5 *brinie* salty 6 *Congeal'd* froze 8 *native* intrinsic 10 *object* the thing looked at 11 *froward* perverse, wilful 13 *pin'de* starved

18 *Boldnesse in love.*

Marke how the bashfull 'morne, in vaine
Courts the amorous Marigold,
With sighing blasts, and weeping raine;
Yet she refuses to unfold.
But when the Planet of the day,
Approacheth with his powerfull ray,

Then she spreads, then she receives
His warmer beames into her virgin leaves.
So shalt thou thrive in love, fond Boy;
If thy teares, and sighes discover
Thy griefe, thou never shalt enjoy
The just reward of a bold lover:
But when with moving accents, thou
Shalt constant faith, and service vow,
Thy *Celia* shall receive those charmes
With open eares, and with unfolded armes.

18 5 *Planet of the day* the sun 13 *accents* speech, or musical notes

JAMES SHIRLEY

19 *To his Mistris confined.*

Think not my *Phebe*, cause a cloud
Doth now thy heavenly beauty shroud,
My wandring eye
Can stoop to common beauties of the sky.
Be thou but kind, and this Eclipse
Shall neither hinder eyes, nor lips;
For we will meet
Within our hearts, and kisse, when none shall see't.

Nor canst thou in thy Prison be,
Without some loving signes of me,
When thou dost spy
A sun-beam peep into thy room, 'tis I,
For I am hid within that flame,
And thus unto thy chamber came,
To let thee see,
In what a Martyrdom I burn for thee.

There's no sad picture that doth dwell
Upon thy Arras wall, but well
resembles me.

No matter though our yeers do not agree,
Love can make old, as well as time,
And he that doth but twenty clime,
If he will prove
As true as I, shews fourscore yeers in love.

19 Title *confined* ill at home 1 *Phebe* Diana, the moon 18 *Arras* wall-hanging, tapestry
22 *clime* attain in years

20 *Goodnight.*

Bid me no more goodnight; because
'Tis dark, must I away?
Love doth acknowledge no such Lawes,
And Love 'tis I obey:
Which blind, doth all your light despise,
And hath no need of eyes
When day is fled:
Besides the Sun, which you
Complain is gone, 'tis true,
Is gone to bed:
Oh let us do so too.

20 5 *blind* see Appendix 1 for the proverbial blindness of Cupid

21 *Upon his M[istris] Dancing.*

I Stood and saw my Mistris dance,
Silent, and with so fixt an eye,
Some might suppose me in a trance,
But being asked why,
By one that knew I was in love,
I could not but impart
My wonder, to behold her move
So nimbly with a marble heart.

KATHERINE, LADY DYER

22 [Epitaph on Sir William Dyer]

M.S. Sir Will: Dyer, Kt: Who put on Immortality Aprill the 29th Anno Domini 1621.

If a large hart: Joyned with a Noble minde
Shewing true worth, unto all good inclin'd,
If faith in freindship, Justice unto all,
Leave such a Memory as we may call
Happy, Thine is: Then pious Marble keepe
His Iust Fame waking, Though his lov'd dost sleepe.
And though Death can devoure all that hath breath,
And Monuments them selves have had a Death,
Nature shan't suffer this, to ruinate,
Nor time demolish't, nor an envious fate,
Rais'd by a Just hand not vaine glorious pride
Who'd be conceal'd, wer't modesty to hide
Such an affection did so long survive
The object of 't: yet lov'd It as alive.
And this grate Blessing to his Name doth give
To make It by his Tombe, and Issue live.

My dearest dust could not thy hasty day
Afford thy drowzy patience leave to stay
One hower longer; so that we might either
Sate up, or gone to bedd together?
But since thy finisht labor hath possest
Thy weary limbs with early rest,
Enjoy it sweetly; and thy widdowe bride
Shall soone repose her by thy slumbring side;
Whose business, now is only to prepare
My nightly dress, and call to prayre:
Mine eyes wax heavy and the day growes old
The dew falls thick, my bloud growes cold;
Draw, draw the closed curtaynes: and make roome;
My deare, my dearest dust; I come, I come.

22 . see no. 14 Title *M.S .memoriae sacrum*: to the sacred memory of... 16 *Issue* children 26 *nightly dress* nightclothes, also shroud 27 *wax* grow

PIARAS FEIRITÉAR

23 [Léig dhíot th'airm, a mhachaoimh mná]

Léig dhíot th'airm, a mhachaoimh mná,
  muna fearr leat cách do lot;
muna léige th'airmse dhíot,
  cuirfead bannaidhe ón rígh ort.

Má chuireann tú th'airm ar gcúl,
  folaigh feasta do chúl cas,
ná léig leis do bhráighe bhán
  nach léig duine chách as.

Má shaoileann tú féin, a bhean,
  nár mharbhais aon theas ná thuaidh,
do mharbh silleadh do shúl mín
  cách uile gan scín gan tuaigh.

Dar leat féin gé maol do ghlún,
  dar leat fós gé húr do ghlac,
do lot gach aon—tuig a chiall—
  ní fearra dhuit scian nó ga.

Folaigh orthu an t-uch mar aol,
  ná faiceadh siad do thaobh bog,
ar ghrádh Chríost ná faiceadh cách
  do chíoch roigheal mar bhláth dos.

Folaigh orthu do rosc liath,
  má théid ar mharbhais riamh leat;
ar ghrádh th'anma dún do bhéal,
  ná faiceadh siad do dhéad geal.

Ní beag shuit ar chuiris d'éag,
  cé shaoile nach cré do chorp;
folaighthear leat th'airm go cóir—
  ná déana níos mó de lot.

Más lór leat ar chuiris tim,
  sula gcuirthear sinn i gcré,
a bhean ará rem ro-chloí,
  na hairmsin díotsa léig.

Do shloinneadh, a mhacaoimh mná,
  ní beag liom ar chách mar cheist:
do chuirffeadh soin th'ainm i gcéill
  dá mbeith a agus é leis.

23 Lay your weapons down, young lady, do you want to ruin us all? Lay your weapons down, or else I'll have you under royal restraint. Put these weapons behind you: hide, henceforth, your curling hair; do not bare that white breast that spares no living man. Lady, do you believe you've never killed, to North or South? Your mild eye-glance has killed at large, without the need of knife or axe. You may think your knee's not sharp, and your palm is soft: to wound a man, believe me, you need no knife or spear! Hide your lime-white bosom, do not show your tender flank. For the love of Christ, let no one see your gleaming breast, a tuft in bloom. Conceal those eyes of grey, if you'd go free for all you've killed. Close your lips to save your soul; do not let your bright teeth be seen. Not a few have you done to death: do you think that you're not mortal clay? In justice, put your weapons down and let us have no further ruin. If you have terrified all you want, lady who seek my downfall, now—before I'm buried in earth—your weapons, lay them down. What your surname is, young lady, is a question worth asking everybody. But add an 'a' and an 'é', and it gives your name away.

36 *dá mbeith a/add an 'a'* Ó Tuama and Kinsella suggest that the lady's name was Husae (Hussey)

ALASDAIR MAC MHURCHAIDH

24 *Is tuirseach dhuinne ri port*

Is tuirseach dhuinne ri port,
  Chan iongnadh mo dhos bhith liath:
Thug mo chridhe troigh ar éis
  Mar Oisean an déidh nam Fiann.

'S mi an déidh Choinnich an àigh,
  Nach ceileadh air chàch an t-òr;
Làmh a mhalairt nan seud:
  Iomadh ceud da dtug sè fòir.

Nì air mhaireann Cailean ùr,
  B'allail a chliù is è òg:
Ge do ghabh sè ruinne fearg,
  Ghiorraich è gu dearbh mo lò.

Nì air mhaireann Ruairidh Mór,
  Bhrostnadh fa trom dhùinn air thùs:
Och òn nach maireann na suinn
  Choisinn le'n lamn dhùinn gach cùis.

Nì air mhaireann Ruairidh Geàrr,
  Do chumadh spàirn ris gach neach;
Laoch nach géilleadh ach 'san chòir:
  B'éibhinn leis slòigh agus creach.

Smuainmid air ceannard an Tùir,
  Bho'n d'fhuaras mùirn is mi òg;
B'éibhinn leis seobhag is cù:
  B'annsa leis a chliù na an t-òr.

Nì air mhaireann mac Ruairidh fhéil,
  Neach nach d'fhuiling beum fo eud;
No fear-taighe Chille Chrìosd:
  Allail an dìs a chaidh eug.

Smuainim aon ogha Eachainn fhéil,
  Neach nach d'eur cara mu nì:
Bu luath leam do ghoin am bàs
  An urra dh' fhàg sè 'na thìr.

Mo chompán 's mo charaid ghaoil,
  Neach nach cuireadh fo sgaoil rùn:
Goirid leam do ghléidh a mhac
  A' ghlac fhuair sè anns an Dùn.

Iomadh duine uasal an Ros
  Nach faod mi a nois chur sìos,
Is cubhaidh leam-s' do dhol eug
  Is mise 'nan déidh gun phrìs.

Nì air mhaireann fir Innse Gall,
  Mór an call domh ri m'aois:
Ceannard an t-slòigh, Dòmhnall Gorm,
  Is Ruairidh nan còrn 's nam pìos.

Nì air mhaireann mac MhicLeòid,
  An Talasgair bha ròd nan cliar:
'San t-Srath do bhì am fear pailt;
  An Ratharsair bha an t-slat fhial.

Nì air mhaireann Eachann Og
  'S mac Ailein nan seòl 's nam pìos;
No Raoghalt bha air Dùn Bhuirbh,
  No Dòmhnall Gorm, tòir do phill.

Iomadh caraid do chaidh bhuam
  Bho faighinn-sa cuairt is lòn,
Ged tharla mi an nochd gun chuirm:
  Mo dheoch is è burn ri òl.

Ta mi gun aighear gun fhonn,
  Mo làmh lom ri dol an cùirt:
A mheud 's a chosg mis' ri càch,
  Gheibhim 'na àit an nochd bùrt.

Do bhì osnaidh da mo ghoin,
  Gun chosnadh air mhuir no tìr;
Dana chrann cha dtugas fonn:
  B'annsa leam long agus fìon.

'S minig dh' òl mi *sause* de 'n fhìon
  As mìlse a thig bho'n Fhraing;
Bho sguir mi sgrìobhadh nan trosg,
  An nochd chan fhiach mo dheoch plaing.

Bidh mi a nis ri mo bheò
   Aig Seòras Og an ceann bhùird:
Le clàrsaich ge ghabhainn dàn,
   Olaim gach tràth làn a' chùirn.

Nì air mhath mo ghnothuch 'na chùirt,
   Nach faighim mùirn bho na mnài.
Ol dhìth 's nach eil mo cruaidh
   'S e gheibhim fuath air son gràidh.

Foghlamar an leabhar bàn
   Anns an gléidhmear gach là tuigs';
Gach uair 'g am bìomar ag osnaidh
   Ochad-òn is mì fo thuirs'.

24 Sad am I kept waiting at the port. No wonder my forelock has greyed: my heart has stepped backwards a foot, like Ossian outliving the Fiann. I outlive Kenneth of success, who hid not his gold from others; hand who paid out in gems, he gave help to many hundreds. Fresh Colin is no more. When but young, his fame was great: though his anger was turned on me, his loss has shortened my days. Great Ruairidh is no more, his encouragement was keen in my youth; alas that the heroes are gone, whose swords won for us in every cause. Short Ruairidh is no more, he who would take on any man: a hero who only yielded when right, his delights were plunder and hosts. Let us think of the chief of the Tower, from whom I gained affection when young. His delights were a hawk and a hound; fame was dearer to him than gold. Generous Ruairidh's son is no more, a man who suffered no jealous blow. The house of Kilchrist's head is no more: noble the pair who have gone with death. Let us think of generous Hector's only grandson. A man who never refused anything to a friend: I consider it quick that death struck the hero that he left in his earth. My comrade and beloved friend, a man who never let a secret spread, I deem it short that his son held the hand that he won in the Dùn. Many a nobleman in Ross whose name I cannot now write down; well do I remember their deaths, while I surviving them have little worth. No more are the Hebridean chiefs, great their loss to me at my age; the leader of the hosts, Donald Gorm, and Ruairidh of the drinking-horns and quaichs. No more is the son of MacLeod: in Talisker was the poets' road, in Strath was the liberal lord, in Raasay was the generous gauge. Young Hector is no more, or the son of Alan of the sails and cups, or Ronald who was on Dùn Buirbh, or Donald Gorm who turned a rout. Many the friend who has left me from whom I'd get a visit and food, though tonight I share no feast, and water is my lot to drink. I am without joy or tune, my hand empty for going to court: mockery is all I get tonight for all that I have spent on others. Sighing over my hurt, with no livelihood on land or sea, I had no love for the plough; dearer to me were a ship and wine. Often I have drunk a sauce of the sweetest wine from France. Since I stopped keeping account of the cod, my drink tonight is not worth a plack. Young George will maintain me at the table-head for the rest of my life now, though I could recite a verse with a harp, let me drink a full horn at every meal. My business at his court is no good, the women hold me in no regard. For lack of my being hard, what I get is aversion and not love. Let me study the fair Book whence I reap understanding each day, sighing all the whiles. Alack and alas, I am sad.

This poem is typologically similar to the *Gododdin*, a very early Welsh poem celebrating a battle at Catterick in the seventh century, which is similarly a lament for a string of fallen heroes by a bard (Aneirin) who survived the conflict. 4 *Oisean/Ossian.* Finn and his warriors (the Fiann) were legendary Irish heroes. Ossian was the poet of the Fiann, and survived both Finn himself and many of his principal supporters 5 *Choinnich/Kenneth* Kenneth MacKenzie, Lord of Kintail and chief of the MacKenzies, died 1611 9 *Cailean/Colin* Colin, First Lord Seaforth, chief of the MacKenzies, died 1633 13 *Ruairidh Mór/great Ruairidh* Sir Roderick MacKenzie of Coigach, Tutor of Kintail, died 1626. 17 *Ruairidh Geàrr/short Ruairidh* possibly Roderick Matheson, fl.1627 21 *ceannard an Tùir/the chief of the Tower* possibly Alexander MacKenzie of Fairburn (the Tower) near Strathpeffer, died c.1620 25 *mac Ruairidh/Ruaridh's son* either Murdoch MacKenzie, second of Redcastle, or Kenneth MacKenzie, third of Davochmalug 27 *fear-taighe Chille Chrìosd/the house of Gilchrist's head* Kenneth MacKenzie, third of Kilchrist, near Muir of Ord 29 *aon ogha Eachainn/Hector's only grandson* probably John Roy MacKenzie, fourth of Gairloch, died 1628 43 *Dòmhnall Gorm/Donald Gorm* Donald Gorm MacDonald of Sleat, Skye, died 1617 44 *Ruairidh* Sir Roderick MacLeod of Harris and Dunvegan, died 1626 45 *mac MhicLeòid/the son of MacLeod* William MacLeod of Talisker 49 *Eachann Og/young Hector* possibly Eachann Og MacLean of Duart, died 1618 50 *mac Ailein/the son of Alan* probably Sir Donald, chief of Clanranald, died 1618 51 *Raoghalt/Ronald* Ranald MacDonald of Benbecula, died 1636 70 *Seòras Og/young George* George MacKenzie, second Lord Seaforth 77 *leabhar bàn/fair Book* the Bible

OWEN FELLTHAM

25 *The Sun and Wind.*

Why think'st thou (fool) thy Beauties rayes,
  Should flame my colder heart;
When thy disdain shall several wayes,
  Such piercing blasts impart?

Seest not those beams that guild the day,
  Though they be hot and fierce,
Yet have nor heat nor power to stay,
  When winds their strength disperse.

So though thy Sun heats my desire,
  Yet know thy coy disdain
Falls like a storm on that young fire,
  So blowes me cool again.

25 5 *guild* gild

26 *This ensuing Copy the late Printer hath been pleased to honour, by mistaking it among those of the most ingenious and too early lost,* Sir John Suckling.

When, Dearest, I but think on thee,
Methinks all things that lovely be
  Are present, and my soul delighted:
For beauties that from worth arise,
Are like the grace of Deities,
  Still present with us, though unsighted.

Thus while I sit and sigh the day,
With all his spreading lights away,
  Till nights black wings do overtake me:
Thinking on thee, thy beauties then,
As sudden lights do sleeping men,
  So they by their bright rayes awake me.

Thus absence dyes, and dying proves
No absence can consist with Loves,
  That do partake of fair perfection:
Since in the darkest night they may
By the quick motion find a way
  To see each other by reflection.

The waving Sea can with such floud,
Bath some high Palace that hath stood
 Far from the Main up in the River:
Oh think not then but love can do
As much, for that's an Ocean too,
 That flows not every day, but ever.

26 21 *Main* sea

WILLIAM HABINGTON

27

To the Dew,
In hope to see CASTARA *walking.*

Bright Dew which dost the field adorne
As th'earth to welcome in the morne,
Would hang a jewell on each corne.

Did not the pittious night, whose eares
Have oft beene conscious of my feares,
Distill you from her eyes as teares?

Or that *Castara* for your zeale,
When she her beauties shall reveale,
Might you to Dyamonds congeale?

If not your pity, yet how ere
Your care I praise, 'gainst she appeare,
To make the wealthy Indies here.

But see she comes. Bright lampe oth' skie,
Put out thy light: the world shall spie,
A fairer Sunne in either eye.

And liquid Pearle, hang heavie now
On every grasse that it may bow
In veneration of her brow.

Yet if the wind should curious be,
And were I here should question thee,
Hee's full of whispers, speake not me.

But if the busie tell-tale day,
Our happy enterview betray;
Lest thou confesse too, melt away.

27 9 *congeale* solidify 12 *Indies* source of riches, especially jewels

28 *To* CASTARA *Upon an embrace.*

'Bout th'husband Oke, the Vine
Thus wreathes to kisse his leavy face:
Their streames thus Rivers joyne,
And lose themselves in the embrace.
But Trees want sence when they infold,
And Waters when they meet, are cold.

Thus Turtles bill, and grone
Their loves into each others eare:
Two flames thus burne in one,
When their curl'd heads to heaven they reare,
But Birds want soule though not desire:
And flames materiall soone expire.

If not prophane; we'll say
When Angels close, their joyes are such.
For we no love obey
That's bastard to a fleshly touch.
Let's close *Castara* then, since thus
We patterne Angels, and they us.

28 1 *Oke* oak 7 *Turtles* doves *bill* kiss 14 *close* embrace 18 *patterne* imitate

SIR WILLIAM DAVENANT

29 *The Philosopher and the Lover; to a Mistress dying.*

SONG.

LOVER.

Your Beauty, ripe, and calm, and fresh;
As Eastern Summers are,
Must now, forsaking Time and Flesh,
Add light to some small Star.

PHILOSOPHER.

Whilst she yet lives, were Stars decay'd,
Their light by hers, relief might find:
But Death will lead her to a shade
Where Love is cold, and Beauty blinde.

LOVER.

Lovers (whose Priests all Poets are)
Think ev'ry Mistress, when she dies,
Is chang'd at least into a Starr:
And who dares doubt the Poets wise?

PHILOSOPHER.

But ask not Bodies doom'd to die,
To what abode they go;
Since Knowledge is but sorrows Spy,
It is not safe to know.

29 14 *abode* home 15 *Spy* forerunner

POETS OF THE TIXALL CIRCLE [COLLECTED BY CATHERINE GAGE, LADY ASTON]

30 A CONFESSION.

Since you will needs my hart possesse,
Tis just to you it should confesse
  The faults to which tis given;
It is to change much more inclin'd
Then women, or the sea, or wind,
  Or ought that's under heaven.

Nor will I hide from you this truth,
It hath been from its very youth
  A most egregious ranger;
And since from me it often fled,
With whom it was both born and bred,
  Twill scarce stay with a stranger.

Therefore, the gay, the blacke, the sad,
Which makes me often thinke twere mad,
  With one kind looke could win it;
Soe naturally it loves to range,
That it hath left successe for change;
  And what was glory in it.

Nay, I to it became a sport,
When I did soundly chide it fort,
  It would in smiles be saying,
Your debts of love you must dispaire
To pay to all thats kind or faire,
  If long with one you're staying.

And now, if you are not affraid,
After these truths which I have said,
  To take this arrant rover;
Be not displeasd if I protest,
I doubt the hart within your breast
  Will prove just such another,

30 6 *ought* aught, anything 9 *egregious* notable 20 *chide* scold *fort* for it 27 *arrant* wandering, or notorious

POETS OF THE TIXALL CIRCLE [GERTRUDE ASTON]

31 TO HER HUSBAND ON NEW YEAR'S DAY, 1651.

How swiftly time doth passe away,
Wher happines compleates the day!
Weeks, months, and years, but moments prove
To those that nobly are in love.
This computation's only knowne
To them that our pure flame can owne.
Succeeding yeares example take
By those are past; ther numbers wake
Envy, whilst with a will resigned,
No will is known till th'other's mind.

31 10 *till* to

EDMUND WALLER

32 *To a Lady in a Garden.*

Sees not my love how Time resumes
The glory which he lent these flowers;
Though none should tast of their perfumes,
        Yet must they live but some few hours,
        Time what we forbear devours.

Had *Hellen*, or the Egyptian Queen,
Been nere so thrifty of their graces,
Those beauties must at length have been
        The spoyle of Age which finds out faces
        In the most retired places.

Should some malignant Planet bring
A barren drought, or ceaseless shower
Upon the Autumn, or the Spring,

And spare us neither fruit nor flower,
Winter would not stay an hour.

Could the resolve of loves neglect
Preserve you from the violation
Of comming years, then more respect
Were due to so divine a fashion,
Nor would I indulge my passion.

32 1 *resumes* takes back 5 *forbear* leave alone 6 *Hellen, Egyptian Queen* see Appendix 1 9 *spoyle* prey 11 *malignant Planet* (astrology) star exerting a negative influence

33 *SONG.*

Go lovely Rose,
Tell her that wasts her time and me,
That now she knows
When I resemble her to thee,
How sweet and fair she seems to be.

Tell her that's young,
And shuns to have her graces spy'd,
That hadst thou sprung
In desarts, where no men abide,
Thou must have uncommended dy'd.

Small is the worth
Of beauty from the light retir'd;
Bid her come forth,
Suffer her self to be desir'd,
And not blush so to be admir'd.

Then die, that she,
The common fate of all things rare,
May read in thee
How small a part of time they share,
That are so wondrous sweet and fair.

33 4 *resemble* compare

34 *To Amoret.*

Amoret, the milky way,
Fram'd of many nameless stars,
The smooth stream where none can say,
He this drop to that prefers;

Amoret, my lovely fo,
Tell me where thy strength does lie,
Where the power that charms us so,
In thy Soul, or in thy eye?

By that snowy neck alone,
Or thy grace in motion seen,
No such wonders could be done:
Yet thy wast is streight and clean,
As *Cupids* shaft, or *Hermes* rod,
And powerfull too, as either God.

34 12 *streight* narrow 13 *shaft* arrow *Cupid, Hermes* see Appendix 1 *rod* caduceus: the god's staff of office

35 *To a very young Lady.*

Why came I so untimely forth
Into a world which wanting thee
Could entertain us with no worth
Or shadow of felicity?
That time should me so far remove
From that which I was born to love.
Yet fairest blossome do not slight
That age which you may know so soon;
The rosie Morn resignes her light,
And milder glory to the Noon:
And then what wonders shall you do,
Whose dawning beauty warms us so?

Hope waits upon the flowry prime,
And Summer though it be less gay,
Yet is not look't on as a time
Of declination or decay.
For with a full hand that do's bring
All that was promis'd by the Spring.

THOMAS CARY

36 [Tell me, *Eutresia*, since my fate]

1.

Tell me, *Eutresia*, since my fate
And thy more powerfull Forme decrees
My heart an Immolation at thy Shrine,
Where it is ever to incline,
How I must love, and at what rate,
And by what steps, and what degrees
I shall my hopes enlarge, and my desires confine?

A.

First when thy flames begin
See they burne all within,
And so, as lookers on may not descry
Smoake in a sigh, or sparkle in an eye
I'de have thy love a good while there
Ere thine own heart should be aware,
And I my selfe would choose to know it
First by thy care and cunning not to show it.

2.

When my flame thine owne way is thus betrayd,
Must it be still afrayd?
May it not be sharpsighted too as well,
And know thou knowst that which it dares not tell,
And by that knowledge finde it may
Tell it selfe ore a lowder way?

B.

Let me alone a while,
For so thou maist beguile
My heart to a consent
Long ere it meant.
For while I dare not disaprove
Least that betray a knowledge of thy love,
I shall be so accustom'd to allow,
That I shall not know how
To be displeas'd when thou shalt it avow.

3.

When by loves powerfull secret sympathy
Our Soules are got thus nigh,
And that by one another seene
There needs no breath to goe betweene,
Though in the maine agreement of our breasts
Our *Hearts* subscribe as *Interests*,
Will it not need
The Tongues signe too as *Witnesse* to the deed?

C.

Speake then, but when you tell the tale
  Of what you ayle,
Let it be so disorder'd that I may
Guesse onely thence what you would say,
  Then to speake sence
    Were an offence,
  And twill thy passion tell the subtlest way
    Not to know what to say.

36 1 *Eutresia* 'Utrechia' MS (Greek) 'beautiful hair'; see Notes on the Text 3 *Immolation* sacrifice 10 *descry* notice 23 *beguile* deceive, trick 36 *Interests* (legal) those with a right or share in a property 40 *you ayle* troubles you

HENRY HARINGTON [attrib. to FRANCIS BEAUMONT]

37 A Charme.

Sleepe old man let silence charme thee
 Dreaminge slumber overtake thee
Quiet thoughts and Darkness arme thee
 let noe Creakeinge doore awake thee
Phoebus hath put out his light
 all in Darknes closeinge
Phoebe lends her hornes to night
 To thy heads disposinge.

Let noe fatall bell nor Clock
 pearce the hollow of thine eare
tongeles be the earlie Cock
 or what els may add a feare.
Let noe ratt noe sillie mouse
 move the senseles rushes
nor a cough disturbe this house
 till Aurora Blushes.

Now my Sweete Corinna come
 laugh and leave thy late deploringe
Sable midnight makes all dumbe
 and thy Jealeous husband snoringe.
to thy sweete perfumed kisses
 entertayne a stranger
for a lovers cheefest blisses
 are gott with greatest danger.

37 5 *Phoebus* Apollo, the sun, see Appendix 1 7 *Phoebe* Diana, the moon 13 *sillie* simple 14 *rushes* as floor covering 16 *Aurora* the dawn 19 *Sable* black

SIR JOHN SUCKLING

38 *Sonnet* I.

1.

Do'st see how unregarded now
that piece of beauty passes?
There was a time when I did vow
to that alone;
but mark the fate of faces;
That red and white works now no more on me
Then if it could not charm or I not see.

2.

And yet the face continues good,
and I have still desires,
Am still the self same flesh and blood,
as apt to melt
and suffer from those fires;
Oh! some kind power unriddle where it lies,
Whether my heart be faulty, or her eyes?

3.

She every day her Man does kill,
and I as often die;
Neither her power then, nor my will
can question'd be,
what is the mystery?
Sure Beauties Empires, like to greater States
Have certain periods set, and hidden fates.

38 15 *kill*, 16 *die* both with connotations of orgasm

39 *Sonnet* III.

1.

Oh! for some honest Lovers ghost,
Some kind unbodied post
Sent from the shades below.
I strangely long to know

Whether the nobler Chaplets wear,
Those that their mistresse scorn did bear,
Or those that were us'd kindly.

2.

For what-so-e're they tell us here
To make those sufferings dear,
'Twill there I fear be found,
That to the being crown'd,
T'have lov'd alone will not suffice,
Unlesse we also have been wise,
And have our Loves enjoy'd.

3.

What posture can we think him in,
That here unlov'd agen
Departs, and's thither gone
Where each sits by his own?
Or how can that *Elizium* be
Where I my Mistresse still must see
Circled in others Armes?

4.

For there the Judges all are just,
And *Sophonisba* must
Be his whom she held dear;
Not his who lov'd her here:
The sweet *Philoclea* since she dy'de
Lies by her *Pirocles* his side,
Not by *Amphialus*.

5.

Some Bayes (perchance) or Myrtle bough
For difference crowns the brow
Of those kind souls that were
The noble Martyrs here;

And if that be the onely odds
As who can tell ye kinder Gods,
Give me the Woman here.

39 2 *post* message or messenger 5 *Chaplets* headdresses, garlands, in religious iconography, a sign of martyrdom; in classical art a sign of victory in martial or artistic trials 19 *Elizium*, 23 *Sophonisba*, 26 *Philoclea*, 27 *Pirocles*, 28 *Amphialus*, see Appendix 1 29 *Bayes*, *Myrtle* laurel expresses victory, myrtle expresses love

40 *A Supplement of an imperfect Copy of Verses of Mr.* Wil. Shakespears, *By the Author.*

1.

One of her hands, one of her cheeks lay under,
Cozening the pillow of a lawful kisse,
Which therefore swel'd, and seem'd to part asunder,
As angry to be rob'd of such a blisse:
The one lookt pale, and for revenge did long,
While t'other blusht, cause it had done the wrong.

2.

Out of the bed the other fair hand was
On a green sattin quilt, whose perfect white
Lookt like a Dazie in a field of grasse,
*And shew'd like unmelt snow unto the sight,
There lay this pretty perdue, safe to keep
The rest oth'body that lay fast asleep.

3.

Her eyes (and therefore it was night) close laid,
Strove to imprison beauty till the morn,
But yet the doors were of such fine stuffe made,
That it broke through, and shew'd it self in scorn.
Throwing a kind of light about the place,
Which turnd to smiles stil as't came neare her face.

4.

Her beams (which some dul men call'd hair) divided
Part with her cheeks, part with her lips did sport,
But these, as rude, her breath put by still; some
Wiselyer downwards sought, but falling short,
Curl'd back in rings, and seem'd to turn agen
To bite the part so unkindly held them in.

* Thus far *Shakespear.*

40 2 *Cozening* cheating 9 *Dazie* daisy 11 *perdue* sentinel 22 *Wiselyer* more wisely

41 *Farewel to Love.*

1.

Well shadow'd Landskip, fare-ye-well:
How I have lov'd you, none can tell,
At least so well
As he that now hates more
Then e're he lov'd before.

2.

But my dear nothings, take your leave,
No longer must you me deceive,
Since I perceive
All the deceit, and know
Whence the mistake did grow.

3.

As he whose quicker eye doth trace
A false star shot to a mark't place,
Do's run apace,
And thinking it to catch,
A gelly up do's snatch.

4.

So our dull souls tasting delight
Far off, by sence, and appetite,
Think what is right
And real good; when yet
'Tis but the Counterfeit.

5.

Oh! how I glory now; that I
Have made this new discovery!
Each wanton eye
Enflam'd before: no more
Will I encrease that score.

6.

If I gaze, now, 'tis but to see
What manner of deaths-head 'twill be,
When it is free
From that fresh upper skin;
The gazers Joy, and sin.

7.

The Gum and glist'ning which with art
And studi'd method, in each part
Hangs down the heart.
Looks (just) as if, that day
Snails there had crawl'd the *Hay*.

8.

The Locks, that curl'd o're each eare be,
Hang like two Master-worms to me,
That (as we see)
Have tasted to the rest
Two holes, where they lik't best.

9.

A quick coarse me-thinks I spy
In ev'ry woman; and mine eye
At passing by,
Check, and is troubled, just
As if it rose from Dust.

10.

They mortifie, not heighten me:
These of my sins the Glasses be:
And here I see
How I have lov'd before.
And so I love no more.

41 1 *Landskip* (landscape) painting 6 (alluding to the Latin tag 'splendidis longum valedico nugis', origin unknown, used by Sidney at the end of his *Certain Sonnets*; by Henry King as motto to his poem 'The Farewell'; and by Sir John Denham appended to the Epistle to his *Poems and Translations*, 1668) 15 *gelly* jelly, jelly-like mass of algae on dry soil after rain, popularly supposed to be the remains of a fallen star or meteor 27 *deaths-head* skull 31 *Gum and glist'ning* cosmetics 35 *Hay* lively country dance 37 *Master-worms* snakes 41 *quick coarse* living corpse 47 *Glasses* mirrors

SIDNEY GODOLPHIN

42 [Noe more unto my thoughts appeare]

Noe more unto my thoughts appeare
  att Least appeare Lesse Fayre
For Crazy tempers Justly Feare
  the goodnesse of the ayre;

Whilst your pure Image hath a place
  in my Impurer Mynde
your very shaddow is the glasse
  wher My defects I finde.

Shall I not Fly that brighter Light
  which makes my Fyres Looke Pale
and put that Vertue out of sight
  which makes Myne none att all.

No, no, your picture doeth impart
  such Valew I not wish
the native Worth to any heart
  that's unadorn'd with this.

Though poorer in desert I make
  My selfe whilst I admyre
the fuell which from hope I take
  I give to my desire.

If this flame lighted from your Eyes
the subject doe Calcine
A Heart may bee your sacrifice
too weake to bee your shrine.

42 17 *desert* deserving 22 *Calcine* burn to ashes

43 [Adieu thys is no cheape ayre]

Adieu thys is no cheape ayre
Tis my soules selfe I thus breathe awaye
Sorrow doth its place supply
It kils butt gives no leave to dy

Griefe which from hence did my life fyrst expell
Hear an usurping soule doth dwell
And I am long lived now how free from fate
Alas is hee whom woe doth animate
Disease is of hys syde, ruin doth fitt
The house to give that soule more roome in itt.

43 1 *Adieu* farewell 9 *ruin* starvation

44 To the tune of, In fayth I cannot keepe my fathers Sheepe.

Cloris, it is not thy disdaine
Can ever Cover with dispaire
Or in cold ashes hide that Care
Which I have fedd with soe long paine
I may perhaps myne Eyes refraine
And fruiteless wordes noe more impart
But yet still serve, still serve thee in my hearte;

What though I spend my haplesse dayes,
In finding Entertainements out
Carelesse of what I goe aboute

Or seeke my peace in skillfull Wayes
Applying to my Eyes new rays
Of Beauty, And another flame
Unto my Heart, my heart is still the same.

Tis true that I could Love noe face
Inhabited by cold disdayne
Taking delight in others paine
Thy Lookes are full of native grace
Since then by chance scorne there hath place
Tis to be hop't I may remove
This scorne one day, one day by Endless Love.

WILLIAM CARTWRIGHT

45
To Chloe *who wish'd her self young enough for me.*

Chloe, why wish you that your years
Would backwards run, till they meet mine,
That perfect Likeness, which endears
Things unto things, might us Combine?
Our Ages so in date agree,
That Twins do differ more than we.

There are two Births, the one when Light
First strikes the new awak'ned sense;
The Other when two Souls unite;
And we must count our life from thence:
When you lov'd me, and I lov'd you,
Then both of us were born anew.

Love then to us did new Souls give,
And in those Souls did plant new pow'rs;
Since when another life we live,
The Breath we breath is his, not ours;
Love makes those young, whom Age doth Chill,
And whom he finds young, keeps young still.

Love, like that Angell that shall call
        Our bodies from the silent Grave,
Unto one Age doth raise us all,
        None too much, none too little have;
Nay that the difference may be none,
He makes two not alike, but One.

And now since you and I are such,
        Tell me what's yours, and what is mine?
Our Eyes, our Ears, our Taste, Smell, Touch,
        Do (like our Souls) in one Combine;
So by this, I as well may be
Too old for you, as you for me.

45 19 *Angell* at the Last Judgement

JAMES GRAHAM, MARQUIS OF MONTROSE

46 *In Praise of Women*

When Heav'ns great *Jove* had made the World's round
  Frame,
Earth, Water, Air, and Fire; above the same,
The ruling Orbs, the Planets, Spheres, and all
The lesser Creatures, in the Earth's vast Ball:
But, as a curious Alchimist, still draws
From grosser Mettals finer, and from those
Extracts another, and from that again
Another that doth far excel the same.
So fram'd he Man of Elements combin'd,
T'excel that Substance where he was refin'd:
But that poor Creature, drawn from his Breast
Excelleth him, as he excell'd the rest:
Or as a stubborn Stalk, whereon there grows
A dainty Lilly or a fragrant Rose;

The Stalk may boast, and set its Vertues forth,
But take away the Flow'r, where is its Worth?
  But yet, fair Ladies, you must know
  Howbeit I adore you so:
  Reciprocal your Flames must prove,
  Or my Ambition scorns to love:
  A Noble Soul doth still abhore
  To strike, but where its Conquerour?

46 1 *Jove* see Appendix 1 3 *ruling Orbs* medieval astronomy has the planets fixed to crystal spheres encircling the earth and influencing human destiny 5 *curious* learned 11 *Creature... Breast* woman, created from Adam's rib in Genesis 2:21

47 [There's nothing in this World can prove]

There's nothing in this World can prove
  So true and real Pleasure,
As perfect Sympathy in Love,
  Which is a real Treasure.

The purest Strain of perfect Love
  In Vertue's Dye and Season,
Is that whose Influence doth move,
  And doth convince our Reason.

Designs attend, Desires give place,
  Hopes had no more availeth;
The Cause remov'd the Effect doth cease,
  Flames not maintain'd soon faileth.

The Conquest then of richest Hearts,
  Well lodg'd and trim'd by Nature,
Is that which true Content imparts,
  Where Worth is join'd with Feature.

Fill'd with sweet Hope then must I still
 Love what's to be admired;
When frowning Aspects cross the Will,
 Desires are more endeared.

Unhappy then unhappy I,
 To joy in tragick Pleasure,
And in so dear and desperate Way
 T'abound yet have no Treasure.

Yet will I not of Fate despair,
 Time oft in End relieveth,
But hopes my Star will change her Air,
 And joy where now she grieveth.

47 6 *Dye* day 19 *frowning Aspects,* both facial expressions and hostile stars 24 *T'abound* to be rich 27 *Air* (Scots 'airt') place

48 Mad on my lady binny

Burst out pour soull in main of tears
and thou my hea[r]t sith tempests mowe
my toung uhich nevers plaints forbear
bot points ut fourth my crossed lawe
combind together all in on
and thunder fourth my tragik mone

bot both poor soull cut breath brak air
can yow my pasion express
no way bot agment my car
in making them apear the Less
Siing bot from small woes wordes doe com
when great ones sing aluays dumb

yow suelling greues the bound your selfs
into the fatall brest yow fill
the centre uher all sorouss duell
the lembicke whence all ils distill

that silint in my paine I may
consume and burst in tears auay

yet that I may contented dye
I only wish befor my death
Transparant that my brest might bei
That or I doe expire my breath
Since sighes plaints tears expres no smart
It may be seine into my heart.

48 Title 'My lady binnis lilt' is the name of the air to which the verses are contrafacted. It is given, in two types of lute tablature, in the Wemyss MS (see Notes on the Text) on f. 26v and f. 45v. 1 *main* sea 2 *sith* such 4 *ut* out *lawe* love 7 *brak* broken 11 *Siing* seeing 13 *greues* griefs 16 *lembicke* flask used in distillation 22 *or* ere

RICHARD CRASHAW

49 *Wishes. To his (supposed) Mistresse.*

Who ere shee bee,
That not impossible shee
That shall command my heart and mee;

Where ere shee lye,
Lock't up from mortall Eye,
In shady leaves of Destiny;

Till that ripe Birth
Of studied fate stand forth,
And teach her faire steps to our Earth;

Till that Divine
Idea, take a shrine
Of Chrystall flesh, through which to shine:

Meet you her my wishes,
Bespeake her to my blisses,
And bee yee call'd my absent kisses.

I wish her Beauty,
That owes not all his Duty
To gaudy Tire, or glistring shoo-ty.

Something more than
Taffata or Tissew can,
Or rampant feather, or rich fan.

More then the spoyle
Of shop, or silkewormes Toyle
Or a bought blush, or a set smile.

A face thats best
By its own beauty drest,
And can alone command the rest.

A face made up
Out of no other shop,
Then what natures white hand sets ope.

A cheeke where Youth,
And Blood, with Pen of Truth
Write, what the Reader sweetly ru'th.

A cheeke where growes
More then a Morning Rose:
Which to no Boxe his being owes.

Lipps, where all Day
A lovers kisse may play,
Yet carry nothing thence away.

Lookes that oppresse
Their richest Tires but dresse
And cloath their simplest Nakednesse.

Eyes, that displaces
The Neighbour Diamond, and our faces
That Sunshine by their own sweet Graces.

Tresses, that weare
Iewells, but to declare
How much themselves more pretious are.

Whose native Ray,
Can tame the wanton Day
Of Gems, that in their bright shades play.

Each Ruby there,
Or Pearle that dare appeare,
Bee its owne blush, bee its owne Teare.

A well tam'd Heart,
For whose more noble smart,
Love may bee long chusing a Dart.

Eyes, that bestow
Full quivers on loves Bow;
Yet pay lesse Arrowes then they owe.

Smiles, that can warme
The blood, yet teach a charme,
That Chastity shall take no harme.

Blushes, that bin
The burnish of no sin,
Nor flames of ought too hot within.

Ioyes, that confesse,
Vertue their Mistresse,
And have no other head to dresse.

Feares, fond and flight,
As the coy Brides, when Night
First does the longing lover right.

Teares, quickly fled,
And vaine, as those are shed
For a dying Maydenhead.

Dayes, that need borrow,
No part of their good Morrow,
From a fore spent night of sorrow.

Dayes, that in spight
Of Darkenesse, by the Light
Of a cleere mind are Day all Night.

Nights, sweet as they,
Made short by lovers play,
Yet long by th'absence of the Day.

Life, that dares send,
A challenge to his end,
And when it comes say *Welcome Friend.*

Sydnaean showers
Of sweet discourse, whose powers
Can Crowne old Winters head with flowers,

Soft silken Houers,
Open sunnes; shady Bowers,
'Bove all; Nothing within that lowres.

What ere Delight
Can make Dayes forehead bright;
Or give Downe to the Wings of Night.

In her whole frame,
Have Nature all the Name,
Art and ornament the shame.

Her flattery,
Picture and Poesy,
Her counsell her owne vertue bee.

I wish, her store
Of worth, may leave her poore
Of wishes; and I wish—No more,

Now if Time knowes
That her whose radiant Browes,
Weave them a Garland of my vowes;

Her whose just Bayes,
My future hopes can raise,
A trophie to her present praise;

Her that dare bee,
What these Lines wish to see:
I seeke no further, it is shee.

'Tis shee, and heere
Lo I uncloath and cleare,
My wishes cloudy Character.

May shee enjoy it,
Whose merit dare apply it,
But Modesty dares still deny it.

Such worth as this is,
Shall fixe my flying wishes,
And determine them to kisses.

Let her full Glory,
My fancyes, fly before yee,
Bee ye my fictions; But her story.

49 18 *Tire* attire, clothes *glistring* shining 20 *Taffata* glossy silk *Tissew* rich fabric, often cloth of gold or silver 22 *spoyle* plunder 23 *Toyle* work 33 *ru'th* longs for, regrets 48 *pretious* precious 60 *then* than 64 *bin* are 66 *ought* aught 70 *fond and flight* deluded and insubstantial 88 *Sydnaean* as in the poetry of Sir Philip Sidney 93 *lowres* scowls 95 *Dayes forehead* morning sky 96 *Downe* wing feathers, soft bedding 109 *Bayes* garland of laurel 126 *story* renown

JOHN CLEVELAND

50 *Upon* Phillis *walking in a morning before Sun-rising.*

The sluggish morne, as yet undrest,
My *Phillis* brake from out her East;
As if shee'd made a match to runne
With *Venus,* Usher to the Sun.

The trees like Yeomen of her Guard,
Serving more for pomp, then ward,
Rank't on each side with loyall duty,
Weave branches to inclose her beauty.
The Plants whose luxury was lopt,
Or age with crutches underpropt;
Whose wooden carkases are grown
To be but coffins of their owne;
Revive, and at her generall dole
Each receives his antient soule.
The winged Choristers began
To chirp their Matins: and the Fan
Of whistling winds, like Organs plai'd,
Untill their Voluntaries made
The wakened earth in odours rise
To be her morning-Sacrifice.
The flowers call'd out of their beds,
Start, and raise up their drowsie heads:
And he that for their colour seeks,
May finde it vaulting in her cheekes,
Where Roses mix: no civill war
Between her *York*, and *Lancaster*.
The Marigold whose Courtiers face
Ecchoes the sunne, and doth unlace
Her at his rise, at his full stop
Packs and shuts up her gawdy shop;
Mistakes her cue, and doth display.
Thus *Phillis* antidates the day.
These miracles had cramp't the sunne,
Who thinking that his kingdom's wonne,
Powders with light his frizled locks,
To see what Saint his lustre mocks.
The trembling leaves through which he plaid,
Dapling the walke with light and shade,
Like lattice-windowes, give the spye
Room but to peep with halfe an eye;
Least her full Orb his sight should dim,
And bids us all good-night in him,
Till she would spend a gentle ray,
To force us a new-fashion'd day.

But what religious Palsie's this
Which makes the boughs divest their bliss?
And that they might her foot-steps strawe,
Drop their leaves with shivering awe.
Phillis perceives, and (least her stay
Should wed October unto May;
And as her beauty caus'd a Spring,
Devotion might an Autumne bring)
With-drew her beames, yet made no night,
But left the Sun her Curate-light.

50 4 *Venus* see Appendix 1 *Usher* escort 13 *dole* distribution 16 *Matins* morning service 25 *civill war* the Wars of the Roses, between York (white) and Lancaster (red) 32 *antidates* anticipates, precedes 35 *frizled* curled 45 *Palsie* shaking, with illness or religious fervour 47 *strawe* scatter 54 *Curate* delegate or understudy, especially for a clergyman

51 *A Faire Nimph scorning a Black Boy Courting her.*

Nymph. Stand off, and let me take the aire,
Why should the smoak pursue the faire?
Boy. My face is smoak, thence may be guest
What flames within have scorch'd my brest.
Nymph. The flame of love I cannot view,
For the dark Lanterne of thy hue.
Boy. And yet this Lanterne keeps loves Taper
Surer then yours, that's of white paper.
Whatever Midnight hath been here,
The Moon-shine of your light can cleare.
Nymph. My Moon of an Eclipse is 'fraid,
If thou should'st interpose thy shade.
Boy. Yet one thing (sweet-heart) I will ask,
Buy me for a new false Mask.
Nymph. Yes: but my bargaine shall be this,
I'le throw my Maske off when I kiss.
Boy. Our curl'd embraces shall delight
To checquer limbs with black, and white.

Nymph. Thy inke, my paper, make me guesse,
Our Nuptiall bed will make a Presse;
And in our sports, if any came,
They'l read a wanton Epigram.
Boy. Why should my Black thy love impaire?
Let the darke shop commend thy ware:
Or if thy love from black forbeares,
I'le strive to wash it off with teares.
Nymph. Spare fruitless teares, since thou must needs
Still weare about thee mourning weeds:
Teares can no more affection win,
Then wash thy Aethiopian skin.

51 See nos. 12 and 13 Title *Nimph* see Appendix 1 7 *Taper* small candle 20 *Presse* printing press 28 *weeds* garments 30 *Aethiopian* see Jeremiah 13: 23 'Can the Ethiopian change his skin, or the leopard his spots?'

52 The Antiplatonick.

For shame, thou everlasting Woer,
Still saying grace, and never falling to her!
Love that's in contemplation plac't,
Is *Venus* drawn but to the wast.
Unlesse your flame confesse it's gender,
And your Parley cause surrender
Y'are Salamanders of a cold desire,
That live untoucht amid the hottest fire.

What though she be a Dame of stone
The Widow of *Pigmalion*;
As hard and un-relenting she,
As the new-crusted *Niobe*;
Or what doth more of statue carry,
A Nunne of the Platonick Quarry?
Love melts the rigour which the rocks have bred,
A flint will break upon a Feather-bed.

For shame you pretty Female Elves,
Cease for to candy up your selves:
No more, you sectaries of the Game,
No more of your calcining flame.
Women commence by *Cupids* Dart,
As a King hunting dubs a Hart,
Loves votaries inthrall each others soul,
Till both of them live but upon Paroll.

Vertue's no more in Woman-kind
But the green sicknesse of the mind.
Philosophy, their new delight,
A kind of Char-coal appetite.
There's no Sophistry prevails,
Where all-convincing love assails;
But the disputing petticoat will warp,
As skilfull gamesters are to seek at sharp.

The souldier, that man of iron,
Whom ribs of *Horror* all inviron;
That's strung with Wire, instead of Veins,
In whose embraces you're in chains,
Let a Magnetick girl appear,
Straight he turns *Cupids* Cuiraseer.
Love storms his lips, and takes the Fortresse in,
For all the Brisled Turn-pikes of his chin.

Since Loves Artillery then checks
The breast-works of the firmest sex,
Come let's in affections riot,
Th'are sickly pleasures keep a Diet:
Give me a lover bold and free,
Not Eunucht with formality;
Like an Embassador that beds a Queen
With the nice Caution of a sword between.

52 Title *Antiplatonick* Cleveland opposes himself here to the cult of chaste or Platonic love which was fashionable at the Stuart court 1 *Woer* wooer 4 *wast* waist 6 *Parley* talk, negotiations 7 *Salamanders* fabulous monsters who live in flames 19 *sectaries* followers of a sect 20 *calcining* reducing to cinders 22 *dubs* makes a knight 23 *votaries* disciples 24 *Paroll* bail

26 *green sicknesse* wasting disease thought to afflict unmarried women 28 *Char-coal appetite* taste for unsuitable foodstuffs thought to characterize pregnancy or sexual frustration 29 *Sophistry* skill in delusive argument 38 *Cuiraseer* soldier 40 *Brisled Turn-pikes* moustache compared to military defences 41 *checks* holds back 42 *breast-works* pun on (military) ramparts 48 *sword between* ceremonial etiquette of a proxy marriage

SAMSON BRIGGS

53 *Song.*

When as the Nightingale chanted the Vesper
And the wild forresters couch'd on the ground
Venus invited me in th'eveninge whisper
Unto a fragrant feild with Roses crown'd
Where she before had sent
My wishes complement
Who to my Soules content
Joy'd with mee on the greene
Never Marke Antonye
Dally'de more wantonly
With the fayre Aegyptian Queene.

First on her cherry cheeks I mine eye feasted
Thence feare of surfetting made me retire
Unto her warmer lippe, which when I tasted
My Spiritts chill were made active as fyre,
This heate againe to calme
Her moyst hand yeilded balme
When wee joyn'd palme to palme,
As if they one had beene,
Never Marke &c.

Into her golden hayre I mine arme twined
She her hand in my locke hoisted againe
As if hayre had beene for fetters assigned
Great-little Cupids loose Captives to chayne
Then wee did often dart
At each anothers hart
Arrows which knew no smart
Sweet looks with smiles betweene
Never &c.

Wanting a glasse to platte those amber tresses
Which for a bracelet deckt richly mine arme
Gawdier then Juno weares, when as she blesses
Jove with embraces more stately than warme.
Shee sweetly peepte in mine
Eyes Humoure Christalline
And by reflexive shine
I in her eye was seene
Never &c.

Mysticall Grammer of amorous glances,
Feeling of pulses, the Physicks of Love,
Rhetoricall Courtings, and Musical daunces
Numbring of kisses Arithmeticke prove.
Eyes light Astronomy,
Streight limbs Geometry
In these arts Ingenye
Our witts were sharpe and keene
Never &c.

53 See Notes on the Text for the attribution of this poem 1 *Vesper* evening prayers 2 *couch'd* slept 10 *Dally'd* flirted, petted 13 *surfetting* overdosing 35 *Humoure Christalline* shining eyes 39–45 run through the students' curriculum of the liberal arts: grammar, physics, rhetoric, music, arithmetic, astronomy, and geometry (mathematics) 45 *Ingenye* skills

SIR JOHN DENHAM

54 *Natura Naturata.*

What gives us that Fantastick Fit,
That all our Judgment and our Wit
To vulgar custom we submit?

Treason, Theft, Murther, all the rest
Of that foul Legion we so detest,
Are in their proper names exprest.

Why is it then thought sin or shame,
Those necessary parts to name,
From whence we went, and whence we came?

Nature, what ere she wants, requires;
With Love enflaming our desires,
Sends Engines fit to quench those fires:

Death she abhors; yet when men die,
We are present; but no stander by
Looks on when we that loss supply:

Forbidden Wares sell twice as dear;
Even Sack prohibited last year,
A most abominable rate did bear.

'Tis plain our eyes and ears are nice,
Only to raise by that device,
Of those Commodities the price.

Thus Reason's shadows us betray
By Tropes and Figures led astray,
From Nature, both her Guide and way.

54 Title *Natura Naturata* nature made natural 17 *Sack* wine, particularly sherry 19 *nice* particular 23 *Tropes* figures of speech

55 *Out of an Epigram of* Martial.

Prithee die and set me free,
Or else be
Kind and brisk, and gay like me;
I pretend not to the wise ones,
To the grave, to the grave,
Or the precise ones.

Tis not Cheeks, nor Lips nor Eyes,
That I prize,
Quick Conceits, or sharp Replies,
If wise thou wilt appear, and knowing,
Repartie, Repartie
To what I'm doing.

Prithee why the Room so dark?
Not a Spark
Left to light me to the mark;
I love day-light and a candle,
And to see, and to see,
As well as handle.

Why so many Bolts and Locks,
Coats and Smocks,
And those Drawers with a Pox?
I could wish, could Nature make it,
Nakedness, Nakedness
It self were naked.

But if a Mistress I must have,
Wise and grave,
Let her so her self behave
All the day long *Susan* Civil,
Pap by night, pap by night
Or such a Divel.

55 This poem is a free and inventive reworking of Martial, *Epigrams,* XI. 104. *Martial* see Appendix 1 4 *pretend* aspire 9 *Conceits* witticisms 11 *Repartie* reply, respond 28 *Susan Civil* maybe a general term for a woman of discreet behaviour, possibly a more specific reference to Susan Fielding, Countess of Denbigh who was a pious member of the exiled court in France 29 *Pap* the primary meanings are breast or gruel, but there may be an irrecoverable contemporary reference cognate with 'Pug' the little devil in Ben Jonson's *The Devil is an Ass*, 1616 30 *Divel* devil

ROBERT HEATH

56 *Seeing Her Dancing.*

Robes loosly flowing, and aspect as free,
A carelesse carriage deckt with modestie;
    A smiling look, but yet severe:
    Such comely Graces 'bout her were.

Her steps with such an evenness she wove,
As shee could hardly be perceiv'd to move;
    Whilst her silk sailes displaied, shee
    Swam like a ship with Majestie.

As when with stedfast eies we view the Sun,
We know it goes though see no motion;
    So undiscern's she mov'd, that we
    Perceiv'd shee stirr'd, but did not see.

56 1 *aspect* appearance

57 *To her, the Storm ceasing.*

How *Neptune* smiles to view this Deitie
Which all the hoarie Gods amaz'd to see,
    Are at a stand and cannot move
    When they behold this Queen of Love!

Thy brow not wrinkled now with fear, the sea
Resumes its smoothness by a Sympathie:
    And whilst thou smil'st the rougher main
    Is levell'd to a verdant plain.

A happy *Halcyon* calmness sits upon
The equal face of all the Ocean:
    And not a wave his head dares show
    While thus in triumph you do go.

With such fair Wind and Weather, oh let me
Sail alwaies! and I ne'r shal sea-sick be!

57 2 *hoarie* grey-haired 4 *Queen of Love* Venus, see Appendix 1 7 *main* sea 8 *verdant* green 9 *Halcyon* see Appendix 1

58 *On* Clarastella *walking in her Garden.*

See how *Flora* smiles to see
This approaching Deitie!
Where each herb looks young and green
In presence of their comming Queen!
Ceres with all her fragrant store,
Could never boast so sweet a flow'r;
While thus in triumph she doth go
The greater Goddess of the two.
Here the Violet bows to greet
Her with homage to her feet;
There the Lilly pales with white
Got by her reflexed light;
Here a Rose in Crimson die
Blushes through her modestie;
There a Pansie hangs his head
'Bout to shrink into his bed,
'Cause so quickly she past by
Not returning suddenly;
Here the Currans red and white
In yon green bush at her sight
Peep through their shady leaves, and cry
Come eat me, as she passes by;
There a bed of Camomil,
When she presseth it doth smel
More fragrant than the perfum'd East,
Or the *Phoenix* spicie nest;
Here the Pinks in rowes do throng
To guard her as she walks along,
There the flexive Turnsole bends
Guided by the raies shee sends

From her bright eies, as if thence
It suckt life by influence;
Whilst She the prime and chiefest flow'r
In all the Garden by her pow'r
And onely life-inspiring breath
Like the warm Sun redeems from death
Their drooping heads, and bids them live
To tel us Shee their sweets did give.

58 1 *Flora*, 5 *Ceres* see Appendix 1 12 *reflexed* reflected 19 *Currans* currants 29 *flexive Turnsole* the marigold, which turns to face the sun 33 *She* i.e. Clarastella

ABRAHAM COWLEY

59 ODE.

In imitation of Horace *his Ode.*

Quis multa gracilis te puer in rosa Perfusus, etc. Lib.I.Od. 5.

1.

To whom now *Pyrrha*, art thou kinde?
To what heart-ravisht Lover,
Dost thou thy golden locks unbinde,
Thy hidden sweets discover,
And with large bounty open set
All the bright stores of thy rich *Cabinet?*

2.

Ah simple *Youth*, how oft will he
Of thy chang'ed *Faith* complain?
And his own *Fortunes* finde to be
So airy and so vain,
Of so *Camaeleon*-like an hew,
That still *their colour* changes with *it* too?

3.

How oft, alas, will he admire
The blackness of the Skies?
Trembling to hear the Winds sound higher,
And see the billows rise;
Poor *unexperienc'ed He*
Who ne're, alas, before had been at *Sea*!

4.

He enjoys thy calmy *Sun-shine* now,
And no breath stirring hears,
In the clear heaven of thy brow,
No smallest *Cloud* appears.
He sees thee gentle, fair, and gay,
And trusts the *faithless April* of thy *May*.

5.

Unhappy! thrice unhappy He,
T'whom *Thou untry'ed* dost shine!
But there's no danger now for *Me*,
Since o're *Loretto*'s *Shrine*
In witness of the *Shipwrack* past
My consecrated *Vessel* hangs at last.

59 Title *Quis multa* etc., the opening line of Horace, *Odes*, I.5. 'What boy adorned with how many graces among the roses' 6 *Cabinet* treasure-house, private room 7 *oft* often 11 *Camaeleon-like* changeable in colour *hew* colour 16 *billows* waves 28 *Loretto's Shrine* Shrine of the Holy House of Loreto near Recanati, Marche, Italy, at this time the chief pilgrimage church of Europe 30 *Vessel* the literal image is of a votive model hung up at the shrine in thanksgiving, but 'vessel' has also a subsidiary meaning of 'penis'

60 *The Spring.*

1.

Though you be absent here, I needs must say
The *Trees* as beauteous are, and *flowers* as gay,
As ever they were wont to be;
Nay the *Birds* rural musick too

Is as Melodious and free,
As if they sung to pleasure you:
I saw a *Rose-Bud* o'pe this morn; I'll swear
The blushing *Morning* open'd not more fair.

2.

How could it be so fair, and you away?
How could the *Trees* be beauteous, *Flowers* so gay?
Could they remember but last year,
How *you* did *Them, They you* delight,
The sprouting leaves which saw you here,
And call'd their *Fellows* to the sight,
Would, looking round for the same sight in vain,
Creep back into their silent *Barks* again.

3.

Where ere you walk'd, trees were as reverend made,
As when of old *Gods* dwelt in every shade.
Is't possible they should not know,
What loss of honor they sustain,
That thus they smile and flourish now,
And still their former pride retain?
Dull *Creatures*! 'tis not without Cause that she,
Who fled the *God of wit*, was made a *Tree*.

4.

In ancient times sure they much wiser were,
When they rejoyc'd the *Thracian* verse to heare;
In vain did *Nature* bid them stay,
When *Orpheus* had his song begun,
They call'd their wondring *roots* away,
And bad them silent to him run.
How would those learned trees have followed you?
You would have drawn *Them*, and their *Poet* too.

5.

But who can blame them now? for, since you're gone,
They're here the *onely Fair*, and *Shine alone*.
You did their *Natural Rights* invade;
Where ever you did walk or sit,

The thickest Bows could make no *shade*,
Although the Sun had granted it:
The fairest *Flowers* could please no more, neer you,
Then *Painted Flowers*, set next to them, could do.

6.

When e're then you come hither, that shall bee
The time, which this to others is, to *Mee*.
The little joys which here are now
The name of Punishments do beare;
When by their fight they let us Know
How we depriv'd of greater are.
'Tis you the best of *Seasons* with you bring;
This is for *Beasts*, and that for *Men* the *Spring*.

60 23 *she* Daphne, 24 *God of wit* Apollo, 26 *Thracian* of Orpheus, see Appendix 1 29 *roots* (of the ambulant trees) 37 *Bows* boughs

61 *Clad all in White.*

1.

Fairest thing that shines below,
Why in this robe dost thou appear?
Wouldst thou a *white* most perfect show,
Thou must at all *no garment* wear:
Thou wilt seem much whiter so,
Then *Winter* when 'tis *clad* with snow.

2.

'Tis not the *Linnen* shews so fair:
Her skin shines through, and makes it bright;
So *clouds* themselves like *Suns* appear,
When the *Sun* pierces them with Light:
So *Lillies* in a glass enclose,
The *Glass* will seem as white as those.

3.

Thou now *one heap* of *beauty* art;
Nought outwards, or within is foul:
Condensed beams make every part;
Thy *Body's Cloathed* like thy *Soul.*
Thy *soul*, which does it self display,
Like a *star* plac'd i'th *Milky* way.

4.

Such robes the *Saints* departed weare,
Woven all with *Light* divine;
Such their exalted *Bodies* are,
And with such full glory shine.
But they regard not mortals pain;
Men *pray*, I fear, to *both* in vain.

5.

Yet seeing thee so gently pure,
My hopes will needs continue still;
Thou wouldst not take this garment sure,
When thou hadst an intent to *kill.*
Of *Peace* and *yielding* who would doubt,
When the white *Flag* he sees hung out?

61 15 *Condensed beams* to reflect the purity of her soul, he imagines her body being made of compacted light 24 *both* (syntax obscure) apparently referring to saints and to his mistress 30 *white Flag* traditional sign of surrender

62 *The Injoyment.*

1.

Then like some wealthy *Island thou* shalt ly;
And like the *Sea* about it, *I*;
Thou like fair *Albion*, to the Sailors Sight,
Spreading her beauteous Bosom all in *White*:
Like the kind *Ocean* I will bee,
With loving *Arms* for ever clasping Thee.

2.

But I'll embrace Thee gentli'er far then so;
As their fresh *Banks* soft *Rivers* do,
Nor shall the *proudest Planet* boast a power
Of making my *full Love* to *ebb* one hour;
It never *dry* or *low* can prove,
Whilst thy unwasted *Fountain* feeds my Love.

3.

Such Heat and Vigour shall our *Kisses* bear,
As if like *Doves* we'engendred there.
No *bound* nor *rule* my pleasures shall endure,
In Love there's none too much an *Epicure*.
Nought shall my hands or Lips controul;
I'll kiss Thee *through*, I'll kiss thy *very Soul*.

4.

Yet nothing, but the *Night* our sports shall know;
Night that's both *blind* and *silent* too.
Alpheus found not a more secret trace,
His lov'd *Sicanian Fountain* to embrace,
Creeping so far beneath the Sea,
Then I will do t'enjoy, and *feast* on Thee.

5.

Men, out of *Wisdom; Women*, out of *Pride*,
The pleasant Thefts of Love do *hide*.
That may secure thee; but thou 'hast yet from Me
A more *infallible Securitie*.
For there's no danger I should tell
The Joys, which are to Me *unspeakable*.

62 1–4 the trope of Britain as the happy island parted from the cares of the world has its origin in Virgil, *Eclogue* I. 66 'et penitus tota divisus orbe Britannos' ('The Britons almost apart from the rest of the world)', see no. 205 3 *Albion* see Appendix 1 9 *proudest Planet* the moon which controls the ebb and flow of tides 14 *engendred* were born: it was believed that certain creatures were born spontaneously from heated matter 16 *Epicure* pleasure-seeker 21 *Alpheus* see Appendix 1

63 DIALOGUE,

After Enjoyment.

1.

She. What have we done? what cruel passion mov'd thee,
Thus to ruine her that lov'd Thee?
Me thou hast *robb'ed*, but what art thou
Thy *Self* the *richer* now?
Shame succeeds the short liv'd *pleasure*;
So soon is spent, and gone, this thy *Ill-gotten*
Treasure.

2.

He. We'have done no harm; nor was it *Theft* in *mee*,
But noblest *Charity* in *Thee*.
I'll the well-gotten *Pleasure*
Safe in my *Memorie* Treasure;
What though the *Flower* it self do wast,
The *Essence* from it drawn does long and sweeter last.

3.

She. No: I'm undone; my *Honor* Thou hast slain,
And nothing can restore't again.
Art and Labour to bestow,
Upon the *Carcase* of it now,
Is but t'embalm a body *dead*,
The *Figure* may remain, the *Life* and *Beautie's* fled.

4.

He. Never, my dear, was *Honor* yet undone,
By Love, but *Indiscretion*.
To th'*wise* it all things does allow;
And cares not *What* we do; but *How*.
Like *Tapers* shut in ancient *Urns*,
Unless it let in *ayr*, for ever *shines* and *burns*.

5.

She. *Thou first* perhaps who didst the fault commit,
Wilt make thy wicked boast of it.
For *Men*, with *Roman pride*, above
The *Conquest* do the *Triumph* love:
Nor think a perfect *Victory* gain'd,
Unless they through the *streets* their *Captive* lead enchain'd.

6.

He. Who e're his secret joys has open laid,
The *Baud* to his own *Wife* is made.
Beside what boast is left for mee,
Whose whole wealth's a *Gift* from *Thee?*
'Tis you the *Conqu'eror* are, 'tis you
Who have not onely *ta'ne*, but *bound*, and *gag'd* me too.

7.

She. Though publique punishment we escape, the *Sin*
Will rack and *torture* us within:
Guilt and *Sin* our bosom bears;
And though fair, yet the *Fruit* appears,
That *Worm* which now the *Core* does wast,
When long t'has gnaw'd within will break the *skin* at last.

8.

He. That *Thirsty Drink*, that *Hungry Food* I sought,
That *wounded Balm*, is all my fault.
And Thou in pity didst apply,
The kind and onely *remedie*:
The *Cause* absolves the *Crime*; since *Mee*
So mighty *Force* did move, so mighty *Goodness Thee*.

9.

She. *Curse* on thine *Arts*! methinks I *Hate* thee now;
And yet I'm sure I *love Thee* too!

I'm *angry*, but my *wrath* will prove,
More *Innocent* then did thy *Love*.
Thou hast *this* day undone me quite;
Yet wilt undo me more, should'st thou not come
at Night.

63 12 *Essence* perfume, essential oil 16 *Carcase* corpse 23 *Tapers* candles: this refers to a persistent belief that ancient magicians (Cicero, Virgil) and some modern magi (the fictitious Christian Rosenkreuz) had the power to make lamps which would burn for ever in a tomb. An archaeological hoax of the 1660s claimed amongst other things to have found such a lamp at a tomb in Colton's Field in Cirencester 28 *Triumph* Roman victories were celebrated with triumphal processions, often imitated in Renaissance Europe 32 *Baud* bawd, pimp

64 *The Chronicle*. A Ballad

1.

Margarita first possest,
If I remember well, my brest,
Margarita first of all;
But when a while the wanton Maid
With my restless Heart had plaid,
Martha took the flying Ball.

2.

Martha soon did it resign
To the beauteous *Catharine*.
Beauteous *Catharine* gave place
(Though loth and angry she to part
With possession of my Heart)
To *Elisa*'s conqu'ering face.

3.

Elisa till this Hour might reign
Had she not *Evil Counsels* ta'ne.
Fundamental Laws she broke,
And still new *Favorites* she chose,
Till up in *Arms* my *Passions* rose,
And cast away her yoke.

4.

Mary then and gentle *Ann*
Both to reign at once began.
Alternately they sway'd,
And sometimes *Mary* was the *Fair*,
And sometimes *Ann* the *Crown* did wear,
And sometimes *Both* I' obey'd

5.

Another *Mary* then arose,
And did rigorous Laws impose.
A mighty *Tyrant* she !
Long, alas, should I have been
Under that *Iron-Scepter'd Queen*,
Had not *Rebecca* set me free.

6.

When fair *Rebecca* set me free,
'Twas then a *golden Time* with mee.
But soon those pleasures fled,
For the gracious Princess dy'd
In her Youth and Beauties pride,
And *Judith* reigned in her sted.

7.

One Month, three Days, and half an hour
Judith held the *Soveraign Power*.
Wondrous beautiful her Face,
But so weak and small her Wit,
That she to govern was unfit,
And so *Susanna* took her place.

8.

But when *Isabella* came
Arm'd with a resistless flame
And th'Artillery of her Eye;
Whilst she proudly marcht about
Greater Conquests to find out,
She beat out *Susan* by the By.

9.

But in her place I then obey'd
Black-ey'd *Besse*, her *Viceroy-Maid*,
To whom ensu'd a *Vacancy*.
Thousand worse *Passions* then possest
The *Interregnum* of my Brest.
Bless me from such an *Anarchy* !

10.

Gentle *Henriette* than
And a third *Mary* next began,
Then *Jone*, and *Jane*, and *Audria*.
And then a pretty *Thomasine*,
And then another *Katharine*,
And then a *long Et caetera*.

11.

But should I now to you relate,
The strength and riches of their *state*,
The *Powder, Patches*, and the *Pins*,
The *Ribbans, Jewels*, and the *Rings*,
The *Lace*, the *Paint*, and *warlike things*,
That make up all their *Magazins*:

12.

If I should tell the politick Arts
To take and keep mens hearts,
The Letters, Embassies, and Spies,
The Frowns, and Smiles, and Flatteries,
The Quarrels, Tears, and Perjuries,
Numberless, *Nameless Mysteries* !

13.

And all the *Little Lime-twigs* laid
By *Matchavil* the *Waiting-Maid*;
I more voluminous should grow
(Chiefly if I like them should tell
All Change of *Weathers* that befell)
Then *Holinshead* or *Stow*.

14.

But I will briefer with them be,
Since few of them were long with Me.
An higher and a nobler strain
My present *Emperess* does claim,
Heleonora, First o'th'Name;
Whom *God grant long to reign*!

64 4 *wanton* careless 6 *flying Ball* his heart, as a toy 10 *loth* reluctant 18 *yoke* metaphorically, her service 21 *sway'd* reigned 29 *Iron-Scepter'd* metaphorically, stern ruling 45 *Artillery* metaphorically, her glances 50 *Viceroy* substitute for a monarch 53 *Interregnum* gap between the rule of two successive monarchs 54 *Anarchy* no rule; period of social chaos 63 *Patches* cosmetic beauty spots 66 *Magazins* stores of weaponry 71 *Perjuries* telling lies under oath 73 *Lime-twigs* used as snares to trap birds 74 *Matchavil* see Appendix 2 78 *Holinshead, Stow* see Appendix 2

RICHARD LOVELACE

65 ELINDA'S GLOVE

SONNET.

I.

Thou snowy Farme with thy five Tenements!
Tell thy white Mistris here was one
That call'd to pay his dayly Rents:
But she a gathering Flowr's and Hearts is gone,
And thou left voyd to rude Possession.

II.

But grieve not pretty *Ermin* Cabinet,
Thy Alablaster Lady will come home;
If not, what Tenant can there fit
The slender turnings of thy narrow Roome,
But must ejected be by his owne dombe?

III.

Then give me leave to leave my Rent with thee;
Five kisses, one unto a place:
For though the *Lute's* too high for me;
Yet Servants knowing Minikin nor Base,
Are still allow'd to fiddle with the Case.

65 1 *snowy* the glove is white *Tenements* lodgings 5 *voyd* untenanted 6 *Ermin* fur, proverbially pure white 7 *Alablaster* pure white marble 10 *dombe* doom, judgement 13 *Lute's* metaphorically, her hand 14 *Minikin, Base* highest and lowest strings of a lute or viol 15 *Case* double-entendre: contemporary slang for vagina

66 *La Bella Bona Roba*

I.

I cannot tell who loves the Skeleton
Of a poor Marmoset, nought but boan, boan.
Give me a nakednesse with her cloath's on.

II.

Such whose white-sattin upper coat of skin,
Cut upon Velvet rich Incarnadin,
Ha's yet a Body (and of Flesh) within.

III.

Sure it is meant good Husbandry in men,
Who do incorporate with Aëry leane,
T'repair their sides, and get their Ribb agen.

IV.

Hard hap unto that Huntsman that Decrees
Fat joys for all his swet, when as he sees,
After his 'Say, nought but his Keepers Fees.

V.

Then Love I beg, when next thou tak'st thy Bow,
Thy angry shafts, and dost Heart-chasing go,
Passe *Rascall Deare*, strike me the largest Doe.

66 Title *Bona Roba* common expression for a harlot, see Shakespeare *2 Henry IV* III. ii. 23, 'And I may say to you wee knew where the *Bona-Roba*'s were, and had the best of them all at commandement' 2 *Marmoset* small monkey 5 *Incarnadin* reddened 7 *Husbandry* use of resources 8 *incorporate* here, mate *Aëry* thin as air 10 *hap* luck 12 *'Say* essay *Keepers Fees* the shoulder and intestines of the deer 14 *Heart-chasing* flirting, also hunting the hart (deer) 15 *Rascall* thin

67 *A Black Patch on* Lucasta'*s Face.*

1.

As I beheld a Winters Evening Air,
Curl'd in her court false locks of living hair,
Butter'd with Jessamine the Sun left there.

2.

Galliard and clinquant she appear'd to give,
A Serenade or Ball to us that grieve,
And teach us *A la mode* more gently live.

3.

But as a *Moor*, who to her Cheeks prefers
White Spots t'allure her black Idolaters,
Me thought she look'd all ore bepatch'd with Stars.

4.

Like the dark front of some *Ethiopian* Queen,
Vailed all ore with Gems of Red, Blew, Green;
Whose ugly Night seem'd masked with days Skreen.

5.

Whilst the fond people offer'd Sacrifice
To Saphyrs 'stead of Veins and Arteries,
And bow'd unto the Diamonds, not her Eyes.

6.

Behold *Lucasta's* Face, how't glows like Noon!
A Sun intire is her complexion,
And form'd of one whole Constellation.

7.

So gently shining, so serene, so cleer,
Her look doth Universal Nature cheer;
Only a cloud or two hangs here and there.

67 Title *Patch* fashionable beauty spot 3 *Butter'd* anointed *Jessamine* jasmine 4 *Galliard* high-spirited *clinquant* adorned with gold or silver 5 *Serenade* music played outdoors 6 *A la mode* fashionably 7 *Moor* African 14 *Saphyrs* sapphires

68 Lucasta *at the Bath.*

I'th'Autumn of a Summers day,
When all the Winds got leave to play;
Lucasta, that fair Ship, is lanch'd,
And from its crust this Almond blanch'd.

Blow then, unruly Northwind, blow,
'Till in their holds your Eyes you show;
And swell your Cheeks, bequeath chill Death:
See! she hath smil'd thee out of Breath.

Court gentle *Zephyr*, court and fan
Her softer breast's carnation'd Wan;
Your charming Rhethorick of Down
Flyes scatter'd from before her frown.

Say, my white Water-Lilly, say,
How is't those warm streams break away?
Cut by thy chast cold breast which dwells
Amidst them arm'd in Isicles.

And the hot floods more raging grown
In flames of Thee, then in their own;
In their distempers wildly glow,
And kisse thy Pillar of fix'd Snow.

No Sulphur, through whose each blew Vein
The thick and lazy Currents strein,
Can cure the Smarting, nor the fell
Blisters of Love wherewith they swell.

These great Physicians of the Blind,
The Lame, and fatal Blains of *Inde*,
In every drop themselves now see
Speckled with a new Leprosie.

As Sick drinks are with old Wine dash'd,
Foul Waters too with Spirits wash'd;
Thou greiv'd, perchance, one tear let'st fall,
Which straight did purifie them all.

And now is cleans'd enough the flood,
Which since runs cleare, as doth thy blood;
Of the wet Pearls uncrown thy hair,
And mantle thee with *Ermin* Air.

Lucasta, hail! fair Conqueresse
Of Fire, Air, Earth, and Seas;
Thou whom all kneel to, yet even thou
Wilt unto Love, thy captive, bow.

68 3 *lanch'd* launched 4 *Almond blanch'd* the almond skinned to expose the white nut 9 *Zephyr* see Appendix 1 10 *carnation'd* reddened *Wan* pallor 21 *Sulphur* naturally sulphurated water was used to treat venereal diseases and skin complaints 26 *Blains* sores *Inde* India 29 *Sick drinks* medicines *dash'd* mixed 36 *Ermin* white fur

69 AMYNTOR *from beyond the Sea to* ALEXIS A Dialogue.

AMYNTOR

ALEXIS! ah ALEXIS! can it be
Though so much wet and drie
Doth drowne our Eye,
Thou keep'st thy winged voice from me?

ALEXIS

AMYNTOR a profounder sea I feare
Hath swallow'd me, where now
My armes do row,
I floate i t'h'Ocean of a Teare.

LUCASTA weepes lest I look back and tread
Your watry Land againe.
AMYNT. I'd through the raine.
Such showrs are quickly over-spread.

IV.

Conceive how Joy after this short divorce
Will circle her with beames,
When like your streames
You shall rowle back with a kinder force

V.

And call the helping winds to vent your thought.
ALEX. AMYNTOR ! CHLORIS where
Or in what Sphere
Say may that glorious faire be sought?

AMYNTOR.

She's now the center of these armes e're blest
Whence may she never move
Till Time and Love
Haste to their everlasting rest.

ALEXIS.

Ah subtle swaine ! doth not my flame rise high
As yours, and burne as hot?
Am not I shot
With the selfe same Artillery?

VIII.

And can I breathe without her air? AMYN. why
then
From thy tempestuous Earth
Where blood and dearth
Raigne 'stead of Kings, agen

Wafte thy self over, and lest stormes from far
Arise, bring in our sight
The Seas delight,
LUCASTA that bright Northerne star.

ALEXIS.

But as we cut the rugged deepe, I feare
The green God stops his fell
Chariot of shell
And smooths the maine to ravish her.

AMYNTOR.

Oh no, the Prince of waters fires are done,
He as his Empire Old
And Rivers Cold,
His Queen now runs a bed to th'Sun;

XII

But all his treasure he shall ope' that day:
TRITONS shall sound, his fleete
In silver meete,
And to her their rich offrings pay.

ALEXIS.

We flye AMYNTOR, nor amazed how sent
By Water, Earth, or Aire:
Or if with her
By Fire, ev'n there
I move in mine owne Element.

69 See nos. 74, 114 5 *profounder* deeper 13 *divorce* parting 38 *green God* Neptune, see Appendix 1 *fell* ominous 40 *maine* sea 44 *His Queen* Amphitrite, see Appendix 1 46 TRITONS see Appendix 1

70 *To* Lucasta

1.

I laugh and sing, but cannot tell
Whether the folly on't sounds well;
But then I groan
Methinks in Tune,
Whilst Grief, Despair, and Fear, dance to the Air
Of my despised Prayer.

2.

A pretty Antick Love does this,
Then strikes a Galliard with a Kiss;
As in the end
The Chords they rend;
So you but with a touch from your fair Hand,
Turn all to Saraband.

70 7 *Antick* clown or lunatic 8 *Galliard* lively court dance 12 *Saraband* stately dance

THOMAS PHILIPOTT

71 *To a Gentlewoman viewing her selfe in her glasse.*

Cruell faire one, think this Glasse,
Wherein you now behold your face,
Was compos'd of one who dyed
For love of you, since he applyed
His liquid and dissolving eyes,
So long with teares to sacrifice
To your disdaine, that to relieve
His Bankrupt and impoverish'd griefe

With a fresh stock of moysture, hee
Melted to a spring, which see
The cold, but charitable North,
(Lest a fountaine of such worth
Should, by vulgar lips, be tasted,
Or profanely be exhausted)
Congeal'd into a Chrystall Masse,
Of which was form'd this Looking-glasse:
And as your Figure faire did rest,
Within this Lovers living brest,
So still you see it doth appeare,
Though turn'd to Chrystall, harbour'd there.

71 See no. 17

72 *On a sparke of fire fixing on a Gentlewomans brest.*

Faire *Julia* sitting by the fire,
An amorous spark, with hot desire,
Flew to her brest, but could not melt
The chast snow there, which when it felt,
And that resistance it did bide,
For griefe it blush'd, and so it di'd.
Yet lest it should prove ought unkind,
It contrite ashes left behind.

72 7 *ought* aught, in some way

THOMAS STANLEY

73 *The Gloworme.*

Stay fairest *Chariessa*, stay and mark
This animated Gem, whose fainter spark
Of fading light, its birth had from the dark.

A Star thought by the erring Passenger,
Which falling from its native Orb dropt here,
And makes the Earth (its Centre,) now its Sphere.

Should many of these sparks together be,
He that the unknown light far off should see
Would think it a terrestrial Galaxie.

Take't up fair Saint; see how it mocks thy fright,
The paler flame doth not yield heat, though light,
Which thus deceives thy Reason, through thy sight.

But see how quickly it (ta'ne up) doth fade,
To shine in darkness onely being made,
By th'brightness of thy light turn'd to a shade;

And burnt to ashes by thy flaming eyes
On the chaste Altar of thy hand it dies,
As to thy greater light a sacrifice.

73 1 *Chariessa* from Greek *charis*, 'grace' 4–6 The image here compares the glow-worm to a star which has shot from its place in heaven, its 'orb', and has taken up its place, 'sphere', on Earth

JOHN HALL

74 *A Sea Dialogue*

Palurus.

My Antinetta though thou be
More white, then fome wherewith a wave
Broke in his wrath besmears the sea;
Yet art thou harder then this cave.

Antinetta.

Though thou be fairer then the light,
Which doubting Pilots onely mind
That they may steere there course aright,
Yet art thou lighter then the wind:

Palurus.

And shall I not be chang'd? when thou
Hast fraught Medorus with thy heart,
And as a-long the sands we go
To gather shells, do's take his part?

Antinetta.

What shall I not congeal to see
Doris the Ballast of thine arms?
(Which have so oft encompass'd me)
Now pinion'd by her faithlesse charms;

Palurus.

What if I henceforth shall disdain
The golden tressed Doris love?
And Antinetta serve again,
And in that service constant prove?

Antinetta.

Though mighty Neptune cannot stand
Before Medorus, and thou be
Restlesse as whirle-pool's, false as sand;
Yet will I live and die with thee,

Palurus.

Nay live, and lest one single death
Should wrack thee, take this life of mine,

Antinetta.

Thou but exchanged with that breath,
Thy Antinetta's soul for thine.

Chorus.

How powerfull's love! which like a flame
That sever'd, reunites more close!
Or like a broken limb in frame
That ever after firmer grows.

74 A very free version of Horace, *Odes*, III. 9 (see nos. 11, 119) 8 *lighter* more fickle

10 *fraught* loaded down 13 *congeal* freeze, turn hard 14 *Ballast* weight carried to balance a ship, sometimes in place of cargo 31 *in frame* mended, in order

75 *Julia Weeping.*

1.

Fairest, when thine eyes did poure
A Christall shower,
I was perswaded that some stone
Had liquid grown;
And thus amazed, sure thought I
When stones are moist some rain is nigh.

2.

Why weep'st thou? cause thou cannot be
More hard to mee?
So Lionesses pitty, so
Do Tygers too:
So doth that Bird, which when she's fed
On all the man, pines o're the Head.

3.

Yet I'le make better Omens till
Event beguile,
Those pearly droppes in time shall be
A precious sea;
And thou shall like thy Corall prove,
Soft under water, hard above.

75 13–14 'I will invent better omens until a good outcome delights us'

CHARLES COTTON

76 Laura *Sleeping.*

ODE.

I.

Winds whisper gently whilst she sleeps,
And fan her with your cooling wings;
Whilst she her drops of Beauty weeps,
From pure, and yet unrivall'd Springs.

II.

Glide over Beauties Field her Face,
To kiss her Lip, and Cheek be bold,
But with a calm, and stealing pace;
Neither too rude; nor yet too cold.

III.

Play in her beams, and crisp her Hair,
With such a gale, as wings soft *Love*
And with so sweet, so rich an Air,
As breaths from the *Arabian* Grove.

IV.

A Breath as hush't as Lovers sigh;
Or that unfolds the Morning door:
Sweet, as the Winds, that gently fly,
To sweep the *Springs* enamell'd Floor.

V.

Murmur soft *Musick* to her Dreams,
That pure, and unpoluted run,
Like to the new-born Christal Streams,
Under the bright enamour'd Sun.

VI.

But when she waking shall display
Her light retire within your bar,
Her Breath is life, her Eyes are day,
And all Mankind her Creatures are.

76 9 *crisp* curl 12 *Arabian Grove* grove of spice-trees

KATHERINE PHILIPS

77 *A Dialogue of Absence 'twixt* Lucasia *and* Orinda. *Set by Mr.* Hen. Lawes.

Luc. Say my *Orinda*, why so sad?
Orin. Absence from thee doth tear my heart;
Which, since with thine it union had,
Each parting splits. *Luc.* And can we part?
Orin. Our Bodies must. *Luc.* But never we:
Our Souls, without the help of Sense,
By wayes more noble and more free
Can meet, and hold intelligence.
Orin. And yet those Souls, when first they met,
Lookt out at windows through the Eyes.
Luc. But soon did such acquaintance get,
Not Fate nor Time can them surprize.
Orin. Absence will rob us of that bliss
To which this Friendship title brings:
Love's fruits and joys are made by this
Useless as Crowns to captiv'd Kings.
Luc. Friendship's a Science, and we know
There Contemplation's most employ'd.
Orin. Religion's so, but practick too,
And both by niceties destroy'd.
Luc. But who ne're parts can never meet,
And so that happiness were lost.

Orin. Thus Pain and Death are sadly sweet,
Since Health and Heav'n such price must cost.

Chorus.

But we shall come where no rude hand shall sever,
And there wee'l meet and part no more for ever.

77 6 *Sense* the physical body

PHILIP AYRES

78 *Invites his Nymph to his Cottage.*

On yon' Hill's Top which this sweet Plain commands,
Fair *Cynthia*, all alone my Cottage stands,
'Gainst storms, and scorching Heats well fortify'd,
With Pines, and spreading Oaks on ev'ry side.

My lovely Garden too adjoyning lyes,
Of sweetest Flowers, and of the richest Dyes:
The Tulip, Jas'min, Emony and Rose
Of which we'll Garlands for thy Head compose.

Nature to make my Fountain, did its Part,
Which ever flows without the help of Art,
A faithful Mirror shall its Waters be,
Where thou may'st sit beneath a shady Tree,

Admiring what above the World I prize,
Thy self, the object of thine own fair Eyes;
And which is greatest let the Spring proclaim,
Thy Powers of Love, or this my Amorous Flame.

78 Title *Nymph* see Appendix 1 7 *Emony* anemone

DANIEL SCARGILL

79 Come Pilgrim to thy Home

Dear Love, one Feathered minute and I come
To lye down in thy darke Retireing Roome
And mingle Dust with thine, that wee may have,
As when alive one Bed, so dead, one Grave:
And may my Soul teare through the vaulted Sky
To be with thine to all Eternitie.
O how our Bloudless Formes will that Day greet
With Love Divine when we again shall meet
Devest of all Contagion of the Flesh
Full filled with everlasting joys and Fresh
In Heaven above (and t'may be) cast an eye
How far Elizium doth beaneath us lye.
Deare, I disbody and away
More swift than Wind
Or flying Hind
I come I come away.

79 See no. 22. 2 *Retireing Roome* private dressing room, here tomb 7 *that Day* Doomsday, when the dead rise for the Last Judgement 9 *Devest* divested

PART TWO

SONG TEXTS AND POEMS ABOUT MUSIC

ANONYMOUS [? SIR FRANCIS FANE]

80 [Rare, and ever to be wisht maye sownde heere]

Rare, and ever to be wisht maye sownde heere
Instruments which fainte sp'rites and muses cheere
Composing for the body, soule and eare
Which sicknes, sadnes and foule spirits feare.

80 See Notes on the Text for possible attribution 3 *Composing* bringing harmony

AURELIAN TOWNSHEND

81 On his hearing her Majesty sing.

I have beene in Heav'n, I thinke,
For I heard an Angell sing,
Notes my thirsty ears did drinke,
Never any earthly thing
Sung so true, so sweet, so cleere,
I was then in Heav'n, not heere.

But the blessed feele no change,
So I may mistake the place,
But mine eyes would think it strange,
Should that be no Angels face;
Powr's above, it seems, designe
Me still Mortal, her Divine.

Till I tread the Milky way,
And I lose my sences quite;
All I wish is that I may
Hear that voice, and see that sight,
Then in types and outward show
I shall have a heav'n below.

81 Title *her Majesty* Queen Henrietta Maria The central idea of this poem is that the power of music can exalt the soul to the point where it has foreknowledge of (a platonic) heaven
17 *types and outward show* earthly manifestations of the platonic 'reality'

JOHN POLWHELE

82 To Mrs M.E. who sange to her Lute.

Noe more of this eare-lecherie! laye bye
that quidled lute!
and let thy sweeter voyce be mute
Tune up those veines for nature's harmony
that everie sinew ye touch
May in our mutuall sympathye be such
as when two vyols by on hand doe move
There is noe musick like consort in Love.

Entreatyes cannot silence, yet extorte
Musical ayres
from harpes strunge with a thousand haires
for the blinde Harper, amarous Cupid's sporte
who steals this waye more hearts
then conquers by his golden-headed darts:
Woemen are his best Instruments to prove
Ther is noe Musick like Consorte in Love.

82 This poem plays continually on ideas of bodies resonating in sympathy like stringed instruments 2 *quidled* from the verb to quiddle: to trifle, with 1567 musical sense of improvising on a set base [*OED*] 5 *sinew* lutestring

LADY MARY WROTH

83 Song.

O me, the time is come to part,
And with it my life-killing smart:
Fond Hope leave me, my deare must goe,
To meete more joy, and I more woe.

Where still of mirth injoy thy fill,
One is enough to suffer ill:
My heart so well to sorrow us'd,
Can better be by new griefes bruis'd.

Thou whom the Heavens themselves like made,
Should never sit in mourning shade:
No, I alone must mourne and end,
Who have a life in griefe to spend.

My swiftest pace to wailings bent,
Shewes joy had but a short time lent,
To bide in mee where woes must dwell,
And charme mee with their cruell spell.

And yett when they their witchcrafts trye,
They only make me wish to dye:
But ere my faith in love they change,
In horrid darknesse will I range.

83 2 *smart* pain 3 *Fond* deluded 9 'The heavens made you like themselves' 20 *range* wander

84 Song.

I that am of all most crost,
Having, and that had have lost,
May with reason thus complaine,
Since love breeds love, and Loves paine.

That which I did most desire,
To allay my loving fire,
I may have, yet now must misse,
Since another Ruler is.

Would that I no Ruler had,
Or the service not so bad,
Then might I with blisse enjoy
That which now my hopes destroy.

And that wicked pleasure got,
Brings with it the sweetest lot:
I that must not taste the best,
Fed, must starve, and restlesse rest.

ROBERT HERRICK

85 *To Musique, to becalme his Fever*

1.

Charm me asleep, and melt me so
With thy Delicious Numbers;
That being ravisht, hence I goe
Away in easie slumbers.
Ease my sick head,
And make my bed,
Thou Power that canst sever
From me this ill:
And quickly still:
Though thou not kill
My Fever.

2.

Thou sweetly canst convert the same
From a consuming fire,
Into a gentle-licking flame,
And make it thus expire.
Then make me weep
My paines asleep;
And give me such reposes,
That I, poore I,
May think, thereby,
I live and die
'Mongst Roses.

3.

Fall on me like a silent dew,
Or like those Maiden showrs,
Which, by the peepe of day, doe strew
A Baptime o're the flowers.
Melt, melt my paines,
With thy soft straines;
That having ease me given,

With full delight,
I leave this light;
And take my flight
For Heaven.

85 2 *Numbers* groups of musical notes, 1598 usage [*OED*] 24 *Maiden showrs* dew 26 *Baptime* baptism

86 *To Musick*

Begin to charme, and as thou stroak'st mine ears
With thy enchantment, melt me into tears.
Then let thy active hand scu'd o're thy Lyre:
And make my spirits frantick with the fire.
That done, sink down into a silv'rie straine;
And make me smooth as Balme, and Oile againe.

86 3 *scu'd* move swiftly 6 *Balme* salve

[? HENRY NOEL]

87 A Song.

Gaze not on swans in whose soft breast
A full hatch'd beauty seems to nest,
Nor snow, which falling from the skye
Hovers in its Virginitie.

Gaze not on Roses though new blowne
Grac'd with a fresh Complexion
Nor Lillyes which no subtle bee
Hath rob'd by Kissing Chymistrie.

Gaze not on that pure milkey way
Where night vy's splendour with the day,
Nor pearles whose silver walls confine
The riches of an Indian mine,

For when my Empresse once appeares,
Swans moulting dye, Snow melts to teares
Roses doe blush, hanging their heads
Pale Lillies shrinke into their beds

The milkey way rides post, to shrowde
Her baffled glory in a clowd
The Pearles do climbe into her eare
To hang themselves for envy there

Thus may you see stars bigge with light
Proove Lanthorns to the moone-ey'd night,
Which when Sols rayes are once display'd
Sinke in their socketts, and decay'd.

87 8 *Kissing Chymistrie* collecting pollen 17 *rides post* speeds, changing horses frequently to speed a journey 18 *baffled* disgraced, confused 23 *Sol* the sun

THOMAS CAREW

88 A Song.

Aske me no more where *Jove* bestowes,
When *June* is past the fading rose:
For in your beauties orient deepe,
These flowers as in their causes, sleepe.

Aske me no more whether doth stray,
The golden Atomes of the day:
For in pure love heaven did prepare,
Those powders to inrich your haire.

Aske me no more whether doth hast,
The Nightingale when May is past:
For in your sweet dividing throat,
She winters and keepes warme her note.

Aske me no more where those starres light,
That downewards fall in dead of night:
For in your eyes they sit and there,
Fixed become as in their sphere.

Aske me no more if East or West,
The Phenix builds her spicy nest:
For unto you at last shee flies,
And in your fragrant bosome dyes.

88 3 *orient* eastern, with connotation of riches 4 *causes* essence, platonic 'first matter' 6 *golden Atomes* dust in sunbeams 11 *dividing* in music, to ornament an existing tune

JAMES SHIRLEY [possibly revised by THOMAS CAREW]

89 Song.

Would you know what's soft? I dare
Not bring you to the downe, or aire:
Nor to starres to shew what's bright,
Nor to snow to teach you white.

Nor if you would Musicke heare,
Call the orbes to take your eare:
Nor to please your sence bring forth,
Bruised Nard or what's more worth.

Or on food were your thoughts plac't,
Bring you Nectar, for a tast;
Would you have all these in one,
Name my mistris, and 'tis done.

89 See Ben Jonson's song 'Have you seene but a bright Lilly grow' in *The Devil is an ass*, 1616 2 *downe* soft feathers 6 *orbes* the planets were believed to circle the earth fixed to crystal spheres each of which emitted a musical note 8 *Nard* spikenard, an aromatic root pounded to release its scent

WILLIAM STRODE

90 The Commendation of musicke.

When whispering straines with creeping winde
distill soft passion through the hart,
and when at every touch wee finde
our pulses beate, and beare a part,
when threads can make
A heart string shake,
philosophie
cannot denye
our soules consist of Harmony:

When unto heavenly Ioyes wee feigne
what ere the soule affecteth most,
which only thus we can explaine
by musicke of the heavenly Hoast,
whose layes me thinkes
make starres to shrinke,
philosophie
may Iudge thereby
our soules consist of Harmony:

Oh Lull me, lull me charming ayre,
my sences rocke with wonder sweete,
like snow on wooll thy fallings are,
soft as a spirits are thy feete;
griefe who neede feare
that hath an eare,
downe let him lye
and slumbring dye,
And change his soule for Harmony.

90 See no. 82 4 *part* i.e. a line within the texture of the music 6 *heart string* the image here is of the emotions resonating like sympathetic strings on a musical instrument 13 *Hoast* company of angels 14 *layes* songs

91 Song

I saw faire Cloris walke alone
    When featherd raine came softly downe
And Jove descended from his Towre
To Court her in a Silver showre.
The wanton Snow flew on her breast
As little birdes unto their nest
  But overcome in whiteness there
  For greife it thawd into a Teare
  Then falling on her garments hemme
  To decke her freezd into a Gemme.

91 4 *Silver showre* Jove wooed Danae in a shower of gold, see Appendix 1 10 *decke* ornament

92 Song.

When Orpheus sweetly did complaine
Upon his lute with heavy straine
How his Euridice was slaine
        The trees to heare
        Obtaind an Eare
And after left it off againe.

At ev'ry stroke and ev'ry stay
The boughes kept Time and nodding lay
And listend bending all one way
        The Aspen Tree
        As fast as He
Began to shake and learn'd to play.

If wood could speake a Tree might heare
If wood could sounde true grief soe neere
A Tree might droppe an Amber teare
        If wood soe well
        Could ring a knell
The Cypresse might condole the beare.

The standing *Nobles* of the Grove
Hearing dead wood soe speake and move
The fatall Axe began to love
They envy'd Death
Which gave such breath
As men alive doe saints above.

92 2 *heavy* sad 7 *stroke* note *stay* pause in the music 12 *shake* trill, musical ornament 18 *Cypresse* funereal tree *beare* bier 19 *Nobles* high trees 20 a common inscription on Renaissance musical instruments is 'Dum vixi tacui, mortuus dulce cano' ('living I was silent, dead I sing sweetly')

93 Song.

Keepe on your maske and hide your Eye
For with beholding you I dye
Your fatall beauty Gorgonlike
Dead with astonishment will strike
Your peircing Eyes if them I see
Are worse then Basiliskes to *me*.

Shutt from mine Eyes those hills of snow
Their melting valley doe not show
Those azure paths leade to dispayre
O vexe me not, forbeare, forbeare
For while I thus in torments dwell
The sight of heavn is worse then hell.

Your dainty voice and warbling breath
Sounds like a Sentence past for death
Your dangling tresses are become
Like Instruments of finall doome
O if an Angell torture soe
When life is donne where *shall I goe?*

93 3 *Gorgonlike* see Appendix 1 9 *azure paths* blue veins, but see also notes to no. 229

SIR WILLIAM DAVENANT

94 *SONG.*

1.

The Lark now leaves his watry Nest
        And climbing, shakes his dewy Wings;
He takes this Window for the East;
        And to implore your Light, he Sings,
Awake, awake, the Morn will never rise,
Till she can dress her Beauty at your Eies.

2.

The Merchant bowes unto the Seamans Star,
        The Ploughman from the Sun his Season takes;
But still the Lover wonders what they are,
        Who look for day before his Mistress wakes.
Awake, awake, break through your Vailes of Lawne!
Then draw your Curtains, and begin the Dawne.

94 7 *Seamans Star* the North (pole) star 11 *Lawne* gauzy fabric 12 *Curtains* bed curtains

95 *SONG.*

Endimion Porter, *and* Olivia.

OLIVIA.

        Before we shall again behold
In his diurnal race the Worlds great Eye,
        We may as silent be and cold.
As are the shades where buried Lovers ly.

ENDIMION.

        Olivia 'tis no fault of Love
To loose our selves in death, but O, I fear,
                When Life and Knowledge is above
Restor'd to us, I shall not know thee there.

OLIVIA.

Call it not Heaven (my Love) where we
Our selves shall see, and yet each other miss:
So much of Heaven I find in thee
As, thou unknown, all else privation is.

ENDIMION.

Why should we doubt, before we go
To find the Knowledge which shall ever last,
That we may there each other know?
Can future Knowledge quite destroy the past?

OLIVIA.

When at the Bowers in the Elizian shade
I first arrive, I shall examine where
They dwel, who love the highest Vertue made?
For I am sure to find *Endimion* there.

ENDIMION.

From this vext World when we shall both retire,
Where all her Lovers, and where all rejoyce;
I need not seek thee in the Heavenly Quire;
For I shall know *Olivia* by her Voice.

95 2 *diurnal race* daily course 17 *Elizian shade* the classical paradise, see Appendix 1. The imagery of the dead lovers amongst the groves draws on Virgil, *Aeneid*, VI 23 *Quire* choir

96 *SONG. The Dying Lover.*

1.

Dear *Love* let me this Evening dy!
O Smile not to prevent it.
Dead with my Rivals let me ly;
Or we shall both repent it.
Frown quickly then, and break my heart;
That so my way of dying
May, though my life was full of smart,
Be worth the Worlds envying.

2.

Some, striving knowledge to refine,
 Consume themselves with thinking;
And some, who Friendship Seal in Wine,
 Are kindly kill'd with drinking.
And some are Wrackt on th'*Indian* Coast;
 Thither by Gain invited:
Some are in smoak of Battels lost;
 Whom Drums, not Lutes delighted.

3.

Alas, how poorly these depart,
 Their Graves still unattended?
Who dies not of a broken heart,
 Is not of death commended.
His memory is only sweet,
 All praise and pitty moving,
Who kindly at his Mistress feet
 Does die with over-loving.

4.

And now thou frown'st, and now I die;
 My Corps by Lovers follow'd;
Which straite shall by dead Lovers ly;
 That Ground is only hallow'd.
If Priests are griev'd, I have a Grave,
 My death not well approving,
The Poets my Estate shall have
 To teach them the Art of Loving.

5.

And now let Lovers ring their Bells,
 For me poor Youth departed,
Who kindly in his love excells
 By dying broken hearted.
My Grave with Flowers let Virgins strow;
 Which, if thy Teares fall near them,
May so transcend in Scent and Show,
 As thou wilt shortly weare them.

6.

Such Flowers how much will Florists prize,
Which on a Lover growing,
Are water'd with his Mistress eyes,
With pitty ever flowing.
A Grave so deckt, will, though thou art
Yet fearful to come nie me,
Provoke thee straite to break thy heart,
And lie down boldly by me.

7.

Then ev'ry where all Bells shall ring,
All Light to Darkness turning,
Whilst ev'ry Quire shall sadly sing,
And Natures self weare mourning.
Yet we hereafter may be found,
By Destinies right placing,
Making, like Flowers, Love under Ground,
Whose Rootes are still embracing.

96 1 *dy* die, also reach orgasm 41 *Florists* botanists, specialist gardeners 45 *deckt* covered, ornamented 51 *Quire* choir

97 SONG. [from *Newes from Plimouth*]

O Thou that sleep'st like *Pigg* in Straw,
Thou *Lady* dear, arise;
Open (to keep the *Sun* in awe)
Thy pretty pinking eyes:
And, having stretcht each Leg and Arme,
Put on your clean white Smock
And then I pray, to keep you warme,
A *Petticote* on *Dock*.

Arise, arise! Why should you sleep,
When you have slept enough?
Long since, French boyes cry'd Chimney-sweep,
And Damsels Kitching-stuffe.

The Shops were open'd long before,
And youngest Prentice goes
To lay at's Mistress Chamber-doore
His Masters shining Shooes.

Arise, arise; your Breakfast stayes,
Good Water-grewell warme,
Or Sugar-sops, which *Galen* sayes
With Mace, will doe no harme.
Arise, arise; when you are up,
You'l find more to your cost,
For Mornings-draught in Caudle-cup,
Good Nutbrown-Ale, and Tost.

97 4 *pinking* winking, half-shut 8 *on Dock* put on 11 *cry'd* shouted, the advertisments of street-vendors and tradesmen 12 *Kitching-stuffe* vegetables 18 *Water-grewell* porridge 19 *Sugar-sop* slices of bread, soaked and sometimes spiced *Galen* Greek physician, still quoted as a medical authority in the early-modern period 20 *Mace* the spice derived from the rind of the nutmeg 23 *Caudle-cup* cup, usually wooden, for drinking gruel mixed with wine or beer 24 *Tost* toast floated on top of beer

ANONYMOUS

98 To Splendora weeping.

Oh now the certaine cause I know
Whence the Rose, and Lillies grow
On your faire Cheeke, those often showers
Which you doe weepe, produce those flowers;
If that the flouds could Venus bring,
And warlike Mars from Juno spring,
Why may not hence two Gods arise,
This from your Cheeke, that from your Eyes?

98 3 *often* frequent 5–6 *Venus, Mars, Juno* see Appendix 1

EDMUND WALLER

99 SONG.

Behold the brand of beauty tost;
See how the motion does dilate the flame:
Delighted love his spoyls does boast,
And triumph in this game.
Fire to no place confin'd,
Is both our wonder and our fear,
Moving the mind,
As lightning hurled through the air.

High heaven the glory does encrease
Of all her shining lamps this artfull way,
The Sun in figures such as these
Joyes with the Moon to play.
To the sweet strains they advance,
Which do result from their own spheres,
As this Nymphs dance,
Moves with the numbers which she hears.

99 1 *brand* burning torch *tost* tossed 11 *figures* patterns of the dance 14 *spheres* the crystal spheres bearing the planets around the earth were thought each to emit a musical note 15-16 the idea of the last lines is that the dance of the woman who is the subject of the poem, the 'nymph', is as fitted to the notes ,'numbers', of the music as is the movement of the heavens

SIR RICHARD FANSHAWE

100 [from *Il Pastor Fido*]

Let us use it whilst wee may;
Snatch those joyes that haste away.
Earth her winter-coat may cast,
And renew her beauty past;

But, our winter come, in vain
We sollicite spring again:
And when our furrows snow shall cover,
Love may return, but never Lover.

100 Title see Notes on the Text 7 *furrows* ploughed in fields, metaphorically, wrinkles of age *snow* metaphorically, white hair

JOHN MILTON

101 At a solemn Musick.

Blest pair of *Sirens*, pledges of Heav'ns joy,
Sphear-born harmonious Sisters, Voice, and Vers,
Wed your divine sounds, and mixt power employ
Dead things with inbreath'd sense able to pierce,
And to our high-rais'd phantasie present,
That undisturbed Song of pure content,
Ay sung before the saphire-colour'd throne
To him that sits thereon
With Saintly shout, and solemn Jubily,
Where the bright Seraphim in burning row
Their loud up-lifted Angel trumpets blow,
And the Cherubick host in thousand quires
Touch their immortal Harps of golden wires,
With those just Spirits that wear victorious Palms,
Hymns devout and holy Psalms
Singing everlastingly:
That we on Earth with undiscording voice
May rightly answer that melodious noise;
As once we did, till disproportion'd sin
Jarr'd against natures chime, and with harsh din
Broke the fair musick that all creatures made
To their great Lord, whose love their motion sway'd
In perfect Diapason, whilst they stood
In first obedience, and their state of good.
O may we soon again renew that Song,
And keep in tune with Heav'n till God ere long

To his celestial consort us unite,
To live with him, and sing in endles morn of light.

101 1 *Sirens* see Appendix 1 2 *Sphear-born* heavenly, but also proceeding from the musical spheres of medieval cosmology 7 *Ay* for ever 9 *Jubily* jubilation, also see Appendix 1 14 *Palms* are the emblems of the martyrs 17 *undiscording* not out of tune 23 *Diapason* concord, harmony 27 *consort* combination of voices, or instruments; here there is an echo of the idea of the universe as musical, a concord ordained by God

SIDNEY GODOLPHIN

102 Song.

Tis affection but dissembled
or dissembled Lyberty,
to pretend thy passion changed
with change of thy Mistresse Eye
following her inconstancy:

Hopes which doe from favour florish
may perhapps as soone Expire
as the Cause which did them nourish
and disdain'd they may retire,
but Love is another fyre.

For if beawty cause thy passion
if a fayre resistlesse Eye
melt thee with its soft impression
then thy hopes will never dye,
nor bee cur'd by cruelty.

Tis not Scorne that can remove thee
for thou Either wilt not see,
Such Lov'd beawty, not to Love thee,
or wilt els consent that Shee
judges as she ought of thee.

Thus thou either canst not sever
hope from what appeares soe fayre
or unhappier thou canst never

Find Contentment in despayre
nor make Love a trifling care.

There are seen but few retyring
stepps in all the pathes of Love
made by such, who in aspiring
meeting scorne, their hopes remove
yet even these ne're change their Love.

ANONYMOUS

103 On a Lady Sleeping.

Calmely as the mornings soft teares shedd
Upon some rose or Violett bedd
May your slumbers fall upon you
All your thoughts sit easy on you
Gently rocking heart and eyes
With their tunefull Lullabyes
While still th'early morrow light
Shall with your dreames have chac'd the night
Like the sick flower which when to bedd
The sun is gonn hangs the faynt head
As every other warmth despising
Will Lye and waite your eyelidds fayre uprising.

ANONYMOUS

104 [No clouds Inhabite where shee dwells]

No clouds Inhabite where shee dwells
All the ayre like perfume smells
No winde or rayne but such as shower
Heere a health, and there a flower.

Where her fayre touch she disposes
Lillyes grow, and Damaske roses,
And in envy of her vaynes
The Vyolett shoots up and raigns.
So these wyther, and decay
When she but turnes her beames away.

104 6 *Damaske roses* species of roses of middle-eastern origin; richly scented, with velvety petals 10 *beames* gaze

SAMSON BRIGGS

105 Song.

See See
See Phoebus falne from his coach
And in Eclipse at Eumorphe's approach
Sicke hee's gone unto his bed
With a sable cover
A cappe of clouds upon his head
Mists about him hover
Wretched mortalls well might feare an everlasting night
Did not shee
Bright as hee
From her eyes resplendancie
Promise unto them new light.

Close, Close
Close up myne eyes do not gaze
Upon so bright and caelestiall rayes
Say my Love an Eaglett bee
It dares not aspire
Fearing doome of bastardie
To gaze on such a fire
Wherefore eyes you shall bee to a dripping fountaine turn'd.
I'le goe weepe
Or else sleepe
Thus perhaps I shall you keepe
From so bright a Sun unburn'd.

105 3 *Eumorphe* see Appendix 1 5 *sable* black (heraldic) 15 *caelestiall* heavenly 16 *Eaglett* young eagle; eagles were proverbially able to out-stare the sun

RICHARD LOVELACE

106 ORPHEUS *to* BEASTS. SONG.
Set by Mr. *Curtes.*

I.

Here, here, oh here *Euridice*,
Here was she slaine;
Her soule's 'still'd through a veine:
The Gods knew lesse
That time Divinitie,
Then ev'n, ev'n these
Of brutishnesse.

II.

Oh could you view the Melodie
Of ev'ry grace,
And Musick of her face,
You'd drop a teare,
Seeing more Harmonie
In her bright eye,
Then now you heare.

106 Title *Orpheus*, 1 *Euridice* see Appendix 1 3 *'still'd* distilled, leaked away

107 *A Dialogue.*
Lute *and* Voice.

L. Sing *Laura*, sing, whilst silent are the Sphears,
And all the eyes of Heaven are turn'd to Ears.

V. Touch thy dead Wood and make each living tree,
Unchain its feet, take arms, and follow thee.

Chorus.

L. Sing. *V*. Touch. O Touch. *L*. O Sing,
Both. It is the Souls, Souls, Sole offering.

V. Touch the Divinity of thy Chords, and make
Each Heart string tremble, and each sinew shake.

L. Whilst with your Voyce you Rarifie the Air.
None but an host of Angels hover here.

Chorus. Sing. Touch, &c.

V. Touch thy soft Lute, and in each gentle thread,
The *Lyon* and the *Panther* captive lead.

L. Sing, and in Heav'n Inthrone deposed Love,
Whilst Angels dance and Fiends in order move.

Double Chorus.

What sacred Charm may this then be
In Harmonie,
That thus can make the Angels wild,
The Devils mild,
And teach low Hell to Heav'n to swell,
And the High Heav'n to stoop to Hell.

107 1 *Sphears* the music supposed to emit from the crystal spheres which bore the planets around the earth 2 *eyes of Heaven* stars 3 the idea of the wood of the musical instrument finding a voice in death was a commonplace often used in inscriptions on actual instruments 9 *Rarifie* refine

ANONYMOUS

108 [Sleepe, sleepe within thy virgin bed]

Sleepe, sleepe within thy virgin bed
That is with virgin curtaines drawne
Where thou maist rest thy love-sicke head
Within those dainty sheets of lawne

And wake not till the morning dawne.
But dreame thou hast him in thine armes
That meanes to shield thee from all harmes.
And when those pleasures thou descries
Entwine him with thy snowy thighs.
Thus those embraces being done
And you could seeme to pant for breath
Awake and espy the glorious sun
Whose beams hath beautifie'd the Earth
What though thy thoughts doe thee surprise
Yet thou shalt still a virgin rise.

108 4 *lawne* fine linen 8 *descries* perceives

ANONYMOUS

109 Epitaph

In depth of waves long hath *Alexus* slept
So choicest jewells are the closest kept:
Whose death the land hath seene, but it appeares
To countervaile his losse men wanted teares.
So here he lies whose dirge each Mermaid sings
For whom the clouds weepe raine, the earth her springs.

109 4 *countervaile* answer, match

ALEXANDER BROME

110 SONG VII
The hard Heart

1.

Still so *hard-hearted*? what may be
The sin thou hast committed?
That now the angry *Deity*
Has to a *Rock* congealed thee,

And thus thy *hardnesse* fitted?
To make one act both *sin* and *curse*,
And plague thy *hardness* with a *worse*.

2.

Till thee there never was but one
Was to a *Rock* translated,
Poor *Niobe* that weeping stone:
She ever did, thou ne're dost, moan,
Nor is thy scorn abated.
The *tears* I send to thee are grown
Of that same nature, and turn *stone*.

3.

Yet I, dear *Rock*, must worship thee,
Love works this *superstition*,
And justifies th'*Idolatry*
That's shown to such a *stone* as thee,
Where it foreruns *fruition*.
Thou'rt so *magnetick*, that I can
No more leave thee than to be *Man*.

4.

But thou, I warrant thee, do'st suppose
This new *design* will *slay* me,
And *ravel* out my life with *woes*
Till death, at last, mine eyes shall close;
Then in thy breast thou'lt lay me,
That all may read, *lo here I ly*
Tomb'd in thy heart, slain by thine eye.

5.

But I, I vow, will be more wise,
And love with such discretion;
When I read coynesse in thy eyes,
I'll *roab* mine with like cruelties,
And kill with *prepossession.*
Then I'll turn *stone*, and so will bee
An endless *monument* to thee.

110 10 *Niobe* see Appendix 1 19 *fruition* sexual consummation 20 *magnetick* metaphorically, even changed to stone she draws him as the magnet does iron 24 *ravel* draw out; metaphor from unwinding wool or thread 32 *roab* clothe 33 *prepossession* literally, being in possession first; pre-emptive action

111 SONG XVII

Mirth.

Out of Anacreon.

When our brains well liquor'd are,
Then we charm asleep our care,
Then we accompt *Machivile* a fool with his plots,
And cry there's no depth, but the bottom o'th'pots,
Then *Hector* compar'd with us will be
But a coward, and *Craesus* beggarly.
Then with songs our voices we raise,
And circle our Temples with bayes,
Then Honour we account but a blast of Wind,
And trample all things in our mind.
The valiant at arms,
That are led by fond charms
Get their honour with harms
While he that takes up
A plentiful cup,
To no danger is brought
But of paying his groat.
Then quickly come Lad and fill our cups full,
For since down we all must be laid,
'Tis held a good rule
In *Bacchus* free-schole
'Tis better lie drunk then dead.

111 Title *Anacreon* see Appendix 1 3 *accompt* account *Machivile* Machiavelli, see Appendix 2 5 *Hector*, 6 *Craesus* proverbially brave and rich respectively, see Appendix 1 8 *bayes* laurel wreaths, not those of the poets, here, but the garlands of the classical banquet or drinking-party 17 *groat* the price of his drink 21 *Bacchus free-schole* the drinking-party

ANONYMOUS

112 [The first concoction perfited]

The first concoction perfited
When wanton fumes were made
    The fancyes theame
My Mistris came unto my Bed
    Transhap't into a Dreame,

Shee stood as naked and as white as Snow,
Not Jove more Beauty could bestowe
    On the faire Swan's beloved skin
Nor Venus could more softnes showe,
    Should she put on hir Cloud ag'in.

112 1–3 see Notes on the Text for an explanation of the medical metaphor of these lines 5 *Transhap't* transformed 7 *Jove*, 8 *Swan* (Leda), 9 *Venus* see Appendix 1; here Venus is referred to as she appeared to her lover Anchises

ANONYMOUS

113 *The* NIGHTINGALE.

Hark how the *Nightingale* displayes
The latest pleasures of her throat,
And dies content, if her poor Note
Might serve but as one step to raise
A Trophie to your Beauties praise.

The Rose, in whose rich Odours lie
The perfum'd Treasures of the Year,
Doth blush to death when you appear,
And Martyr-like towards you doth fly,
To wear your Cheeks fresh Livery.

Aurora weeps to see a light
Outvie her splendour in your Eyes,

The Sun's ashamed to walk the skies;
And th'Envious Moon, grown pale for spight,
Vows ne're to Revel but with Night.

The saucy Wind with senseless care
(Seeming to feel soft sense of bliss)
Steals through your hair, your lips to kiss.
So rivals me, who now despair
To touch your Lip, Cheek, Eye or Hair.

113 10 *Livery* uniform in the master's (or mistress's) heraldic colours 11 *Aurora* see Appendix 1 14 *spight* spite 16 *saucy* insolent

ANONYMOUS

114 Captain *DIGBY*'s Farewell.

And I'le go to my Love where he lies in the Deep,
and in my embraces my Dearest shall sleep:
When we wake, the kind Dolphins together shall throng,
and in Chariots of Shells shall draw us along.

The Orientest Pearl that the Ocean bestowes
We'll mix with the Coral, and a Crown so compose:
The Sea Nimphs shall sigh, and envy our bliss;
We'll teach them to Love, and Cockles to Kiss.

For my Love sleeps now in a Wat'ry Grave,
and hath nothing to shew for his Tomb but a Wave:
I'le kiss his dear lips than the Coral more red,
that grows where he lies in his Wat'ry bed.
Ah! Ah! Ah my Love's dead! There was not a Bell,
but a *Triton*'s Shell to Ring, to Ring out his Knell.

114 Title 'Captain Digby' is unidentified 5 *Orientest* most brilliant, most precious

ANONYMOUS

115 ENDYMION'S *Dream.*

Fall dew of Slumbers in a gentle Stream,
And my *Endymion* bless;
That he i'the Banquet of a Dream
May taste his future Happiness.
Softly, softly;
O let no rude affright
As he lies
Break up his eyes,
But open them to real new Delight.

Blest Seraphins, put on your softest wings;
Glide eas'ly from above:
With blisses Heavens fruition brings
Refresh the panting hopes of Love.
Charm him, Charm him:
Then with a Bee-like Hum
Gently wake
For *Hero*'s sake
Leander from *Elizium.*

115 Title *Endymion* see Appendix 1 12 *fruition* consummation 17 *Hero*, 18 *Leander* see Appendix 1

CHARLES COTTON

116 *SONG.*

Set by Mr. Coleman.

I.

See, how like Twilight *Slumber* falls
T'obscure the glory of those balls,
And, as she sleeps,
See how Light creeps

Thorow the Chinks, and Beautifies
The rayie fringe of her fair *Eyes*.

II.

Observe *Loves* feuds, how fast they fly,
To every heart, from her clos'd Eye,
What then will she,
When waking, be?
A glowing Light for all t'admire,
Such, as would set the *World* on fire.

III.

Then seal her Eye-lids, gentle *Sleep*,
Whiles cares of her mine open keep;
Lock up, I say,
Those Doors of *Day*,
Which with the *Morn* for Lustre strive,
That I may look on her, and live.

116 2 *balls* eyes 6 *rayie fringe* eyelashes

KATHERINE PHILIPS

117 *To Mr* Henry Lawes.

Nature, which is the vast Creation's Soul,
That steddy curious Agent in the whole,
The Art of Heaven, the Order of this Frame,
Is only Number in another name.
For as some King conqu'ring what was his own,
Hath choice of several Titles to his Crown;
So harmony on this score now, that then,
Yet still is all that takes and governs Men.
Beauty is but Composure, and we find
Content is but the concord of the Mind,
Friendship the Unison of well-tun'd Hearts,
Honour the *Chorus* of the noblest parts,

And all the World on which we can reflect
Musick to th'Ear, or to the Intellect.
If then each man a Little World must be,
How many Worlds are copied out in thee,
Who art so richly formed, so compleat
T'epitomize all that is Good and Great;
Whose Stars this brave advantage did impart,
Thy Nature's as harmonious as thy Art?
Thou dost above the Poets praises live,
Who fetch from thee th'Eternity they give.
And as true Reason triumphs over sense,
Yet is subjected to intelligence:
So Poets on the lower World look down,
But *Lawes* on them; his Height is all his own.
For, like Divinity it self, his Lyre
Rewards the Wit it did at first inspire.
And thus by double right Poets allow
His and their Laurel should adorn his brow.
Live then, great Soul of Nature, to asswage
The savage dulness of this sullen Age.
Charm us to Sense; for though Experience fail
And Reason too, thy Numbers may prevail.
Then, like those Ancients, strike, and so command
All Nature to obey thy gen'rous hand.
None will resist but such who needs will be
More stupid than a Stone, a Fish, a Tree.
Be it thy care our Age to new-create:
What built a World may sure repair a State.

117 Title *Mr Henry Lawes* see Appendix 2 4 *Number* musical order 9 *Composure* pun on 'arrangement of features' and 'musical composition' 15 *Little World* the idea is of the human body as the microcosm of the world 23 *sense* physical sensuality 27–8 The sense here is that Lawes, by setting it to music, rewards the poetry which his music inspired 31 *asswage* temper, soften 39–40 Here the conceit is that music could compose chaos into order, lead the beasts and trees as Orpheus did, and so Lawes's music has the capacity to heal the divisions of the Civil War

ANONYMOUS

118 Musick.

Although the Cannon, and the Churlish Drum
Have strook the Quire mute, and the Organs Dumb:
Yet Musicks Art with Ayre and String and Voyce
Makes glad the Sad, and Sorrow to Rejoyce.

118 1 *Churlish* loutish 2 *Quire* choir: the idea of this line stems from the banning of liturgical music from Puritan church services

PART THREE

SPIRITUAL POEMS AND PROPHECIES

119 *Imitatio Horatianae*

Odes 9. donec gratus eram tibi, *Lib. 3.*

A DIALOGUE betwixt GOD *and the* SOUL

Soul.

Whilst my *Souls* eyes beheld no light
But what stream'd from thy gracious sight;
To me the worlds greatest King
Seem'd but some little vulgar thing.

God.

Whilest thou prov'dst pure; and that in thee
I could glass all my Deity:
How glad did I from Heaven depart,
To find a lodging in thy heart!

Soul.

Now Fame and Greatness bear the sway,
('Tis they that hold my prisons Key:)
For whom my soul would dy, might she
Leave them her Immortalitie.

God.

I, and some few pure Souls conspire,
And burn both in a mutual fire,
For whom Il'd die once more, ere they
Should miss of Heavens eternal day.

Soul.

But Lord ! What if I turn again,
And with an adamantine chain
Lock me to thee? What if I chase
The world away to give thee place?

God.

Then though these souls in whom I joy
Are *seraphins*, thou but a toy,

A foolish toy, yet once more I
Would with thee live, and for thee die.

119 This is a sacred imitation of Horace, *Odes*, III. 9 (see nos. 11, 74) 6 *glass* reflect: the idea is that the pure soul can act as a mirror to the primal light, God 9 *sway* control 18 *adamantine* of diamonds, of surpassing hardness 22 *toy* trifle

ROBERT HERRICK

120 The Star-Song: A Carroll to the King; sung at White-Hall.

The Flourish of Musick: then followed the Song.

1

Tell us, thou cleere and heavenly Tongue,
Where is the Babe but lately sprung?
Lies He the Lillie-banks among?

2

Or say, if this new Birth of ours
Sleeps, laid within some Ark of Flowers,
Spangled with deaw-light; thou canst cleere
All doubts, and manifest the where.

3

Declare to us, bright Star, if we shall seek
Him in the Mornings blushing cheek,
Or search the beds of Spices through,
To find him out?

Star. No, this ye need not do;
But only come, and see Him rest
A Princely Babe in's Mothers Brest.

Chor. He's seen, He's seen, why then a Round,
Let's kisse the sweet and holy ground;
And all rejoyce, that we have found
A King, before conception crown'd.

4

Come then, come then, and let us bring
Unto our prettie *Twelfth-Tide King*,
Each one his severall offering.

Chor. And when night comes, wee'l give Him wassailing:
And that His treble Honours may be seen,
Wee'l chuse Him King, and make His Mother Queen.

120 5 *Ark* chest or coffer, but also with a reference to the Ark of the Covenant see Appendix 1 20 *Twelfth-Tide King* The custom on twelfth night was to choose by lot a 'King' and 'Queen' of the feast 22 *wassailing* feasting, more specifically, the carol-singers' serenade

121 The white Island: or place of the Blest

In this world (the *Isle of Dreames*)
While we sit by sorrowes streames,
Teares and terrors are our theames
Reciting:

But when once from hence we flie,
More and more approaching nigh
Unto young Eternitie
Uniting:

In that *whiter Island*, where
Things are evermore sincere;
Candor here, and lustre there
Delighting:

There no monstrous fancies shall
Out of hell an horrour call,
To create (or cause at all)
Affrighting.

There in calm and cooling sleep
We our eyes shall never steep;
But eternall watch shall keep,
Attending

Pleasures, such as shall pursue
Me immortaliz'd, and you;
And fresh joyes, as never too
Have ending.

121 10 *sincere* real, without illusion 11 *Candor* (Latin, 'white') clear brightness, *lustre* bright refracted light

122 *A Meditation for his Mistresse*

1

You are a *Tulip* seen to day,
But (Dearest) of so short a stay;
That where you grew, scarce man can say.

2

You are a lovely *July-flower*,
Yet one rude wind, or ruffling shower,
Will force you hence, (and in an houre.)

3

You are a sparkling *Rose* i'th'bud,
Yet lost, ere that chast flesh and blood
Can shew where you or grew, or stood.

4

You are a full-spread faire-set Vine,
And can with Tendrills love intwine,
Yet dry'd, ere you distill your Wine.

5

You are like Balme inclosed (well)
In *Amber*, or some *Chrystall* shell,
Yet lost ere you transfuse your smell.

6

You are a dainty *Violet*,
Yet wither'd, ere you can be set
Within the Virgins Coronet.

7

You are the *Queen* all flowers among,
But die you must (faire Maid) ere long
As He, the maker of this Song.

122 4 *July-flower* gillyflower, pink or stock 9 *or...or* either...or 13 *Balme* scented ointment or perfume

123 *Ceremonies for Candlemasse Eve*

Down with the Rosemary and Bayes,
Down with the Misleto;
In stead of Holly, now up-raise
The greener Box (for show.)

The Holly hitherto did sway;
Let Box now domineere;
Untill the dancing Easter-day,
Or Easters Eve appeare.

Then youthfull Box which now hath grace,
Your houses to renew;
Grown old, surrender must his place,
Unto the crisped Yew.

When Yew is out, then Birch comes in,
And many Flowers beside;
Both of a fresh, and fragrant kinne
To honour Whitsontide.

Green Rushes then, and sweetest Bents,
With cooler Oken boughs;
Come in for comely ornaments,
To re-adorn the house.
Thus times do shift; each thing his turne do's hold;
New things succeed, as former things grow old.

123 Title *Candlemasse* the Feast of the Purification of the Virgin, the second of February

1–4 *Rosemary, Bayes, Mistleto, Holly* are all evergreen Christmas decorations. Herrick is referring to the medieval practice of garlanding churches for festivals *Box* as the greenest of evergreens carries the symbolic meanings of eternity and resurgence, being used in many countries to represent the palm of Palm Sunday 12 *Yew* is the funeral tree; Herrick also refers to its new growth in spring 16 *Whitsontide* Whit Sunday or Pentecost, the Christian festival celebrating the descent of the Holy Spirit to the first Christians 17 *Rushes* still used to strew floors of houses *Bents* grasses

HENRY KING

124 Sic Vita

Like to the Falling of a Starre;
Or as the Flights of Eagles are;
Or like the fresh Springs gawdy hew;
Or Silver Drops of Morning Dew;
Or like the Wind that chafes the Flood;
Or Bubbles which on Water stood;
Even such is Man whose borrow'd Light
Is streight Call'd in, and paid to Night.
The wind blowes out, The Bubble Dyes.
The Spring entomb'd in Autumne lyes.
The Dew dryes up. The Starre is shott.
The Flight is past. And Man forgott.

124 See no. 130 Title (Latin) 'Life is like these things'

125 *AN ELEGY*

Occasioned by the losse of the most incomparable Lady Stanhope, daughter to the Earl of Northumberland.

Lightned by that dimme Torch our sorrow bears
We sadly trace thy Coffin with our tears;
And though the Ceremonious Rites are past
Since thy fair body into earth was cast;

Though all thy Hatchments into ragges are torne,
Thy Funerall Robes and Ornaments outworn;
We still thy mourners without Shew or Art,
With solemn Blacks hung round about our heart,
Thus constantly the Obsequies renew
Which to thy precious memory are due.

Yet think not that we rudely would invade
The dark recess of thine untroubled shade,
Or give disturbance to that happy peace
Which thou enjoy'st at full since thy release;
Much less in sullen murmurs do complain
Of His decree who took thee back again,
And did e're Fame had spread thy vertues light,
Eclipse and fold thee up in endless night.
This like an act of envy not of grief
Might doubt thy bliss and shake our own belief,
Whose studi'd wishes no proportion bear
With joyes which crown thee now in glories sphere.

Know then blest Soul! we for our selves not thee
Seal our woes dictate by this Elegie:
Wherein our tears united in one streame
Shall to succeeding times convey this theme,
Worth all mens pity who discern how rare
Such early growths of fame and goodness are.
Of these part must thy sexes loss bewail
Maim'd in her noblest Patterns through thy fail;
For 'twould require a double term of life
To match thee as a daughter or a wife:
Both which Northumberlands dear loss improve
And make his sorrow equal to his love.
The rest fall for our selves, who cast behind
Cannot yet reach the Peace which thou dost find;
But slowly follow thee in that dull stage
Which most untimely poasted hence thy age.

Thus like religious Pilgrims who designe
A short salute to their beloved Shrine,
Most sad and humble Votaries we come
To offer up our sighs upon thy Tomb,

And wet thy Marble with our dropping eyes
Which till the spring which feeds their current dries
Resolve each falling night and rising day
This mournfull homage at thy Grave to pay.

125 2 *trace* follow 5 *Hatchments* heraldic blazons displayed at funerals 30 *Patterns* examples 38 *poasted* travelled at speed 40 *salute* greeting, action of worship

THOMAS CAREW

126 To my worthy friend Mr. *George Sandys*.

I presse not to the Quire, nor dare I greet
The holy Place with my unhallow'd feet:
My unwasht Muse pollutes not things Divine,
Nor mingles her prophaner notes with thine;
Here, humbly at the Porch, she listning stayes,
And with glad eares sucks in thy Sacred Layes.
So, devout Penitents of old were wont,
Some without doore, and some beneath the Font,
To stand and heare the Churches Liturgies,
Yet not assist the solemne Exercise.
Sufficeth her, that she a Lay-place gaine,
To trim thy Vestments, or but beare thy traine:
Though nor in Tune, nor Wing, She reach thy Larke,
Her Lyricke feet may dance before the Arke.
Who knowes, but that her wandring eyes, that run
Now hunting Glow-wormes, may adore the Sun.
A pure Flame may, shot by Almighty Power
Into my brest, the earthy flame devoure:
My Eyes, in Penitentiall dew may steepe
That bryne, which they for sensuall love did weepe:
So (though 'gainst Natures course) fire may be quencht
With fire, and water be with water drencht.
Perhaps, my restlesse Soule, tyr'd with pursuit
Of mortall beautie, seeking without fruit
Contentment there; which hath not, when enjoy'd,
Quencht all her thirst, nor satisfi'd, though cloy'd;
Weary of her vaine search below, above

In the first Faire may find th'immortall Love.
Prompted by thy Example then, no more
In moulds of Clay will I my God adore;
But teare those Idols from my Heart, and Write
What his blest Sp'rit, not fond Love, shall endite.
Then, I no more shall court the Verdant Bay,
But the dry leavelesse Trunke on Golgotha:
And rather strive to gaine from thence one Thorne,
Then all the flourishing Wreathes by Laureats worne.

126 1 *Quire* choir, sanctuary of a church 3 *unwasht* in the classical sense: not ritually purified 6 *Layes* songs 8 *without* outside 9 *Liturgies* services following a set form (of the established church) 11 *Lay-place* the nave, where the congregation sit 12 *trim* order, assist in dressing 20 *bryne* salt water, tears 26 *cloy'd* filled, surfeited 30 *moulds of Clay* human bodies 33 *Verdant Bay* green laurels, worn by poets to honour Apollo and the Muses 34 *Trunke* the wood of the Cross 35 *Thorne* here, from Jesus' crown of thorns 36 *Laureats* poets so crowned, themselves being honoured for their writing

KATHERINE, LADY DYER

127 [Epitaph on Sir Cope and Lady D'Oyley]

To the memory of that noble Knight Sr Cope D'Oyley who put on Immortality the IIIIth of August 1633.

Ask not me, who's buried here;
Goe, ask the Commons; ask the Sheire.
Goe, ask the Church; They'l tell thee who,
As well as blubberd eyes can doe;
Goe, ask the Heraulds; Ask the poore;
Thine eares shall heare enough, to ask no more.
Then, if thine eye bedewe this sacred urne
Each drop a pearle will turne
T 'adorne his Tombe, or if thou canst not vent
Thou bringst more Marble to his Monument.

To the memory of that rare example of unstayned Virtue Martha, Wife to the said Sr Cope D'Oyley...who received the crowne of glory in the yeare of Grace 1618.

Wouldst thou, reader, draw to life
The perfect copy of a wife.
Read on; and then redeeme from shame
That lost, that honourable name;
This dust was once in spirit a Jael;
Rebecca in grace; in heart an Abigail
In works, a Dorcas; to the Church a Hanna;
And to her spouse, Susanna;
Prudently simple, providently wary
To th'world a Martha, and to heav'n a Mary.

127 2 *Sheire* shire, county 4 *blubberd* dimmed with tears 9 *vent* in this context, cry 10 The idea here is that those hard-hearted enough to fail to weep his death, must themselves be hard as monumental stone 15–20 *Jael, Rebecca, Abigail, Dorcas, Hanna, Susanna, Martha, Mary* see Appendix 1

ANONYMOUS [? 'LADY LOTHIAN']

128 Ane godlie Instructione for old and young ['The Lady Lothian's Lilt']

On yeir begines ane other endis
Thus Tyme doeth come and goe
All thus to your Instructione tends
Give we culd tak it so
The sommeris heat the winters cold
Quhois seasonis lets us see
Quhan youth is gone and we wax old
Lyk flouris we fade and die.

Men for the most pairt dois rejoyce
Quhan sonis to them ar borne
Quhois weiping noice bevailles thair vois
and folis chanes to scorne

Thes ar the mesengeris to schow
Our tyme is passing fast
Qu[han] We deceas still they do grow
Till death us pairt at last

Now let us learne to spend our dayes
In vertue as we ought
In doing guid mak no delay
put sleuth out of our thought
The sleuthfull nevir yit ateind
To honour wealth nor fame
But many hath by vertue gaind
ane long long lasting name

In spring tyme of our youth we suld
The seidis of learning Saw
Weid furth our vyces give we could
our sinfull lustis overthrow
quha in the pryme of youth taks paines
Thair service to bestow
In harvest of his age againe
The grapes of grace do grow

Thus all tymes begines and ends
No thing bot fame remaines
hapie is he quha wyslie spends
His Tym in Vertues paines
Bot qu[han] the paine is past away
The pleasour sall abyde
Now hapie thryse ar such I say

That taks tyme at the tyd
The tyd of tyme it floweth fast
and quickly ebes away
Bot if our schip lacks saill or mast
Our Voyage mast delay
our bodies ar that brittle barks
That sailles that floodes of fame
Bot if throue sleuth we miss [the] marke
we sinke in seas of schame

Occatione haveth hear befoir
Bot scho is beld behind
Tint tyme no travell can restoir
as many folles may find
the little ant the hony bee
In sommer layeth up stoir
for to provyd for winters stormes
man most and suld do moir

Thus I haue done to pleas your Will
Now let me have my hyre
I have bewray'd my want of skill
In doing your desyre
The Weakness of a Woman's Witt
Is not to natures fault
Bot lack of educatione fitt
Makes nature quhylls to halt.

128 4 *Give* if 6 *Quhois* whose 7 *Quhan* when *wax* grow 12 *folis chanes* folly's chains, the snares of the world 15 *deceas* die 20 *sleuth* sloth, the sin of idleness 36 *paines* endeavours 45 *barks* boats 47 *marke* navigation mark 49–50 The emblematic image of Occasion or Fortune depicts her as having a flowing forelock, her head otherwise bald, signifying the necessity of prompt action, the lack of second chances 50 *beld* bald 51 *travell* also with the meaning of labour 58 *hyre* reward 59 *bewray'd* betrayed 64 *quhylls* at times *halt* limp

CATHAL MAC MHUIRICH

129 [A Sheónóid méadaigh meanma]

A Sheónóid méadaigh meanma;
tuig thrá toil an Tighearna
  do dhéanaimh, a chnú chridhe,
  's tú d'fhéaghain dá oirbhire.

Fuarais roimhe'na ghrís ghoirte
bás Eóin is Iarla Síphoirte;
  is fios a reilge ar n-éag ann,
  ór fhéad nach feirrde bhur bhfulang.

Glac ó Dhia aoibhneas oile
i n-ionadh bhur n-éolchaire;
  beir buidhe do Dhia na ndúl;
  cia ar nach cluine caochlúdh?

Fa ní dá dhoilghe ar domhan
déana Iosa d'adhmoladh;
  gé bheith baoghal dhuid i ndán,
  tuig an saoghal ar seachrán.

Nar chualais riamh do ró gráidh
ó thús tochta an domhnáin—
  's é dá rádh riamh mar oideacht—
  nach biadh crádh 'na chomhuideacht?

Léig do Dhia bhur ndobrón díbh;
tiodhlaic t'inghean don Airdrígh;
  cuir sólais céim tar chumhaidh,
  réim dóláis go ndiúltaighir.

Tréig th'imshníomh ar aigneadh mear,
ar mhuirn, ar mhacnas mhíleadh;
  a shubh fíneamhna, a ghéig ghlain,
  léig do mhímheanma ar mheadhair.

Tuig fós mar do dhearlaig dhúin
Rí na cruinne—is cúis iomthnúidh—
  a Mhac—ní h-é nárbh ionnráidh—
  is glac é mar eisiomláir.

Cuimhnigh mar do-chuaidh sa gcrann
Mac Dé dár ndíon a h-iofrann,
  meanma dár dtaobh mar do ghabh,
  go ndearna a thaobh do tholladh.

Is tuigthe fós dod ghnúis ghil
nach tug Dia dona daoinibh
  acht iasacht ar dhruim dhomhain,
  a dhiasfholt cruinn cladhamhail.

Cubhaidh dhuitse, a rosg ramhall,
dá n-éisde rém uraghall,

laoidh d'fhagháil do chosg cumhadh
's tosd i n-anáir ealadhan.

A dul ar neamh giodh leasg linn,
do Chaitir Fhíona is aoibhinn;
maith an dícheal dá dreich ghlain
bheith san rícheadh do roghain.

Maith an rogha rug sise
triall ón bheathaidh bhréigese
go teagh na gclann gan choire
thall i dteagh na trócaire.

A-tá i measg aingeal is ógh,
'na diadh ní déanta dobrón,
'na mionn shúl, ina gréin ghil
gan phéin i ndún an Dúilimh.

Damadh tarbha dhí nó dhúinn
caoi cridhe fa cúis chaochlúidh
do bhiadh leam cungnamh cumhadh
le geall n-urrlamh n-ealadhan.

Gan mo thagra i n-ainmhibh mh'olc
guidhim Mac Dé le dúthracht
fam shaoradh ó ghuin an gha
ler taomadh fhuil ó Iosa.

129 [O Seonoid be of good cheer]

O Seonoid, be of good cheer; nut of my heart, understand now that you must do his will, and be wary of his displeasure. Before this, you received like burning coals the deaths of Eoin and the Earl of Seaforth; knowledge of their graves after their decease could not have made your suffering easier. From God accept other joy in the place of your longing; give thanks to God of the elements over whom do you not hear of changes coming? However difficult the world give praise to Jesus: though danger for you may be in store, understand the world is in error. Heard you not this about excessive love—recounted ever as a caution—that as long as the world has existed love has been accompanied by agony? For God's sake desist from your grief; to the High King grant your daughter; let mourning give way to joys, may you forsake your course of sorrow. Abandon your care for high mirth, for merriment, for dalliance with champions; O grape of the vine, O pure branch, your dejection supplant with gladness. Understand too how the King of the world gave us—a cause for envy—His Son—a fact worthy of note—take that as example. Remember how He went on the Cross to protect us from Hell, the Son of the Father, how He assumed care for us and let his side be punctured. Let it be understood by you of the fair face, that God granted to mankind only a lease to the surface of the world, O furrowed hair like corn clustered. It is proper for you, O languid eye, if you listen to my discourse, to accept a lay to still grief and be quiet in respect for poetry. Though her going to heaven we deplore, for Catriona it is glorious; good the zeal of her pure face allowing her by choice the Kingdom. Good is the choice she made to depart this life of falsehood for the house of the children without sin yonder in the house of mercy. She is among angels and virgins, we should not sorrow after her, she is a cynosure, a bright sun, without pain in the fort of the Creator. If sadness of heart on account of her death were to her or us any profit I would have by me some help for grief in a ready promise of poems. Not to charge me with the defects of my sins I earnestly beseech the Son of the Father and to redeem me from the wound of the lance by which his blood was spilled from Jesus.

129 Seonoid was the wife of Dòmhnall Gorm Og of Sleat, and the subject of the poem is their daughter Catriona who died between 1635 and 1640. This is a highly professional poem, syllabic, written in a strict metre in use since the seventh century 2(7x+7x+1) (*deibhidhe*), and in Classical Gaelic. 6 Her two brothers: MacKenzie of Lochslin, died 1631, and Cailean, first Earl of Seaforth, died 1633

WILLIAM STRODE

130 Song of Death and the Resurrection.

Like to the rowling of an Eye
Or like a Starre-shott from the skie
Or like a hande upon a Clocke
Or like a wave upon a Rocke
Or like a winde or like a flame
Or like false newes which people frame.
Ev'n such is man of Equall stay
Whose very Growth leades to Decay.
The Eye is turnd the Starre downe bendeth
The Hande doth steale, the wave descendeth
The winde is spent, the flame unfird
The newes disprov'd, mans life expir'd.

Like to an Eye which sleepe doth chaine
Or like a Starre whose fall we faine
Or like the shade on Ahaz watch
Or like a wave which gulfes did snatch
Or like a winde or flame that's past
Or smothered newes confirmd at last
Ev'n soe mans life pawnd in the Grave
Waites for a Rising it must have
The Eye still sees, the Starre still blazeth
The shade goes backe, the Wave escapeth
The winde is turne, the flame reviv'd
The Newes renewed and man new liv'd.

130 See no. 124 2 *Starre-shott* shooting star, comet 7 *Equall stay* lasting no longer 14 *faine* imagine 15 *Ahaz watch* Sundial in 2 Kings 20: 11, which runs backwards by divine intervention 19 *pawnd* left temporarily as security

131 An Epitaph.

Keepe well this sacred Lawne thou bed of stone
For thou must render it a Saint; each bone
Shall be requird, the very Shrowde shall rise
Turnd to a robe of Light. Spende not your Eies
Ye that lov'd her and Vertue; though the mold
Containe them both, though Charity grow cold
Since She is soe, yet know that after sleepe
Shee'l rise more fresh; and Memory will keepe
Due watch about her to preserve her name
Untill her Nature wake. Death cannot tame
The Life of Hope; be sure that where she lies
The Grave is but an Usher to the skies.

131 1 *Lawne* fine linen 2 *render it* give it up as (to God, at the Last Judgement) 4 *Spende* give forth liquid, weep, exhaust 5 *mold* earth 12 *Usher* ceremonial attendant to receive guests

WILLIAM HABINGTON

132 Nox nocti indicat Scientiam

DAVID.

When I survay the bright
Coelestiall spheare:
So rich with jewels hung, that night
Doth like an Æthiop bride appeare.

My soule her wings doth spread
And heaven-ward flies,
Th'Almighty's Mysteries to read
In the large volumes of the skies.

For the bright firmament
Shootes forth no flame
So silent, but is eloquent
In speaking the Creators name.

No unregarded star
Contracts its light
Into so small a Charactar,
Remov'd far from our humane sight:

But if we stedfast looke,
We shall discerne
In it as in some holy booke,
How man may heavenly knowledge learne.

It tells the Conqueror,
That farre-stretcht powre
Which his proud dangers traffique for,
Is but the triumph of an houre.

That from the farthest North;
Some Nation may
Yet undiscovered issue forth,
And ore his new got conquest sway.

Some Nation yet shut in
With hils of ice
May be let out to scourge his sinne
'Till they shall equall him in vice.

And then they likewise shall
Their ruine have,
For as your selves your Empires fall,
And every Kingdome hath a grave.

Thus those Coelestiall fires,
Though seeming mute
The fallacie of our desires
And all the pride of life confute.

For they have watcht since first
The World had birth:
And found sinne in it selfe accurst,
And nothing permanent on earth.

132 Title Psalm 19: 2 'night unto night sheweth knowledge' *DAVID* author of the Psalms 2 *Coelestiall spheare* sky, heavens 4 *Æthiop bride* African woman wearing jewels, a frequent baroque image for the night sky 9 *firmament* sky 15 *Charactar* letter 28 *sway* rule

POETS OF THE TIXALL CIRCLE [GERTRUDE ASTON]

133 TO SIR WILLIAM AND MY LADY PERSALL, UPPON THE DEATH OF THEIR LITTLE FRANKE.

Happy parents, mourne no more,
You this jewell but restore:
Nor yet question Heavens will,
Why he was not lent you still.
As you merited that grace,
So his innocence the place
We all ambition; nor could you
Covet yours to bar his due.
Say in him we know did meete
All was good, and all was sweet,

Does this aggravate your cross?
Your gaine is greater then your loss.
For, alas! what did he here?
Please your eye, delight your eare:
He your senses' welcome guest,
Treates your soules now with a feast.
Tis his powerfull praires give you
All good here, and heaven too.
Yet hence your comfort most will rise,
God loves the child that quickly dies.

133 2 *restore* give back (to God) 7 *ambition* hope for 15–17 Gertrude Aston, a Catholic, works here with the idea of the dead child as a saint in heaven, interceding for his parents

134 ON FAIRE MRS HALL DYING IN HER PRIME.

How soon these faire and forward springs
  Are nip't by some unruly blast!
Whose beuty whilst the poet sings,
  This sadly sighs the blessing past.

Not th'earely violet was more sweet,
  Or new-blowne rose apear'd more faire;
All that was wish'd our senses meet,
  But the quick losse augments our care.

So we rejoice in some kind dream,
  That makes a good as much our owne;
But waking, ebs the flowing stream,
  Sorrow contracts us to her stone.

134 8 *augments* adds to 12 *stone* see Appendix 1, Niobe

GERRARD WINSTANLEY

135 [*from* The Breaking of the Day of God]

Rev.5.13. Commander in Chief, is God himself,
Rev.19.6. who rules the spirits of men,
Joh.14.27 Wait then on him, uproars to quell,
Gen.14.13 and settle peace again.

Luk 17.33 Those that doe rise, for fleshy ends,
1 Sam.23. a kingdome for to trouble,
27. Shall loose their pains, undoe themselves,
Isa 2.22. and vanish like a buble.

Eze 38.19 God's shaking Nations, trying men,
Rev.19. and changing times and customs,
19.20. Ruining the Beast, and saving men,
Psal.124.1,2 amidst these great cumbustions.

John 5.22 Cease striving then, ye sons of men,
Ro.12.19. destroy not one another
Psal.83. God will avenge, him that's opprest,
2. &c. by Christ our elder brother.

Dan.2.44. His turn is next the Realm to take,
Dan.7.26. and rule the sons of men.
27. And Beast and Devil, Pope and Sin,
Rev 16.17 shall never reign again.

Mat 24.12 But yet mens hearts, disquiet are
Dan.7.25. and bitter as we see,
Rom.19. Hot times have been, hot times yet are:
13, &c. but hotter yet may be.

Revel.13, For now the Image of the Beast,
15, &c. appears to act his part,
Dan.8.25. But hee's a falling. And Saints shall sing,
Rev.19.6. Haleluja with joy of heart.

135 See Appendix 1 for Apocalyptic vocabulary 5 *fleshy* worldly 12 *cumbustions* inflammatory upheavals 28 *Haleluja* Hebrew, 'rejoice'

CLEMENT PAMAN

136 *Good Friday*

Almighty Lownesse, whose free power
Can, as it please, contract or spread
Thee to Eternity or an Houre,
Canst be all life and canst be dead
Where shall I seeke thee? If I hope to have
Thee in thy Heaven, Thou'rt shrunk into a Grave.

Yet low as Graves slow Natures foot
First sought and found thee out: In flies
Or wormes, some grasses spire or root
Ere it durst search the stars or skies.
Shall I then ask thy grave? Oh the deafe stone
The dumbe muffling clothes can say, that thou art gone.

But there's a place hollow and darke
Hard too, as Tombes in rocks, yet where
Lifes heat is kept both flame and sparke
Quickning a world with daily care.
Perhaps thou mayst be there, Lend me thy art
And light to search, that place may prove my Heart.

For hearts are every thing, And Thou
Art every where, In hearts which shine
All day Sun-full, In hearts which show
Nightsome as graves. And such is mine
Oh might I find thee there, I'ld beg thy stay
Rise when thou wouldst, thou shouldst not go away.

136 1 *Lownesse* humility; Christ in his humility in suffering death 9 *spire* stalk, stem

137 *On Christmas Day To my Heart.*

To Day,
Hark! Heaven sings:
Stretch, Tune my Heart,
For Hearts have strings
(May beare their Part)
What though thy Lute were Bruis'd ith' Fall?
Bruis'd Hearts may reach an humble Pastorall.

To Day,
Sheepherds reioice,
And Angels doe
Noe more; Thy voice
Can reach That too.
Then bring at least thy Pipe along
And mingle Consort with the Angels song.

To Day,
A shedde thats Thatchd
(Yet strawes can sing)
Holds God; God's match'd
with Beasts; Beasts bring
Their song their way; for shame then Rayse
Thy Notes, Lambes bleat and Oxen bellow Praise.

To Day
God Honour'd Man,
Not Angels, Yet
They sing, And can
Rais'd Man forget?
Praise is our debt to day, nor shall
Angels (man's not soe poore) discharge it All.

To Day
Then screw Thee high,
My Heart, up to
The Angels Key,
Sing Glorie; Doe.

What if thy Strings All crack and fly?
On such a Ground Musick 'twill be to Die.

137 Title *Christmas* feast of the Incarnation of Christ, the commemoration of the Nativity 5 *Part* in a harmony 6 *Fall* of man into sin 7 *Pastorall* here, the song of the shepherds to the Christ child 14 *Consort* choir, combination of instruments 30 *screw* tune by tightening the wooden pegs of a stringed instrument 35 *Ground* musical sequence forming the basis for variations, therefore matter or subject

138 *On Christmas Day 1661*

Praeludium.
Mysterious Day! which no time can
Cleere up to Angel or to man

Antiphone.
Angels: We reach it not; but we aspire
Men: We understand not; But Admire.
Ang: We pry,
Men: We spy;
Ang: More than we,
Men: Yet you see.
Ang: Reproach us not for yours the gain:
Men: Yet you rayse first in song and strein.
Ang: We sung your parts. *Men*: More high your own.
Ang: But peace on earth. *Men*: That's little known.

Chorus
Agree, agree, Fix'd Angels will
Live on and sing theire glory still
While we poor men must gladly die
To meet their Quire in Eternitie:
Then upon Times sunset shall display
The untold riddles of this Day.

138 *Praeludium* prelude, prologue *Antiphone* answering voices 10 *strein* tune 16 *Quire* choir 17–18 the full paradoxical mystery of the Incarnation of Christ will not be understood until his second coming

139 *On his death*

No, no, Hee's gone, I hear'd the Angells sing
And call him Throne there, who was here a King.
Gone like the Tyde that drown'd him, and in vaine
We looke for hym till the world Tydes againe.
For all mankind hath ebbd ere since the fall
And twon't be *full Sea* till the *Generall*,
When glory quickens out of mudd, and when
A whales or sea-horse slime shall spawne a man.
When too this aery body now impal'd
In the seas armes shan't rise but be exhal'd,
Till when would but all Gold and pearles which have
Been drown'd like him, and ly without a grave
Meete and consult his monument; In this
They should be their own tombe by being His.
Diamonds should cutt his Epitaph, *Here lyes*
Whom jewells gave a Tombe, he them their prise.
But cursed rock! Who'le be thy Sexton? wee
But in thy *ruines* would not bury *thee*.
The Earth disclaimes thee and each vulgar wave
Shall pisse upon thy dust and drown thy grave.
But what cars't thou for buryall? who wer't sent
To th'world a Stone, and *borne* a monument.
Then weep not, stone, thy dust shaln't be despis'd
Thou shalt not be interr'd, but canoniz'd
As well as all those Jesuites have been
Which have sunk Kings like thee, and live unseene.
Yett thou must be a lesse Saint, for thou'rt content
To kill some men, They the Commandment.
But we forgive thee—Blest and gainfull too
Was't for our earth, that he descended so;
Had th'land contriv'd his grave, He there as here
Had torne her ribs, and rent with him the Sphaere
Isles are but Natures barkes, as his, our Isle
Had shipwrackt in the Sea and faln his Pile.
Greatnes can't dye alone. But oh! you men,
You mariners, whom nature curs'd ev'n then
When first she made you soe; brought up to dwell
Probationers, here for ferrymen, in Hell.

You that ner'e prayed since Jonah's time, who ne're
Are nam'd but in a storme, and then left there.
Whose very *scaping's* guilty and who fall
Condemn'd, cause freed, by the Seas Ordeall,
Had thou but fir'd the Vatican, although
With the seare leaves snatcht from the Sybils bough
Your sin perhaps had turn'd a *Sacrifice*
And you *zealotts* for burning Heresies.
Or had you but drown'd Frankford, had it bin
On the Mart-day, when th'list of books comes in
Like bills o'th'sickness, where a man may heare
What controversie sickd and dyde that yeare,
Why I had lov'd you; Books inflame, not cure
And heal an Ague with a Calenture.
   But to sinke all the Artes, all Volumes, All
The stamps of learning with the minerall,
(While you (yee papers principles, ragge) are found
Floating like leaves false printed and unbound;)
Was not to kill but to annihilate
And to force destiny on arts and fate.
For Pallas lyes with Thetis now, and wee
Must send for Arts to this Colledg in the Sea,
They'le nere returne till you thee boatswaines call
And in vaine whistle to that rock to fall
And hide your Guilt, which for *your* sin not *hers*
Now stands a party at that precious hearse.
   And now the *Route's* beate back; unfold the Sceane
Where sitts the waters newborne Cherubin:
The Sea has now *her* Hierarchy, and brings forth
Fayre images of Heaven as well as Earth,
Here Neptunes Sceptre swaies the Scaly powres
From Pythagoreans turn'd to Confessors,
Who sung before but in dumb Anthems now
Their voyce paies what their silence did but vow.
There the wise Porpoise, and the Dolphins move
Sea Angels both of *Knowledg* and of *Love*;
Here is the Holy whale, which once, you know,
Was both a Prophets house and Temple too.
Here are cold Virgin Sea nymphs, who are plac't
So, that (like Heaven) the place even makes them chast.

Amidst which traine our young Sea-Saint putts on
Deaths sayst robes of Sea-translation.
As Enoch who because he died before
Just time, tis said, That he was seen no more.
And is't not pretty Iustice there should bee
Heaven in the Sea, as well as there's a Sea
In Heaven above? Is not the seas cleare shine
Nearer of kin to th' Heavenly Christalline
Than the dark earths, yett her black face can show
Not only shapes of Heaven but hell too
(Like tables o'th' Pope and Christ). It was the Sea
Lent us all primitive Divinity.
From her Heavens cheife discoverers were sent
And planters too; but oh they were but lent,
She now askes payment; Peter from the maine
Rose like the Sun and there goes downe againe,
In our Apostlet here, who at his fall
Was Text and preacher at's own Funerall,
Whose death was a convincing Text, whence we
May prove and feele the worlds mortality.
In his decay, whose lips had power to have
Converted all but Saylers and the waves.
I'm sure the passengers all hung about
His parting words and soule, as they had thought
Were but theire Soules found Patentees with his
In his wide patent, drowning were a blisse.
He made their noyse devout, while they implore
And cry by shipwrack to be sett on shore,
While he first burnt in zeale then drown'd in teares
Dyes his own Martyr and descends the Spheares,
Works miracles in all, At's parting, where
His Ship turnes Church, his Pulpitt and his biere.
But I thus break the slumbers of his tombe
Who shan't be wept in Items but the summe;
Hee's the History of life and death, where's none
Found ever liv'd soe long, yet dy'd so soone;
Glory attend his dust, and till's Returne
Give him the seas wide vaults but for his urne,
While th'inch of ashes of our mighty spans
Our balm'd and cear-cloth'd land-Leviathans

Clos'd in their petty sand-boxes, shall lye
To dry the teares of his wept Elegie.
Whose life shall overlive their bedrid fame
And death *baptise* the waters with his **name.*

*The Kings Seas J. Selden's Mare Clausum

139 Title The second of two poems lamenting the death of Edward King, Fellow of Christ's College, Cambridge, drowned in the Irish Sea in 1637. Elegies for him were written by many Cambridge poets, most notably John Milton's *Lycidas* 2 *Throne* one of the nine orders of angels 4 *world Tydes* 6 *Generall* Last Judgement, when the boies of the dead will rise 13 *consult* compose 17 *rock* on which King's ship foundered *Sexton* gravedigger 25 *Jesuites* here Paman images the guilty rock as being as worthy of a place in heaven as are (in his opinion) those Jesuits (popularly supposed to be great political conspirators) martyred in England 27 *Saint* extreme Puritan, political radical 28 *Commandment* the sixth: Thou shalt not kill 32 *her ribs* of Mother Earth 33 *barkes* boats 34 *Had* would have *Pile* monument 38 *ferrymen, in Hell* here the sailors , blamed for the shipwreck, are apprentices to Charon, see Appendix 1 41 *scaping* escape 43 *fir'd* set alight *Vatican* the largest library of the early-modern world 44 *seare* dry 47 *Frankford* Frankfurt, all the books of the annual international book fair 52 *Ague* cold shivering fever *Calenture* hot burning fever 56 *leaves false printed* the rejects of the printer's workshop 59 *Pallas...Thetis* see Appendix 1 65 *Route* way, now cleared 69 *Neptune* see Appendix 1 *Scaly powres* the sea-creatures 70 *Pythagoreans* believers in reincarnation, see Appendix 1 *Confessors* witnesses to Christianity 75 *Holy whale* Old Testament, *Jonah* 1: 17 *et seq.* 80 *sayst* from French 'sayette', 'sayon', a kind of mixed silk 81 *Enoch* see Appendix 1 84–5 Genesis 1: 7-8 'And God...divided the waters which were...above the firmament...and God called the firmament Heaven' 89 *tables o'th' Pope and Christ* there appears to be reference here to the sorts of propaganda print which were reversible: showing, in one example, the Pope when held upright, and the devil when reversed 90 *primitive Divinity* the original Christian Church of the Apostles, seen by Paman in the following lines as now represented on earth by the Church of England, the Church Catholic purged of Roman errors and accretions 91 *Heavens cheife discoverers* the apostles, who began as fishermen 93–4 King is seen here as exemplary Christian, sinking below the waters of the sea, as St Peter had walked on them 103 *Patentees* literally, co-holders of a royal warrant, here, King's fellow believers 117–20 King's grave is the wide sea; those buried on land in coffins will also rise at the last day, but are at present as confined as the sand used to blot wet ink, here imagined blotting the tears of those who weep for King 118 *balm'd* embalmed *cear-cloth'd* shrouded *Leviathans* see Appendix 1

RICHARD CRASHAW

140 IN THE GLORIOUS ASSUMPTION OF OUR BLESSED LADY. THE HYMN.

Hark! she is call'd, the parting houre is come
Take thy Farewell, poor world! heavn must goe home.
A peice of heav'nly earth; Purer and brighter
Then the chast starres, whose choise lamps come to light her
While through the crystall orbes, clearer than they
She climbes; and makes a farre more milkey way.
She's call'd. Hark, how the dear immortall dove
Sighes to his sylver mate rise up, my love!
Rise up, my fair, my spottlesse one!
The winter's past, the rain is gone.
The spring is come, the flowrs appear
No sweets, but thou, are wanting here.
Come away, my love!
Come away, my dove! cast off delay,
The court of heav'n is come
To wait upon thee home; Come come away!

The flowrs appear.
Or quickly would, wert thou once here
The spring is come, or if it stay,
'Tis to keep time with thy delay.
The rain is gone, except so much as we
Detain in needfull teares to weep the want of thee.
The winter's past.
or if he makes less hast,
His answer is, why she does so.
If sommer come not, how can winter goe.
Come away, come away.
The shrill winds chide, the waters weep thy stay;
The fountains murmur; and each loftyest tree
Bowes low'st his heavy top, to look for thee.
Come away, my love.
Come away, my dove &c.
She's call'd again. And will she goe?
When heavn bidds come, who can say no?

Heavn calls her, and she must away.
Heavn will not, and she cannot stay.
GOE then; goe GLORIOUS.
    On the golden wings
Of the bright youth of heavn, that sings
Under so sweet a Burthen. Goe,
Since thy dread son will have it so.
And while thou goest, our song and we
Will, as we may, reach after thee.
HAIL, holy Queen of humble hearts!
We in thy prayse will have our parts.
    Thy pretious name shall be
    Thy self to us; and we
    With holy care will keep it by us.
    We to the last
    Will hold it fast
    And no ASSUMPTION shall deny us.
    All the sweetest showres
    Of our fairest flowrs
    Will we strow upon it.
    Though our sweets cannot make
    It sweeter; they can take
    Themselves new sweetness from it.
MARIA, men and Angels sing
MARIA, mother of our KING.
   Live, rosy princesse, LIVE. And may the bright
Crown of a most incomparable light
Embrace thy radiant browes. O may the best
Of everlasting joyes bath thy white brest.
LIVE, our chast love, the holy mirth
Of heavn; the humble pride of earth.
Live, crown of woemen; Queen of men.
Live mistresse of our song. And when
Our weak desires have done their best,
Sweet Angels come, and sing the rest.

140 Title *ASSUMPTION* the Catholic doctrine that the Blessed Virgin Mary was taken up body and soul into heaven; this doctrine was widely believed from the fourth century, but was only defined by Pius XII in the 1950s 5 *crystall orbes* the planets, fixed to the crystal spheres circling the earth 7 *immortall dove* Holy Spirit, the following sacred love song draws heavily on the Song of Solomon from the Old Testament, parts of which were traditionally applied both to Christ and his bride the Church and, particularly in the 'Litany of Loreto', to the Virgin as Queen of Heaven 22 *want* lack, absence 40 *Burthen* burden, pun on musical ground or chorus 41 *dread son* Christ 44 paraphrasing the traditional prayer to the Virgin, the *Salve Regina* 60 *rosy* roseate, but also as, in varying phases of Counter-Reformation devotion, 'Queen of the Most Holy Rosary'

141 A HYMN TO THE NAME AND HONOR OF THE ADMIRABLE SAINTE TERESA, FOUNDERESSE of the Reformation of the Discalced CARMELITES, both men and Women; A WOMAN for Angellicall heigth of speculation, for Masculine courage of performance, more then a woman. WHO Yet a child, out ran maturity, and durst plott a Martyrdome; THE HYMNE.

Love, thou art Absolute sole lord
OF LIFE AND DEATH. To prove the word.
Wee'l now appeal to none of all
Those thy old Souldiers, Great and tall,
Ripe Men of Martyrdom, that could reach down
With strong armes, their triumphant crown;
Such as could with lusty breath
Speak lowd into the face of death
Their Great LORD'S glorious name, to none
Of those whose spatious Bosomes spread a throne
For LOVE at larg to fill, spare blood and sweat;
And see him take a private seat,
Making his mansion in the mild
And milky soul of a soft child
  Scarce has she learn't to lisp the name
Of Martyr; yet she thinks it shame
Life should so long play with that breath
Which spent can buy so brave a death.
She never undertook to know
What death with love should have to do;
Nor has she e're yet understood
Why to show love, she should shed blood
Yet though she cannot tell you why,
She can LOVE, and she can DY.

Scarce has she Blood enough to make
A guilty sword blush for her sake;
Yet has she'a HEART dares hope to prove
How much lesse strong is DEATH then LOVE.
Be love but there; let poor six yeares
Be pos'd with the maturest Feares
Man trembles at, you straight shall find
LOVE knowes no nonage, nor the MIND.
'Tis LOVE, not YEARES or LIMBS that can
Make the martyr, or the man.
LOVE touch't her HEART, and lo it beates
High, and burnes with such brave heates;
Such thirsts to dy, as dares drink up,
A thousand cold deaths in one cup.
Good reason. For she breathes All fire.
Her white breast heaves with strong desire
Of what she may with fruitles wishes
Seek for amongst her MOTHER'S kisses.
Since 'tis not to be had at home
She'l travail to a Martyrdom.
No home for hers confesses she
But where she may a Martyr be.
She'l to the Moores; And trade with them,
For this unvalued Diadem.
She'l offer them her dearest Breath,
With CHRIST'S Name in't, in change for death.
She'l bargain with them; and will give
Them GOD; teach them how to live
In him: or, if they this deny,
For him she'l teach them how to DY.
So shall she leave amongst them sown
Her LORD'S Blood; or at lest her own.
FAREWEL then, all the world! Adieu.
TERESA is no more for you.
Farewell, all pleasures, sports, and joyes,
(Never till now esteemed toyes)
[Farewell whatever deare may bee,]
MOTHER'S armes or FATHER'S knee
Farewell house, and farewell home!
SHE'S for the Moores, and MARTYRDOM.

SWEET, not so fast! lo thy fair Spouse
Whom thou seekst with so swift vowes,
Calls thee back, and bidds thee come
T'embrace a milder MARTYRDOM
Blest powres forbid, Thy tender life
Should bleed upon a barborous knife;
Or some base hand have power to race
Thy Brest's chast cabinet, and uncase
A soul kept there so sweet, ô no;
Wise heavn will never have it so
THOU art love's victime; and must dy
A death more mysticall and high.
Into love's armes thou shalt let fall
A still-surviving funerall.
His is the DART must make the DEATH
Whose stroke shall tast thy hallow'd breath;
A Dart thrice dip't in that rich flame
Which writes thy spouse's radiant Name
Upon the roof of Heav'n; where ay
It shines, and with a soveraign ray
Beates bright upon the burning faces
Of soules which in that name's sweet graces
Find everlasting smiles. So rare,
So spirituall, pure and fair
Must be th'immortall instrument
Upon whose choice point shall be sent
A life so lov'd; And that there be
Fitt executioners for Thee.
The fair'st and first-born sons of fire
Blest SERAPHIM, shall leave their quire
And turn love's souldiers, upon THEE
To exercise their archerie.
O how oft shalt thou complain
Of a sweet and subtle PAIN.
Of intolerable JOYES;
Of a DEATH, in which who dyes
Loves his death, and dyes again.
And would for ever so be slain.
And lives, and dyes; and knowes not why
To live, But that he thus may never leave to DY.

How kindly will thy gentle HEART
Kisse the sweetly-killing DART!
And close in his embraces keep
Those delicious Wounds, that weep
Balsom to heal themselves with thus
When These thy DEATHS, so numerous,
Shall all at last dy into one,
And melt thy Soul's sweet mansion;
Like a soft lump of incense, hasted
By too hott a fire, and wasted
Into perfuming clouds, so fast
Shalt thou exhale to Heavn at last
In a resolving SIGH, and then
O what? Ask not the Tongues of men.
Angells cannot tell, suffice,
Thy selfe shall feel thine own full joyes
And hold them fast for ever there
So soon as you first appear,
The MOON of maiden starrs, thy white
MISTRESSE, attended by such bright
Soules as thy shining self, shall come
And in her first rankes make thee room;
Where 'mongst her snowy family
Immortall wellcomes wait for thee.
O what delight, when reveal'd LIFE shall stand
And teach thy lipps heav'n with his hand;
On which thou now maist to thy wishes
Heap up thy consecrated kisses.
What joyes shall seize thy soul, when she
Bending her blessed eyes on thee
(Those second Smiles of Heav'n) shall dart
Her mild rayes through thy melting heart!
Angels, thy old freinds, there shall greet thee
Glad at their own home now to meet thee.
All thy good WORKES which went before
And waited for thee, at the door,
Shall own thee there; and all in one
Weave a constellation
Of CROWNS, with which the KING thy spouse
Shall build up thy triumphant browes.

All thy old woes shall now smile on thee
And thy paines sitt bright upon thee
[All thy sorrows here shall shine]
All thy SUFFERINGS be divine.
TEARES shall take comfort, and turn gemms
And WRONGS repent to Diademms.
Ev'n thy DEATH shall live; and new
Dresse the soul that erst they slew.
Thy wounds shall blush to such bright scarres
As keep account of the LAMB'S warres.
Those rare WORKES where thou shalt leave writt.
Love's noble history, with witt
Taught thee by none but him, while here
They feed our soules, shall cloth THINE there.
Each heavnly word by whose hid flame
Our hard Hearts shall strike fire, the same
Shall flourish on thy browes, and be
Both fire to us and flame to thee;
Whose light shall live bright in thy FACE
By glory, in our hearts by grace.
Thou shalt look round about, and see
Thousands of crown'd Soules throng to be
Themselves thy crown. Sons of thy vowes
The virgin-births with which thy soveraign spouse
Made fruitfull thy fair soul, goe now
And with them all about thee bow
To Him, put on (hee'l say) put on
(My rosy love) That thy rich zone
Sparkling with the sacred flames
Of thousand soules, whose happy names
Heav'n keep upon thy score. (Thy bright
Life brought them first to kisse the light
That kindled them to starrs.) and so
Thou with the LAMB, thy lord, shalt goe;
And whereso'ere he setts his white
Stepps, walk with HIM those wayes of light
Which who in death would live to see,
Must learn in life to dy like thee.

141 See Appendix 2 for St Teresa; see Notes on the Text for the changes which Crashaw made to the text between its publication in England and its publication on the Continent 18 *spent* poured out (as at the moment of death) *brave* in the modern sense, but also fine, beautiful 32 *nonage* extreme youth 48 *Diadem* martyr's crown 60 *toyes* trivial things 65 *Spouse* Christ, her mystic husband 71 *race* cut 79 *DART* in St Teresa's own writings (and in the famous statue by Bernini) the Love of God is imaged as a burning arrow 94 *quire* choir 123 *MOON of maiden starrs* the Virgin Mary 127 *snowy* pure 154 *LAMB'S warres* Christ the Lamb of God 167 *Sons of thy vowes* the members of the order which she founded 172 *zone* (Latin) girdle 175 *score* literally, 'account', here, 'by your intercession'

142 JOANN 2.: Aquae in vinum versae

Unde rubor vestris, et non sua purpura lymphis,
  Quae rosa mirantes tam nova mutat aquas?

Numen (convivae) praesens agnoscite Numen:
  Nympha pudica Deum vidit, et erubuit.

142 JOHN 2: Water turned into wine.

Whence your rosiness, and the purple of your waters which is not your own? into what new rose now does the wondering water change? The genius of the feast, present there, acknowledge God! The chaste nymph saw God and blushed.

143 Pontio lavanti

Non satis est caedes, nisi stuprum hoc insuper addas,
  Et tam virginae sis violator aquae?

Nympha, quidem pura haec et *honesti filia fontis*
  Inget, adulterio jam temerata tuo.

Casta verecundo properat cum murmure gutta,
  Nec satis in lacrymam se putat esse suam.

Desine tam nitidos stuprare (ah, desine) rores.
  Aut dic, quare miseras unda lavabit aquas.

143 Pontius [Pilate] washing [his hands]

The fall is not sufficient, unless you add defilement on top of it, that you should be such a ravisher of virgin water. The nymph, this pure creature and daughter of noble spring, moans having been polluted by your adulteration. A chaste drop hurries with a modest murmur, nor does she think herself to be sufficiently in tears. Cease, ah, cease to defile such shining dews, or say how the waves may wash the unhappy water.

143 The poem is a meditation or commentary on the incident recorded in Matthew 27: 24

THOMAS JORDAN

144 An Epitaph on a Childe.

Ladies that are young and wise,
Shall I tell ye of a *Prize*?
Here a *Box of Beauty* lies.

A *Jewel* hid from vulgar view,
Whose excellency if you knew,
Your eyes would drop like morning dew.

Dame-Nature's Diamond, which when
She saw it was too high for men,
Shew'd it, and shut it up agen.

MARTIN LLUELYN

145 Epitaph on [ ] borne tenne weekes before his time, died at three Quarters.

Griev'd at the *World* and *Crimes*, this early Bloome
Look'd round, and sigh'd, and stole into his *Tombe*,
His fall was like his *Birth*, too quicke, this *Rose*
Made hast to *spread*, and the same hast to *close*:

Here lyes his *Dust*, but his best Tombe's fled hence,
For *Marble* cannot last like *Innocence*.

145 4 *spread* open

LAURENCE CLARKSON

146 [*from* A Single Eye, All Light, no Darkness]

Behold, the King of glory now is come
T'reduce God and the Devil to their Doom;
For both of them are servants unto Me
That lives, and rules in perfect Majesty:
Though called God, yet that is not my Name,
True, I be both, yet am I not the same:
Therefore a wonder am I to you all,
So that to titul'd Gods ye pray and call,
Oh then my Creature, let me speak to thee;
Thy Worship, and thy God, shall dy truly.
Why dote ye Worldlings? up and down being hurl'd
As he is, so are we even in this World;
And so are all things perfect, just and good;
Yea, all are sav'd by's Cross, his wounds and blood.
Where else is heaven, but in our present peace
From him? or hell, but when that this doth cease?
Fie then for shame, look not above the Skies
For God, or Heaven; for here your Treasure lies
Even in these Forms, Eternal Will will reigne,
Through him are all things, onely One, not Twain:
Sure he's the Fountain from which everything
Both good and ill (so term'd) appears to spring.
Unto this Single Eye, though Adams two
Cannot perceive, to Such, to All
Adieu.

146 In so far as it is internally consistent, the theology which Clarkson appears to be setting forth concerns itself with Christ as advocate and champion of humanity against a remote and hostile God the Father. The first person of the poem is shifting and unstable, but would appear to be the voice of Christ in at least ll. 1–10 6 *both* both God and man 8 *titul'd* so-called 11 *Worldlings* mortals 20 The idea here is that the division of God and Devil, light and dark, is ultimately meaningless in the eternal present of Christ

JOSEPH BEAUMONT

147 Jesus inter Ubera Mariae
Cantcl. 6.

(To a Base and 2 Trebles.)

In the coolnesse of the day
The old Worlds Even, *God* all undrest went downe
Without His Roab, without His Crowne,
Into His private garden, there to lay
On spicey Bed
His Sweeter Head.

There He found two Beds of Spice,
A double Mount of Lillies, in whose Top
Two milkie Fountaines bubled up.
He soon resolv'd: and well I like, He cries,
My table spread
Upon my Bed.

Scarcely had He 'gun to feed,
When troops of *Cherubs* hover'd round about;
And on their golden Wings they brought
All *Edens* flowers. But We cry'd out; No need
Of flowers heere;
Sweet Spirits, forbeare.

True, He needs no Sweets, say They,
But Sweets have need of Him, to keep them so.
Now *Paradise* springs new with you,
Old *Edens* Beautie's all inclin'd this way;
And We are come
To bring them home.

Paradise springs new with you,
Where 'twixt those Beds of Lillies you may see
Of Life the Everlasting Tree.
Sweet is your reason, then said Wee, come strow
Your pious showres
Of Easterne Flowres.

CHORUS

Winds awake, and with soft Gale
Awake the Odours of our Garden too;
By which your selv's perfumed goe
Through every Quarter of your World, that All
Your sound may heare,
And breathe your Aire.

147 Title 'Jesus between Mary's Breasts'; the imagery of this poem, poising the sacred and the erotic, draws heavily on the Song of Solomon 2 *Even* evening: Genesis 3: 8 'And they heard the voice of the LORD God walking in the garden in the cool of the day.' Two descents of God are put in parallel: the angry God coming to Adam and Eve, and Christ as Redeemer coming to the Virgin in the Incarnation 4 *private garden* 'hortus conclusus', the Virgin's body, but also recalls the Garden of Eden 28 *strow* scatter 31–6 Song of Solomon 4: 16 'Awake, O north wind; and come, thou south; blow upon my garden, that the spices thereof may flow out'

148 The Gardin

June 12.

The Gardins quit with me: as yesterday
I walked in that, to day that walks in me;
Through all my memorie
It sweetly wanders, and has found a way
To make me honestly possess
What still Anothers is.

Yet this Gains dainty sence doth gall my Minde
With the remembrance of a bitter Loss.
Alas, how odd and cross

Are earths Delights, in which the Soule can finde
No Honey, but withall some Sting
To check the pleasing thing!

For now I'm haunted with the thought of that
Heavn-planted Gardin, where felicitie
Flourished on every Tree.
Lost, lost it is; for at the guarded gate
A flaming Sword forbiddeth Sin
(That's I,) to enter in.

O Paradise! when I was turned out
Hadst thou but kept the Serpent still within,
My banishment had been
Less sad and dangerous: but round about
This wide world runneth rageing He
To banish me from me:

I feel that through my soule he death hath shott;
And thou, alas, hast locked up Lifes Tree.
O Miserable Me,
What help were left, had JESUS'S Pity not
Shewd me another Tree, which can
Enliven dying Man.

That Tree, made Fertile by his own dear blood;
And by his Death with quickning virtue fraught.
I now dread not the thought
Of barracado'd Eden, since as good
A Paradise I planted see
On open Calvarie.

148 1 *quit* equal, even 7 *gall* embitter 11 *withall* always 13 *hanted* haunted 14 *Gardin* of Eden 29 *another Tree* the Cross, set in parallel with the Tree of Knowledge in the Garden of Eden 32 *quickning* life-giving 34 *barracado'd* barricaded, forbidden

ABRAHAM COWLEY

149 *On the Death of Mr.* Crashaw

Poet and *Saint*! to thee alone are given
The two most sacred *Names* of *Earth* and *Heaven*.
The hard and rarest *Union* which can be
Next that of *Godhead* with *Humanitie*.
Long did the *Muses* banisht *Slaves* abide,
And built vain *Pyramids* to mortal pride;
Like *Moses* Thou (though Spells and Charms withstand)
Hast brought them nobly home back to their *Holy Land*.
  Ah wretched *We, Poets* of *Earth*! but *Thou*
Wert *Living* the same *Poet* which thou'rt *Now*.
Whilst *Angels* sing to thee their ayres divine,
And joy in an applause so great as *thine*.
Equal society with them to hold,
Thou need'st not make *new Songs*, but say the *Old*.
And they (kind Spirits!) shall all rejoyce to see
How little less than *They, Exalted Man* may be.
Still the old *Heathen Gods* in *Numbers* dwell,
The *Heav'enliest* thing on Earth still keeps up *Hell*.
Nor have we yet quite purg'd the *Christian Land*;
Still *Idols* here, like *Calves* at *Bethel* stand.
And though *Pans Death* long since all *Oracles* breaks,
Yet still in Rhyme the *Fiend Apollo* speaks.
Nay with the worst of Heathen dotage We
(Vain Men!) the *Monster Woman Deifie*.
Find *Stars*, and tye our *Fates* there in a *Face*,
And *Paradise* in them by whom we *lost* it, place.
What different faults corrupt our *Muses* thus?
Wanton as *Girles*, as *old Wives, Fabulous*!
  Thy spotless *Muse*, like *Mary*, did contain
The boundless *Godhead*; she did well disdain
That her *eternal Verse* employ'd should be
On a less subject than *Eternitie*.
And for a sacred *Mistress* scorn'd to take,
But her whom *God* himself scorn'd not his *Spouse* to make.

It (in a kind) *her Miracle* did do;
A fruitful *Mother* was, and *Virgin* too.
   *How well (blest Swan) did Fate contrive thy death;
And made thee render up thy tuneful breath
In thy great *Mistress* Arms? thou most divine
And richest *Off 'ering* of *Loretto's Shrine*!
Where like some holy *Sacrifice* t'expire,
A *Fever* burns thee, and *Love* lights the *Fire*.
Angels (they say) brought the fam'ed *Chapel* there,
And bore the sacred Load in Triumph through the aire.
'Tis surer much they brought thee there, and *They*,
And *Thou*, their charge, went *singing* all the way.
   Pardon, my *Mother Church*, if I consent
That *Angels* led him when from thee he went,
For even in *Error* sure no *Danger* is
When joyn'd with so much *Piety* as *His*.
Ah, mighty *God*, with shame I speak't, and grief
Ah that our greatest *Faults* were in *Belief*!
And our weak *Reason* were ev'en weaker yet,
Rather than thus our *Wills* too strong for it.
His *Faith* perhaps in some nice Tenents might
Be wrong; his *Life*, I'm sure, was *in the right*.
And I my self a *Catholick* will be,
So far at least, great *Saint*, to *Pray* to thee.
   Hail, *Bard Triumphant*! and some care bestow
On *us*, the *Poets Militant* Below!
Oppos'ed by our old En'emy, adverse *Chance*,
Attacqu'ed by *Envy*, and by *Ignorance*,
Enchain'd by *Beauty*, tortur'd by *Desires*,
Expos'd by *Tyrant-Love* to savage *Beasts* and *Fires*.
Thou from low earth in nobler *Flames* did rise,
And like *Elijah*, mount *Alive* the skies.
Elisha-like (but with a wish much less,
More fit thy *Greatness*, and my *Littleness*)
Lo here I beg (I whom thou once didst prove
So humble to *Esteem*, so Good to *Love*)
Not that thy *Spirit* might on me *Doubled* be,
I ask but *Half* thy mighty *Spirit* for Me.

And when my *Muse* soars with so strong a Wing,
'Twill learn of things *Divine*, and first of *Thee* to sing.

* M. Crashaw died of a Fever at Loretto, being newly chosen Canon of that Church.

149 See Appendix 3 for Crashaw (see also nos. 49, 140–3) 5–8 The restriction of poetry to secular, neoclassical subjects is compared to the servitude of Israel in Egypt, the Muses being the slaves 18 *keeps up Hell* supports the work of the devil (by writing exclusively within a heathen or profane frame of reference) 20 *Calves at Bethel* a famous instance of idolatry in 1 Kings 12: 28 24–5 love poetry and astrology are both seen here as vanity, idolatry 28 *Fabulous* full of tales, fables 37 *Swan* Crashaw; swans proverbially only sang at death 38-9 *Mistress* Both the Catholic Church and the Blessed Virgin, to whom Crashaw had written in terms poised between the chivalric and the erotic (see no. 140) 40 *Loretto's Shrine* The Shrine of the Holy House, at Loreto, the chief place of Marian pilgrimage in early-modern Europe. Crashaw died shortly after he was installed as a Canon there 43–4 From the basis in fact that the stones of a palaeo-Christian church in Nazareth had been transported to Italy by a returning Crusader called possibly 'di Angelis', the legend grew that the structure (identified with the house of the Holy Family) had literally been transported through the air by angels 55 *nice* scrupulous, pedantic 59 *Triumphant* the Church and Saints already in heaven are victorious 60 *Militant* the faithful still embattled in life on earth 66–7 *Elijah*, *Elisha* see Appendix 1

150 *On the Death of Mr.* William Hervey

Immodicis brevis est aetas, & rara senectus, Mart.

1.

It was a dismal, and a fearful night,
Scarce could the Morn drive on th'unwilling Light,
When *Sleep*, *Deaths Image*, left my troubled brest,
By something *liker Death* possest.
My eyes with Tears did uncommanded flow,
And on my Soul hung the dull weight
Of some *Intolerable Fate*.
What Bell was that? Ah me! Too much I know.

2.

My sweet *Companion*, and my gentle *Peere*,
Why hast thou left me thus unkindely here,
Thy *end* for ever, and my *Life* to moan;
O thou hast left me all alone!
Thy *Soul* and *Body* when *Deaths Agonie*
Besieg'd around thy noble heart,
Did not with more reluctance part
Then I, my dearest *Friend*, do part from *Thee*.

3.

My dearest *Friend*, would I had dy'ed for thee!
Life and this *World* henceforth will tedious bee.
Nor shall I know hereafter what to do
If once my *Griefs* prove *tedious* too.
Silent and sad I walk about all day,
As sullen *Ghosts* stalk speechless by
Where their hid *Treasures* ly;
Alas, my *Treasure's* gone, why do I stay?

4.

He was my *Friend*, the truest *Friend* on earth;
A strong and mighty *Influence* joyn'd our *Birth*.
Nor did we envy the most sounding *Name*
By *Friendship* giv'en of old to *Fame*.
None but his *Brethren* he, and *Sisters* knew,
Whom the kind youth preferr'd to Me;
And ev'n in that we did agree,
For much above my self I lov'd them too.

5.

Say, for you saw us, ye immortal *Lights*,
How oft unweari'ed have we spent the Nights?
Till the *Ledaean Stars* so fam'd for *Love*,
Wondred at us from above.
We spent them not in toys, in lusts, or wine;
But search of deep *Philosophy*,
Wit, *Eloquence*, and *Poetry*,
Arts which I lov'ed, for they, my *Friend*, were *Thine*.

6.

Ye fields of *Cambridge*, our dear *Cambridge*, say,
Have ye not seen us walking every day?
Was there a *Tree* about which did not know
The *Love* betwixt us two?
Henceforth, ye gentle *Trees*, for ever fade;
Or your sad branches thicker joyn,
And into darksome shades combine,
Dark as the *Grave* wherein my *Friend* is laid.

7.

Henceforth no learned *Youths* beneath you sing,
Til all the tuneful *Birds* to 'your boughs they bring;
No tuneful *Birds* play with their wonted chear,
And call the learned *Youths* to hear,
No whistling *Winds* through the glad branches fly,
But all with sad solemnitie,
Mute and unmoved be,
Mute as the *Grave* wherein my *Friend* does ly.

8.

To him my *Muse* made haste with every strain
Whilst it was new, and *warm* yet from the *Brain*.
He lov'd my worthless *Rhymes*, and like a *Friend*
Would finde out something to *commend*.
Hence now, my *Muse*, thou canst not me delight;
Be this my latest verse
With which I now adorn his *Herse*,
And this my *Grief*, without *thy* help shall write.

9.

Had I a wreath of *Bays* about my brow,
I should contemn that flourishing honor now,
Contemn it to the *Fire*, and joy to hear
It rage and crackle there.
Instead of *Bays*, crown with sad *Cypress* me;
Cypress which *Tombs* does beautifie;
Not *Phoebus* griev'd so much as I
For him, who first was made that mournful *Tree*.

10.

Large was his *Soul*; as large a *Soul* as ere
Submitted to *Inform* a *Body* here.
High as the Place 'twas shortly' in *Heav'en* to have,
But low, and humble, as his *Grave*.
So *high* that all the *Virtues* there did come
As to their chiefest seat
Conspicuous, and great;
So *low* that for *Me* too it made a roome.

11.

He scorn'd this busie world below, and all
That we, *Mistaken Mortals*, Pleasure call;
Was fill'd with inn'ocent *Gallantry* and *Truth*,
Triumphant ore the sins of *Youth*.
He like the *Stars*, to which he now is gone,
That shine with beams like *Flame*
Yet burn not with the same,
Had all the *Light* of *Youth*, of the *Fire* none.

12.

Knowledge he onely sought, and so soon caught,
As if for him *Knowledge* had rather *sought*.
Nor did more *Learning* ever crowded lie
In such a short *Mortalitie*.
When ere the skilful *Youth* discourst or writ,
Still did the *Notions* throng
About his eloquent *Toung*,
Nor could his *Ink* flow faster than his *Wit*.

13.

So strong a *Wit* did *Nature* to him frame,
As all things but his *Judgment* overcame;
His *Judgment* like the heav'nly *Moon* did show,
Temp'ring that mighty *Sea* below.
Oh had he liv'd in *Learnings World*, what bound
Would have been able to controul
His over-powering Soul?
We 'have lost in him *Arts* that not yet are *found*.

14.

His *Mirth* was the pure *Spirits* of various Wit,
Yet never did his *God* or *Friends* forget.
And when deep talk and wisdom came in view,
Retir'ed and gave to them their due.
For the rich help of *Books* he always took,
Though his own searching mind before
Was so with *Notions* written ore
As if wise *Nature* had made that her *Book*.

15.

So many *Virtues* joyn'd in him, as we
Can scarce pick here and there in *Historie*.
More then old *Writers Practice* ere could reach,
As much as they could ever teach.
These did *Religion, Queen* of Virtues sway,
And all their sacred *Motions* stear,
Just like the First and *Highest Sphaere*
Which wheels about, and turns all *Heav'en* one way.

16.

With as much Zeal, Devotion, Pietie,
He always *Liv'ed*, as other Saints do *Dye*.
Still with his Soul severe account he kept,
Weeping all *Debts* out ere he slept.
Then down in peace and innocence he lay,
Like the *Suns* laborious light,
Which still in *Water* sets at Night,
Unsullied with his *Journey* of the *Day*.

17.

Wondrous young Man, why wert thou made so good,
To be snatcht hence ere better *understood*?
Snatcht before half of thee enough was seen!
Thou Ripe, and yet thy *Life* but *Green*!
Nor could thy Friends take their last sad Farewel,
But Danger and *Infectious Death*
Malitiously seiz'd on that Breath
Where *Life, Spirit, Pleasure* always us'd to dwell.

18.

But happy Thou, ta'ne from this frantick age,
Where *Igno'rance* and *Hypocrisie* does rage!
A fitter *time* for Heav'n no soul ere chose,
The place now only free from those.
There 'mong the *Blest* thou dost for ever shine,
And wheresoere thou casts thy view
Upon that white and radiant crew,
See'st not a *Soul* cloath'd with more *Light* then *Thine*.

19.

And if the glorious *Saints* cease not to know
Their wretched Friends who *fight* with *Life* below;
Thy Flame to *Me* does still the same abide,
Onely more pure and rarifie'd.
There whilst immortal Hymns thou dost reherse
Thou dost with holy pity see
Our dull and earthly *Poesie*,
Where *Grief* and *Mis'ery* can be join'd with *Verse*.

150 Epigraph Martial, *Epigrams*, VI. 29 'the life of those who live to the full is short, rarely do they grow old' 9 *Peere* contemporary 17 2 Samuel 18: 33 'O my son Absalom, my son, my son Absalom! would God I had died for thee' 26 *Influence* (astrology) combination of stars determining the pattern of the life of the individual born under them 27 *sounding* celebrated 35 *Ledaean Stars* see Appendix 1 37 *toys* trivial things 51 *wonted* usual 65 *Bays* the poet's laurel 72 *Him* Cyparissus, a youth changed to a Cypress tree in Ovid, *Metamorphoses*, X. 121 *et seq.* 119 *First and Highest Sphaere* in the medieval cosmological tradition, the 'primum mobile', the sphere which moves the whole machine of the universe 145 *if* despite his later crypto-Catholic position on the fate of the virtuous after death (see no. 149) here Cowley is reflecting Anglican ambiguity on this issue: unsure whether the soul of one recently dead has passed straight to its reward, and if so, whether it can intercede for those still alive

HENRY VAUGHAN

151 The Brittish Church.

Ah! he is fled!
And while these here their *mists*, and *shadowes* hatch,
My glorious head
Doth on those hills of Myrrhe, and Incense watch.
Hast, hast my dear,
The Souldiers here
Cast in their lotts againe
That seamless coat
The Jewes touch'd not,
These dare divide, and staine.

O get thee wings!
Or if as yet (until these clouds depart,
And the day springs,)
Thou think'st it good to tarry where thou art,
Write in thy bookes
My ravish'd looks
Slain flock, and pillag'd fleeces,
And hast thee so
As a young Roe
Upon the mounts of spices.

O Rosa Campi! O lilium Convallium! quomodò nunc facta es pabulum Aprorum!

151 Title the Church speaks the poem in the first person 1 *he* in the Anglican interpretation of the Song of Solomon in the Authorized (King James) version of the Bible, Christ is the bridegroom of the Christian Church 14 *tarry* linger, stay 19 *Roe* deer, metaphorically Christ as in Song of Solomon 8: 14–20 'be thou like to a roe or to a young hart upon the mountains of spices'; also motto: 'O flower of the field, o lily of the valleys, now you are made the food of wild boars'. To express his outrage at the attack on the Church of England by the parliamentarians, Vaughan combines an epithet for the Church, again from the Song of Solomon 2: 1 'I am the rose of Sharon, and the lily of the valleys' with an image of destruction from Virgil, *Eclogue* II. 58–9 'the north wind destroys the flowers, the boars pollute the fountain'

152 The Lampe.

'Tis dead night round about: Horrour doth creepe
And move on with the shades; stars nod, and sleepe,
And through the dark aire spin a firie thread
Such as doth gild the lazie glow-worms bed.
 Yet, burn'st thou here, a full day; while I spend
My rest in Cares, and to the dark world lend
These flames, as thou dost thine to me; I watch
That houre, which must thy life, and mine dispatch;
But still thou doest out-goe me, I can see
Met in thy flames, all acts of piety;
Thy light, is *Charity*; Thy heat, is *Zeale*;
And thy aspiring, active fires reveale
Devotion still on wing; Then, thou dost weepe
Still as thou burn'st, and the warme droppings creepe
To measure out thy length, as if thou'dst know
What stock, and how much time were left thee now;
Nor dost thou spend one teare in vain, for still
As thou dissolv'st to them, and they distill,
They're stor'd up in the socket, where they lye,
When all is spent, thy last, and sure supply,
And such is true repentance, ev'ry breath
Wee spend in sighes, is treasure after death;
Only, one point escapes thee; That thy Oile
Is still out with thy flame, and so both faile;
But whensoe're I'm out, both shalbe in,
And where thou mad'st an end, there I'le begin.

Mark Cap. 13. ver. 35.

Watch you therefore, for you know not when the master of the house commeth, at Even, or at mid-night, or at the Cock-crowing, or in the morning.

152 5 *thou* addresses the lamp 16 *stock* store (of fuel) 24 *out with* separate from

153 The Retreate.

Happy those early dayes! when I
Shin'd in my Angell-infancy.
Before I understood this place
Appointed for my second race,
Or taught my soul to fancy ought
But a white, Celestiall thought,
When yet I had not walkt above
A mile, or two, from my first love,
And looking back (at that short space,)
Could see a glimpse of his bright-face;
When on some *gilded Cloud*, or *flowre*
My gazing soul would dwell an houre,
And in those weaker glories spy
Some shadows of eternity;
Before I taught my tongue to wound
My Conscience with a sinfull sound,
Or had the black art to dispence
A sev'rall sinne to ev'ry sence,
But felt through all this fleshly dresse
Bright *shootes* of everlastingnesse.
O how I long to travell back
And tread again that ancient track!
That I might once more reach that plaine,
Where first I left my glorious traine,
From whence th'Inlightned spirit sees
That shady City of Palme trees;
But (ah!) my soul with too much stay
Is drunk, and staggers in the way.
Some men a forward motion love,
But I by backward steps would move,
And when this dust falls to the urn
In that state I came return.

153 4 *second race* his life on earth 5 *ought* anything 8 *first love* proximity of the unborn soul to God 26 *Palme trees* as emblems of martyrs, often seen in depictions of Heaven. The palm has a vastly complex range of emblematic meanings: the chief connotations are endurance, fidelity, victory

154 Midnight

When to my eyes
(Whilst deep sleep others catches,)
Thine hoast of spyes
The starres shine in their watches,
I doe survey
Each busie Ray,
And how they work, and wind,
And wish each beame
My soul doth streame,
With the like ardour shin'd;
What Emanations,
Quick vibrations
And bright stirs are there?
What thin Ejections,
Cold Affections,
And slow motions here?

2.

Thy heav'ns (some say,)
Are a firie-liquid light,
Which mingling aye
Streames, and flames thus to the sight.
Come then, my god!
Shine on this bloud,
And water in one beame,
And thou shalt see
Kindled by thee
Both liquors burne, and streame.
O what bright quicknes,
Active brightnes,
And celestiall flowes
Will follow after
On that water,
Which thy spirit blowes!

Matth. Cap. 3. ver. xi.

I indeed baptize you with water unto repentance, but he that commeth after me, is mightier than I, whose shooes I am not worthy to beare, he shall baptize you with the holy Ghost, and with fire.

154 3 *hoast* army 11 *Emanations* i.e. starlight 19 *aye* ever

155 Unprofitablenes.

How rich, O Lord! how fresh thy visits are!
'Twas but Just now my bleak leaves hopeles hung
Sullyed with dust and mud;
Each snarling blast shot through me, and did share
Their Youth, and beauty, Cold showres nipt, and wrung
Their spiciness, and bloud;
But since thou didst in one sweet glance survey
Their sad decays, I flourish, and once more
Breath all perfumes, and spice;
I smell a dew like *Myrrh*, and all the day
Wear in my bosome a full Sun; such store
Hath one beame from thy Eys.
But, ah, my God! what fruit hast thou of this?
What one poor leaf did ever I yet fall
To wait upon thy wreath?
Thus thou all day a thankless weed doest dress,
And when th'hast done, a stench, or fog is all
The odour I bequeath.

155 3 *Sullyed* stained 10 *Myrrh* see Appendix 1 15 *wreath* i.e. by his works Vaughan feels that he has done nothing to repay God for so many mercies

THOMAS VAUGHAN

156 On the Death of Mr WILLIAM CARTWRIGHT

So! we are now beyond the spleen of Fate,
Our miseries have made us fortunate:
The Grave was Physick here; Death speaks us free,
Her malice now is spent as well as we;

Nay, now our ruin doth so much displease,
That to strike more is to her a disease.
None can deserve her Envy, her Contempt
Exceeds her former anger, she hath spent
No Arrows but on pretious lives, and we
Are but the leavings of her tyranny:
Such, whom when she hath taken from the Prease
Cannot requite the Expence of a disease.
He fell a nobler ruine; we that live
Owe our short lives, but to a base Reprieve.
He, when as yet in death he was not lost,
Made Fate suspect her Jurisdiction crost,
'Cause Learning knew no destiny; 'twas He
Whose Studies bordered on Eternity.
Our Speculations were too poor to have
With thee the equall glory of a Grave,
And share a fair mortality that we
Might be thought wise, because we fell with Thee.
Death had thee hence, lest thy large Phansy might
In time take Wing, and with a saving flight
Rove Thee beyond the World into a State
Too high, and so outrun the reach of Fate.
Thou wert so richly good, so great, that we
The Church in Thee ev'n at one view might see;
Saints that so long possess'd the quiet Earth,
And slept out Centuries, were at thy Birth
Regenerate, They liv'd again in thee,
And did outdo their former Piety:
And as their Souls contracted in thine own
Did thus forestall the Resurrection,
So in thy Death they met a second Fate,
Nature in Thee did recapitulate.
So fraught wert thou with Learning, that we can
Stile Thee almost a breathing *Vatican*,
A Library not fram'd of stone and wood,
But animate and Cemented with bloud:
All Arts so suffer'd in thy Fall, that We
May call thy Grave an *University*,
And look our Schooles out there, as if that now
Eternall *BODLEY* did descend below

To gratifie thy Dust. O! that we might
Install thee Lecturer again, and right
The injur'd *Metaphysicks* like to be
Eclipsed with their own obscurity
Robb'd of thy Light: and yet they are content
To mourn the ruine of their Ornament.
When He did read, how did we flock to hear!
Sure some Professors became Pupils there:
He would refine *Abstractions*, it was He
That gave the Text all its authority;
As if the *Stagyrite* resign'd his Pen,
And took his *Censure* not his *Comment* then:
And though with some the Science goes for pelf,
His Lectures made it to *transcend* it self:
He us'd the Creatures as a Scale to storm
The spirituall World, and though 'twas torn,
And broken with uncertainties, yet He
By Reason as by Faith a Deity
Could apprehend and reach. Thus having trac'd
These secondary things, his soul made haste
To view the Cause, and there began to plod,
Nothing being left to puzzle him but God;
Whose Mysteries he reach'd, as far as He
Of his great self had made discovery:
He plunderd not the Heavens, nor brought he down
Secrets from thence, which were before unknown:
Yet some there are beleeve their Wits so ripe,
That they can draw a Map of the Arch-Type,
And with strange Opticks tutor'd they can view
The Emanations of the *Mystique Jew*;
In this his pious Ignorance was best,
And did excell his knowledge of the rest:
But he is gone, and Providence took him
To add to Heaven another *Cherubim*.
This to our Tears may minister relief,
'Tis his Preferment, that does cause our Grief.

156 Title see Appendix 3 for Cartwright 1 *spleen* traditionally the seat of envy 3 *Physick* medicine 11 *Prease* press, humankind 19 *Speculations* thoughts 20–50 *thee* the poet addresses Cartwright 23 *Phansy* imagination 31 *Regenerate* born again, almost reincarnated

34 *forestall* anticipate 36 *recapitulate* not in the modern sense, here 'sum up all (the Saints) in one' 37 *fraught* made full 38 *Vatican* as the largest library of early-modern Europe 43 *Schooles* faculties, departments 44 *BODLEY* the Bodleian Library of the University of Oxford 53 *refine Abstractions* clarify or condense philosophical terms 55 *Stagyrite* see Appendix 1, Aristotle 57 *pelf* reward 72 *Arch-Type* the invisible essences of Plato, which are the real reality of which experience is but a reflection 73 *strange Opticks* telescopes 74 *Emanations* rays proceeding from God, out of which matter was created (a theory contrary to the idea of creation out of nothing) *Mystique Jew* Philo Judaeus (first to second century) 80 *Preferment* promotion, advancement

157 [Lord God! This was a *stone*]

Lord God! This was a *stone*,
as *hard* as any *One*
Thy *Laws* in *Nature* fram'd:
Tis now a *springing Well*,
and many *Drops* can tell,
Since it by *Art* was tam'd.
My God! my *Heart* is so,
'tis all of *Flint*, and no
Extract of *Teares* will yeeld:
Dissolve it with thy *Fire*,
that something may *aspire*,
And *grow* up in my *Field*,
Bare Teares Ile not intreat,
but let thy *Spirits seate*
Upon those *Waters* bee,
Then I *new form'd* with *Light*
shall move without all *Night*,
Or *Excentricity*.

157 The central idea of this emblematic poem is similar to the emblem-image which gives its title to Henry Vaughan's *Silex Scintillans* ('The Flint Sparkling'). The flint (the obdurate heart) struck by God's fire (grace, repentance) gives forth the sparks which fly upwards to God. Here Thomas Vaughan combines this image with that of the rock miraculously producing water for Moses in the desert, Numbers 20: 11 18 *Excentricity* (astronomy) of wavering or irregular orbit

VAVASOUR POWELL

158 18 Decemb.1653 His Hymn at Christ-Church

To *Christ* our *King*, let us *praise* sing,
Who is our *Saviour* dear,
Who is our *Protector*, and our *Rock*,
Who will *come, and soon appear.*

To *humble* his, and *try* their *hearts*,
And make them *clean* and *pure*,
To set his *Kingdom* upon *Earth*,
Which ever shall *endure:*

His *Saints* shall *reign* with him on *Earth,*
And *great ones* then shall *bow*,
The *Battle*, and the *Battle ax*,
And *men* of *War* shall know

That he will *arise*, and he will *rule*,
And their *power* will *fall*,
And *Christ* our great *Commander*, He
Shall be our *General.*

Hast *Lord, come* quickly *down*,
Thy *Saints* do *wait*, and *pray*,
And men would faign, if they knew how,
Thy *prophets* kill and slay:

But they shall live and eke stand up,
And give their *Testimony*
Against the *Monarchs* of the *Earth*,
That *sit*, and *reign* on *high*.

158 3 *Rock* Christ himself, 1 Corinthians 10: 4 19 *faign* with pleasure 21 *eke* also

ANNA TRAPNEL

159 [*from* The Cry of a Stone or a Relation of Something spoken in Whitehall]

Oh glorious Lord, thou dost break forth
Unto thy servant here,
Oh the glorious shine of the great God
Most lovely doth appear.

Oh the Seal of God is glorious,
It is a Seal abides,
Oh, it doth seal the soul to thee
That art its running tydes.

Oh a Seal of the mightie Lord,
When others are gone there comes
The fresh discoveries of that seal,
Given forth by thee the Sun.

A broad seal sure, oh Lord it is,
Which none can break in sunder,
Yet is a seal that is within,
No foe can come it plunder.

A seal that is not by men here,
To be melted at all,
But it is a seal which thou dost keep,
It never here shall fall.

Thy servant Lord shall be preserv'd
By this thy seal of Love,
Which over and over thou bringest down,
From the Eternal Love.

Oh that all thine may know what tis,
That so they might up mount,
To magnifie the Lord their God,
And give of this Account.

For who can Lord, shew forth, but those
To whom thou dost it bring,
Oh, who can with language set forth
The sealing of their King?

Oh, thou dear Christ, first sealed was,
That sealed One indeed,
And through thes thine they do partake
A sealing in their need.

When they are in great despairings,
And in great temptations lye,
Oh then comes forth the seal to them,
And draws them through the skie.

Through all Clouds they most swiftly fly
Unto their Saviour great,
Which bids them welcome unto him,
And to his Mercy Seat.

Where they shall see his loving heart,
And his embracing arms,
Where they shall be for evermore,
Taken up from all these harms.

159 1 *break forth* reveal 5 *Seal* see Revelation, chapters 5–8 *passim*, also Appendix 1, Seals 14 *in sunder* in pieces 27 *magnifie* praise greatly

160 [*from* The twenty ninth day of the tenth Moneth 1657]

...O therefore lord unto thy will
I humbly do submit,
For however thy dispensation be,
For thy children's good is it.
O therefore for thy will, the voice
Shall cry against all those
That do not with thy will, O Lord
Nor thy outgoings close.

O the voice it doth cry against
Those that would thy utterings deface;
And humbly submit unto thy will,
And to thy royal grace.
The voice it doth come down and cast
All that is of self away;
But what's of Christ it doth show forth;
For it is that must bear sway.
That voice which is mine, pass sentence on;
But what is of the Lord,
Do thou most sweetly utter forth,
And O spread it abroad.
That voice which is mine, is very dross,
It is filthy dregs also:
But what is of the Lord Christ, is that
For which the Spirit doth blow.
Voice that is mine, throw to the pit,
It's worthy to have no other place:
But what is of the Lord shall be advanced
In its most lovely grace.
What is of me is mixed, and
Its defilement is great:
But what is of the Lord is pure,
And cometh from his seat.
Voice which is mine, bury under ground,
And let it no more come:
But what is of the Lord, let it run forth
With a mighty discovering tongue.
Voice that is mine, O do thou bury,
And lay it in the grave;
But what is thine, do thou raise up,
A glorious resurrection to have.
Voice which is mine, let the dunghil have,
It's fit for no other place:
But what is the Lord Christ's, O sing forth;
That tells of his rich grace.
Voice that is mine, I am very sure
The best of it is vile;
But what is of Christ, O let it be shewn,
For nothing can it defile.

That voice which is mine can do no good,
What can the creature do?
But thine comes with a power and efficacy
That is very abiding and true.
Voice that is mine, it is odious,
I care not of it to speak:
But spirit, thy words are Christ's, which is
Risen to his glorious seat.
Voice that is mine, is very impure,
For I, O Lord, am vile:
But pray discover of Jesus Christ,
Whom on my heart doth smile.
That voice which is mine shall decay,
That which is of him shall abide:
It shall still grow higher O Lord,
It must encrease and thrive.
It is not tied to me or any other;
But it hath a power free,
In this or that, or where it will,
Triumphantly to be.
For the word bloweth where it listeth,
It bloweth up and down
With a witness of Jesus Christ,
And of his precious crown.

160 3 *dispensation* divine Providence 8 *outgoings* divine grace *close* assent: this seems quite simple within the terms of post-Calvinist discourse—the individual must be open to the free operation of the grace of God 16 *sway* power 29 *mixed* impure 51 *efficacy* power 69 alludes to John 3: 8 'The wind bloweth where it listeth [wishes], and thou hearest the sound thereof, but canst not tell whence it cometh, and whither it goeth: so is every one that is born of the Spirit'

161 [*from* the fourth day of the sixth moneth, upon the fourth day of the week 1658]

O Spirit, thou commandst a voice,
And a voice thou shalt have:
O thou hast chosen a poor fool
That shall sing to the grave.

Thou hast commanded one that's weak
But thy power and grace thou dost bring
To me, that even to the last breath
In Spirit shall of thee sing.
Thou hast commanded a poor low thing,
In vision to sing of thee;
And thou hast p[r]ovided tongue and voice
To declare thy rich glory.
O Spirit, thou hast a care of that
Which is a piece of clay:
A poor, low, empty and mean thing
Whereon nothing doth lie.
O this sound it is very sweet,
It is not in a mixed way
As that which comes from Beast and Whore
To children in this day.

161 3 *fool* simpleton 18 *mixed* impure 19 *Beast and Whore* see Appendix 1, Revelation

ELIZABETH MAJOR

162 *Elisabeth Maior.*

Annagram: *O I am a blest Heir*

What? an Heir and blest, my soul! what honor's here
To a poor subject! Draw near my soul, draw near
With Songs of Praise, let low born thoughts expire,
Let love-inflamed zeal break out as fire
Into the praises of the King of Kings,
Soar thou above these low inferior things:
Try how the wings of faith will rise above
The towering Eagle, or the mounting Dove:
What? an Heir and blest! Doth not this eccho ring,
Shall I do ill, and Heir to such a King?
O no, assist me Lord, then shall I flie
Sins soiled ways, and to my self shall die;

But live to thee, in whom I'm Heir and blest,
Till thou transport me to thy eternal rest.

162 The author's name (written as Elisabeth Maior) gives the anagram of the title 1 *honor* providence making her name capable of such an anagram is construed as a sign of divine favour 4 *zeal* extreme religious fervour

ANNA ALCOX

163 [All you that are to mirth Inclin'd]

All you that are to mirth Inclin'd
consider well and bare in mind
What our Good God hath for us don
in sending his beloved sonne
for to redeeme our sowles from thrall
who is the saviour of us all.

Let all your songs and praises bee
Unto his heavenly maiestie
And evermore amongst your mirth
remember christ our saviours birth

The twenty fift Day of December
Good cause have we for to remember
In bethlem upon that morne
there was our blest messias borne

That night before the happie tyde
the spotlesse virgin and her guide
Went long time seeking up and downe
to find their lodging in the towne

But marke how all things came to passe
the Inns and lodgings so fild was
that they could have no roome at all
but in a sillie oxes stall

That night the virgin mary milde
Was safe delivered of a childe
According unto heavens Decree
mans sweete salvation for to bee

Neere bethlem then did sheepheards keepe
Their heards and flocks of feeding sheepe
to them Gods angells did appeare
which put the sheepheards in great feare

Prepare and goe the Angells sayd
to bethlehem bee not affraid
theire shall you find this bleassed morne
the princly babe sweete Jesus borne

With thankfull harts and Joyfull minds
the sheepheards went this babe to find
And as the heavenly angells told
they did our saviour Christ behold

all in a manger was he layd
the virgin mary by him stay'd
attending on the lord of life
being both mother, maide, and wife

Three easterne wisemen from a farre
Directed by a gloryous starre
came bodily and made no stay
untill they came where Jesus lay

And being come into that place
Where as our blest messias was
they humbly layd before his feete
their gifts of gold and odoures sweet

No costly robes nor rich attire
did Jesus christ our Lord Desire
no musicke nor sweete harmony
till glorious angells from on high
did in a melodious maner sing
praises unto our heavenly king

All honour glory might and power
be unto christ for evermore
he raised lazarus from his grave
and to the sicke thir health he gave

he gave the blind their perfect sight
and made the lame to goe upright
he cur'd the leperous of their evills
And by his power cast out divills
And to redeeme our soules from thrall
became a saviour to us all.

163 5 *thrall* captivity 22 *sillie* simple

JOHN COLLOP

164 *To the Soul.*

Dull soul aspire,
Thou art not earth, mount higher:
Heav'n gave the spark, to it return the fire.

Let sin ne're quench,
Thy high flam'd Spirit hence
The earth the heat, to heaven the flame dispence.

Rejoyce, rejoyce,
Turn, turn each part a voice:
While to the heart-strings tun'd ye all rejoyce.

The house is swept,
Which sin so long foul kept:
The peny's found for which the loser wept.

And purg'd with tears,
Gods Image re-appears,
The peny truly shews whose stamp it bears.

The sheep long lost,
Sins wilderness oft crost,
Is found, regain'd, return'd; spare, spare no cost.

'Tis heav'ns own suit,
Hark how it woo's you to't:
When Angels needs must speak, shall man be mute?

164 2 *earth* common metaphor for mortal flesh 10–12 allusion to Luke 15: 8–10 'Either what woman having ten pieces of silver, if she lose one piece, doth not light a candle, and sweep the house, and seek diligently till she find it? And when she hath found it, she calleth her friends and her neighbours together, saying, Rejoice with me; for I have found the piece which I had lost. Likewise, I say unto you, there is joy in the presence of the angels of God, over one sinner that repenteth' 14 *Gods Image* himself, mankind: Genesis 1: 27 'So God created man in his own image, in image of God created he him, male and female created he them' 16 Luke 15: 4–6 'What man of you, having an hundred sheep, if he lose one of them, doth not leave the ninety and nine in the wilderness, and go after that which is lost, until he find it? And when he hath found it, he layeth it on his shoulders, rejoicing. And when he cometh home, he calleth together his friends and neighbours, saying unto them, Rejoice with me; for I have found my sheep which was lost' 19 *suit* request

165 The Leper cleans'd.

Hear, Lord, hear
The Rhet'rick of a tear:
Hear, hear my brest;
While I knock there, Lord take no rest.

Open! ah open wide,
Thou art the door, Lord, open; hide
My sin; a spear once entred at thy side.

See! ah see
A *Na'mans* leprosie!
Yet here appears
A cleansing *Jordan* in my tears.

Lord, let the faithless see
Miracles ceas'd, revive in me.
The Leper cleans'd, Blinde heal'd, Dead rais'd by thee.

Whither? ah whither shall I fly,
To heav'n? my sins, ah sins there cry!
Yet mercy, Lord, O mercy! hear
Th'atoning incense of my prayer.

A broken heart thoul't not despise.
See! see a Contrites sacrifice!

Keep, keep, viols of wrath keep still:
I'le viols Lord of Odors fill:
O[f] prayers, sighs, grones, and tears a shower;
This precious ointment forth i'le power:
I'le 'noint, wash, wipe, kisse, wash, wipe, weep;
My tears Lord in thy bottle keep.
Lest flames of lust, and fond desire,
Kindle fresh fuel for thine ire,
Which tears must quench, like *Magdalene*,
I'le wash thee Lord, till I be clean.

165 Title *Leper* Christ cleanses (heals) a leper in Matthew 8: 2 and Mark 1: 40; gives the same power to his disciples in Matthew 10: 8 2 *Rhet'rick* rhetoric, the language of formal persuasion 6 *door* John 10: 9 'I am the door: by me if any man enter in, he shall be saved' 7 *spear* at the Crucifixion, John 19: 34 9 *Na'mans leprosie* see Appendix 1 21 *viols* vials, bottles 22-30 the poet compares his penitence to that of Mary Magdalene and emulates her anointing of Christ in John 12: 3. The figure of Mary Magdalene in the tradition of meditation is a composite character derived from linking the John 12 incident with Mary, the sister of Martha in Luke 10: 39–42, and the woman taken in adultery in John 8: 3

ELIZABETH CAVENDISH, COUNTESS OF BRIDGEWATER

166 On my Boy Henry.

Here lyes a Boy the finest Child from me
Which makes my Heart and Soule sigh for to see
Nor can I think of any thought, but greeve,
For joy or pleasure could me not releeve,
It lived dayes as many as my years,
No more, which caused my greeved teares;
Twenty and Nine was the number;
And death hath parted us asunder,
But thou art happy, Sweetst on High,
I mourne not for thy Birth, nor Cry.

PART FOUR

HALCYON DAYES: PEACE AND THE GOOD LIFE

SIR HENRY WOTTON

167 *On his Mistris, the* Queen *of* Bohemia.

You meaner *Beauties* of the *Night*,
That poorly satisfie our *Eyes*
More by your *number*, than your *light*,—
You *common people* of the skies;
What are you when the *Sun* shall rise?

You curious Chanters of the Wood,
That warble forth *Dame Natures* layes,
Thinking your *Voyces* understood
By your weak *accents*; what's your praise
When *Philomel* her voyce shall raise?

You *Violets*, that first appear,
By your *pure purple mantles* known,
Like the proud *Virgins* of the *year*,
As if the *Spring* were all your own;
What are you when the *Rose is blown*?

So, when my *Mistris* shall be seen
In *Form* and *Beauty* of her *mind*,
By *Vertue* first, then *Choyce* a *Queen*,
Tell me, if *she* were not design'd
Th'*Eclypse* and *Glory* of her kind?

167 Title *Queen of Bohemia* Elizabeth Stuart, see Appendix 2 1 *meaner beauties* lesser, in this context, stars compared to the sun 6 *Chanters* singers 7 *layes* songs 10 *Philomel* usual poetical name for the nightingale 12 *mantles* cloaks 15 *blown* in full flower

RICHARD CORBET

168 *To his sonne* Vincent Corbet.

What I shall leave thee none can tell,
But all shall say I wish thee well;
I wish thee (*Vin*) before all wealth,
Both bodily and ghostly health;

Nor too much wealth, nor wit come to thee,
So much of either may undoe thee.
I wish thee learning, not for show,
Enough for to instruct, and know;
Not such as Gentlemen require
To prate at Table, or at Fire.
I wish thee all thy mothers graces,
Thy fathers fortunes, and his places.
I wish thee friends, and one at Court
Not to build on, but support;
To keepe thee, not in doing many
Oppressions, but from suffering any.
I wish thee peace in all thy wayes,
Nor Lazy nor contentious dayes;
And when thy soule and body part,
As innocent as now thou art.

168 4 *ghostly* spiritual 10 *prate* prattle 12 *places* appointments (rather than premises)

AURELIAN TOWNSHEND

169 [*from* Albion's Triumph] *The Eighth Song.*

Armes are layd by: Earely and late,
The Traveller goes safe to Bed:
Men eate and Drinke in Massie Plate,
And are with Deinties dayly fed.
Why should this Ile above the rest,
Be made (great Gods) the Halcions nest?

The five Deities

Imperious peace her selfe Descends

The foure Gods

Then here our search, and wonder ends,
Wee'l steale away

Peace

Earths Rulers, stay!

The foure Gods
Doth soft Peace call?
Peace
Yes: and will streight employ yee All.
The foure Gods
How, and wherein?
The five Deities
Give eare, your Charge doth now begin.
Peace
Neptune to Sea, And let no Sayle,
Meete ALBIONS Fleete, But make it veile.
Bellona Arme, That Foes may see,
Their Lillies kept by Lyons be.
Their fruitfull fields (*Cebele*) make
Pay Centuple for all they take.
And let Both Indes (*Pluto*) meete,
And lay their wealth at ALBAS feete.
The foure Gods
When *Peace* commands such pleasing things,
From *Love* and *Time* wee'l steale their wings.
Chorus
Loaden with Wealth and Honor may,
These Gods returne to crowne this Day,
And MARY-CHARLES whose mindes within,
And Bodyes make by *Hymens Twin*,
Long live they so, And Brest, to Brest,
May Angels sing them to their Rest.

169 See Notes on the Text for the masque; for *Albion* and *The four Gods*, Neptune, Bellona, Cebele, and Pluto, see Appendix 1 3 *Massie Plate* substantial domestic silver 4 *Deinties* delicacies 5 *Ile* island 6 *Halcion* kingfisher, bearer of good fortune, fair weather 12 *streight* immediately 15 *Sayle* ship 16 *veile* lower flags or sails in sign of respect 18 *Lillies* emblems of the French king *Lyons* of England 20 *Centuple* a hundredfold 21 *Both Indes* East and West Indies 22 *ALBA* Albion, Britain 27 *MARY-CHARLES* Queen Henrietta Maria and King Charles, united in marriage

170 Aurelian Tounsend to Thomas Carew upon the death of the King of Sweden.

I had, and have a purpose to be kind
To thee Tom Carew, for where meritts binde,
My court of consience will a right decree
To one that brings no advocate nor fee,
I love thy persoun which being large and tall,
Containes a sperritt that full mans it all;
I love thy witt, that chooses to be sweete
Rather than sharpe, therefore in Lirique feete
Steales to thy mistris; letting others write
Rough footed Satires that in kissing bite.
I love thy Celia if shee did infuse
That fire into thee which begott thy Muse,
And all thy Lovers that with listening eares
Sipp in and relish thy Ambrosian teares,
Which as they fell like manna on the hearse
Of devine Donne feeding us all in verse.
So when the windes from every corner bring
The too true nuse of the dead conquering King,
Let our Land waters meeting by consent
The showres descending from the Firmament;
Make a new floode; one whose teares swelling face
Clos'd in an arke of fatall Cyprisse, place
Gustavus bodie, wound about with bayes;
And while a constant gale of sighes conveyes
This world of wonder to the muses hill,
Each sacred swann in his immortall bill
Shall beare his name, in witnesse of that wracke
His snowe white plumes transforme to sable black
His sword shall like a fierie piller stand,
Or like that graspt in the angrie Angells hand,
Before his herse: needing no other light
But what hee gave it to make day of night.
Princes ambitius of renoune shall still
Strive for his spures to helpe them up the hill.
His gloryus gauntletts shall unquestiond lye,
Till handes are found fitt for a monarchie.

Minerva may without her gorgon com
To beare his sheld, the shield of Christendom
And the Sunn rising to his daly taske
Would showe the brighter if he wore his caske.
Lett solem silence and darke night be there
Making a morner of the hemisphere.
And when upon Pernassus double Toppe
His corpes is come lett the Prosession stopp;
And sleeping in the Muses cradell lay
This child of Honor. Till at peepe of day
Fame like a Phenix from his ashes rise
Courting that new borne bird of Paradice,
And then each spring to his exhausted head
It back retyrd, if out of slime be bredd
Any foule monster over chargd with gall
One drame of his will make the Pithon fall;
For though this Lyon can no more prescribe
Detraction bounds, then that of Judas tribe,
If in the toyle of tongues his feareles name
Be cought by such as would perplex his fame;
A mouse may free him from those Aspes that lye
Hissing in holes till they truth-bitten dye.

170 See no. 180 Title *King of Sweden* see Appendix 2 6 *sperritt* spirit 8 *Lirique feete* lyric metre, the poetry of songs 10 *Rough footed Satires* satire named for the goat-footed satyrs of classical myth, also an improvised, irregular poem 14 *Ambrosian teares* see Appendix 1, ambrosia 15 *manna* food from heaven 16 *devine Donne* John Donne was a divine (cleric) and an inspired poet 18 *nuse* news 20 *Firmament* sky, heavens 22 *fatall* used for funerals, symbolic of death 25 *muses hill* see Appendix 1, Parnassus 27 *wracke* wreck 30 *angrie Angells* see Genesis 3: 24 'and he placed at the east of the garden of Eden Cherubims, and a flaming sword' 40 *caske* helmet 51 *gall* bitter poison 55 *toyle* trap, net: reference to Aesop's fable of the Mouse and the Lion: Townshend is the mouse

ROBERT HERRICK

171 Corinna's *going a Maying.*

Get up, get up for shame, the Blooming Morne
Upon her wings presents the god unshorne.
 See how *Aurora* throwes her faire
 Fresh-quilted colours through the aire:

Get up, sweet-Slug-a-bed, and see
The Dew bespangling Herbe and Tree.
Each Flower has wept, and bow'd toward the East,
Above an houre since; yet you not drest,
Nay! not so much as out of bed?
When all the Birds have Mattens seyd,
And sung their thankfull Hymnes: 'tis sin,
Nay, profanation to keep in,
When as a thousand Virgins on this day,
Spring, sooner then the Lark, to fetch in May.

Rise; and put on your Foliage, and be seene
To come forth, like the Spring-time, fresh and greene;
And sweet as *Flora*. Take no care
For Jewels for your Gowne, or Haire:
Feare not; the leaves will strew
Gemms in abundance upon you:
Besides, the childhood of the Day has kept,
Against you come, some *Orient Pearls* unwept:
Come, and receive them while the light
Hangs on the Dew-locks of the night:
And *Titan* on the Eastern hill
Retires himselfe, or else stands still
Till you come forth. Wash, dresse, be briefe in praying:
Few Beads are best, when once we goe a Maying.

Come, my *Corinna*, come; and comming, marke
How each field turns a street; each street a Parke
Made green, and trimm'd with trees: see how
Devotion gives each House a Bough,
Or Branch: Each Porch, each doore, ere this,
An Arke a Tabernacle is
Made up of white-thorn neatly enterwove;
As if here were those cooler shades of love.
Can such delights be in the street,
And open fields, and we not see't?
Come, we'll abroad; and let's obay
The Proclamation made for May:
And sin no more, as we have done, by staying:
But my *Corinna*, come, let's goe a Maying.

There's not a budding Boy, or Girle, this day,
But is got up, and gone to bring in May.
A deale of Youth, ere this, is come
Ba
ck, and with *White-thorn* laden home.
Some have dispatcht their Cakes and Creame,
Before that we have left to dreame:
And some have wept, and woo'd, and plighted Troth,
And chose their Priest, ere we can cast off sloth:
Many a green-gown has been given;
Many a kisse, both odde and even:
Many a glance too has been sent
From out the eye, Loves Firmament:
Many a jest told of the Keyes betraying
This night, and Locks pickt, yet w'are not a Maying.

Come, let us goe, while we are in our prime;
And take the harmlesse follie of the time.
We shall grow old apace, and die
Before we know our liberty.
Our life is short; and our dayes run
As fast away as do's the Sunne:
And as a vapour, or a drop of raine
Once lost, can ne'r be found againe:
So when or you or I are made
A fable, song, or fleeting shade;
All love, all liking, all delight
Lies drown'd with us in endlesse night.
Then while time serves, and we are but decaying;
Come, my *Corinna*, come, let's goe a Maying.

171 Title *Maying* May-day celebrations, bringing home the may (hawthorn) to decorate houses 2 *the god unshorne* the sun-god with his bright rays (hair) 10 *Mattens* Matins, the church's morning service 22 *Orient Pearls* common conceit for dewdrops 28 *Beads* both prayers and knops 34 *Arke, Tabernacle* holy places, here arbours of green branches 40 *Proclamation* Book of Sports issued by James I, 1618, renewed by Charles I, 1633, upholding traditional festivities against Puritan attacks 41 *staying* lingering 51 *green gown* from rolling in the grass 55 *Keyes* keys exchanged, assignations made 59 *apace* quickly 65 *or...or* either...or

172 *The Hock-cart*, or *Harvest home: To the Right Honourable* Mildmay, *Earle of* Westmorland.

Come Sons of Summer, by whose toile,
We are the Lords of Wine and Oile:
By whose tough labours, and rough hands,
We rip up first, then reap our lands.
Crown'd with the eares of corne, now come,
And, to the Pipe, sing Harvest home.
Come forth, my Lord, and see the Cart
Drest up with all the Country Art.
See, here a *Maukin*, there a sheet,
As spotlesse pure, as it is sweet:
The Horses, Mares, and frisking Fillies,
(Clad, all, in Linnen, white as Lillies.)
The Harvest Swaines, and Wenches bound
For joy, to see the *Hock-cart* crown'd.
About the Cart, heare, how the Rout
Of Rurall Younglings raise the shout;
Pressing before, some coming after,
Those with a shout, and these with laughter.
Some blesse the Cart; some kisse the sheaves;
Some prank them up with Oaken leaves:
Some crosse the Fill-horse; some with great
Devotion, stroak the home-borne wheat:
While other Rusticks, lesse attent
To Prayers, then to Merryment,
Run after with their breeches rent.
Well, on, brave boyes, to your Lords Hearth,
Glitt'ring with fire; where, for your mirth,
Ye shall see first the large and cheefe
Foundation of your Feast, Fat Beefe:
With Upper Stories, Mutton, Veale
And Bacon, (which makes full the meale)
With sev'rall dishes standing by,
As here a Custard, there a Pie,
And here all tempting Frumentie.
And for to make the merry cheere,
If smirking Wine be wanting here,
There's that, which drowns all care, stout Beere;

Which freely drink to your Lords health,
Then to the Plough, (the Common-wealth)
Next to your Flailes, your Fanes, your Fatts;
Then to the Maids with Wheaten Hats:
To the rough Sickle, and crookt Sythe,
Drink frollick boyes, till all be blythe.
Feed, and grow fat; and as ye eat,
Be mindfull, that the lab'ring Neat
(As you) may have their fill of meat.
And know, besides, ye must revoke
The patient Oxe unto the Yoke,
And all goe back unto the Plough
And Harrow, (though they'r hang'd up now.)
And, you must know, your Lords word's true,
Feed him ye must, whose food fils you.
And that this pleasure is like raine,
Not sent ye for to drowne your paine.
But for to make it spring againe.

172 Title *Hock-cart* harvest-cart *Mildmay Fane, Earl of Westmorland* see Appendix 3, also see nos. 185, 249 1 *Sons of Summer* harvesters 9 *Maukin* mop, bundle of rags, here, corn-dolly 15 *Rout* unruly crowd 20 *prank* dress up 21 *Fill-horse* (not in *OED*) in some parts of Britain, the last sheaf to be harvested is still called 'the horse' 25 *rent* ripped 34 *Frumentie* drink of oatmeal and ale or wine 40 *Flailes, Fanes, Fatts* all tools for winnowing grain 45 *Neat* cattle 46 *meat* food generally 47 *revoke* literally, call back

173 *The Amber Bead.*

I saw a Flie within a Beade
Of Amber cleanly buried:
The Urne was little, but the room
More rich then *Cleopatra's* Tombe.

173 4 *Cleopatra* see Appendix 1

174 *His Grange.*

How well contented in this private *Grange*
Spend I my life (that's subject unto change:)
Under whose Roofe with *Mosse-worke* wrought, there I
Kisse my *Brown wife*, and *black Posterity*.

174 A riddle: answer, a blackbird

175 TO THE QUEENE

GODDESSE of Youth, and Lady of the Spring,
(Most fit to be the Consort to a King)
Be pleas'd to rest you in *This Sacred Grove*,
Beset with *Mirtles*; whose each leafe drops Love.
Many a sweet-fac'd *Wood-Nymph* here is seene,
Of which chast *Order You* are now the *Queene*:
Witness their *Homage*, when they come and strew
Your Walks with Flowers, and give their Crowns to you.
Your Leavie-Throne (with *Lilly*-work) possesse;
And be both *Princesse* here, and *Poetresse*.

175 4 *Mirtles* sacred to Venus, see Appendix 1

176 *To the Water Nymphs, drinking at the Fountain*

1.

Reach, with your whiter hands, to me,
Some Christall of the Spring;
And I, about the Cup shall see
Fresh Lillies flourishing.

2.

Or else sweet Nimphs do you but this;
To'th'Glasse your lips encline;

And I shall see by that one kisse,
The Water turn'd to Wine.

176 See no. 143 6 *encline* bend

177 To Meddowes.

1.

Ye have been fresh and green,
Ye have been fill'd with flowers:
And ye the Walks have been
Where Maids have spent their houres.

2.

You have beheld, how they
With *Wicker Arks* did come
To kisse, and beare away
The richer Couslips home.

3.

Y'ave heard them sweetly sing,
And seen them in a Round:
Each Virgin, like a Spring,
With Hony-succles crown'd.

4.

But now, we see, none here,
Whose silv'rie feet did tread,
And with dishevell'd Haire,
Adorn'd this smoother Mead.

5.

Like Unthrifts, having spent,
Your stock, and needy grown,
Y'are left here to lament
Your poore estates, alone.

177 6 *Wicker Arks* baskets 10 *Round* song arranged for several voices singing in canon
17 *Unthrifts* wastrels

178 *To live merrily, and to trust to Good verses*

Now is the time for mirth,
Nor cheek, or tongue be dumbe:
For with the flowrie earth,
The golden pomp is come.

The golden Pomp is come;
For now each tree do's weare
(Made of her Pap and Gum)
Rich beads of *Amber* here.

Now raignes the *Rose*, and now
Th' *Arabian* Dew besmears
My uncontrolled brow,
And my retorted haires.

Homer, this Health to thee,
In Sack of such a kind,
That it wo'd make thee see,
Though thou wert ne'r so blind.

Next, *Virgil*, Ile call forth,
To pledge this second Health
In Wine, whose each cup's worth
An Indian Common-wealth.

A Goblet next Ile drink
To *Ovid*; and suppose,
Made he the pledge, he'd think
The world had all *one Nose*.

Then this immensive cup
Of *Aromatick* wine,
Catullus, I quaffe up
To that Terce Muse of thine.

Wild I am now with heat;
O *Bacchus!* coole thy Raies!
Or frantick I shall eate
Thy *Thyrse,* and bite the *Bayes.*

Round, round, the roof do's run;
And being ravisht thus,
Come, I will drink a Tun
To my *Propertius.*

Now, to *Tibullus*, next,
This flood I drink to thee:
But stay; I see a Text,
That this present to me.

Behold, *Tibullus* lies
Here burnt, whose smal return
Of ashes, scarce suffice
To fill a little Urne.

Trust to good Verses then;
They onely will aspire,
When Pyramids, as men,
Are lost, i'th'funerall fire.

And when all Bodies meet
In *Lethe* to be drown'd;
Then onely Numbers sweet,
With endless life are crown'd.

178 10 *Arabian* see Appendix 1 12 *retorted* curled back 13 *Homer* see Appendix 1 14 *Sack* sherry 17 *Virgil,* 22 *Ovid,* 27 *Catullus,* 30 *Bacchus* see Appendix 1 32 *Thyrse* thyrsus, Bacchus' rod 35 *Tun* barrel 36 *Propertius,* 37 *Tibullus,* 50 *Lethe* see Appendix 1

THOMAS CAREW

179 To Saxham.

Though frost, and snow, lockt from mine eyes,
That beautie which without dore lyes;
Thy gardens, orchards, walkes, that so
I might not all thy pleasures know;
Yet (*Saxham*) thou within thy gate,
Art of thy selfe so delicate;

So full of native sweets, that blesse
Thy roofe with inward happinesse;
As neither from, nor to thy store
Winter takes ought, or Spring addes more;
The cold and frozen ayre had sterv'd
Much poore, if not by thee preserv'd;
Whose prayers have made thy Table blest
With plenty, far above the rest.
The season hardly did afford
Course cates unto thy neighbours board,
Yet thou hadst daintyes, as the skie
Had only been thy Volarie;
Or else the birds, fearing the snow
Might to another deluge grow:
The Pheasant, Partiridge, and the Larke,
Flew to thy house, as to the Arke.
The willing Oxe, of himselfe came
Home to the slaughter, with the Lambe,
And every beast did thither bring
Himselfe, to be an offering.
The scalie herd, more pleasure tooke,
Bath'd in thy dish, then in the brooke:
Water, Earth, Ayre, did all conspire,
To pay their tributes to thy fire,
Whose cherishing flames themselves divide
Through every roome, where they deride
The night, and cold abroad; whilst they
Like suns within, keepe endlesse day.
Those chearfull beames send forth their light,
To all that wander in the night,
And seeme to becken from aloofe,
The weary Pilgrim to thy roofe;
Where if refresh't, he will away,
Hee's fairly welcome, or if stay
Farre more, which he shall hearty find,
Both from the Master, and the Hinde.
The strangers welcome, each man there
Stamp'd on his chearfull brow, doth weare;
Nor doth this welcome, or this cheere
Grow lesse, 'cause he stays longer here:

There's none observes (much lesse repines)
How often this man sups or dines.
Thou hast no Porter at the doore
T'examine, or keep back the poore;
Nor locks, nor bolts; thy gates have bin
Made onely to let strangers in;
Untaught to shut, they doe not feare
To stand wide open all the yeare;
Carelesse who enters, for they know,
Thou never didst deserve a foe;
And as for theeves, thy bountie's such;
They cannot steale, thou giv'st so much.

179 Title *Saxham* Little Saxham, near Bury St Edmunds, Suffolk, belonged to the Crofts family. John Crofts, son of Sir John Crofts, was with Carew in France in 1619 attending Lord Herbert of Cherbury 10 *ought* anything 11 *sterv'd* killed 16 *Course cates* plain foods 18 *Volarie* aviary 27 *scalie herd* fish 42 *Hinde* labourer 47 *repines* grieves, complains

180 *In answer of an Elegiacall Letter upon the death of the King of Sweden from* Aurelian Townsend, *inviting me to write on that subject.*

Why dost thou sound, my dear *Aurelian*,
In so shrill accents, from thy *Barbican*,
A loude allarum to my drowsie eyes,
Bidding them wake in teares and Elegies
For mightie *Swedens* fall? Alas! how may
My Lyrique feet, that of the smooth soft way
Of Love, and Beautie, onely know the tread,
In dancing paces celebrate the dead
Victorious King, or his Majesticke Hearse
Prophane with th'humble touch of their low verse?
Virgil, nor *Lucan*, no, nor *Tasso* more
Then both, not *Donne*, worth all that went before,
With the united labour of their wit
Could a just Poem to this subject fit,
His actions were too mighty to be rais'd
Higher by Verse, let him in prose be prays'd,

In modest faithfull story, which his deedes
Shall turne to Poems: when the next Age reades
Of *Frankfort, Leipsigh, Worsburgh*, of the *Rhyne*;
The *Leck*, the *Danube, Tilly, Wallestein,*
Bavaria, Papenheim, Lutzenfield, where Hee
Gain'd after death a posthume Victorie,
They'le thinke his Acts things rather feign'd than done
Like our Romances of the Knight o'th'Sun.
Leave we him then to the grave Chronicler,
Who though to Annals he can not refer
His too-briefe storie, yet his Journals may
Stand by the *Caesars* yeares, and every day
Cut into minutes, each, shall more containe
Of great designement then an Emperours raigne;
And (since 'twas but his Church-yard) let him have
For his owne ashes now no narrower Grave
Then the whole *German* Continents vast wombe,
Whilst all her Cities doe but make his Tombe.
Let us to supreame providence commit
The fate of Monarchs, which first thought it fit
To rend the Empire from the *Austrian* graspe,
And next from *Swedens*, even when he did claspe
Within his dying armes the Soveraigntie
Of all those Provinces, that men might see
The Divine wisedome would not leave that Land
Subject to any one Kings sole command.
Then let the Germans feare if *Caesar* shall,
Or the United Princes, rise, and fall,
But let us that in myrtle bowers sit
Under secure shades, use the benefit
Of peace and plenty, which the blessed hand
Of our good King gives this obdurate Land,
Let us of Revels sing, and let thy breath
(Which fill'd Fames trumpet with *Gustavus* death,
Blowing his name to heaven) gently inspire
Thy past'rall pipe, till all our swaines admire
Thy song and subject, whilst they both comprise
The beauties of the *SHEPHERDS PARADISE*;

For who like thee (whose loose discourse is farre
More neate and polisht then our Poems are,
Whose very gate's more gracefull then our dance)
In sweetly flowing numbers may advance
The glorious night? When, not to act foule rapes,
Like birds, or beasts, but in their Angel-shapes
A troope of Deities came downe to guide
Our steerelesse barkes in passions swelling tide
By vertues Carde, and brought us from above
A patterne of their owne celestiall love.
Nor lay it in darke sullen precepts drown'd
But with rich fancie, and cleare Action crown'd
Through a misterious fable (that was drawne
Like a transparent veyle of purest Lawne
Before their dazelling beauties) the divine
Venus, did with her heavenly *Cupid* shine.
The stories curious web, the Masculine stile;
The subtile sence, did Time and sleepe beguile,
Pinnion'd and charm'd they stood to gaze upon
Th'Angellike formes, gestures, and motion.
To heare those ravishing sounds that did dispence
Knowledge and pleasure, to the soule, and sense.
It fill'd us with amazement to behold
Love made all spirit, his corporeall mold
Dissected into Atomes melt away
To empty ayre, and from the grosse allay
Of mixtures, and compounding Accidents
Refin'd to immateriall Elements,
But when the Queene of Beautie did inspire
The ayre with perfumes, and our hearts with fire,
Breathing from her celestiall Organ sweet
Harmonious notes, our soules fell at her feet,
And did with humble reverend dutie, more
Her rare perfections, then high state adore.
These harmlesse pastimes let my *Townsend* sing
To rurall tunes; not that thy Muse wants wing
To soare a loftier pitch, for she hath made
A noble flight, and plac'd th'Heroique shade
Above the reach of our faint flagging ryme;
But these are subjects proper to our clyme.

Tourneyes, Masques, Theaters, better become
Our *Halcyon* dayes; what though the German Drum
Bellow for freedome and revenge, the noyse
Concernes not us, nor should divert our joyes;
Nor ought the thunder of their Carabins
Drowne the sweet Ayres of our tun'd Violins;
Beleeve me friend, if their prevailing powers
Gaine them a calme securitie like ours,
They'le hang their Armes up on the Olive bough,
And dance, and revell then, as we doe now.

180 See no. 170 Title King of Sweden, see Appendix 2 2 *Barbican* i.e. in London 11 *Virgil, Lucan* see Appendix 1 *Tasso* see Appendix 2 19–20 locations of the King's victories *Tilly, Wallestein* see Appendix 2 21 sites of further battles in the Thirty Years' War 22 *posthume* posthumous 24 *Knight o'th'Sun* hero of fictional epic romance 45 *myrtle* sacred to Venus 52 *past'rall pipe* Pan pipes played by shepherds in arcadian fantasies 54 *SHEPHERDS PARADISE* a pastoral drama by Walter Montagu performed at the Queen's court, here referring to the fortunate and peaceful state of England 56 *our* Carew's and Townsend's 57 *gate* gait, movement 62 *barkes* boats 63 *Carde* navigator's card to find directions at sea 68 *Lawne* delicate fabric 71 *web* plot, thread of story 73 *Pinnion'd* trapped, tied 78–83 this passage makes use of technical alchemical terminology 78 *corporeall mold* mortal body 80 *allay* alloy 95 *Tourneyes* jousting tournaments *Masques* formal and elaborate musical court entertainments 96 *Halcyon dayes* days of peace and prosperity; anciently, the halcyon (kingfisher) was thought to bring fair weather 99 *Carabins* guns 103 *Olive bough* sign of peace

181 The second Song. [from *Coelum Britannicum*]

KINGDOMES.

Here are shapes form'd fit for heaven,
Those move gracefully and even,
Here the Ayre and paces meet
So just, as if the skilfull feet
Had struck the Vials. So the Eare
Might the tunefull footing heare.

CHORUS.

And had the Musicke silent beene,
The eye a moving tune had seene.

GENIUS.

These must in the unpeopled skie
Succeed, and governe Destinie,
Jove is temp'ring purer fire,
And will with brighter flames attire
These glorious lights. I must ascend
And helpe the Worke.

KINGDOMES.

We cannot lend
Heaven so much treasure. Nor that pay
But rendring what it takes away.
Why should they that here can move
So well, be ever-fix'd above?

CHORUS.

Or be to one eternall posture ty'd,
That can into such various figures slide.

GENIUS.

Jove shall not, to enrich the Skie,
Beggar the Earth, their Fame shall fly
From hence alone, and in the Spheare
Kindle new Starres, whilst they rest here.

KINGDOMES.

How can the shaft stay in the quiver,
Yet hit the marke?

GENIUS.

Did not the River
Eridanus, the grace acquire
In Heaven and Earth to flow,
Above in streames of golden fire,
In silver waves below?

KINGDOMES.

But shall not we, now thou art gone
Who wert our Nature, wither,
Or breake that triple Union
Which thy soule held together?

GENIUS.

In Concords pure immortall spring
I will my force renew,
And a more active Vertue bring
At my returne. Adieu.

KINGDOMES adieu, CHORUS adieu.

181 Title *Coelum Britannicum* the British heaven, see Notes on the Text 5 *Vials* viols, stringed instruments 11 *Jove* see Appendix 1 *temp'ring* forging, refining 23 *Spheare* celestial sphere, the heavens 27 *Eridanus* see Appendix 1 33 *triple Union* of England, Scotland, and Ireland 35 *Concords* of peace

JAMES SHIRLEY

182 *The Garden.*

This Garden does not take my eyes,
Though here you shew how art of men
Can purchase Nature at a price
Could stock old Paradise agen.

These glories while you dote upon,
I envie not your Spring nor pride,
Nay boast the Summer all your own,
My thoughts with lesse are satisfied.

Give me a little plot of ground,
Where might I with the Sun agree,
Though every day he walk the Round,
My Garden he should seldom see.

Those Tulips that such wealth display,
To court my eye, shall lose their name,
Though now they listen, as if they
Expected I should praise their flame.

But I would see my self appear
Within the Violets drooping head,
On which a melancholy tear
The discontented Morne hath shed.

Within their budds let Roses sleep,
And virgin Lillies on their stemme,
Till sighes from Lovers glide, and creep
Into their leaves to open them.

Ith' Center of my ground compose
Of Bayes and Ewe my Summer room,
Which may so oft as I repose,
Present my Arbour, and my Tombe.

No woman here shall find me out,
Or if a chance do bring one hither,
Ile be secure, for round about
Ile moat it with my eyes foul weather.

No Bird shall live within my pale,
To charme me with their shames of Art,
Unlesse some wandring Nightingale
Come here to sing, and break her heart.

Upon whose death I'le try to write
An Epitaph in some funeral stone,
So sad, and true, it may invite
My self to die, and prove mine owne.

182 4 *old Paradise* Eden, see Appendix 1 11 *Round* circuit 26 *Bayes* suitable for a poet's arbour *Ewe* funereal yew, suitable for a tomb 32 *moat* surround (with tears)

WILLIAM STRODE

183 On Westwell Downes.

When Westwell Downes I gan to treade
  Where cleanly windes the Greene doe sweepe,
Me thought a Landskipp there was spread
  Here a bush and there a sheepe
The pleated wrinkles on the face
Of wave-swoln Earth did lend such grace
As shaddowings in Imagrie
Which both deceave and please the Eye.

The sheepe sometimes doe treade a Mase
  By often winding in and in,
And sometimes rounde about they trace,
  Which Milke-maids call a Fairy ring
Such Semicircles they have run,
Such lines acrosse soe trimly spun
That sheapheards learne whenere they please
A new Geometry with Ease.

The slender foode upon the Downe
  As allway even, allway bare,
Which nether spring nor winters frowne
  Can ought improve or ought impayre
Such is the barren Eunuchs chin
Which thus doth evermore begin
With tender downe to be orecast
Which never comes to hayre at last.

Here and there two hilly Crests
  Amidst them hugg a pleasant Greene
And these are like two swelling brests
  That close a tender Vale betweene
Here could I reade or sleepe or play
From Early morne till flight of Day
But harke a Sheeps-bell calls me up
Like Oxford Colledg bells to supp.

183 See nos. 215, 223 Title *Westwell Downes* see Notes on the Text
3 *Landskipp* landscape 7 *Imagrie* painting 9 *Mase* maze 23 *downe* fluff
32 *supp* have supper

RALPH KNEVET

184 The Vote.

The Helmett now an hive for Bees becomes,
And hilts of swords may serve for Spiders loomes,
Sharp pikes may make,
Teeth for a rake:
And the keene blade, th'arch enemy of life,
Shall bee digraded to a pruneing knife:
The rusticke spade,
Which first was made
For honest agriculture, shall retake
It's primitive imployment, and forsake
The rampires steepe,
And trenches deepe.
Tame conyes in our brazen gunnes shall breed,
Or gentle Doves, their yong-ones there shall feede:
In musket barrells,
Mice shall raise quarrells
For their quarters: The ventriloquious drumme
(Like Lawyers in vacations) shall be dumme:
Now all recrutes
(But those of fruites)
Shall bee forgott: and th'unarm'd Soldier
Shall only boast of what Hee did whilere,
In chimneys ends
Among his freinds.
If good effects shall happy signes ensue,
I shall rejoyce, and my prediction's true.

184 Title *Vote* literal translation of Latin 'votum', an offering made to a shrine, here the weapons and armour of a retiring soldier. This poem uses a series of emblematic commonplaces expressing peace after war. It also draws on Isaiah 2: 4 'and they shall beat their swords into plowshares, and their spears into pruninghooks: nation shall not lift up sword against nation, neither shall they learn war any more' 6 *digraded* demoted, relegated 11 *rampires* ramparts 13 *conyes* rabbits 17 *ventriloquious* reverberating; literally, speaking from its stomach 22 *whilere* formerly

MILDMAY FANE, EARL OF WESTMORLAND

185 *To Sir* John Wentworth, *upon his Curiosities and Courteous entertainment at* Summerly *in* Lovingland.

When thou the choice of Natures wealth hast skan'd,
And brought it to compare with *Lovingland*;
Know, that thou maist as well make wonder less,
By fancying of two Timbering Phoenixes
At the same time: and dream two Suns to rise
At once, to cast fire 'midst those Spiceries:
(Pregnant She is) yet that must not deny
The purest Gold to come from *Barbary*,
Diamonds and Pearl from th'*Indies*, to confer
On every Clime some thing peculier,
(For so She hath:) And like a sum to all
That Curious is, seems here most liberall,
Affording in Epitome at least,
What ere the world can boast of, or call best.
Now as contracted vertue doth excell
In power and force, This seems a Miracle;
Wherein all Travailers may truly say,
They never saw so much in little way:
And thence conclude their folly, that did steer
To seek for that abroad, at home was neer
In more perfection: Wouldst thou *Phoebe* meet,
Apollo, or the *Muses*? not in *Creet*
And *Greece*, but Here, at *Summerly*, those are
Remov'd to dwell, under a Patrons care,
Who can as much Civility express,
As *Candie* lies, or *Grecia* Barbarousness:
Wouldst thou be sheltred under *Daphnes* groves,
Or choose to live in *Tempe*, or make loves

To any place where Shepherds wont to lie
Upon the Hills, Piping security
Unto their flocks? here the sweet Park contains
More eevenness than the *Arcadian* Plains:
Nor yet enchanted by those shadowed rings,
Some say the Fairies print with Revellings,
But's all in one dye clad, and doth appear
Like the Springs Favourite throughout the year.
The usefull Ash, and sturdy Oak are set
At distance, and obey; the Brambles met
Embracing twine int'Arbours, to conceal
And harbour such as stock this Common-weal;
Untill their Master please they should delight
His, or his Friends desire and appetite:
All tales of Satyrs banish'd are from hence,
And fabled Goblins that delude the sence;
'Tis reall Ven'son and abroad, in paste
Alike may satisfie both eye and taste.
The Nobler Plants, as Firre Deal, and the Pine
Weeping out Rozen, bleeding Turpentine;
Like the Life-guard, upon the Hall attend
At nearer distance; where the Gods descend
To keep their Courts, and either Globe's devis'd,
To grasp the Elements Epitomis'd.
    The Sun-beams steady Fire, with the Aire
    Of the inconstant winds Indiall'd are.
    So whilst the one, the Houre doth infer,
    The Other Points a rule for th'Mariner;
    Earth here's Embroydered into Walks, some strait,
    Others like Serpents are, or worms to bait
    Occasions hook till every humor come,
    And feed here fat as in Elysium.
    Nor is there water wanting in this wood,
    Clear as if running, Calm as if it stood,
    And so contriv'd by Natures helper Art,
    There's no appearance from the whole or part,
    That any sullen Sluce to malice bent
    Can open, to impair that Element;
    Nor yet th'Ambition of a Springs ore'flow,
    Cause it t'exceed, or Limits overthrow.

Thus like a gold Chain link'd, or Bracelet strung,
From Carkanet Pleasures on Pleasures hung,
And such delightfull objects did descry
Pursuing of each other, that the ey
Astonish'd at such wonder, did crave rest,
For fear of Forfeiting its interest
In so great bliss, for over-dazled 't grew,
And dim of sight made by each object new.
So there's a parley granted, and some space
To gather strength 'twix This and t'other place
But very short, not half a Mile at most,
We landed were again, and made a Coast;
Where if all ancient Poets were to write,
They'd need no other fountain to indite
Story of kindes with, but dip their pen,
Then swear the Muses more then nine, were ten;
For here dwelt one whose Magick could infuse
A fluency beyond all other Muse,
And Court the Soil, with so much Art applide,
That all the world seems Barbarous beside.
Here Fish and Fowl inhabit with such state,
As Lords and Ladies wont when serv'd in Plate,
Rich Arras, or the like, Bill, Breed, and swim
In all delightfull solace to the brim.
Decoy'd by so much rapture, on we pass
Unto a Castle that enchanted was
By th'magick spell of Musick; till there set
We found a Cod like to *Euterpe*'s net,
To catch all Passengers, the *Lesbian* Lute,
O'rcome in harmony became there mute:
Whilst as for Table to the Song-books serv'd
The Crystall fountain: so have I observ'd,
When walking near a stream, the heavens to be
Beneath my feet, to ease Astronomie:
There tell the *Gammuth* of the Stars, and crack
Of all their motions even with *Tychobrack*.
The Fablers of old, I guess, might finde
Some Objects t'help invention, but the minde
Was sure Prophetick, for what ever is
Describ'd for rare by them, 'twas meant by this.

And yet this falls short too, when He to whom
The Cost and Care Owes tribute, 's there to sum
Up all, with such humanity, and press
Of crowded Favours, and heap'd Curtesies,
As Friendship were a Jeweller the while,
His welcome seem'd the Diamond, Those the foile.

185 Title The Hall at Somerleyton in the part of Suffolk now called Lothingland was the seat of the parliamentarian Sir John Wentworth, d. 1651. There is now no trace of the house and the park described in the poem. 1 *skan'd* scanned, looked over 4 *Timbering* nest-building *Phoenixes* see Appendix 1 7 *She* Nature 8 *Barbary* North Africa 9 *confer* bestow 10 *Clime* part of the world 13 *Epitome* summary 26 *Candie* Crete: Cretans were proverbially liars 28 *Tempe*, 33 *Arcadian* see Appendix 1 43 *Satyrs* see Appendix 1 45 *in paste* in a pie 47 *Firre Deal* fir trees yielding deal timber 48 *Rozen* resin 51 *either Globe* celestial and terrestrial globes presumably ornamenting the courtyard of the house 54 *Indiall'd* recorded on the dial 57 *Walks* paths 59 *Occasion* fortune 65 *Sluce* artificial dam, mechanical water-gate 70 *Carkanet* ornamental chain 82 *indite* write down 91 *Arras* tapestry hangings 103 *Gammuth* gamut, whole range 104 *Tychobrack* see Appendix 2, Brahe 114 *foile* thin metal set behind a gem to enhance its lustre

WILLIAM HABINGTON

186 A Dialogue betweene ARAPHILL and CASTARA:

ARAPH.

Castara, you too fondly court
The silken peace with which we cover'd are,
Unquiet time may for his sport,
Up from its iron den rowse sleepy warre.

CAST.

Then in the language of the drum,
I will instruct my yet afrighted eare,
All women shall in me be dumbe;
If I but with my *Araphill* be there!

ARAPH.

If fate like an unfaithfull gale,
Which having vow'd to th'ship a faire event,
Oth'sudden rends her hopefull saile;
Blow ruine; will *Castara* then repent?

CAST.

Love shall in that tempestuous showre
Her brightest blossome like the black-thorne show:
Weake friendship prospers by the powre
Of fortunes Sunne. I'le in her winter grow.

ARAPH.

If on my skin the noysome skar
I should o'th'leprosie, or canker weare;
Or if the sulph'rous breath of warre
Should blast my youth; should I not be thy feare?

CAST.

In flesh may sicknesse horror move,
But heavenly zeale will be by it refin'd,
For then wee'd like two Angels love,
Without a sense; imbrace each others mind.

ARAPH.

Were it not impious to repine;
'Gainst rigid Fate I should direct my breath,
That two must be, whom heaven did joyne
In such a happy one, disjoyn'd by death.

CAST.

That's no divource. Then shall we see
The rites in life, were tipes o'th'marriage state,
Our soules on earth contracted be;
But they in heaven their nuptials consumate.

186 11 *rends* rips 17 *noysome* foul-smelling 20 *feare* beloved 22 *zeale* fervour, passion 23 *two Angels* incorporeal, in the mind alone 25 *repine* lament 30 *tipes* patterns, ideal examples

THOMAS RANDOLPH

187 Upon his Picture.

When age hath made me what I am not now;
And every wrinckle tels me where the plow
Of time hath furrowed; when an Ice shall flow
Through every vein, and all my head wear snow:
When death displayes his coldnesse in my cheeke,
And I, my selfe in my owne Picture seeke.
Not finding what I am, but what I was,
In doubt which to beleive, this, or my glasse:
Yet though I alter, this remaines the same
As it was drawne, retaines the primitive frame,
And first complexion; Here will still be seen
Blood on the cheeke, and Downe upon the chin.
Here the smooth brow will stay, the lively eye,
The ruddy Lip, and haire of youthfull dye.
Behold what frailty we in man may see,
Whose Shaddow is lesse given to change then hee.

187 8 *this* the picture *glasse* mirror 16 *Shaddow* his image in the picture

188 An Ode to Mr Anthony Stafford to hasten him into the Country.

Come spurre away,
I have no patience for a longer stay;
But must goe downe,
And leave the chargeable noise of this great Towne.
I will the country see;
Where old simplicity,
Though hid in gray
Doth looke more gay
Then foppery in plush and scarlat clad.
Farewell you City-wits that are
Almost at Civill warre;
'Tis time that I grow wise, when all the world grows mad.

More of my dayes
I will not spend to gaine an Idiots praise;
Or to make sport
For some slight Punie of the Innes of Court.
Then worthy *Stafford* say
How shall we spend the day.
With what delights,
Shorten the nights?
When from this tumult we are got secure;
Where mirth with all her freedome goes,
Yet shall no finger loose;
Where every word is thought, and every thought is pure.

There from the tree
Wee'l cherries plucke, and pick the strawbery.
And every day
Go see the wholesome Country Girles make hay.
whose browne hath lovlier grace,
Then any painted face,
That I doe know
Hide-Parke can show.
Where I had rather gaine a kisse then meet
Though some of them in greater state
Might court my love with plate,
The beauties of the *Cheape*, and wives of *Lumbardstreet*.

But thinke upon
Some other pleasures, these to me are none,
Why doe I prate
Of woemen, that are things against my fate
I never meane to wed,
That torture to my bed.
My Muse is shee
My Love shall bee.
Let Clownes get wealth, and heires; when I am gone,
And the great Bugbeare grisly death
Shall take this idle breath,
If I a Poem leave, that Poem is my Sonne.

Of this no more;
Wee'd rather tast the bright *Pomona*'s store.
No fruit shall scape
Our pallats, from the damsen, to the grape.
Then full we'l seek a shade,
And heare what musique's made;
How Philomell
Her tale doth tell:
And how the other Birds doe fill the quire;
The Thrush and Blackbird lend their throats
warbling melodious notes;
Wee will all sports enjoy, which others but desire.

Ours is the skie,
Whereat what fowle we please our Hauke shall flye;
Nor will we spare
To hunt the crafty foxe, or timorous hare,
But let our hounds runne loose
In any ground they'l choose,
The Bucke shall fall,
The stagge and all:
Our pleasures must from their owne warrants bee,
For to my *Muse*, if not to mee,
I'me sure all game is free;
Heaven, Earth, are all but parts of her great Royalty.

And when we meane
To tast of *Bacchus* blessings now and then,
And drink by stealth
A cup or two to noble *Barkleys* health.
I'le take my pipe and try
The *Phrygian* melody;
Which he that heares
Lets through his eares
A madnesse to distemper all the braine.

Then I another pipe will take
And *Dorique* musique make,
To Civilize with graver notes our wits againe.

188 7 *gray* woollen cloth 16 *Punie* a negligible person *Innes of Court* the lawyers' colleges in London 35 *plate* domestic silver 55 *Philomell* nightingale, see Appendix 1 57 *quire* choir 69 *warrants* i.e. our pleasures are their own justification 77 *pipe* pastoral Pan pipes 78 *Phrygian* the mode or scale of Greek music said by Aristotle to be orgiastic and emotional 81 *distemper* fever 83 *Dorique* the mode or scale of Greek music said by Aristotle to be ethical and steady

189 On the Death of a Nightingale.

Goe solitary wood, and henceforth be
Acquainted with no other Harmonie,
Then the Pyes chattering, or the shreeking note
Of bodeing Owles, and fatall Ravens throate.
Thy sweetest Chanters dead, that warbled forth
Layes, that might tempests calme, and still the North;
And call downe Angels from their glorious Spheare
To heare her Songs, and learne new Anthems there.
That soule is fled, and to *Elisium* gone;
Thou a poore desert left; goe then and runne,
Begge there to stand a grove, and if shee please
To sing againe beneath thy shadowy Trees;
The soules of happy Lovers crown'd with blisses
Shall flock about thee, and keepe time with kisses.

189 3 *Pyes* magpies 4 *bodeing* ill-omened 5 *Chanter* singer 10 *desert* barren place

190 The milk-maids Epithalamium.

Joy to the Bridegroome and the Bride
That lye by one anothers side!
O fie upon the Virgin Bedds,
No losse is gain but Maiden heads.
Love quickly send the time may be
When I shall deal my Rosemary!

I long to simper at a feast,
To dance, and kisse, and doe the rest.
When I shall wed, and Bedded be
O then the qualme comes over me,
And tells the sweetnesse of a Theame
That I ne're knew but in a dreame.

You Ladies have the blessed nights,
I pine in hope of such delights,
And silly Dam'sell only can
Milk the cowes teats and think on man:
And sigh and wish to tast and prove
The wholesome Sillibub of Love.

Make hast, at once twin-Brothers beare;
And leave new matter for a starre.
Woemen and ships are never shown
So fair as when their sayles be blown.
Then when the Midwife hears your moane,
I'le sigh for grief that I have none.

And you, deare Knight, whose every kisse
Reapes the the full crop of *Cupids* blisse,
Now you have found, confesse and tell
That single sheets doe make up hell.
And then so charitable be
To get a man to pitty me.

190 Title *Epithalamium* marriage-song 6 *Rosemary* as wedding keepsakes 10 *qualme* sickness, erotic stimulation 20 *starre* see Appendix 1, Castor and Pollux

SIR WILLIAM DAVENANT

191 TO THE QUEENE,

entertain'd at night by the Countesse of *Anglesey*.

Faire as unshaded Light; or as the Day
In its first birth, when all the Yeare was May;
Sweet, as the Altars smoake, or as the new
Unfolded Bud, swell'd by the early Dew;

Smooth, as the face of Waters first appear'd,
Ere Tides began to strive, or Winds were heard;
Kind, as the willing Saints, and calmer farre,
Than in their sleepes forgiven Hermits are:
You that are more, than our discreeter feare
Dares praise, with such dull Art, what make you here?
Here, where the Sommer is so little seene,
That Leaves (her cheapest wealth) scarce reach at greene;
You come, as if the silver Planet were
Misled a while from her much injur'd Spheare,
And t'ease the travailes of her beames tonight,
In this small Lanthorn would contract her light.

191 3 *smoake* incense 13 *silver Planet* moon 16 *Lanthorn* lantern

192 For the Lady, *Olivia* Porter. A present, upon a New-yeares day.

Goe! hunt the whiter Ermine! and present
His wealthy skin, as this dayes Tribute sent
To my *Endimion's* Love; Though she be farre
More gently smooth, more soft than Ermines are!
Goe! climbe that Rock! and when thou there hast found
A Starre, contracted in a Diamond,
Give it *Endimion's* Love; whose lasting Eyes,
Out-looke the Starry Jewells of the Skies!
Goe! dive into the Southern Sea! and when
Th'ast found (to trouble the nice sight of Men)
A swelling Pearle; and such whose single worth
Boasts all the wonders which the Seas bring forth;
Give it *Endimion's* Love! whose ev'ry Teare,
Would more enrich the skillfull Jeweller.
How I command? how slowly they obey?
The churlish *Tartar*, will not hunt to day:
Nor will that lazy, sallow-*Indian* strive
To climbe the Rock, nor that dull *Negro* dive.
Thus Poets like to Kings (by trust deceiv'd)
Give oftner what is heard of, than receiv'd.

192 1 *Ermine* white fur pelt traditionally emblematic of chastity 6 *contracted in* shrunk into

193 THE QUEENE,

returning to London after a long absence.

How had you walk'd in Mists of Sea-coale-smoke,
Such as your ever teeming Wives would choak,
(False Sonnes of thrift!) did not her beauties light,
Dispell your Clouds, and quicken your dull sight?
As when, th'illustrious Officer of Day,
(First worship'd in the East) 'gins to display
The glory of his beames; then Buds unfold
Their chary Leafes; each dew-drownd Marigold
Insensibly doth stirre it selfe, and spread;
Each Violet lifts up the pensive Head;
So when the Rayes of her faire Eyes appeare,
To warme, and guild your clouded Hemispheare;
Those Flow'rs which in your narrow Gardens grow,
(Narrow as Turfs, which you a Lark allow
In's wicker Cage) rejoyce upon their stalks;
Imbellishing your sommer inch-broad walks:
But she remov'd, what all your weary'd lives,
You plant in German pots, to please your Wives,
Shall fade; scarce in your Climate shall be seene
Enough of Spring to make your Tansies green.
Nor shall your blew-Ey'd Daughters more appeare
(Though in the hopefull'st season of the Yeare)
In the dark street, where *Tantlin's* Temple stands,
With Time, and Marg'rom Posies in their hands.
Wee know (distrustfull Bergainers!) you most
Love sacrifice, that puts you least to cost;
Give her your prayers then: that her Lookes may
After long nights, restore you unto Day.
Though Ringing be some charge, and Wood grow deere
In troth; it will become you once a yeare,
To offer Bells, and Bonfires too, alltho'
You couzen't out in Silks, next publique Show.

193 2 *teeming* fertile 8 *chary* cautious 14 *Turfs* in the bottom of a birdcage 18 *German pots* flower pots 20 *Tansies* bitter herbs used to make a curdled milk pudding, traditionally eaten at Easter 24 *Time* thyme *Marg'rom* marjoram 32 *couzen't* trick

194 To *Tho: Carew*.

1

Upon my conscience whensoe're thou dy'st
(Though in the black, the mourning time of Lent)
There will be seene, in Kings-street (where thou ly'st)
More triumphs, than in dayes of Parl'ament.

2

How glad, and gaudy then will Lovers be?
For ev'ry Lover that can Verses read,
Hath beene so injur'd by thy Muse, and thee,
Ten Thousand, Thousand times, he wish'd thee dead.

3

Not but thy Verses are as smooth, and high,
As Glory, Love or Wine, from Wit can rayse;
But now the Devill take such destinie!
What should commend them, turnes to their disprayse.

4

Thy Wit's chiefe Virtue, is become its Vice;
For ev'ry Beauty thou hast rays'd so high,
That now course-Faces carry such a price,
As must undoe a Lover, if he buy.

5

Scarce any of the Sex, admits commerce;
It shames mee much to urge this in a Friend;
But more, that they should so mistake thy Verse,
Which meant to conquer, whom it did commend.

194 2 *Though* even 17 *commerce* relationships in love

195 Sung as a Prologue when 'the faithful Shepherdess' was Presented.

Priest.

A Broyling Lamb on *Pan*'s chief Altar lies,
My Wreath, my Censor, Virge, and Incense by:
But I delay'd the precious Sacrifice,
To shew thee here a gentler Deity.

Nymph.

Nor was I to thy Sacred Summons slow,
Hither I came swift as the Eagles wing.
Or threat'ning Shaft from vext *Diana*'s Bow.
Pan sends his offering to this Islands King.

Priest.

Bless then that Queen whose Eies have brought that light
  Which hither led and stays him here;
  He now doth shine within her Sphear,
And must obey her Scepter half this night.

Nymph.

Sing we such welcomes as shall make her sway
Seem easie to him, though it last till day.

Chorus *of both.*

Welcome as Peace to wealthy Cities when
Famine and Sword have left more Graves then Men;
As Spring to Birds, or *Phebus* to the old
Poor Mountain *Muscovite* congeal'd with cold;
As Shore to Pilots in a safe-known Coast,
Their Cards being broken and their Rudders lost.

195 Title *the faithful Shepherdess* see Notes on the Text 2 *Virge* wand, staff of office 10 *stays* keeps 11 *Sphear* the moon, identified with Diana, see Appendix 1 20 *Cards* navigation charts for seamen

POETS OF THE TIXALL CIRCLE [POEMS COLLECTED BY HERBERT ASTON]

196 A GLASS LAMPE BROKEN.

This vestall flame might ever burne,
Closd in so pure a virgin urne,
Had not the frost outmatch'd the fire,
And taught how beauty may expire.
I know thy blazing beautye's might,
I feele the heate, I see the light;

Thy soule, unto my eyes though dimme,
Transpares, I grant, through every limbe;
But age's frost comes on a pace,
And that may crack thy christall case.

196 1–2 for lamps in tombs, see note on no. 63 1 *vestall flame* see Appendix 1 8 *Transpares* shows through

197 A GLASSE CHAYNE BROKEN.

Cease to proclayme the victory,
And trophy of your either eye;
Vaunt me no more your captive there,
Enchayned in a single haire:
Thees were glorious fetters too,
And every linke as strong as you;
And yet you see the chayne is broke,
And I in tyme may slip the yoake.

197 3 *Vaunt* boast

198 A GLASSE RING BROKEN.

Behold this broken ring, and spy
An embleme of your false eternity.
We think our joys must have no bound,
Because they come about so cleare and round.
The circle of our happynesse
Must brake itself in tyme as well as this;
And then the ring of all the mirth we have,
Must only serve to wed our spousall grave.

198 2 *embleme* image 8 *spousall* wedded

POETS OF THE TIXALL CIRCLE [GERTRUDE ASTON]

199 TO THE LADY ELIZABETH THIMELBY, ON NEW-YEARES-DAY, 1655, LOOKING DAYLY FOR HER SONNE FROM TRAVAILE.

Past is the winter absence of the sunne,
The welcome embleame of your joys begunne,
Your sonne's returning, to make good the trope,
Tis he presents this new-years horiscope.
Tis his returne and presence doth salute,
First in the flowre, and after in the fruite.
For by a rich concurrence he doth bring
Profit and pleasure, harvest-home in spring.
O, happy travailes! that with even paces
Leade, hand in hand, the muses with the graces:
And put you to the study whether hee
Hath more o' th' court or th' university.
To me, at distance, the result is cleare,
All notions meete to crowne your happy yeare.
Madam, observe a poets crafty thrift,
That makes anothers stock his new-yeares-guift.

199 2 *embleame* image 3 *trope* figure of speech, set comparison 9 *travailes* sufferings 16 *stock* store of poetic commonplaces *his* refers to the returning son of the title

EDMUND WALLER

200 *From a Childe.*

Madam,

As in some Climes the warmer Sun
Makes it full Summer ere the Spring's begun,
And with ripe fruit the bending boughs can load,
Before our Violets dare look abroad:
So measure not by any common use,
The early love your brighter eyes produce;

When lately your fair hand in womans weed,
Wrap't my glad head, I wish't me so indeed,
That hasty time might never make me grow
Out of those favours you afford me now;
That I might ever such indulgence finde,
And you not blush, or think your self too kind,
Who now I fear while I these joyes express,
Begin to think how you may make them less;
The sound of love makes your soft heart affraid,
And guard it self, though but a child invade,
And innocently at your white breast throw
A dart as white, a Ball of new faln snow.

200 8 *weed* clothing 9 *Wrap't* wrapped

201 *Puerperium.*

You Gods that have the power,
To trouble, and compose
All that's beneath your bower,
Calm silence on the Seas, on Earth impose.

Fair *Venus* in thy soft arms,
The God of rage confine,
For thy whispers are the charms
Which only can divert his fierce design.

What though he frown, and to tumult do incline,
Thou the flame,
Kindled in his breast can'st tame,
With that snow which unmelted lies on thine?

Great Goddess give this thy sacred Island rest,
Make Heaven smile,
That no storm disturb us, while
Thy chief care our *Halcyon* builds her nest.

Great *Gloriana*, fair *Gloriana*,
Bright as high Heaven is, and fertile as Earth,
Whose beauty relieves us,
Whose Royal bed gives us
Both glory and peace.
Our present joy, and all our hopes increase.

201 Title *Puerperium* Latin 'childbirth' 6 *the God of rage* Mars, see Appendix 1 16 *Halcyon* here applied to the Queen, see Appendix 1 17 *Gloriana* poetic name for Elizabeth I, here applied to Henrietta Maria

202 Chloris *and* Hilas. *Made to a Sarabran.*

Chl. Hilas, o Hilas, why sit we mute,
Now that each Bird saluteth the Spring?
Wind up the slackned strings of thy Lute,
Never canst thou want matter to sing:
For love thy Brest does fill with such a fire,
That whatso'er is fair, moves thy desire.

Hil. Sweetest you know, the sweetest of things,
Of various flowers the Bees do compose,
Yet no particular taste it brings
Of Violet, Woodbind, Pink, or Rose:
So love the resultance is of all the graces
Which flow from a thousand several faces.

Chl. Hilas, the Birds which chant in this Grove,
Could we but know the Language they use,
They would instruct us better in love,
And reprehend thy inconstant muse:
For love their Brests does fill with such a fire,
That what they once do chuse, bounds their desire,

Hil. Chloris, this change the Birds do approve,
Which the warm season hither does bring;
Time from your self does further remove
You, than the Winter from the gay Spring:

She that like lightning shin'd while her face lasted,
The Oak now resembles which lightning hath blasted.

202 Title: *Sarabran* saraband, slow dance 4 *matter* subject 13 *chant* sing

203 The Battell of the *Summer Islands*.

Canto. I.

What fruits they have, and how heaven smiles
Upon those late discovered Isles.

Aid me *Bellona* while the dreadfull fight
Betwixt a Nation, and two Whales I write:
Seas stain'd with goar, I sing, advent'rous toyl,
And how these Monsters did disarm an Isle.
Bermudas wall'd with Rocks, who does not know
That happy Island where huge Lemons grow,
And Orange Trees which golden fruit do bear,
Th'Hesperian Garden boasts of none so fair?
Where shining Pearl, Coral, and many a pound
On the rich shore, of Amber-greece is found:
The lofty Cedar which to Heaven aspires,
The Prince of Trees, is fewel for their fires:
The smoak by which their loaded spits do turn,
For incense might, on sacred Altars burn.
There privat roofs on od'rous timber born,
Such as might Palaces for Kings adorn:
The sweet *Palmettas*, a new *Bacchus* yield
With leaves as ample as the broadest shield:
Under the shadow of whose friendly boughs
They sit carrowsing, where their liquor grows:
Figs there unplanted through the fields do grow,
Such as fierce *Cato* did the Romans show,
With the rare fruit inviting them to spoyl
Carthage the mistris of so rich a soyl:
The naked rocks are not unfruitfull there,
But at some constant seasons every year,

Their barren tops with luscious food abound,
And with the eggs of various fowls are crown'd:
Tobacco is the worst of things which they
To English Land-lords as their Tribute pay:
Such is the mould, that the blest Tenant feeds
On pretious fruits, and payes his rent in weeds:
With candid Plantines, and the jucy Pine,
On choicest Melons and sweet Grapes they dine
And with Potatoes fat their wanton Swine:
Nature these Cates with such a lavish hand
Pours out among them, that our coarser Land
Tastes of that bounty, and does Cloath return,
Which not for Warmth, but Ornament is worn:
For the kind Spring which but salutes us here
Inhabits there, and courts them all the year:
Ripe fruits and blossoms on the same Trees live,
At once they promise what at once they give,
So sweet the aire, so moderate the clime,
None sickly lives, or dies before his time.
Heaven sure has kept this spot of earth uncurst
To shew how all things were created first.
The tardy plants in our cold Orchards plac't,
Reserve their fruits, for the next ages taste:
There a small grain in some few months will be
A firm, a lofty, and a spacious Tree:
The *Palma Christi*, and the fair *Papah*,
Now but a seed (preventing Natures law)
In half the circle of the hasty year
Project a shade, and lovely fruits do wear:
And as their Trees in our dull Region set
But faintly grow, and no perfection get;
So in this Northern tract our hoarser throats
Utter unripe and ill-constrained notes,
Where the supporter of the Poets stile,
Phoebus on them eternally does smile.
O how I long my careless limbs to lay
Under the Plantanes shade, and all the day
With am'rous aires my fancy entertain,
Invoke the Muses, and improve my vein!

No passion there in my free breast should move,
None but the sweet and best of passions Love:
There while I sing, if gentle Love be by
That tunes my Lute, and winds the Strings so high,
With the sweet sound of *Sacharissa*'s name,
I'll make the listning savages grow tame.
  But while I do these pleasing dreams indite,
  I am diverted from the promis'd fight.

Canto II.

Of their alarm, and how their foes
Discovered were, this Canto shows.

Though Rocks so high about this Iland rise,
That well they may the num'rous Turk despise,
Yet is no humane fate exempt from fear
Which shakes their hearts, while through the Ile they hear
A lasting noise, as horrid and as loud
As thunder makes, before it breaks the cloud.
Three days they dread this murmur, e're they know
From what blind cause th'unwonted sound may grow.
At length two Monsters of unequal size,
Hard by the shore a fisher-man espies;
Two mighty Whales, which swelling Seas had tost,
And left them prisoners on the rocky coast;
One as a Mountain vast, and with her came
A Cub not much inferior to his Dam:
Here in a pool among the Rocks ingag'd,
They roar'd like Lions, caught in toyls and rag'd:
The man knew what they were, who heretofore
Had seen the like lye murdered on the shore,
By the wild fury of some tempest cast
The fate of ships and shipwrackt men to tast;
As careless dames whom wine and sleep betray
To frantick dreams their Infants overlay:
So there sometimes the raging Ocean fails,
And her own brood exposes, when the Whales
Against sharp Rocks like reeling vessels quash't,
Though huge as Mountains, are in pieces dash't;

Along the shore their dreadfull limbs lie scatter'd,
Like Hills with Earthquaks shaken, torn and shatter'd:
Hearts sure of brass they had who tempted first,
Rude Seas that spare not what themselves have nurst.
   The welcome news through all the Nation spread,
   To sudden joy and hope converts their dread.
What lately was their publick terror, they
Behold with glad eyes as a certain prey;
Dispose already of th'untaken spoyl,
And as the purchase of their future toyl,
These share the bones, and they divide the Oyl;
So was the Huntsman by the Bear opprest,
Whose hide he sold before he caught the beast.
   They man their Boats, and all their young men arm
With whatsover may the Monsters harm;
Pikes, Holberts, Spits, and Darts that wound so far,
The Tools of Peace, and Instruments of War:
Now was the time for vig'rous lads to show
What love or honor could invite them too;
A goodly Theatre where Rocks are round
With reverend age, and lovely lasses crown'd:
Such was the lake which held this dreadfull pair
Within the bounds of noble *Warwicks* share:
Warwicks bold Earl, than which no title bears
A greater sound among our British Peers;
And worthy he the memory to renew,
The fate and honor, to that title due;
Whose brave adventures have transferr'd his name,
And through the new world spread his growing fame.
   But how they fought, and what their valour gain'd,
   Shall in another Canto be contain'd.

Canto III.

The bloody fight, successless toyl,
And how the fishes sack'd the Isle.

The Boat which on the first assault did go
Struck with a harping Iron the younger so;

Who when he felt his side so rudely goar'd
Loud as the Sea that nourish't him he roar'd;
As a broad Bream to please some curious tast,
While yet alive in boyling water cast,
Vex't with unwonted heat, boyls, flings about
The scorching brass, and hurls the liquor out:
So with the barbed Javeling stung, he raves,
And scourges with his tayl the suffering waves:
Like *Spencer's Talus* with his iron flayl,
He threatens ruine with his pondrous tayl;
Dissolving at one strok the battered Boat,
And down the men fall drenched in the Moat:
With every fierce encounter they are forc't
To quit their Boats, and fare like men unhorst.
  The bigger Whale like some huge Carrack lay,
Which wanteth Sea room, with her foes to play;
Slowly she swims, and when provok'd she wo'd
Advance her tail, her head salutes the mudd,
The shallow water doth her force infringe,
And renders vain her tails impetuous swinge.
The shining steel her tender sides receive,
And there like Bees they all their weapons leave.
  This sees the Cub, and does himself oppose
Betwixt his cumbred mother and her foes:
With desperate courage he receives her wounds,
And men and boats his active tayl confounds.
Their forces joyn'd, the Seas with billows fill,
And make a tempest, though the winds be still.
  Now would the men with half their hoped prey
Be well content, and wish this Cub away:
Their wish they have, he to direct his dam
Unto the gap through which they thither came,
Before her swims, and quits the hostile lake,
A pris'ner there, but for his mothers sake.
She by the Rocks compell'd to stay behind,
Is by the vastness of her bulk confin'd.
They shout for joy, and now on her alone
Their fury falls, and all their darts are thrown,
Their Lances spent; one bolder than the rest
With his broad sword provok'd the sluggish beast:

Her oily side devours both blad and heft,
And there his Steel the bold Bermudian left.
Courage the rest from his example take,
And now they change the colour of the lake:
Blood flows in Rivers from her wounded side,
As if they would prevent the tardy tide;
And raise the flood to that propitious height,
As might convey her from this fatal streight.
She swims in blood, and blood do's spouting throw
To Heaven, that Heaven mens cruelties might know.
Their fixed Javelins in her side she wears,
And on her back a grove of pikes appears.
You would have thought had you the monster seen
Thus drest, she had another Island been:
Roaring she tears the air with such a noise,
(As well resembled the conspiring voice
Of routed Armies, when the field is won)
To reach the ears of her escaped son.
He (though a league removed from the fo)
Hastes to her aid, the pious Trojan so
Neglecting for *Creusas* life his own,
Repeats the danger of the burning Town;
The men amazed blush to see the seed
Of monsters; humane piety exceed,
Well proves this kindness what the Grecians sung,
That Loves bright mother from the Ocean sprung.
Their courage droops, and hopeless now they wish
For composition with th'unconquer'd fish:
So she their weapons would restore again,
Through rocks they'd hew her passage to the main.
But how instructed in each others minde,
Or what commerce can men with monsters finde?
Not daring to aproach their wounded fo,
Whom her couragious son protected so,
They charge their Muskets, and with hot desire
Of fell revenge, renew the fight with fire.
Standing a looff with lead they bruise the scales,
And tear the flesh of the incensed Whales.
But no success their fierce endeavors found,
Nor this way could they give one fatal wound.

Now to their Fort they are about to send
For the loud Engines which their Isle defend.
But what those pieces fram'd to batter walls
Would have effected on those mighty Whales,
Great *Neptune* will not have us know, who sends
A tyde so high, that it relieves his friends.
And thus they parted with exchange of harms;
Much blood the Monsters lost, and they their Arms.

203 Canto I 1 *Bellona* see Appendix 1 10 *Amber-greece* ambergris 15 *od'rous* scented 17 *Palmettas* palm trees 33 *candid* white, sweet *Plantines* plantains, bananas *Pine* pineapple 36 *Cates* delicacies 44 *clime* climate 52 *Palma Christi* palm of Christ, date palm *Papah* paw-paw 64 *aires* tunes or songs 65 *vein* style 70 *Sacharissa* 'sweetest', his name for his mistress 72 *indite* write, compose Canto II 10 *Hard by* close to 14 *inferior* smaller 22 *overlay* suffocate 25 *quash't* squashed, crushed 42 *Holberts* halbards, spears 49 *Warwick* Earl of Warwick, see Appendix 2 Canto III 5 *Bream* type of fish 11 *Spencer's Talus* in Spenser's *Faerie Queene*, see Appendices 1 and 2 12 *pondrous* large and heavy 17 *Carrack* large boat 19 *wo'd* would 26 *cumbred* encumbered 33 *dam* mother 43 *blad and heft* blade and handle 62 *pious Trojan* Aeneas, see Appendix 1 65 *seed* offspring 68 *Loves bright mother* Venus, see Appendix 1 70 *composition* truce 72 *main* sea 85 *pieces* cannon

204 *To* Vandike.

Rare *Artisan*, whose Pencil moves
Not our Delights alone, but Loves:
From thy Shop of Beauty, we
Slaves return that enter'd free.
The heedless Lover does not know
Whose eyes they are that wound him so:
But confounded with thy art,
Inquires her name that has his Heart:
Another who did long refrain,
Feels his Old wound bleed fresh again,
With dear remembrance of that face,
Where now he reads new hopes of grace:
Nor Scorn, nor Cruelty does find,
But gladly suffers a false wind
To blow the ashes of Despair
From the reviving brand of care:

Fool that forgets her stubborn look,
This softness from thy finger took:
Strange that thy hand should not inspire
The beauty only, but the fire:
Not the form alone, and grace,
But act and power of a face:
May'st thou yet thy self as well,
As all the world besides excell;
So you th'unfeigned truth rehearse,
(That I may make it Live in Verse)
Why thou couldst not at one assay,
That face to after times convey,
Which this admires; was it thy wit
To make her oft before thee sit?
Confess, and wee'l forgive thee this,
For who would not repeat that bliss,
And frequent sight of such a Dame,
Buy with the hazard of his Fame?
Yet who can tax thy blameless skill,
Though thy good hand had failed still?
When natures self so often errs,
She for this many thousand years
Seems to have practis'd with much care,
To frame the Race of Women fair;
Yet never could a perfect birth
Produce before to grace the Earth:
Which waxed old ere it could see
Her that amaz'd thy art and thee.
 But now 'tis done, O let me know
Where those Immortal Colours grow,
That could this Deathless piece compose
In Lillies, or the fading Rose?
No, for this Theft thou hast clim'd higher
Than did *Prometheus* for his fire.

204 Title for *Vandike* see Appendix 2 27 *assay* attempt 43 *waxed* grew 50 *Prometheus*, see Appendix 1

SIR RICHARD FANSHAWE

205 AN ODE Upon occasion of His MAJESTIES Proclamation in the yeare 1630. Commanding the Gentry to reside upon their Estates in the Country

Now warre is all the world about,
And everywhere *Erynnis* raignes,
Or else the Torch so late put out
The stench remaines.

Holland for many yeares hath beene
Of Christian tragedies the stage,
Yet seldome hath she play'd a Scene
Of bloudyer rage.

And *France* that was not long compos'd
With civill Drummes againe resounds,
And ere the old are fully clos'd
Receives new wounds.

The great *Gustavus* in the west
Plucks the Imperiall Eagles wing,
Than whom the earth did ne're invest
A fiercer King.

Revenging lost *Bohemia*,
And the proud wrongs which *Tilly* dud,
And tempereth the German clay
With Spanish bloud.

What should I tell of Polish Bands,
And the blouds boyling in the North?
Gainst whom the furred Russians
Their Troops bring forth,

Both confident: This in his purse,
And needy valour set on worke;
He is his Axe; which oft did worse
Th'invading Turke.

Who now sustaines a Persian storme:
There hell (that made it) suffers schisme
This warre (forsooth) was to reforme
    Mahumetisme.

Onely the Island which wee sowe,
(A world without the world) so farre
From present wounds, it cannot showe
    An ancient skarre.

White Peace (the beautiful'st of things)
Seemes here her everlasting rest
To fix, and spreads her downy wings
    Over the nest.

As when great *Jove* usurping Reigne
From the plagu'd world did her exile
And ty'd her with a golden chaine
    To one blest Isle:

Which in a sea of plenty swamme
And Turtles sang on ev'ry bowgh,
A safe retreat to all that came
    As ours is now.

Yet wee, as if some foe were here,
Leave the despised Fields to clownes,
And come to save our selves as twere
    In walled Townes.

Hither we bring Wives, Babes, rich clothes
And Gemms; Till now my Soveraigne
The growing evill doth oppose:
    Counting in vaine

His care preserves us from annoy
Of enemyes his Realmes to'invade,
Unlesse hee force us to enjoy
    The peace hee made.

To rowle themselves in envy'd leasure
He therefore sends the Landed Heyres,
Whilst hee proclaimes not his owne pleasure
So much as theirs.

The sapp and bloud o'the land, which fled
Into the roote, and choackt the heart,
Are bid their quickning pow'r to spread
Through ev'ry part.

O, 'twas an act, not for my muse
To celebrate, nor the dull Age
Untill the country aire infuse
A purer rage!

And if the Fields as thankfull prove
For benefits receiv'd, as seed,
They will, to quite so great a love,
A *Virgill* breed;

A *Tytirus*, that shall not cease
Th' *Augustus* of our world to praise
In equall verse, author of peace
And *Halcyon* dayes.

Nor let the Gentry grudge to goe
Into those places whence they grew,
But thinke them blest they may doe so
Who would pursue

The smoaky glory of the Towne,
That may goe till his native earth,
And by the shining fire sit downe
Of his owne hearth,

Free from the griping Scriveners bands,
And the more byting Mercers books;
Free from the bayt of oyled hands
And painted looks?

The country too ev'n chopps for raine:
You that exhale it by your power
Let the fat dropps fall downe againe
In a full showre.

And you bright beautyes of the time,
That waste yourselves here in a blaze,
Fixe to your Orbe and proper clime
Your wandring rayes.

Let no darke corner of the land
Be unimbellisht with one Gemme,
And those which here too thick doe stand
Sprinkle on them.

Beleeve me Ladies you will finde
In that sweet life, more solid joyes
More true contentment to the minde
Than all Town-toyes.

Nor *Cupid* there lesse bloud doth spill,
But heads his shafts with chaster love,
Not feathered with a Sparrowes quill
But of a Dove.

There shall you hear the Nightingale
(The harmeless Syren of the wood)
How prettily she tells a tale
Of rape and blood.

The lyrricke Larke, with all beside
Of nature's feathered quire: and all
The Common-wealth of Flowres int's pride
Behold you shall.

The Lillie (Queene) the (Royall) Rose,
The Gilyflowre (Prince of the bloud)
The (Courtyer) Tulip (gay in clothes)
The (Regall) Budd

The Vilet (purple Senatour)
How they doe mock the pompe of State,
And all that at the surly doore
Of great ones waite.

Plant Trees you may, and see them shoote
Up with your Children, to be serv'd
To your cleane boards, and the fair'st Fruite
To be preserv'd:

And learne to use their severall gummes,
'Tis innocence in the sweet blood
Of Cherryes, Apricocks and Plummes
To be imbru'd.

205 See Notes on the Text for the historical background to this 2 *Erynnis* see Appendix 1 13 *Gustavus* King of Sweden, see Appendix 2 14 *Imperiall Eagle* arms of the Holy Roman Emperor 18 *Tilly* see Appendix 2 *dud* did 30 *schisme* religious division 33 *sowe* plant crops 39 *downy wings* Peace is winged, either as the dove of the Holy Spirit, or as personification 46 *Turtles* turtle doves 62 *Heyres* heirs 67 *quickning* life-giving 76 *Virgill*, 77 *Tytirus*, 78 *Augustus* see Appendix 1 80 *Halcyon dayes* see note on no. 180 89 *griping* greedy *Scrivener* copyist 90 *Mercer* haberdasher 93 *chopps* cracks open 99 *Orbe* orbit *proper clime* own place: this stanza addresses (court) beauties as stars or suns, advising them to go back to their homes, like planets in their own spheres, and cease blazing out of their proper orbits like comets 111 *Sparrowes* symbol of lechery 116 *rape and blood* see Appendix 1, Philomel 117 *lyrricke* musical, tuneful 122 *Gilyflowre* carnation or stock (usage imprecise) 125 *Senatour* senators of ancient Rome wore purple, like the violet 131 *boards* dining tables 136 *imbru'd* steeped

206 [That virgin-Rose, which, while she grew (though crown'd]

That virgin-Rose, which, while she grew (though crown'd
With prickles sweet) was glorie of the Vale
Dandled by wanton winds, fainting and pale
Yeelds up her purple honour to the ground.
The fragrancies she had, remaine in death;
Or may it not be sayd, she doth but rest
Against the Earth, like flowers, with rayne opprest.
How is she dead, that hath not lost her breath?

Her bloudlesse Leaves, her native *Betis* mournes;
But not her sweetnes; groveling on his sands,
Exhausted *Tagus*, his hidd gold up-turnes.
She's now transplanted by the Maker's hands,
Amongst those flowers a better Morne adornes,
Whose fading deaw are the bright starrie Bands.

206 9 *Betis*, 11 *Tagus* see Appendix 1

JOHN MILTON

207 Elegia quinta, Anno aetatis 20.

In adventum veris.

In se perpetuo Tempus revolubile gyro
Jam revocat Zephyros vere tepente novos.
Induiturque brevem Tellus reparata juventam,
Jamque soluta gelu dulce virescit humus.
Fallor? an et nobis redeunt in carmina vires,
Ingeniumque mihi munere veris adest?
Munere veris adest, iterumque vigescit ab illo
(Quis putet) atque aliquod jam sibi poscit opus.
Castalis ante oculos, bifidumque cacumen oberrat,
Et mihi Pyrenen somnia nocte ferunt.
Concitaque arcano fervent mihi pectora motu,
Et furor, et sonitus me sacer intus agit.
Delius ipse venit, video Peneide lauro
Implicitos crines, Delius ipse venit.
Jam mihi mens liquidi raptatur in ardua coeli,
Perque vagas nubes corpore liber eo.
Perque umbras, perque antra feror penetralia vatum,
Et mihi fana patent interiora Deum.
Intuiturque animus toto quid agatur Olympo,
Nec fugiunt oculos Tartara caeca meos.
Quid tam grande sonat distento spiritus ore?
Quid parit haec rabies, quid sacer iste furor?
Ver mihi, quod dedit ingenium, cantabitur illo;
Profuerint isto reddita dona modo.

Jam Philomela tuos foliis adoperta novellis
Instituis modulos, dum silet omne nemus.
Urbe ego, tu sylva simul incipiamus utrique,
Et simul adventum veris uterque canat.
Veris io rediere vices, celebremus honores
Veris, et hoc subeat Musa quotannis opus.
Jam sol Aethiopas fugiens Tithoniaque arva,
Flectit ad Arctoas aurea lora plagas.
Est breve noctis iter, brevis est mora noctis opacae
Horrida cum tenebris exulat illa suis.
Jamque Lycaonius plaustrum caeleste Bootes
Non longa sequitur fessus ut ante via,
Nunc etiam solitas circum Jovis atria toto
Excubias agitant sydera rara polo.
Nam dolus et caedes, et vis cum nocte recessit,
Neve Giganteum Dii timuere scelus.
Forte aliquis scopuli recubans in vertice pastor,
Roscida cum primo sole rubescit humus,
Hac, ait, hac certe caruisti nocte puella
Phoebe tua, celeres quae retineret equos.
Laeta suas repetit sylvas, pharetramque resumit
Cynthia, Luciferas ut videt alta rotas,
Et tenues ponens radios gaudere videtur
Officium fieri tam breve fratris ope,
Desere, Phoebus ait, thalamos Aurora seniles,
Quid juvat effeto procubuisse toro?
Te manet Aeolides viridi venator in herba,
Surge, tuos ignes altus Hymettus habet.
Flava verecundo dea crimen in ore fatetur,
Et matutinos ocyus urget equos.
Exuit invisam Tellus rediviva senectam,
Et cupit amplexus Phoebe subire tuos;
Et cupit, et digna est, quid enim formosius illa,
Pandit ut omniferos luxuriosa sinus,
Atque Arabum spirat messes, et ab ore venusto
Mitia cum Paphiis fundit aroma rosis.
Ecce coronatur sacro frons ardua luco,
Cingit ut Idaeam pinea turris Opim;
Et vario madidos intexit flore capillos,
Floribus et visa est posse placere suis.

Floribus effusos ut erat redimita capillos
  Taenario placuit diva Sicana Deo.
Aspice Phoebe tibi faciles hortantur amores,
  Mellitasque movent flamina verna preces.
Cinnamea Zephyrus leve plaudit odorifer ala,
  Blanditiasque tibi ferre videntur aves.
Nec sine dote tuos temeraria quaerit amores
  Terra, nec optatos poscit egena toros,
Alma salutiferum medicos tibi gramen in usus
  Praebet, et hinc titulos adjuvat ipsa tuos.
Quod si te pretium, si te fulgentia tangunt
  Munera, (muneribus saepe coemptus Amor)
Illa tibi osteneat quascunque sub aequore vasto,
  Et superinjectis montibus abdit opes.
Ah quoties cum tu clivoso fessus Olympo
  In vespertinas praecipitaris aquas,
Cur te, inquit, cursu languentem Phoebe diurno
  Hesperiis recipit Caerula mater aquis?
Quid tibi cum Tethy? Quid cum Tartesside lympha,
  Dia quid immundo perluis ora salo?
Frigora Phoebe mea melius captabis in umbra,
  Huc ades, ardentes imbue rore comas.
Mollior egelida veniet tibi somnus in herba
  Huc ades, et gremio lumina pone meo.
Quaque jaces circum mulcebit lene susurrans
  Aura per humentes corpora fusa rosas.
Nec me (crede mihi) terrent Semeleia fata,
  Nec Phaetonteo fumidus axis equo;
Cum tu Phoebe tuo sapientius uteris igni,
  Huc ades et gremio lumina pone meo.
Sic Tellus lasciva suos suspirat amores;
  Matris in exemplum caetera turba ruunt.
Nunc etenim toto currit vagus orbe Cupido,
  Languentesque fovet solis ab igne faces.
Insonuere novis lethalia cornua nervis,
  Triste micant ferro tela corusca novo.
Jamque vel invictam tentat superasse Dianam,
  Quaeque sedet sacro Vesta pudica foco.
Ipsa senescentem reparat Venus annua formam,
  Atque iterum tepido creditur orta mari.

Marmoreas juvenes clamant Hymenaee per urbes,
Litus io Hymen, et cava saxa sonant.
Cultior ille venit tunicaque decentior apta,
Puniceum redolet vestis odora crocum.
Egrediturque frequens ad amoeni gaudia veris
Virgineas auro cincta puella sinus.
Votum est cuique suum, votum est tamen omnibus unum,
Ut sibi quem cupiat, det Cytherea virum.
Nunc quoque septena modulatur arundine pastor,
Et sua quae jungat carmina Phyllis habet.
Navita nocturno placat sua sydera cantu,
Delphinasque leves ad vada summa vocat.
Jupiter iste alto cum conjuge ludit Olympo,
Convocat et famulos ad sua festa Deos.
Nunc etiam Satyri cum sera crepuscula surgunt,
Pervolitant celeri florea rura choro,
Sylvanusque sua Cyparissi fronde revinctus,
Semicaperque Deus, semideusque caper.
Quaeque sub arboribus Dryades latuere vetustis
Per juga, per solos expatiantur agros.
Per sata luxuriat fruticetaque Maenalius Pan,
Vix Cybele mater, vix sibi tuta Ceres,
Atque aliquam cupidus praedatur Oreada Faunus,
Consulit in trepidos dum sibi Nympha pedes,
Jamque latet, latitansque cupit male tecta videri,
Et fugit, et fugiens pervelit ipsa capi.
Dii quoque non dubitant caelo praeponere sylvas,
Et sua quisque sibi numina lucus habet.
Et sua quisque diu sibi numina lucus habeto,
Nec vos arborea dii precor ite domo.
Te referant miseris te Jupiter aurea terris
Saecla, quid ad nimbos aspera tela redis?
Tu saltem lente rapidos age Phoebe jugales
Qua potes, et sensim tempora veris eant.
Brumaque productas tarde ferat hispida noctes,
Ingruat et nostro serior umbra polo.

207 Fifth Elegy, written when he was 20. On the Coming of Spring

Revolving in its perpetual round, Time calls back the zephyrs as the spring grows warm. Mother Earth, restored, enters her short-lived youth: the frost has melted, the ground grows sweet and green. Am I deceived or is the strength of song also coming back to me, and has inspiration returned as the gift of the spring? It has come indeed as the gift of the spring and gains in strength again (who would believe it?) and now it seeks for work to do. The hill of Castalia, the twin-peaked mountain, floats before my eyes, and the [Muses'] fountain of Pirene comes to me at night in dreams. My heart is stirred and burns with hidden fire, and poetic rage and holy thunder stir within me. Delian Apollo himself appears—I see his hair entwined with the laurel of the daughter of Peneus [Daphne]—Delian Apollo himself appears. Now my mind is carried up to the heights of the lucid sky, and, freed from the body, I pass amongst the wandering clouds. I am carried through the shadows and through caverns, the secret shrines of poets, and the hidden shrines of the gods are revealed to me. My spirit sees everything which is done on Olympus and dark Tartarus is not hidden from my eyes. What great song will my spirit pour forth from my open mouth? What will this madness and holy fury bring to birth? I will sing of the spring which has brought this inspiration, I will return the gift to the giver.

Now, Philomela, you begin your song among the newly opened leaves, while the whole wood is still. You in the wood, I in the city, let us begin together, let us sing of the arrival of spring. The spring (rejoice) has come again, let us celebrate the triumphs of spring, and may the Muse sustain her yearly task. Now the sun, leaving the Ethiopian lands and the territories of Tithonus, steers his golden reins towards the northern lands. The night's journey is short, short is the stay of the dark night, her fears are banished with the darkness. Now Lyconian Bootes no longer wearily follows the celestial plough. Now only a few stars keep watch around the halls of Jove in the skies: murder, violence, and treachery have vanished with the night and the gods fear no attack from the giants. Perhaps some shepherd reclining amongst the mountain rocks, as the dewy earth reddens with the first light, will say, 'O Phoebus, it is certain that your love was not with you this night to hold back your fleet horses.' Cynthia returns happily to her forest and takes her quiver up again, when from on high she sees the chariot of the sun, and putting aside her thin light, she rejoices to see her task thus shortened by her brother. 'Leave', says Apollo, 'leave, Aurora, the halls of your ancient husband, it serves you nothing to lie in that exhausted bed. The Aeolian hunter [Cephalus] waits for you in the green fields. Arise, your fire is already on high Hymettus.' The goddess of dawn blushes red, in admission of her fault, and urges on the horses of the morning.

Earth, reviving, throws off hated age, and longs, Phoebus, for your embraces. She longs for them, and is worthy of them, for what is lovelier than she is as she lays bare her fruitful breasts and breathes forth Arabian perfumes, and from her lovely mouth pours forth balsam and Paphian roses. See, her high forehead is crowned with a sacred grove, as a tower of pines encircles Idean Opis. She weaves coloured flowers into her dewy hair, and with her flowers is seen to be pleasing, as the Sicanian goddess [Persephone] charmed the Taenarian god [Pluto] with poured-forth flowers entwining flowing hair. Phoebus, look, the willing loves call to you, and honeyed prayers are borne on the winds of spring. Scent-bearing Zephyrus gently fans with his cinnamon wings and the birds seem to bring you their blandishments. Earth does not seek your love boldly without a dowry: nor empty-handed does she claim the longed-for bridal. She gracefully offers you healing herbs and with these adds to your fame. If splendour or reward can move you (and love is often bought with gifts) she lays before you the riches hidden in the broad ocean and under the piled-up mountains. Alas, how often has she said, when you tired from steep Olympus [the sky] have hurled yourself into the evening waters, 'Why, O Phoebus, when you are tired from your daily journey, does the blue mother receive you into the western sea? What is your business with Tethys? And what is your interest in Tartessian waters? Why do you steep your godly face in foul salt water? You would do better to enjoy my cool shades, come to me to steep your burning hair in dew. Softer sleep will come to you on the cool grass. Come to me and lay your brightness on my breast. Where you lie, whispering breezes will soothe us as we lie on beds of dewy roses. Believe me, the fate of Semele does not frighten me, nor the smoking axle of the chariot of Phaeton. When, Phoebus, you will use your fire more wisely, you will come to me and lay your brightness on my breast.'

Thus the desirous Earth pours forth her love, and all creatures follow the example of their mother. Now Cupid runs unchecked over the earth, lighting his guttering torch at the fire of the sun. His unerring bow resounds with new strings, and the iron of his new arrows shines with a fatal gleam. Now would he attempt to overcome the unconquered Diana, or the chaste Vesta sitting by the sacred hearth. And Venus herself restores her ageing beauty, and seems once again newly risen from the warm sea. Through the marble cities the young men cry forth *Hymenaeus*; *Io Hymen* echoes back from the shore and from the hollow rocks. The worshipped one appears himself in his appropriate tunic, his scented garment which is scented with the purple crocus. The virgin girls go forth to enjoy the delights of the spring, their breasts girded with gold. Each one has her prayer, they all share the same prayer, that Venus may grant them the man whom they desire.

Now the shephed plays on his seven-reeded pipe and his Phyllis joins with her own songs. The sailor sings to the stars of the night sky and draws the lithe dolphins to the surface of the waves. On high Olympus, Jove pleases himself with his queen, and calls the servant gods to his feast. When twilight comes the bands of satyrs whirl rapidly through the flowery countryside, with Sylvanus crowned with cypress: half-goat god, half-god goat. Those Dryads who have been hiding in the shades of the ancient trees, wander on the hills and in the deserted fields. Maenalian Pan rejoices in the seeded fields and the orchards, hardly are mother Cybele or Ceres safe from him. The lustful Faunus seeks to seize upon the Oread, while the nymph flees him on trembling feet. Now she hides, and half-hidden, wishes to be seen, and flees and fleeing wishes to be caught. The gods themselves hurry to leave the heavens for the woods, and every grove has its deity. Long may every grove thus have its god; Gods, I pray, do not leave your woodland home. O Jupiter, may the golden age return you to the miserable earth, why leave it for your harsh armoury in the clouds? Phoebus, drive your rapid team slowly under their yoke, as much as you can, and let the springtime pass slowly. Let fur-clad winter be slow in bringing its long nights and may the shadows fall later than usual upon our sky.

207 For classical names, see Appendix 1 *passim*

SIR JOHN SUCKLING

208 *Upon my Lady* Carliles *walking in* Hampton Court garden.

Dialogue.

T.C.
J.S.

Thom.

Didst thou not find the place inspir'd,
And flow'rs as if they had desir'd
No other Sun, start from their beds,
And for a sight steal out their heads?
Heardst thou not musick when she talk't?
And didst not find that as she walkt
She threw rare perfumes all about
Such as bean-blossoms newly out,
Or chafed spices give?——

J.S.

I must confesse those perfumes (*Tom*)
I did not smell; nor found that from
Her passing by, ought sprung up new,
The flow'rs had all their birth from you;

For I pass't o're the self same walk,
And did not find one single stalk
Of any thing that was to bring
This unknown after after spring.

Thom.

Dull and insensible, could'st see
A thing so near a Deity
Move up and down, and feel no change?

J.S.

None, and so great, were alike strange,
I had my Thoughts, but not your way,
All are not born (Sir) to the Bay;
Alas! *Tom*, I am flesh and blood,
And was consulting how I could
In spite of masks and hoods descry
The parts deni'd unto the eye;
I was undoing all she wore,
And had she walkt but one turn more,
Eve in her first state had not been
More naked, or more plainly seen.

Thom.

'Twas well for thee she left the place,
There is great danger in that face;
But had'st thou view'd her legg and thigh,
And upon that discovery
Search't after parts that are more dear
(As Fancy seldom stops so near)
No time or age had ever seen
So lost a thing as thou hadst been.

208 Title *Lady Carlile* see Appendix 2 *Thom/ T.C.* Thomas Carew, see Appendix 3
23 *Bay* emblem of poetry and poets

WILLIAM CARTWRIGHT

209 Sadness.

Whiles I this standing Lake,
Swath'd up with Ewe and Cypress Boughs,
Do move by Sighs and Vows,
Let Sadness only wake;
That whiles thick Darkness blots the Light,
My thoughts may cast another Night:
In which double Shade,
By Heav'n and Me made,
O let me weep,
And fall asleep,
And forgotten fade.

Heark! from yond' hollow Tree
Sadly sing two Anchoret Owles,
Whiles the Hermit Wolf howls,
And all bewailing me,
The Raven hovers o'r my Bier,
The Bittern on a Reed I hear
Pipes my Elegy,
And warns me to dye;
Whiles from yond' Graves
My wrong'd Love craves
My sad Company.

Cease *Hylas*, cease thy Call;
Such, O such was thy parting Groan,
Breath'd out to me alone
When thou disdain'd didst fall.
Loe thus unto thy silent Tomb,
In my sad Winding Sheet, I come,
Creeping o'r dead Bones,
And cold Marble Stones,
That I may mourn
Over thy Urn,
And appease thy Groans.

209 2 *Ewe* yew, with cypress, symbolic of death and funerals 13 *Anchoret* anchorite, hermit

210 *Love but one.*

See these two little Brooks that slowly creep
In Snaky windings through the Plains,
I knew them once one River, swift and deep,
Blessing and blest by Poets strains.

Then touch'd with Aw, we thought some God did powr
Those flouds from out his sacred Jar,
Transforming every Weed into a Flow'r
And every Flower into a Star.

But since it broke it self, and double glides,
The Naked Banks no dress have worn,
And yon dry barren Mountain now derides
These valleys which lost glories mourn.

O Chloris! think how this presents thy Love,
Which when it ran but in one Streame,
We happy Shepheards thence did thrive and prove,
And thou wast mine and all Mens Theme.

But since't hath been imparted to one more,
And in two Streams doth weakly creep,
Our Common Muse is thence grown low, and poor,
And mine as lean as these my Sheep.

But think withall what honour thou hast lost,
Which we did to thy full Stream pay,
Whiles now that Swain that swears he loves thee most,
Slakes but his Thirst, and goes away?

O in what narrow waies our Minds must move!
We may not Hate, nor yet diffuse our Love!

SIR THOMAS URQUHART

211 The First Epigram To the King

Great monarch, since the Worlds Nativitie,
no mind, nor body had so divine parts
to grace the State of Sov'rain Majestie,
as hath your Royal person, whose deserts
  Soare higher 'bove the reach of other kings
  then the bright Sun transcends terrestrial things.

CLEMENT PAMAN

212 *The Distill'd Rose*

I once the flower of flowers, The starre
Which lead each eye my follower;
I whom Queens breasts have nurst 'till I
Grew big to judge of Victorie
I who have spar'd Lovers my leaves
To mend their Tales, but not Deceive,
Who like their Mistresses am best
When I'me thus naked and undrest;
(For what's a distill'd tortured Rose
But scarlett stript out of its cloaths?)
I who have help'd dresse many an herse,
Whom Poets beg'd into their verse;
Almighty Homer wold not scorne
To woe my hand to paint his Morne;
The *Stella's Celia's*, thousands more
Ne're blush or breath but on my score,
Or if they weep or smile, t'is my
Wardrobe must lend them Propertye.
I whose Constant sweets noe fate
Not fire or Death can violate;
I who in case my trifling Beere
Should want a Mourner, turn'd a Teare,

And if the East should spare mee none
I bring Embalments of my owne.
I, who of all my Beautyes have
Nought left me, but this Christall grave,
When now by an unusuall doome
My Body must keepe sweet my Tombe.
Live still and breath more whole delights.
Thus Separation more unites!
The Phaenix Riddle here's unty'de,
She and I live because we dide.
Sometimes to burne a City builds
And those Flames ruine not but guilde.
So Tyrants when they Martyre, trye
But Cruell wayes to Glorify.

212 Title *Distill'd* into perfume 18 *Propertye* literally, clothing, the poets borrow attributes of the rose to describe their mistresses 19 *sweets* delights 26 *Christall grave* perfume bottle 32 *dide* died

SAMSON BRIGGS

213 [Songs of Shephards and rusticall roundelayes]

Songs of Shephards and rusticall roundelayes
Formed of Fancies and whistled on reeds
Sung to solace the Nymphs upon Holydayes
Are to unworthy for wonderfull deedes.
Phoebus ingenious
And witty Silenus
The lofty Genius
May seem to declare
In verse better coyned
And voice more refined
How States divined
Hunted the hare.

Stars inamour'd with pastime Olympicall
Stars and Planetts that beautyfull shone

Would no longer that earthly men only shall
Swim in their pleasures and they but look on.
Round about horned
Lucina thay swarmed
And her informed
How minded they were
Each God and Goddesse
To take humane bodies
Like Lords and Ladies
To follow the hare.

Chaste Diana applauded the motion
And pale Proserpina sate in her place
To lighten the welken and govern the Ocean
While she conducted her Nephews in chase
Who by her example
Their Father to trample
The old and ample
Earth, leaved the Ayre
Neptune the water
The wine Liber Pater
And Mars the slaughter
To follow the hare.

Light God Cupid was hors't upon Pegasus
Borrow'd of Muses with kisses and prayres.
Stout Alcides upon clowdy Caucasus
Mounts a Centaure which proudly him beares
Postillion of the skie
Light heeled Mercury
Maketh his Courser flye
Fleete as the Aire
Yellow Apollo
The Kenell to follow
With Whoop and Hollow
After the hare.

Hymen ushers the Ladyes, Astraea
The just takes hand with Minerva the bold
Ceres the brown with the bright Cytherea
With Thetis the Wanton Bellona the old.

Shamfact Aurora
With subtle Pandora
And Maia with Flora
Did company beare
Juno was stated
Too high to be mated
But ô she hated
Not hunting the hare.

Drown'd Narcissus from his Metamorphosis
Rowsed with Eccho new manhood did take
Snoring Somnus up started in Cimeris
Who for this thousand years was not awake
To see Clubfooted
Old Mulciber booted
And Pan Promooted
To Chirons mare
Proud Faunus powted
Lowd Aeolus showted
And Momus flowted
Yet follow the hare.

Deepe Melampus with cunning Ichnobates,
Nape and Tiger and Harper the Skies
Rend with roaring while hunterlike Hercules
Winded his plentifull horne to theire cryes.
Till with varietyes
Having solac'd their pietyes
The weary Deities
Repos'd them where
Wee shepheards were seated
While that wee repeated
What wee conceited
Of hunting the hare.

Young Amintas suppos'd the Gods came to breath
After some battle themselves on the ground
Thirsis thought the stars came to dwell here beneath
And that hereafter the earth shold go round
Corydon aged
With Phillis ingaged

Was much enraged
With jealous despaire
But fury vaded
And he was perswaded
And I applauded
The hunting the hare.

Stars but shaddows were, State was but sorrow
Had they no motion or that no delight
Joyes are Joviall, Delight is the marrow
Of life, and action the axle of might.
Pleasure depends
Upon no other freinds
And yet freely tends
To each virtue a share
Only I measure
The jewell of pleasure
Of pleasure the treasure
Is hunting the hare.

Fowre broad bowls to th'Olympicall Rector
His Troyeborne Eagle presents on his knee
Jove to Phoebus carowsed in Nectar
And he to Hermes and Hermes to mee
Wherewith infused
I pip'd and I mused
In songs unused
This sport to declare
And now the rouse of Jove
Round as his sphere shall move
A Health to all that love
Hunting the hare.

213 For all classical names, see Appendix 1 1 *roundelayes* songs 2 *reeds* pan pipes 9 *coyned* composed 27 *welken* sky 34 *Liber Pater* Bacchus 37 *Light* flirtatious 39 *Caucasus* mountain range 41 *Postillion* rider (messenger) 43 *Courser* horse 45 *Yellow* as the sun god 46 *Kenell* pack of hounds 53 *Shamfact* blushing 57 *stated* of status 58 *mated* matched, partnered 71 *flowted* joked 74 *Nape* hound name, from Ovid, *Metamorphoses*, III. 214, meaning 'wooded valley' 78 *solac'd* comforted 83 *conceited* thought 93 *vaded* faded

JOHN CLEVELAND

214 *Square-Cap*

Come hither *Apollo's* bouncing Girle,
And in a whole *Hippocrene* of Sherry
Let's drink a round till our braines do whirle,
Tuning our pipes to make our selves merry.
A Cambridge-Lasse, *Venus*-like, borne of the froth
Of an old half-fill'd Jug of Barley broth,
She, she is my Mistris, her Suiters are many,
But shee'l have a *Square-cap* if ere she have any.

And first for the Plush-sake the *Monmouth-cap* coms,
Shaking his head like an empty bottle;
With his new-fangled Oath, *By Iupiter's thumbs*,
That to her health hee'l begin a pottle:
He tells her that after the death of his Grannam,
He shall have—God knowes what *per annum*:
But still she replies, good Sir La-bee,
If ever I have a man, *Square-cap* for mee.

Then Calot-*Leather-cap* strongly pleads,
And faine would derive the pedigree of fashion:
The *Antipodes* weare their shoes on their heads,
And why may not we in their imitation?
Oh, how this foot-ball noddle would please,
If it were but well tost on *S. Thomas* his Lees.
But still she replied, good Sir La-bee,
If ever I have a man, *Square-cap* for me.

Next comes the Puritan in a *wrought-Cap*,
With a long-wasted conscience towards a Sister,
And making a Chappell of Ease of her lap,
First he said grace, and then he kist her.
Beloved, quoth he, thou art my Text,
Then falls he to Use and Application next:
But then she replied, your Text (Sir) I'le be,
For then I'm sure you'l ne'r handle me.

But see where *Sattin-Cap* scouts about,
And faine would this wench in his fellowship marry,
He told her how such a man was not put out,
Because his wedding he closely did carry.
Hee'l purchase Induction by Simonie,
And offers her money her Incumbent to be.
But still she replied, good Sir La-bee,
If ever I have a man *Square-cap* for me.

The Lawyer's a Sophister by his *round-cap*,
Nor in their fallacies are they divided;
The one milks the pocket, the other the tap,
And yet this wench he faine would have brided.
Come leave these thred-bare Schollers, quoth he,
And give me livery and season of thee:
But peace *John-a-Nokes*, and leave your Oration,
For I never will be your Impropriation.
I pray you therefore good Sir La-bee;
For if ever I have a man *Square-cap* for me.

214 1 *Apollo* 2 *Hippocrene* see Appendix 1 8 *Square-cap* university graduate 9 *Monmouth-cap* a soldier 12 *pottle* a half-gallon measure, hence, a large libation 15.*La-bee* let it be, stop it 17 *Calot-Leather-cap* a lawyer 21 *noddle* head 22 *S. Thomas his Lees* playing-field 33 *Sattin-cap* a Clerk in Holy Orders (who loses his College Fellowship if he marries) 37 *Induction by Simonie* pun: 'a Church living' or 'right of entrance' 38 *Incumbent* pun: 'beneficed clergyman' or 'physical possessor' 47 *John-a-Nokes* proverbial name for the common man 48 *Impropriation* (legal) the action of taking possession of, particularly, a church benefice or its revenues

SIR JOHN DENHAM

215 COOPERS HILL.

Sure there are Poets which did never dream
Upon *Parnassus*, nor did tast the stream
Of *Helicon*, we therefore may suppose
Those made not Poets, but the Poets those.
And as Courts make not Kings, but Kings the Court,
So where the Muses and their train resort,

Parnassus stands; if I can be to thee
A Poet, thou *Parnassus* art to me.
Nor wonder, if (advantag'd in my flight,
By taking wing from thy auspicious height)
Through untrac't ways, and aery paths I fly,
More boundless in my Fancy than my eie:
My eye, which swift as thought contracts the space
That lies between, and first salutes the place
Crown'd with that sacred pile, so vast, so high,
That whether 'tis a part of Earth, or sky,
Uncertain seems, and may be thought a proud
Aspiring mountain, or descending cloud,
Pauls, the late theme of such a Muse whose flight M.*W.*
Has bravely reach't and soar'd above thy height:
Now shalt thou stand though sword, or time, or fire,
Or zeal more fierce than they, thy fall conspire,
Secure, whilst thee the best of Poets sings,
Preserv'd from ruine by the best of Kings.
Under his proud survey the City lies,
And like a mist beneath a hill doth rise;
Whose fate and wealth the business and the crowd,
Seems at this distance but a darker cloud:
And is to him who rightly things esteems,
No other in effect than what it seems:
Where, with like hast, though several ways, they run
Some to undo, and some to be undone;
While luxury, and wealth, like war and peace,
Are each the others ruine, and increase;
As Rivers lost in Seas some secret vein
Thence reconveighs, there to be lost again.
Oh happiness of sweet retir'd content!
To be at once secure, and innocent.
Windsor the next (where *Mars* with *Venus* dwells. *Windsor*;
Beauty with strength) above the Valley swells
Into my eye, and doth it self present
With such an easie and unforc't ascent,
That no stupendious precipice denies
Access, no horror turns away our eyes:
But such a Rise, as doth at once invite
A pleasure, and a reverence from the sight.

Thy mighty Masters Embleme, in whose face
Sate meekness, heightned with Majestick Grace
Such seems thy gentle height, made only proud
To be the basis of that pompous load,
Than which, a nobler weight no Mountain bears,
But *Atlas* only that supports the Sphears.
When Natures hand this ground did thus advance,
'Twas guided by a wiser power than Chance;
Mark't out for such a use, as if 'twere meant
T'invite the builder, and his choice prevent.
Nor can we call it choice, when what we chuse
Folly, or blindness only could refuse.
A Crown of such Majestick towrs doth Grace
The Gods great Mother, when her heavenly race
Do homage to her, yet she cannot boast
Amongst that numerous, and Celestial host,
More *Hero's* than can *Windsor*, nor doth Fames
Immortal book record more noble names.
Not to look back so far, to whom this Isle
Owes the first Glory of so brave a pile,
Whether to *Caesar, Albanact,* or *Brute*,
The British *Arthur*, or the Danish *Knute*,
(Though this of old no less contest did move,
Then when for *Homers* birth seven Cities strove)
(Like him in birth, thou should'st be like in fame,
As thine his fate, if mine had been his Flame)
But whosoere it was, Nature design'd
First a brave place, and then as brave a mind.
Not to recount those several Kings, to whom
It gave a Cradle, or to whom a Tombe,
But thee (great *Edward*) and thy greater son,
(The lillies which his Father wore, he won)
And thy *Bellona*, who the Consort came
Not only to thy Bed, but to thy Fame,
She to thy Triumph led one Captive King
And brought that son, which did the second bring.
Then didst thou found that Order (whither love
Or victory thy Royal thoughts did move)
Each was a noble cause, and nothing less,
Than the design, has been the great success:

Edward the third and the *Black Prince*.

Queen *Philip*

The Kings of *France* and *Scotland*

Which forraign Kings, and Emperors esteem
The second honour to their Diadem.
Had thy great Destiny but given thee skill,
To know as well, as power to act her will,
That from those Kings, who then thy captives were,
In after-times should spring a Royal pair
Who should possess all that thy mighty power,
Or thy desires more mighty, did devour;
To whom their better Fate reserves what ere
The Victor hopes for, or the Vanquisht fear;
That bloud, which thou and thy great Grandsire shed,
And all that since these sister Nations bled,
Had been unspilt, had happy *Edward* known
That all the bloud he spilt, had been his own.
When he that Patron chose, in whom are joyn'd
Souldier and Martyr, and his arms confin'd
Within the Azure Circle, he did seem
But to foretell, and prophesie of him,
Who to his Realms that Azure round hath joyn'd,
Which Nature for their bound at first design'd.
That bound, which to the Worlds extreamest ends,
Endless it self, its liquid arms extends;
Nor doth he need those Emblemes which we paint,
But is himself the Souldier and the Saint.
Here should my wonder dwell, and here my praise,
But my fixt thoughts my wandring eye betrays,
Viewing a neighbouring hill, whose top of late
A Chappel crown'd, till in the Common Fate,
The adjoyning Abby fell: (may no such storm
Fall on our times, where ruine must reform.)
Tell me (my Muse) what monstrous dire offence,
What crime could any Christian King incense
To such a rage? was't Luxury, or Lust?
Was he so temperate, so chast, so just?
Were these their crimes? they were his own much more:
But wealth is Crime enough to him that's poor,
Who having spent the Treasures of his Crown,
Condemns their Luxury to feed his own.
And yet this Act, to varnish o're the shame
Of sacriledge, must bear devotions name.

No Crime so bold, but would be understood
A real, or at least a seeming good.
Who fears not to do ill, yet fears the Name,
And free from Conscience, is a slave to Fame.
Thus he the Church at once protects, and spoils:
But Princes swords are sharper than their stiles.
And thus to th'ages past he makes amends,
Their Charity destroys, their Faith defends.
Then did Religion in a lazy Cell,
In empty, airy contemplations dwell;
And like the block, unmoved lay: but ours,
As much too active, like the stork devours.
Is there no temperate Region can be known,
Betwixt their Frigid, and our Torrid Zone?
Could we not wake from that Lethargick dream,
But to be restless in a worse extream?
And for that Lethargy was there no cure,
But to be cast into a Calenture?
Can knowledge have no bound, but must advance
So far, to make us wish for ignorance?
And rather in the dark to grope our way,
Than led by a false guide to erre by day?
Who sees these dismal heaps, but would demand
What barbarous Invader sackt the land?
But when he hears, no Goth, no Turk did bring
This desolation, but a Christian King;
When nothing, but the Name of Zeal, appears
'Twixt our best actions and the worst of theirs,
What does he think our Sacriledge would spare,
When such th'effects of our devotions are?
Parting from thence 'twixt anger, shame, and fear,
Those for whats past, and this for whats too near:
My eye descending from the Hill, surveys
Where *Thames* amongst the wanton vallies strays. *Thames.*
Thames, the most lov'd of all the Oceans sons,
By his old Sire to his embraces runs,
Hasting to pay his tribute to the Sea,
Like mortal life to meet Eternity.
Though with those streams he no resemblance hold,
Whose foam is Amber, and their Gravel Gold;

His genuine, and less guilty wealth t'explore,
Search not his bottom, but survey his shore;
Ore which he kindly spreads his spacious wing,
And hatches plenty for th'ensuing Spring.
Nor then destroys it with too fond a stay,
Like Mothers which their Infants overlay.
Nor with a sudden and impetuous wave,
Like profuse Kings, resumes the wealth he gave.
No unexpected inundations spoyl
The mowers hopes, nor mock the plowmans toyl:
But God-like his unwearied Bounty flows;
First loves to do, then loves the Good he does.
Nor are his Blessings to his banks confin'd,
But free, and common, as the Sea or Wind;
When he to boast, or to disperse his stores
Full of the tributes of his grateful shores,
Visits the world, and in his flying towers
Brings home to us, and makes both *Indies* ours;
Finds wealth where 'tis, bestows it where it wants
Cities in deserts, woods in Cities plants.
So that to us no thing, no place is strange,
While his fair bosom is the worlds exchange.
O could I flow like thee, and make thy stream
My great example, as it is my theme!
Though deep, yet clear, though gentle, yet not dull,
Strong without rage, without ore-flowing full.
Heaven her *Eridanus* no more shall boast,
Whose Fame in thine, like lesser Currents lost,
Thy Nobler streams shall visit *Jove's* aboads,
To shine amongst the Stars, and bath the Gods,
Here Nature, whether more intent to please   The Forrest
Us or her self, with strange varieties,
(For things of wonder give no less delight
To the wise Maker's, than beholders sight.
Though these delights from several causes move
For so our children, thus our friends we love)
Wisely she knew, the harmony of things,
As well as that of sounds, from discords springs.
Such was the discord, which did first disperse
Form, order, beauty through the Universe;

While driness moysture, coldness heat resists,
All that we have, and that we are, subsists.
While the steep horrid roughness of the Wood
Strives with the gentle calmness of the flood.
Such huge extreams when Nature doth unite,
Wonder from thence results, from thence delight
The stream is so transparent, pure, and clear, *Narcissus*
That had the self-enamour'd youth gaz'd here,
So fatally deceiv'd he had not been,
While he the bottom, not his face had seen.
But his proud head the aery Mountain hides
Among the Clouds; his shoulders, and his sides
A shady mantle cloaths; his curled brows
Frown on the gentle stream, which calmly flows,
While winds and storms his lofty forehead beat:
The common fate of all that's high or great.
Low at his foot a spacious plain is plac't,
Between the mountain and the stream embrac't:
Which shade and shelter from the Hill derives,
While the kind river wealth and beauty gives;
And in the mixture of all these appears
Variety, which all the rest indears.
This scene had some bold Greek, or Brittish Bard
Beheld of old, what stories had we heard,
Of Fairies, Satyrs, and the Nymphs their Dames,
Their feasts, their revels, and their amorous flames
'Tis still the same, although their aery shape
All but a quick Poetick sight escape.
There *Faunus* and *Sylvanus* keep their Courts,
And thither all the horned hoast resorts,
To graze the ranker mead, that noble heard
On whose sublime and shady fronts is rear'd
Natures great Master-piece; to shew how soon
Great things are made, but sooner are undone.
Here have I seen the King, when great affairs
Give leave to slacken, and unbend his cares,
Attended to the Chase by all the flower
Of youth, whose hopes a Nobler prey devour:
Pleasure with Prayse, and danger, they would buy,
And wish a foe that would not only fly.

The stagg now conscious of his fatal Growth,
At once indulgent to his fear and sloth,
To some dark covert his retreat had made,
Where nor mans eye, nor heavens should invade
His soft repose; when th'unexpected sound
Of dogs, and men, his wakeful ear doth wound.
Rouz'd with the noise, he scarce believes his ear,
Willing to think th'illusions of his fear
Had given this false Alarm, but straight his view
Confirms, that more than all he fears is true.
Betray'd in all his strength, the wood beset,
All instruments, all Arts of ruine met;
He calls to mind his strength, and then his speed,
His winged heels, and then his armed head;
With these t'avoid, with that his Fate to meet:
But fear prevails, and bids him trust his feet.
So fast he flyes, that his reviewing eye
Has lost the chasers, and his ear the cry;
Exulting, till he finds, their Nobler sense
Their disproportion'd speed does recompense.
Then curses his conspiring feet, whose scent
Betrays that safety which their swiftness lent.
Then tries his friends, among the baser herd,
Where he so lately was obey'd, and fear'd,
His safety seeks: the herd, unkindly wise,
Or chases him from thence, or from him flies.
Like a declining States-man, left forlorn
To his friends pity, and pursuers scorn,
With shame remembers, while himself was one
Of the same herd, himself the same had done.
Thence to the coverts, and the conscious Groves,
The scenes of his past triumphs, and his loves;
Sadly surveying where he rang'd alone
Prince of the soyl, and all the herd his own;
And like a bold Knight Errant did proclaim
Combat to all, and bore away the Dame;
And taught the woods to eccho to the stream
His dreadful challenge, and his clashing beam.
Yet faintly now declines the fatal strife;
So much his love was dearer than his life.

Now every leaf, and every moving breath
Presents a foe, and every foe a death.
Wearied, forsaken, and pursu'd, at last
All safety in despair of safety plac'd,
Courage he thence resumes, resolv'd to bear
All their assaults, since 'tis in vain to fear.
And now too late he wishes for the fight
That strength he wasted in Ignoble flight:
But when he sees the eager chase renew'd,
Himself by dogs, the dogs by men pursu'd:
He straight revokes his bold resolve, and more
Repents his courage, than his fear before;
Finds that uncertain waies unsafest are,
And Doubt a greater mischief than Despair.
Then to the stream, when neither friends, nor force,
Nor speed, nor Art avail, he shapes his course;
Thinks not their rage so desperate t'assay
An Element more merciless than they.
But fearless they pursue, nor can the floud
Quench their dire thirst; alas, they thirst for bloud.
So towards a Ship the oarefin'd Gallies ply,
Which wanting Sea to ride, or wind to fly,
Stands but to fall reveng'd on those that dare
Tempt the last fury of extream despair.
So fares the Stagg among th'enraged Hounds,
Repels their force, and wounds returns for wounds.
And as a Hero, whom his baser foes
In troops surround, now these assails, now those,
Though prodigal of life, disdains to die
By common hands; but if he can descry
Some nobler foes approach, to him he calls,
And begs his Fate, and then contented falls.
So when the King a mortal shaft lets fly
From his unerring hand, then glad to dy,
Proud of the wound, to it resigns his bloud,
And stains the Crystal with a Purple floud.
This a more Innocent, and happy chase,
Than when of old, but in the self-same place
Fair liberty pursu'd, and meant a Prey *Runny Mead where that Great Charter was first sealed*
To lawless power, here turn'd, and stood at bay.

When in that remedy all hope was plac't
Which was, or should have been at least, the last.
Here was that Charter seal'd, wherein the Crown *Magna Charta*
All marks of Arbitrary power lays down:
Tyrant and slave, those names of hate and fear,
The happier stile of King and Subject bear:
Happy, when both to the same Center move,
When Kings give liberty, and Subjects love.
Therefore not long in force this Charter stood;
Wanting that seal, it must be seal'd in bloud.
The Subjects arm'd, the more their Princes gave,
Th'advantage only took the more to crave.
Till Kings by giving, give themselves away,
And even that power, that should deny, betray.
"Who gives constrain'd, but his own fear reviles
"Not thank't, but scorn'd; nor are they gifts, but spoils.
Thus Kings, by grasping more than they could hold,
First made their Subjects by oppression bold:
And popular sway, by forcing Kings to give
More than was fit for Subjects to receive,
Ran to the same extreams; and one excess
Made both, by striving to be greater, less.
When a calm River rais'd with sudden rains,
Or Snows dissolv'd, oreflows th'adjoyning Plains,
The Husbandmen with high-rais'd banks secure
Their greedy hopes, and this he can endure.
But if with Bays and Dams they strive to force
His channel to a new, or narrow course;
No longer then within his banks he dwells,
First to a Torrent, then a Deluge swells:
Stronger, and fiercer by restraint he roars,
And knows no bound, but makes his power his shores.

215 Title *Coopers Hill* in Surrey, near Egham, close to Windsor and Runnymede: a good place from which to contemplate the tensions of Charles's reign. Windsor is the visible symbol of Royal power, Runnymede the site of the signing of the 'constitutional' Magna Carta 2 *Parnassus*, 3 *Helicon* see Appendix 1 10 *auspicious* lucky 15 *pile* building 19 side-note *M.W.* Edmund Waller, in his poem 'Upon his *Majesties* repairing of *Pauls*' 39 *Mars*, *Venus* see Appendix 1 47 *Masters Embleme* Windsor Hill and Castle are Charles I's public visual signifiers, but also the site, inviting 'pleasure' and 'reverence', expresses the nature of the King 50 *pompous* dignified 60 *Mother* Cybele, see Appendix 1 67–8 lists the legendary founders of the castle 78 *lillies* fleur-de-lys, emblem of France: Edward III first quartered the arms of England and France, to assert his claim to France 79 side-note *Queen Philip* see Appendix 2 81 *Captive King* David of Scotland, captured 1356 82 *the second* John of France, captured 1356 83 *that Order* The Order of the Garter, founded 1349 92 *Royal pair* Charles I was descended from the royal house of Scotland, Henrietta Maria from the Bourbons of France 97 *great Grandsire* Edward I 101 *that Patron* St George 102–3 The insignia of the Garter: St George and the dragon within the blue garter of the order 104 *him* Charles I: the following lines develop the kinds of public imagery which surrounded the launch of Charles's great ship 'The Sovereign of the Seas' in 1637 109 Rubens's painting of Charles as St George dates from 1629 113 *neighbouring hill* St Anne's hill, Chertsey 115 *Abby* Chertsey Abbey 118 *King* Henry VIII 131 The title of 'Defender of the Faith' *Fidei defensor* had been conferred by the Pope on the young Henry VIII 132 *stiles* titles, pens 137-8 Aesop's fable of the frogs and their king: dissatisfied with a log, the frogs appeal to Zeus for a new king, he sends a stork which devours them 144 *Calenture* burning fever: delirium 148 *erre* be mistaken, wander 149 *dismal heaps* the ruins of Chertsey 165 *those streams* Tagus and Pactolus 172 *overlay* suffocate asleep 209 *horrid* shaggy 223 *spacious plain* Egham Mead, including Runnymede and Long Mead 237 *ranker* with longer grass 284 *beam* the main trunk of a stag's antlers 303 *assay* try 307 *oarefin'd* with oars like fins 325 side-note King John signed the Magna Carta at Runnymede in 1215: retrospective wishful thinking from the seventeenth century onwards chose to view it as a charter of 'English Liberty' 341–2 The marginal inverted commas indicate sententiae; maxims, detachable proverbs 353 *Bays* embankments

MARY McLEOD

216 *Marbhrann do Fhear na Comraich*

Tha mise air leaghadh le bròn
O'n là dh'eug thu 's nach beò
Mu m'fhiùran faidhidneach còir
Uasal aighearach òg
As uaisle shuidheadh mu bhòrd:
Mo chreach t'fhaighinn gun treòir éirigh.

Is tu an laoch gun laigse gun leòn
Macan mìngheal gun sgleò;
Fearail fìnealta an t-òg
De shliochd nam fear mór
D'am bu dual a bhith còir,
'S gum b'fhiù faiteal do bheòil éisdeachd.

Is tu clann na h-irghinn a b'fheàrr,
Glan an fhriamh as an d'fhàs,
Càirdeas rìgh anns gach ball,
Bha sud sgrìobht' leat am bann
Fo làiṃh duine gun mheang
Ach thu lìonta de àrdan euchdach.

A Ruairidh aigeanntaich àird
O Chomraich ghreadhnaich an àigh,
Mhic an fhir bu mhór gàir
Nan lann guineach cruaidh garg,
Ort cha d'fhuaradh riamh cearb,
Iarogha Uilleam nan long bréidgheal.

Fhuair mi m'àilleagan ùr
Is e gun smal air gun smùr,
Bu bhreac mìndearg do ghnùis,
Bu ghorm laghach do shùil,
Bu ghlan sliasaid is glùn,
Bu deas daingeann an lùb ghleusta thu.

A lùb abhall nam buadh,
Is mairg a tharladh ort uair
Mu Ghlaic Fhionnlaigh so shuas
Air each crodhanta luath,
Nàmhaid romhad 'na ruaig,
Air dhòigh buille cha b'uair éis e.

Ach fhir as curanta làmh
Thug gach duine gu cràdh,
Is truagh nach d'fhuirich thu slàn
Ri uair cumaisg no blàir
Thoirt tilleadh as do nàmh;
Bu leat urram an là cheutaich.

Bu tù an sgoilear gun dìobradh,
Meoir as grinne nì sgriobhadh,
Uasal faidhidneach cinnteach,
Bu leat lagh an tigh-sgrìobhaidh,
Is tu nach mùchadh an fhìrinn;
Sgeul mo chreiche so! shil do chreuchdan.

Stad air m'aighear an dé;
Dh'falbh mo mharcanta féin;
Chuir mi an ciste an teud;
Dhiùlt an gobha dhomh gleus;
Dh'fhairtlich sud orm 's gach léigh,
Is chaid m'onoir, is, mo rìgh, dh'eug thu.

Thuit a'chraobh as a bàrr,
Fhrois an gràinne gu làr,
Lot thu an cinneadh is chràdh
Air an robh thu mar bhàrr
'Gan dìonadh gach là,
Is mo chreach, bhuinig am bàs teum ort.

An àm suidhe 'nad sheòmar
Chaidh do bhuidheann an òrdugh,
Cha b'ann mu aighear do phòsaidh
Le nighean Iarla Chlann Dòmhnaill
As do dhéidh mar bu chòir dhi;
Is ann chaidh do thasgaidh 'san t-sròl fo d'léine.

Ach gur mise that bochd truagh,
Fiamh a' ghuil air mo ghruaidh;
Is goirt an gradan a fhuair,
Marcach deas nan each luath,
Sàr cheannard air sluagh,
Mo chreach, t'fhàgail ri uair m'fheime.

Ach fhuair mi m'àilleagan òg
Mar nach b'àbhaist gun cheòl,
Saoir ri spìonadh an fheòir,
Fir gun tàilisg gun cheòl;
Gur bochd fulang mo sgeòil éisdeachd.

An uair a thionail an sluagh
Is ann bha an t-iomsgaradh cruaidh
Mar ghàir sheillean am bruaich
An déidh ne meala thoirt uath;
Is ann bha an t-eireadh bochd truagh
Is iad mu cheannas an t-sluaigh threubhaich.

216 Elegy for the Laird of Applecross

Since you are dead and no longer living, I am melted with grief for my kindly patient youth, noble, merry, and young, that sat as the stateliest around a table: alas, to find you without strength to rise. You were a warrior without feebleness or hurt, a smooth, fair-skinned gallant without boasting, a high-souled manly scion of the stock of great men; it was native to you to be true, and the speech of your mouth was worthy to hear. You were a child of the noblest lady, the stock from which you grew was pure; kinship with kings showed in your every member, and you held that charter under the seal of a man without guile; you were filled with the pride of prowess. You, noble towering Roderick out of majestic, blessed Applecross, son of the loud-shouting hero of tough, stern, wounding swordblades, never a blemish was found on you, grandson of William of the white-sailed galleys. I found that my fresh, young darling was without spot, without gloom, his face was freckled, smooth and ruddy, his eye blue and charming, his knee and thigh were shapely, he was a trim youth, comely and firm. Scion of the apple-tree of virtues, woe to him who once happened upon you on your swift, strong-hoofed horse here by Finlay's Hollow! Your enemy fled in rout before you, it was no time for him to linger, for dread of your smiting. But you, whose warlike hand brought every foe to anguish, alas that you have not remained hale and strong against the hour of battle-tumult, to put your enemies to flight; you would win the honour of that glorious day. You were an unfailing scholar, your fingers skilled to write; you were noble, patient, steadfast; you knew the rules of the writing-house, you would not stifle the truth—to hear that your wounds have dripped blood is news of my own despoiling.

Yesterday my gladness came to a close; my dear knight departed, I laid aside my harp, music was denied me; I and every physician were baffled, and so my honour is departed and you, my king, are dead. The tree has fallen headlong, the grain has showered to earth, the people over whom you stood pre-eminent, protecting them at all times, are wounded and anguished for your sake; alas, death has inflicted his bite upon you. When they sat in your chamber, your company arrayed themselves not in readiness for the joy of your wedding, with the daughter of the earl of Clan Donald seeking after you as was right—not so; you were arrayed in a satin shroud beneath your shirt. O it is I that am sad and sorrowful, the tinge of weeping is on my cheek! Sore is the bitter pang that I have suffered; comely rider of swift steeds, prime leader over a host, alas that you have forsaken me in my time of need! But I have found my young dear one without music, as was not the custom, carpenters making your coffin, the women plucking grass, the men without music or chess-playing; it is grievous to hear the sorrow of my news. When the folk gathered, there they suffered a bitter parting, as bees in a bank cry loudly when their honey has been taken from them; as they surrounded the captain of the heroic host, mournful and wretched was their burden.

216 Title *Fhear na Comraich / Lord of Applecross* Roderick MacKenzie of Applecross, died 1646 13 *h-irghinn a b'fheàrr / the noblest lady* Annabella, daughter of Murdoch MacKenzie of Fairburn 21 *fhir bu mhór gàir / the loud-shouting hero* Alexander MacKenzie of Coul and Applecross, whose son predeceased him

ABRAHAM COWLEY

217 *The Swallow*

Foolish *Prater*, what do'st thou
So early at my window do
With thy tuneless *Serenade*?
Well t'had been had *Tereus* made
Thee as *Dumb* as *Philomel*;
There his Knife had done but well.
In thy undiscover'ed Nest
Thou dost all the winter rest,
And dream'est ore thy summer joys
Free from the stormy seasons noise:
Free from th'Ill thou'st done to me;
Who disturbs, or seeks out *Thee*?
Had'st thou all the charming notes
Of all the woods *Poetick Throats*,
All thy art could never pay
What thou'st ta'ne from me away;
Cruel *Bird*, thou'st ta'ne away
A *Dream* out of my arms to day,
A *Dream* that ne're must equal'd bee
By all that *waking Eyes* may see.
Thou this damage to repaire,
Nothing half so sweet or faire,
Nothing half so good can'st bring,
Though men say, *Thou bring'st the Spring*.

217 A translation from the Greek of Anacreon, a poem also translated by Thomas Stanley 1 *Prater* chatterer 3 *Serenade* song below the window of the beloved, an evening song

ALEXANDER BROME

218 SONG XV

To his Friend that had vow'd Small-Bear.

1.

Leave off fond *Hermite*, leave thy vow,
And fall again to *drinking*
That *beautie* that wont *sack* allow,
Is hardly worth thy thinking,
Dry love or *small* can never hold,
And without *Bacchus Venus* soon grows cold.

2.

Doest think by turning *Anchorite*;
Or a dull *small-Bear* sinner,
Thy cold embraces can invite,
Or sprightless *Courtship* win her?
No, 'tis *Canary* that inspires,
'Tis *Sack*, like *Oyle*, gives *Flames* to am'rous *Fiers*.

3.

This makes thee *chant* thy Mistresse name,
And to the heavens to raise her;
And range this universal frame
For *Epithets* to praise her.
Low liquours render brains unwitty,
And ne're provoke to *love*, but move to pity.

4.

Then be thy self, and take thy *Glasse*,
Leave off this dry *Devotion*,
Thou must like *Neptune* court thy lass,
Wallowing in *Nectars* Ocean,
Let's offer at each Ladies shrine,
A full crown'd bowl, first here's a health to thine.

218 Title *Small-Bear* thin, weak beer: the friend has presumably forsworn all stronger drink at the instigation of his mistress 3 *sack* strong wine 6 a widely used Latin tag 'Sine Cerere et Baccho friget Venus': 'Without Ceres (food) and Bacchus (wine) Venus (love) grows cold', Terence, *Eunuchus*, 732 7 *Anchorite* recluse, hermit 11 *Canary* sweet fortified wine from the Canary Islands 13 *chant* sing 21 *Neptune* see Appendix 1 22 *Nectar* the drink of the classical gods

MARGARET CAVENDISH, DUCHESS OF NEWCASTLE

219 *The Poetresses hasty Resolution*

Reading my Verses, I like't them so well,
Selfe-love did make my *Iudgement* to rebell.
Thinking them so good, I thought more to write;
Considering not how others would them like.
I writ so fast, I thought, if I liv'd long,
A *Pyramid* of *Fame* to build thereon.
Reason observing which way I was bent,
Did stay my hand, and ask't me what I meant;
Will you, said shee, thus waste your time in vaine,
On that which in the World small praise shall gaine?
For shame leave off, sayd shee, the *Printer* spare,
Hee'le loose by your *ill Poetry*, I feare
Besides the World hath already such a *weight*
Of uselesse Bookes, as it is over fraught.
Then pitty take, doe the World a good turne,
And all you write cast in the fire, and burne.
Angry I was, and *Reason* strook away,
When I did heare, what shee to me did say.
Then all in haste I to the *Presse* it sent,
Fearing *Perswasion* might my *Book* prevent:
But now 'tis done, with greife repent doe I,
Hang down my *head* with *shame, blush sigh*, and *cry*.
Take pitty, and my drooping *Spirits* raise,
Wipe off my *teares* with *Handkerchiefes* of *Praise*.

219 6 *Pyramid* monument; this line echoes the famous opening of Horace, *Odes*, III. 30 'Exegi monumentum aere perennius': 'I have made (in my poetry) a monument which will outlast bronze' 14 *fraught* laden 17 *strook* struck, brushed

220 *An excuse for so much writ upon my Verses.*

Condemne me not for making such a coyle
About my *Book*, alas it is my *Childe*.
Just like a *Bird*, when her *Young* are in Nest,
Goes in, and out, and hops and takes no Rest;
But when their *Young* are fledg'd, their heads out peep,
Lord what a chirping does the *Old* one keep.
So I, for feare my *Strengthlesse Childe* should fall
Against a doore, or stoole, aloud I call,
Bid have a care of such a dangerous place:
Thus write I much, to hinder all *disgrace*.

220 1 *coyle* fuss

MATTHEW STEVENSON

221 *The Song* [for the Florists' Feast at Norwich]

Stay! O stay! ye winged howers,
The windes that ransack East and West,
Have breathed perfumes upon our flowers,
More fragrant then the *Phoenix* nest:
Then stay! O stay sweet howers! that yee,
May witnesse that, which time nere see.

Stay a while, thou featherd Syth-man,
And attend the Queen of flowers,
Show thyself for once a blyth man,
Come dispence with a few howers:
Else we our selves will stay a while,
And make our pastime, *Time* beguile.

This day is deignd to *Floras* use,
If yee will revel too, to night
Weel presse the Grape, to lend ye juyce,
Shall make a deluge of delight:

And when yee cant hold up your heads,
Our Garden shall afford ye beds.

221 See Notes on the Text for the occasion of this poem 7 *featherd Syth-man* Time, personified with wings and a scythe 13 *Flora* goddess of flowers 16 *deluge* flood

222 *In prayse of winter*

Honour and Age inhabit the same spheare,
Winter is the antiquity of the yeare:
Grave signiour Hyems, so his hoary pate,
And snowy beard, denounce his aged state.
See but how like a statlye traveller,
Northward hee comes; Autumne's his harbinger,
That bids the trees unmask, unveyle their creasts,
That he may read submission on their breasts;
Whilst their green offspring lowly fall, to greet
The potent presence of his stable feet.
The gawdy bankes pack up alas! here comes
No midwife *Aprill*, to unteeme their wombs.
Nay here the showr'd down waters, stand amaz'd,
Rivers are Chrystallin'd, *Neptune's* hall is glaz'd,
Spouts have their pendents, paultry thatch receives
Translucent Chrystall, And adornes his Eaves.
Leda's a fable, but I here presume
To justifie, that *Jove* descends in plume.
And that the stupid earth may know he comes,
The Heavens send down whole showers of Sugar plums,
Whilst streets are pav'd with Pearl: Let summer boast
Such pomp, such cates, and all my praise is lost.
But here's not all of winter: you shall see
His providence for mortall wights, whilst hee
Locks up the graine in bosome of the Earth,
Till *Ceres* blesse it with a thriving birth.
How would the blade endure th'Aeolian tugge,
But winter guards it with his snow-white rugge?

We may conclude his power, in that he can
Enjoyne the Alps a pennance as a man.
The saucie Dust checkt into mud, and mire,
Merits no mention, our reports are higher:
Summer breeds surfets, and infects the bloud,
Winter is haile againe, and makes all good:
Is beauty of esteem? then winter can
Boast, hee abstergeth Summers freckled tan:
Ladies so spruce to captivate mens sight,
Borrow March winds to make that spruceness white.
Winter makes men couragious, who dare
Dance upon *Thetis* lap at midsummer.
In Summers dayes even length, and lazinesse meet,
Winters are short, The Proverbs, short and sweet.
Theres none so bad to be call'd dog-dayes here,
No no we move not in so base a spheare:
No scorching Sun offends, any man may
With a good faggot make a Summers day.
What entertainment to a winters toast?
What Christmasse, pray, can *June* or *July* boast?
Summer alas hath no Aeolian breath,
To rescue his perishing souls from death,
Flame-coloured hearth, even ready to expire,
Looks pale as ashes, Sol puts out the fire,
Trees strait are lopt then and their verdant locks
Borrow'd to border out the Chymnie stocks;
Set out with trunks of trees, stumps, armes and all,
As if the Chymnie were some Hospitall:
In winter time the hearth stands alter wise,
And men with hands erected sacrifice.
Whilst in a round the priests of *Bacchus* sing
Ingenious Anthems, to their grape-crownd King:
In winter men at cold meat make a pish,
In Summer they are glad of such a dish;
Winter hath boyld, and bak't, and roast, Alas!
Summer turnes men, as men do beasts, to grasse.
Winter makes warres oft cease, who would not that
If peace and plenty have no praise, then what?
I might enlarge myself, but thus farre may,
Suffice to travell on a winters day.

Who likes not this, a gods name let him run
Out of Gods blessings, into the warm sun.

222 3 *Hyems* (Latin) winter personified, see Appendix 1 *hoary* grizzled 6 *harbinger* advance rider bringing warning of arrivals 9 *green offspring* leaves 12 *unteeme* deliver 18 *plume* shower of snow, like the shower of gold in which Jove descended to Danae, like the swan's feathers in which he descended to Leda, see Appendix 1 22 *cates* delights, delicacies 24 *wights* beings, men 27 *Aeolian tugge* the pull of the wind 30 that is, cause them to dress in the white sheet of the penitent 33 *surfets* excesses 36 *abstergeth* cleanses 40 *Thetis lap* the sea, see Appendix 1 42 *Proverbs* winter days, like proverbs, are short and sweet 46 *faggot* bundle of firewood 53 *verdant* green 54 *Chymnie stocks* fire-irons 60 *Ingenious* inspired 61 *pish* expression of scorn

ANNE KEMP

223 A Contemplation on Bassets down-Hill* by the most Sacred adorer of the Muses Mrs. A. K.

If that exact Appelles now did live,
And would a picture of Elizium give;
He might portrai'ct the prospect which this Hill
Doth show; and make the eie command at will.
Heer's many a shire whose pleasauntries for sight
Doth yield to the Spectators great delight.
Ther's a large Feild guilded with Ceres gold;
Here a green mead doth many Heifers hold:
Ther's pasture growne with virdant grass, whose store,
Of Argent-sheep shews th'owner is not poore.
Here springs doe intricate Meanders make
Excelling farr oblivion's Lethe Lake.
There woods and coppises harbour as many
And sweet melodious Choristers, as any
Elizium yields; whose Philomel'an laies
Merit the highest of the Lyrick's praise
Heer's Flora deckt with robes of Or, and Azur,
Fragrantly smelling yeild's two senses pleasure.
Hence Zephirus doth breath his gentle gales
Coole on the Hills, and sweet throughout the vales

How happy are they that in this climate dwell?
Alas! they can't their owne sweet welfare tell;
Scarce I myselfe whil'st I am here doe know it
Till I see its Antithesis to shew it.
Here are no smoaking streets, nor howling cryes,
Deafning the eares, nor blinding of the eyes,
No noys orre smells t'infect, and choake the aire,
Breeding diseases envious to the faire.
Deceipt is here exil'd from Flesh, and Bloud:
(Strife only reigns, for all strive to be good.)
With Will his verse, I here will make an end
And as the crab doth alwaies backward bend
So, thogh from this sweet place I goe away
My loyal heart will in this Climate stay.
Thus heartless doth my worthless body rest
Whilest my hart liveth with the ever blest.

* neare Meysay Hampton or Down-Ampney in Glocestershire

223 1 *Appelles* 2 *Elizium* see Appendix 1 7 *Ceres gold* ripe corn 8 *mead* meadow 9 *virdant* green 10 *Argent* heraldic term for silver(-fleeced) 15 *Philomel'an* like Philomel (the nightingale) 17 *Or, Azur* heraldic terms for gold and blue 19 *Zephirus* see Appendix 1 30 *Strife* discord *strive* try hard 31 *Will* this is unclear, possibly the preceding couplet is a quotation from another poet in Anne Kemp's circle; possibly Will is a generic shepherd who is supposed to have spoken a number of the preceding lines 34 *loyal heart* there is an implication here that her removal from Gloucestershire is in some way enforced by the circumstances of the times

THOMAS STANLEY

224 SYLVIA'S PARK.

Apollo (Poets say) his Beam
On all that court his Name bestows;
And knowledg in his vales smooth stream,
Into their quickned Spirits flows;
But our chaste Muse is unbeguil'd,
Phoebus eternally exil'd

From her sublimer Poesy;
Those Temples now are overthrown,
And all the Daemons they did own
In their dumb ruines buried ly.

Those dark Impostors shall no more
Intrap us in their dangerous snares;
A Power Celestial We implore,
Enthron'd above the highest Starres:
From this Divinity alone
(The Bound of all Devotion)
Have I receiv'd a hallowed flame,
Which learns my humble Soul to rise,
And bids her aim at such a Prize,
As may inherit deathlesse Fame.

Then we an Image so divine
Of his bright Glories will reherse,
That Heav'n it self shall gladly joyn,
To justifie our sacred Verse.
For next the Altar, at whose fire
Falls prostrate the Seraphick Quire,
And Eccho their harmonious Layes,
We with a thought as innocent,
To a chaste Beauty may present
The fragrant Incense of our Praise.

Thus *Sylvia* from the just presage
Of my unspotted vows, shall claim
That lasting sound, which every Age
To come, a second Life will name,
But if cross Fate my verse cast down,
Ecclipsing by some Potent frown
The sacred Reliques of her Glory,
These Waters, every Rock, and Grove,
Assuming Soul, and Speech, will prove
Faithful Recorders of her Story.

If Trees that were of old renown'd
By impious Adoration, took
New spirit, and articulate sound,
From weak *Diana's* sickly look;
If Rivers, as along they glide,
Spoke in the Murmurs of their Tide,
What Fauns, or Fairies did inspire;
If Stubborn Rocks and senseless Stones,
Could melt with Pitty, and in Grones
Keep time with *Orpheus* charming Lyre.

What stranger hardness must possess
The object by my Princess grac'd,
If quickned by that happiness,
To voice its Joyes it do not haste?
Through this proud structures daz'ling Hight,
Through this sweet Walks secure delight,
What Marble can so solid be,
But is transparent to her Eye?
What Trees and Fountains stealing by,
But her own for a Deity?

Those Oaks that most obdurate are,
Shall willingly their arms unwind;
And by themselves ungraven wear
My verse upon their Leaves, and Rind:
And every Tree, whose Top prefers
To Heaven these sacred Characters,
No storms shall offer to invade.
For whilst thus charm'd, the rough Winds may
Hope with more ease, to snatch away
Their fastned Roots, or fleeting shade.

These floating Mirrours, on whose Brow
Their various figures gently glide,
For love of her shall gently grow,
In faithful Icy fetters ty'd.
This cheerful Brooks unwrinkled face,
Shall smile within its Christal case,
To see it self made permanent,
And from Times rage secur'd, the deep

Impression of my Cyphers keep,
  And my fair Princess form present.

But her unequal Praise requires
  More Pens then ours to set her forth:
Behold how Heaven it self conspires
  O're all the World to paint her forth!
In the bright Sun her eyes are drawn;
In the fresh Beauties of the Dawn,
  Those of her blushing cheek appear:
No Power her Vertues can deface,
Until the Heavens forsake their place,
  And darkned Stars drop from their sphear.

One evening, when the Azure Main
  Its softer Litter did prepare
For the bright Steeds which draw the Wain
  Of weary Day's declining Star,
By chance the Bed I did survey
Whereon a sleeping Naiad lay,
  And *Sylvia* angling in the Brook:
There I beheld the Fishes strife,
Which first should sacrifice its life,
  To be the Trophey of her Hook.

Whilst with one hand the Line she cast,
  Commanding Silence with the other,
Her signe the Day obeying, past
  More slily by her dusky Brother.
The doubtful Sun with equal awe,
Fear'd to approach or to withdraw:
  The intentive Stars suspend their glowing.
No Rage the quiet Billows swell'd,
Favonius his soft breath withheld,
  The listning Grass refrain'd from growing.

Her sparkling Eyes, a subtle fire
  Through the undreaded streams transmit:
Whose radiant flame the waves admire,
  Not daring to extinguish it.

These warring Elements (their wild
Dissention gladly reconcil'd)
   Submit to her imperious Eye:
Her anger fearing to excite,
Lay down their own, forgetting quite
   Their old inherent Enmity.

Soon as the Tritons her bright face
   Did through their fluid windows view,
The flaming object did displace
   Their humid forms, to give them new,
Whilst, with amazement extaside,
About them creeps a Stags rough hide,
   And their devested figure vails:
Now wondring whence their young horns sprout,
Or how their rugged coat buds out,
   Through the smooth hardness of their scales.

Griev'd at this Fate unkindly strange,
   Which fixing branches on their brows,
These Deities to Beasts doth change,
   And down their bashful foreheads bows;
The treacherous water they forsake,
And to the Land themselves betake,
   Where trees their gloomy lodging shade,
There walk with discontented look,
Their shadow onely to that Brook
   Now trusting, which themselves betray'd.

The Suns bright sister, Poets say,
   Nature with newer power enclosed;
And in this figure did array
   Acteon, his old shape depos'd.
The same inglorious punishment
Which to a Man, a Goddess sent,
   For his profanely curious sight,
The Gods themselves have suffer'd here;
Who with bold eyes ventur'd too near
   Our chaste *Dianas* greater light.

These dear pursued by fear, and shame,
   Which from the walks and alleys drive them,
Their own deceitful fortunes blame,
   That of their wonted cold deprive them.
Their hearts are now of moisture drain'd,
Nor but with timerousness restrain'd,
   Look they to Heaven, or on Earth tread:
For oft as *Sylvia* passeth by,
She lightning darts from her black eye,
   Threatning the war which still they dread.

Yet happy, and o'rejoyd are they,
   To breath the air which she respires;
Living subjected to her sway,
   Fate now exceeds their proud desires.
The Princess, when she did devest
Their ancient forms, of new possest,
   A snowy whiteness made them bear:
Kindly bestowing on their grief,
The priviledge of this relief,
   They alwayes should her livery wear.

Here a close Valley Trees protect,
   With twisted branches overlai'd:
To which the Sun bears much respect,
   He never violates their shade.
To wait on whom, on either side,
Two purling Rivers gently glide.
   A lazy Lake sleeps at his feet,
Rous'd from his sluggish dreams by these
Self-chasing sister-Naïades,
   Who kindly in his Bosom meet.

A thousand little Cupids here,
   Aside their Bows and Quivers laid,
When Night is by their eyes made cleer,
   Into the glittering Water wade.
Hither the *Nereïds* resort,
To bath their purer Limbs, to sport,

And with the Loves raise harmless wars,
Diana from her silver Wain
Descending, leaves her drowsie Swain,
To swim amongst these naked Stars.

Ith midst is plac'd a little Isle,
Crownd by an Arbours shady Crest,
Where Spring eternal seems to smile,
With flowers by careful Nature drest.
Hither each morn, and night, repair
The featherd Choristers oth'air,
To give their various passions vent:
The Nightingale above the rest,
Her joyes in this soft language drest,
Doth to fair *Sylvias* ear present.

I, who so oft the Eastern Bowers
Visit, my sacred Hymns to sing;
And view the spicy sweets, the Flowers,
With all the rich Embellishing
Of Gold, Pearls, Rubies, which the Morn
Takes her fair Tresses to adorn;
And that bright flame with which she dies
(Stoln from the Sun) her pale Cheeks,
When she to seem most lovely seeks
In her deer *Cephalus* his Eyes.

Daily the Woods fair Queen I see
With nimble feet the Thickets trace,
Who, list'ning to my Harmony,
Stands often still, and leaves the Chace.
But I the Heavens, and Gods attest,
By whom with Life and Musick blest;
Thy Eyes, in their least glance, disclose
More Beauties, a diviner fire,
And in my Song more Life inspire,
Then all the Grace that either owes.

Enough, enough, sweet *Philomel*!
  We now this happy Park must leave;
In every part such Beauties dwell,
  As our too bold attempt deceive.
Each drop that from these Fountains flows,
Each Flower that in these Gardens grows,
  The fruit on every Tree or Wall,
Are the just subject of all praise:
What then must be the glorious raies,
  Of *Sylvias* Eyes, that guild them all.

224 Title see Notes on the Text 1 *Beam* sunbeam, poetic inspiration 5 *chaste Muse* Christian muse, refusing the pagan machinery of Baroque poetry *unbeguil'd* not deceived 18 *learns* teaches 26 *Seraphick Quire* choir of angels 27 *Layes* songs 42 *impious Adoration* pagan worship of nature 44 *Diana's* pale moonlight 53 *quickned* brought to life 61 *obdurate* stubborn 64 *Rind* bark 79 *Cyphers* writings; words of power because dedicated to his patroness 91 *Azure Main* blue sea 92 *Litter* the stabling for the horses which draw the chariot of the sun 93 *Steeds* horses *Wain* cart, chariot 104 *dusky Brother* night 109 *Favonius* the west wind, see Appendix 1 127 *devested* unclothed (of their familiar shape) *vails* covers 130 *scales* the fish-tails of the Tritons now changing into deer 144 *Acteon* see Appendix 1 146 *a Goddess* Diana, see Appendix 1 151 *dear* deer 154 *wonted* usual 170 *livery* uniform of her (heraldic) colours 176 *purling* moving with the sound of water 189 *Swain* Endymion, see Appendix 1 190 *Stars* the water nymphs 210 *deer* beloved *Cephalus* see Appendix 1 214 *Chace* hunt 221 *Philomel* the nightingale 230 *guild* gild

CHARLES COTTON

225 *To my dear and most worthy Friend, Mr.* Isaac Walton.

Whilst in this cold and blust'ring Clime,
    Where bleak winds howl, and Tempests roar,
We pass away the roughest time
    Has been of many years before;

Whilst from the most tempest'ous Nooks
    The chillest Blasts our peace invade,
And by great Rains our smallest Brooks
    Are almost navigable made;

Whilst all the ills are so improv'd
        Of this dead quarter of the year,
That even you, so much belov'd,
        We would not now wish with us here;

In this estate, I say, it is
        Some comfort to us to suppose,
That in a better Clime than this
        You our dear Friend have more repose;

And some delight to me the while,
        Though nature now does weep in Rain,
To think that I have seen her smile,
        And haply may I do again.

If the all-ruling Power please
        We live to see another *May*,
We'll recompence an Age of these
        Foul days in one fine fishing day:

We then shall have a day or two,
        Perhaps a week, wherein to try,
What the best Master's hand can doe
        With the most deadly killing Flie:

A day without too bright a Beam,
        A warm, but not a scorching Sun,
A Southern gale to curl the Stream,
        And (Master) half our work is done.

There whilst behind some bush we wait
        The Scaly People to betray,
We'll prove it just with treach'rous Bait
        To make the preying Trout our prey;

And think our selves in such an hour
        Happier than those, though not so high,
Who, like Leviathans, devour
        Of meaner men the smaller Fry.

This (my best Friend) at my poor Home
Shall be our Pastime and our Theme,
But then should you not deign to come
You make all this a flatt'ring Dream.

225 This poem, with its half-reference to Horace, *Odes*, I. 9 (see no. 296), is still a poem of the years of peace, though the same nexus of imagery frequently occurs in royalist poems of consolation in adversity 8 *navigable* deep enough to sail on 20 *haply* maybe 34 *Scaly People* fish 39 *Leviathans* sea monsters 40 *Fry* the smallest fish

226 *The Retirement. Stanzes Irreguliers.* To Mr. *Isaak Walton.*

I.

Farewell thou busie World, and may
We never meet again:
Here I can eat, and sleep, and pray,
And doe more good in one short day,
Than he who his whole Age out-wears
Upon thy most conspicuous theatres,
Where nought but Vice and Vanity do reign.

II.

Good God! how sweet are all things here!
How beautifull the Fields appear!
How cleanly do we feed and lie!
Lord! what good hours do we keep!
How quietly we sleep!
What Peace! what Unanimity!
How innocent from the leud Fashion,
Is all our bus'ness, all our Conversation!

III.

Oh how happy here's our leisure!
Oh how innocent our pleasure!
Oh ye Vallies, oh ye Mountains,
Oh ye Groves and Chrystall Fountains,
How I love at liberty,
By turn to come and visit ye!

IV.

O Solitude, the Soul's best Friend,
That man acquainted with himself dost make,
And all his Maker's Wonders to intend;
With thee I here converse at will,
And would be glad to do so still;
For it is thou alone that keep'st the Soul awake.

V.

How calm and quiet a delight
It is alone
To read, and meditate, and write,
By none offended, nor offending none;
To walk, ride, sit, or sleep at one's own ease,
And pleasing a man's self, none other to displease!

VI.

Oh my beloved Nymph! fair Dove,
Princess of Rivers, how I love
Upon thy flow'ry Banks to lie,
And view thy Silver stream,
When gilded by a Summer's Beam,
And in it all thy wanton Fry
Playing at liberty,
And with my Angle upon them,
The All of Treachery
I ever learn'd to practise and to try!

VII.

Such streams *Rome*'s yellow *Tiber* cannot show,
Th'*Iberian Tagus*, nor *Ligurian Po*;
The *Meuse*, the *Danube*, and the *Rhine*,
Are puddle-water all compar'd with thine;
And *Loire*'s pure streams yet too polluted are
With thine much purer to compare:
The rapid *Garonne*, and the winding *Seine*
Are both too mean,
Beloved Dove, with thee
To vie Priority:

Nay, *Tame* and *Isis*, when conjoyn'd, submit,
And lay their Trophies at thy Silver Feet.

VIII.

Oh my beloved Rocks! that rise
To awe the Earth, and brave the Skies,
From some aspiring Mountain's crown
How dearly do I love,
Giddy with pleasure, to look down,
And from the Vales to view the noble heights above!

IX.

Oh my beloved Caves! from Dog-star heats,
And hotter Persecution safe Retreats,
What safety, privacy, what true delight
In the artificial Night
Your gloomy entrails make,
Have I taken, do I take!
How oft, when grief has made me fly
To hide me from Society,
Even of my dearest Friends, have I
In your recesses friendly shade
All my sorrows open laid,
And my most secret woes entrusted to your privacy!

X.

Lord! would men let me alone,
What an over-happy one
Should I think my self to be,
Might I in this desart place,
Which most men by their voice disgrace,
Live but undisturb'd and free!
Here in this despis'd recess
Would I maugre Winter's cold,
And the Summer's worst excess,
Try to live out to sixty full years old,
And all the while
Without an envious eye

On any thriving under Fortune's smile,
Contented live, and then contented die.

226 Title *Irreguliers* verses with lines of uneven length 34 *Dove* the river Dove, in Derbyshire 42 *The All* i.e. deceiving the fish while angling is the only deceit which he knows 44–50 the chief rivers of Europe: *Po* and *Tiber* in Italy; *Tagus* in Spain and Portugal; *Meuse*, *Danube*, and *Rhine* in the Low Countries and Germany; *Loire*, *Garonne*, and *Seine* in France 53 *Priority* precedence 54 *Tame and Isis* which join at Oxford to make the Thames 62 *Dog-star* the star Sirius, anciently thought to produce conditions of unhealthy summer heat when it rose in conjunction with the sun 77 *desart* deserted, uncultivated 81 *maugre* despite

KATHERINE PHILIPS

227 *Invitation to the Country*

Be kind, my dear *Rosania*, though 'tis true
Thy Friendship will become thy Penance too;
Though there be nothing can reward the pain,
Nothing to satisfie or entertain;
Though all be empty, wild, and like to me,
Who make new Troubles in my Company:
Yet is the action more obliging great;
'Tis Hardship only makes Desert complete.
But yet to prove Mixtures all things compound,
There may in this be some advantage found;
For a Retirement from the noise of Towns,
Is that for which some Kings have left their Crowns:
And Conquerours, whose Laurel prest the brow,
Have chang'd it for the quiet Myrtle-bow.
For Titles, Honours, and the World's Address,
Are things too cheap to make up Happiness;
The easie Tribute of a giddy race,
And pay'd less to the Person then the place.
So false reflected and so short content
Is that which Fortune and Opinion lent,

That who most try'd it have of Fate complain'd,
With Titles burthen'd and to greatness chain'd.
For they alone enjoy'd what they possest,
Who relisht most and understood it best.
And yet that understanding made them know
The empty swift dispatch of all below.
So that what most can outward things endear,
Is the best means to make them disappear:
And even the Tyrant (Sense) doth these destroy,
As more officious to our Grief then Joy.
Thus all the glittering World is but a cheat,
Obtruding on our Sense things Gross for Great.
But he that can enquire and undisguise,
Will soon perceive the sting that hidden lies;
And find no Joys merit esteem but those
Whose Scene lies only at our own dispose.
Man unconcern'd without himself may be
His own both Prospect and Security.
Kings may be Slaves by their own Passions hurl'd,
But who commands himself commands the World.
A Country-life assists this study best,
Where no distractions do the Soul arrest:
There Heav'n and Earth lie open to our view,
There we search Nature and its Author too;
Possest with Freedom and a real State
Look down on Vice, and Vanity, and Fate.
There (my *Rosania*) will we, mingling Souls,
Pity the Folly which the World controuls;
And all those *Grandeurs* which the World do prize
We either can enjoy, or will despise.

227 1 *Rosania* invented name 8 *Desert* deserving 14 *quiet Myrtle-bow* wreath of myrtle, see Appendix 1 32 *Obtruding* forcing 49 *Grandeurs* (French) splendours

PART FIVE

POEMS OF WAR AND REVOLUTION

228 *A Letany for the New-year*

From all and more than I have written here,
I wish you well protected this *New-year*,
From *Civil* war, and such *uncivil* things
As ruine *Law* and *Gospel, Priests* and *Kings;*
From those who for *self-ends* would all betray,
And such new *Saints* that *Pistol* when they *pray*,
From flattering *Faces* with infernal *Souls*,
From new *Reformers*, such as pull down *Pauls*,
From *Linsywoolsy Lords*, from *Town* betrayers,
From *Apron Preachers*, and *extempore* Prayers,
From *Pulpit*-blasphemy and bold *Rebellion*,
From *Bloud* and—somethings else that I could tell ye on.
From new false *Teachers* which destroy the *old*,
From those that turn the *Gospel* into *Gold,*
From that black *Pack* where Clubs are alwayes *Trump*
From *Bodies Politique* and from the *Rump*,
From those that *ruine* when they should *repair*,
From such as cut off *Heads* instead of *Hair*,
From twelve months *Taxes* and abortive *Votes,*
From chargeable *Nurse-Children* in *red Coats*,
From such as sell their *Souls* to save their *Sums*,
From City *Charters* that make Heads for *Drums*,
From *Magistrates* which have not truth or knowledge
From the *red students* now in *Gresham* Colledge,
From Governments elected by the *Rabble*,
From sweet sir *Arthurs* Knights of the Round Table,
From City-Saints whose *Anagram* is *Stains*,
From *Plots* and being choak'd with our own *Chains*,
    From these, and ten times more which may ensue,
    The *Poet* prays, *Good Lord deliver you.*

228 See Appendix 4 for the events of the winter of 1658–9 Title *Letany* litany, formal order of prayer in the established church 5 *self-ends* selfish interest 6 *Saints* Puritans (their own term) 8 *Pauls* St Paul's Cathedral 9 *Linsywoolsy* cheap woollen cloth: parliamentarian Lords 10 *Apron Preachers* tradesman (or women) preachers *extempore* Puritan improvised

prayer, as opposed to Anglican set liturgy 20 *chargeable* maintained at the public expense 24 *red students* soldiers *Gresham Colledge* in London, founded by Sir Thomas Gresham (1518–79) in 1575, later the meeting-place of the Royal Society 26 *sir Arthur* (Haselrigg) see Appendix 2

RICHARD CORBET

229 *The Distracted Puritane*

Am I madd, o noble Festus,
When zeale and godly knowledge
Have put me in hope
To deale with the Pope,
As well as the best in the Colledge?
Boldly I preach, hate a Crosse, hate a Surplice,
Miters, Copes, and Rotchets:
Come heare mee pray nine times a day,
And fill your heads with Crotchets.

In the howse of pure Emanuel
I had my Education;
Where my friends surmise
I dazeld mine Eyes,
With the light of Revelation.
Boldly I preach, etc.

They bound me like a Bedlam,
They lash't my foure poore quarters:
Whilst this I endure
Faith makes mee sure
To be One of Foxes Martyrs.
Boldly I preach, etc.

These injuryes I suffer
Through Anti-Christs perswasions:
Take of this Chaine,
Neither Rome nor Spaine
Can resist my strong invasions.
Boldly I preach, etc.

Of the Beasts ten hornes (God blesse us)
I have knock't of three allready:
If they let me alone,
I'le leave him none;
But they say I am too heady.
   Boldly I preach, etc.

When I sack'd the Seaven-hilld Citty
I mett the great redd Dragon:
I kept him aloofe
With the armour of proofe,
Though here I have never a rag on.
   Boldly I preach, etc.

With a fiery Sword and Target
There fought I with this monster:
But the sonnes of pride
My zeale deride,
And all my deedes misconster.
   Boldly I preach, etc.

I unhorst the whore of Babel
With a Launce of Inspirations:
I made her stinke,
And spill her drinck
In the Cupp of Abominations.
   Boldly I preach, etc.

I have seene two in a Vision,
With a Flying Booke betweene them:
I have bin in dispaire
Five times a yeare,
And cur'd by reading Greenham.
   Boldly I preach, etc.

I observ'd in Perkins Tables
The black Lines of Damnation:
Those crooked veines
Soe struck in my braines,
That I fear'd my Reprobation.
  Boldly I preach, etc.

In the holy tongue of Chanaan
I plac'd my chiefest pleasure:
Till I prickt my foote
With an Hebrew roote,
That I bled beyond all measure.
  Boldly I preach, etc.

I appear'd before the Arch-Bishopp,
And all the high Commission:
I gave him noe Grace,
But told him to his face
That he favour'd Superstition.
  Boldly I preach, hate a Crosse, hate a Surplice,
    Miters, Copes, and Rotchets:
  Come heare mee pray nine times a day,
    And fill your heads with Crotchets.

229 See Notes on the Text for a fuller context 1 *Festus* the judge before whom St Paul appears, Acts 25–6 5 *Colledge* Sacred College, the Roman Cardinals 6–9 *Surplice, Miters, Copes, Rotchets* priestly vestments of Catholic origin, revived for Anglican use in the 1620s and 1630s 10 *Emanuel* Emmanuel College, Cambridge, a Puritan stronghold 16 *Bedlam* lunatic, from the name of the London madhouse (This poem fits to the tune of 'Tom o'Bedlam', the most enduring mad song of the early-modern period.) 20 *Foxes Martyrs* John Foxe, author of *Actes and Monuments*, the exhaustive protestant martyrology of the persecutions under Mary Tudor, first printed in English in 1563 and continually expanded thereafter 32 *heady* headstrong 43 *deride* mock, scorn 44 *misconster* misconstrue, misinterpret 56 *Greenham* Richard Greenham, Puritan divine; 58 *Perkins Tables* William Perkins, Cambridge Puritan, see Notes on the Text 62 *Reprobation* preordained damnation 72 *noe Grace* failed to address him by his episcopal title

EDWARD HERBERT, LORD HERBERT OF CHERBURY

230 *October* 14. 1644.

Enraging Griefs, though you most divers be,
In your first Causes, you may yet agree
  To take an equal share within my heart,
  Since if each grief strive for the greatest part,
You needs must vex your selves as well as me.

For your own sakes and mine then make an end,
In vain you do about a Heart contend,
Which though it seem in greatness to dilate,
Is but a tumor, which in this its state
The choicest remedies would but offend.

Then storm't at once, I neither feel constraint
Scorning your worst, nor suffer any taint
Dying by multitudes, though if you strive,
I fear my heart may thus be kept alive,
Until it under its own burden faint.

What is't not done? Why then, my God, I find,
Would have me use you to reform my mind:
Since through his help I may from you extract
An essence pure, so spriteful and compact,
As it will be from grosser parts refin'd:

Which b'ing again converted by his Grace
To godly sorrow, I may both efface
Those sins first caus'd you, and together have
Your pow'r to kill turn'd to a power to save,
And bring my Soul to its desired place.

230 Title On the outbreak of the Civil War, Herbert of Cherbury sided, half-heartedly, with the royalists, but compounded with the parliament and accepted a pension in 1644
1 *divers* varied 19 *spriteful* lively

WILLIAM DRUMMOND OF HAWTHORNDEN

231 EPIGRAM 2

Against the King, Sir, now why would ye fight
Forsooth, because he dubb'd me not a Knight?
And ye (My Lords,) why arm ye 'gainst King *Charles*?
Because of Lords he would not make us Earls.
Earls, why do ye lead forth these Warlike Bands?
Because we will not quit the Church's Lands.

Most Holy Church-men, what is your Intent?
The King our Stipends largely did augment.
Commons to Tumult thus, why are you driven?
Priests us persuade it is the Way to Heaven.
Are these just Cause of War, (good People,) grant:
Hoe! Plunder! Thou ne're swore our Covenant.

Give me a Thousand Cov'nants, I'le subscrive
Them all, and more, if more ye can contrive,
Of Rage and Malice; and let every one
Black Treason bear, not bare Rebellion.
I'le not be mockt, hiss'd, plunder'd, banish'd hence
For more Years standing for a ... Prince.
His Castles are all taken, and his Crown,
His sword, and scepter, Ensign of Renown,
With that Lieutenant, Fame did so extol,
And Captives carried to the Capital,
I'le not die Martyr for a mortal Thing,
'Tis enough to be Confessor for a King.
Will this you give Contentment, Honest-men?
I've written Rebels; Pox upon the Pen.

231 See Notes on the Text for the events of 1639 in Scotland 8 *augment* increase 12 *Covenant* National Covenant, see Notes on the Text 13 *subscrive* sign 20 *Ensign* royal standard, flag 24 *Confessor* one who gives testimony to a faith without being martyred for it 26 *Pox* venereal disease, here, 'curse'

RICHARD BROME

232 Prologue
[*from* A Joviall Crew; or, The Merry Beggars]

Presented in a Comedie at the Cock-Pit in Drury-Lane in the yeer 1641

The Title of our *Play*, A Joviall Crew,
May seem to promise Mirth: which were a new,
And forc'd thing, in these sad and tragick daies
For you to finde, or we expresse in *Playes*.

We wish you, then, would change that expectation,
Since Joviall Mirth is now grown out of fashion.
Or much not to expect; For, now it chances,
(Our comick Writer, finding that *Romances*
Of lovers, through much travell and distresse,
Till it be thought, no Power can redresse
Th'afflicted Wanderers, though stout chevalry
Lend all his aid for their delivery;
Till, lastly, some impossibility
Concludes all strife, and makes a Comedie)
Finding (he saies) such stories bear the sway,
Near as he could, he has compos'd a *Play*,
Of *Fortune-tellers*, Damsels, and their *Squires*,
Expos'd to strange Adventures, through the Briers
Of *Love* and *Fate*. But why need I forestall
What shall so soon be obvious to you all:
But wish the dullnesse may make no Man sleep,
Nor sadnesse of it any Woman weep.

232 See nos. 233, 239, see also Notes on the Text 2 *were* (subjunctive) would be 3 *forc'd* strained, contrived 11 *chevalry* chivalry, knightly heroics 18 *Briers* thorny bushes

THOMAS JORDAN

233 *The Players Petition to the Parliament*

Heroic Sirs, you glorious nine or ten,
That can depose the King, and the Kings men,
Who by your Sublime Rhetorick agree,
That prisons are the Subjects libertie:
And though we sent in silver at great rates,
You plunder, to secure us our Estates.
Your serious subtilty is grown so grave,
We dare not tell you how much power you have,
At least you dare not hear us; how you frown
If we but say, King *Pym* wears *Charles* his Crown,
Such a word's *Treason*, and you dare not hear it,
Treason to speak it, and yet not to wear it.

O wise mysterious Synod, what shall we
Do for such men as you e're forty three
Be half expir'd, and an unlucky season
Shall set a period to *Triennial Treason*,
When the fields pitcht, and some, for all their skill,
Shall fight a Bloody Battle on *Tower-Hill*;
Where Master *Pym*, your wise judicious Schollar,
Ascends his Throne, and takes his Crown in Coller;
When *Canterbury* coming forth shall wonder
You have so long secur'd him from the Thunder
Of King-hunting Prentices, and the Mayor
Shall jussel zealous *Isaack* from his Chair.
Fore-seeing *Brookes*, thou drewst a happy lot;
'Twas a wise Bolt, although 'twas quickly shot;
But whilst you live, our loude Petition craves,
That we the true Subjects, and the true Slaves,
May in our Comick mirth and Tragick rage,
Set up the Theatre, and shew the Stage,
The shop of truth and fancy, and we vow
Not to Act any thing you disallow:
We will not dare at your strange Votes to Jear,
Nor personate King *Pym* with his State-flear;
Aspiring *Cataline* shall be forgot,
Bloody *Sejanus*, or who e're would Plot
Confusion to a State; the Warrs betwixt
The Parliament, and just *Henry* the sixt,
Shall have no thought or mention, cause their power,
Not only plac'd, but left him in the *Tower*;
Nor yet the Grave advice of Learned *Pym*,
Make a Malignant, and then Plunder him.
All these and such like actions as may mar
Your soaring Plots, and shew you what you are,
We will omit, lest that your mention shake'um,
Why should the men be wiser then you make'um.
Methinks there should not such a difference be
'Twixt our profession and your quality,
You meet, plot, talk, consult, with minds immense,
The like with us, but only we speak sense

Inferiour unto you; we can tell how
To depose kings, there we are more than you,
Although not more then what you would; then we
Likewise in our vast Privilege agree,
Only yours are the longer; and controules,
Not only Lives and Fortunes, but mens Souls;
For you declare by Aenigmatick sense,
A Privilege over mens Conscience,
As if the *Trinity* would not consent
To save a Soul without the Parliament.
Wee make the People laugh at some vain shew,
And as they laugh at us, they doe at you;
But then i'th'Contrary we disagree,
For you can make them cry faster then wee:
Your *Tragedies* more really are exprest,
You murder men in *Earnest*, wee in *Jest*.
There we come short: But if you follow't thus,
Some wise men fear you will come short of us.
Now humbly, as we did begin, Wee pray,
Dear *School-masters,* you'd give us leave to play
Quickly before the King come, for we wou'd
Be glad to say y'ave done a little good
Since you have sate, your Play is almost done,
As well as ours, would have it ne're begun;
For we shall see e're the last Act be spent,
Enter the King, *Exeunt* the Parliament.
And hey, then up go we, who by the frown
Of guilty Consciences have been kept down:
So may you still remain, and sit and Vote,
And through your own beam see your brothers mote,
Until a legal trial do shew how
You us'd the King and hey then up goe you:
So pray your humble *Slaves* with all their powers,
That they may have their due, and you have yours.

233 See Notes on the Text 1 *nine or ten* Pym's junta, the inner council of the parliament 2 *Kings men* most celebrated public acting company (formerly Shakespeare's) 13 *Synod* religious forum 14 *forty three* in the context of exponential abrogation of power by the parliament, these lines are asking if any liberties will be left to the subject by the end of the year 16 *Triennial* acts instituting parliaments, see Appendix 4 20 *Coller* choler, anger

21 *Canterbury* Archbishop Laud, imprisoned 1641, tried 1644, beheaded 1645; see Appendix 2 25 *Brookes* Robert Greville, Lord Brookes, fled with his regiment from Brentford as it was stormed by Prince Rupert on 12 November 1642 26 *Bolt* arrow 33–4 things obviously too controversial for any stage representation 34 *flear* sneer, grimace 35–6 *Catiline, Sejanus* (1611 and 1603 respectively) Roman tragedies by Ben Jonson, both with uncomfortable republican undercurrents 38 *Henry the sixt* Shakespeare's series of histories portraying the downfall of a just but weak king 57 *Aenigmatick* obscure 71–6 these lines make rhetorical play with the anticipated brevity of parliamentary rule 73 *sate* sat, as a parliament 77 *hey, then up go we* see the refrain of no. 240 80 *beam...mote* alludes to parable in Matthew 7: 3 and Luke 6: 41 82 *hey then up goe you* on the gallows

ROBERT HERRICK

234 *His Cavalier*

Give me that man, that dares bestride
The active Sea-horse, and with pride,
Through that huge field of waters ride:
Who, with his looks too, can appease
The ruffling winds and raging Seas,
In mid'st of all their outrages.
This, this a virtuous man can doe,
Saile against rocks, and split them too;
I! and a world of Pikes passe through.

234 5 *ruffling* turbulent, troublesome 5–10 for this emblem of specifically Royal endurance, see no. 311 9 *I!* aye *Pikes* both predatory fish and infantry weapons

235 *A Pastorall sung to the King:* Montano, Silvio, *and* Mirtillo, *Shepheards.*

Mon. Bad are the times. *Sil.* And wors then they are we,
Mon. Troth, bad are both; worse fruit, and ill the tree:
The feast of Shepheards fail. *Sil.* None crowns the cup
Of *Wassaile* now, or sets the *quintell* up:

And He, who us'd to leade the Country-round,
Youthfull *Mirtillo*, Here he comes, Grief drownd.
Ambo Lets cheer him up. *Sil.* Behold him weeping ripe.
Mirt. Ah! *Amarillis*, farewell mirth and pipe;
Since thou art gone, no more I mean to play,
To these smooth Lawns, my mirthfull Roundelay.
Dear *Amarillis*! *Mon.*Hark! *Sil.*mark: *Mir.*this earth grew sweet
Where, *Amarillis*, Thou didst set thy feet.
Ambo. Poor pittied youth! *Mir.* And here the breth of kine
And sheep, grew more sweet, by that breth of Thine,
This flock of wooll, and this rich lock of hair,
This ball of *Cow-slips*, thesė she gave me here.
Sil. Words sweet as Love it self. *Montano*, Hark.
Mirt. This way she came, and this way too she went;
How each thing smells divinely redolent!
Like to a field of beans, when newly blown;
Or like a medow being lately mown.
Mon. A sweet-sad passion.——
Mirt. In dewie-mornings when she came this way,
Sweet Bents wode bow, to give my Love the day:
And when at night, she folded had her sheep,
Daysies wo'd shut, and closing, sigh and weep.
Besides (Ai me!) since she went hence to dwell,
The voices Daughter nea'r spake syllable.
But she is gone. *Sil. Mirtillo*, tell us whether,
Mirt. Where she and I shall never meet together.
Mont. Fore-fend it *Pan*, and *Pales* do thou please
To give an end: *Mir.* To what? *Sil.* Such griefs as these.
Mirt. Never, O never! Still I may endure
The wound I suffer, never find a cure.
Mont. Love for thy sake will bring her to these hills
And dales again: *Mir.* No I will languish still;
And all the while my part shall be to weepe;
And with my sighs, call home my bleating sheep:
And in the Rind of every comely tree
Ile carve thy name, and in that name kisse thee:
Mont. Set with the Sunne, thy woes: *Sil.* The day grows old:
And time it is our full-fed flocks to fold.

Chor. The shades grow great; but greater growes our sorrow;
But lets go steepe
Our eyes in sleepe;
And meet to weepe
To morrow.

235 See Notes on the Text 4 *Wassaile* celebration *quintell* quintain for jousting practice 7 *Ambo* Latin, 'both' 10 *Roundelay* song 13 *kine* cattle 16 *ball of Cow-slips* flower-heads threaded together as a ball 24 *Bents* blades of grass 28 *voices Daughter* Echo 39 *Rind* bark

236 *Farwell Frost, or welcome the Spring*

Fled are the Frosts, and now the Fields appeare
Re-cloth'd in fresh and verdant Diaper.
Thaw'd are the snowes, and now the lusty Spring
Gives to each Mead a neat enameling.
The Palms put forth their Gemmes, and every Tree
Now swaggers in her Leavy gallantry.
The while the *Daulian Minstrell* sweetly sings,
With warbling Notes, her *Tyrrean* sufferings.
What gentle Winds perspire? As if here
Never had been the *Northern Plunderer*
To strip the Trees, and Fields, to their distresse,
Leaving them to a pittied nakednesse.
And look how when a frantick Storme doth tear
A stubborn Oake, or Holme (long growing there)
But lul'd to calmnesse, then succeeds a breeze
That scarcely stirs the nodding leaves of Trees:
So when this War (which tempest-like doth spoil
Our salt, our Corn, our Honie, Wine, and Oile)
Falls to a temper, and doth mildly cast
His inconsiderate Frenzie off (at last)
The gentle Dove may, when these turmoils cease,
Bring in her Bill, once more, *the Branch of Peace*.

236 2 *verdant Diaper* green cover (lit. cloth with a repeat pattern, here flowers spread all over the field) 4 *Mead* meadow 5 *Palms* willows *Gemmes* catkins 7 *Daulian Minstrell*

Philomela, the nightingale, see Appendix 1 9 *perspire* literally, blow through 10 *Northern Plunderer* winter wind 18 *Honie* honey 19 *Falls to a temper* abates into mildness

237 TO THE KING

Upon his comming with his Army into the West

Welcome, most welcome to our Vowes and us,
Most great, and universall *Genius*!
The Drooping West, which hitherto has stood
As one, in long-lamented-widow-hood;
Looks like a Bride now, or a bed of flowers,
Newly refresh't, both by the Sun, and showers.
War, which before was horrid, now appears
Lovely in you, brave Prince of Cavaliers!
A deale of courage in each bosome springs
By your accesse; (*O you the best of Kings!*)
Ride on with all white *Omens*; so, that where
Your Standard's up, we fix a Conquest there.

237 Title Written in Devon in 1645: after the defeat at Naseby, the King travelled into the west, arriving at Raglan in early July, at Cardiff by 22 July. Armies were mustering for the King at Taunton and Barnstaple. Herrick seems to be sanguine in anticipating any victory at a point where events had begun to work against the royalists 3 *Drooping* discouraged 10 *accesse* arrival 11 *white Omens* (Latinism) good omens

238 *The bad season makes the Poet sad*

Dull to my selfe, and almost dead to these
My many fresh and fragrant Mistresses:
Lost to all Musick now; since every thing
Puts on the semblance here of sorrowing.
Sick is the Land to'th'heart; and doth endure
More dangerous faintings by her desp'rate cure.
But if that golden Age wo'd come again,
And *Charles* here Rule, as he before did Raign;

If smooth and unperplext the Seasons were,
As when the *Sweet Maria* lived here:
I sho'd delight to have my Curles halfe drown'd
In *Tyrian Dewes*, and Head with Roses crown'd.
And once more yet (ere I am laid out dead)
Knock at a Starre with my exalted Head.

238 4 *semblance* appearance 6 *desp'rate cure* the image here is of blood-letting (the war) which weakens the patient (England) without effecting a cure 10 *Maria* Queen Henrietta Maria 12 *Tyrian* ointments, as for a classical feast *Roses* garlands of the classical reveller

WILLIAM CAVENDISH, DUKE OF NEWCASTLE

239 *A Songe*

Sweet harte we are beggers, our Comforts tis seene
That we are undunne, for the Kinge, and the Queene
Which doth make us rejoice, with Royall braggs
That now we doe foote it, with Royall raggs
Wee can not borrow, nor take up of Trust
So water weele drinke, and bite a hard Cruste
Lett Care goe kill Catts, what Comfort's in Sorrow
Therefore lett to Morrow, care for to Morrow.

In a Gray Mornings dew thy Coates thou wilt dagg
Whilst thou bearest the bottle and I beare the bagg
And then when the wether growes cold and rawe
Weel into the Barne, and tumble in Straw
And when the Springe on our love setts an Edge
Weel kisse, and wee'l play, under Evry Hedge
Though Nothinge we have, yett nothing we lack
A Staffe in your hand, A childe att your back.

This Diett will make us both looke pale and wanne
Your Hatt band of Inkle and Buttermilk Canne
Or for a doale att a great mans gate sitt
Exspectinge the Porter your Stockings ther knitt

Whilst his Inrag'ed black staffe ther some rapps
Bee thou then busie in stealinge of Scrapps
And when our *Olio* of Almes tubb is cleere
Our hands be our Cupps the river our beere.
For all these blessings lett's Merrily singe
Give God the Prayse and to Charles our brave Kinge.

239 See no. 232 3 *braggs* boasts 5 *Trust* credit 7 *kill Catts* proverb: let us be happy despite our circumstances 9 *dagg* to trail through drizzle and mud 18 *Inkle* common type of linen tape 19 *doale* charitable distribution of food 23 *Olio* stew made of scraps

FRANCIS QUARLES

240 [Know then my brethren, heav'n is cleare]

Know then my brethren, heav'n is cleare
   And all the Clouds are gon;
The Righteous now shall flourish, and
   Good dayes are comming on;
Come then, my Brethren, and be glad
   And eke rejoyce with me;
Lawn sleeves and Rochets shal go down,
   And, hey! then up go we.

Wee'l breake the windowes which the whore
   Of Babilon hath painted,
And when the Popish Saints are downe
   Then *Barow* shal be Sainted;
Ther's neither Crosse nor Crucifixe
   Shall stand for men to see;
Romes trash and trumperies shall goe down,
   And, hey! then up go we.

What ere the Popish hands have built
   Our Hammers shall undoe;
Wee'l breake their Pipes and burne their Copes,
   And pull downe Churches too:
Wee'l exercise within the Groves,

And teach beneath a Tree,
Wee'l make a Pulpit of a Cart,
And, hey! then up we go.

Wee'l downe with all the *Varsities*
Where Larning is profest,
Because they practise and maintaine
The language of the Beast:
Wee'l drive the Doctors out of doores,
And Arts what ere they be,
Wee'l cry both Arts and Larning downe,
And, hey! then up go we.

Wee'l down with Deanes and Prebends too,
But I rejoyce to tell ye,
How then we will eate Pig our fill,
And Capon by the belly:
Wee'l burne the Fathers witty Tomes,
And make the Schoole-men flee,
Wee'l down with all that smels of wit,
And, hey! then up go we.

If once that Antichristian crew
Be crusht and overthrowne,
Wee'l teach the Nobles how to croutch,
And keep the Gentry downe;
Good manners have an evill report,
And turnes to pride we see,
Wee'l therfore cry good manners down,
And, hey! then up go we.

The name of Lord shall be abhor'd,
For every man's a brother,
No reason why in Church or State,
One man should rule another:
But when the change of Government
Shall set our fingers free,
Wee'l make the wanton Sisters stoope,
And, hey! then up go we.

Our Coblers shall translate their Soules
From Caves obscure and shady,
Wee'l make *Tom T*—— as good as my Lord,
And *Joane* as good as my Lady.
Wee'l crush and fling the marriage Ring
Into the Roman See;
Wee'l ask no bands, but even clap hands,
And hey! then up go we.

240 This is a fair example of the process of 'othering' the opposition 7 *Lawn sleeves* as worn by senior Anglican clergy *Rochets* type of linen surplice worn by bishops 9–10 *Whore of Babilon* common ultra-Protestant term for the Catholic Church, see Appendix 1 10 *painted* Puritans regarded all images in churches, including stained glass, as idolatrous 12 *Barow* Henry Barow, Elizabethan radical protestant, executed in 1593, thus a Separatist 'martyr' 15 *trumperies* gaudy trivia 19 *Pipes* organ pipes *Copes* church vestments 28 *The language of the Beast* Latin, used by the Catholic Church, also used in Anglican services in Oxford and Cambridge; see Appendix 1, Beast 33 *Deanes Prebends* ranks of Anglican clerics 37 *witty Tomes* the ingenious books of the earliest Christian scholars condemned by Puritans, who based their faith solely and directly on the Scriptures 38 *Schoole-men* medieval theologians 59–60 *Tom T[urd], Joane* proverbially lower-class names 62 *See* sea, and ecclesiastical jurisdiction

JAMES SHIRLEY

241 Epitaph on the Duke of *BUCKINGHAM*.

Here lies the best and worst of Fate,
Two Kings delight, the peoples hate,
The Courtiers star, the Kingdoms eye,
A man to draw an Angel by.
Fears despiser, *Villiers* glory,
The Great mans volume, all times story.

241 See Appendix 2 for George Villiers, Duke of Buckingham

ANONYMOUS

242 *London* sad *London*. AN ECCHO.

What wants thee, that thou art in this sad taking?
A King
What made him first remove hence his residing?
syding.
Did any here deny him satisfaction?
Faction.
Tell me whereon this strength of Faction lyes?
On lyes.
What didst thou do when the King left Parliament?
Lament.
What terms would'st give to gain his Company?
Any.
But how wouldst serve him, with thy best endeavour?
Ever.
What wouldst thou do if here thou couldst behold him?
Hold him.
But if he comes not what becomes of *London*?
Undone.

242 See Notes on the Text 1 *taking* condition of distress 4 *syding* divisions

MARTIN PARKER

243 Upon defacing of *White-hall*

1.

What *Booker* doth prognosticate
Concerning Kings or Kingdoms state,
I think my self to be as wise,
As some that gazeth on the skyes:
My skill goes beyond, the depth of a *Pond*,
Or *Rivers* in the greatest rain,
Whereby I *can tell, all things will be well,*
When the King enjoys his own again.

2.

There's neither *Swallow, Dove,* nor *Dade,*
Can soar more high, nor deeper wade;
Nor shew a reason from the stars,
What causeth Peace or Civil Wars:
The man in the Moon, may wear out his shoo'n
By runing after *Charls* his Wain,
But all's to no end, for the times will not mend
Till the King, etc.

3.

Full forty years this Royal Crown
Hath been his fathers and his own:
And is there anyone but He,
That in the same should sharers be?
For who better may, the Scepter sway,
Than he that hath such right to reign?
Then let's hope for a peace, for the Wars will not cease
Till the King enjoys, etc.

4.

Though for a time we see *White-hall*
With Cobweb-hangings on the wall,
Instead of gold and silver brave,
Which formerly 'twas wont to have,
With rich perfume in every room,
Delightful to the Princely Train,
Which again shall be, when the time you see,
That the King enjoys, etc.

5.

Did *Walker* no predictions lack
In *Hammonds* bloody Almanack?
Foretelling things that would ensue,
That all proves right, if lies be true:
But why should not he, the pillory foresee,
Wherein poor *Toby* once was ta'ne?
And also foreknow, to th'Gallows he must go,
When the King enjoys, etc.

6.

Till then upon Ararats-hill,
My hope shall cast his Anchor still,
Untill I see some peaceful *Dove *Gen. *Monck*
Bring home the Branch I dearly love:
Then will I wait till the waters abate,
Which most disturbs my troubled brain,
Else never rejoyce till I hear the voice,
That the King enjoys his own again.

243 1–9 *Booker, Pond, Rivers, Swallow, Dove, Dade* all puns on the primary meanings of the names (a 'dade' is a wading-bird) but also the surnames of astrologers and almanac-writers of the first half of the seventeenth century 14 *Charls his Wain* another name for the constellation of the Plough, frequently played on by Caroline poets 30 *Princely Train* the Court 33 *Walker* Henry Walker, parliamentarian journalist 34 *Hammonds bloody Almanack* John Hammond, Presbyterian ballad-maker, issued the highly political *The new bloody almanack for this insuing yeare* in 1644 38 *poor Toby* Henry Walker was pilloried in July 1642 for incitement to rebellion. John Taylor's 1642 satire *A seasonable lecture* puts an absurd sermon on Tobias's dog (Tobit 5: 16, the only pet dog in Scripture) into his mouth 41 *Ararats-hill* where Noah's ark came to rest after the flood, where the dove brought him the olive-branch of hope and peace (Genesis 8: 4–11) 42 *Anchor* traditional emblem of the virtue of Hope

POEMS ATTRIBUTED TO CHARLES STUART, KING CHARLES I

244 MAJESTY in MISERY:

or, *An Imploration to the KING of Kings.*
Written by His late Majesty King *CHARLES* the First, during His Captivity at *Carisbrook* Castle, *Anno Dom.* 1648.

Great Monarch of the World, from whose Power Springs
The Potency and Power of Kings,
Record the Royal Woe my Suffering sings;

And teach my tongue, that ever did confine
Its faculties in Truths Seraphick Line,
To track the Treasons of thy foes and mine.

Nature and Law, by thy Divine Decree
(The only Root of Righteous Royaltie)
With this dim Diadem invested me,

With it, the sacred Scepter, Purple Robe,
The Holy Unction, and the Royal Globe.
Yet am I levell'd with the life of *Job*.

The fiercest Furies, that do daily tread
Upon my Grief, my Gray Dis-crowned Head,
Are those that owe my Bounty for their Bread.

They raise a War, and Christen it, *The Cause*,
Whilst sacrilegious hands have best applause,
Plunder and Murder are the Kingdoms Laws;

Tyranny bears the Title of *Taxation*,
Revenge and Robbery are *Reformation*,
Oppression gains the name of *Sequestration*.

My Loyal Subjects who in this bad season
Attend me (by the Law of God and Reason)
They dare impeach, and punish for High Treason.

Next at the Clergy do their Furies frown,
Pious Episcopacy must go down,
They will destroy the Crosier and the Crown.

Church-men are chain'd, and Schismaticks are free'd,
Mechanicks preach, and Holy Fathers bleed,
The Crown is crucified with the Creed.

The Church of *England* doth all Faction foster,
The Pulpit is usurpt by each Impostor,
Ex tempore excludes the *Pater noster*.

The *Presbyter* and *Independent* Seed
Springs with broad blades; to make Religion bleed,
Herod and *Pontius Pilate* are agreed.

The Corner-stone's misplac'd by every Pavier;
With such a bloody method and behaviour,
Their Ancestors did crucifie our Saviour.

My Royal Consort, from whose fruitful Womb
So many Princes legally have come,
Is forc'd in Pilgrimage to seek a Tomb.

Great *Britain*'s Heir is forced into *France*,
Whilst on his Father's head his foes advance:
Poor Child! He weeps out his Inheritance.

With my own Power my Majesty they wound,
In the King's Name the King himself 's uncrowned:
So doth the Dust destroy the Diamond.

With Propositions daily they enchant
My Peoples ears, such as do Reason daunt,
And the Almighty will not let me grant.

They promise to erect my Royal Stem,
To make Me great, t'advance my Diadem,
If I will first fall down, and worship them;

But for refusal they devour my Thrones,
Distress my Children, and destroy my bones,
I fear they'l force me to make bread of stones.

My Life they prize at such a slender rate,
That in my absence they draw Bills of hate,
To prove the King a Traytor to the State.

Felons obtain more priviledge than I,
They are allow'd to answer e're they die,
'Tis death for me to ask the reason, Why.

But, Sacred Saviour, with thy words I woo
Thee to forgive, and not be bitter to
Such, as thou know'st do not know what they do.

For since they from their Lord are so disjointed,
As to contemn those Edicts he appointed,
How can they prize the Power of his Anointed?

Augment my Patience, nullifie my Hate,
Preserve my Issue, and inspire my Mate,
Yet though We perish, bless this Church and State.

244 5 *Seraphick* angelic 9 *Diadem* crown 11 *Unction* oil, used in the ceremony of anointing at a coronation *Globe* orb, symbol of royal power in the regalia 21 *Sequestration* confiscation of goods by parliamentary decree 27 *Crosier* bishop's ceremonial staff 28 *Schismaticks* nonconformist sects 33 *Ex tempore* spontaneous, improvised prayer favoured by Puritans *Pater noster* the Our Father, representing the traditional Anglican liturgy 37 *Corner-stone* St Paul's description of Christ in Ephesians 2: 20 *Pavier* paviour, layer of pavements 52 *Stem* heirs, descendants 54, 57 both referring to the temptation of Christ by Satan in the wilderness in Matthew 4: 3–9 66 echo of Christ's words from the Cross, Luke 23: 34 68 *Edicts* laws 69 *Anointed* the king

245 King *Charles*'s Lament.

You Gods and Goddesses that rules in *Helicon*,
Look me upon;
Help to relieve a Pris'ner out of Thrall,
Let not these savage Hearts, as Furies sent from Hell,
Torment me still,
Who have in Store no Mercy, none at all.
Alcides come for to defend me,
And wave thy Club about,
Or else they will my Person kill
Before they let me out.
For wicked *Cerberus*, my Porter,
Doth bear me great Despite,
And seeks by Death to stop my breath;
He can both bark and bite.

To me most patient pensive Pris'ner left
Of Joy bereft;
My Griefs and Troubles cannot numbred be:
A hopeless, helpless, harmless Man lies here forlorn,
And held in Scorn,

By those who once were Subjects unto me;
Who through the Mercies that I used
While I was in full Power,
Most merc'lessly oppress they me,
And vex me every Hour:
I have released many bond Slaves,
And set the Pris'ners free,
Yet helpless I in Prison ly,
Without all Remedy.

'Twould make a Heart of Flint relent to see my Woes
Done by my Foes,
Who once had all Things at my own Command;
No Cloaths to wear, no Food for me to eat,
No Drink or Meat,
But what is given by my En'mies Hand.
My Friends are all from me departed,
Though sore against their Will:
Not one is here that comes me near,
But those that wish me ill.
A Thousand Ways they do practise
To work my Life's Decay.
Hap Well, hap Wo, it must be so,
The bond Man must obey.

To try and vex my Patience, to my Charge they lay,
Day after Day,
Such horrid Crimes, of which I never knew.
Their Tongues like poys'ning Asps or double edged Swords,
Speak byting Words,
Which are as false as any Thing is true.
Even so with their false Accusations,
They raise a deadly StrIfe,
To separate and breed Debate
Betwixt me and my Wife;
My Children also are abus'd,
As to the World is known,
And others they do now enjoy
That which was once my own.

Besides my Keepers Cruelty is over much,
Never was such
A Captive Pris'ner kept in Slavery.
There is no Friend dare come my Person near,
And that for Fear,
Without Admittance from my Enemy.
Each Day and Hour I stand in Danger
Of these my desperate Foes,
Who do not spare, 'tis known they dare
To give me bloody Blows,
If they but say I do offend them,
Though I know not the Cause;
They show their Might, and with me fight.
These are their new made Laws.

Thus am I ev'ry Day most barbarously used,
Basely abused
By some of them, for whom I have done good,
And some in whom I put my Trust,
Have prov'd unjust,
And are most ready for to shed my Blood.
Ev'n as that cursed Traitor *Judas*
His Master did betray;
So my false Friends for their own Ends,
Have sold my Life away.
No faithful Friend dare come me near
At all too take my Part,
But ev'ry Man doth what he can
To break my wounded Heart.

How happy is the Man that labours all the Day
For little Pay,
For he at Night may safely go to Rest;
And he that travails up and down, and takes most Pains
Receives the Gains,
And takes his Lodging where it likes him best.
These Men have Liberty to labour,
A sweet and pleasant Thing;
And in their Fare more happy are
Than is a troubled King.

The Country Swains, the silly Shepherds,
And Tradesmen eek also,
Have Liberty, while here I ly
In Sorrow and in Wo.

Is't not a Father's chiefest Comfort for to see
These Things to be,
His own dear Children, ever in his Sight?
Is't not the Mirror of a Husband's Life
To see his Wife,
And have her in his Presence Day and Night.
All these sweet Pleasures are kept from me,
While I on Earth remain,
Except the Wind will prove so kind,
As to turn the Tide again:
Till then with Patience will I wait,
Wishing Health, Wealth and Peace
To these that be at Liberty,
And wish for my Release.

245 1 *Helicon* 7 *Alcides* 11 *Cerberus* see Appendix 1 3 *Thrall* captivity 41 *Hap Well, hap Wo* whether things turn well or ill 95 *silly* simple

246 His Majesties Complaint to his Subjects.

Are wee your King? A King of griefe 'tis true,
A Title strange, yet all wee have from you:
Our other honours you usurp as due.
Never was King so griev'd.

Our Scepter's broke, our Lawes lie trodden downe,
The Revenues belonging to our Crowne
Are all but purchasers of your renowne.
Never was griefe like Ours.

Our Wif 's debar'd us, Our deare Children too,
Our *Conscience* must be subject unto *you*:
Why don't you vote to *part our garments too?*
Was ever griefe, &c.

With Clubs and Staves you to our Court did rune
Alas! What haste you made to be undone:
Although but Glow-wormes, you'd out-shine the Sun.
Never was griefe, &c.

Must you accuse us with dispitefulnesse,
Vying your malice with Our gentilenesse,
Pick Quarrells with your only happinesse?
Never was griefe, &c.

You in High Counsell sit, Whilst wee by-stand,
Voting us with a censorious hand:
Wee must obey, that should all you command.
Was ever griefe, &c.

Yet you your selves; that now at us doe brave,
Are become worse than an Egyptian slave;
Using that power against us which we gave.
Was ever griefe, &c.

You cannot thinke we had an ill intent
In granting a Trieniall Parliament,
Though you by it usurp our government.
Never was griefe, &c.

Plots, feares and jealousies indeed you had
To blind the vulgar, and to make them sad,
A thiefe at his owne shadow may run mad.
Was ever case like mine.

When he has mist his aime in doing ill,
And so despairing to effect his will
For feare or shame himselfe himselfe may kill.
Never was griefe like mine.

Arme, arme ye people: quickly make a head
Against the King: for we may wish him dead
Whose evill counsell hath him thus mislead.
Was ever griefe, &c.

Thus by your witchcraft, rebellion
You charm'd our subjects, gull'd the whole Nation,
Blessed effects of such a Reformation.
Never was King so, &c.

Your holy League with th'Scots must next advance
Your treachery: Then mount your Ordinance,
'Tis but the breach of your Allegiance.
Never was griefe, &c.

Your Nationall Covenant must next agree
Between your deare brethren the Scots and yee,
To rob my subjects of their liberty.
Never was griefe, &c.

I have been truckt for, bought and sold, yet I
Am King (though prisoner) pray tell my why
I am removed now from Holdenby?
Never was griefe, &c.

To Newmarket now I am by your Army led,
They'l sell me better then your brethren did,
Else seek to make me shorter by the head.
Never was griefe, &c.

Religion, our life, our Crowne, our glory,
By you exchanged for a Directory,
Never was read the like in any story,
Nor griefe like ours.

You have abandoned both Law and liberty,
And studied to root out Monarchie
To create an arbitrary Tyranny.
Never was griefe, &c.

Your cholerique Synod stood you in great stead
To make you new Commandements and Creed,
They'l make you a new God too, if you have need.
Never was griefe, &c.

Both God and King, both Church and Nation,
Are all comprised in your Declaration,
You sure are both Saviour and salvation,
Never was griefe, &c.

With watry Rivelets both mine eyes oreflow
To thinke my people should be ruined so
By them that did pretend their weale, not woe,
Never was griefe, &c.

For my wrong'd Kingdomes sake: my very griefe
Doth breake my heart, untill I finde reliefe,
Ile sue to heav'n, Mercy from God my chiefe.
Never was griefe, &c.

Causelesse they like a bird have chased me,
Behold, O Lord, looke downe from heaven and see,
Thou that hearest prisoners prayers, heare me.
Never was griefe, &c.

They have rebelled, and falne away from thee,
O pardon them, even for thy clemencie,
Looke downe from heaven and our afflictions see.
Never was griefe, &c.

Compassion as thy mercy is infinite,
Else we had been ere this consumed quite,
But we thee pray, that thou our cause wilt right.
Never was griefe, &c.

Thou know'st my wrongs; their vengeance they have wrought,
Their reproaches thou hast heard, and what they thought,
And now hast all their counsells brought to nought.
Never was griefe like, &c.

I was their song whether they rise or sit,
Give them rewards, Lord, for their working fit,
Sorrow of heart, thy curse; and with thy might
Follow, and from under heaven destroy them quite.

246 See Notes on the Text for the relation of this poem to George Herbert's 'The Sacrifice' 26 *Egyptian slave* the sufferings of the Israelites in Egypt are narrated in Exodus 5–8 30 *Trieniall Parliament* Charles's concession for parliaments every three years, rather than called as infrequently as the King wished 41 *make a head* like a boil rising to a head, the people have thrown up leaders against the King 50 *Ordinance* the 'Ordinance' of February 1644 established the Committee of Both Kingdoms to direct the war against the King 57 *truckt* traded for 66 *Directory* the 'Directory of Public Worship' of 1644 set forth rules on a Presbyterian model for all public church services 73 *cholerique* hot-tempered *Synod* the Westminster Assembly of divines, whose deliberations resulted in the 1644 'Directory'

247 King CHARLES His Speech, and last Farewell to the World, made upon the Scaffold at White-hall-gate, on Tuesday, January 30. 1648.

To the Tune of, *Weladay*.

Faire Englands joy is fled,
Weladay, weladay,
Our Noble King is dead,
Sweet Prince of love;
This heavy news so bad,
Hath made three Kingdoms sad,
No comfort to be had,
But from above.

On Tuesday last his Grace,
Chearfully, chearfully,
Went to his dying place,
to end all strife,
Where many a weeping eye
With groans unto the skie,
To see his Majesty
there end his life.

His Foes he did forgive,
Graciously, graciously,
And wisht we all might live
in quiet peace.
He wisht what ere was past,
That he might be the last,
No sorrow we might taste,
but wars might cease.

Theres nothing griev'd him so,
Weladay, weladay,
As when he thought that woe
might light on all.
The tears stood in his eyes
To heare the peoples cries,
And think what miscarries
on us should fall.

Upon the Scaffold then,
Weladay, weladay,
In hearing of all men
this he made knowne,
That Hee was innocent
of all the blood was spent,
He strove with Parliament
but for his owne.

Quoth he, themselves confest,
Weladay, weladay,
And thus much have exprest
in mine owne hearing,
The *Militia* in mine hand
was granted by the land
To be at my command,
none with me sharing.

The keeping of the same,
Weladay, weladay,
I know not who to blame,
they did desire.

Which made us disagree,
The fault's now laid on me,
This all the world may see
set all on fire.

247 2 *Weladay* alas 9 *his Grace* an older title than 'his Majesty' 31 *miscarries* calamities 41 *Quoth* said 45 *Militia* army

THOMAS JORDAN

248 *The New State described.*

Lo here a Glorious *Realm* subverted stands,
Just *Tumbler*-like upon the *Feet* and *Hands*;
Once *Europes Pride* and *Envy*, now their *Scoff*,
Since the base *Entrayles* cut the *Head* on't off,
The *Body* lost its form, and's turn'd a *Lump;*
Now all the *Limbs* are *Vassals* to the *Rump*,
Which all the *Nutriture* devour'd and spent,
Yields nothing back but *stink* and *excrement*,
And all *returns* that ever this doth send us,
Serves only to *defile* us and *offend* us;
'Tis by much *pampering* grown a strange *Disease,*
Which all *receives*, and *gives* nor food nor ease
To th'pining *Body*, but is craving still;
And we by *feeding* it our selves do *kill*;
Which nothing lives by that has any worth,
But those base *vermin* which its *stink* brought forth.
If every *Member* in this Body would
Withdraw its *strength* and influence, as they should,
This nasty *Highness* quickly must abate,
And yield to th' *Head* which only saves the *State.*

248 The metaphor of the state as 'body politic', as a human body, is frequently used in the seventeenth century, perhaps the best-known instance being Shakespeare's *Coriolanus*, I. i 2 *Tumbler* acrobat 4 *Head* Charles I 6 *Vassals* servants; *Rump* the Rump Parliament, see Appendix 4 19 *nasty* filthy *Highness* (pun) stench, political authority 20 *Head* king (head of state)

MILDMAY FANE, EARL OF WESTMORLAND

249 *Upon the Times*

Awake thou best of sence,
Intelligence,
And let no Fancy-vapour steer
Thy Contemplation t'think that peace is neer,
Whilst war in words we doe bemone,
There's nothing less left in Intention.

England that was, not Is,
Unless in Metamorphosis,
Chang'd from the Bower of bliss and rest,
To become now *Bellonaes* Interest,
In danger of a Funerall Pile,
Unless some happy Swift means reconcile.

Which how to bring to pass,
Beyond Mans hoopes, alass,
Therefore be pleas'd (Thou) who didst make
Atonement for His sake,
To silence this unnaturall spell,
As Thou didst once the Delphian Oracle.

249 3 *Fancy-vapour* illusion 8 *Metamorphosis* transformation 9 *Bower of Bliss* a loose citation of Spenser's *Faerie Queene*, II. xii: Fane clearly intends to suggest here that, compared to its state after the wars, the England of the 1630s enjoyed a golden age. Spenser's 'Bower of Bliss', however, is an ambiguous place, superficially beautiful, but in fact artificial, seductive, and rightly destroyed by Sir Guyon 10 *Bellonaes Interest* the domain of the goddess of war, see Appendix 1 15 *Thou* Christ 16 *Atonement* Christ's sacrifice on the Cross for the sins of mankind 18 see Appendix 1, Pan

ANONYMOUS

250 *The Power of the Sword*

Lay by your Pleading, Law lies a Bleeding,
Burn all your Studies down, and throw away your
Reading;

Small Power the Word has, and can afford us
Not half so many Privileges as the Sword has:

It fosters your Masters, it plasters Disasters,
And makes your Servants, quickly greater than their
    Masters;
It venters, it enters, it circles, it centers,
And makes a Prentice free in spight of his Indentures.

This takes off tall Things, and sets up small Things,
This masters Money, though Money Masters all Things;
'Tis not in Season, to talk of Reason,
Or call it Legal, when the Sword will have it Treason.

It conquers the Crown too, the Furrs and the Gown too,
This set up a Presbyter, and this pull'd him down too;
This subtil Deceiver, turn'd Bonnet to Beaver,
Down drops a Bishop, and up starts a Weaver.

This fits a Lay-man to Preach and pray Man,
'Tis this can make a Lord of him that was a Dray-man;
Forth from the dull Pit, of Follies full Pit,
This brought an *Hebrew* Iron-monger to the Pulpit:

Such pittiful Things be, more happier than Kings be,
This got the Heraldry of *Thimblebee* and *Slingsbee*;
No Gospel can guide it, no Law can decide it,
In Church or State, until the Sword hath sanctify'd it.

Down goes the Law-tricks, for from that Matrix
Sprung holy *Hewson's* Power, and tumbled down
    St. *Patrick's*.
The Sword prevails so highly in *Wales* too,
Shinkin-ap-Powel cries, and swears Cuts-plutter
    a- nails too;

In *Scotland* this Waster, did make such Disaster,
They sent their Money back for which they sold their
    Master;
It batter'd so their *Dunkirk*, and did so the *Don* firk,
That he is fled, and swears the Devil is in *Dunkirk*.

He that can tower o'er him that is lower,
Would be but thought a Fool to put away his Power;
Take Books and rent 'um, who would invent 'um,
When as the Sword replies, *Negatur argumentum*:

Your grand College Butlers, must stoop to your Sutlers,
There's not a Library living like the Cutlers;
The Blood that is spilt, Sir, hath gain'd all the gilt, Sir,
Thus have you seen me run the Sword up to the hilt, Sir.

250 Title see Notes on the Text 1 *Pleading* lawsuits 5 *plasters* heals 7 *venters* seeks out, possible secondary meaning of 'stabs' 8 *Indentures* formal contract binding apprentices to a term of service with a master 13 *Furrs and the Gown* the Peers and the Clergy 14 *Presbyter* Presbyterian minister 15 *Bonnet* hat of a civilian *Beaver* helmet of a soldier 16 *Weaver* the working-class Puritan lay-preacher 18 *Dray-man* carter 22 *Thimblebee and Slingsbee* possibly Sir John Thimelby, head of a large royalist and partly Catholic family in Yorkshire and Lincolnshire, subjected by the Parliament to punitive confiscation of their estates; and Sir Henry Slingsby (1602–58), who was executed by the parliament for his part in a royalist conspiracy to seize Hull for the exiled Charles II 25 *Matrix* source of power 26 *Hewson's...St. Patrick's* see Appendix 2 28 *Shinkin-ap-Powel* derogatory name for a Welshman *Cuts-plutter-a-nails* pseudo Anglo-Welsh 'God's blood and nails' 30 see Appendix 4 31 *Dunkirk* won back from the Spaniards in 1658 *Don* derogatory name for a Spaniard *firk* stab, prick 36 *Negatur argumentum* the argument is refuted 37 *Sutlers* tradesmen supplying the army, or a soldier's servants 38 *Cutlers* makers of knives and swords

SIR WILLIAM DAVENANT

251 *The Countess of* ANGLESEY *led Captive by the Rebels, at the Disforresting of* Pewsam. SONG.

1.

O whither will you lead the Fair,
    And spicy Daughter of the Morne?
Those Manacles of her soft Haire,
    Princes, though free, would faine have worn.

2.

What is her crime? what has she done?
Did she, by breaking Beauty stay,
Or from his Course mislead the Sun;
So robb'd your Harvest of a Day?

3.

Or did her voyce, divinely clear!
(Since lately in your Forrest bred)
Make all the Trees dance after her,
And so your Woods disforrested?

4.

Run, Run! Pursue this Gothick Rout,
Who rudely Love in bondage keep;
Sure all old Lovers have the Goute,
The young are overwatcht and sleep.

251 Title see Notes on the Text *Disforresting* bringing forest into cultivation, thus depriving local inhabitants of their rights in the forest 2 *spicy* fragrant 13 *Gothick* barbaric: the earliest recorded use in *OED* is 1695 15 *Goute* disabling disease, causing swelling particularly in the legs

252 Chorus of Women [*from* The Siege of Rhodes]

1.

Let us live, live! for being dead,
The pretty Spots,
Ribbands and Knots,
And the fine French dress for the Head;
No Lady wears upon her
In the cold, cold, Bed of Honour.
Beat down our Grottoes, and hew down our Bowers,
Dig up our Arbours, and root up our Flowers.
Our Gardens are Bulwarks and Bastions become:
Then hang up our Lutes, we must sing to the Drum.

2.

Our Patches and our Curls
(So exact in each station)
Our Powders and our Purls
Are now out of fashion.
Hence with our Needles, and give us your Spades;
We, that were Ladies, grow coorse as our Maids.
Our Coaches have drove us to Balls at the Court,
We now must drive Barrows to earth up the Port.

252 2 *Spots* beauty spots 9 *Bulwarks, Bastions* fortifications. There is an interesting play with ideas here: a number of early-modern gardens throughout northern Europe were laid out in deliberate imitation of military earthworks 10 See the conclusion of no. 180 for the inversion of this image 11 *Patches* beauty spots 18 *Port* either as the modern meaning, or a gate in a fortified wall

POETS OF THE TIXALL CIRCLE [POEMS COLLECTED BY HERBERT ASTON]

253 A New Remonstrance to His Malignant Mistresse.

Since Beauty's such a tyrant growne
In thee, I'l now discover,
What grievances can ne'ere be borne
By any freeborne lover.

Nor is my hart rebellious growne:
Since thou art still betraying
The trust and power of Beauty's throne,
It finds no more obaying.

My loves benevolence, I say,
Though deue was freely given;
Without a parlament, I'l pay
No subsidy to Heaven.

A routed faith, a plundred love,
And a sequestred deuty,
Are taxe and impost good enough
For thy delinquent beauty.

Call not my harts free homage, scant
Allegiance pay'd unto thee,
Least it engage, and covenant,
New fealtys to undoe thee.

Revoake not back the lyfe you give,
I'l die no doating martyr,
But question thy prerogative,
If thou repeale my charter.

Strive not thy Babell towre to build,
Or arme gainst loves free citty;
Scorne's high commission-court may yeeld
To freedomes grand committy.

Tempt not with thy new minion's pride
My love to wrath abetted;
Felton had not a knife more tryed,
Nor Pymme a toung more whetted.

Nor thinke thy force, or thy deceipt,
Of art or arme can out me:
Love has his Ferfaxes to beat,
And Crumwells too to rowt thee.

253 Title see Appendix 4 for the context of this poem, which uses the vocabulary of the war playfully for the quarrel of the lovers *Malignant* parliamentarian term for royalists 14 *sequestred* confiscated 19 *covenant* make a binding agreement 29 *minion* lover, favourite 30 *abetted* assisted 31 *Felton* see Appendix 2 32 *Pymme* see Appendix 2 *whetted* sharpened 35 *Ferfax* , 36 *Crumwell* see Appendix 2 *rowt* drive from the field of battle, defeat

EDMUND WALLER

254 *To* Chloris.

Chloris since first our calm of peace
Was frighted hence, this good we find,
Your favours with your fears increase,
And growing mischiefs make you kind:
So the fayr tree which still preserves
Her fruit and state whilst no wind blows,
In storms from that uprightness swerves,
And the glad earth about her strows
With treasure from her yielding boughs.

254 4 *kind* sexually accommodating

SIR RICHARD FANSHAWE

255 *The Praise of the Winde*

If words are winde, which (guilt with eloquence)
Like windes at sea, doe mens affections turne
Which way they list, and (lin'd with noble sense)
To highest place preferre the meanest borne
If that preferrement's winde, and all those Arts
To which these gallant Spiritts are inclin'd:
If life was winde, is winde, to winde converts,
And Beautie is the Musick of that winde:
If warre-begotten Honour be no more
Nor Vertue in her mortall morall part,
Nor a good Name (although deserv'd before)
Nor all the Heart desires, or decks the Heart:
Let us esteeme the Winde then, since we finde,
That the world's firmest Glorie, it is Winde.

255 1 *guilt* gilded 3 *list* choose 5 *preferrement* advancement 12 *decks* adorns

256 Horace, Ode IV, 9.

To LOLLIO.

That his writings shall never perish: Vertue without the help of Verses is buried in Oblivion. That he will sing Lollio's praises, whose vertues he now also celebrates.

Least Thou shouldst think the words which I
(By sounding *Aufid* born) compile
To marry with the Lute b'a skill
Never before reveal'd, shall die:
  Though *Homer* lead the Van, the Muse
Of *Pindar*, nor *Alcaeus* heights,
Grave *Stesichore*, nor *Caean* sighs,
Are silenc't, or worn out of use.
  Nor what of old *Anacreon* plaid,
Hath time defac't: *Love* lights his Fire,
And with his Quiver weares the Lyre
Of the yet fresh *Aeolian* Maid.
  Helen was not the onely she
A curled Gallant did enflame,
The Splendour of his Royal Traine,
And Gold and Pearles Embroyderie.
  Nor *Teucer* first that drew a strong
Cydonian Bow. *Trojans* had fought
Before: nor that age onely wrought
Deeds worthy of the *Muses* song.
  Nor valiant *Hector*, and the brave
Deiphob, were the onely men
Receiv'd deep wounds upon them then,
Their Children and chast Wives to save.
  Men slasht ere *Diomed* was made:
But all are in oblivion drown'd,
And put unmourn'd into the Ground,
For lack of Sacred *Poets* Aide.
  Vertue that's buried, and dead Sloth,
Differ not much. Un-understood
Thou shalt not die; nor so much good
As thou hast acted feed the Moth.

Lollio Thou art a man hast skill
To fathome things: that being tride
In either Fortune, couldst abide
In both up-right, and *Lollio* still.
Of covetous Fraud a scourge severe
On whom the All-attracting Gold
Could with its Tenters ne'r take hold:
Nor Consul of one year. When ere
A vertuous Magistrate, and true,
Shall call good, gain, bid Bribes Avaunt:
Upon Opposers' bellies plant
His conqu'ring Flags: *Lollio*, That's You.
He is not happy that hath much:
But who so can his minde dispose
To use aright what Heav'n bestows,
He justly is accounted such:
If he know how hard want to bear:
And fear a crime, more then his end.
If for his Country, or his Friend
To stake his life he doth not fear.

256 For names throughout, see Appendix 1 5 *Van* advance party 39 *Tenters* hooks
40 *Consul* public office held annually in ancient Rome

WILLIAM FOWLER [rev. ?THOMAS CARY]

257 [Farewell faire Saint, let not the Seas and wind]

Farewell faire Saint, let not the Seas and wind
Swell like the eyes and hearts you leave behind.
But smooth and gentle as the lookes you beare
Smile in your face, and whisper in your eare.
May no bold Billow venture to arise
That it may neerer gaze upon your eyes,
Least Wind and Waves enamour'd of your forme
Should crowd and throng themselves into a storme.

But if it be your fate (vast Seas) to love,
Of my becalmed breast learne how to move.
Move then, but in a gentle lovers pace,
No wrinckle nor no furrough in your face.
And you (Fierce winds) see that you tell your tale
In such a breath as may but fill her Sayle.
So whilst you court her each your severall way
You may her safely to her Port convey,
And loose her by the noblest way of wooing
Whilst both contribute to your own undoing.

257 Ssee Notes on the Text for attribution and for a radically variant Scots-spelling version 5 *Billow* wave 12 *furrough* furrow

JOHN MILTON

258 To the Lord Generall Cromwell May 1652 On the proposals of certaine ministers at the Commitee for Propagation of the Gospell

Cromwell, our cheif of men, who through a cloud
Not of warr onely, but detractions rude,
Guided by faith and matchless Fortitude
To peace and truth thy glorious way hast plough'd,
And on the neck of crowned Fortune proud
Hast reard Gods Trophies and his work pursu'd,
While Darwen stream with blood of Scotts imbru'd,
And Dunbarr feild resounds thy praises loud,
And Worsters laureat wreath; yet much remaines
To conquer still; peace hath her victories
No less renownd then warr, new foes aries
Threatning to bind our soules with secular chaines:
Helpe us to save free Conscience from the paw
Of hireling wolves whose Gospell is their maw.

258 5 *crowned Fortune* Charles I, Charles II 7 *Darwen* the river near Preston, Lancashire, where the Scots were defeated by Cromwell in August 1648 8 *Dunbarr* Dunbar, East

Lothian, where Cromwell defeated the Scots in September 1650 9 *Worster* Worcester, where Cromwell defeated the Scots under Charles II, September 1651, see Appendix 4 14 *maw* stomach

259 Sonnet VIII.

Captain or Colonel, or Knight in Arms,
  Whose chance on these defenceless dores may sease,
  If ever deed of honour did thee please,
  Guard them, and him within protect from harms,
He can requite thee, for he knows the charms
  That call Fame on such gentle acts as these,
  And he can spred thy Name o're Lands and Seas,
  What ever clime the Suns bright circle warms.
Lift not thy spear against the Muses Bowre,
  The great *Emathian* Conqueror bid spare
  The house of *Pindarus*, when Temple and Towre
Went to the ground: And the repeated air
  Of sad *Electra*'s Poet had the power
  To save th'*Athenian* Walls from ruine bare.

259 2 *sease* seize 10 *Emathian Conqueror* Alexander 13 *Poet* Euripides: in 404 BC, according to Plutarch, an Athenian officer saved the city from Spartan aggressors by singing the first chorus from Euripides' *Electra*: Milton may possibly be developing intertextually from an apparent ambiguity in Plutarch. The first Chorus of the *Electra* is a long lyric account of boats turned to sea-nymphs, and not apparently relevant to the condition of a besieged town. In Book X of Virgil's *Aeneid*, however, Cybele turns Aeneas' fleet to sea-nymphs, in sign of settlement and eventual peace

GERRARD WINSTANLEY

260 [*from* A Mite cast into the Common Treasury]

Though we have been sad
  yet now are glad
To see such a joyfull time,

Our Miseries they,
Are passing away,
And truth beginneth to clime.
We shall
be freed from thrall
When Righteousnesse reigneth as King,
The Glory so bright
Shall darken the light
Which comes from the Man of sinne.

Though men do us hate,
yet we in this state
Do suffer joyfully,
Though stripes we receive,
We do them forgive,
Which acts such cruelty.
For we
with them must agree,
Who seeketh our blood to spill,
And thus we may
Their cruelty slay,
Yea thus we shall envy kill.

The Poore long
have suffered wrong,
By the Gentry of this Nation,
The Clergy they
Have bore a great sway
By their base insultation.
But they shall
Lye levell with all
They have corrupted our Fountaines;
And then we shall see
Brave Community,
When Vallies lye levell with Mountains.

Tyranny have
made many a slave
Within this Land of ours,

But he must packe
For his Power doth cracke
And the day it will be ours.
The Priests ball,
and after him call
Saying, you must with us abide,
For if you do goe
Then cometh our woe,
And we shall have no more Tythe.

The Gentry are
fil'd with the like care,
How they shall their Power maintaine,
For they know
If Tyranny go,
They must packe to *France* or to *Spaine*.
Therefore they
will this gallant stay,
And hide him under a backe Gowne,
Or else in a Coach
Will keepe him very close,
Fearing he should be found.

The time indeed
that this cursed seed
Doth as closely in all men;
But chiefly in those
Who are *Englands* foes,
And we do very well know them.
But the light
that shineth so bright
Revileth this wickednesse,
And it must go
I very well know
To a Land of forgetfullnesse.

The time is nigh
that this mystery
Shall be no more obscure,

And then we shall see
Such community
As shall alwayes indure.
The Rich and Poore
shall love each other
Respecting of Persons shall fall,
The Father alone
That sits in his Throne
Shall honoured be of all.

The glorious State
which I do relate
Unspeakable comfort shall bring,
The Corne will be greene
And the Flowers seene
Our store-houses they will be fill'd
The Birds will rejoyce
with a merry voice
All things shall yield sweet increase
Then let us all sing
And joy in our King,
Which causeth all sorrowes to cease.

260 Title *Mite* small coin, the parable of 'the widow's mite' is in Mark 12: 41–4 and Luke 21: 1–4 8 *thrall* captivity 29 *sway* power, influence 36 see Isaiah 40:4 prophesying the coming of the Messiah: here the key image of Leveller belief 40 *packe* go 43 *ball* bawl, weep 48 *Tythe* the church's ten per cent 57 *backe* possibly misprint for 'black' 82 *Father* God the Father 87 *Unspeakable* indescribable, beyond telling 95 *King* Christ

261 THE DIGGERS SONG 1649

You noble diggers all stand up now
you noble diggers all stand up now
the wast land to maintaine seeing Cavaleirs by name
your digging does disdaine and persons all defame
Stand up now stand up now

Your houses they pull down: stand up now stand up now,
your houses they etc.
your houses they pull down to fright poore men in town,
but the gentry must come down, and the poor shall wear
the Crown
Stand up now diggers all.

With spades and hoes and plowes: stand up now, stand
up now,
with spades and hoes etc.
your freedome to uphold seeing Cavaleirs are bold
to kill you if they could and rights from you to hold
Stand up now diggers all.

There self will is theire law, stand up now stand up now,
theire self will etc.
since Tyrany came in, they count it now no sin
to make a Gaole a gin, to sterve poor men therein
Stand up now stand up now.

The Gentrye are all round, stand up now stand up now
the gentrie are all round etc.
the Gentrye are all round on each side they are found
there wisdomes so profound, to cheat us of our ground
Stand up now stand up now.

The Lawyers they conjoyne, stand up now stand up now,
the lawyers they etc.
to Arrest you they advise, such fury they devise
the devill in them lies, and hath blinded both their eyes.
Stand up now stand up now.

The Clergy they come in stand up now stand up now,
the Clergy they etc.
the Clergy they come in, and say it is a sin
that we should now begin, our freedom for to win.
Stand up now diggers all

The Tiths they yet will have, stand up now stand up now,
the tiths they etc.
the tithes they yet will have, and Lawyers their fees crave
and this they say is brave, to make the poor their slave
Stand up now diggers all.

'Gainst lawyers and the Priests, stand up now, stand up now,
'gainst Lawyers etc.
for Tyrants they are both, even flatt against their oath
to grant us they are loth, free meat and drinke and cloth
Stand uppe now diggers all.

The Club is all their Law, stand uppe now, stand uppe now
The Club is all their Law, stand uppe now,
The Club is all their Law to keepe men in awe,
but they noe vision saw to maintaine such a Law.
Stand uppe now diggers all.

The Cavaleers are foes, stand uppe now, stand uppe now,
The Cavaleers are foes stand uppe now
The Cavaleers are foes, themselves they do disclose
by verses nott in prose, To please the singing boyes
Stand uppe now diggers all.

To conquer them by Love, come in now, come in now,
To conquer them by love, come in now,
To conquer them by Love, as itt does you behove,
for hee is Kinge above, and noe power like to Love.
Glory heere diggers all.

261 See Notes on the Text for the probable occasion of the poem 19 *gin* snare, trap 26 *conjoyne* join with 46 *Club* metaphorically, violence, as well as with specific reference to beatings of Diggers and their stock

262 [*from* The Law of Freedom]

The Winter's past, the Spring time now appears,
Be gone thou Kingly Tyrant, with all thy Cavaliers.
Thy day is past, and sure thou dost appear
To be the bonds-mans son, and not the free-born Heir

Matt.15.13

262 5 Matthew 15: 13 Christ's words: 'Every plant, which my heavenly Father hath not planted, shall be rooted up'

WILLIAM CARTWRIGHT

263 *A New-years Gift*

Although Propriety be Crost,
By those that cry't up most,
No Vote hath yet pass'd to put down
The pious fires
Of good desires,
Our wishes are as yet our own.

Bless'd be the day then, 'tis *New year's*,
Natures knows no such fears
As those which do our hearts divide,
In spight of Force
Times keep their Course,
The Seasons run not on their side.

I send my (Muse) to one that knows
What each Relation ows,
One who keeps waking in his Breast
No other sense
But Conscience,
That only is his Interest.

Though to be Moderate, in this time,
Be thought almost a Crime,
That vertue yet is his so much,
That they who make
All whom they take
Guilty, durst never Call him such.

He wishes Peace, that Publike Good,
Dry Peace, not bought with Bloud,
Yet such as Honour may maintain,
And such the Crown
Would gladly own.
Wish o'r that Wish to him again.

He wishes that this Storm Subside,
Hush'd by a turn of Tide,
That one fix'd Calm would smooth the Main,
As Winds relent
When Furie's spent.
O wish that Wish to him again.

The Joys that Solemn Victories Crown,
When we not slay our own,
Joys that deserve a generall Song
When the day's gain'd
And no Sword stain'd,
Press on and round him in a Throng.

Thoughts rescue, and his danger kiss'd,
Being found as soon as miss'd,
Wish him not taken as before,
Hazard can ne'r
Make him more dear.
We must not fear so long once more.

Twist then in one most Glorious Wreath
All Joys you can bequeath,
And see them on the Kingdom thrown,

When there they dwell
He's pleas'd as well,
As if they sate on him alone.

Go, and return, and for his sake
Less noise and Tumult make,
Than Stars when they do run their Rounds;
Though Swords and Spears
Late fill'd his Eares,
He silence Loves, or Gentle Sounds.

263 33 *Main* sea

264 NOVEMBER.

Thou *Sun* that shed'st the Dayes, looke downe and see
A Month more shining by Events, than thee;
1. Day, is All Saints
Departed *Saints* and *Souls* sign'd it before,
But now the living signe it more.
2. All Souls.
Persons and *Actions* meet, All meant for Joy,
But some build up, and some destroy.
Bate us That Ushering Curse so dearly knowne,
And then the Month is All our Owne.
So, at the First, Darkenesse was throwne about
Th'unshapen Earth, and Light was thence strooke out.

3. Day, The Assembling of the unhappy Parliament
Draw the first Curtaine and the Scene is then
A Triple State of Cull'd and Trusted Men:
Men, in whose Hands 'twas once t'have giv'n us more
Then our Bold Fathers Askd before:
Who, had they us'd their Prince's Grace, had got
What no Armes could, and Theirs will not.
What more then Witchcraft did our Blessing Curse
And made the Cure make Evills worse?
'Tis the *Third* Day; throw in the Blackest Stone,
Mark it for Curs'd, and let it stand Alone.

4. Day, The Birth of the Princesse MARY.

But, hold! speake gentler things! This *Fourth* was seene
The softest Image of our Beauteous *Queene*.
Bring me a Lambe, not us'd to Elder Food,
That h'as as yet more Milke than Blood,
That to the Honour of this Early Bride
(Like *Thetis* joynd to *Peleus* side,)
Some Tender Thing may fall; though none can be
So White, so Tender, as is She.
Whiles we at home our Little Turfe debate,
She spreads our Glories to another State.

5. Day, Our Delivery from the Papists Conspiracy.

NEXT view a Treason of the worst Intent,
Had not our Owne *done* more, then Strangers *meant*;
Religion is the Thing both sides pretend,
But either to a different End:
They, out of Zeale, labour to reare their owne,
These, out of Zeale to pull All downe.
Blesse Us from These, as Them! but yet compare
Those in the Vault, These in the Chayre.
Though the just Lot of unsuccessful sin
Fix their's Without, you'l finde Worse Heads within.

12. Day, The Kings Victory at *Brainford*.

But hearke! What Thunder's that? and who hose men
Flying tow'rds Heav'n, but falling downe agen?
Whose those Blacke Corps cast on the Guilty Shore?
'Tis sin that swimmes to its owne Dore.
'Tis the Third scourge of Rebells, which allow'd
Our Army, like the Prophets Cloud
Did from an Handfull rise, Untill at last
Their Sky was by it Overcast.
But (as Snakes Hisse after th'have lost their Sting)
The Traytor call'd This Treachery in the King.

16. Day, The Birth of our gracious Q.

Away, and view the Graces and the Houres Hov'ring aloofe
and dropping mingled Flowres Upon a Cradle, where an

MARY Infant lay
More Grace, more Goddesse then were they;
Thrice did they destine Her to passe the seas;
(Love made Her Thrice to pass with ease)
To raise a strength of Princes first, and then
To raise Another strength of Men.
Most Fruitful Queene! we boast Both Gifts, and thus
The Day was meant to You, the Joy to Us.

17. Day, The begin- ning of Q. *Elizabeths* Raigne.

Next to this *Mother* stands a *Virgin Queene*,
Courting and Courted wheresoever seen;
The Peoples Love first from Her Troubles grew;
Her Reigne then made That Love her Due.
That Comely Order, which did then adorne
Both Fabricks, now by Facion's torne;
That *Forme*, by her allow'd, of *Common Pray'r*
Is styl'd *vaine Beating of the Ayre*.
How doe they Honour, how forsake Her Crowne!
Her Times are still Cry'd up, but Practis'd Downe.

19. Day, The Birth of our gracious King CHARLES.

Reach last, the Whitest Stone the World yet knew,
White as the Soule, to whom the Day is due.
Sonne of the peaceful *James*, how is he blest
With All his Blessings, but His Rest!
Though undeserved Times call All His Pow'rs,
And Troubles season Other Hour's,
Let this Day flow to Him as void of Care,
As Feasts to Gods, and Poets are:
The Wish is Just, O Heavens! As our strife
Hath added to His *Cares*, adde Yee to His *Life*.

And now, since His Large Heart with Hers is met,
Whose Day the starres on purpose neare His set;
NOVEMBER shall to me for ever shine,
Red in its Inke, Redder in Wine.
And since the *Third* (which almost hath made shift
T'Absolve the Treason of the *Fift*)
Cannot be well Remembred, or Forgot
By Loyall Hearts, as if 'twere not;

The *Last* extreame, against the *First* wee'l bring:
That gave us *Many Tyrants*, This a *KING*.

264 See Appendix 4 for the developing events related to the Royal Family described in this poem 7 *Bate* spare *Ushering* entering, beginning 11 side-note *unhappy Parliament* the Long Parliament assembled on 3 November 1640 21 side-note *Princesse Mary* was born on 4 November 1630 26 *Thetis, Peleus* see Appendix 1 29 *Turfe* small patch of earth 38 *Vault* cellars at Westminster where the conspirators attempted to blow up King James in Parliament in 1605 39 *Lot* reward 41 side-note *Brainford* Royalist victory at Brentford 12 November 1642 46 see 1 Kings 18: 44–5 51 side-note *Queen Mary* Henrietta Maria 65 *Comely* attractive 66 *Both Fabricks* ambiguous, possibly Church and State 70 *Cry'd up* fondly remembered, cited as a golden age 71 *Whitest Stone* a monument of white stone, classically commemorating a fortunate event 84 *Red in its Inke* rubrication in, for example, *The Book of Common Prayer* marking the day of a festival 86 *Fift* the date of the Gunpowder Plot

SIR THOMAS URQUHART

265 A non covenanters opinion of the violent, and impetuous disposition of some of our Puritans in Scotland.

By knocking down of Churches, Knox gave edge
t'opinions, fuller of blind zeal, then doubt:
Which hardly can be curbed in our age,
if some new Knocks come not, and knock them out.

265 1 *Knox* John Knox, see Appendix 2

THOMAS, LORD FAIRFAX

266 On the Fatal day. Jan: 30 1648

Oh Lett that Day from time be blotted quite
And lett beleefe of 't in next Age be waved
In deepest silence th'Act Concealed might

Soe that the King-doms-credit might be saved
But if the Power devine permitted this
His Will's the Law and ours must acquiesse.

Curae loquuntur Leves
Ingentes stupent

266 Title *Fatal day* the day of the execution of Charles I 6 *acquiesse* consent 7–8 'Light cares may be spoken, great [troubles] render dumb'

ANONYMOUS

267 COMPLAINT

Wise men suffer, good men grieve,
Knaves devise, and Fools believe;
Help, O Lord, send aid unto us,
Else Knaves and Fools will quite undo us.

ATTRIBUTED TO JAMES GRAHAM, MARQUIS OF MONTROSE

268 [My dear and only Love...]

My dear and only Love, I pray
 This Noble World of thee,
Be govern'd by no other Sway
 But purest Monarchie.

For if Confusion have a Part,
 Which vertuous Souls abhore,
And hold a Synod in thy Heart,
 I'll never love thee more.

Like *Alexander* I will reign,
 And I will reign alone,
My Thoughts shall evermore disdain
 A Rival on my Throne.

He either fears his Fate too much,
Or his Deserts are small,
That puts it not unto the Touch,
To win or lose it all.

But I must rule and govern still,
And always give the Law,
And have each Subject at my Will,
And all to stand in awe.

But 'gainst my Battery if I find
Thou shun'st the Prize so sore,
As that thou set'st me up a Blind,
I'll never love thee more.

Or in the Empire of thy Heart,
Where I should solely be,
Another do pretend a Part,
And dares to Vie with me,

Or if Committees thou erect,
And goes on such a Score,
I'll sing and laugh at thy Neglect,
And never love thee more.

But if thou wilt be constant then,
And faithful of thy Word,
I'll make thee glorious by my Pen,
And famous by my Sword.

I'll serve thee in such noble Ways,
Was never heard before:
I'll crown and deck thee all with Bays,
And love thee evermore.

268 1 *Love* there has been much speculation as to who, or what, is addressed here. A majority of critics favour the interpretation that this poem, inverting the strategy of no. 253, is an address to Scotland, appropriating the discourse of amatory poetry in a way. This produces the difficulty that, if the poem is in Montrose's own persona, it makes extravagant claims for his status. It is at least possible that it is in the persona of the King, appropriating the Gaelic and Irish trope of the ruler married to his (personified) kingdom 7 *Synod* meeting of churchmen, parliament 15 *Touch* test, alluding to the testing of gold or silver with a touchstone 21 *Battery* gun-emplacement 23 *Blind* technical term of fortification: a

screen or other structure to give protection from enemy fire 28 *Vie* compete 30 *Score* ambiguous: probably, 'in such a way', but *OED* records an early ninteenth-century usage 'to go off at score' for a horse running out of control

269 *On Humane Inconstancy*

The world's a tennis Court, man is the ball
Toss'd at the wall
High soareing thoughts, and languishing despaire
The rackets are
Content the line, our straynes oft ore and under
Like balls of thunder.
Bid all who build their hopes on towers of Aire
Take heed, since fall they must, their falls be faire.

Last night I looked up to promotions skie
There did I spy
A star whose greatness was with glory mixt
But twas not fixt
For when the Pleiades begun to play
It shrunke away
And taught Astrologers by this to know
That meteors are no substance, but a show.

From thence to Church I went to thinke to pray
Twas holy day
But from afarr the high priests ghost did cry
Oh come not nigh
Our sanctuary is with Blood defild
And truth's exiled
Bethel Bethanen is. Doeg treads downe
The Preistly miter, and Imperiall Crowne.

Affrighted with these florrid shews at last
Mine eyes I cast
Up to Great Charles his wayne, and soon I finde
That Boreas winde
Hym blasted, all his hopes, and made him try
The uncertaynety

Of Humane glory, which with Flattering smiles
At first Embraces, but i'th'end beguiles.

Tis strange to see how spiders oft doe spin
A Trifling gin
To trap a gnat, but man with anxious Care
Contrives a snare
For his owne foot, and whilst that wretched he
Strives to fre
In vayne he toyles for who cairs him a fall
When heaven writes mene Tekel on the wall?

Aideu then Brainsick pleasures, get you gone
Let me alone
Ile drinke o'th'brooke, and Eate o'th'hony comb
In peace at home
Not striveing to be greate, but good, for Loe
The event doth show
That outward guilding cannot serve to hide
The Ruines of a rottin Inward side.

269 See Notes on the Text for the possible authorship of this poem, and for the tennis metaphor in 1–6. 5 *straynes* stretchings, exertions to return the ball 19 *high priest* Archbishop Laud, see Appendix 2 23 *Bethel Bethanen...Doeg* see Appendix 1 27 *Great Charles his wayne* the constellation the Plough (*wayne* wain, wagon) 28 *Boreas* the north wind, see Appendix 1; here, metaphorically, perhaps the Scots army 34 *gin* trap 40 *mene Tekel* see Appendix 1 47 *guilding* gilding

270 [Unhappy is the Man]

Unhappy is the Man
In whose Breast is confin'd
The Sorrows and Distresses all
Of an afflicted Mind.

The Extremity is great,
He dies if he conceal,
The World's so void of secret Friends,
Betray'd if he reveal.

Then break afflicted Hearts,
And live not in these Days,
When all prove Merchants of their Faith,
None trusts what other says.

For when the Sun doth shine,
Then Shadows do appear;
But when the Sun doth hide his Face,
They with the Sun retire.

Some friends as Shadows are,
And Fortune as the Sun;
They never proffer any Help
Till fortune first begin.

But if in any Case
Fortune shall first decay,
Then they as Shadows of the Sun
With Fortune run away.

270 7 *secret* to be trusted with a confidence

271 *Upon the Death of King Charles the First*

Great! Good! and Just! could I but rate
My griefs, and thy too rigid fate,
I'de weep the world to such a strain,
As it should Deluge once again,
But since thy loud-tongu'd bloud demands supplies
More from *Briareus* hands, than *Argus* eyes,
I'le sing thy Obsequies, with Trumpet sounds,
And write thy Epitaph with *Bloud* and *Wounds*.

Montrose

Written with the point of his Sword.

271 1 *rate* equal 4 *Deluge* flood 6 *Briareus, Argus* see Appendix 1

272 *Some Lynes one the killing of the Earle of Newcastells Sonnes doge by the Marques Hamilton in the Quiens Garden at Yorke. Wrettin then by The Earl of Montrois.*

Heir Layes a doge quhosse qualities did plead
Such fatall end from a Renowned blade,
And Blame him not, though he Succumed Now
For Hercules could not Combat 'gainst too,
For quhillst he one hes foe revenge did take
He manfully was killed behind his backe.
Then say to Eternise the Curr thats gone
He flech't the Mayden Sword of Hamiltone.

272 1 *quhosse* whose 3 *Succumed* was defeated 4 *Hercules* see Appendix 1 *too* two 5 *quhillst* while 7 *Eternise* immortalize 8 *flech't* fleshed, blooded, in the sense of initiated with a first kill

273 [Can little Beasts with Lions roar]

Can little Beasts with Lions roar,
And little Birds with Eagles soar;

Can shallow Streams command the Seas,
And little Aunts the humming Bees?
No, no, no, no, it is not meet
The Head should stoup unto the Feet.

273 4 *Aunts* ants

274 *On Himself, upon hearing what was his Sentence.*

Let them bestow on ev'ry Airth a Limb;
Open all my Veins, that I may swim
To Thee my Saviour, in that Crimson Lake;
Then place my purboil'd Head upon a Stake;

Scatter my Ashes, throw them in the Air:
Lord (Since Thou know'st where all these Atoms are)
I'm hopeful, once Thou'lt recollect my Dust,
And confident Thou'lt raise me with the Just.

274 1 *Airth* modern Scots 'airt', region: the poem in 1–5 reflects on the public display of the dismembered bodies of executed criminals 4 *purboil'd* parboiled 7 *recollect* reassemble

CLEMENT PAMAN

275 *Epitaph on the Earl of* Strafford

Here lies Wise and Valiant Dust,
Huddled up 'twixt Fit and Just:
Strafford, who was hurried hence
'Twixt Treason and Convenience.
He spent his Time here in a Mist;
A *Papist*, yet a *Calvinist*.
His Prince's nearest Joy, and Grief.
He had, yet wanted all Reliefe.
The Prop and Ruine of the State;
The People's violent Love, and Hate:
One in extreames lov'd and abhor'd.
Riddles lie here; or in a word,
Here lies Blood; and let it lie
Speechlesse still, and never crie.

275 See Notes on the Text for discussion of Paman's authorship, Appendix 2 for Thomas Wentworth, Earl of Strafford 2 'Dealt with summarily, with a mixture of justice and expediency' 3 *hurried* to execution

276 *The teares*

Leave mee all other busines but teares,
A sadder busines than both houses feares,
And a much holyer concernment, Cou'd
Our eyes but wash our hands and purge that blood

Which stain'd Edgehill, where some of our men lye,
And what should save the rest, our Charity.
Compassion dide there gasping in a wound
And stretchd out in a sinew, where she found
Death and a grave, while the cold gore relents
And weeps ageal'd into her Monument.
Oh! had she not dyde there we had not kept
A feast for that for which our good Kinge wept,
Whose Heavenly breast doth dayly entertaine
More real visions then others feigne
For here 'Tis true the feild is found agen,
And his hart bleeds the blood was was squander'd then.
Here *Lindsey, Varney* fall anew and lye
Brave scenes of an unhappy Loyalty.
Whose virtue shall beare out their fortune; And
Fame teare their chronicle from chances hand
Whose blinder hand knoweth no different dresse
'Twixt valour and Rebellious successe.
Here too fall St. John, Essex punisht more
By the Kings pitty now than's force before.
Whose mercy mornes his Justice, greivd to see
His sword do more than can his clemency
A Royall pitty where the conquerors Eyes
Weepe and upbrayd his Enemyes obsequies
And that because they're Enemies, and strive
To kill that life which keepeth them alive
To kill their owne souls too. This stayes his hand;
Thence come his treaty's. Hee'le have none bee damn'd.
O you hott zealotts, learne from that good King
You lye and rayle on, Mercy, not to fling
Souls down to Hell extempore, Stand and weigh
What a life cost before you throw't away,
Tis dearer than your prayers. They cost nought,
But soules (stand and bethinke yourselves) were bought;
Bought with that blood you shed. For Christs blood may
Adapt that Brothers veines whom thou dost slay,
Valew the cause. 'Tis Ceremony. Can
A shadow ere dost think be worth a man?
Or which is the more ghastly Rubrick, looke
Thou on Edgehill, or on The Service booke

Noe, pray that Devill out you have preacht in
Beg pardon for your new Originall sin
Which staines and kills us and Posterity.
You'le eate the apple, though the people dye.
Oh; Muster up yourselves and spare your men,
Repent your Buffs to quiett gowns agen:
Silence your Trumpets and unbrace your drums.
Cannons and these wern't Christ's voice. He was dumbe,
Meeke as his Gosple. It was the old law
That spoke in fyre, and it became the Awe
Well of a killing letter. Th'news still-borne
Still as the dew teem'd from the wombe of Morne,
Your patent too's for peace. Oh go not on
To rend both her and your Commission.
Fighting with what should keep you quiett, and
Suborning just Religion to stand
A wittnes gainst herselfe, and to defend
That as her act which is by her condemn'd,
Whose unarm'd Conquests Holy Fame hath spread
More for the blood she lost, than that she shead.
Remember Iudgement and that trumpe which shall
Sound to your Keinton Trumps to wake and call
The ashes up, and theirs who but for you
Had beene as loath to fight as they'le be now
To rise, and 'fore the dreadfull bench appeare
When they'le now run away as you did here
Oh! Melt your harts to teares, and in them draw
A map of that great Courts unbribed awe
Where no demure Religious pretence
Compounds for Treason, nor makes your offence
Lesse cause you sinn'd for Gods sake, for his cause
While men are preacht to death and slaine by lawes.
Next, draw a sea of blood, Twere not amisse
To draw't in such a teare where let there rise
A constellation of Martyrs who
Gott crownes for suffering that which you would doe.
Draw them amaz'd to see men wiser growne
Then to buy God so deare as Martyrdome.
Here in a line apart draw out St Paul
Dreadfull with his damnation to all

That resist higher powers, Thinke he askes
Who gave you licence Then? not he, your maskes
Are not of his but your owne making, who
Thus cheate his doctrine and example too
Then draw a sigh. A sigh made up of flame
Fearfull as that which sooted *Nero's* name
And burnt his Rome. In that white flame let fall
Some ruddy streaks of blood drawn from St Paul.
In which gay torment lett the Tyrant lye
Folded in penance for his crueltye
Cursing that coward fury which slew those
Whose hands were bound and taught not to oppose
And last among your *Martyrs* or amonge
The *Confessors* at least let our Kinges wrongs
And what are great as they his virtues stand
With Peace and Plenty upon either hand
Draw too his Crime. He was not tyrant, This
Though in bad Kings a virtue, was his vice
Who has no fault but that is too good
And hazardeth his owne to save your blood
The unborne blood whilst this his wise defence
Conquers a Civill war and three yeares hence
Not by his Peoples feet lett this Deare head
Suffer almost those ills which Nero did.
And now read o're this table and compare
Paul, Martyrs, Nero, Charles, your case will there
None, Paul may not resist the worst of men,
You may the best of Kings, Pauls ravisht pen
Writes God on Nero, but your zealous spite
Blasphemes the people into God, and writes
Them King of Kings, Kings of a King whose name
Shall live your infamy, and when by fame
His life and your Sermons shall be read o're
(Sermons, enough to fyre the world before
Her tyme) Our easy nephews will suspect
Th'whole story for a libell gainst the Sect:
But stay'der heads will curse that pious lie
Which feign'd Gods hand to signe disloyalty.
  Good then be wise betimes. Go not about
By new untrod distractions to cutt out

The broad way wider, it is plaine enough,
Wee need no guides, tis the first way we knew
Although you have found out a narrower track
To murder Kings in, than Ravilliack
Yet at the all seeing day you will be told
The path indeed was new, the way was old,
And twill be then but a cold boast to tell
You first discover'd this new way to Hell.
Oh come, lett's mingle teares untill they grow
A sea, on whose calms bosome we may row
Peace home in tryumph, and at each oare sing
Hymns to two mighty mercyes, Gods and the Kings.

276 The poem is a complex lament for the hardening of attitudes on both sides following the indecisive battle of Edgehill, 22 October 1642, a battle claimed as a victory by the royalists 2 *both houses* Lords and Commons, but also royalists and parliamentarians 7–10 The allegory laments the death of Compassion in England, killed at Edgehill and buried below a monument of congealed blood 8 *sinew* muscle 9 *gore* blood 11 *she* Compassion 12 Contemporary propaganda asserted that Charles was haunted by spectres of those who had died at Edgehill (*The Great Eclipse of the Sun, or Charles his Waine Over-clouded*, 30 August 1644). Paman states obliquely that it would be better if all of England were haunted by the real implications of the battle 17 *Lindsey, Varney* the Earl of Lindsey resigned as the commander-in-chief of the royalist troops on the morning of Edgehill, but died at the head of his Royal Foot Guards. Sir Edmund Verney, the royal standard bearer, was killed at Edgehill, defending the Standard 21 *dresse* uniform: Fame records the deaths of royalist and rebel impartially. 23 *St. John, Essex* Oliver St John (1603–42) the younger, died from wounds received at Edgehill; the Earl of Essex commanded the parliamentary forces, see Appendix 2 25 *mornes* mourns 25–36 Paman expounds Charles's actions as motivated by pity for his subjects and desire for peace, as opposed to the utterances of the Puritan clergy who incite their hearers to war 28 *upbrayd* reproach 34 *rayle on* denounce 41–65 Paman asserts that the cause of the war is no more than disagreement about the form of public worship and contrasts the hardened attitudes of the Puritan clergy with the forgiveness and compassion preached by Christ 43 *Rubrick* literally 'that written in red': the directions for observance in the Anglican Prayer Book (the 'Ceremony' of 41) The choice is between red ink and red blood 48 *eate the apple* man's first sin of disobedience 49 *Muster* gather together 50 *Buffs* Buff Coats: uniforms 51 *unbrace* slacken the drumheads, metaphorically, silence the drums 55 *killing letter* The pre-Christian codes of revenge of the Old Testament; opposed to Paul's exposition of the new, merciful Christian covenant in 2 Corinthians 3: 6. 57 *patent* literally 'licence', metaphorically duty as a Christian minister 66 *Keinton Trumps* the parliamentarian forces who fled to Kineton before the royalist cavalry charge 68 *dreadfull bench* the Last Judgement 83 *St. Paul* the reference here is to St Paul's assertion in Ephesians 6 that all people should live in decent subjection in their place in society 90 The Emperor Nero, a persecutor of Christians, was asserted to have ordered that much of Rome should be destroyed by fire that he might enjoy the spectacle as an aesthetic experience. 97–8 *Martyrs...Confessors* those saints who died for, or proclaimed, their faith. 108 *ded* did 113 St Paul commands no resistance, even to the worst of tyrants 119 *easy* living at ease, after the wars 121 *stay'der* more sensible 128 *Ravilliack* François Ravilliac assassinated Henri IV of France in 1610 129 *all seeing day* Judgement Day, contrasted with the imagined judgement of posterity in 109–22.

THOMAS JORDAN

277 *An Allarme in* 1645.

Bring a Light, the Foe's in sight;
Prethee forgive me,
That I must thus leave thee in the Night;
My Bliss, Take this, and this,
Sleep well, I'le keep 'till
My happy returne, a parting kisse,
Thou wouldst free my life from feares,
Yet thy wet Eye
Drownes me with teares,
Wipe those faire pearles from thine eye,
And heare thy Souldiers
Lullaby.

Sweet sleep, lye still my Deare,
Dangers be strangers
For ever, unto thy eye or eare
No sounds, or wo for wounds,
Numbers thy slumbers,
Or dare to approach within thy bounds;
But such Songs as *Seraphs* sing,
Which move by Love
Unto their King.
That thy sight, touch, tast, or smells
May say, all joy
In hearing dwells.

And when thou wakest agen,
Fortune importune
Thy senses to see us happy Men,
That we may so agree,
Dangers of strangers
May never destroy our Unity:
So shall Peace ascend her Throne,
For than each man
May claime his owne;
We like raging seas will run,
That meet and fight
Then flow in one.

So shall all sweete Joyes content thee,
That Ayre, Earth, or sea affords,
Tables shall be spread with plenty,
Sickles shall be made of swords:
Horses shall no more weare Armour,
That were plunder'd from the Plow,
Whilst the doubtfull frighted Farmour,
Questiond is, *For whom are you?*

Private jarres shall be relinquish'd,
Every man shall have his owne.
Thine and mine shall be distinguish'd,
And no Seeds of sorrow sowne;
Comfort come to all complayners,
That were frighted back with frowns,
Governours no more be gayners,
Which are now the Kings of Townes.

Mountains shall no more grow myrish
With so many noble bloods,
Fickle French and idle Irish
That come over for our Goods,
And have had so much enjoyment
In the ruine of the Land,
Shall be set to fit employment
By the power of strong Command.

Bulwarks then shall all be slighted
To let in our Trades encrease,
Church and State shall be united
'Tis the Paradise of Peace;
Merchants feare no navall dangers
Or from their own Colours go,
But hold free Commerce with strangers,
Neighbour-nations should do so.

Midnight calls, and I must leave thee,
This shall purchase my release,
May not such sweet dreames deceive thee
That pretend a prudent Peace?
War with this dark night fly over
And all joy rise with the Light:
Thus thy Lipps with mine I cover
One kiss more, and then Good night.

277 19 *Seraphs* see Appendix 1 26 *importune* solicit 40 see Isaiah 2: 4 45 *jarres* quarrels 53 *myrish* marshy 61 *Bulwarks* fortifications *slighted* demolished 66 *Colours* ships' ensigns

278 *The Farewell*

1.

Fair *Fidelia* leave me now,
I may no more
Thy Deity adore,
Nor offer to thy shrine,
I serve one more divine,
And greater far then you;
Hark, the trumpets call away,
I must go,
Lest the foe
Lose the King and win the day.
Let's march bravely on,
Charge them in the Van,
Our Cause Gods is,
Though the ods is
Ten times ten to one.

2.

Tempt no more, I may not yield,
Although thy eyes
A Kingdom might surprize;
Leave off thy wanton tales,
The high-born Prince of *Wales*
Is mounted in the Field,
Where the loyal Gentry flock,
Though forlorn,
Nobly born,
Of a near decaying stock,
Cornish boyes be bold,
Never lose your hold,
He that loiters,
Is by Traytors
Basely bought and sold.

3.

One kiss more, and then farewell,
Nay now give o're,
I prethee fool no more;
Why cloud'st thou so thy beams?
I see by these extreams
A woman's heaven or hell.
Pray the King may have his own,
That the Queen
May be seen
With her Babes on *Englands* Throne;
Rally up your men,
One shall vanquish ten:
Victory we
Come to try thy
Favour once agen.

278 10 *Lose* fail to see; Jordan implies that the mere sight of Charles commands obedience 12 *Van* vanguard, first line of assault 34 *beams* from her weeping eyes

279 [*from* The Cheaters Cheated]

Souldiers fight and Hectors rant on
  Whilst poor Wenches go to rack,
Who would be a wicked wanton
  Onely for Suppers, Songs and Sack,
To endure the alteration
  Of these times that are so dead;
Thus to lead a long vacation
  Without Money, Beer, or Bread.

Farewel *Bloomsberry* and *Sodom*,
  Lukeners-lane and *Turnbull-street*,
Woe was me when first I trod'em
  With my wilde unwary feet.
I was bred a Gentlewoman,
  But our family did fall
When the Gentry's coin grew common,
  And the Souldiers shar'd it all.

279 Title see Notes on the Text. This is a song from a semi-dramatic entertainment, sung by a fallen gentlewoman turned prostitute. 1 *Hectors* bullies 2 *rack* ruin 4 *Sack* sherry wine 9 *Bloomsberry* then a disreputable area *Sodom* a comparable den of iniquity in the Bible, or a part of London so called 10 *Lukeners-lane*, *Turnbull-street* again streets in London frequented by prostitutes

280 *The Resolution.* 1642.

1.

Ask me no more why there appears
Daily such troops of Dragoneers,
Since it is requisite you know
They rob *cum Privilegio.*

2.

Ask me not why the Gaole confines
Our Hierarchy of best Divines,
Since 'twas allow'd by full consent,
The Priviledge of Parliament.

3.

Ask me no more why from *Blackwall*
Such tumults come unto *White-hall*,
Since some in Parliament agree,
'Tis for the Subjects Liberty.

4.

Ask me not why to *London* comes
So many Muskets, Pikes, and Drums,
So that we fear they'l never cease,
'Tis to procure the Kingdoms Peace.

5.

Ask me no more why little *Finch*
From Parliament began to flinch,
Since such as dare to Hawk at Kings,
May easily clip a Finches wings.

6.

Ask me no more why *Strafford*'s dead,
Or why they aim'd so at his head;
Faith all the reason I can give,
'Tis thought he was too wise to live.

7.

Ask me no more where's all the Plate
Brought in at such an easie rate,
It to the owners back they'l bring,
In case it fall not to the King.

8.

Ask me not why the House delights
Not in our two wise Kentish Knights,
Their Counsels never were thought good,
Because they were not understood.

9.

Ask me no more why *Livesey* goes
To ceaze all rich men as his foes,
Whilst Countrey Farmers sigh and sob,
Yeomen may beg when Knights do rob.

10.

Ask me no more by what strange slight
London's Lord Mayor was made a Knight.
Since there's a strength sprung out of war
That can at once both make and mar.

11.

Ask me no more why in this age
I sing so free without a cage,
My answer is, I need not fear,
All *England* doth the burthen bear.

12.

Ask me no more (for I grow dull),
Why *Hotham* keeps the Town of *Hull.*
I'le answer ye one word for all,
All things are thus when Kings do fall.

280 A parody of no. 88: the rhetorical strategy is to set forth the public pronouncements of parliament, revealing them by context as increasingly disengenuous. See Appendix 4. 2 *Draguneers* dragoons, troops 4 *cum Privilegio* 'with the Privilege' [of the parliament] 9–10 the London mob, attempting to intervene in the government 17 *Finch*, see Appendix 2 21 *Strafford* see Appendix 2 and no. 275 25 *Plate* precious metal wares 30 *Kentish Knights* The Kentish Petition, 'for restoring the King to his Rights and for setling the Government', was delivered to the House of Commons on 30 April 1642: Richard Lovelace and Sir William Boteler were both imprisoned for delivering it 33 *Livesey* see Appendix 2 34 *ceaze* seize 38 *London's Lord Mayor* see Appendix 2, under Pennington 44 *doth the burthen bear* pun, as modern sense, but also 'sings this chorus' 46 *Hotham* see Appendix 2

ANONYMOUS

281 *The Passage of a Coach travelling to Dover.*

The Foundation of the Coach, a *Guilty Conscience.*
The Axeltree, *Ambition* and *Cruelty.*
The Wheels, *Fears* and *Jealousies.*
The Reins, *too much liberty and licentiousness.*
The six Horses, *five Members* and *K—*

The Postillion, *Captain Venne.*
The Coach-man, *Isaac Pennington* Lord Maior:
In the two ends of the Coach sate *Essex* and *B—*
In the Boots sate *Say* and *Seal*, and the *silent Speaker.*
On the hinder part of the Coach was written this Anagram.

Robert Devereux General
Never duller Oxe greater Rebel.

After the Coach follows *Straffords* Ghost, crying,
Drive on, Drive on, Revenge, revenge.

As this Coach was going through the City it was staid by a *Court of Guard*, who cry'd, *Where's our Mony? Where's our Plate?* the Speaker said, *Ye have the Publick Faith for't.* Whereupon they passed towards *Gravesend*, where they stayed at the Sign of the *Hope*, where was the Earl of *Warwick*, with a Ship called the *Carry-Knave.*

281 See Appendix 4, for the year 1642 2 *Axeltree* the beam attaching the wheels 5 *five members and K—* the five Members of Parliament and Lord Kimbolton, see Appendix 2 6 *Postillion* groom, riding one of the coach horses 6 *Venne;* 8 *Essex and B—* [Lord Brooke] see Appendix 2 9 *Boots* a low outside compartment behind the main body of a closed coach *Say and Seal, silent Speaker* [Lenthall]; 13 *Strafford* see Appendix 2 17 *Plate* precious metal wares 19 *Sign* inn, identified with and by its painted emblem 20 *Warwick* see Appendix 2

SIR JOHN DENHAM

282 Sarpedon's *Speech to* Glaucus *in the 12th book of* Homer.

Thus to *Glaucus* spake

Divine *Sarpedon*, since he did not find
Others as great in Place, as great in Mind.
Above the rest, why is our Pomp, our Power?
Our flocks, our herds, and our possessions more?
Why all the Tributes Land and Sea affords
Heap'd in great Chargers, load our sumptuous boards?

Our chearful Guests carowse the sparkling tears
Of the rich Grape, whilst Musick charms their ears.
Why as we pass, do those on *Xanthus* shore,
As Gods behold us, and as Gods adore?
But that as well in danger, as degree,
We stand the first; that when our *Lycians* see
Our brave examples, they admiring say,
Behold our Gallant Leaders! These are They
Deserve the Greatness; and un-envied stand:
Since what they act, transcends what they command.
Could the declining of this Fate (oh friend)
Our Date to Immortality extend?
Or if Death sought not them, who seek not Death,
Would I advance? Or should my vainer breath
With such a Glorious Folly thee inspire?
But since with Fortune Nature doth conspire,
Since Age, Disease, or some less noble End,
Though not less certain, doth our days attend;
Since 'Tis decreed, and to this period lead,
A thousand ways the noblest path we'll tread;
And bravely on, till they, or we, or all,
A common Sacrifice to Honour fall.

282 A free translation of Homer, *Iliad*, XII. 310–28 6 *Chargers* serving dishes 7 *carowse* quaff, drink 9 *Xanthus* see Appendix 1 12 *Lycians* see Appendix 1

SIR ROGER L'ESTRANGE

283 *Mr. Le Strange his verses in the Prison at Linn*

Beat on proud billows, Boreas blow,
  Swell curled waves high as Joves roofe,
Your incivillity shall know,
  That innosence is tempest proofe:
    Thou surely Nereus roare, my thoughts are calm,
    Then strike affliction, for thy wounds are balm.

That which the world miscalls a Gaole,
A private closet is to me,
Whilst a good conscience is my baile,
And innocense my liberty:
Locks, barres, lonlinesse, together mett,
Make me no prisoner, but an Anchorett.

I, while I wisht to be retir'd,
Into this private roome was turn'd,
As if theire wisdomes had conspir'd,
A Salamander should be burn'd.
Or like those Sophies that would drowne a fish,
I am constrain'd to suffer what I wish.

So he that strocke at Iasons life,
Thinking to make his purpose sure,
By a malicious friendly knife,
Did only wound him to a cure:
Malice I see wants witt, for what it ment,
Mischiefe oftimes proves favour in th'event.

These manacles upon mine arme,
I as my sweet-hearts favours weare,
And then to keepe mine ancles warme,
I have some iron shackles there;
Contentment cannot smart, Stoicks we see
Make torments easie by theire apathie.

Here sin for want of food doth starve,
Where tempting objects are not seen,
And these strong walls do only serve
To keepe vice out, and keepe me in:
Malice of late grows charitable sure,
I'me not comitted, but I'm kept secure.

When once my Prince affliction hath,
Prosperity doth treason seeme;
And then to smooth so rough a path,
I can learne patience, e'en from him:
Now not to suffer shews no loyall heart;
When Kings want ease, subjects must learne to smart.

What though I cannot see my King
  Either in his Person or his Coine;
Yet contemplation is a thing
  Will render what I have not, mine.
    My King from me what adamant can part,
    Whom I doe weare engraven in my heart.

My soule's as free as th'ambient aire,
  Although my baser parts immur'd,
While loyall thoughts do still repaire,
  T'accompany my sollitude:
    And though rebellion doe my body bind,
    My King can only captivate my mind.

Have you beheld the nightingale,
  A pilgrime turn'd into a cage;
How still shee tells her wonted taile,
  In this her private hermitage:
    E'en there her chanting melody doth prove
    That all her barres are trees, her cage a grove.

I am the bird whom they combine,
  Thus to deprive of liberty;
And though they doe my corps confine,
  Yet maugre hate, my soule is free:
    And though imur'd, yet here I'le chirp and sing,
    Disgrace to rebells, glory to my King.

283 1 *billows* waves *Boreas* see Appendix 1 2 *Joves roofe* the sky 6 *balm* soothing ointment 8 *closet* room 12 *Anchorett* hermit 16 *Salamander* mythical fire-lizard 17 *Sophies* Persian rulers, infamous as cruel despots 19 Iason see Appendix 1 30 *apathie* here, philosophical subjugation of emotion 44 *Coine* the king's face on minted money 47 *adamant* diamond, the strongest cutting edge 49 *ambient* encircling 50–4 see no. 290 57 *wonted* usual 61 *combine* conspire 64 *maugre* in spite of 65 *imur'd* imprisoned

MARTIN LLUELYN

284 *Caroll*, Sung to His Majesty on Christmas day, 1645.

Great *Copie* of this *Solemne Day*,
Which you transcribe afresh,
And make *afflictions* your *array*,
As God made *his* of *flesh*.
God humbled *best* by afflicted Kings *is showne*,
Because their height is *nearest* to his own.

Though in his *Traine* the *Oxe* appeare,
And to his *Court* intrude,
It was no *breach* of *Reverence* there,
What's *Nature* is not Rude.
This Act the Oxe *with Innocence befell*
They cannot sinne, who know not to doe well.

But some into your *Pallace* gat,
And rear'd a threatning head,
Some, whom your *Pastures* have made fat,
And your owne *Cribbe* hath fed.
The wanton Beasts *which to this temper rise*,
Are ripe *and* fit *to fall a Sacrifice.*

The Beasts which to his *cradle* came,
There at his *manger* stood,
Not to *build triumphs* on his shame,
But to *receive* their *food.*
But here the Herd *now surfieted doth stand*,
And being full, *learnes to* despise *the hand.*

But as the *Treasure* in the *Mine*,
Is *treasure* still though *trodde*,
So in this *Cloud* our Sun *you* shine,
And *God* in *flesh* was *God.*

For *God* and *Kings* are still beyond us plac't,
And *highest* still though ne're so *low debas't*.

284 1 *Copie* literally, copy of a text: the central idea of this poem is that Charles I in adversity is like Christ humbling himself to take on humanity 3 *array* clothes 16 *Cribbe* manger

ABRAHAM COWLEY

285 *SORS VIRGILIANA*

Aeneid Lib. 4 v. 615

By a bold peoples stubborn armes opprest,
Forc'd to forsake the land which he possest
Torn from his dearest son, let him in vain
Beg help, and see his friends unjustly slain:
Let him to bold unequal Termes submit,
In hopes to save his Crown; but loose both it
And life at once: untimely let him dye
And on an open stage unburied lye.

285 See Notes on the Text for the context of the poem

286 *To the Lord Falkland. For his safe Return from the Northern Expedition against the* Scots.

Great is thy *Charge, O North*; be wise and just,
England Commits her *Falkland* to thy trust;
Return him safe: *Learning* would rather choose
Her *Bodley*, or her *Vatican* to loose.
All things that are but *writ* or *printed* there,
In his unbounded Breast *engraven* are.
There all the *Sciences* together meet,
And every *Art* does all her *Kindred* greet.
Yet justle not, nor quarrel; but as well
Agree as in some *Common Principle*.

So in an *Army* govern'd right we see
(Though out of several Countrys rais'd it be)
That all their Order and their Place maintain,
The *English, Dutch*, the *Frenchman* and the *Dane*.
So thousand diverse *Species* fill the aire,
Yet neither crowd nor mix confus'dly there,
Beasts, Houses, Trees, and Men together lye,
Yet enter *undisturb'd* into the Eye.
  And this great *Prince of Knowledge* is by Fate
Thrust into th'noise and business of a State,
All *Virtues*, and some *Customs* of the *Court*,
Other mens *Labour*, are at least his *Sport*.
Whilst we who can no action undertake,
Whom *Idleness* it self might *Learned* make,
Who hear of nothing, and as yet scarce know,
Whether the *Scots* in *England* be or no,
Pace dully on, oft tire, and often stay,
Yet see his nimble *Pegasus* fly away.
'Tis *Natures* fault who did thus partial grow,
And her *Estate* of *Wit* on *One* bestow.
Whilst we like *younger Brothers*, get at best
But a *small Stock*, and must *work* out the rest.
How could he answer't, should the State think fit
To question a *Monopoly* of *Wit*?
  Such is the *Man* whom we require the same
We lent the *North*; untoucht as is his *Fame*.
He is too good for *War*, and ought to be
As far from *Danger*, as from *Fear* he's free.
Those *Men* alone (and those are useful too)
Whose *Valour* is the only *Art* they know,
Were for sad *War* and bloody *Battels* born,
Let *Them* the *State Defend*, and *He Adorn*.

286 Title see Appendix 2 4 *Bodley* Bodleian Library in Oxford *Vatican* the Papal library in Rome 6 *engraven* carved, fixed 28 *Pegasus* see Appendix 1 32 *Stock* inheritance, as the main share goes to the firstborn 34 *Monopoly* exclusive possession of a commodity

287 The Civill Warre.
The second Booke.

Thus like a *Deluge War* came roaring forth,
The bending *West* orewhelm'd, and riseing *North.*
A *Deluge* there; and high red *Tides* the while
Oreflowd all parts of *Albions* bleeding *Ile.*
For dire *Alecto*, ris'en from *Stygian* strand,
Had scatterd *Strife* and *Armes* through all the Land.
In a black hollow Clowd, by ill Windes driven,
Shee sat; oreshadow'ed *Earth* and frighted *Heaven.*
Thus like *Triptol'emus* through wide aire shee rode;
And all the fertill glebe with discords sow'ed.
The fatall seede still dropt shee as shee went,
And her owne clowds with a shrill *Trumpet* rent.
Great *Brittaines* aged *Genius* heard the sound,
Shooke his gray head, and sunck into the ground.
The'astonisht *Plowmen* the sad noyse did heare,
Look'ed up in vaine, and left their worke for feare.
Pale *woemen* heard it from afarr, and prest
The crying *Babes* close to their panting brest.
The nightborne *Virgin* stopt on *Hopton* heath;
Thrice filld the balefull *Trumpe* with deadly breath;
Scarce had the fatall sound thrice strooke the aire,
When strait her owne deare *Gell* and *Brereton's* there.
Men whom she lov'ed, and twice had sav'ed before
From *Hastings* sword, when thowsand fates it bore
On the keene point; when from his dropping blade
Warme *Soules* reek'ed out, and *mists* around him made.
Just as the Sword raisd it selfe up to'his pray,
In a blind Clowd shee snatcht them both away.
Let now (said Shee) lesse villaines fill their roome,
Theise have a *Race* of *Mischeifes* still to come.
They have; and now meet here by her drad call,
To beare the *Curse* of great *Northamptons* fall.
Up marcht the loyall *Earle*, and joy'd to see
Their *Numbers*, and vaine *Odds* for *Victoree.*

Still as hee march'd gay *Conquest* neere him kept;
But still (Ah mee!) shee *Sighd*, and still shee *Wept*.
Up to their Horse our Troopes advance; and see
The power of *Custome!* at first charge they flee.
Their proud-mouthd *Canon* all forsaken lay;
Gap'ed with wide horrour, but had nought to say,
Why doe the conquering Troopes soe farr persue,
And *Edgehills* almost-*Victory* renew?
Whilst the brave *Earle* engaged with Enemies round,
Still *gives* a *Death*, and still *receives* a *Wound?*
O *God*! his Horse is shot; it falls, and throwes
The noble burden into'a Crowd of Foes.
Yet still hee fought, till hee on every side
With slaughter'ed corps had almost *fortified*
The place hee stood in; for each blow hee strooke,
Cut out a *Life*, and *Name* from *Fates* large *Booke*.
At last hee groanes and reeles with many'a stroake,
The *Brambles* round all dread the tottering *Oake*.
They proffer *Life*, but hee to them disdaines
To owe one drop in all his generous veines.
Hee scornes to'accept the safety of his *Head*
From *Villaines*, who their owne had forfeited.
The fetterd Soules below of those hee slew,
Curst his free *Spirit*, whilst up through aire it flew.
Looke back, great *Spirit*, as thow doest mounting goe;
And see *thyselfe* againe i'the feild below.
Midst the lowd Throng behold thy gallant *Sonne*,
Cut out his way to *Fame* as thow hast *donne*.
Like thee, in all but *Death*, the brave *Youth*'s found,
In that too, comes too neere *Thee* by a *wound*.
O stay, bright *Planet*, stay a while, and veiw,
Our just revenge set more in *red* then *Yow*.
'Tis gonne, and Shades drop downe on all; by *Night*
The Rebells *now* are sav'ed; at *Morne*, by *Flight*.
  Yee bold *Cornavian* race, from hence begin
Your *Lesson*, from hence dread th'Effects of *Sinne*.
Ope wide your gates; great *Rupert* is come downe;
What wilt thow doe, black *Vulcans* noysy *Towne*

Old *Bremigham* ? lowd Fame to thee affords
A title from the *Make*, not *Use* of *Swords*.
Did ere *Pyracmon* and big *Brontes* prove
The new-made *Thunders* force against their *Jove?*
The high borne *Welch* disdaine a stop soe base;
Downe falls the barbarous *Cyclops* sooty race.
They knock the Earth, and every cave around
Ecchoes as lowd, as to their *Anviles* sound.
How bravely there the noble *Denby* lead?
Till, oh, wide *Death* gap'ed in his wounded Head.
An old and youthfull Souldier! O sad sight!
The crimson streame all staines his reverent *White*!
Goe burne the wicked *Towne*, and let it all
Bee one bright *Pire* for his great *Funerall.*
Into one glowing *Forge* the whole streets turne;
Soe *Aetna, Vulcans* other *Shop*, does burne.
Too late the foolish Rebells peace desire;
Like *Paris* Lust quencht when his *Troyes* on fire.
The *Ghosts* see flames beneath, as they drop downe,
And wondring thinke that still they veiw their *Towne.*
The neighboring *Rea* starts back with pale affright,
To see his waves peirc'ed through with dreadfull Light.
  Lichfeilds strong *Close* beheld this light afarre;
Beheld in vaine, and still praepar'ed for *Warre.*
Hence, yee profane; this is a sacred place;
Long hallow'ed by the peacefull *Miter'ed* race
Of reverent *Duina*; feare t'offend this *Sea,*
Founded at first, and built by *Victoree.*
Not here, oh, doe not here proud Ensignes spread,
To'affright the *Ghost* of *Canonized Ced.*
The soules of thowsand *Bishops* midst yee stand,
And with heard prayers adde strength to *Ruperts* hand.
Rupert is come, and the place stormed round;
All shapes of active mischeife fill the ground.
Some whilst the walls (bold men!) they'attempt to scale,
Drop downe by'a leaden storme of deadly haile.
Some with huge stones are crusht to dust beneath,
And from their hasty *Tombes* receive their *Death.*

Some leave their parted hands on th'highest wall,
The joynts hold fast a while, then quake, and fall.
Nature and *Art* did *Cowrage* overpower,
And the proud *Wall* at last grew *Conquerour.*
The'unwearied *Prince* scornes to bee conquer'd soe;
The labouring Spade and Pick-axe sound below.
With a dire noyse the earth and wall is rent,
High into aire th'unwilling Stones are sent,
Twice all about, the ground did tremble there,
First with the violent *shock*, and next with *Feare.*
The wicked *Guards* thought t'had some *Earthquake*
binne,
Their Soules confest the guilt of *Korahs* Sinne.
A *Breach* is made, and enter'd; but, oh, stay;
Sell not your valours and high Fates for pray.
Whilst yee seeke that, behold our soldiers ta'ne,
The matchless *Digby* hurt, and *Usher* slaine,
The rest driven back by their despairing Steele,
Achilles like, our Vict'ory slaine i'the Heele.
Yet when their boyling veines did once begin
To coole and let some *Thought* and *Providence* in;
When *Ruperts* Spirit they weighd, a Spirit no lesse
Driven on by *Ill*, then spurd by *good successe,*
They yeild the place and their *Lives forfeit* save;
Reserv'd by *Fate* for some *lesse hallow'ed Grave.*
Unhappy men! who can your curses tell?
Damn'd, and infam'ed for fighting *ill soe well!*
Such fate and edge did Lincolne Rebells feele
[ ] flameing Steele
Oft did the noble *youth* whole Armies chase;
Hector in his *Hands*, and *Paris* in his *Face.*
Oft from his sword the vanquisht *Parnham* fled;
The *Man* lookd big, and joyd when hee was dead.
At last old *Gainesbrow* his sad fall beheld;
And all along *Trents* mournfull waters swelld.
Too few the teares of its owne *Spring* hee thought,
Too few the waves that thirty *Rivers* brought.
The sullen Streame crept silent by his shore,
Mute as the *Fish* his populous current bore.

Whilst Hee, with thowsand foes strow'ed lifelesse by,
In all the *triumphs* of brave *Death* did ly.
Like some fair *Flower*, which *Morne* saw freshly gay,
In the feilds generall ruine mowne away.
The *Hyacinth*, or purple *Violet*,
Just languishing, his colourd *Light* just set.
Ill mixt it lies amidst th'ignobler *Grasse;*
The country *daughters* sigh as by'it they passe.
  Meanewhile the *Essexian Army* marcht about;
Their *Redding Blaze* by *Chalgroves storme* blowne out.
Downe towards their Campe avenging *Angells* move;
Before them *Clowds* of pale *Diseases* drove;
Faintnesse, and *Thirst, Madnesse*, and sickly *Heats;*
The brood *Gods wrath* joynd with *mans sinne* begets.
Armd with this strength *Death* sets at once on all
The *Quarters*; their proud boasts grow weake, and fall.
Oxford, a prisoner *King* and wealthy *pray,*
(Bold, seely hopes) sunck into aire away.
A deadly dampe does their stiffe veines surprize,
And leaden fate sits in their fixed eyes.
The sacred flame wanes in their torturd heads,
From thence through all the bones and marrow spreads.
Their feeble hands the weapons burden hate,
And trembling knees deceive their bodies waight.
Some fell like sickly *Autumnes* yellowish Leaves,
Their *deaths* as silent *then*, as *now* their *Graves.*
Some madly talke, blaspheme, and rave about,
The *Feinds* and *Furies scourge* their *Spirits* out.
The pent-up *fire* in their wild heads does swell;
And their scorch'd *Soules* drop *roaring* into *Hell.*
Great *God*, thine hosts from such a curse defend;
May none but *Rebells* lives soe sadly end!
Some whilst the watch and *sentinells* they keepe,
Nod into'a black and everlasting sleepe.
Some, as they move, their ranks and lives forsake,
And a quick march to'aeternall *Quarters* make.
Their fellowes gaze around, amas'ed to'espy
Soe many fall, and yet noe *Rupert* nigh.

Th'*Essexian Ghosts* below all woundring stood,
To see whole *Troopes* come downe unstain'd with blood.
In vaine they oft remove, change oft the aire,
Up march the vengefull *Angells* in their Reare.
Infection's brought them in by every *wind;*
And *swarmes* of country *Curses* crowd behind.
Towards *Londons* frantick Towne the *tawny Host*
Retreats, and their sighs forth a fruitlesse boast.
Before from *Keinton* such torne pride they brought,
Then *God* and *Man*, but *God alone* now fought.
  At the same time hee fought almost alone,
When *Wallers* boastfull powers were overthrown.
Both to their *Dens*, well worried both, retreat,
There snarle, and grinne, and brag which *lest* was beat.
When (loe!) two *Armies* by two *Princes* lead,
At *Bristow Walles* their conquering *Crosses* spread.
Where beawteous *Frome* weds *Avons* wealthy tide,
(*Avon* stout *Bridegroome, Frome* a lovely *Bride)*
Bristow, the goodly *Cyty*, stands alone;
And sees two *Countries*, but submits to none.
Herselfe alone a *Province* large and wide,
For what in *Land* shee wants, in *Sea's* supply'ed.
The farthest *Easterne* waves her *Armes* can tell,
And *Magellanick Fishes* know them well.
Noe where can *Thetis* her blew head upreare,
Noe where looke round, and not see *Bristow* there.
All *Nature* was her owne by wide commerce,
And her rich streets saw all the *Universe.*
Thus streames of wealth flow'ed in with every *Tide,*
But in too rusht *Fulnesse* of *Bread*, and *Pride.*
Strait they the bonds of *freest duty* broke,
And from their necks cast *Charles* his gentle yoake.
Instead of him whom Heaven did highest place,
The *Sonne* of two great *Kingdomes* crowned race,
Whom did theise *sencelesse Sinners* choose to obey,
Whom but th'unworthy seed of factious *Say*?
At once their *Faith* and *Reason* they forsooke;
The *Devill* for *God*, and *Fines* for *Charles* they tooke.

In vaine their strong-built *Castle* makes them bold,
In vaine, though't boast a Pris'oner *King* of old.
In vaine, alas, they trust the workes they have made,
And thinke our *Sword* lesse powerfull then the *Spade.*
Should Fates againe give *Briareus* a birth
And all those great first *Rebells* of the *Earth,*
(Should they assist your armes as sure they'de doe)
And cast workes of *Hills* on *Hills* for yow.
Not those would guard this cause in which yee fight,
Nor *Fines* guard them although his *Cause* were *right.*
Rupert this side, and *Maurice* that, assaile;
Nere yet did *Rupert*, nere did *Maurice* faile
In what their Swords were drawne for; at first sight
Of their keene blades did Fate our Victory write.
On this side *Maurice* with the nimble might
Of strong-limm'd *Westerne* Youth, begins the fight.
They scorne the grimmest dangers of the place;
Still *Lansdowne, Stratton* still's before their face.
They joy to *kill* their foes, they joy to *Dy;*
In the deepe *Trenches proud* and *gasping* ly,
Glad ev'en in *Death*, if they can *fill* them *soe;*
A streame of Enemies blood does downewards flow.
But, oh, what Devill misled those shot soe right;
And added *Fate* to their uncertaine flight,
By which they *Slaning*, and *Trevanion* found?
They could not sure have ment soe proud a wound.
Both hit, as if they'de both a mind to spare;
Both in the *Thigh*; but, oh, *Death* crept in *there* !
Both matchlesse men! and *Freinds* soe neerely growne,
That each felt least that wound which was his owne.
Meanewhile great *Rupert* by maine force possest
Their blood-dyed *workes*, and on to Vict'ory prest
Into the streets they breake; and all around
The groanes of men, and shreikes of woemen sound.
There valiant *Lunsford*, there the *Hero* fell,
And with rich blood did their base *channels* swell
The'accursed bullet his strong hart peirc'ed through;
Away his *Spirit*, swift as the *Bullet*, flew.

O sad! two minutes more had conquest showne;
Just now they beg their *lives*, and yeild their *Towne.*
They march unarm'ed away; the *Conqu'erours* give
A *Pardon*, but *Fate* onely a *Repreive.*
Then first did *Fines* his *Conscience* ake and smart,
Then first the vengefull *Serpents* stung his heart.
His guilty Soule shooke with each blast of winde;
The tread of *Rupert's* Horse still sounds behinde.
Still on each side his *Murthers* vex his sight,
Bourchier on th'*left*, and *Yeomans* on the *right.*
Halters and *brands* the angry *Figure* shakes;
The *palfry* starts, the *Rider* sweats and quakes.
Thus happy now was *Bristol* forc'ed to bee;
And *Charles* lay'd here fast hold uppon his *Sea.*
  From hence great *Maurice* with his westerne force,
To *Isca's* stubborne seidge turne back their course
Isca an ancient, strong, and factious Towne;
Peace gave it *Wealth*, and often *Warrs, Renowne.*
Here did the race of *Saxon* triumphs stay,
Troyes fatall seed they drove from hence away.
Hether the *Danes* victorious *Poleaxe* came;
It felt great *Suenoes* rage in blood and flame.
Yet they the swelling *Norman* durst oppose,
Till *Heaven* it selfe, declar'ed which side t'had chose.
Downe at his feet, downe fell th'unbatterd Wall;
The *Cities Stones* did *Homage* first of all.
Strange was the sight; yet not soe strange a show
That they fell then, as that they fell not now.
Thrice since that time did they a Seidge sustaine;
First *Courtneys* wrath here tyr'ed it selfe in vaine.
In vaine did *Warbecks tragick Pageant* here,
With *Armes* as weake, as his false *clayme*, appeare.
The *Painted Rose* was here discern'ed too well,
All his false *Leaves* soone lost their hue and fell.
Much of white fame did this good action get;
And *Henries Sword* beares witnesse still of it.
Alas, thow wisest *King*, what hast thow donne?
They'le use it 'gainst thy best and greatest Sonne.

Againe they prove their faith, and nobly fight
'Gainst *Sword*, and *Famine*, and the *Cornish might.*
The *Cornish* then *rebell*, the *Cornish fall*;
Their strength (wee see) and boldnes is not all.
The *Causes* change now changes both their doomes;
Isca rebells, and *Cornwall* overcomes.
Warwick, the Publick *Pyrat*, brings them ayde,
And dares, like an high *Tyde*, the Land invade.
Hee seekes his prey both uppon *earth* and *Sea;*
Soe lives the doubtfull *Crocodile*, and Hee.
What dares not hee who can, like *Jonas*, sleepe,
In midst of his *Rebellion*, and the *Deepe.*
Who can a Mind constant in Sinne retaine,
Amidst those dreadfull *wonders* of the *Mayne,*
Who feares noe *Shipwrack*, which the *Stormes* foretell
When mutinous *waves rise up*, and *Windes rebell!*
And yet on *Exes* streames hee learnt to feare,
There rose a new and deadlier *Tempest* there.
The *Canons* murthering blasts from ether shore,
Their canoas pride, and thin-built safety tore.
Here a tall Ship sunck by degrees below,
The decks yet seene, now masts, and nothing now.
[Here floate the Armes,] and there the *Men* about;
In rush the *Waves*, and crowd their wet *Soules* out.
Some feele hot wounds shot through the dashing flood,
They drinke in *Water*, and supply't with *Blood.*
Some, not yet slaine, are caught by *Fish* beneath,
And feele their painfull *Buriall* ere their *Death.*
Here on the *Streame* two Ships for *waters* call;
The *Streame* lookes on, and brings noe helpe at all.
A naturall hate though to the *Flame* hee bore,
Hee will not quench't; but hates the *Rebells* more.
Soe *Cold* and *Heat* on *Aetna's* top conspire,
Here *Frosts* ly bound, and by them breakes out *Fire.*
A secure peace the faithfull *neighbours* keepe;
Th'emboldned *Snow* next to the *Flame* does sleepe.
Some to avoyde the *fires* embrase a *wave;*
Some, burning planks, from *waves* there life to save.

What helpe, alas, could in this Change appeare?
Onely the death thats next them, that they feare.
Warwick beholds dead corps around him swimme,
And their last breath heard, when it cursed him.
Hee dares not longer his just fortune try;
In hast, but slow, the batterd *Vessels* fly.
How was the hopeing *Towne* that night dismayde,
When the next *Tide* cast up to them their *ayde*.
Thus happy *Charles* obtain'ed without the *Sea*
And without *Ships* a *Navall Victorie*.
This timely blow well broke th'*Excestrian pride;*
Nor could they long our feirce assaults abide.
With *Bristols* fate *Stamford* the *Towne* resignes;
Noe precedent soe fit for *Him*, as *Fines*!
Beware next *Plymmouth*; for if future thinges,
Nere faile my prophesying *Muse*, in what shee sings,
Thy conquest soone fame from my pen shall git;
Meanwhile a sadder *Vict'ry* calls for it.
  Th'Imperiall Hoast before proud *Gloc'ester* lay;
From all parts *Conquest* did her beames display.
Feare, Sadnesse, Guilt, Despaire at *London* meete;
And in black Smoakes fly thick through ev'ery Street
Their best Townes lost, noe Army left to fight!
Charles strong in *Power, invincible* in *Right!*
If hee march up, what shall theise wretches dow?
They're trowbled all, and Hell was troubled too.
  Beneath the silent Chambers of the Earth,
Where the Suns fruitfull beames give Metalls birth.
Where hee the growth of fatall Gold does see,
Gold, which above more Influence has then Hee.
Beneath the dens, where unflecht Tempests ly,
And infant Windes their tender voyces try.
Beneath the mighty Oceans wealthy caves;
Beneath th'aeternall Fountaine of all waves,
Where their vast Court the mother waters keepe,
And undisturb'd by Moones in silence sleepe.
There is a place, deepe, wondrous deepe below,
Which genuine night and horrour does oreflow.

Noe bound controules th'unwearied space; but Hell,
Endlesse as those dire paines which in it dwell.
Here noe deare glimpse of the Suns lovely face,
Strikes through the solid darknesse of the place.
Noe dawning Morne does her kind reds display;
One slight, weake beame, would here bee thought
the Day.
Noe gentle Starrs with their faire drops of light
Offend the tyrannous and unquestion'ed Night.
Here Rebell Minds in envious torments ly;
Must here forever Live, forever Dy.
Here Lucifer, the mighty Captive reignes,
Proud midst his Woes, and Tyrant in his Chaines.
Once Generall of a guilded Hoast of Spr'ites,
Like Hesper, leading on the spangled nights
But downe like Lightning, which him strooke, hee came,
And roar'd at his first plunge into the flame.
Myriads of Spirits fell wounded round him there;
With dropping Lights thick shone the singed aire.
Since then the dismall solace of their woe,
Has onely binne weake mankind to undoe.
Round the fond earth their thin-wrought nets they
throw;
Worlds of mad Soules come crowding downe below.
But their deare Sinne, the Sinne themselves dare boast,
The Sinne they love in man, and punish most,
Is proud Rebellion, their great Sonne, and Sire;
Which kindled first, now blowes the'aeternall fire.
A tall and dreadfull Feind! with double Face,
One virgin like, and full of painted Grace.
Faire seem'd her hew, and modest seemd her guise;
Her Eyne cast up towards Heaven in holy wise.
From her false mouth kind words did always fly,
Religion, Reformation, Liberty!
Oft sung shee Psalmes, and oft made zealous prayers;
All long and lowd, to cheat th'unknowing eares.
Her other face was grisly black of hew,
And from her stareing eyes feirce Lightning flew.
Her wicked Mouth spoke proud and bitter things,
Blasphem'ed Gods Church, and curst anoynted Kings.

Thowsand wild Lyes from her bold lipps there came;
Her Words were Bullets, and her Breath was Flame.
Thus as shee went, shee'enrag'ed the beastly rout,
And hurld unbounded ruine all about.
Like a rough Wind all rest and peace shee hates,
And joyes in th'Earth-quakes of well-grounded States.
Good God! what hoasts has this worst Feind of Death,
Sent mangled to th'unlovely Lands beneath.
There factious Korah and his murm'urers roare;
Still curse great Moses, but themselves much more.
Through gapeing gulfs thether alive they fell;
And skipt o're the first death, with hast to Hell.
By them, an Hoast of plague-strooke Rebells lay;
Noe endlesse fires purge the raw sores away.
By them, the men, whose factious hisse and sting,
Did the just scourge of forked Serpents bring.
How did their new-come Soules start back with feare,
Meeting againe theire firy Serpents here!
Davids proud Sonne hangs up in flames by th'haire;
A thowsand Feinds stand round and wound him there.
Still with fresh darts his dropping limmes they tore,
As Joab, and the young men did before.
By him, the Pol'itick wretch, soe fondly wise,
Forever hangs; and as hee dy'ed, hee dyes.
To them old Shimei from his stake does call,
And curses both, and Hell, and Heaven, and all.
By them still Sheba does his Trumpet sound;
Foole! for it calls the torturing Feinds around.
And there ly those, who cut old Jacobs Stemme,
And rent in twaine the Jess'ian Diadem.
What though the Tyr'annous King their prayers denide?
What though God spoake't, and Fate was on their side?
They who their Princes scourge disdain'd to beare,
Are by worse Tyrants lasht with Scorpions there.
There Baashas head weares still a burning Crowne,
And Zimri, whose wild Spirit came smoaking downe.
In such feirce flames the Traytour now is fried,
That hee thinkes those scarce warme, in which hee died.
What Toung can all these dismall Starrs of Hell,
(As numberlesse, as those Heaven shines with) tell?

But of all Lands, (though all send millions in)
More bountifull then Albion none hath bin.
There thowsand stubborne Barons fetterd ly,
And curse their old vaine noyse of Liberty.
They who their angry Soveraigne to oppose,
The hatefull yoake of France and Lewis chose.
A vaine pretence from Johns bad acts they bring;
John was a fond wild man, but yet their King.
Next them their Sonnes, who vext old Henries Crowne,
Blunted his Sword, and his high Throne pluckt downe.
Who lopt all branches from the royall Oake,
And into many parts the Scepter broke.
Montford the cheife, that falsest sonne of earth,
Till theise ungodly times gave [Cromwell] birth.
They, who unhappy Edward cast soe low,
His wicked Queene, around whose head does grow
A Crowne of torturing Flame, that shines, and burnes,
Her Mortimer close by forever mournes.
Their scorching lusts, and all their hot desires,
Are now extinguisht quite by greater fires.
Th'unchristian Bishop too, who first did preach,
What now theise Bishop-haters boldlier teach.
Tormenting heats his subtle braine surprize,
Oh mine head akes, still, mine head akes, hee cryes.
But all the art and rage of Death, does still
Matrevers Sp'irit, and barb'arous Gourneys kill.
The paines that dying Edward felt before,
Would seeme his heav'en, if onely those they bore.
Nor did the second Richards dolefull end,
A lesser troope to theise black mansions send.
Hether his Lords, hether his Commons come;
Noe Priveledge can save them from the doome.
There Warwick lyes, who like a God awhile,
Raisd and pulld downe the Kings of Albions Ile.
There Gloc'ester, whom noe sacred life withstood,
(Blood-thirsty man!) is drown'd in boyling blood.
The deform'd wretch grinning with paine does show,
Farr ouglier now then any Feind below.
There too an endlesse multitude is spread,
By Kets, and Cades, and Tylers thether lead.

Long darknesse now their Ign'orance does repay;
Blind, stubborne men, that hether groap'd their way!
Th'accursed powder-traitours there remayne,
(Ne're yet did Hell, nere shall such Sinners gaine)
Still by swift flames they're torne, and blowne up high,
Still those swift flames the nimbler Feinds supply.
But nere did the large Threshing-floore below,
A richer Crop then this yeares Harvest know.
At once whole feilds of ripened Traytours fell;
'Tis onely Peace breeds Scarcity in Hell.
Which that the Stygian Tyrant might prevent,
Hee calls below a dreadfull Parlament.
Deepe in a dismall den, Bel-zebubs Hall,
The Feinds all meet at their grimme Soveraignes call.
From every part of that wide Land they come;
The Soules awhile rest from their endlesse doome.
They rest awhile; but woe to man above!
For none but mighty ills theise Sessions move,
The change of a Religion or a State,
Mischeifes of greatest consequence, and weight.
Th'affaires of bleeding Brittaine calld them now;
Alas, unhappy Ile, what wilt thow doe!
They all set round, and from his direfull throne
Of burnisht Flames the Tyrant rose alone.
Much anger in his words, much in his looke;
The Feinds themselves, and all Hells Empire shooke.
My Freinds, and fellow Gods,
I need not, I suppose, the desperate state,
Of all our Brittish hopes to yow relate.
Yow'have heard and seene't, and are asham'ed, I know,
To see our bold Confoederates falne soe low,
Since coward Fines did from lost Bristol flee,
Against those solemne Oaths to'his God and Mee.
Which shall wee'endure? shall wee sit tame and still,
Suff'ering a Cause soe'unjust to thrive soe ill?
Shall wee behold long sleepy peace againe,
The ills of Charles his dull and godly raigne?
Shall wee againe the Bishops pride behold,
Which sixteene hundred yeares hath us controul'd?

It must not bee; by my great selfe, I sweare,
Had I another Heav'en I'de venture't here;
The Cause is ours, ours the cheife gaine will bee;
Is Say, or Pym concern'd soe much as Wee?
Goe then, hast all to Luds seditious Towne;
Yee know, and love't, scarce Hell is more your owne.
There's nothing now your great designe to stay,
God, and his troubl'esome Spir'its are gonne away.
I heard the voyce, I heard it bid them goe;
'Twas a good sound! they left Jerus'alem soe!
Seeke first the men who our high bus'ines sway,
Saint-Johns, the Vanes, Kimbolton, Pym, and Say.
Without a noyse possesse their Soules, get in
As subtly, as the close Originall Sinne
Seazes the new-form'd Infant in the wombe;
And let your acts shew first that yow are come.
Urge their lowd Feares, unmaske their ougly Guilt;
Too shallow's yet the Streame of blood they've spilt;
Tell them they all on dang'erous Rocks are cast,
And some high Tide must bring them off at last.
Bid them rush on, breake through all sins their way;
Vengeance behind oretakes them if they stay.
With such bold deeds let them the world amaze,
That men shall find noe leysure to dispraise.
Tell them what mighty Names they're like to grow,
Whilst modest Catiline blushes here below;
With shame and envy their high acts hee sees,
And seemes a Cic'ero, when compar'ed with these.
Tell them how brave a Funerall they may have,
They, and three Kingdomes with them in one grave.
When they shall say to Fate, yow owe us more,
Then all your Famins, and sick Yeares before,
When each shall publick ruine round him see,
And as hee falls, cry out, 'Twas donne by Mee.
Theyr gallant deeds (my Freinds) will ours excell;
Wee, wee our selves from Heav'en lesse nobly fell.
This at the worst; then brighter things suggest;
All the bold hopes that swell a Traytours brest,
Conquest with Slaughter (else 'twill make noe show),
The Crowne cast downe to Earth, the King more low,

The Churches Lands (alas, what's that? 'Tis lesse,
Then will suffice their very Wantonnesse,
Much lesse their Av'arice), all the Kingdomes Wealth,
Theires, not, as now, by borr'owing, plunder, stealth,
But openly, confest, and by a Law;
For such shall Votes bee then, and such their awe.
Th'Estates and Lives shall bee theyr owne of all
Whom they by'unpopular Names but please to call,
Their rage and furious Av'arice shall appeare,
Boundlesse as Marius Sword, and Sylla's Speare.
If in their misty Soules there chance to shine
The smallest peacefull glimpse of Light divine,
Raise up new fogs, and thicked clowds apace,
Till all our Night of Hell confuse the place.
Next to their Preists; use here all art and care;
Bee you to Them, what they to th'People are.
Their sordid soules with dull rewards enflame,
Large feasts, and larger Gifts and popular fame.
But sometimes shake the Halter and the chaine,
Shew them their Ilands, and new World againe.
Bid them now groane, and knock the pulpit more,
Pray longer, and preach lowder then before,
Bid them renew old blasphemies, and fling
All Texts of wicked Princes at their King,
Bid them their mouth-Granadoes cast about,
Till their owne fires ceaze all the catching rout.
Then into every street your force divide,
Swarme like the Plagues that scourgd old Pharaos pride,
Mens brests with thirst of blood, and fury fill.
Spare not, for t'will bee thought Gods Spirit still.
Strengthen weake Rebells, and confirme the bold,
Adde fewell to the hot, flame to the cold.
In different shapes to differing mindes appeare,
In shapes of hope, and zeale, and hate, and feare.
Learne this wise art from your grand en'emy Paul,
And to gaine some, doe yow turne all to all.
Pluck from their hearts each mild and sober thought,
Till warr and publick woe with joy bee bought
Ev'en by the Covetu'ous, till pale Cowards fight,
And all men crowd to ruine with delight.

Cease not, my Freinds, till yow their ensignes spy,
Advanc'ed 'gainst Charles his Army, and the Sky.
The rest, when once their banners spread yee see,
Leave to th'aeternall Justice, and to Mee.

287 See Notes on the Text for context and date of composition 5 *Alecto* a fury, inciter of Civil War in Virgil, *Aeneid*, VII 9 *Triptol'emus* see Appendix 1 19 *Hopton* at the indecisive battle of Hopton Heath near Stafford, 19 March 1643, the Earl of Northampton, commander of the royalist forces, was killed 22 *Gell and Brereton* Sir John Gell commanded the parliamentary forces at Hopton, Sir William Brereton commanded the reinforcements which turned the battle in Parliament's favour 24 *Hastings* Colonel Henry Hastings held Ashby-de-la-Zouch against Gell and Brereton in 1643 42 *Edgehill* 22 October 1642. A cavalry charge led by Prince Rupert scattered the parliament infantry, but the battle, like Hopton, was abandoned at nightfall 65 *Northampton*, in apotheosis, is identified with the planet Mars 69 *Cornavian* of the Midlands, from the tribe occupying Warwickshire and adjacent counties in antiquity 73 *Bremigham* Birmingham, famous for the manufacture of weapons 77 Welsh troops in Prince Rupert's army were prominent in the attack on Birmingham 81 William Fielding, first Earl of Denbigh, died from wounds sustained in the attack 101 *Ced* Ceadda, died 672, first bishop of Lichfield 126 in the royalist attempt on the wall of Lichfield Close, 20 April 1643, Colonel James Usher was killed and George, Lord Digby, was wounded 139 *noble youth* Charles Cavendish, son of the Earl of Devonshire, killed July 1643 at Gainsborough 141 *Parnham* Francis, Lord Willoughby of Parnham, parliamentary ommander-in-chief in Lincolnshire 157 *Essexian* Essex had captured Reading on 26 April. His advance on Oxford was halted by a partial defeat by Prince Rupert at Chalgrove on 18 June. The parliamentary army, camped around Thame in Oxfordshire, was prey to sickness 195 *Keinton* Kineton, Warwickshire, the northern limit of the battlefield of Edgehill 201 Princes Rupert and Maurice besieged Bristol on 23 July, taking the city three days later 206 Bristol was both City and county 222 *Say* Nathaniel Fiennes (Fines), the Governor of Bristol, was the second son of the parliamentarian Viscount Saye and Sele 226 Edward II had been imprisoned in Bristol Castle 242 *Lansdowne Stratton* Earlier royalist victories in the Western campaign 249 *Slaning, and Trevanion* Sir Nicholas Slanning and Colonel John Trevanion died in Maurice's assault on Bristol 256 *workes* earthworks, ramparts 259 *Lunsford* Colonel Henry Lunsford was shot just before the royalist troops obtained victory 272 Robert Yeomans and John Bourchier had been leaders of a plot in 1643 to deliver Bristol to the royalists; although they were civilians, Fiennes tried them by court martial and executed them 278 *Isca* Isca Dumnoniorum, Exeter 285–98 in 1003, Exeter fell to the Danish king Sweyn Forkbeard; surrendered to William the Conquerer in 1068; was besieged in 1470 by the Yorkist Sir Hugh Courtney and in 1497 by the pretender Perkin Warbeck when it was relieved by a force sent by Henry VII who presented his sword to the Mayor 302–3 in 1549 Exeter had been besieged by Catholic rebels of Devon and Cornwall; many of the royalist troops in 1643 were Cornish 307 *Warwick* Robert Rich, Earl of Warwick (1587-1658) the Admiral of the parliamentary fleet, had attempted to relieve the siege by navigating the River Exe 320 *canoas* skiffs, rowing-boats 351 Exeter was surrendered on 4 September by the Earl of Stamford, Parliament's General 353 Plymouth was one of the few Western towns still held for Parliament 357 the royalists laid siege to Gloucester on 10 August 1643 369 *unfletcht* unfledged 401-2 the rebellion of Satan is seen

as the parent of all subsequent sins 423 *Korah* Korah, Dathan, and Abiram (Numbers 16) led a rebellion against Moses and were swallowed by the earth 433 *Davids proud Sonne* Absalom (2 Samuel 18) rebelled against his father and was killed by Joab and the youth of Israel 437 *Pol'itick wretch* Ahithophel, a counsellor of Absalom's in his revolt against his father, who suggested executing David. He committed suicide by hanging himself (2 Samuel 17) 439 *Shimei* he cursed and stoned David (2 Samuel 16) and was executed by Solomon (1 Kings 2) 441 *Sheba* also a rebel against David (2 Samuel 20) 443–4 (1 Kings 12) the northern Rebels who forced a division of Israel 449 *Baasha* (1 Kings 15) Baasha, King of Israel, deposed and had murdered King Nadab 450 *Zimri* (1 Kings 16) this King of Israel also murdered his predecessor and died in his palace which he had fired 457 the barons of England who forced King John to sign Magna Carta allied themselves in 1216 with Prince Louis of France 463 the barons led by Simon de Montfort revolted against Henry III, and curtailed his power after their victory at Lewes in 1264 470–6 Isabella of France overpowered her husband Edward II in 1326, assisted by her lover Roger Mortimer. The king was put to death in the following year. They were supported by Adam of Orlton, bishop of Winchester 480 Sir John Maltravers and Thomas Gourney were the reputed murderers of Edward II 487 *Warwick* Richard Neville, Earl of Warwick (1428–71), both put Edward IV on the throne and deposed him in favour of Henry VI 489 Richard, Duke of Gloucester, usurped the throne as Richard III in 1483 494 *Kets, and Cades, and Tylers rebels*: William Ket led the Norfolk rising of 1594; John Cade the Kentish Rebellion of 1450, Wat Tyler the Peasants' Revolt of 1381 497 the gunpowder plotters of 1605 538 *Luds seditious Towne* London, from its mythical founder 545 the chief leaders of the parliamentary 'war party'; see Appendix 2 593 *Ilands* the leaders of the 'war party' were among the promoters of a settlement in Providence Island in the Caribbean 598 *Granadoes* grenades 608 A distortion of 1 Corinthians 9: 22 'I am made all things to all men, that I might by all means save som'

ANONYMOUS

288 *The Encounter A SONG*

1.

Hang the Presbyters Gill,
Bring a Pinte of Sack *Will*,
More Orthodox of the two;
Though a slender dispute
Will strike the Elfe mute,
Hees one of the honester Crue.

2.

In a Pinte there's small heart,
Sirrah, bring us a Quart,
There's substance and vigor met,
'Twill hold us in Play,
Some part of the day,
But we'll suck him before Sun-set.

3.

The dareing old Pottle
Does now bid us Battle;
Let's try what his strength can do;
Keep your Ranks and your Files:
And for all his Wiles,
Wee'l tumble him down Staires too.

4.

The Stout-breasted Lumberd,
His Brains ne'er encumber'd
With drinking of Gallons three;
Tricongius was named,
And by *Caesar* famed,
Who dubbed him Knight Cap-a-pe.

5.

If then Honour be in't,
Why a pox should we stint
Our selves of the fullness it bears?
H'has lesse wit than an Ape
In the blood of the Grape,
Will not plunge himself o're head and ears.

6.

Then summon thc Gallon,
A stout Foe, and a tall One,
And likely to hold us to't;
Keep Coyn in your Purse,
The Word is disburse,
I'le warrant he falls at your foot.

7.

See, the bold Foe appears,
May he fall that him fears;
Keep you but close Order, and then,
We will give him the Rout,
Be he never so stout,
And prepare for his Rallying agen.

8.

Wee'l dreyn the whole Cellar
Pipes, Butts, and the Dweller,
If the Wine does flow no faster;
Will, when thou does slack us,
By Warrant from *Bacchus*,
Wee'l Cane thy Tun-belly'd Master.

288 1 *Presbyters* Presbyterian, parliamentarian *Gill* quarter of a pint 2 *Sack* sherry wine 3 *Orthodox* the pint is the Anglican, Cavalier measure 5 *Elfe* rogue 13 *Pottle* half-gallon measure 19 *Lumberd* Lombard 22 *Tricongius* invented name 'three wine-measures' 24 *Cap-a-pe* head to foot 35 *disburse* pay out 40 *give him the Rout* put to flight (continuing the image of doing battle with the various wine-measures) 42 *Rallying* regrouping forces 44 *Pipes, Butts* both large casks for storing wine *Dweller* the cellarer 48 *Tun* large barrel (252 old wine gallons)

RICHARD LOVELACE

289

Song. Set by Mr. *John Laniere.*
TO LUCASTA, *Going to the Wars.*

I.

Tell me not (Sweet) I am unkinde,
That from the Nunnery
Of thy chaste breast, and quiet minde,
To War and Armes I flie.

II.

True; a new Mistresse now I chase,
The first Foe in the Field;
And with a stronger Faith imbrace
A Sword, a Horse, a Shield.

III.

Yet this Inconstancy is such,
As you too shall adore;
I could not love thee (Deare) so much,
Lov'd I not Honour more.

289 Compare no. 268 7 *imbrace* embrace 9 *Inconstancy* infidelity

290 TO ALTHEA *From Prison.* Song. Set by Dr. *John Wilson.*

I.

When Love with unconfined wings
Hovers within my Gates;
And my divine *Althea* brings
To whisper at the Grates:
When I lye tangled in her haire,
And fetterd to her eye;
The *Gods* that wanton in the Aire,
Know no such Liberty.

II.

When flowing Cups run swiftly round
With no allaying *Thames*,
Our carelesse heads with Roses bound,
Our hearts with Loyall Flames;
When thirsty griefe in Wine we steepe,
When Healths and draughts go free,
Fishes that tipple in the Deepe,
Know no such Libertie.

III.

When (like committed Linnets) I
  With shriller throat shall sing
The sweetnes, Mercy, Majesty,
  And glories of my KING;
When I shall voyce aloud, how Good
  He is, how Great should be;
Inlarged Winds that curle the Flood,
  Know no such Liberty.

IV.

Stone Walls doe not a Prison make,
  Nor Iron bars a Cage;
Mindes innocent and quiet take
  That for an Hermitage;
If I have freedome in my Love,
  And in my soule am free;
Angels alone that sore above,
  Injoy such Liberty.

290 Compare no. 283 Title *Althea* name meaning 'truth' (Greek) 7 *wanton* frolic 10 *allaying* diluting 11 *Roses* Romans wore rose garlands at banquets 13 *steepe* soak 17 *committed* imprisoned 23 *Inlarged* liberated

291 TO LUCASTA. *From Prison.*

An Epode.

I.

Long in thy Shackels, liberty,
  I ask not from these walls, but thee;
Left for a while anothers Bride
  To fancy all the world beside.

II.

Yet e're I doe begin to love,
  See! How I all my objects prove;
Then my free Soule to that confine,
  'Twere possible I might call mine.

III.

First I would be in love with *Peace*,
And her rich swelling breasts increase;
But how alas! how may that be
Despising Earth, she will love me?

IV.

Faine would I be in love with *War*,
As my deare Just avenging star;
But War is lov'd so ev'ry where,
Ev'n He disdaines a Lodging here.

V.

Thee and thy wounds I would bemoane
Faire thorough-shot *Religion*;
But he lives only that kills thee,
And who so bindes thy hands, is free.

VI.

I would love a *Parliament*
As a maine Prop from Heav'n sent;
But ah! Who's he that would be wedded
To th'fairest body that's beheaded?

VII.

Next would I court my *Liberty*,
And then my Birth-right, *Property*;
But can that be, when it is knowne
There's nothing you can call your owne?

VIII.

A *Reformation* I would have,
As for our griefes a *Sov'raigne* salve;
That is, a cleansing of each wheele
Of State, that yet some rust doth feele:

IX.

But not a Reformation so,
As to reforme were to ore'throw;
Like Watches by unskilfull men
Disjoynted, and set ill againe.

X.

The *Publick Faith* I would adore,
  But she is banke-rupt of her store;
Nor how to trust her can I see,
  For she that couzens all, must me.

XI.

Since then none of these can be
  Fit objects for my Love and me;
What then remaines, but th'only spring
  Of all our loves and joyes? The KING.

XII.

He who being the whole Ball
  Of Day on Earth, lends it to all;
When seeking to ecclipse his right,
  Blinded, we stand in our owne light.

XIII.

And now an universall mist
  Of Error is spread or'e each breast,
With such a fury edg'd, as is
  Not found in th'inwards of th'Abysse.

XIV.

Oh from thy glorious Starry Waine
  Dispense on me one sacred Beame
To light me where I soone may see
  How to serve you, and you trust me.

291 This poem examines the terms of the public discourse of the 1640s in a similar way to no. 280, a poem in which Lovelace is mentioned, and one which he may have known
12 *Despising Earth* Astrea (Justice, Peace), see Appendix 1 22 *Prop* support 24 *beheaded* deprived of its rightful head, the King 30 *salve* ointment, cure 40 *couzens* deceives
43 *spring* source 45–6 *Ball Of Day* the sun 53 *Starry Waine* the King identified again with 'Charles's Wain', the constellation of the Plough

292 *Calling* LUCASTA *from her Retirement.*

ODE.

I.

From the dire Monument of thy black roome
Wher now that vestal flame thou dost intombe
As in the inmost Cell of all Earths Wombe.

II.

Sacred LUCASTA like the pow'rfull ray
Of Heavenly Truth passe this Cimmerian way,
Whilst all the Standards of your beames display.

III.

Arise and climbe our whitest highest Hill,
These your sad thoughts with joy and wonder fill.
And see Seas calme as Earth, Earth as your Will.

IV.

Behold how lightning like a Taper flyes
And guilds your Chari't, but ashamed dyes
Seeing it selfe out-gloried by your Eyes.

V.

Threatning and boystrous tempests gently bow,
And to your steps part in soft paths, when now
There no where hangs a Cloud, but on your brow.

VI.

No showrs but 'twixt your lids, nor gelid snow,
But what your whiter chaster brest doth ow,
Whilst winds in Chains colder your sorrow blow.

VII.

Shrill Trumpets doe only sound to Eate
Artillery hath loaden ev'ry dish with meate.
And Drums at ev'ry Health Alarmes beate.

VIII.

All Things LUCASTA, but LUCASTA call,
Trees borrow Tongues, Waters in accents fall,
The Aire doth sing, and Fire's Musicall.

IX.

Awake from the dead Vault in which you dwell,
All's Loyall here, except your thoughts rebell,
Which so let loose, often their Gen'rall quell.

X.

See! She obeys! by all obeyed thus;
No storms, heats, Colds, no soules contentious,
Nor Civill War is found—I meane, to us.

XI.

Lovers and Angels, though in Heav'n they show
And see the Woes and Discords here below
What they not feele, must not be said to know.

292 1–3 the image is of Lucasta buried alive, attended by the ever-burning lamp erroneously supposed to have been placed in classical sepulchres 5 *Cimmerian* proverbially dark 6 *standards* banners, flags 10 *Taper* candle 16 *gelid* frozen 23 *accents* poetical metre

293 *The Ant*

1.

Forbear thou great good Husband, little Ant
  A little respite from thy flood of sweat;
Thou, thine own Horse and Cart under this Plant
  Thy spacious tent, fan thy prodigious heat;
Down with thy double load of that one grain;
It is a Granarie for all thy Train.

2.

Cease large example of wise thrift a while,
  (For thy example is become our Law)
And teach thy frowns a seasonable smile:

So *Cato* sometimes the nak'd Florals saw.
And thou almighty foe, lay by thy sting,
Whilst thy unpay'd Musicians, Crickets, sing.

3.

Lucasta, She that holy makes the Day,
And 'stills new Life in fields of Fueillemort:
Hath back restor'd their Verdure with one Ray,
And with her Eye bid all to play and sport,
Ant to work still; Age will Thee Truant call;
And to save now, th'art worse than prodigal.

4.

Austere and *Cynick*! not one hour t'allow,
To lose with pleasure what thou got'st with pain:
But drive on sacred Festivals, thy Plow;
Tearing high-ways with thy ore charged Wain.
Not all thy life time one poor Minute live,
And thy o're labour'd Bulk with mirth relieve?

5.

Look up then miserable Ant, and spie
Thy fatall foes, for breaking of her Law:
Hov'ring above thee, Madam, *Margaret Pie*,
And her fierce Servant, Meagre, Sir *John Daw*:
Thy Self and Storehouse now they do store up,
And thy whole Harvest too within their Crop.

6.

Thus we unthrifty thrive within Earths Tomb,
For some more rav'nous and ambitious Jaw:
The *Grain* in th'*Ants*, the *Ants* in the *Pies* womb
The *Pie* in th'*Hawks*, the *Hawks* ith' *Eagles* maw
So scattering to hord 'gainst a long Day,
Hording to save all, we cast all away.

293 1 *Husband* farmer, also provident man 6 *Train* all the ants 9 *seasonable* timely 10 *Cato* see Appendix 1 *Florals* dancers at the ancient Roman feast of the Floralia 14 *'stills* instils, gives *Fueillemort* the colour of dead leaves, a cloth of that colour 15 *Verdure* greenness 19 *Austere* self-denying 22 *Wain* wagon, cart 27 *Margaret Pie* magpie 28 *John Daw* jackdaw 30 *Crop* stomach

294 *The* Vintage *to the* Dungeon. A Song. Set by Mr. *William Lawes.*

I.

Sing out pent Soules, sing cheerefully!
Care Shakles you in Liberty,
Mirth frees you in Captivity:
Would you double fetters adde?
Else why so sadde?

Chorus.

Besides your pinion'd armes you'l find
Grief too can manekell the minde.

II.

Live then Pris'ners uncontrol'd;
Drinke oth'strong, the Rich, the Old,
Till Wine too hath your Wits in hold;
Then if still your Jollitie,
And Throats are free;

Chorus.

Tryumph in your Bonds and Paines,
And daunce to th'Musick of your Chaines.

294 Title *Vintage* wine 1 *pent* captive 6 *pinion'd* tied behind the back 7 *manekell* manacle, chain

295 *The Falcon*

Fair Princesse of the spacious Air,
That hast vouchsaf'd acquaintance here,
With us are quarter'd below stairs,
That can reach Heav'n with nought but Pray'rs;

Who when our activ'st wings we try,
Advance a foot into the Sky.

Bright Heir t'th'Bird Imperial,
From whose avenging penons fall
Thunder and Lightning twisted Spun;
Brave Cousin-german to the Sun,
That didst forsake thy throne and Sphere,
To be an humble Pris'ner here;
And for a pirch of her soft hand
Resign the Royal Woods command.

How often would'st thou shoot Heav'ns Ark,
Then mount thy self into a Lark;
And after our short faint eyes call,
When now a Fly, now nought at all;
Then stoop so swift unto our Sence,
As thou wert sent Intelligence.

Free beauteous Slave, thy happy feet
In silver Fetters vervails meet,
And trample on that noble Wrist
The Gods have kneel'd in vain t'have kist:
But gaze not, bold deceived Spye,
Too much oth'lustre of her Eye;
The Sun, thou dost out-stare, alas!
Winks at the glory of her Face.

Be safe then in thy Velvet helm,
Her looks are calms that do orewhelm,
Then the *Arabian* bird more blest,
Chafe in the spicery of her breast,
And loose you in her Breath, a wind
Sow'rs the delicious gales of *Inde*.

But now a quill from thine own Wing
I pluck, thy lofty fate to sing;
Whilst we behold the various fight,
With mingled pleasure and affright,

The humbler Hinds do fall to pray'r,
As when an Army's seen i'th'Air
And the prophetick Spannels run,
And howle thy *Epicedium*.

The *Heron* mounted doth appear
On his own Peg'sus a Lanceer,
And seems on earth, when he doth hut,
A proper Halberdier on foot;
Secure i'th'Moore, about to sup,
The Dogs have beat his Quarters up.

And now he takes the open air,
Drawes up his Wings with Tactick care;
Whilst th'expert *Falcon* swift doth climbe,
In subtle Mazes serpentine;
And to advantage closely twin'd
She gets the upper Sky and Wind,
Where she dissembles to invade,
And lies a pol'tick Ambuscade.

The hedg'd-in *Heron*, whom the Foe
Awaits above, and Dogs below,
In his fortification lies,
And makes him ready for surprize;
When roused with a shrill alarm,
Was shouted from beneath, they arm.

The *Falcon* charges at first view
With her brigade of Talons; through
Whose Shoots, the wary *Heron* beat,
With a well counterwheel'd retreat.
But the bold Gen'ral never lost,
Hath won again her airy Post;
Who wild in this affront, now fryes,
Then gives a Volley of her Eyes.

The desp'rate *Heron* now contracts,
In one design all former facts,

Noble he is resolv'd to fall
His and his En'mies funerall,
And (to be rid of her) to dy
A publick Martyr of the Sky.

When now he turns his last to wreak
The palizadoes of his Beak;
The raging foe impatient
Wrack'd with revenge, and fury rent,
Swift as the Thunderbolt he strikes,
Too sure upon the stand of Pikes,
There she his naked breast doth hit
And on the case of Rapiers's split.

But ev'n in her expiring pangs
The *Heron*'s pounc'd within her Phangs,
And so above she stoops to rise
A Trophee and a Sacrifice;
Whilst her own Bells in the sad fall
Ring out the double Funerall.

Ah Victory! unhap'ly wonne,
Weeping and Red is set the Sun,
Whilst the whole Field floats in one tear,
And all the Air doth mourning wear:
Close hooded all thy kindred come
To pay their Vows upon thy Tombe;
The *Hobby* and the *Musket* too,
Do march to take their last adieu.

The *Lanner* and the *Lanneret*,
Thy Colours bear as Banneret;
The *Goshawk* and her *Terceel* rows'd,
With Tears attend thee as new bows'd,
All these are in their dark array
Led by the various *Herald-Jay*.

But thy eternal name shall live
Whilst Quills from Ashes fame reprieve,

Whilst open stands Renown's wide dore,
And Wings are left on which to soar;
Doctor *Robbin*, the Prelate *Pye*,
And the poetick *Swan* shall dye,
Only to sing thy Elegie.

295 3 *quarter'd* housed 7 *Bird Imperial* Jove's eagle 8 *penons* feathers 10 *Sun* eagles were thought, classically, to look on the sun with open eyes 15 *Heav'ns Ark* arch, the sky 19 *stoop* dive 22 *vervails* thongs round the hawk's legs 29 *helm* helmet 31 *Arabian bird* phoenix 34 *Sow'rs* sours 35 *quill* feather, to make a pen 39 *Hinds* countrymen 41 *Spannels* spaniels 42 *Epicedium* funeral song, lament 44 mounted on his own wings as if on the winged horse Pegasus, see Appendix 1. The heron's lance is his beak: several early-modern treatises on hawking affirm that a heron will stab a falcon as in this poem 45 *hut* take up his quarters: the combat between the falcon and the heron employs an extended military metaphor 56 *Ambuscade* ambush 69 *fryes* rages 78 *palizadoes* palisades, sharpened stakes 97 *Hobby Musket,* 99 *Lanner Lanneret,* kinds of hawk 100 *banneret* Knight dubbed on the field of battle, squire 101 *Goshawk, Terceel* the female and male respectively of the largest of the broad-winged hawks (considered less noble than falcons) 102 *bows'd* (technical term of falconry) having drunk 104 *Herald-Jay* its bright plumage recalls a herald's tabard 106 *Quills* pens, hence commemorative poems 109–10 *Robbin* its red breast seems blood-stained like a surgeon *Pye* magpie, coloured black and white like a cleric *Swan* the swan was supposed to sing only at the approach of its death

296 *The Grasse-hopper*. To my Noble Friend, Mr. CHARLES COTTON. Ode.

I.

Oh thou that swing'st upon the waving haire
Of some well-filled Oaten Beard,
Drunke ev'ry night with a Delicious teare
Dropt thee from Heav'n, where now th'art reard.

II.

The Joyes of Earth and Ayre are thine intire,
That with thy feet and wings dost hop and flye;
And when thy Poppy workes thou dost retire
To thy Carv'd Acorn-bed to lye.

III.

Up with the Day, the Sun thou welcomst then,
Sports in the guilt-plats of his Beames,
And all these merry dayes mak'st merry men,
Thy selfe, and Melancholy streames.

IV.

But ah the Sickle! Golden Eares are Cropt;
Ceres and *Bacchus* bid good night;
Sharpe frosty fingers all your Flowr's have topt,
And what sithes spar'd, Winds shave off quite.

V.

Poore verdant foole! and now green Ice! thy Joys
Large and as lasting, as thy Peirch of Grasse,
Bid us lay in 'gainst Winter, Raine, and poize
Their flouds, with an o'reflowing glasse.

VI.

Thou best of *Men* and *Friends*! we will create
A Genuine Summer in each others breast;
And spite of this cold Time and frozen Fate
Thaw us a warme seate to our rest.

VII.

Our sacred harthes shall burne eternally
As Vestall Flames, the North-wind, he
Shall strike his frost-stretch'd Winges, dissolve and flye
This *Aetna* in Epitome.

VIII.

Dropping *December* shall come weeping in,
Bewayle th'usurping of his Raigne;
But when in show'rs of old Greeke we beginne,
Shall crie, he hath his Crowne againe!

IX.

Night as cleare *Hesper* shall our Tapers whip
From the light Casements where we play,

And the darke Hagge from her black mantle strip,
And sticke there everlasting Day.

X.

Thus richer then untempted Kings are we,
That asking nothing, nothing need:
Though Lord of all what Seas imbrace; yet he
That wants himselfe, is poore indeed.

296 3 *teare* dewdrop 7 *Poppy* sleeping draught 17 *verdant* green 19 *poize* balance, correct 28 *Epitome* miniature or condensed version 34 *Casements* windows 35 *Hagge* night as a witch *mantle* cloak

MORGAN LLWYD O WYNEDD

297 1648

A spring in spring
Poore birds now sing
Our head is high
Our sumer nigh.

297 Compare no. 262

298 THE HARVEST

1. A depth. A depth in things to come!
man is a shallow shell
The scripture closetts lord unlocke,
else, none thy mind can tell.

2. Christs coming, and end of the world
are two distinctive times
This busy harvest makes short worke
with doctrines, tares and crimes.

3. The field is large, the barne at hand
the reapers quicke and wise
The stubble flames and sinfull soules
lye doune and never rise

4. In summer Christ is all in all
as Pope in winter was.
But after harvest God is all
Then, never turn our glasse.

5. In Gog and Magog hell shall spew
that last and filthy fome
and before winter comes againe
wee shall bee all at home.

6. No eye hath seene, no eare hath heard
no man can well conceave
How God will angells Christ and saincts
into himselfe receave.

7. Now I have given a sparing hint
for wisemen to enlarge
lett fooles sleepe on, and Atheists laugh
yee saincts, Advance and charge.

8. I tyre thee friend, I make an end
But see thou bend thy line
and heart to sing in this thy spring
of Christ thy king and mine.

298 8 *tares* the weeds, like the doctrines of the established church, must be cleared from the field as Christ comes as harvester 17 *Gog and Magog* see Appendix 1

299 CWYNFAN, CYSSUR, CRYFDER Y FFYDDLONIAID YNGHYMRU YNGHANOL Y RHYFELOEDD

1. Mae honom ychydig, o blant cystuddiedig
 a adawyd yn unig ynghymru.
ynghanol ein cystydd, yn cwyno iw gilydd
 an calon sydd beynydd yn pallu.

2. Hawddfyd ir hen ddyddiau, ar holl ordinhadau
 pan oedd ein heneidiau ni'n llwyddo
Hawddfyd in dyscawdwyr, hawddfyd in holl frodyr
 Mae'r enaid yn rhywyr yn cwyno.

3. Mae'r defaid ar wasgar, mewn tristwch a galar
 mae rhai yn y carchar yn pydru.
Mae rhai wedi ymadel, gan gymryd hir ffarwel
 mae rhai yn y dirgel yn llechu.

4. Mae rhyfedd newidiad, dros wyneb yr hollwlad
 Ple ceir dim gwir gariad mewn undyn.
y byd a dywyllodd, y ddayar a grynnodd,
 ar nefoedd a dduodd in herbyn.

5. Ni fedrem weddio, ni garem ymprydio
 ni geisiem gynt rodio 'n gyssurus,
tra fu gair y bywyd, yn cadw mewn iechyd
 yr enaid gwan nychlyd galarus.

6. Diffoddwyd pob canwyll, holl gymru sydd dywyll,
 ple ceir undyn didwyll drwy'r hollwlad.
fe gwympodd rhai cryfion, fe ballodd y moddion
 fe oerodd ein calon an cariad.

7. yn'r Arglwydd bostiasom, ei -ddewid credasom,
 ei ras a geisiasom in helpu.
Ei wyneb a guddiodd, ei foliant a gollodd,
 Ei Deyrnas a gwympodd ynghymru.

8. yn lle yr hir heddwch, yn lle'r hen ddiddanwch
yn lle'r holl lonyddwch a gawsom,
y Drwmm sydd yn taro, ar udcorn yn seinio
ar rhyfel yn rhuthro ('n wyllt) arnom.

9. yn lle canu Psalmu, a gofyn Qwestiwnau
a son am resymau ysbrydol,
Mae swn ein gelynion, yn blino ein calon,
ai geiriau coeg beilchion uffernol.

10. Ond hyn an hamdwyodd, y Pechod an daliodd
a dynion an denodd or diwedd.
Ei -hwllys nhwy wnaethpwyd, ai llw a gymerwyd
an henaid a faglwyd yn rhyfedd.

11. Mae Duw wedi digio, cydwybod sy'n pigo,
ar cythrel sy'n temptio yn ddibaid.
heb un in cynghori, heb neb in rheoli,
heb fugail in porthi sydd weiniaid.

12. Pa ddyn na thosturie, pa lygaid nad wyle
pa galon na waede gan ddolur?
Wrth weled ein galar, an gwae ar y ddayar
an hiraeth digymar digyssur.

13. Pan ddaeth ir wlad unwaith, waredwyr a gobaith
fei troes Duw nhwy eilwaith oddiwrthym
Ond etto er cynted, y bom ni llawn addfed
fe droir ein caethiwed ni'n gyflym.

14. Er maint ydiw'n gofid, ni gredwn ei -ddewid
ni feiddiwn ni newid mon harglwydd.
Or diwedd fe'n cofia, fe'n cynnal, fe'n nertha
fe ddaw ag an helpa ni'n cbrwydd.

15. Er bod y tywyllwch, y gauaf ar tristwch,
y nos ar anailwwch ynghymru
yr haul a fyn godi, y wawr a fyn dorri,
a Christ fyn reoli heb pallu.

16. Er trymmed ein haflwydd, ein gofid an gwradwydd
Dros eraill mae'r Arglwydd yn gweithio
Mae'r delwaddoliaeth, mae'r ofer wasanaeth
Mae'r dynion anhywaeth yn cwympo.

17. Ag Oen nhw ryfelant, gorchfygu nis gallant
ni chyll Christ nai foliant nai fwriad.
Cans brenin brenhinoedd, rheolwr teyrnasoedd
iw Arglwydd y lluoedd yn wastad.

18. Disgwiliwn am dano, drwy ffydd glynwn wrtho
na wadwn byth mono drwy gelwydd.
Cawn weled ei wrthiau, cawn gyfwrdd ai seintiau
cawn gadw'n eneidiau'n dragywdd.

19. Tra fo ein tafodau, yn rhydd yn ein genau
ni ganwn ganiadau gogoniant.
Ar Duw a fu'n magu ei ddefaid ynghymru
an ceidw ni i fynu iw foliant.

20. Hyd ddiwedd ein dyddiau, nis mynd honom ninnau
ir bedd at ein tadau i gysgu
Ni gwynwn, ni ganwn, ni griwn, ni gredwn,
ni garwn, ni gofiwn Ghrist Iesu.

299 The Desolation, Lamentation, and Resolution of the Welsh Saints in the Late Wars. Sung in 1643

We are but a few afflicted children who are left alone in Wales; in the midst of our suffering, complaining to one another and our heart daily faltering. Farewell to the old days, and all the ordinances when our souls prospered; Farewell to our teachers, farewell to all our brothers for whom the soul too late laments. The sheep are astray, in sadness and mourning, some rot in prison; some have left, taking a long farewell, some cower in secret. A strange change has come over the face of the whole land where no true love is found in any man; the world has grown dark, the earth has shaken, and the heavens have darkened against us. We could pray, we loved to fast, we tried [oncc] to walk in comfort, while the world of life sustained in health the feeble, sickening, mournful soul. Every candle is extinguished, all Wales is dark, where no trustworthy man is to be found throughout the country. The strong have fallen, the medicine has failed. Our heart and our love have grown cold. In the Lord we trusted, we believed his promise, we sought his grace to help us. He hid his face, his praise was lost, his kingdom fell in Wales. Instead of the long peace, instead of the old merriment, instead of the tranquillity we had, the drum beats and the trumpet sounds and the war rushes (wildly) upon us. Instead of the singing of Psalms and the asking of questions and talk of spiritual matters, is the sound of our enemies troubling our heart with their vain, proud, hellish words. But this wounded us: sin caught us and men drew us to them at last. Their will was done, the oath was sworn and our soul was thoroughly trapped. God is angry, conscience pricks, and the devil tempts [us] ceaselessly; with none to counsel us, with none to rule us, with no shepherds to feed those who are weak. What man would not pity, what eye would not weep, what heart would not bleed in pain in seeing our distress, and our woe upon earth and our matchless, comfortless longing? When saviours and hope came once to the land, God turned them once more away from us; yet as soon as we are fully ready our enslavement will be quickly overturned. However great our grief, we believe his promise, we would not dare to change our lord. At last he will remember us, uphold us, strengthen us, [One] who will help us will come swiftly. Despite the darkness, the winter and the sadness, the night and the wilderness in Wales, the sun must rise, the dawn must break, and Christ must reign without faltering. However heavy our defeat, our grief and our shame, the Lord is working for others. The worship of idols, vain service [and] intractable men are falling. And the Lamb will wage war against them, they cannot overcome, Christ will lose neither praise nor purpose since the king of kings, the ruler of kingdoms is the Lord to his hosts forever. We shall [Let us] wait for him, attach ourselves to him in faith; we shall [let us] never deny him through lies. We shall see his miracles, we shall touch his saints, we shall save our souls for eternity. While our tongues are free in our mouths, we shall sing hymns of glory. And may God who has nursed his sheep in Wales, make us worthy to praise him. Until the end of our days, until we too go to sleep in the graves of our fathers, we shall lament, we shall sing, we shall cry, we shall believe, we shall love, we shall remember Christ Jesus.

ALEXANDER BROME

300 *To his Mistres affrighted in the wars*

1.

Come sigh no more, but kiss again,
  These troubles shall never trouble me;
Your sighs are but wind, and your sorrows vain;
  They'l never the sooner for us agree.

Let *Canons* keep roaring
And bullets still fly;
While I am adoring
Thee, my deity.
Hang this wealth! let money flee,
They cannot undo me, while I have thee.

2.

I'll be thy *Champion* to defend
Thy person from all these dangers and harms;
No Army's so sure as a real friend,
Nor Castle defends like a lover's arms.
But if I can't daunt 'um,
By valour and might
Your face shall enchant 'um,
For beauty can fight.
There's no armour can men free
From the naked pow'r of such beauties as thee.

3.

I *Venus* serve, a fig for *Mars*,
Loves arrows may wound, but never kill me;
Me thinks there's no pleasure in bloody wars,
But I long to be wounded and taken by thee.
When our bullets are kisses,
And our field is a bed,
And the top of our bliss is
A pure maidenhead.
Both will strive to lose the day,
And both shall be conquer'd and yet not run away.

300 11 *Champion* under chivalric law, since a women could not fight a duel, she could appoint a man to fight on her behalf 21 *fig for* I care nothing for 28 *maidenhead* virginity

301 *The Royalist*

Written in 1646

1.

Come, pass about the *bowl* to me,
    A health to our distressed *King*;
Though we're in hold, let cups go free,
Birds in a cage may freely sing.
The ground does tipple healths apace,
    When *stormes* do fall, and shall not we,
A sorrow dares not shew its face,
    When we are *ships* and sack's the *sea*.

2.

Pox on this grief, hang *wealth*, let's *sing*,
    Shall's kill ourselves for fear of death?
We'l live by th'*aire* which songs do bring,
    Our *sighing* does but wast our breath.
Then let us not be discontent,
    Nor drink a glass the lesse of *Wine*;
In Vain they'l think their plagues are spent,
When once they see we don't *repine*.

3.

We do not suffer here alone,
    Though we are beggar'd, so's the *King*,
'Tis sin t'have wealth, when he has none,
    Tush! poverty's a *Royal* thing!
When we are *larded* well with drink,
    Our *heads* shall turn as *round* as theirs,
Our *feet* shall rise, our *bodies* sink
Clean down the wind, like *Caveliers*.

4.

Fill this unnatural *quart* with *sack*,
    Nature all vacuums doth decline,
Ourselves will be a *Zodiack*,
    And every mouth shall be a sign.

Me thinks the *Travels* of the glasse,
Are circular like *Plato's* year;
Where every thing is as it was,
Let's tipple round; and so 'tis here.

301 5 *tipple* drink 8 *sack* sherry wine 10 *Shall's* shall we (not an unusual usage) 16 *repine* lose heart 21 *larded* stuffed 24 *Clean down the wind* be unfortunate 25 *quart* two-pint measure, also quarter, perhaps here quarter of the year 26 *vacuum* proverbial phrase: 'nature abhors a vacuum' 27 *Zodiack* the astrological sky with its circle of anthropomorphic constellations (signs) 30 *Plato's year* an astronomical concept: the point at which the various movements of all stars brought them round in a complete cycle to where they started

302 *For the Generalls entertainment*

1.

Farewell all *cares* and *fears*, let *Gladness* come,
Let's all strive which shall most rejoyce,
No more the *Trumpet*, or the Thundring *Drum*,
Shall interrupt our peace with *noise*,
But all their *Offices* shall be
Inherited by sprightly melody.
Th'inchanting *Lute* and the melodious *Lyre*,
With well-tun'd souls does make
a full harmonious Quire.

2.

In vain do we ourselves, ourselves destroy,
In vain do *English*, *English* beat,
Contests are cruel, we must now wear joy,
And all in love, each other greet.
Our civil *discords* now shall cease,
And lose *themselves* in a desired *peace*.
All things by war are in a *Chaos* hurl'd,
But love alone first made,
and still preserves the World.

3.

The *Trophies* of the *Conquerours* of old,
And all the *spoils* with which they'r *crown'd*,
Were all but *types* of what we do behold,
What they did seek for, we have found.
Here peace and plenty sweetly kist,
And both with *loyalty* and *vertue* twist,
Then let our joy rise high that all may share it,
Let wealth and honour meet desert,
he that wins Gold may wear it.

302 5 *Offices* duties 7 *Lute* Renaissance stringed instrument *Lyre* stringed instrument of classical times 9 *Quire* choir 20 *spoils* plunder 21 *types* prototypes, examples 26 *desert* the reward they deserve

303 SONG II: *The Commoners*

Written in 1645

1.

Come your wayes
Bonny Boyes,
Of the *Town*,
For now is your time or never,
Shall your fears
Or your cares
Cast you down?
Hang your wealth
And your health,
Get renown,
We all are undone for ever.
Now the *King* and the *crown*
Are tumbling down,
And the *realm* doth groan with *disasters*,
And the scum of the land,
Are the men that command,
And our *slaves* are become our *masters*.

2.

Now our lives
Children, wives
And Estate,
Are a prey to the lust and plunder,
To the rage
Of our age.
And the fate
Of our land
Is at hand,
'Tis too late
To tread these *Usurpers* down
First down goes the *crown*,
Then follows the *gown*,
Thus levell'd are we by the *Roundhead*,
While *Church* and *State* must
Feed their *pride* and their *lust*,
And the *Kingdom* and *King* confounded.

3.

Shall we still
Suffer ill
And be dumb?
And let every *Varlet* undo us?
Shall we doubt
Of each Lowt,
That doth come,
With a voice
Like the noise
Of a Drum,
And a *sword* or a *Buffe-coate* to us?
Shall we lose our estates
By *plunder* and *rates*
To bedeck those proud upstarts that *swagger*?
Rather fight for your meat,
Which those *Locusts* do eat,
Now every man's a beggar.

303 30 *gown* the Anglican Church 38 *Varlet* low-born rogue 39 *doubt* be afraid 45 *Buffe-coate* uniform of parliamentary troops 50 *Locusts* in Exodus 10: 12, a plague of locusts consumes all the crops of the Egyptians at the instigation of Moses: therefore those who destroy and devour a land

304 SONG XXV:
Upon the Cavaleers departing out of London

1.

Now fare thee well *London,*
Thou next must be undone,
'Cause thou hast undone us before;
This *cause* and this *tyrant,*
Had never plaid this high rant
Wer't not for thy *argent* and *Or.*

2.

Now we must desert thee,
With the lines that begirt thee,
And the red-coated Saints domineer,
Who with liberty fool thee,
While a Monster doth rule thee,
And thou feelst what before thou didst fear.

3.

Now *justice* and *freedom*
With the *laws* that did breed'um,
Are sent to *Jamaica* for gold,
And those that upheld'um,
Have power but seldom,
For justice is barter'd and sold.

4.

Now the Christian Religion
Must seek a new Region,
And the old Saints give way to the new;
And we that are loyal
Vail to those that destroy all,
When the Christian gives place to the Jew.

5.

But this is our glory
In this wretched story,
  Calamities fall on the best;
And those that destroy us
Do better employ us,
  To sing till they are supprest.

304 5 *Had* would have 6 *argent* silver *Or* gold 8 *begirt* surround 9 *red-coated Saints* the parliamentary army 15 *Jamaica* used as a dumping-ground for criminals and dissidents, 'planted' with settlers by parliament during the Interregnum 24 *Jew* nickname for Cromwell

305 SONG XXX: *The New Gentry*

1.

Enough for shame! leave off this fooling,
  Prithee cring no more
  Nor admire the illgotten store
Of the upstart *Mushrooms* of our Nation
With blind and *groundlesse* adoration,
If thy nature still wants schooling,
  As thou dost grow old grow wise,
  For age can easily advise,
    And make thee know
    'Tis only such as thou
That bring and keep both fools and knaves in fashion.

2.

We make each other proud and knavish,
  For where ever we
  Great abundance chance to see,
There we fling both power and honour
As if wealth were the only donour,
And our natures are so slavish,
  That we tamely will submit,
  All our reason strength and wit,

And pay and pray,
Great men in power, that they
Will take our *Liberty* and *trample* on *her*.

3.

What is't makes all men so much covet,
Toyling more and more,
To increase a needless store,
So violently tugg and *hall* for't
Ventering body soul and *all* for't?
The rich are flatter'd and they love it
We obey their *shalls* and *musts*,
And to gratifie their lusts,
We madly strive
Who first our selves shall give
And all that is ours to them, if they'l but *call* for't.

4.

If we did take no notice of them,
Like not, nor applaud
Their *spoyles obtaind* by *force* and *fraud*
But would live content and jolly
Laughing at their painful folly,
And would neither fear nor love them,
Underneath their loads, they'ld groan,
Or with shame would throw them down,
And live as free
From needless cares as we,
Slight *pompe* and *wealth*, that makes men *melancholly*.

5.

Pray what are all these gaudy *bubbles*
That so boast and rant,
Of what they think they *have* but *hant*?
But men that had the luck of living,
And made other's fall their *thriving*,
Hailstones got in stormes of troubles;
That for *valour* are as fit
For *Knights*, as to be *Squires* for wit

Inspir'd with pride,
Did what good men defied,
Grown great by *Protean* turning and conniving

6.

That man that would have me adore him,
With my heart, he must
Be *noble, pow'rful, wise* and *just*,
And improve his parts and power
To *support* not to *devour*,
Nor *pride* nor *lust* must e're rule o're him.
Th'*bugbeare* greatnesse without this
An idle, empty *pageant* is,
He that doth rise
And is not good and wise,
I honour not, but pity and deplore him.

305 2 *cring* cringe 4 *Mushrooms* because they spring up overnight 24 *Toyling* working 26 *hall* haul, heave 27 *Ventering* adventuring, risking 36 *spoyles* plunder 44 *Slight* despise 50 *Hailstones* able to do damage, but liable to melt 55 *Protean* shape-changing, see Appendix 1 62 *bugbeare* monster

ANONYMOUS

306 *A Hue and Cry after the Reformation*

When Temples lye like batter'd Quarrs,
Rich in their ruin'd Sepulchers,
When Saints forsake their painted Glasse
To meet their worship as they passe,
When Altars grow luxurious with the dye
Of humane bloud,
Is this the floud
Of Christianity?

When Kings are cup-boarded like cheese,
Sights to be seen for pence a piece,
When Dyadems, like Brokers tire,

Are custom'd reliques set to hire,
When Soveraignty and Scepters loose their names,
Stream'd into words,
Carv'd out by swords
Are these refining flames?

When Subjects and Religion stir
Like Meteors in the Metaphor,
When zealous hinting and the yawn
Excize our *Miniver* and *Lawn*;
When blue digressions fill the troubled ayr,
And the Pulpit's let
To every Set
That will usurp the Chair?

Call ye me this the night's farewell,
When our noon day's as dark as Hell?
How can we lesse than term such lights
Ecclesiastick Heteroclites?
Bold sons of *Adam* when in fire you crawl,
Thus high to be,
Perch'd on the tree,
Remember but the fall.

Was it the glory of a King
To make him great by suffering?
Was there no way to build God's House
But rendring of it infamous ?
If this be then the merry ghostly trade?
To work in gall?
Pray take it all
Good brother of the blade.

Call it no more the Reformation,
According to the new translation:
Why will you wrack the common brain
With words of an unwonted strain?
As Plunder? or a phrase in senses cleft?
When things more nigh
May well supply
And call it down-right theft.

Here all the *School-men* and *Divines*
Consent, and swear the naked lines
Want no expounding or contest,
Or *Bellarmine* to break a jest.
Since then the Heroes of the pen with me
Nere scrue the sense
With difference
We all agree agree.

306 Title *Hue and Cry* outcry calling for the pursuit of a criminal 1 *Quarrs* quarries, or building-blocks 2 *Sepulchers* tombs 3–4 *Saints forsake...to meet* Puritans rejected the cult of saints, but adopted the name for themselves 9 *cup-boarded* unceremoniously locked up 11 *Dyadems* crowns; *Brokers tire* merchants' clothes 17 *stir* move, quarrel 18 *Meteors* shooting-stars, presaging ill luck and bad weather 20 *Miniver* ermine, worn by peers *Lawn* fine linen, symbolizing bishops 21 *blue* associated with the Covenanters 23 *Set* group of people, sect 28 *Heteroclites* abnormal and eccentric deviants 29 *sons of Adam* mere men *fire* one of the four elements, unsuited to supporting human life, also the fire of Hell 32 *fall* of Adam 37 *ghostly* spiritual 38 *gall* bitterness 44 *unwonted* uncommon 49 *School-men* academics, more precisely, medieval theologians 52 *Bellarmine* see Appendix 2

MARCHAMONT NEDHAM

307 [*from* A Short History of the English Rebellion]

O happy *Nation* heretofore,
When Seas our Walls have been;
Unhappy now we see no shore,
But are all Sea within.

Factions, like *Billows*, rage and toss,
And *Death* mounts ev'ry *Wave*;
Yet in this *Storm* we are so cross,
We will no *Pilot* have.

Just such a *Tempest* seiz'd upon
Blest *Paul*, the *Scripture* says,
When he had seen no *Sun* or *Moon*,
Nor *Stars* for many days.

Our *Sun* and *Moon* no beams create,
Our *Stars* disperst we see:
Such as was his, shall be our *Fate*,
We must all *shipwrackt* be.

A glorious *Prince* this *Parliament*
The *King* should be, did swear;
But now we understand they meant
In *Heaven*, and not *here*.

Let them invade the *Throne*, and part
His *Crown*, and vote his *Fate*;
Yet know, in each true *Noble Heart*,
He keeps his *Chair of State*.

Princes may be, like other Men,
Imprison'd and kept under
A while, as *fire in clouds*, but then
At length appear in *Thunder*.

And as in hidden *Caves* the *wind*
Sad *tremblings* doth create;
So *Monarchs*, by their own confin'd,
Cause *Earthquakes* in the *State*

Farewel the *Glory* of our *Land*;
For, now the *Free-born Blades*,
Our *Lives* and our *Estates* command,
And ride us all like *Jades*.

Faith and *Religion* bleeding lie,
And *Liberty* grows faint;
No *Gospel*, but pure *Treachery*,
And *Treason* make the *Saint*.

Oh ! 'tis a heavenly *Cause* (I trow)
Which first baptiz'd the *Round-head*
In *Noble Strafford's Blood* ! but now
Must on the *Kings* be founded.

Yet know, that *Kings* are *Gods* on Earth;
And those which pull them down,
Shall find it is no less than Death
To tamper with a *Crown*.

307 5 *Billows* waves 7 *cross* perverse 9–12 alludes to Acts 27, describing St Paul's stormy voyage to Rome 36 *Jades* nags 41 *trow* believe, trust 43 *Strafford* see Appendix 2

308 [*from* A Short History of the English Rebellion]

Poor CHARLES pursu'd in *Forty one*,
Unking'd in *Forty-seven*;
The *Eighth* will place him on his *Throne*,
In *Earth*, or else in *Heaven*.

Three *Kingdoms* brought to a fine pass;
Whilst that our *Saviours* Rule,
The Country is become an *Ass*,
The City but a *Mule*.

Each *University* now pines,
The *Church* may hang and rot;
They banish all our true *Divines*,
The *Lawyers* too must trot.

Come, *Sirs*, more *Sacks* unto the *Mill*,
More *Taxes*, more *Free-quarter*;
'Tis fit our *Laws* be your *bare Will*,
And the *Excise* our *Charter*.

God speed the Plough: plague *Rooks and Crows*,
And send us years more cheap:
For I am sure, whoever *sows*,
The *Houses* mean to *reap*.

Money, the *Soul* of *Man* and *Wit,*
But yet no *Saint* of mine !
While th'*Houses* vote, and *Synod* sit,
Thou ne're shalt want a *Shrine.*

Reforming is a dull *Device*,
Dreads naught but strife and rage:
Thou putt'st us into *Paradice*,
And bring'st the *Golden Age.*

Thou art *Religion, God* and all
That we may call *Divine*:
Thy *Temple* is *Westminster-Hall*,
And all our *Priests* are thine.

Tush, tell us not the way to *Heav'n*,
Thou juggling *Clergy-Elf*,
That sett'st the World at *six* and *seven's*;
Money is *Heav'n* it self.

Betwixt those *Atheists* feign'd of old,
And ours, there is no odds;
For, both this one opinion hold,
That *Fear did first make Gods.*

Hell now is thought an idle *Dream*
To fright Men from their *Crimes*:
Religion but a crafty *Theam*,
Made to *Bug-bear* the *Times.*

The *Bible* and great *Babels Whore,*
May booth together burn;
For the *Religious Fit* is o're
Now they have serv'd their turn.

Only, one *Text* may scape their hands,
Since they have ta'en such pains,
To lay their *Lords in Iron Bands,*
And bind their *Kings in Chains.*

308 5 *Three Kingdoms* England, Scotland, Ireland 13 (send) *Sacks unto the Mill* take advantage of abundance 17 *Rooks and Crows* scavengers on carrion 20 *Houses* of Parliament 23 *Synod* church council 28 *Golden Age* play on age worshipping gold, and the Golden Age proper: see Appendix 1 31 *Westminster-Hall* seat of the parliament 34 *Clergy-Elf* rogue of a (presumably Puritan) minister 40 *fear did first make Gods*, first formulated by the notoriously frivolous and irreverent Petronius (*Fragment* 27.1), and repeated by other writers, including Chaucer (*Troilus* IV. 1408) 44 *Bug-bear* frighten 45 *Babels Whore* the Whore of Babylon, see Appendix 1 52 Psalm 149: 5–8 'Let the saints be joyful...and a two edged sword in their hand; to execute vengeance upon the heathen...To bind their kings with chains, and their nobles with fetters of iron'

309 [*from* A Short History of the English Rebellion]

Religion but a Pack-horse is
  To carry on *Designes*:
The *Bible* like a *Juglers Box*
  Us'd by our *State-Divines*.

Texts are tormented one by one
  Like *Votes*, now here, now there:
Thus *Hocus-Pocus* is out-done
  By them of *Westminster*.

309 3 *Juglers Box* conjuror's equipment 7 *Hocus-Pocus* conjuror's magic formula derived from the supposedly superstitious words of the Latin Mass *Hoc est Corpus* 8 the Westminster Assembly, the governing body of the English Presbyterian Church

310 [*from* A Short History of the English Rebellion]

No *Lord*, no *Knight*, no *Gentleman*,
  For *Honours* now are Crimes:
The *Saints* will form us (if they can)
  All to the *Prim'tive times*.

Brave days when *Adam* was a king,
  Without *Crown, Lands* or *Riches*!
So, stript of *Royal Robes*, they'll bring
  Great CHARLES, to *Fig-leave Breeches*.

Princes with *Plowmen* rank shall pass;
  Ladies, like the first *Woman*,
Must spin, or else be turn'd to Grass,
  Now all things are in *common*.

Thus *Cov'nanting* and *Levelling*,
  Three *Kingdoms* have o'rethrown,
And made all fellows with their *King*,
  A *Foot-ball* of the *Crown*.

310 3 *form* conform or reform 4 *Prim'tive times* the earthly paradise before the Fall 8 *Fig-leave* like Adam and Eve who in Genesis 3: 7 'sewed fig leaves together, and made themselves aprons' 11 *turn'd to Grass* killed 14 *Three Kingdoms* England, Scotland, Ireland 15 *fellows* equals

ANDREW MARVELL

311 *The unfortunate Lover*

1.

Alas, how pleasant are their dayes
With whom the infant Love yet playes!
Sorted by pairs, they still are seen
By Fountains cool, and Shadows green.
But soon these Flames do lose their light,
Like Meteors of a Summer's night:
Nor can they to that Region climb,
To make impression upon Time.

2.

'Twas in a Shipwrack, when the Seas
Ruled, and the Winds did what they please,
That my poor Lover floating lay,
And, e're brought forth, was cast away:
Till at the last the master-Wave
Upon the Rock his Mother drave;
And there she split against the Stone,
In a *Cesarean section*.

3.

The Sea him lent those bitter Tears
Which at his Eyes he alwaies bears.
And from the Winds the Sighs he bore,
Which through his surging Breast do roar.
No Day he saw but that which breaks
Through frighted Clouds in forkèd streaks.
While round the ratling Thunder hurl'd,
As at the Fun'ral of the World.

4.

While Nature to his Birth presents
This masque of quarrelling Elements,
A num'rous fleet of Corm'rants black,
That sail'd insulting o'er the Wrack,
Receiv'd into their cruel Care
Th'unfortunate and abject Heir:
Guardians most fit to entertain
The Orphan of the *Hurricane*.

5.

They fed him up with Hopes and Air,
Which soon digested to Despair.
And as one Corm'rant fed him, still
Another on his Heart did bill,
Thus while they famish him, and feast,
He both consumed, and increast:
And languished with doubtful Breath,
The *Amphibium* of Life and Death.

6.

And now, when angry Heaven wou'd
Behold a spectacle of Blood,
Fortune and He are call'd to play
At sharp before it all the day:
And Tyrant Love his brest does ply
With all his wing'd Artillery.
Whilst he, betwixt the Flames and Waves,
Like Ajax, the mad Tempest braves.

7.

See how he nak'd and fierce does stand,
Cuffing the Thunder with one hand;
While with the other he does lock,
And grapple, with the stubborn Rock:
From which he with each Wave rebounds,
Torn into Flames, and ragg'd with Wounds.
And all he saies, a Lover dressed
In his own Blood does relish best.

8.

This is the only *Banneret*
That ever Love created yet:
Who though, by the Malignant Starrs,
Forced to live in Storms and Wars,
Yet dying leaves a Perfume here,
And Musick within every Ear:
And he in Story only rules,
In a field *Sable* a Lover *Gules*.

311 9 *Shipwreck* of a metaphorical 'ship of state' 16 *Cesarian section* like a child born by surgery rather than naturally, also pun on 'the cutting (section) of a King (Caesar) a reference to the beheading of Charles I 26 *masque* courtly entertainment, often on allegorical themes 27 *Corm'rants* proverbially greedy and destructive 40 *Amphibium* double life 55 *saies* essays, attempts 57 *Banneret* knight created on the field of battle 63 *Story* 1610 usage recorded by *OED* 'a painting or sculpture of an event' 64 the line correctly blazons (describes) a coat of arms: *field Sable...lover Gules* a black shield charged (decorated) with a red lover

312 *The Nymph complaining for the death of her* Faun.

The wanton Troopers riding by
Have shot my Faun and it will dye.
Ungentle men! They cannot thrive
To kill thee. Thou neer didst alive
Them any harm: alas nor cou'd
Thy death yet do them any good.

I'me sure I never wisht them ill;
Nor do I for all this; nor will:
But, if my simple Pray'rs may yet
Prevail with Heaven to forget
Thy murder, I will Joyn my Tears
Rather then fail. But, O my fears!
It cannot dye so. Heavens King
Keeps register of every thing:
And nothing may we use in vain.
Ev'n Beasts must be with justice slain;
Else Men are made their *Deodands*.
Though they should wash their guilty hands
In this warm life blood, which doth part
From thine, and wound me to the Heart,
Yet could they not be clean: their Stain
Is dy'd in such a Purple Grain.
There is not such another in
The World, to offer for their Sin.
  Unconstant *Sylvio*, when yet
I had not found him counterfeit,
One morning (I remember well)
Ty'd in this silver Chain and Bell,
Gave it to me: nay and I know
What he said then; I'me sure I do.
Said He, look how your Huntsman here
Hath taught a Faun to hunt his *Dear*.
But *Sylvio* soon had me beguil'd.
This waxed tame; while he grew wild,
And quite regardless of my Smart,
Left me his Faun, but took his Heart.
  Thenceforth I set my self to play
My solitary time away,
With this: and very well content,
Could so mine idle Life have spent.
For it was full of sport; and light
Of foot, and heart; and did invite
Me to its game: it seem'd to bles
Its self in me. How could I les
Than love it? O I cannot be
Unkind, t'a Beast that loveth me.

Had it liv'd long, I do not know
Whether it too might have done so
As *Sylvio* did: his Gifts might be
Perhaps as false or more than he.
But I am sure, for ought that I
Could in so short a time espie,
Thy Love was far more better then
The love of false and cruel men.
With sweetest milk, and sugar, first
I it at mine own fingers nurst.
And as it grew, so every day
It wax'd more white and sweet than they.
It had so sweet a Breath! And oft
I blusht to see its foot more soft
And white, (shall I say then my hand?)
NAY any Ladies of the Land.
It is a wond'rous thing, how fleet
'Twas on those little silver feet.
With what a pretty skipping grace,
It oft would challenge me the Race:
And when 'thad left me far away,
'Twould stay, and run again, and stay.
For it was nimbler much than Hindes;
And trod, as on the four Winds.
I have a Garden of my own,
But so with Roses over grown,
And Lillies, that you would it guess
To be a little Wilderness.
And all the Spring time of the year
It onely loved to be there.
Among the beds of Lillyes, I
Have sought it oft, where it should lye;
Yet could not, till it self would rise,
Find it, although before mine Eyes.
For, in the flaxen Lillies shade,
It like a bank of Lillies laid.
Upon the Roses it would feed,
Until its Lips ev'n seem'd to bleed:
And then to me 'twould boldly trip,
And print those Roses on my Lip.

But all its chief delight was still
On Roses thus its self to fill:
And its pure virgin Limbs to fold
In whitest sheets of Lillies cold.
Had it liv'd long, it would have been
Lillies without, Roses within.
  O help! O help! I see it faint:
And dye as calmely as a Saint.
See how it weeps. The Tears do come
Sad, slowly dropping like a Gumme.
So weeps the wounded Balsome: so
The holy Frankincense doth flow.
The brotherless *Heliades*
Melt in such Amber Tears as these.
  I in a golden Vial will
Keep these two crystal Tears; and fill
It till it do o'reflow with mine;
Then place it in *Diana's* Shrine.
  Now my sweet Faun is vanish'd to
Whether the Swans and Turtles go
In fair *Elizium* to endure,
With milk-white Lambs, and Ermins pure.
O do not run too fast: for I
Will but bespeak thy Grave, and dye.
  First my unhappy Statue shall
Be cut in Marble; and withal,
Let it be weeping too: but there
Th'Engraver sure his Art may spare;
For I so truly thee bemoane,
That I shall weep though I be Stone:
Until my Tears, still dropping, wear
My breast, themselves engraving there.
There at my feet shalt thou be laid,
Of purest Alabaster made:
For I would have thine Image be
White as I can, though not as Thee.

312 1 *wanton* careless 17 *Deodands* an animal which killed a human being was forfeited by its owner and became a deodand ('given to God') 29 *it* the faun 34 *waxed* grew 36 *Heart* pun on hart (deer) 63 *fleet* nimble, swift 69 *Hindes* female deer or shepherds 81 *flaxen* pale blonde, the colour of flax 97 *wounded Balsome* balm 98 *holy Frankincense* gum resin, used for making church incense 99 *Heliades* see Appendix 1 106 *Turtles* turtle-doves 120 *Alabaster* finest white marble

313 *An* Horatian *Ode upon* Cromwel's *Return from* Ireland.

The forward Youth that would appear
Must now forsake his *Muses* dear,
Nor in the Shadows sing
His Numbers languishing.
'Tis time to leave the Books in dust,
And oyl th'unused Armours rust:
Removing from the Wall
The Corslet of the Hall.
So restless *Cromwel* could not cease
In the inglorious Arts of Peace,
But through adventrous War
Urged his active Star.
And, like the three-fork'd Lightning, first
Breaking the Clouds where it was nurst,
Did thorough his own Side
His fiery way divide.
For 'tis all one to Courage high
The Emulous or Enemy;
And with such to inclose
Is more then to oppose.
Then burning through the Air he went,
And Pallaces and Temples rent:
And *Caesars* head at last
Did through his Laurels blast.
'Tis Madness to resist or blame
The force of angry Heavens flame:
And, if we would speak true,
Much to the Man is due.
Who, from his private Gardens, where
He liv'd reserv'd and austere,

  As if his highest plot
  To plant the Bergamot,
Could by industrious Valour climbe
To ruine the great Work of Time,
  And cast the Kingdome old
  Into another Mold.
Though Justice against Fate complain,
And plead the antient Rights in vain:
  But those do hold or break
  As Men are strong or weak.
Nature that hateth emptiness,
Allows of penetration less:
  And therefore must make room
  Where greater Spirits come.
What Field of all the Civil Wars,
Where his were not the deepest Scars?
  And *Hampton* shows what part
  He had of wiser Art.
Where, twining subtile fears with hope,
He wove a Net of such a scope,
  That *Charles* himself might chase
  To *Caresbrooks* narrow case.
That thence the *Royal Actor* born
The *Tragick Scaffold* might adorn
  While round the armed Bands
  Did clap their bloody hands.
He nothing common did or mean
Upon that memorable Scene:
  But with his keener Eye
  The Axes edge did try:
Nor call'd the *Gods* with vulgar spight
To vindicate his helpless Right,
  But bow'd his comely Head,
  Down as upon a Bed.
This was that memorable Hour
Which first assur'd the forced Pow'r.
  So when they did design
  The *Capitols* first Line,
A bleeding Head where they begun,
Did fright the Architects to run;

And yet in that the *State*
Foresaw it's happy Fate.
And now the *Irish* are asham'd
To see themselves in one Year tam'd:
So much one Man can do,
That does both act and know.
They can affirm his Praises best,
And have, though overcome, confest
How good he is, how just,
And fit for highest Trust:
Nor yet grown stiffer with Command,
But still in the *Republick's* hand:
How fit he is to sway
That can so well obey.
He to the *Commons Feet* presents
A *Kingdome*, for his first years rents:
And, what he may, forbears
His Fame to make it theirs:
And has his Sword and Spoyls ungirt,
To lay them at the *Publick's* skirt.
So when the Falcon high
Falls heavy from the Sky,
She, having kill'd, no more does search,
But on the next green Bow to pearch;
Where, when he first does lure,
The Falckner has her sure.
What may not then our *Isle* presume
While Victory his Crest does plume!
What may not others fear
If thus he crown each Year!
A *Caesar* he ere long to *Gaul*,
To *Italy* an *Hannibal*,
And to all States not free
Shall *Clymacterick* be.
The *Pict* no shelter now shall find
Within his party-colour'd Mind;
But from this Valour sad
Shrink underneath the Plad:

Happy if in the tufted brake
The *English Hunter* him mistake;
  Nor lay his Hounds in near
  The *Caledonian* Deer.
But thou the Wars and Fortunes Son
March indefatigably on;
  And for the last effect
  Still keep thy Sword erect:
Besides the force it has to fright
The Spirits of the shady Night,
  The same *Arts* that did *gain*
  A *Pow'r* must it *maintain.*

313 Title *Horatian Ode* not only an imitation of the manner of the Roman poet, particularly his *Odes*, IV. 4, but also an imitation of the strategy of his poetry which presents the reader with sometimes conflicting ideas, leaving the reader to resolve them 8 *Corslet* breastplate of armour 18 *Emulous* jealous 19 *inclose* limit, restrain 23 *Caesars* the king's 32 *Bergamot* herb, a variety of pear 47 *Hampton* negotiations at Hampton Court (the 'Hampton Propositions') in the late summer of 1647, in the course of which the King rejected the 'Heads of Proposals' presented by the army in July, regarded as the work of Cromwell among other army leaders 52 *Caresbrooks* Carisbrook Castle, where Charles was held 68 *Capitols first Line* a story from Livy, *Annals*, I. 55. 6 83 *sway* rule 89 *Spoyls* plunder, trophies 94 *Bow* bough 101 *Caesar* Julius Caesar 102 *Hannibal* see Appendix 1 104 *Clymacterick* a fateful, dangerous, or pivotal point 105 *Pict* Scot 106 *party-colour'd* duplicitous 108 *Plad* distinctively Scottish loose cloak, forerunner of the kilt 109 *tufted* beaten through by the 'tuft-hounds', who start the deer 110 *mistake* to cross onto the scent of a fresh deer 112 *Caledonian* Scots 115 *last effect* the hunting metaphor is still running: Cromwell the huntsman ought to dispatch the deer with his sword. The hunt appears to have gone wrong 117–19 compare Aeneas, drawing his sword to keep the ghosts at bay, *Aeneid*, VI. 294

ANONYMOUS

314 Cromwell's *Coronation*

Oliver, Oliver, take up thy Crown,
For now thou hast made three Kingdoms thine own;
Call thee a Conclave of thy own creation,
  To ride us to ruine, who dare thee oppose:
Whilst we thy good people are at thy Devotion,
  To fall down and worship thy terrible Nose.

To thee and thy Mermydons, *Oliver*, we,
Do tender our homage as fits thy degree,
We'll pay the Excise and Taxes, God blesse us,
   With fear and contrition, as penitents should,
Whilst you, great Sir, vouchsafe to oppresse us,
   Not daring so much as in private to scold.

We bow down, as cow'd down, to thee and thy Sword,
For now thou hast made thy self *Englands* sole Lord,
By Mandate of Scripture, and Heavenly warrant,
   The Oath of Allegiance, and Covenant too;
To *Charles* and his Kingdoms thou art heir apparent,
   And born to rule over the *Turk* and the *Jew*.

Then *Oliver, Oliver,* get up and ride,
Whilst Lords, Knights and Gentry do run by thy side;
The Maulters and Brewers account it their glory,
   Great God of the Grain-tub's compared to thee:
And Rebells of old are lost in their story,
   Till thou plod'st along to the *Padington*-tree.

314 3 *Conclave* council of cardinals called to elect a pope, here the sense is of a closed council, held in secret 6 *Nose* Cromwell's nose was famous for its gross size 7 *Mermydons* soldiers, after Achilles' personal regiment in Homer's *Iliad* 15 *Mandate* order 18 *Turk* notorious for cruelty *Jew* Cromwell himself was called a Jew because of his nose 21 *Maulters* maltsters: suppliers of malt for making beer 24 *Padington-tree* Tyburn gallows, in the parish of Paddington

315 *The States New Coin*

1.

Saw you the States mony new come from the Mint?
Some People do say it is wonderous fine;
And that you may read a great mystery in't,
Of mighty King *Nol*, the Lord of the *Coyn*.

2.

They have quite omitted his Politick head,
His worshipfull face, and his excellent Nose;
But the better to tempt the sisters to bed,
They have fixed upon it the print of his Hose.

3.

For, if they had set up his Picture there,
They needs must ha' crown'd him in *Charles* his stead;
But 'twas cunningly done, that they did forbear,
And rather would set up his Ar— than his head.

4.

'Tis monstrous strange, and yet it is true,
In this Reformation we should ha' such luck
That Crosses were alwaies distained by you,
Who before pull'd them down, should now set them up.

5.

On this side they have circumscrib'd *God with us*,
And in this stamp and Coyn they confide;
Common-wealth on the other, by which we may guess
That *God* and the *States* were not both of a side.

6.

On this side they have a Crosse and Harp,
And only a Crosse on the other set forth;
By which we may learn it falls to our part
Two Crosses to have for one fit of Mirth.

7.

A Country-man hearing this, straight way did think,
That he would procure such a piece of his own;
And knowing it like his Wifes Butter-print,
She should ha't for a Token when as he came home.

8.

Then since that this is the Parliament coyn,
Now *Lilly* by thy mysterous charms,
Or Heralds, pray tell us if these ha'not been
Carmen or Fiddlers before by their Arms.

315 4 *Nol* diminutive of Oliver 8 *Hose* stockings. The arrangement of two shields on the reverse of Cromwell's coinage suggested buttocks to the satirically minded 12 *Ar*— arse 17 *circumscrib'd* literally, written round 24 *Crosses* trials, frustrations 27 *Butter-print* simple design stamped on butter pats 30 *Lilly* astrologer, see Appendix 2

HENRY VAUGHAN

316 To my worthy friend Master *T. Lewes*.

Sees not my friend, what a deep snow
Candies our Countries woody brow?
The yeelding branch his load scarse bears
Opprest with snow, and *frozen tears*,
While the *dumb* rivers slowly float,
All bound up in an *Icie Coat*.
  Let us meet then! and while this world
In wild *Excentricks* now is hurld,
Keep wee, like nature, the same *Key*,
And walk in our forefathers way;
Why any more cast wee an Eye
On what *may come*, not what is *nigh*?
Why vex our selves with *feare*, or *hope*
And cares beyond our *Horoscope*?
Who into future times would peere
Looks oft beyond his terme set here,
And cannot goe into those grounds
But through a *Church-yard* which them bounds;
Sorrows and sighes and searches spend
And draw our bottome to an end,
But discreet Joyes lengthen the lease
Without which life were a disease,

And who this age a Mourner goes,
Doth with his tears but feed his foes.

316 See no. 296, another consolatory adaptation of Horace, *Odes*, I. 9; this poem also includes elements from *Ode* I. 11 2 *Candies* with frost like sugar-coating 8 *Excentricks* erratic orbits 9 *Key* as in music 20 *bottome* ship, metaphorically reaching harbour

MARGARET CAVENDISH, DUCHESS OF NEWCASTLE

317 *A Description of Civil Wars*

A Kingdome which long time had lived in Peace,
Her People rich with Plenty, fat with Ease,
With Pride were haughty grown, Pride Envy bred,
From Envy Factions grew, then Mischief spread;
And Libels every where were strew'd about,
Which after soon a Civil War broke out.
Some for the Commons fought, some for the King,
And great disorder was 'mongst every thing;
Battles were lost and won on either side,
Where Fortune ebb'd and flow'd, like to a Tide;
At last the Commons won, and then astride
Fierce Tyrannie on Noble Necks did ride;
All Monuments pull'd down, that stood long time,
And Ornaments were then thought a great Crime;
No Law did plead, unless the Martial Law,
The Sword did rule, and keep them all in aw;
No Prayers offer'd to the Gods on high,
All Ceremony in the Dust did lye;
Nothing was done in Order, Truth, and Right,
Nought govern'd then but Malice, Spleen, and Spight.
But mark how justly Gods do punish Men
To make them humble, and to bow to them;
Though they had Plenty, and thereof did eat,
They relish'd not that good and savoury Meat;
Because their Conscience did them so torment,
For all their Plenty they were discontent;

They took no rest, Cares so oppress'd their Minde,
No Joy nor Comfort in the World could finde.
When drowsie sleep upon their eyes did set,
Then fearfull visions in their dreams they met;
In Life no pleasure take, yet fear to dye,
No mercy can they hope from Gods on high.
O serve the Gods, and then the Minde will be
Allwayes in peace, and sweet tranquillity.

317 13 *Monuments* religious statuary 20 *Spight* spite

318 *An antient* Cross

An antient Cross liv'd in our Fathers time,
With as much Fame, as did the Worthyes nine;
No harm it did, nor injury to none,
But dwelt in peace, and quietly alone;
On Times nor Government did not complain,
But stood stone-still, not stirr'd in no Kings reign;
Both Winters Snow, and Summers scorching Sun
He did endure, and urin'd was upon:
Yet peacefull Nature, nor yet humble Minde,
Shall not avoyd rude Ignorance that's blinde,
That superstitiously beats down all things
Which smell but of Antiquity, or springs
From Noble Deeds, nor love, nor take delight
In Laws, or Justice, hating Truth and Right;
But Innovations love, for that seems fine,
And what is new, adore they as divine;
That makes them so neglect the Gods above,
For time doth waste both their respect and love.
And so this Cross, poor Cross, all in a rage
They pull'd down quite, the fault was onely Age.
Had it been gilded gloriously and brave,
Then Vanity for an excuse might have:
But he was poor, his Morter all off worn,
Which time had eaten off, as Dogs had torn
The flesh from bones of Hares, or harmless Sheep,
Or like to Skeletons, that Scholars keep.

If they had pious been, it might have stood
To mollifie the Minds of Men to good:
But they were wicked, hating every thing
That by example might to goodness bring:
Then down they pull'd it, leaving not one stone
Upon another, for it to be known
To after Ages, for the Ground lyes bare,
That none can know once Antient Cross stood there.

318 2 *Worthyes nine* group of heroes, see Appendix 1 28 *mollifie* soften

ANONYMOUS

319 *A Free-Parliament Letany.*

To the Tune of, *An old Soldier of the Queen's.*

More Ballads;—here's a spick-and-span new *Supplication*;
By Order of a Committee for the Reformation,
To be read in all Churches and Chapels of this Nation,
Upon Pain of Slavery, and Sequestration.
From Fools *and* Knaves, *in our Parliament-free*,
Libera nos Domine.

From those that ha' more Religion, and less Conscience than their Fellows;
From a Representative, that's *Fearful*, and *Jealous*;
From a starting Jadish People, that is troubled with the *Yellows*,
And a Priest that blows the Coal—(a Turd in the Bellows.)
From Fools *and* Knaves, etc.

From Shepherds, that lead their Flocks into the Briers;
And then, Fleece 'um.—From *Vow-breakers*, and *King-tryers*:
Of *Church* and *Crown-lands* from both Sellers and Buyers:
From the Children of him, that's the Father of *Lyars*.
From Fools *and* Knaves, etc.

From the Doctrine and Discipline of *now, and anon*:
Preserve *us*, and our *Wives*: from ||John T. and Saint †John
Like Master, like Man, every way but one:
The Master has a large Conscience, and the Man has none.
From Fools *and* Knaves, etc.

From Major Generals,—Army-Officers; and that Phanatick Crew:
From the parboil'd Pimp *Scot*; and from *Good-face* the *Jew*:
From old *Mildmay*, that in *Cheapside* mistook his **Quean*,
And from him that won't *Pledge—give the Devil his due*.
From Fools *and* Knaves, etc.

From long-winded Speeches, and not a wise Word,
From a Gospel-Ministry settled by th'Sword,
From the Act of a *Rump*, that stinks when 'tis stir'd;
From a *Knight of the Post*, and a *Cobling Lord*.
From Fools *and* Knaves, etc.

From all the rich People that ha' made us all Poor;
From a Speaker that creeps to the House by a Back-door:
From that Badger *Robinson*, that limps, and bites sore:
And that Dog in a doublet *Arthur*,—that will do so no more.
From Fools *and* Knaves, etc.

From a certain *sly Knave* with a Beastly Name:
From a Parl'ment that's wild, and People that's tame,
From *Skippon, Titchbourne, Ireton*,—and another of the Same;
From a Dunghill Cock, and a Hen of the Game:
From Fools *and* Knaves, etc.

From all those that sate in the High Court of Justice;
From Usurpers, that stile themselves the *People's Trustees*;
From an *old Rump*, in which neither Profit nor Gust is;
And from the *Recov'ry* of that which now in the Dust is.
From Fools *and* Knaves, etc.

From a back-sliding Saint, that pretends t'acquiesce;
From crossing of Proverbs (let 'um *Hang* that confess)
From a *Snivelling Cause* in a *Pontifical Dress*;
And two Lawyer's, with the Devil, and his Dam in a Mess.
From Fools *and* Knaves, etc.

From those, that trouble the Water to mend the Fishing;
And fight the Lord's Battles, under the Devil's Commission:
Such as eat up the Nation, while the Government's a Dishing,
And from a People when it should be Doing stands Wishing.
From Fools *and* Knaves, etc.

From an *everlasting* Mock-Parliament;—and from *none*;
From *Strafford's* Old Friends,—*Harry, Jack* and *John*,
From the *Sollicitor's* Wolf Law, deliver our *King's* Son:
And from the Resurrection of the *Rump* that is *dead* and *gone*.
From Fools *and* Knaves, etc.

From Foreign Invasion and Commotions at Home,
From our present Distraction, and from worse to come:
From the same Hand again, *Smectymnius*, to the *Bum*:
And from taking *Geneva* in our way to *Rome*.
From Fools *and* Knaves, etc.

From a hundred thousand Pound Tax, to maintain Knaves and Whores:
(But it is well given to These, that turn'd Those out of Doors)
From undoing ourselves, in plast'ring old Sores:
He that set them to work, let him pay their Scores.
From Fools *and* Knaves, etc.

From Saints, and Tender-Consciences in Buff;
From *Mounson* in a Foam; and *Haslerigg* in a Huff;
From both Men and Women that think they never have enough,
And from a Fool's Head that looks through a Chain and a Ruff.
From Fools *and* Knaves, etc.

From those that would divide the *Gen'ral* and the *City*;
From *Harry Martin's Whore*, that was neither Sound nor
Pretty;
From a Faction, that has neither Brain, nor Pity;
From the Mercy of a Phanatick Committee.
From Fools *and* Knaves, etc.

Preserve us good Heaven from intrusting those,
That ha' much to Get, and little to Loos;
That Murther'd the *Father*, and the *Son* would Depose,
(Sure they cann't be Our Friends, that are their Country's
Foes,)
From Fools *and* Knaves, etc.

From *Bradshaw's* Presumption, and from *Hoyle's* Despaires;
From rotten Members; blind Guides, Preaching Aldermen and false
May'rs;
From Long Knives, Long Ears, Long Parliaments, and Long
Pray'rs,
In Mercy to this Nation,—Deliver us and our *Heirs*.
From Fools *and* Knaves, *in our Parliament-free,*
Libera nos Domine.

| | *John a Nokes.*
† *John a Styles.*
* Repulsed by a Citizen's Wife.

319 For references to contemporary names, see Appendix 2 Title *Letany* litany, prayer 4 *Sequestration* confiscation of property 6 *Libera nos Domine* Lord deliver us (standard response in a litany) 9 *Jadish* like a wayward horse *Yellows* a form of jaundice affecting horses 15 *Father of Lyars* Satan 18 *John T. and Saint John* John Thurlow and Oliver St John, see Appendix 2; the glosses *John a Nokes, John a Styles* identify them with proverbial comic common men 22 *Phanatick* fanatical 23 *Good-face the Jew* Cromwell, see Appendix 2 24 *Cheapside* street by St Paul's 25 *Pledge* swear loyalty to the king 29 *Rump* Parliament, also backside 30 *Knight of the Post* perjurer *Cobling Lord* Hewson 33 *Speaker* Lenthall 35 *Dog in a doublet Arthur* Haslerigg 40 *Dunghill Cock* whoremaster *Hen of the Game* prostitute 44 *Gust* savour, zest, but with a pun on gust of wind 49 *Pontifical* papal; the 'cause' of English republicanism is described as having been betrayed by those who would make it as authoritarian as the former hierarchic church 50 *Dam* mother 59 *Wolf Law*

arbitrary law 64 *Smectymnius* see Appendix 2 *Bum* Rump (Parliament), also suggesting a suitable use for the controversialists' works 65 *Geneva* home of Calvinism *Rome* home of Catholicism 69 *plast'ring* treating, healing 72 *Buff* uniform 75 *Chain and a Ruff* insignia of the Lord Mayor 78 *Sound* free of disease 89 *Long Ears* donkeys

320 *A New Kickshaw for the queasie Stomack of Sathan and all those that fight under his Banner.*

To the Tune of *Cook Laurell.*

You pitifull Rimers now be you all dumb;
Let no Dames of the Dunghill sing Ditties about
St. *George* and the Dragon, and little *Tom Thumb*,
With *Wallingford* House and the Rump are worn out.
Here's an Ola Polidra *so pleasant and new,*
The Tayle of the State had n'ere such a Hogooe.
With a hey down down, &c.

Come listen you Cooks and learn my new Dish,
'Tis that that will fill your Guests bellyes with laughter
'Tis a meat neither made of flesh nor fish,
But will make all that tast it to lick their lips after.
Here's an Ola, &c.

First take you three Farts from the parliament-Breech,
The head of an Onion to rubb on your Platter,
The Hums and the Ha's of Mr. *Scots* speech,
Spoke twice to no purpose, and mince not the matter,
Here's an Ola, &c.

Take the Linings of Alderman *Atkins* his Hose,
Some oth'cobling Collonel Shooe-makers wax,
The juice of *Tichburns* and *Iretons* Toes,
'Twill settle your Stomacks, and strengthen your backs.
Here's an Ola, &c.

If an Independent Sermon you hear,
Be sure you take all that is spoke to the Text,
Some of my Lord *Pride* his zeal for a Fear,
And a Prayer by the Spirit made by that Part comes next.
Here's an Ola, &c.

Take *Munson*s chaste motions towards a Wench,
The Sword of the Spirit handled by a *Gough*,
The fear of the Judges that sate on the Bench
When the Head of this Isle by the Tayle was lopt off.
Here's an Ola, &c.

Take all the old Speaker's Honesty whole;
For if it be lessen'd 'twill prove little or none
And, if you have room, you may stop up the hole
With the Knighthood and Wisedom of Sir *John* his Son.
Here's an Ola, &c.

Take one of Sir *Arthur*s passionate dumps,
Sir *Harry Vane*'s hearty Prayers for *Monck*,
The froth of the *Good Old Cause* worn to the stumps.
And modest *Harry Martins* discourse for a Punk.
Here's an Ola, &c.

Of Publick Faith an Ounce if you can get it,
Stew'd well in an Honest Committee mans skull,
Then with the Coales of *Hugh Peter*'s Devotion beat it,
'Twill give all the Devills in Hell belly full.
Here's an Ola, &c.

Take the Whites of a Puritans lifted-up eyes,
And the Saffron engendred on a Presbyters gums,
Mr *William Lillye*s Astrological Lyes,
And the meditations of *Salloway* biting his thumbs.
Here's an Ola, &c.

Of *Lamberts* Religion as much as a Nut,
And of his Wive's Honesty much thereabout,
With the spirit that moveth holy Brethren to rut,
And maketh the holy Sisters hold out.
Here's an Ola, &c.

Stow it in an Excise-mans Conscience well sear'd,
And in a French-man's Codpiece 2. hours let it stew,
Then strow it o're with a Puritan's beard;
'Tis a dish for the Devil and for his Dam too.
Here's an Ola, &c.

But then if it want a Man to say grace,
It must be done by one that's a Sinner,
An Independent Doctor just turn'd out on's place,
Must needs be most fit to give thanks for this Dinner.

320 For all contemporary names, see Appendix 2 Title *Kickshaw* trifling delicacy 3–4 *St. George... Tom Thumb... Wallingford* all subjects of popular ballads 5 *Ola Polidra* mixed stew of scraps 6 *Hogooe* highly flavoured sauce, sometimes concealing strong or tainted meat 13 *Breech* rump 19 *cobling Collonel* Hewson 25 *Pride* Colonel Pride 38 *Sir Arthur* Haslerigg 51 *Salloway* Major Robert Salloway or Salway

IAIN LOM MACDONALD

321 SORAIDH DO'N GHRÀMACH

1. Soraidh do'n Ghràmach
Tha air mhàrsal air fògradh,
Ge tamall o làimh e,
Ta dhàil ri theachd oirnne;
Ge bè ionad do'n champa,
Anns an Spàin no 'san Olaind,
Aon neach leis am b'àill i,
Deoch-slàinte Mhontròsa.

2. Nan tigeadh Montròs'
Ann ar còmhdhail a dh'Eirinn,
Le trì fichead long sgòdach
'S buill chòrcaich mar shréin orr',
Le'm brataichibh sròil
Agus òdugh Rìgh Seurlas,
Thug an fhàistinn ud beò sinn
Mar dh'òrdaich Tom Reumhair.

3. 'N uair thig Alasdair tharainn
Le carraid mu earball,
Naoi mìle fear fallain
'Gan tarraing air fairge,
Uibhir eile bhith mar ris
Nach mealladh 'na earbs' e,
De luchd nan cùl geala
'S nan tarrainnean dearga.

4. Ta seirce 'nad ghruaidhean,
Ta uaisle, ta féile,
Ta maise mhic Rìgh annt';
Dà nì cha tug géill diot,
Bha tapadh is strìth annt'—
Nar dhìobradh each sréin' thu;
Dh'fhàg thu falt is fuil bhrùite
Mu shùilibh luchd Beurla.

5. 'S lìonmhor mac chinneadh t'athar
Sheasadh faidhir gun ghealtachd,
'S a rùisgeadh a chlaidheamh
Mum faigheadh tu masladh;
'N uair a bheireadh tu cunnta
Bu dùbailt do phacaid;
Bu leat Mac Gill' Eathain,
Fir Atholl, Clann Chatain.

6. Gun éireadh sud leatsa,
Ge bè leis am b'olc e,
Clann Laghmain, Clann Lachlainn,
'S gach neach thig 'nan compairt;
Sìol Ilpin, Sìol Ailpin,
An comunn nach trocadh,
Eòin Stiùbhart o'n Apainn,
Mac an Ab' a Gleann Dochart.

7. Clann Dòmhnaill nan sgapall,
Nam bratach, nam pìcean,
Nan lùireach, nan clogad,
Nan ceannbhearta rìoghail,
Nan geurlanna glasa
Leis an caisgte na strìthean,
Gum b'e adhbhar ur gearain
Gun do reic iad an Rìgh uaibh.

8. Clann Dòmhnaill nam bàtan
'S nan àrdlonga luatha,
Ged a tha sibh mar tha sibh
An tràth-s' air an uair-sa,
Tha 'n fhuil ri bhith pàighte.
Cha sàl a thug uainn i.
Dia dùileach tha làidir:
Tha dàil ri bhith 'n uachdar.

9. Is oil leam a' chinnte
Bh'aig Iarla na fàidheachd
Gun chaill sibh an fhiacail
A b'fheàrr grìd bha 'san àlach:
Sàr mharcaich eich-strìthe
Nach dìobradh an àithne,
Làmh threun bha gun tuisleadh
A thuit am Blàr Aford.

10. Gur mór mo chuid éislein
O'n sgeul-s' tha mi clàistinn,
Sibh bhith togail ur léigeard
'N retreut chum na fàsaich;

Thig marcaich a Eirinn
An éirig na dh'fhàg iad,
'S bidh luchd nan each ceumnach
Ag éigheach a' phàrlaidh.

321 Success to the Graham

Success to the Graham who is on the march in exile, though some distance away. His tryst is to meet us; wherever the camp is, in Spain or in Holland, let everyone who so wills drink to the health of Montrose. If Montrose were to come to join us in Ireland with three-score rigged ships with hempen ropes like reins, with their silken banners and King Charles's command, that prophecy would bring us alive as Thomas the Rhymer. When Alasdair crosses over to us, with trouble in his wake, nine thousand strong warriors being ferried over the sea, may as many again be with him who would not betray him in his trust of the men of the fair curling locks and the red shield bosses. There is beauty in your countenance, there is nobility, there is generosity, there is the comeliness of a King's son; two qualities have not forsaken you—the courage and mettlesomeness that were in it; let not a bridled horse fail you, you left hair and bruised blood about the eyes of English-speakers. Many a man of your father's kin would muster at fair-ground without dread and would bare his sword before you would suffer humiliation; when you gave out the pay your measure was double; supporting you were Maclean, the men of Atholl and Clan Chattan. These would rise with you, no matter who objected, Clan Lamont and MacLachlan and all who are allied to them, the seed of Ilpin and Alpin, the company that would not parley, John Stewart from Appin, MacNab from GlenDochart. Clan Donald of the scapulars, the banners, the pikes, the breast-plates, the helmets, the regal head-gear, the sharp grey blades that bring an end to contention; the cause of your complaint was they had sold off your King. Clan Donald of the galleys and the tall swift ships, though you stand as you do at the present time, the blood must be paid for. It was not the sea that took it from us. God of the Elements is strong; there is a decree for victory. Offensive to me is the assertion made by the soothsaying Earl that you have lost from the set the tooth of the finest quality, an excellent rider of a battle-horse who would not fail a command, a brave unfaltering hand, who fell in the Battle of Alford. Great is my sorrow at this news I am hearing, that you are leaving your siege camp and retreating to the wilderness. Horsemen will come from Ireland in revenge of those who have left them, and the men of the prancing steeds will be calling for parley.

321 1 *'n Ghràmach/The Graham* Montrose, see Appendix 3 16 *Tom Reumhair/Thomas the Rhymer* Famous visionary and prophet (1220–97) of Erceldoun in Berwickshire, in Highland tradition inhabitant of the fairy mound at Tomnahurich near Inverness, prophesied eventual victory for the Gaels over the English 17 *Alasdair* Alasdair mac Colla, Montrose's principal Highland ally, see Appendix 2 25 *ghruaidhean/your countenance* the addressee changes here

from Montrose to Alasdair mac Colla 72 *Blàr Aford/The Battle of Alford* fought in July 1645, a victory for Montrose over the Covenanting army

322 CUMHA MHONTROIS

1. Mi gabhail Srath Dhruim-uachdair,
   'S beag m'aighear anns an uair so,
   Tha 'n lath' air dol gu gruamachd,
   'S chan e tha buain mo sproc.

2. Ge duilich leam 's ge dìobhail
   M'fhear-cinnidh math bhith dhìth orm,
   Chan fhasa leam an sgrìob-s'
   Thàinig air an rìoghachd bhochd.

3. Tha Alba dol fo chìoschain
   Aig farbhalaich gun fhìrinn,
   Bhàrr a' chalpa dhìrich—
   'S e cuid de m'dhìobhail ghoirt.

4. Tha Sasannaich 'gar faireigneadh,
   'Gar creach 'gar murt 's 'gar marbhadh,
   Gun ghabh ar n-Athair fearg ruinn,
   Gur dearmad dhuinn 's gur bochd.

5. Mar bha Cloinn Israéil
   Fo bhruid aig Rìgh na h-Eiphit,
   Tha sinn' air a' chor cheudna,
   Chan éigh iad ruinn ach "Seóc".

6. Ar Rìgh an déis a chrùnadh,
   Mun gann a leum e ùrfhas
   'Na thaisdealach bochd rùisgte,
   Gun gheàrd gun chùirt gun choisd.

7. 'Ga fharfhuadach as àite
Gun duine leis de chàirdean,
Mar luing air uachdar sàile
Gun stiùir gun ràmh gun phort.

8. Cha téid mi do Dhùn Eideann
O dhòirteadh fuil a' Ghreumaich,
An leómhann fearail treubhach
'Ga cheusadh air a' chroich.

9. B'e sud am fìor dhuin' uasal
Nach robh de'n lìnne shuaraich,
Bu ro mhath rudhadh gruaidhe
'N am tarrainn suas gu trod;

10. Deud chailc bu ro mhath dlùthadh
Fo mhala chaoil gun mhùgaich,
Ge tric do dhàil 'gam dhùsgadh,
Cha rùisg mi chàch e nochd.

11. Mhic Nèill a Asaint chianail,
Nan glacainn ann mo lìon thu,
Bhiodh m'fhacal air do bhìnne,
'S cha dìobrainn thu o'n chroich.

12. Nan tachrainn is tu féin
Ann am boglachan Beinn Eite,
Bhiodh uisge dubh na féithe
Dol troimh a chéile 's ploc.

13. Thu féin is t'athair-céile,
Fear-taighe sin na Léime,
Ged chrochta sibh le chéile
Cha b'éirig air mo lochd.

14. Craobh rùisgt' de'n abhall bhreugach,
Gun mheas gun chliù gun cheutaidh,
Bha riamh ri murt a chéile,
'Nur fuidheall bheum is chorc.

15. Marbhfhaisg ort féin, a dhìmheis,
    Mar olc a reic thu 'n fhìrinn
  Air son na mine Lìtich
    Agus dà thrian dith goirt.

322 Lament for Montrose

As I travel Drumochter Pass, little is my joy at this time: the day has turned grim and does not lift my spirits. Although it is very distressing for me to have lost my good clansman, no easier to bear is this calamity that has fallen on the kingdom. Scotland is being subjected by dishonest foreigners to pay excessive tribute—that is part of my sore distress. The English are tyrannizing us, pillaging, murdering, and slaying us; our Father has been angered by us for we are miserable and neglected. As the Children of Israel were held captive by the King of Egypt, so are we in the same state, 'Jock' is all they yell at us. Our king, after being crowned and barely before reaching maturity, is a poor naked wanderer, without guard, without court, without assembly. Driven from his land without any of his companions, he is like a ship on the ocean, without rudder, without oar, without harbour. I will not go to Edinburgh since the Graham's blood has been spilt, the mighty valiant lion tortured on the gallows. That was the true nobleman, he was not of the petty line, splendid was the flushing of his cheek when drawing up to fight. Teeth of chalk, regularly set, below slender eyebrows without frown, though often a tryst with you would waken me I will not expose it to others tonight. Son of Neill from dreary Assynt, if I could catch you in my net, my word would condemn you, and I would not banish you from the gallows. If you and I were to meet in the bogs of Ben Etive, the black water of the quagmire would be churning up with sods. You and your father-in-law, that Goodman of Lemlair, even if you were both hanged together it would not make up the blood-price for my loss. Bare branch of the faithless apple tree, without fruit, without honour, without beauty, always killing one another, you are the leavings of dirks and sword thrusts. A shroud on you, you contemptible wretch, for wrongly you have sold the truth for Leith meal, with two-thirds of it gone rancid.

322 6 *fhear-cinnidh/clansman* Alasdair mac Colla, died 1647: the poem was composed by a fellow MacDonald 8 *an rìoghachd/the kingdom* 17 *Cloinn Israéil/Children of Israel* Exodus 1: 12 20 *Seóc/Jock* a Scot (from John), properly a Lowland Scot 41 *Mhic Nèill a Asaint/Son of Neill from...Assynt* Neil MacLeod, Lord of Ardvreck, betrayed Montrose to the Covenanters: his reward of 25,000 pounds Scots was to be paid as £20,000 in cash, with the balance in sour meal 50 *Fear-taighe sin na Léime/Goodman of Lemlair* John Munro of Lemlair 59 *mine Lìtich/Leith meal* oatmeal imported via the harbour of Leith, on the Forth

323 Oran air Latha Blàir Inbhir Lóchaidh eadar Clann Dòmhnaill agus na Caimbeulaich

Hì him ro ho, hò ro leatha,
Hì him ro ho, hò ro leatha,
Hì him ro ho, hò ro leatha,
Chaidh an latha le Clann Dòmhnaill.

'N cuala sibh-se an tionnadadh duineil
Thug an camp bha an Cille Chuimein?
'S fada chuaidh ainm air an urram:
Thug iad as an naimhdean iomain.

Dhìrich mi moch madainn Dòmhnaich
Gu bràigh caisteal Inbhir Lòchaidh,
Chunnaic mi an t-arm dol an òrdugh
'S bha buaidh a' bhlàir le Clann Dòmhnaill.

Dìreadh a-mach glùn Chùil Eachaidh,
Dh'aithnich mi oirbh sùrd bhur tapaidh;
Ged bha mo dhùthaich na lasair
'S èirig air a' chùis mar thachair.

Ged bhitheadh iarlachd a' Bhràghad
An seachd bliadhna so màr tha e,
Gun chur gun chliathadh gun àiteach,
'S math an riadh o bheil sinn pàighte.

Air do làimh-se, a Thighearna Labhair,
Ge mòr do bhòsd as do chlaidheamh
'S iomadh òglach chinne t'athar
Tha an Inbhir Lòchaidh na laighe.

'S iomadh fear gòrsaid is pillein,
Chomh math 's a bha riamh de d' chinneach,
Nach d'fhaod a bhòtainn thoirt tioram
Ach foghlam snàmh air bun Nibheis.

Sgeul a b'aite nuair a thigeadh
Air Caimbeulaich nam beul sligneach,
H-uile dream dhiubh mar a thigeadh
La bualadh lann an ceann gam bristeadh.

'N latha sin shaoil leo dhol leotha
'S ann bha laoich gan ruith air reodhadh;
'S iomadh slaodanach mòr odhar
Bha na shìneadh air Ach an Todhair.

Ge be dhìreadh Tom na h-Aire,
Bu lìonmhor spòg ùr bh'ann air dhroch shailleadh;
Neul marbh air an sùil gun anam
An dèidh an sgiùrsadh le lannan.

Thug sibh toiteal teth mu Lòchaidh,
Bhith gam bualadh mu na sròna;
Bu lìonmhor claidheamh claisghorm còmhnard
Bha bualadh an lamhan Chlann Dòmhnaill.

Sin 'n uair chruinnich mòr-dragh na falachd
'N àm rùsgadh nan greidlein tana:
Bha iongnan nan Guibhneach ri talamh
An dèidh an lùithean a ghearradh.

'S lìonmhor corp nochdte gun aodach
Tha nan sìneadh air chnocain fhraoiche
On bhlàr an greaste na saoidhean
Gu ceann Leitir Blàr a' Chaorainn.

Dh'innsinn sgeul eile le fìrinn
Cho math 's a nì clèireach a sgrìobhath:
Chaïdh na laoich ud gu'n dìcheall
'S chuir iad maoim air luchd am mìoruin.

Iain Mhùideartaich nan seòl soilleir
Sheòladh an cuan ri là doilleir,
Ort cha d'fhuaradh bristeadh coinne:
'S ait leam Barra-breac fo d' chomas.

Cha b'e sud an siubhal cearbach
A thug Alasdair do dh'Albainn,
Creachadh, losgadh agus marbhadh,
'S leagadh leis Coileach Srath Bhalgaidh.

An t-eun dona chaill a cheuta
An Sasann, an Albainn 's an Eirinn,
Ite à cùrr na sgèithe:
Gur misde leam ona ghèill e.

Alasdair nan geurlann sgaiteach,
Gheall thu an dè bhith cur as doibh;
Chuir thu an raitreuta seach an caisteal—
Seòladh glè mhath air an leantainn.

Alasdair nan geurlann guineach,
Nam biodh agad àrmainn Mhuile
Thug thu air na dh'fhalbh dhiubh fuireach,
'S raitreut air pràbar an duilisg.

Alasdair mhic Colla ghasda,
Làmh dheas a sgoltadh nan caisteal,
Chuir thu an ruaig air Ghallaibh glasa
'S ma dh'òl iad càl gun d' chuir thu asda e.

'M b'aithne dhuibh-se an Goirtein Odhar?
'S math a bha e air a thodhar:
Chan inneir chaorach no ghobhar
Ach fuil Ghuibhneach an dèidh reodhaidh.

Sgrios oirbh mas truagh leam ur càradh,
'G èisdeachd anshocair ur pàisdean,
Caoidh a' phannail bha anns an àraich,
Donnalaich bhan Earra-Ghàidheal.

323 The Battle of Inverlochy

Hì him ro ho, hò ro leatha, hì him ro ho, hò ro leatha, hì him ro ho, hò ro leatha, the day was a victory for Clan Donald.

Have you heard about the bold return-march made by the army that camped at Cille Chuimein? Far has fame of their distinction been published: they forced their enemies on before them. I climbed early on Sunday morning the brae of the Castle of Inverlochy, I saw the army get into order and victory on the field was with Clan Donald. As you ascended the spur of Culachy, I recognized in you the frenzy of your courage; though the land of my kindred was burning, what happened was compensation for the matter. Even if the earldom of Brae Lochaber remained for seven years as it now is, without sowing or harrowing or ploughing, good is the interest by which we are compensated. As for you, O Lord of Lawers, though great your boasting of your broadsword, many a warrior of your father's people is lying there at Inverlochy. Many a fellow with cuirass and saddle as fine as ever was in your kindred was not allowed to get away dry-shod, but learned to swim in the mouth of the Nevis.

Yet more pleasing news kept coming, concerning the fate of the wry-mouthed Campbells: as each of their bands made its appearance, their heads were battered in by sword-blows. The day they had thought they would be triumphant, warriors were chasing them on frozen uplands; there was many a great sallow sloucher lying stretched out on Ach an Todhair. Anyone who climbed the Look-out Hillock could see many fresh paws badly salted; death's blankness over their lifeless eyes, after the slashing they got from sword-blades. You made a hot attack around Lochy, belabouring them hard on their noses; many the sword, well-balanced, blue-fluted, being wielded in the hands of Clan Donald. Then there arose the great blood-letting at the time of the drawing of slender rapiers: the claws of the Campbells stuck into farmland after the severing of their sinews. Many the stripped corpse without clothing, lying sprawled over heathery hillocks, from the battle where the heroes were incited right to the end of Leitir Blar a' Chaorainn. I could faithfully tell another story as well as any cleric will write it: those warriors did their utmost, and left their enemies utterly stricken. Iain of the sparkling sails of Moidart, who on a gloomy day would sail the ocean, you were never found to break a promise: I am delighted you hold Barbreck in your power.

That was no faulted manoeuvre Alasdair mac Colla made to Scotland, burning, killing, wreaking destruction: the Cock of Strathbogie was broken by him. The wretched bird that lost its appearance in England, in Scotland, and in Ireland, he is a feather from the wing-pit: I am disgusted since he has submitted. Alasdair of the sharp lopping sword-blades, yesterday you promised you would destroy them; you sent their retreat past the castle—that was an excellent way to chase them. Alasdair of the pointed sword-blades, if you had with you the Mull heroes, you could have stopped those ones of the dulse-fed rabble escaping when retreating. Alasdair, son of generous Colla, a skilled hand at splitting castles, you routed the Lowland cowards and you made them skitter the kale they drank.

Did you know the Goirtein Odhar? it has received a fine manuring: neither with sheep-dung nor goat-dung, but with Campbell blood after congealing. Destruction take you if I pity your condition, as I listen to the misery of your children, lamenting the mob who were in the battle, the howling of the women of Argyll.

323 Title The Battle of Inverlochy was fought 2 February 1645 near the present town of Fort William between the royalist forces led by Alasdair mac Colla and Montrose, and the Covenanting army, led by Campbell of Auchinbreck for the Earl of Argyll 30 *beul sligneach/wry-mouthed* Campbell means 'crooked-mouthed' 62 *Alasdair* Alasdair mac Colla, son of Colkitto, the ally of Montrose

AN ANONYMOUS WOMAN OF CLAN CAMPBELL

324 Oran air blàr Inbhir Lóchaidh

O, gur mi a th'air mo leònadh,
Na hì ri ri ri hó hò;
O, gur mise th'air mo leònadh,
Na hì ri ri 's o ho ró.

Bho latha Blàr Inbhir Lòchaidh,
Na hì ri ri ri hó hò;
Bho latha Blàr Inbhir Lòchaidh,
Na hì ri ri 's ri o ho ró.

Bho ruaig nan eireannach dhoithte
Tháinig a dh'Albainn gun stòras,
Le bha dh'earras air an cleòcaibh,
Thug iad spionnadh do Chlann Dòmhnaill,
Mharbh iad m'athair is m'fhear pòsda,

'S mo cheathrar bhràithrean 'gan stròiceadh,
'S mo cheathrar mhacanan òga,
'S mo naoinear chodhaltan bòidheach;
Mharbh iad mo chrodh mór gu feòlach,
'S mo chaoirich gheala 'gan ròsladh,
Loisg iad mo chuid coirc' is eòrna.

O, gur mi a th'air mo chlaoidheadh
Mu mhac Dhunnchaidh Gleanna Faochan,
Tha gach fear a's tìr 'gad chaoineadh
Thall 's a bhos mu Inbhir Aora,
Mhathan 's a bhasraich 's am falt sgaoilte.

O, gur mi a th'air mo mhilleadh
Mu mharcaich' nan strian 's nam pillein,
Thuit 'sa chaonnaig le chuid ghillean;
Thug Mac Cailein Mór an linn'air,
'S leag e 'n sgrìob ud air a chinne!

324 On the Battle of Inverlochy.

O, I have been wounded by the day of Inverlochy, from the charge of the grim Irish who came to Scotland without anything but what they had on their cloaks; they added strength to Clan Donald. They killed my father and my husband, they struck down my four brothers, they killed my four young sons and my nine handsome foster-children; they slaughtered my great cattle, and my white sheep they roasted, they burnt my oats and my barley.

O, I have been anguished by the death of Duncan of Glen Faochan, whom all in the land are lamenting round about Inverary, women beating their hands, dishevelled.

O, I have been devastated, for the horsemen of reins and bridles who fell with his men in the battle; the Earl of Argyll took to the water and let that blow fall on his kin!

324 This song, composed by a Campbell, gives the opposing view of the battle described in no. 323 3 *eireannach/Irish* Alasdair mac Colla had raised troops in Ireland for the royalists 22–3 the Earl of Argyll had taken to sea before the battle

FEAR DORCHA Ó MEALLÁIN

325 *An Díbirt go Connachta*

In ainm an Athar go mbuaidh,
in ainm an Mhic guair an phian,
in ainm an Spioraid Naoimh le neart,
Muire 's a Mac linn ag triall.

Mícheal feartach ár gcuid stóir,
 Muire Ógh 's an dá aspal déag,
Brighid, Pádraig agus Eoin—
 is maith an lón creideamh Dé.

Colam Cille feartach caomh,
 's Colmán mhac Aoidh, ceann na gcliar,
beid linn uile ar aon tslí
 's ná bígí ag caoi fá dhul siar.

Nach dtuigeann sibh, a bhráithre gaoil
 cúrsaí an tsaoil le fada buan?
gé mór atá 'nár seilbh,
 beag bheas linn ag dul san uaigh.

Uirscéal as sin tuigthear libh:
 clann Israel a bhean le Dia,
san Éigipt cé bhí i mbroid,
 furthacht go grod a fuair siad.

Do-chuadar tríd an mhuir mhóir,
 go ndearnadh dhóibh ród nár ghann,
gur éirigh an fhairrge ghlas
 mar charraig 'mach os a gceann.

Iar ndul dhóibhsin fó thír
 fuair siad cóir ó Rí na rann,
furtacht, cabhair agus biadh
 ón Dia bhí riamh is tá ann.

Fuaradar ó neamh mar lón
 cruithneachta mhór—stór nár bheag—
mil dá chur mar cheo,
 uisce go leor ag teacht as creig.

Amhlaidh sin do-ghéanfar libh:
 do-ghéabhaidh sibh gach maith ar dtús;
atá bhur ndúithche ar neamh,
 's ná bígí leamh in bhur gcúis.

A chlann chroí, déanaigh seasamh,
's ná bígí ag ceasnamh le hanró;
Maoise a fuair ar agaill—
cead a chreidimh ó Pharó.

Ionann Dia dhúinn agus dhóibh,
aon Dia fós do bhí 'gus tá;
ionann Dia abhus agus thiar,
aon Dia riamh is bheas go bráth.

Má ghoirthear dhaoibhse Páipis,
cuiridh fáilte re bhur ngairm;
tugaidh foighead don Ardrí—
Deo gratias, maith an t'ainm.

A Dhia atá fial, a thriath na mbeannachta,
féach na Gaeil go léir gan bharanta;
má táimid ag triall siar go Connachta,
fágmaid 'nar ndiaidh fó chian ar seanchairde.

325 The Exodus to Connacht

In the name of the Father full of virtue, in the name of the Son who suffered pain, in the name of the Holy Ghost in power, Mary and her Son be with us. Our sole possessions: Michael of miracles, the virgin Mary, the twelve apostles, Brigit, Patrick, and Saint John—and fine rations: faith in God. Sweet Columcille of miracles too, and Colmán mac Aoidh, poets' patron, will all be with us on our way. Do not bewail our journey West. Brothers mine, do you not see the ways of the world a while now? However much we may possess, we'll go with little into the grave. Consider a parable of this: Israel's people, God's own, although they were in bonds in Egypt, found in time a prompt release. Through the mighty sea they passed, an ample road was made for them, then the grey-green ocean rose out there above them like a rock. When they came to dry land the King of Heaven minded them—relief, succour and nourishment from the God who ever was and is. Food from Heaven they received: great wheat, in no small measure, honey settling like a mist, abundant water out of rock. Likewise it shall be done to you: all good things shall first be yours. Heaven is your inheritance. Be not faint-hearted in your faith. People of my heart, stand steady, don't complain of your distress. Moses got what he requested, religious freedom—and freedom from Pharaoh. Identical their God and ours. One God there was, and still remains. Here or Westward God is one, one God ever, and shall be. If they call you

'Papishes' accept it gladly for a title. Patience, for the High King's sake. *Deo gratias*, good the name! God who art generous, Prince of Blessings, behold the Gael, stripped of authority. Now as we journey Westward into Connacht, old friends we'll leave behind us in their grief.

325 In 1652, by act of parliament all Irish people living to the east of the river Shannon were commanded to remove to the west of that river, into the kingdom of Connacht before 1 May 1654, on pain of death. This enforced a winter journey, on which many died 1–8 This is a version of a traditional prayer before undertaking a journey. Mícheal (Michael) is the Archangel, Muire is the Virgin Mary, Brighid, Pádraig (Brigit and Patrick) two of the three patrons of Ireland, Eoin (John) is St John the Baptist 9 *Colam Cille* St Columba of Iona, with St Patrick and St Brigit, one of the three patrons of Ireland 10 *Colmán mhac Aoidh* a sixth-century Irish saint associated with Ardbó, on Lough Neagh 18 *clann Israel/Israel's people* see Exodus 14 29 *Fuaradar ó neamh/Food from Heaven* Exodus 16: 12–21

THOMAS STANLEY

326 *Upon the various events of War, Victories, and Defeats.*

With ready joy oh let me, Lord! agree
To be orecome when thou wilt have it so:
Instruct me in the noblest Victory,
By patience to subdue my self, and foe;
Conquest like Christs, a Christian King best shew:

Mold us to Piety betwixt thy Hands,
Prest by thy left, supported by thy right;
Pardon the pride of our succesfull Bands,
And the repinings of our luckless Fight,
When (trusting in our own) deny'd thy might:

When we are ought, or nothing, be thou All;
That thy wide glory's the whole World may fill,
Or in our Conquest, or inglorious fall.
Thou know'st with what Regret I suffer ill,
From those whose Good's the scope of all my will.

The Ills they force me to inflict, I bear;
And in their punishments, my own embrace,
Victor or vanquish'd? since a double share
Of certain suffering doth my Hope displace,
Grant me a double Portion of thy Grace.

As most afflicted, Lord, reform me most,
To see our Peace, and to restore it blest.
That all subdu'd by reasons power, may boast,
A mutuall Conquest, common strife suppress
In publick Union, our joynt Interest.

But if as sins of Peace provok'd this War,
Peace for the sins of War thou shouldst deny,
Making our miseries more circular:
Yet let thy servant midst these broyles enjoy
That Peace the World nor gives, nor can destroy.

To me impute not, Lord! the purple Flood,
Shed with unwilling grief in my defence.
But wash me in my Saviours precious blood:
By whom my troubles hope a quick dispence;
For short are impious joy's, and Confidence.

326 Written in the persona of Charles I: 16–35 constitute a loose refutation of the chief charges brought against Charles at his trial: *The charge of the commons of England Against Charls Stuart, King of England, Of High Treason, and other High Crimes, exhibited to the High Court of Justice, By John Cook Esquire, Solicitor General, appointed by the said Court, for, and on behalf of the People of England*, 1648, pp. 3–8.

MURDO MACKENZIE OF ACHILTY

327 Crosanachd do rinneadh le Murchadh Mac Mhic Mhurchaidh 'san àm 'na reiceadh Righ Teàrlach, Anno: 1648.

1. Olc an t-aobhar uabhair,
Ghlac an saoghal àmhghar;
Ni 'm bheil se ach nuadharr
Mar dhuille géig 'san dàmhair.

2. Mar dhuille na géig;
No cop tuinne air fairge;
Mar mhuin blàthbréig;
Mar bheum sruth ri cairge.

3. Mar dhealt romh nòin;
No sneachd an àm gréin;
'S minic saoi fo dhòruinn,
Is daoi gun mhóran péin.

4. Mar sin cor an t-saoghail;
Cealgach e gu leòr;
Thig e air neach sìothmhuil;
Ach 'ga shìor-ruith àmhghar.

5. Cuirim druim ri chomain:
Cuirm iomluath nach fanadh;
Aobhar beud do 'n anam
Gràdh do na bhréig-s', a cholunn.

6. Gràdh an òir 's an ealaidh
A th' aig na slòigh gan dealadh,
Bho chàirdeas gun cheannach
Gu àrdan 's gu geanach.

7. Craos a' bheach-meala
Th' aig an deamhan ullamh
Chun an t-slòigh a mhealladh
Do'n an iath gun toradh.

8. Ceud achd an tasdail bréig:
Cois-cheumaibh na fairge;
Lagh nam foireann fairgnidh:
Bhith brath an rìgh chionn airgid.

9. Is dall gach neach nach cuala
Beachd an sgeòil mar thàrladh;
Bho ghlac an troich oirnn uachdar
Gu'm foghainn croich d'a dhìoladh.

10. Gu'm b'e 'n t-Iudas fallsa
Is ùghdar do na ghnìomhsa;
Bhuail e ploc 'san uailse;
'S dògh gur olc a dhìol-sa.

11. Mar sin is truagh a' chluip
A dh' fhàs gu buan 'nan corp:
'G òl "An Rìgh" le glut:
M'uil-chridhe dhaibh olc.

327 A poem that was composed by Murdo Mackenzie Mhurchaids at the time that King Charles was betrayed, Anno 1648

Evil the cause for pride. The world has seized strife, it is only gloomy, like a tree's leaves in October. Like the leaves of the tree or spume on ocean, like false blossom of bramble, like current's thud against cliff. Like dew before noon or snow in sunshine, many a righteous man is suffering and wicked man is without much pain. Thus is the state of the world, it is deceitful enough; it comes on a person peacefully, but with strife ever following. I turn my back on society, it is a fickle feast that will not last; love of this life, oh body, is a cause of harm to the soul. Love of gold and craft is what turns the people from friendship that cannot be bought off to haughtiness and greed. It is the gluttony of the honey-bee that the devil displays, ready to entice the people into a fruitless land. The first act of the false trial is foot-steps over the ocean; it is the law of the hacking crew to be betraying the king for money. Every man is blind who has not heard an account of the story as it happened. Since the wretch has seized dominion over us, the gallows would serve him right. False Judas was author of this affair, he struck a blow at the nobility. Certainly his reward is evil. Therefore the deceit is wretched that grows enduringly in their bodies; drinking to 'The King' with gluttony, my whole heart wishes them evil.

328 Roinn eile do rinneadh leis 'san àm an d' fhògradh an dàrla Rìgh Teàrlach.

1. Is deas duinn cobhair Mhic Dhé;
Le threis taghar gach rìgh;
'S leis gun strìth a' chruinne-cé;
Gach duine réidh le bhuille nì.

2. Rìgha dh' fhòirinneas gach cùis,
   Tha faicsinn dòruinn is càis,
Dìon T' òglach bho luchd-craois,
   Ri m' aois, tha fòirneartach dhà-s'.

3. Dìon T' fhìor-eun bho'n ealta bhorb
   Tha streap, le mìorun 's le ceilg,
Nar corun ri dibhearg:
   Uime earb le toradh T' fheirg.

4. Caisg an cumhachdan 's am beachd,
   Bho 's gnìomh aṇ-cubhaidh an iochd;
An leóghann bu rìogha reachd,
   Gun cheart a chur riadh le shliochd.

5. Deas-làmh an t-slànuigheir chaoimh
   Bhith leis 'na chòirean g'a dhìon,
A thriall gun aon fhoill 'na chrìdh,
   Gun chrìoch-ce 's ciall iorghuill dìbh.

6. Fògair linn foill-'na-chùis;
   Binn ciall fòst daibh is duais;
Dòrainn r'a faicsinn an gnùis
   Gach trùth nach facain a chàs.

7. A Rìgh chumhachdaich nan cleas,
   Gach tì biodh umhailt do d' thoil-s';
'S tu phill gach fine bho sgrios,
   'Nam fhios, gun bhi leinn gu deas.

328 Other verses that were composed by him at the time of the exile of King Charles II

Near for us is the help of the son of God. Every king is chosen by His strength, the world is His without contention, He will make everyone level at his stroke. A King who helps in every affair, who sees sorrow and hardship, protect Thy servant from gluttons, all my life has been tyrannical to him. Protect Thy eagle from the barbaric flock that is vindictively climbing, with malice and deceit, into our crown, give a command about it with the fruit of Thy wrath. Check their powers and their intention, since clemency is an unfitting measure when the lion of the most royal authority is without the right ever to impose tax on his people.

The right hand of the gentle Saviour be with him in his rights, protecting him so that he may travel without any wrong in his heart, without end—whatever is their idea of horror. Expel for us the treachery in his affair, sweet the idea and reward for them yet. May pain be seen in the face of every wretch who does not bemoan his predicament. Oh omnipotent and all-powerful King, may everyone be obedient to Thy will, it is Thou who turned back every tribe from destruction, I know, without being near.

ANONYMOUS

329 The Ladies Lamentation for the losse of her Land-lord.

The Tune, *Highlanders Ma[r]ch.*

All in a fair morning for sweet recreation,
I heard a fair Lady was making great moan,
Sighing and sobbing with sad lamentation
saying, her Black-bird (most Royall) is gone.
O Fates that have me deceived
with sorrow much grieved,
Ile be reprieved,
from sad misery.
Else I, as duty doth bind me,
and *Cupid* assign'd me,
Ile find out my true love,
where ever he be.

Once with much excellency my Love did fleurish,
And was the chief flower that *England* did spring,
All vertue bequeath'd him his person to nourish,
as if he by lineage had come from a King.
But now this fond fickle Fortune
whose wheel is uncertaine,
That causes this parting
betwixt him and me.
If he alive doe remaine
in *France* or in *Spain*
Ile find out my true love
where ever he be.

The birds in the green woods are mated together
the Turtle is chosen to be with the Dove,
So I am resolved come fair or foul weather,
this Spring for to find out my Lord and my love,
Tis he that is my hearts treasure,
my joy, and my pleasure,
And having such leisure
most sweetly Ile flee,
For he is valiant and kind,
and faithfull in mind,
Ile find out my true love
where ever he be.

Both youngmen and maidens now chuse by election,
then why should not I and my true love be joyn'd?
To heaven I will pray for a blessed protection,
to make me successfull my Landlord to find,
His wings are fatally clipped
and absolutely stripped,
With thier woes nipped,
which humbleth me.
If he his fame do advance
in *Spain*, or in *France*
Ile find out my true love
where ever he be.

The second part to the same Tune.

In *Scotland* my dearest and I were together,
while he was couragious and noble in heart,
A wo is the time when last we came hither,
O then he was forced away to depart.
Though he in *Scotland* was deemed,
and Royall esteemed,
A Stranger seemed
in *England* to bee,
But I as duty doth bind me
and *Cupid* assign'd me,
Ile find out my true love
where ever he be.

At *Worster* being routed, O sad lamentation,
for sorrow amongst us was wonderfull rife,
Dispersed and scattered quite thorow the Nation,
tis well that he scaped away with his life.
Else he had layn with his father
intered together,
So leaving his mother
in sad misery,
If he alive do remain
in *France* or in *Spain*,
Ile find out my true love
where ever he be.

If that the Fowlers my Black-bird had takene,
then sighing and sobbing had been all my tune,
Although for a while he hath me forsaken,
I hope for to find him in *May* or in *June*.
Ile go thorow water and fire,
throw mud, and thorow mire
My love is intire
in every degree.
I know he is valiant and kind,
and faithfull in mind,
Ile find out my true love
where ever he be.

It is not the Ocean shall fear me with danger,
for now like a pilgrim ile wander forlorn,
A man may find more love from one that's a stranger
then he that is native, an *English-man* born.
Ile pray that heaven may be gracious
to *England* so spacious,
Though some be audacious
to him and to me.
If he his fame do advance
in *Spain* or in *France*.
Ile find out my true love
where ever he be.

329 4 *Black-bird* public perception of Charles II frequently draws attention to his swarthy complexion 16 *lineage* descent 26 *Turtle* turtle-dove 61 *Worster* Battle of Worcester, see

Appendix 4 *routed* defeated 63 *thorow* through 73 *Fowlers* bird-catchers (parliamentarians) 78 *mire* swamp 85 *fear* frighten

CHARLES COTTON

330 *To* Chloris. ODE.

Farewel, *My Sweet*, until I come,
Improv'd in *Merit*, for thy sake,
With *Characters* of *Honour* home,
Such, as thou canst not then but take.

To *Loyalty* my love must bow,
My *Honour* too calls to the *Field*,
Where, for a *Ladies* busk, I now
Must keen, and sturdy Iron wield.

Yet, when I rush into those *Arms*,
Where *Death*, and *Danger* do combine,
I shall less subject be to harms,
Than to those killing *Eyes* of thine.

Since I could live in thy *Disdain*,
Thou art so far become my *Fate*,
That I by nothing can be slain,
Until thy *Sentence* speaks my *Date*.

But, if I seem to fall in *War*,
T'excuse the murder you commit,
Be to my Memory just so far,
As in thy Heart t'acknowledg it;

That's all, I ask; which thou must give
To him, that dying, takes a pride
It is for thee; and would not live
Sole *Prince* of all the world beside.

330 7 *for* instead of *busk* corset 16 *Date* the date of my death

331 *ODE.*

I.

The *Day* is set did *Earth* adorn,
To drink the brewing of the *Main*,
And, hot with travel, will e're Morn
Carouse it to an ebb again,

Then let us drink, *Time* to improve,
Secure of *Cromwel* and his Spies,
Night will conceal our *Healths*, and *Love*
For all her thousand thousand *Eyes*.

Cho: *Then let us drink secure of spies*
To Phaebus, *and his Second rise.*

II.

Without the Evening dew, and show'rs,
The *Earth* would be a barren place,
Of *Trees*, and *Plants*, of *Herbs*, and *Flow'rs*,
To crown her now enamell'd *Face*;

Nor can *Wit* spring, or *Fancies* grow,
Unless we dew our heads in Wine,
Plump *Autumn's* wealthy overflow,
And sprightly Issue of the *Vine*.

Cho: *Then let us drink secure of spies*
To Phaebus, *and his Second rise.*

III.

Wine is the cure of *Cares*, and *Sloth*,
That rust the Metal of the *Mind*,
The *Juice*, that *Man* to *Man* does, both
In *Freedom*, and in *Friendship* bind.

This clears the *Monarch's* cloudy brows,
And chears the Hearts of sullen *Swains*,
To wearied Souls repose allows,
And makes *Slaves* caper in their chains.

Cho: *Then let us drink secure of spies*
To Phaebus, *and his Second rise.*

IV.

Wine, that distributes to each part
Its heat and *Motion*, is the *Spring*,
The *Poets* Head, the *Subjects* Heart,
'T was Wine made old *Anacreon* sing.

Then let us quaff it, whilst the *Night*
Serves but to hide such guilty Souls,
As fly the beauty of the *Light*;
Or dare not pledge our *Loyal Bowls*.

Cho: *Then let us Revel, Quaff, and Sing,*
Health, and his Scepter to the King.

331 2–4 The metaphor requires the sun to retire to the sea, there to drink of the full tide, until the sea has been drunk to an ebb by morning 10 *Phaebus* Apollo, metaphorically, Charles II 34 *Anacreon* see Appendix 1, and no. 217

332 *Song. Montross.*

I.

Ask not, why sorrow shades my brow;
Nor why my sprightly looks decay.
Alas! what need I Beauty now,
Since he, that lov'd it, dy'd to day?

II.

Can ye have Ears, and yet not know,
Mirtillo, brave *Mirtillo*'s slain?
Can ye have Eyes, and they not flow,
Or Hearts, that do not share my pain?

III.

He's gone! he's gone! and I will go;
For in my Breast, such Wars I have,
And thoughts of him perplex me so
That the whole *World* appears my grave.

IV.

But I'le go to him, though he lie
Wrapt in the cold, cold Arms of *Death*:
And under yon sad *Cypress-tree*,
I'le mourn, I'le mourn away my Breath.

332 The Marquis of Montrose was executed in Edinburgh on 18 May 1650 (see no. 274). There is little apart from the title to connect this poem to the event; it is one of Cotton's strangest pieces, like a set of distanced scraps of popular song 6 *Mirtillo* see Appendix 1

KATHERINE PHILIPS

333 *Upon the double Murther of K.* CHARLES I. *in Answer to a Libellous Copy of Rimes by* Vavasor Powell.

I think not on the State, nor am concern'd
Which way soever the great Helm is turn'd:
But as that son whose father's danger nigh
Did force his native dumbness, and untie
The fetter'd organs; so this is a cause
That will excuse the breach of Nature's laws.
Silence were now a sin, nay Passion now
Wise men themselves for Merit would allow.
What noble eye could see (and careless pass)
The dying Lion kick'd by every Ass?
Has *Charles* so *broke God's Laws*, he must not have
A quiet Crown, nor yet a quiet Grave?
Tombs have been Sanctuaries; Thieves lie there
Secure from all their penalty and fear.
Great *Charles* his double misery was *this*,
Unfaithful Friends, ignoble Enemies.

Had any Heathen been this Prince's foe,
He would have wept to see him injur'd so.
His Title was his Crime, they reason'd good
To quarrel at the Right they had withstood.
He broke God's Laws, and therefore he must die;
And what shall then become of thee and I?
Slander must follow Treason; but yet stay,
Take not our Reason with our King away.
Though you have seiz'd upon all our defence,
Yet do not sequester our common Sense.
Christ will be King, but I ne're understood
His Subjects built his Kingdom up with blood,
Except their own; or that he would dispence
With his commands, though for his own defence.
Oh! to what height of horrour are they come
Who dare pull down a crown, tear up a Tomb?

333 Title see Notes on the Text

THOMAS SHIPMAN

334 The OLD MAN. 1658.

An Epitaph upon my Gr. Mr. T.S.

Here lies an aged *Corps*, which late
Incag'd a *Soul*; whom neither fate,
Nor Times, could change from its first State.

Opprest more with Age than cares:
Respected more for *Silver hairs*
Than *Gold*; for Wisdom more than Years.

Happy in every *Child* he had;
Happy in self, and only sad,
Being born in good days, but deceas'd in bad.

334 Subtitle *Gr.* 'grandfather'

ANONYMOUS

335 *Burdún*

Do threascair an saol is shéid an ghaoth mar smál
Alastrann, Caesar, 's an méid sin a bhí 'na bpáirt;
tá an Teamhair 'na féar, is féach an Traoi mar tá,
is na Sasanaigh féin do b'fhéidir go bhfaíghidís bás!

335 Epigram

The world laid low, and the wind blew—like a dust—Alexander, Caesar, and all their followers. Tara is grass; and look how it stands with Troy, and even the English—maybe they might die!

335 3 *Teamhair/Tara* anciently the seat of the high king of Ireland

PART SIX

RESTORATION POEMS

336 To the KING, upon his Majesties Happy Return

The rising Sun complies with our weak Sight,
First guilds the Clouds, then shews his globe of light
At such a distance from our eyes, as though
He knew what harm his hasty Beams would do.

But Your full MAJESTY at once breaks forth
In the Meridian of Your Reign, Your worth,
Your youth, and all the splendor of Your State,
Wrapt up, till now in clouds of adverse fate,
With such a floud of light invade our eyes,
And our spread Hearts with so great joy surprise,
That, if Your Grace incline that we should live,
You must not (SIR) too hastily forgive.
Our guilt preserves us from th'excess of joy,
Which scatters spirits, and would life destroy.

All are obnoxious, and this faulty Land
Like fainting *Hester* doth before you stand,
Watching Your Scepter, the revolted Sea
Trembles to think she did Your Foes obey.

Great *Britain*, like blind *Polipheme*, of late
In a wild rage became the scorne and hate
Of her proud Neighbours, who began to think,
She, with the weight of her own force, would sink:
But You are come, and all their hopes are vain,
This Gyant-Isle has got her Eye again;
Now she might spare the Ocean, and oppose
Your conduct to the fiercest of her Foes:
Naked, the Graces guarded You from all
Danger abroad, and now Your Thunder shall.
Princes, that saw You, different passions prove,
For now they dread the Object of their love;
Nor without envy can behold this height,
Whose Conversation was their late delight.

So *Semele* contented with the rape
Of *Jove*, disguised in a mortal shape,
When she beheld his hands with lightning fill'd
And his bright rayes, was with amazement kill'd.

And though it be our sorrow and our crime
To have accepted life so long a time
Without you here, yet does this absence gain
No small advantage to Your present Reign:
For, having view'd the persons and the things
The Councils, State and strength of *Europe's* Kings,
You know your work; Ambition to restrain,
And set them bounds, as Heav'n does to the Main.
We have you now with ruling wisdom fraught,
Not such as Books, but such as Practice taught:
So the lost Sun, while least by us enjoy'd,
Is the whole night, for our concerns imploy'd:
He ripens spices, fruit and precious Gums,
Which from remotest Regions hither comes.

This fear of Yours, from th'other world remov'd,
Had *Archimides* known, he might have prov'd
His Engine's force, fixt here, your power and skill
Make the worlds motion wait upon your will.
Much suffering Monarch, the first English born
That has the crown of these three Nations born
How has Your patience, with the barbarous rage
Of your own soyl contended half an age?
Till (Your try'd virtue and Your sacred word,
At last preventing Your unwilling sword)
Armies and Fleets, which kept You out so long,
Own'd their great Sovereign, and redrest this wrong.
When straight the People by no force compell'd,
Nor longer from their inclination held,
Break forth at once, like Powder set on fire,
And with a noble rage their *KING* require.

So th'injured sea, which from her wonted course
To gain some rich ground, avarice did force,
If the new Banks, neglected once, decay,
No longer will from her old Channel stay,

Raging the late-got Land, she overflowes,
And all that's built upon't to ruine goes.

Offenders now, the chiefest, do begin
To strive for Grace, and expiate their sin:
All winds blow fair, that did the world imbroyle,
Your Vipers Treacle yield, and Scorpions Oyle.

If then such praise the *Macedonian* got,
For having rudely cut the *Gordian* Knot;
What glory's due to him that could divide
Such ravell'd interests, has the knot unty'd,
And without stroke so smooth a passage made,
Where craft and malice such impeachments laid?

But while we praise You, You ascribe it all
To his high hand, which through the untouch't wall
Of self-demolisht *Jerico* so low:
His Angel 'twas that did before You go.
Tam'd savage hearts, and made affections yield,
Like Ears of Corn when wind salutes the field.

Thus patience crown'd like *Job's*, your trouble ends,
Having your Foes to pardon and your Friends:
For, though your Courage were so firm a rock,
What private vertue could endure the shock?
Like your great Master you the storm withstood,
And pitied those which Love with Frailty shew'd.

Rude *Indians* torturing all the Royal race,
Him with the Throne and dear-bought Scepter grace
That suffers best: what Region could be found
Where Your heroick head had not been crown'd?

The next experience of Your mighty mind,
Is, how You combate Fortune now she's kind;
And this way too, you are victorious found;
She flatters with the same successe she frown'd;
Whilc to your self severe, to others kind
With power unbounded, and a will confin'd.
Of this vast Empire You possess the care,
The softer part falls to the People's share:

Safety and equal Government are things
Which Subjects make, as happy, as their Kings.

Faith, Law and Piety, that banisht train;
Justice and Truth, with You return again;
The Cities Trade, and Countries easie life
Once more shall flourish without fraud or strife.
Your reign no less assures the Ploughman's peace,
Than the warm sun advances his increase:
And does the Shepheards as securely keep
From all their fears, as they preserve their Sheep.

But above all, the Muse-inspired train
Triumph, and raise their drooping heads again;
Kind Heav'n at once has in Your Person sent
Their sacred Judge, their Guard and Argument.

336 2 *guilds* gilds 6 *Meridian* noonday: Charles had technically succeeded at the moment of his father's death 16 *Hester* see Appendix 1 19 *Polipheme* see Appendix 1 33 *Semele* 34 *Jove* see Appendix 1 44 *Main* sea 52 *Archimides* see Appendix 1 67 *wonted* usual 76 *Treacle* a cure-all (instead of poison) *Oyle* the antidote to scorpion's venom 77–78 see Appendix 1, Gordian Knot 85 *Jerico* the walls of Jericho fell at the sound of the trumpet of Joshua, Hebrews 11: 30 89 *Job* see Appendix 1 95 *Indians* here savages, notorious for the torture of captives

RACHEL JEVON

337 Exultationis Carmen

TO THE KINGS MOST EXCELLENT MAJESTY
UPON HIS MOST Desired Return

By Rachel Jevon, Presented with her own Hand, Aug. 16th

TO THE *MOST PIOUS* and *MOST SERENE* OF KINGS,
The Unworthiest of His MAJESTIES HAND-MAIDS With all Humility
Offers this Congratulatory Poem.

Dread Soveraign *CHARLES!* O King of Most Renown!
Your Countries Father; and your Kingdoms Crown;
More Splendid made by dark Afflictions Night;
Live ever Monarch in Coelestial Light:

Before Your Sacred Feet these Lines I lay,
Humbly imploring, That, with Gracious Ray,
You'l daign these first unworthy Fruits to view,
Of my dead Muse, which from her Urn You drew.
Though for my Sexes sake I should deny,
Yet EXULTATION makes the verse, not I;
And shouting cryes, *Live Ever* CHARLES, and *Be*
Most Dear unto Thy People, They to Thee.

Welcome Milde *Caesar*, born of Heav'nly Race,
A Branch most Worthy of your Stock and Place,
The Splendour of Your Ancestors, whose Star
Long since out-shin'd the golden *Phoebus* far;
The living Image of our Martyr'd King,
For us His People freely suffering;
Sprung from the *Rose* and *Flower-de-luce* most fair,
The Spacious World ne're boasted such an Heir.
Ye Pious Pens, pluckt from a Seraphs Wing,
Of His high Fame, teach future Times to sing.
Ye lofty Muses of *Parnassus* Hill,
Auspicious be to my unlearned Quill,
Vouchsafing leave the Travels to recite
Of this Great Prince, long Banish'd from His Right;
Which Valiant He, did stoutly undertake
For his Religion, and His Countries sake.
After the murther of our CHARLEMAIN,
(Whose lasting Honour ne're shall know a Wane,
But to the Skies Triumphantly ascend,
As His bright Soul did to *Elizium* tend,)
The Scots our CHARLES th'undoubted Heir recall,
And with His Grandsires Glory Him Install;
But after this *(O cruel Fates !)* betray'd
He was to th'English, who with a rage assay'd
Him to accost, throughout this British Isle;
Could ever Rebels act a part so vile?
Hence, hence sad sorrows, and all past annoys,
Let nought approach You but tryumphant Joys;
And let us now remember with delight
Your strange escape from *Worc'sters* bloody fight,

Through Thundring Troops of armed foes, whose strife
Was to bereave You of Your sacred life.
Where many thousand *Brittains* spilt their blood,
Weltring in gore, for King and Countries good:
How oft have I Your cruel fates bewail'd?
How oft to Heaven have our Devotions sail'd,
Through tides of briny tears, and blown with gales
Of mournful sighes, which daily fil'd the Sails?
That Heaven it's sacred Off-spring would defend,
And to their sorrows put a joyful end.
Propitious were the Heavens to our just Prayer:
You on their Wings the blessed Angels bare
Through thousand dangers, which by Land You past,
Till suddenly into the Sea being cast,
The Deities of *Pontus* flowing Stream,
Did unto You than men far milder seem.
Great *Aeolus* himself hasts You to meet
Prostrates the winds before Your Sacred Feet;
Then with his power commands the fiercer Gales,
Into their Den, lest they disturb Your Sails:
Neptune straight calms the raging of the Sea,
Before Your Stem the pleasant *Dolphins* play;
The surly Waves appeas'd, most gladly bore,
The happy Vessel to the happier Shore.
Then wandring through inhospitable Lands,
Still seeking rest, the world amazed stands
To see Him banished from every part
Of its great Orb, Yet from His Faith not start;
Nor to regain His Fathers Rights would He,
From th'ancient Worship of His Fathers flee,
For every Kingdom He subdu'd by Charms
Of Love and Piety, more strong than Armes.
France with her hair dishevel'd, torn and sad,
With bloody Robes of civil War beclad,
With joy receives this Deity of peace
Who having caus'd those civil Wars to cease,
The barbarous Vine the *Royal Oak* refus'd,
To please the Tyrants, natures bands she loos'd;
But He unmov'd in faith their *Lillies* fled,
And to th'unstable Willows wandered.

Who most ungratefully did Him reject,
That them the rebel brambles might protect.
The *Royal Oak* by storms of leaves bereav'd,
The generous *Olive* to its soil receiv'd;
Streight follows peace, its Deity being come,
Aside they lay their Arms, Sword, Pike and Drum;
The other Trees all shivering as a Reed,
To make a League with th'*Royal Oak* agreed;
At length *Druina* ravished with love,
Humbly recalls Him to His native *Grove*,
In peace to tryumph, and to Reign a Lord
O're hearts subdu'd by Love, not by the Sword.
His Native Country faint and languishing,
Humbly implores the presence of her King:
Loe how the late revolted Sea obeys,
How gladly it the Billows prostrate lays
Before Your Royal Navy, proud to bring
Three widdow'd Kingdoms their espous'd King!
How do the winds contend, the spreading Sails
Of Your blest Ships, to fill with prosperous Gales;
The Fates are kind; Conduct You to the Shoar,
To welcome You the Thundring Canons roar;
Your ravisht Subjects over-joy'd do stand,
To see the stranger, *(PEACE)* with You to land,
With You to earth *Astraea* fair is coome,
And Golden times in Iron ages room:
Much Honour hath both Church and State adorn'd,
Since You, our Faiths Defender, are return'd;
For of the Church the Honour and Renown,
Are unto Kings the strongest Towre and Crown:

Behold how *Thames* doth smooth her silver Waves!
How gladly she, Your gilded Bark receives;
Mark how the courteous Stream her Arms doth spread,
Proud to receive You to her watry Bed.
The old *Metropolis* by Tyrants torn,
Your presence doth with beauteous youth adorn.
On You how doe the ravish't people gaze ?
How do the thronging Troops all in a maze

Shout loud for joy, their King to entertain,
How do their Streets with Triumphs ring again.

Great CHARLS, Terrestrial God, Off-Spring of Heaven,
You we adore, to us poor mortals given,
That You *(Our Life)* may quicken us again,
Who by our Royal MARTYRS death were slain:
For we on earth as Corps inanimate lay,
Till You *(Our Breath)* repaired our decay:
Loe how old *Tellus* courts Your Sacred Feet,
Array'd with flowery Carpets peace to greet;
As *Phoebus* when with glorious Lamp he views,
Earth after Winter, tender grass renews;
So through the world Your radiant Vertues Shine,
Enlightening all to bring forth Fruits Divine:
Or as the drops distil'd by *April* showrs,
Produce from dryest earth imprison'd flowers;
So Your sad Fates sprinkled with holy eyes,
Plung'd in Your Kingly tears, have reacht the skies,
And from the appeased Deity brought down;
T'adorn Your Sacred Temples many a Crown.
The first of glory which shall ever last,
In Heaven of Heavens, when all the rest are past;
The Second shines with Virtues richly wrought
Upon Your Soul, with Graces wholy fraught.
The Third resplendent with your peoples Loves,
Their Hearts by joy being knit like Turtle-Doves.
The Forth's compleat by Your high Charity,
Which hath subdu'd and pardon'd th'enemy.
The Fifth shall shine with Gold and Jewels bright,
Upon Your Head, *O Monarch*! our Delight;
Where the Almighty grant it flourish may,
Until in Heaven You shine with Glorious Ray.
Who doth not stand amazed thus to see
The spotless Turtle Dove Espous'd to be
Unto a Bride whose Robes with blood are foul;
Loe Lovely CHARLES with Dove-like Galless Soul,
(Coming to th'Ark of His blood delug'd Land,
With peaceful Olive in His Sacred Hand)

Espoused is to *Albion* dy'd in gore;
And to her Princely Beauty doth restore;
Then celebrate the Espousals of our King,
With us let far and near all Nations Sing;
Let all the World shout loud perpetually,
LET CHARLES LIVE LOV'D UNTO ETERNITY.
Rejoyce ye Forrests, your choice pleasures yeild,
Thee Royal Hunter Crowns the verdant field:
And Leap for joy ye Beasts of every Plain,
Behold Your King (the Lion) comes to Reign.
Let shady Woods and Groves together dance
To see the *Royal Oak* to them advance,
Whilst Nymphs resound, O thrice, thrice happy they!
Who have the Honour, their faint Limbs to lay
Under the shadow of th'Illustrious *Oak*
Expanded, to depell from Saints the Stroak
Of Tyrants tempests, and a Pillar (squar'd
By Crosses) for the Church of God prepar'd;
Where we may live to sing aloud His Praise,
With heart and voice, and Organs sweetest Lays,
Who hath our DAVIDS Prayer not withstood,
But made his Off-spring, CHARLES the *Great*, and *Good*;
And banishing all sorrow from His Seed,
Highly Enthron'd Him in His Fathers stead;
That He may shine a Splendid Star to damp
Throughout the world at noon bright *Phoebus* Lamp;
And trample down those Tyrants with His Might,
Who dare contemn His Universal Right;
At length Your rip'ned Years being Crown'd with Glory,
Justice and Peace, unparallel'd by story:
Coelestial CHARLES Triumphantly Ascend
T'enjoy the Heavens in Bliss without all End.

GLORY TO GOD ALONE
THRICE BLESSED THREE IN ONE

337 Title 'song of joy' 16 *Phoebus* see Appendix 1, compare no. 331 19 *Rose...Flower-de-luce* emblems of England and France 23 *Parnassus* see Appendix 1 29 *CHARLEMAIN* the early medieval hero, one of the nine worthies, here Charles I 30 *Wane* pun on the constellation 'Charles his Wain' and 'wane' dwindling 32 *Elizium* see Appendix 1 34 *Grandsire* James VI and I 42 *Worc'sters* see Appendix 4 57 *Pontus* 59 *Aeolus*

63 *Neptune* see Appendix 1 75–93 tree-allegories, following from the identification of Charles II with the 'Royal Oak' in which he hid after the battle of Worcester. Rejected by the 'Vine' and 'Lillies' of France, despite his ties of blood with the French royal family, Charles progresses to the 'Willows' of the Netherlands, but there does not find acceptance, because they are harbouring their fellow Calvinist 'brambles', until the treaty of peace 'olive' secures his return to Britain, 'Druina's Grove' 107 *Astraea* see Appendix 1 126 *MARTYRS* Charles I: the iconography of the Interregnum presented Charles as a martyr; after the Restoration a form of commemoration of him remained in the *Book of Common Prayer* of the Church of England, and, although the Anglican Church has no official form of canonization, there are at least two churches dedicated to 'Charles the Martyr', one in Portsmouth and one in Tunbridge Wells 129 *Tellus* the earth 156 *Galless* without bitterness: pigeons have no gall-bladder 159 *Albion* Britain, see Appendix 1 174 *depell* drive away 175–6 *squar'd By Crosses* strengthened by adversity 178 organs had been forbidden during the Interregnum, see no. 118 183 *damp* eclipse 188 *story* history

HUW MORYS

338 *Croeso i'r Arglwydd Mwnc i Lundain yn y flwyddyn 1660.*

Moliant fo i ti, Arglwydd, drwy ffrwythydd burffydd bwnc,
O roi cleddyf grym cyfiawnder yn nwylo'r arglwydd Mwnc;
Ei nerth pan ga'dd yn chwyrn fe chwra'dd, i ddial lladd y llew,
I chwilio ffau'r llwynogod a gwalau'r tyrchod tew.

Gwae yddfau'r hen gigyddion,
Dywalltodd wirion waed;
Fel rhew'n yr haul mae'r rheini
Yn toddi oddi ar eu traed.

Mwnc, trwy bwyll a synnwyr, a dwyllodd dwyllwyr dig,
Fe gwympodd falchder Llundain, fel dail dan bren o'r brig;
Fe faglodd nerth traeturieth, anhyweth oedd ry hy,
Fe dorrodd saethau'r trawsion, a'r bwa creulon cry'.

Gwae yddfau, &c.

Y glân Brentisiaid lysti, y rheini wnaent eu rhan,
Cym'rasant boen a chyffro, i rwystro gwyro'r gwan;
Er gwaetha' 'r Siri mawrffrwyth a'r Capten crinbwyth crydd,
Hwy gurent gyda'r Goron i'w rhadlon roi yn rhydd.

Gwae yddfau, &c.

Trwy gariad a chywirdeb, nod undeb yn ein dydd,
Yn glo cadarna' i'r deyrnas ein brenin Siarlas sydd;
Duc James yn wir a Harri a ddoent o'r drysni a'r drain,
Fel gwinwydd ffraethwydd ffrwythau, rhinweddau Duw i'r rhain.

Gwae yddfau, &c.

Wel, dyna'r tri aur biler, yn Lloeger cânt eu lle,
Yn Sgotland wyrdd a'r Werddon, yn union dan y Ne';
I'n brenin y mae'r bonedd mawr rinwedd yn ymroi,
A'r cnafiaid a fu'n cneifio, rhag iddo 'u ffinio, 'n ffoi.

Gwae yddfau, &c.

Mae'n Llundain seinio clychau, y drymau a'r gynnau ar gân,
Mae miwsig pawb a'u moesau o groeso i'r gleiniau glân,
Cusanu dwylo a dilyn ein brenin braf o bryd;
Y rhod a drodd drwy rasol fodd i ryngu bodd y byd.

Gwae yddfau, &c.

Mae heddwch mawr yng Nghymru a glân brydyddu doeth
O gael gwared y traeturied, a'r ffeils Gapteinied poeth;
Y gwan a'r cry', a'r hen yn hy, eill fynd o'i dy i'w daith;
Pan ffaelodd yr ysbeilwyr, fe ddarfu'r gwyr eu gwaith.

Gwae yddfau, &c.

Tybiasant gan eu mawredd y llynedd yr âi'r llyn,
Drwy nerth y cleddyf llydan, fel brân i fol y bryn;
Ni eill y ffynnon groywdeg fawr redeg fry i'r allt,
I'r pant y rhed yr afon, geill pob rhyw ddynion ddallt.

Gwae yddfau, &c.

Gwnaed meistr y tir yn denant i lawer teurant taer,
A'r tenant a fu tano, eill eto nofio'n aer;
Ar gefn y geldin rhawn-grych, heb sôn am eurych mwy,
Gwnaeth hwnnw wrth chwarae'r tincer fawr bleser yn ei blwy'.

Gwae yddfau, &c.

Wel dyma gyfnewidiad, i ddysgu i fagad fyw,
Chwi ellwch gymryd siamplau y gorau 'i raddau a'i ryw;
Gwnaed pawb yn orau y gallo, rhag cneifio o'r eiddo'r un,
Hynny a brifia'n brafiach, a harddach iddo ei hun.
Na chwerddwch, ond gweddïwch am heddwch a mawrhad,
Y moliant a'r gogoniant fo ar gynnydd i Dduw'r Tad.

338 To Welcome Lord Monck to London in the year 1660

Praise be to you, Lord, through the fruits of purest faith, For putting the sword of the power of justice in the hands of the Lord Monck; When he received his strength he played rapidly, to avenge the killing of the lion, to search the foxes' den and the hiding-places of the fat moles. *Woe to the throats of the old butchers, who spilled innocent blood; like ice in the sun they melt whilst on their feet.* Monck, through discretion and sense, deceived angry deceivers, he felled the pride of London, like leaves from the crown of a tree; he undid the force of wild treachery which was too impudent, he broke the arrows of the upstarts, and the strong, cruel bow. *Woe to the throats...*The faithful lusty Apprentices, they also played their part, they suffered pain and upset, to prevent the submission of the weak; despite the overblown Sheriff, and the wizened, thin stitched Captain, they were victorious with the Crown generously to set them [the weak] free. *Woe to the throats...*Through love and fidelity, the sign of unity in our day, our king Charles is the strongest lock on the kingdom; Duke James indeed and Henry who came through wilderness and thorns [are] like a vineyard of choicest fruit, the blessings of God to [for] these. *Woe to the throats...*Well, these are the three gold pillars, in England they shall have their place, in green Scotland and in Ireland, under heaven's gaze; for the king the gentry do service of great goodness and the villains who had been fleecing flee lest he approach. *Woe to the throats*...In London bells sound, drums and guns sing, the music and courtesy of all is a welcome to the fair jewels,there is kissing of hands and following our fair-featured king; the wheel has turned through gracious means to satisfy the world. *Woe to the throats*...There is great peace in London and beautiful wise versifying because of the dumping of the traitors and the false, hot-tempered Captains; both weak and strong, old and eager, can leave his house to walk abroad; When the marauders failed, the work of these men was done. *Woe to the throats*...Last year they supposed in their greatness that the lake would reach by the strength of the broad sword, like a crow to the top of the hill; The fair, clear fountain can scarcely run up the slope, the river runs to the valley, as all men can understand. *Woe to the throats*...The landowner has been made a tenant to many an importunate tyrant, and the tenant who has suffered can again swim free [? this could read as 'become an heir']; On the back of the curly-maned gelding, without mention of any other tinker, in playing the tinker he caused great pleasure to his parish. *Woe to the throats*...Well, here is a turn in fortune to teach a living band, you can learn from the examples of the best [man] in status and kind; let each one do the best he may, for fear of fleecing another's property, that will bring finer and greater rewards for himself. Do not laugh, but pray for peace and greatness; Let glory and praise to God the Father increase.

338 See Appendix 4, 1659–60; Appendix 2

JOHN OGILBY

339 [*from* The Relation of his Majesties Entertainment Passing through the City of London to His Coronation, London,1661]

Rebellion addresses to his Majesty the Following Speech.

Stand! Stand! who'ere You are! This stage is Ours,
The Names of Princes are inscribed on Flow'rs,
And wither them! Stand! You must me know,
To Kings, and *Monarchy* a deadly Fo;
Me, who dare bid You midst Your Triumphs Stand,
In the Great City of your Native Land:
I am Hell's Daughter, *Satan's* Eldest childe,
When I first cry'd, the Pow'rs of Darkness smil'd,
And my Glad Father, Thun'dring at my Birth,
Unhing'd the Poles, and shook the fixed Earth.

My dear *Rebellion* (that shall be thy Name,
Said He) Thou Emperors and Kings shalt tame,
No Right so good, Succession none so long,
But thou shalt Vanquish by thy Popular Throng:
Those Legions, which t'enlarge our Pow'r we send
Throughout the World, shall Thee (My Dear) attend.
Our Mighty Champions, the Sev'n Deadly Sins,
By Malice, Profit, Pleasure, all their Gins,
Bring to our Kingdom some few Spotted Souls;
Thou shalt by Treason hurry them in Shoals.
   Would you know now what Int'rest I have here?
Hydra I ride: great Cities are my Sphear;
I Sorc'ry use, And Hag men in their Beds,
With Common-Wealths, and *Rotas* fill their Heads,
Making the Vulgar in Fanatique Swarms,
Court Civill War, and Dote on Horrid Arms;
'Twas I, who, in the late unnatural Broils,
Engag'd three Kingdoms, and two Wealthy Isles:
I hope at last, to march with Flags unfurl'd,
And tread down *Monarchy* through all the world.

At which words, Monarchy *and* Loyalty, *unveiling themselves,* Rebellion *starts as affrighted, but recollecting herself, concludes her Speech thus.*

Ah! *Britain,* Ah stand'st thou Triumphant there,
Monarchick Isle? I shake with horrid Fear.
Are thy Wounds whole? Upon thy cheek such Smiles?
Is Joy restor'd to these late mournful Isles?
Ah! must He enter, and a King be Crown'd?
Then, as He riseth, sink we under Ground.

339 2–3 ambiguous: either 'the names of princes are inscribed on the (temporary) flowers, rather than the (permanent) trees: may they wither', or 'the institution of monarchy withers their heraldic flowers' 18 *Gins* traps 23 *Hag* enchant, oppress with nightmare 24 *Rotas* a political club founded by John Harington in 1659, to promote rotation of the offices of government

IAIN LOM MACDONALD

340 Crùnadh an dara Righ Teàrlach

Mi'n so air m'uilinn
An àrdghleann munaidh,
'S mór fàth mo shulais ri gàire.

'S ge fad am thosd mi,
Mas e 's olc leibh,
Thig an sop a m'bhràghad.

On bha sheanns oirnne chluinntinn,
Ged bu teann a bha chuing oirnn,
Gun do thionndaidh a'chuibhle mar b'àill leinn.

An ceum so air choiseachd
Le m'bhata 's le m' phoca
'S an làmh 'ga stopadh gu sàrmhaith.

Gur h-olc an nì dhuinn
Bhith stad am prìosan
'N am theachd an Rìgh gu àite.

Thug Dia dhuinn furtachd
As na cliabhan druidte
'N uair dh'iarr sinn iuchair a ghàrraidh.

'S a Theàrlaich òig Stiùbhairt,
Ma chuaidh an crùn ort,
Dia 'na fhear-stiùiridh air t'àrdraich;

Ma chuaidh thu 'sa' chathair
Gun aon bhuille claidheimh
An ainm an Athar 's an Ardrigh;

'S thu thighinn dhachaidh gu d' rìoghachd
Mar a b'oil le d' luchd mìoruin
An coinne ri mìle ceud fàilte.

'S iomadh subseig mhór mhisgeach
'S miosa run duit na mise,
Tha cur staigh am *petition* an dràsda;

Luchd nan torrchaisteal liatha
Air an stormadh le iarann,
B'olc na lorgairean riamh ann do gheàrd iad.

Cha b'fhas' an dùsgadh a'n cadal
Na madadh-ruadh chur a braclaich,
'N uair a fhuaradh thu lag, ach bhith t'àicheadh.

Na mèirlich uile chuaidh dh'aontaobh,
Gheàrr muineal Mhorair Hunndaidh,
'S math a choisinn le bunndaist am pàigheadh.

Leam is éibhinn mar thachair,
Mar dh'éirich do'n bhraich ud,
Bha gach ceann dith 'na bachlagan bàna.

Cha robh uibhir nan cairtean
Nach robh tionndadh mì-cheart orr',
Bha mo shùilean 'gam faicinn an tràth ud.

'S olc an leasan Di-ciadaoin,
Mura furtaich thu Dhia air,
Tha feitheadh an Iarla neo-bhàidheil.

'N am rusgadh a choileir
Théid an ceann deth o cholainn—
Glòir agus moladh do'n Ardrigh—

Le maighdean sgorshuileach smachdail
Dh'fhàgas giallan gun mheartainn,
Dhùineas fiaras a' Mharcuis mhì-chàirdeil.

'S ged 's e thùs chan e dheireadh
Do luchd dhùsgadh an teine,
'S mar mo run do'n chuid eile d'a chàirdean.

Mar bha Lusaifear tamall,
'N déidh air thùs bhith 'na Aingeal,
Chaidh a sgiùrsadh le h-ainiochd a Phàrais,

Bidh tu nis ann ad dheomhain
Dol timcheall an domhain,
Bhrìgh coltais toirt coimhfhillteachd dhàsan.

'S mór a b'fheàrr dhuit na móran,
No na chruinnich thu stòras,
Bhith tional an òtraich gu d' ghàrradh,

Na thu fhéin 's do gheàrd misgeach
Bhith 'n àit as nach tig sibh
mar sgàile a' phioctuir 'san sgàthan:

Na farbhalaich bhreaca
Bha tarraing uainn ar cuid beartais,
A chuir an Righ mach a *Whitehall* dhuinn.

340 The Crowning of King Charles II

As I lie on my elbow in a high mountain glen, I have good reason to find joy in laughter. Although I have long been silent, if that is what displeases you most, I will remove the silencing wisp out of my throat, since, although the yoke was tight upon us, we have chanced to hear that the wheel (of fortune) has turned propitiously for us. Here is a journey afoot for me, with my stick and my bag by my hand stuffed full tight. Surely it is unfitting for us to stay in prison at the time when the King is coming to his own. God has given us succour from the closed pens, when we asked of Him the key of His garden. And young Charles Stuart, if you have been crowned, may God be the helmsman of your ship (of state); if you have ascended the throne without one sword-blow in the name of the Father and the King on high; since you have returned to your kingdom, to the chagrin of your enemies, to be greeted by a hundred thousand welcomes. Many a great drunken subject, ill-disposed to you as I am not, is now sending in his 'petition' to you: those from the massive grey castles reinforced with iron bars were ever but poor followers in your guard. It was no easier to rouse them from their lethargy than to drive a fox from its den, when you were considered weak: nay, rather they denied you. They were thieves one and all who joined one party; they cut the throat of the Marquis of Huntly, well did they earn their pay with a bounty. What befell pleases me—the accident that happened to that notorious fermented grain—each individual grain had white sprouts from it. Even the cards, when they turned them up, proved to be unlucky ones, I saw them with my own eyes. Dire is the lesson, unless, O God, thou dost succour him, that awaits the merciless Earl on Wednesday. When his collar is torn off, his head will be severed from his body, all glory and praise be to the King on high, by a sharp-eyed austere maiden that leaves jaws powerless, and will close for ever the malevolent Marquis's squint. Although it is the beginning, it is not the end for those who set the fire alight. May the rest of his friends fare as I wish. Just like the plight of Lucifer once upon a time, after being an Angel at first, he was mercilessly ejected from Paradise: so will you now roam as a demon throughout the world, an accomplice of his, according to all appearances. It had been better for you than much, better than all the wealth you have accumulated, to have been gathering refuse for your garden, than that you and your drunken guard should be in a place whence there is no escape, like the reflection of a picture in a mirror: the pock-marked foreigners who were depriving us of our own wealth, which the King apportioned to us from Whitehall.

340 6 *an sop/silencing wisp* the poet will break long silence now that the Restoration has come 7 *chluinntin/journey* now he can travel freely 30 *petition* referring to those noblemen who abandoned the King during the Interregnum, but sought his favour at the Restoration 48 *an Iarla/the Earl* The Marquis of Argyll was summoned by the Scots parliament to answer charges of treason on 13 February 1661 52 *maighdean/maiden* the guillotine in Edinburgh 65 *na chruinnich thu stòras/the wealth you have accumulated* the Marquis of Argyll had received forty-five thousand pounds for damages to his lands during the Montrose campaigns.

KATHERINE PHILIPS

341 Arion *on a Dolphin,*

To his majesty at his passage into England.

Whom does this stately Navy bring?
O! 'tis *Great Britain's* Glorious King.
Convey him then, ye Winds and Seas,
Swift as Desire and calm as Peace.
In your Respect let him survey
What all his other Subjects pay;
And prophesie to them again
The splendid smoothness of his Reign.

Charles and his mighty hopes you bear:
A greater now than *Caesar's* here;
Whose veins a richer Purple boast
Than ever Hero's yet engrost;
Sprung from a Father so august,
He triumphs in his very dust.
In him two Miracles we view,
His Vertue and his Safety too:
For when compell'd by Traitors crimes
To breathe and bow in forreign Climes,
Expos'd to all the rigid fate
That does on wither'd Greatness wait,
Plots against Life and Conscience laid,
By Foes pursu'd, by Friends betray'd;
Then Heaven, his secret potent friend,
Did him from Drugs and Stabs defend;
And, what's more yet, kept him upright
'Midst flattering Hope and bloudy Fight.
Cromwell his whole Right never gain'd,
Defender of the Faith remain'd,
For which his Predecessors fought
And writ, but none so dearly bought.
Never was Prince so much besieged,
At home provok'd, abroad obliged;
Nor ever Man resisted thus,
No not great *Athanasius*.
No help of Friends could, or Foes spight,
To fierce Invasion him invite.
Revenge to him no pleasure is,
He spar'd their bloud who gap'd for his;
Blush'd any hands the English Crown
Should fasten on him but their own.
As Peace and Freedom with him went,
With him they came from Banishment.
That he might his Dominions win,
He with himself did first begin:
And, that best victory obtain'd,
His Kingdom quickly he regain'd.
Th'illustrious suff'rings of this Prince
Did all reduce, and all convince.

He only liv'd with such success,
That the whole world would fight with less.
Assistant Kings could but subdue
Those Foes which he can pardon too.
He thinks no Slaughter-trophees good,
Nor Laurels dipt in Subjects blood;
But with a sweet resistless art
Disarms the hand, and wins the heart;
And like a God doth rescue those
Who did themselves and his oppose.

Go, wondrous Prince, adorn that Throne
Which Birth and Merit make your own;
And in your Mercy brighter shine
Than in the Glories of your Line:
Find Love at home, and abroad Fear,
And veneration every where.
Th'united world will you allow
Their Chief, to whom the *English* bow:
And Monarchs shall to yours resort,
As *Sheba's* Queen to *Judah's* Court;
Returning thence constrained more
To wonder, envy and adore.
Discovered *Rome* will hate your Crown,
But she shall tremble at your Frown.
For *England* shall (rul'd and restor'd by You)
The suppliant world protect, or else subdue.

341 13 *Father* Charles I 34 *Athanasius* see Appendix 1 54 *Laurels* emblem of victory 68 *Sheba's...Judah's* see Appendix 1

GEORGE WITHER

342 [from *Speculum Speculativum*]

A *bloodless Massacre* here is already
Begun among us, and it will be bloody
When you perceive admittance of those *Strangers*,
Who first begun our plagues, renew our dangers;

And then, they who suppos'd their persons free,
Will with the rest, in equal perils be:
For, *boundless lustings*, mischiefs will beget,
Which lie within the womb unheeded yet,
Where *Sin* and *Death* are Twins conceiv'd together,
Though born a little while before each other;
And, will in very ugly shapes be found
In many places, ere this year goes round;
Portended and attended in strange wise,
With *Ominous Events*, and *Prodigies:*
We shall see *Gown-men* tread on *Men of War,*
High Courts of Justice called to the *Bar*;
Those, of whom no man lately stood in dread,
Arraign the Living, and condemn the Dead:
Make *Martyrs, Saints* and *Reprobates* of those
Whose good or bad condition no man knows;
And act such things, as never yet were done
Within this *Clymate* since the world begun.
Yet, heed this, you, who with a sober minde
Seek *peace*, and are not factionally inclinde,
(And you, whose *principle* is to repair
What is decay'd, with no worse Tools then *pray'r*)
With *Christian patience* bear the *Visitation*
Which is alotted to this Generation;
And know, that as now *Nature* runs the race
By her designed, so shall also *Grace*
Pursue her *course,* to purge us in these *fires*
For that perfection whereto Faith aspires.
Strive by renewing of your *self-denials*,
To bear with constancy your *fiery tryals,*
Which must be undergone; for they appear
In shew more painful then in proof they are;
As their experience found, who in times past
Have into *Babels* Fornaces ben cast
When they were seven times heated; and as we
May peradventure find, ere long 'twill be.
Be not afraid of your own *sins*; for they
On your repentance will be done away:

Nor be discouraged, though your Foes at large
Shall sum them up, and lay unto your charge
False Imputations also: for, with ease
Both *Saints* and *Reprobates* of whom they please
The *Vulgar* make: and, if *prophane men* shall
Be Judges betwixt *David* and King *Saul,*
The sins of *David* might be made appear
As many, and much greater then *Sauls* were;
And He, upon whose side GOD sentence gave,
Amongst most men, the least esteem would have.
But, GOD observ'd his heart; purg'd what did flow
From *humane frailty*, as he purgeth now.
With sharp corrections, the late crying crimes
Of *Saints* prevaricating in these times.
Judgement, in our days, at GOD's *house* begins,
Who takes such notice of our many sins,
That since we would not mend when we were chidden,
He will no longer now let them be hidden
Or go unpunish'd: but we, that each other
Provok'd to sin, shall punish one another.
Me blame not then, if I touch here and there
Those failings on all sides which causes were
Of what we suffer: for, GOD will be known
By doing Justice; and we ought to own
Our great Transgressions, and not seek to hide
Those Crimes, for which he layes ev'n Kings aside,
As well as other men; that all may know
He giveth *equal dooms* to high and low.
Though, therefore, we sometimes a vaile may cast
O'er *faulty Rulers*, whilst their *pow'r* doth last,
To keep them from contempt, lest their disgrace
May cause infringement of the *Common Peace*,
We must not counter-act what GOD will do,
When he reproves them, and removes them too:
But, suff'ring with them by commiseration,
As being worthy of like condemnation,
Give GOD the glory, with our Pens and Breath,
For what's intended by their shame or death.
A sickness which is *Epidemical*

(In some degree) hath seized upon all,
And, ease we cannot have, till that hath wrought,
Which to procure a Remedy is brought.
When *Cures* are to *distempers* first appli'd,
We must expect, more torments to abide
Then if we felt our *Maladies* alone,
Without a *Medicine* working thereupon.
Of our *malignant humours* to be eas'd,
To take some poys'nous Drugs we must be pleas'd;
For, our *Physitian*, who doth truly know
Their and our Natures, hath prescribed so.
Diseases otherwise need *letting blood*,
Though with what is corrupt, that which is good
Seems also lost: *Gangrenes* require sometimes
To save the *Whole*, by cutting off of *Limbs*.
Yea, otherwhile a welfare doth redound
In common, when that suffers which is found;
And, once when sick to death the *Body* lay,
'Twas cur'd by taking of the Head away.

342 3 *Strangers* the exiled royalists returning with Charles II 15 'clergymen and lawyers will take vengeance on the army' 38 *Babels Fornaces* the fiery furnace in Daniel 3 48 *David...Saul* see Appendix 1 81–100 the closing metaphor is of a terminal illness, gone into remission through timely amputation in 1649, having remained in remission through the Interregnum, and now broken out again as bad as at first

NOTES ON THE TEXT

1 Text: From the monument of Lord Chief Justice Tanfield, died 1625, in the North Chapel of the Church of St John Baptist, Burford, Oxfordshire. Edition: ed. Alastair Fowler, *The New Oxford Book of Seventeenth Century Verse*, Oxford and New York, 1992, p. 1. This poem, at first apparently simple and grammatically opaque, resolves itself upon inspection into an artefact at once more complex and more lucid. The 'shadow' and the pronoun 'she' refer, in the first two stanzas to the effigies on the monument.

2 Text: Sir Francis Kynaston, *Leoline and Sydanis...together with sundry affectionate addresses to his Mistress under the name of Cynthia*, 1642, pp. 128–9. Edition: ed. George Saintsbury, *Minor Poets of the Caroline Period*, 3 vols. Oxford, 1905–21, ii. 159–60.

3 Text: Sir Francis Kynaston, *Leoline and Sydanis*, 1642, see no. 2, pp. 148–9. Edition: ed. George Saintsbury, see no. 2, ii. 171–2.

4 Text: Lady Mary Wroth, *The Countesse of Montgomery's Urania*, 1621 (separate pagination *Pamphilia To Amphilianthus*), pp. 4–5. Edition: ed. Josephine A. Roberts, *The Poems of Lady Mary Wroth*, Baton Rouge and London, 1983, p. 90. The copy-text here is the printed edition of 1621. The edition of Josephine A. Roberts follows Folger Shakespeare Library, Washington, DC, MS V.a.104 (*Pamphilia to Amphilianthus*), an autograph manuscript perhaps dating from the first period of the circulation of the texts in 1613–20. This text exhibits a process of authorial revision moving towards the 1621 printed text. It did not, however, serve as the copy-text for the printed edition. At the expense of authorial accidentals, the text of 1621 would appear to represent Mary Wroth's final intentions for the poems themselves.

5 Text: Lady Mary Wroth, *Urania*, see no. 4, p. 15. Edition: ed. Josephine A. Roberts, see no. 4, p. 103.

6 Text: Lady Mary Wroth, *Urania*, see no. 4, p. 32. Edition: ed. Josephine A. Roberts, see no. 4, pp. 122–3.

7 Text: Lady Mary Wroth, *Urania*, see no. 4, pp. 45–46. Edition: ed. Josephine A. Roberts, see no. 4, p. 140.

8 Text: Robert Herrick, *Hesperides: or, The Works both Humane and Divine of Robert Herrick Esq.*, 1648, p. 35; Scolar Press facsimile, Menston, 1969. Edition: ed. L. C. Martin, *The Poetical Works of Robert Herrick*, Oxford, 1956, p. 34.

9 Text: *Hesperides*, 1648, see no. 8, p. 42. Edition: ed. L. C. Martin, see no. 8, p. 40.

10 Text: *Hesperides*, 1648, see no. 8, p. 294. Edition: ed. L. C. Martin, see no. 8, p. 250.

11 Text: *Hesperides*, 1648, see no. 8, pp. 76–7. Edition: ed. L. C. Martin, see no. 8, p. 70.

12 Text: Henry King, Cambridge University Library, Additional MS 8471, p. 29. Edition: ed. Margaret Crum, *The Poems of Henry King*, Oxford, 1965, p. 151.
The printed edition of 1657, *Poems, Elegies, Paradoxes and Sonnets*, was printed without the author's consent. It is clear that King himself circulated his poems in scribal copies, first in Bodleian MS Eng. Poet. E. 30, which was corrected by King himself, and in Bodleian MS Malone 22, which is in a hand associated with the earlier manuscript. The manuscript from which the text is taken is formerly Phillips MS 9325, now Cambridge University Library, Additional MS 8471. Although its copyist is less meticulous than the scribes of the earlier two manuscripts, its readings are generally in agreement with the earlier manuscripts. It clearly embodies the last state of the poems, dating, it is conjectured, from 1641–8. This manuscript incorporates revisions and some new poems. The poem by Henry Reinolds which King answers is itself a translation of a Latin poem by George Herbert, 'Aethiopissa ambit Cestum Diversi Coloris Virum', printed in *Ecclesiastes Solomonis. Auctore Joan. Viviano*, Cambridge, 1662.

13 Text: Cambridge University Library, Additional MS 8471, see no. 12, p. 30. Edition: ed. Margaret Crum, see no. 12, p. 151.

14 Text: Cambridge University Library, Additional MS 8471, see no. 12, pp. 37–42. Edition: ed. Margaret Crum, see no 12, pp. 68–72.

15 Text: British Library, Additional MS 32,497, *The Phanseys of the Marquesse of Newcastle, Sett by him in verse att Paris...[1645]*, f. 17r–v. Edition: ed. Douglas Grant, *The Phanseys of William Cavendish Marquis of Newcastle*, London, 1956, p. 21.

16 Text: Thomas Carew, *Poems. By Thomas Carew Esquire*, 1640, pp. 21–2; Scolar Press facsimile, Menston, 1969. Edition: ed. Rhodes Dunlap, *The Poems of Thomas Carew with his Masque Coelum Britannicum*, Oxford, 1949, p. 14.

17 Text: Thomas Carew, *Poems*, 1640, see no. 16, p. 30. Edition: ed. Rhodes Dunlap, see no. 16, p. 19.

18 Text: Thomas Carew, *Poems*, 1640, see no. 16, p. 71. Edition: ed. Rhodes Dunlap, see no. 16, p. 42.

19 Text: James Shirley, *Poems &c by James Shirley*, 1646, p. 6; Scolar Press facsimile, Menston, 1970. Edition: ed. Ray Livingstone Armstrong, *The Poems of James Shirley*, Morningside Heights, New York, 1941, p. 2.

20 Text: James Shirley, *Poems*, 1646, see no. 19, p. 8. Edition: ed. Ray Livingstone Armstrong, see no. 19, p. 2.

21 Text: James Shirley, *Poems*, 1646, see no. 19, p. 17. Edition: ed. Ray Livingstone Armstrong, see no. 19, p.5.

22 Text: From the monument in St Denis's Church, Colmworth, Bedfordshire. It is possible that the stonecutter has introduced error into ll. 19–20. The text here is given literally from the monument: 'have' needs to be understood as an auxiliary to 'sate up'.

23 Text: ed. Seán Ó Tuama and Thomas Kinsella, *An Duanaire, 1600–1900: Poems of the Dispossessed*, Dolmen, Mountrath, 1981, pp. 96–101.

24 Text: Donnchadh Mac Rath, Fernaig MS, 1688–93, Glasgow University MS Gen. 85, Vol. 1, ff. 29v–30v. [Composed c.1642] Editions: Calum MacPharlain, *Lamh-Sgriobhainn Mhic Rath*, Dundee, 1923, p. 142; W. J. Watson, *Bardachd Ghaidhlig*, Stirling, 1932, p. 230; this edition and translation: Meg Bateman.

25 Text: Owen Felltham, *Resolves, the eighth Impression, With New, and Severall other Additions both in Prose and Verse*, [second title-page] *Lusoria: or Occasional Pieces. with a taste of some Letters*, 1661, p. 6. Edition: ed. Ted-Larry Pebworth and Claude J. Summers, *The Poems of Owen Felltham*, University Park, Pennsylvania, 1973, p. 25.

26 Text: Owen Felltham, *Resolves*, 1661, see no. 25, p. 30. Edition: ed. Ted-Larry Pebworth and Claude J. Summers, see no. 25, p. 48.

27 Text: William Habington, *Castara* [the third edition, corrected and augmented], 1640, pp. 44–5. Edition: ed. Kenneth Allott, *The Poems of William Habington*, Liverpool and London, 1948, p. 38.

28 Text: William Habington, *Castara*, 1640, see no. 27, pp. 115–16 [misprinted as 113]. Edition: ed. Kenneth Allott, see no. 27, p. 81.

29 Text: Sir William Davenant, *The Works of Sir William Davenant Kt.*, 1673, [internal title-page] *Poems on Several Occasions Never before Printed*, 1672, p. 321. Edition: ed. A. M. Gibbs, *Sir William Davenant: The Shorter Poems and Songs from the Plays and Masques*, Oxford, 1972, p. 175.

An early version of the poem appears in Davenant's play *The Just Italian*, 1630, V. i., sig. H2.

30 Text: *Tixall Poetry*, ed. Arthur Clifford, Edinburgh, 1813, pp. 153–4. The Aston family of Tixall in Staffordshire formed the centre of a circle of cultivated Recusant families. Their activities as poets and compilers of poetic commonplace books extend throughout the seventeenth century. While their Catholicism to an extent marginalized them within English society, it also gave them regular access to continental culture (many women of the family ended their lives as nuns in the exiled convents of the Low Countries; at least two men of the family served as diplomats). Following what begins to appear as a distinct trend of early-modern Recusant culture, the daughters of the family were educated and encouraged to write themselves and to compile poetic collections. Two manuscripts survive: James Marshall and Marie-Louise Osborn Collection, Beinecke Library, Yale University, MS B4.1634 (compiled by Herbert Aston), and Huntington MS HM 904 (compiled by Constantia Aston, later Fowler.)

However, for the majority of the poetry written and compiled by the Aston family circle, the only available source is Arthur Clifford's apparently meticulous transcription of 1813 from manuscript material then in his possession which now appears to be dispersed and lost. There are no modern editions of any of this material. While individual authors can be identified for some of the poems, it seems useful also to identify all Tixall material by its origin, to give some idea of the way in which poetry worked and circulated independently of the publishing trade and the metropolis. In this connection, see also no. 82.

This poem is placed by Clifford amongst those collected by Catherine Gage (d. 1720), second wife of the third Lord Aston. Its stylistic resemblance to the poetry of the mid-century may simply reflect the literary conservatism of some members of the Tixall circle and the poem may date from the 1660s or 1670s.

31 Text: *Tixall Poetry*, 1813, see no. 30, p. 86. This poem is placed by Clifford amongst those which appear to be the work of Gertrude Aston (Mrs Henry Thimelby), daughter of Walter Aston, first Lord Aston of Forfar, and Gertrude Sadler. On the evidence of *Tixall Poetry*, pp. 213–15, she would seem to have been in her early twenties in 1636, when Sir Richard Fanshawe visited Tixall and wrote poems of compliment to her and her sister Constantia. She married Sir Henry Thimelby, who predeceased her in the 1650s. Her only child died soon after her husband and she became a nun in Louvain. Some forthright and affectionate letters addressed to her family in England are preserved by Clifford in his *Tixall Letters*, 1815. The date of her death is unknown.

32 Text: Edmund Waller, *Poems, &c. Written Upon Several Occasions, And To Several Persons*, 1664, pp. 45–6. Edition: ed. G. Thorn Drury, *The Poems of Edmund Waller*, 2 vols. [1905], i. 113.

33 Text: Edmund Waller, *Poems*, 1664, see no. 32, pp. 53–5. Edition: ed. G. Thorn Drury, see no. 32, i. 128.

34 Text: Edmund Waller, *Poems*, 1664, see no. 32, pp. 80–1. Edition: ed. G. Thorn Drury, see no. 32, i. 83.

35 Text: Edmund Waller, *Poems*, 1664, see no. 32, pp. 100–1. Edition: ed. G. Thorn Drury, see no. 32, i. 57.

36 Text: Sir Richard Fanshawe, *Il Pastor Fido The faithfull Shepheard with An Addition of divers other Poems...*, 1648, pp. 250–2. Fanshawe reproduces this poem facing his own translation of it into Latin. The 'Mr. T.C.' in question would appear, on the evidence of Bodleian Library MS Malone 13, f. 24v [p. 45], to have been Thomas Cary, Gentleman of the Bedchamber to Charles I. There are copies in Bodleian MS Malone 13, f. 24v (with the variant 'Utrechia' for the name of the addressee) and in Henry Lawes, *Ayres and Dialogues*, Book I, 1653, p. 10.

37 Text: Bodleian Library, MS Eng. Poet. C.50, f. 33r. The poem has been attributed both to John and to Francis Beaumont, and printed as the latter's in his *Poems*, 1640, sig. H4v. Alexander Dyce's edition of *The Works of Beaumont and Fletcher*, 11 vols., 1843–6, rejects it from the canon (xi. 442) and ascribes it to Henry Harington.

38 Text: Sir John Suckling, *Fragmenta Aurea*, 1646, pp. 14–15. Edition: ed. Thomas Clayton, *The Works of Sir John Suckling: The Non-dramatic Works*, Oxford 1971, pp. 47–8.

39 Text: Sir John Suckling, *Fragmenta Aurea*, 1646, see no. 38, pp. 16–17. Edition: ed. Thomas Clayton, see no. 38, pp. 49–50.

40 Text: Sir John Suckling, *Fragmenta Aurea*, 1646, see no. 38, pp. 29–30. Edition: ed. Thomas Clayton, see no. 38, p. 16. Lines 1–9 of Suckling's poem are a corrupt version of Shakespeare's *The Rape of Lucrece*, ll. 386–95.

41 Text: Sir John Suckling, *Fragmenta Aurea*, 1646, see no. 38, pp. 47–9. Edition: ed. Thomas Clayton, see no. 38, pp. 66–8.

42 Text: Bodleian Library, MS Malone 13, p. 65. Edition: ed. William Dighton, *The Poems of Sidney Godolphin*, Oxford, 1931, pp. 23–4.

43 Text: Bodleian Library, MS Malone 13, see no. 42, p. 91. Edition: ed. William Dighton, see no. 42, p. 30.

44 Text: Bodleian Library, MS Malone 13, see no. 42, p. 83. Edition: ed. William Dighton, see no. 42, pp. 27–8.

45 Text: William Cartwright, *Comedies, Tragi-comedies. With other Poems*, 1651, pp. 244–5. Edition: ed. G. Blakemore Evans, *The Plays and Poems of William Cartwright*, Madison, Wisconsin, 1951, p. 493.

46 Text: *A Choice Collection of Comic and Serious Scots Poems both Ancient and Modern*, 3 vols., Edinburgh, 1706–11, iii.,. 88. Edition: ed. Harriet Harvey Wood, *James Watson's Choice Collection of Comic and Serious Scots Poems*, 2 vols. (STS 4th ser., nos. 10 and 20), Edinburgh 1977–91, I., iii.88. [Partial editions in Mark Napier, *The Life and Times of Montrose*, Edinburgh, 1840; modernised text ed. Robin Graham, *The Collected Poems of James Graham, First Marquis of Montrose*, New York, 1970.]

Of all the surviving poems which have been attributed to Montrose, only three exist in texts which derive reasonably closely from a possible authorial original. 'Upon the Death of King Charles the First' (no. 271) was printed within five years of its presumed date of composition and 'Some Lynes one the killing of the Earle of Newcastells Sonnes doge...' (no. 272) is preserved in a manuscript copy which appears to have some authority, to the extent of preserving plausibly Scots spelling. 'Burst out pour soull in main of tears' (no. 48) is found in the 'Lady Margaret Wemyss Music Manuscript' which dates from the 1640s. For the other poems, the editor is in the uncertain territory of 'traditional' attributions; anonymous broadsheet ballads; manuscript copies clearly made from memory; and printed copy of unknown provenance, separated from the composition of the poems by a gap of half a century.

Despite all these difficulties, it is attempted for the first time in this anthology to give all those poems which constitute the central canon of works attributed to Montrose, and to give them, with all their imperfections, in the earliest available texts. In several cases, particularly nos. 269 and 274, Montrose's authorship is most unlikely, but the point of interest here is as much the propagandist and crypto-hagiographic attribution of works to Montrose, as it is his possible authorship.

47 Text: *A Choice Collection*, 1706–11, see no. 46, iii. 112–113. Edition: ed. Harriet Harvey Wood, see no. 46, I. iii. 112–3.

48 Text: Edinburgh, National Library of Scotland, Sutherland Papers, Dep. 314/23, f.14r–v, 'The Music Book of Lady Margaret Wemyss' compiled in the 1640s. For a discussion of the MS, see Matthew Spring, 'The Lady Margaret Wemyss Manuscript', *Journal of the Lute Society*, 27 (1987), pp. 5–29.

I am indebted to Victoria Burke for bringing this text to my notice. Variants from *A Choice Collection*, see no. 46, iii, 114–15, as follows:

1 pour] my 2 sith tempests] Sighs Tempest 3 uhich nevers] let never 4 bot points ut fourth...lowe] But murmure still...Love 5 combind] Combine 7 bot both poor soull] But, tush, poor Drop 8 pasion] Passions 9 no way] No: rather 12 when...sing] And...they sing 13] My swelling Griefs then bend your self 14 into the...yow] This...of mine to 16 lembicke whence...ils] Limbeck where...Griefs 17 in my paine] thus in Plaints 18 burst in tears] melt my self 21 might] may 22 That or] E're that 23 plaints tears] Tears, Plaints 24 may] might

The degree of variation recorded here should serve at least as a possible index of the degree to which the texts of the other poems attributed to Montrose may have been adapted and anglicized, before they appeared in print in *Watson's Choice Collection*.

49 Text: Richard Crashaw, *Steps to the Temple...with other Delights of the Muses*, 1646, pp. 134–8; Scolar Press facsimile, Menston, 1970. Edition: ed. L. C. Martin, *The Poems, English, Latin and Greek of Richard Crashaw*, 2nd edn, Oxford, 1957, pp. 195–8. This poem was first published in an abbreviated form in *Wit's Recreations*, 1641.

50 Text: John Cleveland, *The Character of A London-Diurnall, with severall select Poems. By the same author*, 1647 ['optima et novissima Editio'], pp. 16–18. Edition: ed. Brian Morris and Eleanor Withington, *The Poems of John Cleveland*, Oxford, 1967, pp. 14–15.

51 Text: John Cleveland, *The Character of A London-Diurnall*, 1647, see no. 50, pp. 25–6. Edition: ed. Brian Morris and Eleanor Withington, see no. 50, pp. 22–3.

52 Text: John Cleveland, *Poems. by J. C. With Additions, never before Printed*, 1654, pp. 75–6. Edition: ed. Brian Morris and Eleanor Withington, see no. 50, pp. 54–6.

53 Text: Bodleian Library, MS Rawlinson Poet. 147, p. 219; John Cleveland, *The Character of a London-Diurnall*, 1647, see no. 50, pp. 9–10. Edition: [as Cleveland's] ed. Brian Morris and Eleanor Withington, see no. 50, pp. 40–1. This accomplished poem has long been attributed to John Cleveland, with whose parodic answer (undoubtedly Cleveland's) it has appeared since the revised state of the first edition of *The Character of a London-Diurnall* in 1647. However, in that publication and in the many subsequent reprints, it seems clear that it is printed to demonstrate exactly what it is that Cleveland is parodying in the following poem, 'The Authours Mock-Song to Marke Anthony'. Indeed, the stress on 'the Authours' in the title of the parody seems to disclaim the song itself. MS Rawlinson 147 attributes the

poem to Samson Briggs. This manuscript is the source for nearly all of Briggs's surviving poems. It was compiled in Cambridge by Henry Some who was admitted a scholar from Eton to King's College, Cambridge, in 1646. Briggs had come from Eton to King's in 1630 and he had been a Fellow from 1633 until the early 1640s: the attribution to Briggs would seem to carry some authority. The poem may have circulated independently as a ballad broadsheet: *A Transcript of the Registers of the Worshipful Company of Stationers 1640–1708*, 1913, reprint, New York, 1950, I, I, records '4 Nov. 1640 Entered...3 ballads under the hand of Master HANSLEY, viz. *Never Marke Anthony*...' Here, and with other poems by Briggs and Paman, this manuscript has been preferred as copy-text, not only because of its satisfactory provenance, but also to give the reader some feel of another circle of poets and how their poems were copied and presented: in this case a circle of University wits, to contrast to the provincial circles of the Astons of Tixall (see no. 30) and John Polwhele (see no. 82) in the West Country.

54 Text: Sir John Denham, *Poems and Translations, with the Sophy*, 1668, pp. 76–7. Edition: ed. Theodore Howard Banks, Jr., *The Poetical Works of Sir John Denham*, New Haven and London, 1923, p. 106. The copy of the 1668 edition in the James Marshall and Marie-Louise Osborn Collection, Beinecke Library, Yale University, contains a quantity of manuscript material in Denham's autograph. While this adds only to the text of *Coopers Hill* (no. 215), it serves more generally to endorse this edition as having the poet's approval.

55 Text: Sir John Denham, *Poems and Translations*, 1668, see no. 54, pp. 80–1. Edition: ed. Theodore Howard Banks, Jr., see no. 54, pp. 180–1.

56 Text: Robert Heath, *Clarastella*, 1650, pp. 11–12. Edition: ed. F. H. Candelaria, *Clarastella*, Gainesville, Florida, 1970, pp. 15–16.

57 Text: Robert Heath, *Clarastella*, 1650, see no. 56, p. 42. Edition: ed. F. H. Candelaria, see no. 56, p. 46.

58 Text: Robert Heath, *Clarastella*, 1650, see no. 56, pp. 42–3. Edition: ed. F. H. Candelaria, see no. 56, pp. 46–7.

59 Text: Abraham Cowley, *Poems*, 1656, [internal heading] *Miscellanies*, pp. 20–1; Scolar Press facsimile, Menston, 1971. Edition: ed. John Sparrow, *The Mistress and Other Select Poems of Abraham Cowley*, 1926, pp. 42–3.

All texts of Cowley are taken from the Bodleian Library copy: C.2.21.Art. This copy was presented by Cowley in July 1656. Bound in before the printed text is his poem of dedication: 'Pindarique Ode. The Book Humbly presenting it selfe to the Universitie Librarie at Oxford.' This 1656 folio edition of Cowley's poems has a series of internal sections, paginated separately, under different headings: the first, *Miscellanies*, is identified in the titling alone; subsequent sections have internal title-pages.

60 Text: Abraham Cowley, *Poems*, 1656, [internal title-page] *The Mistress; or several copies of Love-Verses.*, see no. 59, pp. 8–9. Edition: ed. John Sparrow, see no. 59, pp. 66–8.

61 Text: Abraham Cowley, *Poems*, 1656, [*The Mistress*] see no. 59, pp. 13–14. Edition: ed. John Sparrow, see no. 59, pp. 73–4.

62 Text: Abraham Cowley, *Poems*, 1656, [*The Mistress*] see no. 59, pp. 46–7. Edition: ed. John Sparrow, see no. 59, pp. 112–3.

63 Text: Abraham Cowley, *Poems*, 1656, [*The Mistress*] see no. 59, pp. 76–7. Edition: ed. John Sparrow, see no. 59, pp. 147–9.

64 Text: Abraham Cowley, *Poems*, 1656, [*Miscellanies*] pp. 22–4. Edition: ed. John Sparrow, see no. 59, pp. 43–6.

65 Text: Richard Lovelace, *Lucasta*, 1649, pp. 63–4.; Scolar Press facsimile, Menston, 1972. Edition: ed. C. H. Wilkinson, *The Poems of Richard Lovelace*, Oxford, 1930, pp. 58–9.

66 Text: Richard Lovelace, *Lucasta*, 1649, see no. 65, pp. 128–9. Edition: ed. C. H. Wilkinson, see no. 65, p. 96. The title is erroneously printed on p.126 of the 1649 edition, at the head of a poem 'To my Lady H. Ode.' to which it clearly cannot apply; this poem begins on p. 128 without a title.

The nexus of vocabulary and references in this poem seem to relate to the Falstaff scenes in Acts II and III of Shakespeare's *The Second Part of Henry the Fourth*.

67 Text: Richard Lovelace, *Lucasta. Posthume Poems of Richard Lovelace Esq*, 1659 [Bodleian Library copy, Malone 372, has a presentation inscription from the poet's brother: 'For the Worthiest of Freindes Mrs Elizabeth Hales From the Unworthiest of Servants. Dudley Posthumus-Lovelace.'], pp. 9–10. Edition: ed. C. H. Wilkinson, see no. 65, pp. 130–1. The preceding poem is titled 'A Black Patch on Lucasta's Face', this one 'Another'.

68 Text: Richard Lovelace, *Lucasta. Posthume Poems*, 1659, see no. 67, pp. 11–13. Edition: ed. C. H. Wilkinson, see no. 65, pp. 132–4.

69 Text: Richard Lovelace, *Lucasta*, 1649, see no. 65, pp. 136–9. Edition: ed. C.H. Wilkinson, see no. 65, pp. 101–3.

70 Text: Richard Lovelace, *Lucasta. Posthume Poems*, 1659, see no. 67, p. 10. Edition: ed. C. H. Wilkinson, see no. 65, p. 131.

71 Text: Thomas Philipott, *Poems*, 1646, p. 25. Edition: ed. L. C. Martin, Liverpool, 1950, p. 25.

72 Text: Thomas Philipott, *Poems*, 1646, see no. 71, p. 33. Edition: ed. L. C. Martin, see no. 71, p. 33.

73 Text: Thomas Stanley, *Poems by Thomas Stanley, Esquire*, 1651, pp. 5–6. Edition: ed. Galbraith Miller Crump, *The Poems and Translations of Thomas Stanley*, Oxford, 1962, pp. 2–3.

74 Text: John Hall, *Poems*, Cambridge, 1646, pp. 15–16. Edition: ed. George Saintsbury, see no. 2, ii. 191.

75 Text: John Hall, *Poems*, 1646, see no. 74, p. 33. Edition: ed. George Saintsbury, see no. 2, ii. 197.

76 Text: Charles Cotton, *Poems on Several Occasions*, 1689, pp. 519–21. Rather like the 1648 poems of Sir Richard Fanshawe (see no. 205), there are two chief sources for Charles Cotton's poems, neither of them wholly satisfactory. The printed text of 1689 was published posthumously and without the authority of Cotton's family. The 'Derby Manuscript' (Derby Central Library, fmss. 8470) is a scribal manuscript in the hands of four copyists, with the authority of corrections in Cotton's autograph. It did not serve as the copy-text for the 1689 printing, and does not contain all the poems which appear in the printed text. It provides an authoritative witness for an earlier state of a number of the poems. Copy-text throughout this book is, inevitably, the 1689 edition, with substantive variants from the Derby manuscript. There is no text of this poem in the Derby MS.

77 Text: Katherine Philips, *Poems by the most deservedly admired Mrs. Katherine Philips the Matchless Orinda*, 1667, pp. 25–6. Edition: ed. Patrick Thomas, *The Collected Works of Katherine Philips The Matchless Orinda. Volume 1: The Poems*, Stump Cross, Essex, 1990, pp. 94–5.

78 Text: Philip Ayres, *Lyric Poems. Made in Imitation of the Italian of which, many are Translations From Other Languages*, 1687, p. 28. Edition: ed. George Saintsbury, see no. 2, ii. 284.

79 Text: From the inscription in the Church of St Mary Magdalen, Mulbarton, Norfolk. Edition: ed. Peter Davidson, *Notes and Queries*, new series 33, 1 (1986), p. 41. This epitaph on Mrs Sarah Scargill (b.1650) was written by her husband in 1680–1. It seems to echo strongly poems by Andrew Marvell which were not published until 1681.

80 Text: From the plaster inscription in the Long Gallery, Apethorpe, Northamptonshire. Royal Commission on Ancient and Historical Monuments, *An Inventory of the Historical Monuments in the County of Northampton*, HMSO, 1984, vi. 13. It is likely that the poem was written by or for Sir Francis Fane, who acquired the estate in 1617, and was raised to the Earldom of Westmorland in 1624. The presence of an Earl's coronet as part of the same scheme of plasterwork as these verses would suggest a date after 1624; the verses are part of an emblematic scheme which suggests both positive and negative possibilities of music, with representations both of King David and of the Sirens.

81 Text: Henry Lawes, *The Second Book of Ayres and Dialogues*, 1655, p. 21. Edition: ed. Cedric C. Brown, *The Poems and Masques of Aurelian Townshend*, Reading, 1983, p. 47.

82 Text: Bodleian Library, MS Eng. Poet. F. 16, f. 2. This manuscript, hitherto unpublished, appears to be the commonplace collection of John Polwhele (1586–1648), a clergyman in Devon. Poems by Polwhele himself form the greater part of the contents of the MS. The poems are very uneven in quality, but give a clear instance of the kinds of poetic activity which were sustained throughout the period covered by this anthology, in provincial centres and virtually independently of metropolitan literary culture. Polwhele's contact with the literary mainstream can only be deduced from poems addressed to Ben Jonson and George Herbert: otherwise the poems are translations and commemorations of strictly local deaths and weddings.

83 Text: Lady Mary Wroth, *The Countesse of Montgomery's Urania*, 1621 (separate pagination *Pamphilia To Amphilianthus)*, see no. 4, p. 26. Edition: ed. Josephine A. Roberts, see no. 4, p. 116.

84 Text: Lady Mary Wroth, *Pamphilia To Amphilianthus*, see no. 4, p. 27. Edition: ed. Josephine A. Roberts, see no. 4, p. 117.

85 Text: Robert Herrick, *Hesperides*, 1648, see no. 8, pp. 106–7. Edition: ed. L. C. Martin, see no. 8, p. 95.

86 Text: Robert Herrick, *Hesperides*, 1648, see no. 8, pp. 46–7. Edition: ed. L. C. Martin, see no. 8, p. 67.

87 Text: Bodleian Library, MS Rawlinson Poet. 147, p. 93. Attributed to Henry Noel, son to the Lord Viscount Cambden; text also in Henry Lawes, *Ayres and Dialogues*, 2 vols., 1653, i. 15, with the same attribution; reprinted Henry Lawes, *Select Ayres and Dialogues to sing to the Theorbo lute or Basse-Viol*, 1669, p. 10, titled 'BEAUTIES *Excellency*'. It is, however, attributed, to a Doctor Richard Love in both Bodleian Library, MS Eng. Poet. D.152, and in Bodleian Library, MS Lat. Misc. C.19. Text: [as Strode's] ed. Bertram Dobell, *The Poetical Works of William Strode*, 1907, pp. 128–9. Samuel Pepys was painted holding the MS of his musical setting of this poem: see entries in his *Diary* for 24 February 1662, *et seq.*

88 Text: Thomas Carew, *Poems*, 1640, see no. 16, pp. 180–1. Edition: ed. Rhodes Dunlap, see no. 16, pp. 102–3. This poem was obviously popular in the 1640s and circulated in a number of variant versions. British Library MSS, Add. MS 30,982; Sloane 1446 and 1792; Harley 3511 arrange the stanzas 2,3,1,4,5. British Library, Add. MS 23,229 offers what looks like an early draft of the poem:

Aske mee no more where Jove bestowes
When June is past, the damaske Rose
For on your Cheekes and lips they bee
Fresher then on anie tree.

Aske mee no more where those starres light
That downewards fall in darke of night,
For in your Eyes they sitt and theare
Fixed become, as in their spheare.

Aske mee no more where Nightingale
When June is past puts forth her tale,
For in your sweete deuidinge throate
Shee winters and keepes warme her note.

Nor aske mee whether East or west,
The Phoenix builds her spiced nest
For unto you shee allwaies flies,
And in your fragrant bosome lies.

89 Text: Thomas Carew, *Poems*, 1640, see no. 16, p. 181. Edition: ed. Rhodes Dunlap, see no. 16, p. 197. James Shirley claims the poem in his *Poems*, 1646 (see no. 19), both by printing a version of it as his own and in his complaint in 'A Postscript to the Reader' that his poems have been 'mingled with other mens (some Eminent) conceptions in print'. The text in Shirley's *Poems* differs considerably from that printed as Carew's:

Would you know what's soft? I dare
Remit you to the Down, or Ayre:
The Stars we all acknowledge bright,
The Snow too is exceeding white:
To please your sent, 't will not be hard
To present you bruised Nard:
And would you heavenly musick hear,
I'le call the Orbes to take your ear,
If old *Pythagoras* sing true.
But *Ambrosia*, heavenly dew
Divinely must affect your taste,
And Nectar is your drink at last.
   But would you have all these delights in one,
   Know but the fair *Odelia*, and 'tis done.

It seems unlikely that these two texts are radically variant versions of a single original. It would seem more probable that the version printed as Carew's represents something much more like a deliberate recasting of the material offered by Shirley's poem. In so far as style can offer an indication, comparison with no. 88 and with other of Carew's lyrics would suggest that the recasting might well be Carew's own work.

90 British Library, MS Harley 6917, f. 32 [51]; copy in Bodleian Library, MS Rawl. Poet. 147, see no. 53, pp. 80–1, titled 'In the prayse of Musicke by W. Strode.' Edition: ed. Bertram Dobell, see no. 87, pp. 2–3. The source for the majority of Strode's poems is Corpus Christi College, Oxford, MS 325; a few are found in the Harleian MSS in the British Library. Their appearance in print in the seventeenth century was sporadic, mostly in miscellanies and song-books.

91 Text: Corpus Christi College, Oxford, MS 325, f. 64r. Edition: ed. Bertram Dobell, see no. 87, p. 41.

92 Text: Corpus Christi College, Oxford, MS 325, see no. 91, f. 69v. The poem also appears in *Poems written by Wil: Shake-speare*, 1640, and *Parnassus Biceps*, 1656. Edition: ed. Bertram Dobell, see no. 87, p. 1.

93 Text: Corpus Christi College, Oxford, MS 325, see no. 91, f. 70r. Edition: ed. Bertram Dobell, see no. 87, p. 3.

94 Text: Sir William Davenant, *Works*, 1673 [internal title-page] *Poems*, 1672, see no. 29, p. 320. Edition: ed. A. M. Gibbs, see no. 29, p. 173.

4 To] so *1672*

95 Text: Sir William Davenant, *Works*, 1673, [internal title-page] *Poems*, 1672, see no. 29, pp. 320–1. Edition: ed. A.M. Gibbs, see no. 29, pp. 173–4.

96 Text: Sir William Davenant, *Works*, 1673, [internal title-page] *Poems*, 1672, see no. 29, pp. 317–18. Edition: ed. A. M. Gibbs, see no. 29, pp. 168–70.

97 Text: Sir William Davenant, *Works*, 1673, see no. 29, [new pagination] *News from Plimouth* (Act III, sc. i), p. 14. Edition: ed. A. M. Gibbs, see no. 29, pp. 215–16.

98 Text: British Library, Harleian MS 6917, f. 77r.

99 Text: Edmund Waller, *Poems*, 1664, see no. 32, pp. 103–4. Edition: ed. G. Thorn Drury, see no. 32, i. 126.

100 Text: Sir Richard Fanshawe, *Il Pastor Fido*, 1648, see no. 36, p. 101. Edition: ed. Walter F. Staton, Jr., and William E. Simeone, *A Critical Edition of Sir Richard Fanshawe's 1647 Translation of Giovanni Battista Guarini's Il Pastor Fido*, Oxford, 1964, p. 81.

Il Pastor Fido ('The Faithful Shepherd') by Baptista Guarini, a political pastoral which enjoyed European success, was translated by Fanshawe in 1647. Fanshawe's translation develops the idea of a spoiled and devastated Arcadia, in which the play is set, to reflect on the Britain of the Civil War and to express hopes for a peaceful resolution focused on the figure of Charles, Prince of Wales. This song comes from Act III, Sc. v.

101 Text: John Milton, *Poems of Mr John Milton, both English and Latin, Compos'd at several times*, 1645, pp. 22–3; Scolar Press facsimile, Menston, 1970. Edition: ed. John Carey and Alastair Fowler, *The Poems of John Milton*, 1968, pp. 162–5.

102 Text: Bodleian Library, MS Malone 13, see no. 42, pp. 7–8. Edition: ed. William Dighton, see no. 42, pp. 10–11.

103 Text: British Library, Additional MS 25,707, f. 67r; also in Dr John Wilson's music manuscript, Bodleian Library, MS Mus. b.1, f. 58.

104 Text: British Library, Additional MS 25,707, f. 95v.

105 Text: Bodleian Library, MS Rawlinson Poet. 147, see no. 53, p. 253 [p. 221].

106 Text: Richard Lovelace, *Lucasta*, 1649, see no. 65, p. 32. Edition: ed. C. H. Wilkinson, see no. 65, p. 37.

107 Text: Richard Lovelace, *Lucasta. Posthume Poems*, 1659, see no. 67, pp. 39–40. Edition: ed. C. H. Wilkinson, see no. 65, pp. 160–1

108 Text: British Library, Harleian MS 3511, f. 49v.

109 Text: British Library, Harleian MS 3511, f. 77v.

110 Text: Alexander Brome, *Songs and Other Poems*, 1661, p. 10. Edition: ed. Roman R. Dubinski, *Alexander Brome: Poems*, 2 vols., Toronto, Buffalo and London, 1982, i. 76–7.

111 Text: Alexander Brome, *Songs*, 1661, see no. 110, p. 68. Edition: ed. Roman R. Dubinski, see no. 110, i. 138.

112 Text: Bodleian Library, MS Mus. b.1., f. 133v. Edition: ed. J. P. Cutts and Frank Kermode, *Seventeenth Century Songs. Now first printed from a Bodleian Manuscript*, Reading, 1956, p. 27.

This poem plays on two levels of meaning. On the simpler, 'concoction perfited' is simply 'digestion accomplished': the rising digestive vapours inspire the lover to the vision of his mistress. There seems also to be rather vague reference to the imagery which alchemists used as metaphors for the transmutation of metals: fumes, clouds, the naked goddess.

113 Text: Henry Lawes, *Select Ayres and Dialogues to sing to the Theorbo-lute or Basse-Viol*, 1669, p. 38.

114 Text: ed. John Playford, *Choice Ayres, Songs and Dialogues to sing to the Theorbo-Lute or Bass-Viol. Being most of the newest Ayres and Songs, sung at Court and at the Public Theatres*, 1675, p. 10; also in ed. John Playford, *Choice Songs and Ayres for one Voyce to sing to a Theorbo-Lute or Bass-Viol*, 1673, p. 14. The music given in both the Playford collections is by 'R. Smith'. There is a late text in *Tixall Poetry*, see no. 30, p. 132.

115 Text: Henry Lawes, *Select Ayres and Dialogues*, 1669, see no. 113, p. 64. Music by 'Mr Alphonsus Marsh'.

10 Blest] Drest *1669*

116 Text: Charles Cotton, *Poems on Several Occasions*, 1689, see no. 76, pp. 353–4. In Derby Central Library, fmss 8470, see no. 76, pp. 17–18.

Title SONG] Sonnet

117 Text: Katherine Philips, *Poems*, 1667, see no. 77, pp. 18–19. Edition: ed. Patrick Thomas, see no. 77, pp. 87–8.

118 Text: Manuscript adversarium to *Select Ayres and Dialogues for One, Two and Three Voyces; to the Theorbo-Lute or Basse-Viol*, 1659 [Fitzwilliam Museum Library, Cambridge]. The text is located on the flyleaf beneath the engraving of the personification of music. This copy also contains an eighteenth-century answer to this adversarium:

> Tho' modern Ears, by Art inform'd, require
> More perfect strains from Arrigoni's Lyre;
> Rude as they are, these antiquated Layes
> Were dear to Waller's Muse, were grac'd by Milton's Praise.

(NH St. Alban's 26th May 1732.)

119 Text: Sir Henry Wotton, *Reliquiae Wottonianae or a collection of lives, letters, poems, With characters of Sundry Personages: And other Incomparable Pieces of Language and Art* ['The second Edition with large Additions'], 1654, pp. 508–9. The first edition of *Reliquiae Wottonianae*, edited by Izaak Walton, appeared in 1651, the second, enlarged edition in 1654, was reprinted in 1672, and appeared with further additions in 1685. [Text not reprinted in ed. Logan Pearsall Smith, *The Life and Letters of Sir Henry Wotton*, Oxford, 1907.]

120 Text: *Hesperides*, 1648, [second title-page] *His Noble Numbers or his pious pieces*, 1647, pp. 35–6. Edition: ed. L. C. Martin, see no. 8, pp. 367–8.

121 Text: *Hesperides* [*His Noble Numbers*], 1648, see no. 120, pp. 46–7. Edition: ed. L. C. Martin, see no. 8, pp. 376–7

This very subtle poem, which only declares its ambiguous status as both spiritual and erotic poem in the penultimate line, develops a complex of ideas frequently worked over in the poetry of the mid-seventeenth century. The line in Virgil's first *Eclogue* 'et penitus toto divisos orbe Britannos' (l. 65) gave rise to the trope of the apartness of Britain, as an island of felicity contrasted to the warring Europe of the 1630s. (See nos. 170, 205.) Herrick here transfers the trope to an anticipated neoclassical heaven, relegating the island of Britain (lit. Albion, see Appendix 1) to the status of a place only of illusion.

122 Text: *Hesperides* [*His Noble Numbers*], 1648, see no. 120, p. 98. Edition: ed. L. C. Martin, see no. 8, pp. 87–8.

123 Text: *Hesperides*, 1648, see no. 8, p. 337. Edition: ed. L. C. Martin, see no. 8, p. 285.

124 Text: Cambridge University Library, Additional MS 8471, see no. 12, p. 24. Edition: ed. Margaret Crum, see no. 12, pp. 148–9.

125 Text: Henry King, *Poems, Elegies, Paradoxes and Sonnets*, 1657, pp. 149–51; Scolar Press facsimile, Menston, 1973. Edition: ed. Margaret Crum, see no. 12, pp. 132–3.

126 Text: George Sandys, *A Paraphrase upon the Divine Poems*, sig. **2v–**3r, [2nd edn., 1638, sig A8v–B1r]. Edition: ed. Rhodes Dunlap, see no. 16, pp. 93–4.

127 Text: From the monument in St Mary's Church, Hambleden, Buckinghamshire.

128 Text: Aberdeen University Library, MS 28, ff. 26r–27r ['The Commonplace Book of Andrew Melville']; collated with National Library of Scotland, Advocates MS 5.2.14, f. 9r–v ['William Stirling's Cantus part book 1639', formerly called 'John Leyden's Vocal MS']. Edition of tune: ed. William Dauney, *Ancient Scottish Melodies from a manuscript of the Reign of King James VI*, Edinburgh and London, 1838, pp. 222, 264. Partial edition of text and tune: ed. Kenneth Elliott and Helena Mennie Shire, *Music of Scotland 1500–1700*, Musica Britannica XV, London, 1957, p. 188. This set of verses bearing as they do strong resemblances both to almanac verses and to folk-song 'floaters' is firmly associated with the name of a Lady Lothian. The most likely candidate would seem to be Lady Lothian, spouse of Mark Kerr, Commendator of Newbottle, who was created Earl of Lothian in 1606 and died in 1609. There was also a Lady Loudon at this time (daughter of the Master of Loudon) who was married to Sir John Campbell of Sawers, one of the Glenurchy family, in 1620. But as the name 'Laudian'—the common way at that time of spelling Lothian—is very distinctly written in the Edinburgh MS, the former was more likely to have been the person to whom the air related. The Edinburgh MS contains the following variants:

2 Thus...come] our...passe 3 thus] this 9 dois...to them ar] doe...are to them 11] Whose weiping eyes bewaill there woes 12 and folis chanes] Our sinfulnes 13 Thes...to schow] they...of deathe 14 passing] posting 15] Till at the houre of fading breath 16 Till...pairt] Then...parts 17 Now let us] Thus must we 20 put] set 21 nevir yit] yet never 23 hath] have 25 spring] prime 28 our...overthrow] And...downe throw 29 quha in the pryme] he that in tyme 30 Thair service] his vertue 32 do] shall 33] Since all thing Creat have an end 35 quha...spends] cane...spend 36 Vertues] vertuous 37 Bot quhan...is past] For soone...shall passe 38 The pleasour] And pleasures 39] O happy happy thryse are they 40 That taks] Who tak 41 it floweth fast] doth flow full fast 45 that] the 46 That sailles that] Which saile the 47 marke] marks 51 Tint] lost 52 may] doe 53 ant the...bee] Ants and...bees 54 layeth] lay 56 and suld do] to doe Much 58 my] mine 62 to] through 64 quhylls] oft

129 Text: Cathal MacMhuirich, RIA MS 778, pp. 20–1 [post-1649]. Editions: Angus Matheson, *Eigse,* vol. xi, Dublin, 1964, pp. 7–10; this edition and translation: Colm O Baoill and Meg Bateman, *Gàir nan Clàrsach*, Edinburgh, 1994, no. XVIII, pp. 94–9.

130 Text: Corpus Christi College, Oxford, MS 325, see no. 91, ff. 64v–65r. Edition: ed. Bertram Dobell, see no. 87, p. 55. The first verse of this very widely-distributed poem is all *memento mori*, the second verse all hope of resurrection. It is reminiscent of the genre of folk-song which derives love-riddles from the paradoxical description of nature. See for instance: 'I have a yong suster, Fer beyonden the se...', ed. R. T. Davis *Mediaeval English Lyrics*, 1963, p. 164; 'Captain Wedderburn's courtship', ed. F. J. Child, *The English and Scottish Popular Ballads*, 5 vols., New York, 1882–98, no. 46, i. 415–25; 'Scarborough Fair', ed. Iona and Peter Opie, *The Oxford Dictionary of Nursery Rhymes*, 1951, pp. 386–8.

131 Text: Corpus Christi College, Oxford, MS 325, see no. 91, f. 89v. Edition: ed. Bertram Dobell, see no. 87, p. 62.

132 Text: William Habington, *Castara*, 1640, see no. 27, pp. 192–4. Edition: ed. Kenneth Allott, see no. 27, pp. 127–8.

133 Text: *Tixall Poetry*, 1813, see no. 30, pp. 99–100. This and the following poem are by Gertrude Aston, see no.31.

134 Text: *Tixall Poetry*, 1813, see no. 30, p. 98.

135 Text: Gerrard Winstanley, *The Breaking of the Day of God*, 1648, p. 128. Edition: Christopher Hill, *Winstanley*, 1983, pp. 390–1. The passages of scripture cited in the marginal glosses are very loosely parallel to the lines of the poem against which they stand.

The poet has assembled a loose scriptural citation in support of his eschatological political verses.

136 Text: Bodleian Library, MS Rawl. Poet. 147, p. 157.

137 Text: Bodleian Library, MS Rawl. D. 945, f. 2; British Library, Additional MS 18,220, f. 11v.

138 Text: British Library, Additional MS 18,220, see no. 137, f. 12v.

139 Text: Bodleian Library, MS Rawl. Poet. 147, see no. 136, pp. 147–50.
Marginal alternative readings:
l. 10+ When scatter'd man's summd up, and when the Sea
Brings in her Bills of dead at th'Auditt day.
Then shall this body now some fishes guest,
Rise from his bed of dust and court the East.
l. 29 But he not curse thee, wise and happy too
ll. 31–4 For had
The land enspir'd his death why he had torne
Her bowells, like his ships, to'attend his urne.
l. 44 With its owne Manuscripts, there are enow
l. 58 And to teach Arts with thee to withstand Fate
l. 80 Those easy robes of Death; Translation.

140 Text: Richard Crashaw, *Carmen Deo Nostro te decet hymnus*, Paris, 1652, pp. 81–3. Edition: ed. L. C. Martin, see no. 49, pp. 304–6; [1646 text] pp. 139–41. This poem was first printed in Crashaw's *Steps to the Temple*, 1646, and reprinted in its final version in the 1652 *Carmen Deo nostro*. The problem with these poems is that while the 1646 edition represents faithfully Crashaw's earlier intentions for his poems, the 1652 edition undoubtedly represents a further stage of the text, and one important in terms of Crashaw's development in that, between the two editions, he had become both an exile and a professed Catholic.

The 1652 edition was printed by a printer with at best an imperfect knowledge of English: it displays dropped lines and other imperfections. At the same time it incorporates what seem clearly authorial revisions and new material. The texts here are given from 1652, with corrections and substantial variants from 1646. It can be argued that the very imperfections of the 1652 text have an eloquence of their own, speaking of the realities of the situation of Crashaw and the other Civil War exiles.

Title] On the Assumption 3 earth] Light 7] Shee's call'd againe, harke how th'immortall Dove 12 but thou, are] since thou art 17–32] *not in 1646* 41 dread] great

45+ And though thy dearest lookes must now be light
To none but the blest heavens, whose bright
Beholders lost in sweet delight,
Feed for ever their faire sight
With those divinest eyes, which wee
And our darke world no more shall see.
Though, our poore joyes are parted so,
Yet shall our lips never let goe

Thy gracious name, but to the last,
Our Loving song shall hold it fast.

48 care] cares 58 MARIA] Mary 60 rosy princesse, LIVE. And] rarest Princesse, and 61 a most] an

141 Text: Richard Crashaw, *Carmen Deo Nostro*, 1652, see no. 140, pp. 93–100. Edition: ed. L. C. Martin, see no. 49, pp. 317–21. Lines 61 and 147, missing in *Carmen Deo Nostro*, supplied from *Steps to the Temple*, 1646. Variants from 1646.

The changes to ll. 129–30 are particularly significant, changing the sense from Our Lady welcoming St Teresa into heaven to Teresa's mystic marriage with Christ.

Title] In memory of the Vertuous and Learned Lady Madre de Teresa that sought an early Martyrdome. 3 now appeal] need to goe 4 Great] stout 5 Men of Martyrdom] and full growne 8 into] unto 10 spatious Bosomes spread] large breasts built 11] For love their Lord, glorious and great, 12 And] Weell 13 Making] And Make 15 the] a 25 has] had 37 dares] dare 40 white] weake 45 hers] her 49 She'l offer] Shee offers 52 GOD;] God, and 61] *not in 1652; from 1646* 77 armes] hand 90 sent] spent 93 and first] and the first 94 SERAPHIM] Seraphims 104] To live, but that he still may dy. 117 resolving] disolving 122 you] thou shalt 128 for] on 129 reveal'd LIFE] shee 130 his] her 133 joyes] joy 147] *not in 1652; from 1646* 151 DEATH] Deaths 152 that erst] which late 168 thy soveraign] thy

142 Text: Richard Crashaw, *Epigrammatum Sacrorum Liber*, Cambridge, 1634, p. 37. Edition: ed. L. C. Martin, see no. 49, p. 38.

143 Text: Richard Crashaw, *Epigrammatum Sacrorum Liber*, Cambridge, 1634, see no. 142, p. 69. Edition: ed. L. C. Martin, see no. 49, p. 57.

144 Text: Thomas Jordan, *A Royal Arbor of Loyal Poesie consisting of Poems and Songs*, n.d. [Bodleian Library, Malone 451; a note in Malone's hand on the flyleaf supplies the date 1663], p. 71. Variant text in Thomas Jordan, *Divinity and Morality in Robes of Poetry* [n.d.], sig. SSS1v.

Title] *The Epitaph.* 8 high] bright

145 Text: Martin Lluelyn, *Men-Miracles with other Poemes*, 1656, p. 96.

146 Text: Laurence Clarkson, *A single eye all light, no darkness; or light and darkness one* [1650], sig. A1v. Edition: ed. Nigel Smith, *A Collection of Ranter Writings from the Seventeenth Century*, London, 1983, p. 162.

147 Text: ed. E. Robinson, *The Minor Poems of Joseph Beaumont*, 1914, pp. 16–17. This edition claims to be a diplomatic transcription of Beaumont's autograph MS (corrected by John Gee, Master of Peterhouse, who printed some of the poems in 1749) which has since been unavailable. It was bought by Herbert Palmer of Harvard in 1911 from the Phillipps collection via the dealer Dobell. The MS was not made available to Norman Ault in 1927, but Palmer vouched for the accuracy of the transcription made by Eloise Robinson, whose edition is used as copy-text here. This poem collated with Bodleian Library, MS. Rawl. Poet. 62, f. 18r–v.

3 Roab] robes *MS* 13] Scarce he begun to feede 22 inclin'd] enclyne 34 your] the

148 Text: ed. E. Robinson, see no. 147, pp. 450–1.

149 Text: Abraham Cowley, *Poems*, 1656 [Bodleian Library C.2.21.Art], see no. 59, [internal heading] *Miscellanies*, pp. 29–30. Edition: ed. John Sparrow, see no. 59, pp. 46–8.

150 Text: Abraham Cowley, *Poems*, 1656, [Bodleian Library C.2.21.Art] see no. 59, [internal heading] *Miscellanies*, pp. 16–20. Edition: ed. John Sparrow, see no. 59, pp. 36–41.

151 Text: Henry Vaughan, *Silex Scintillans: or sacred poems and private ejaculations by Henry Vaughan Silurist*, 1650, p. 22; Scolar Press facsimile, Menston, 1968. Edition: ed. Alan Rudrum, *Henry Vaughan: The Complete Poems*, Harmondsworth, 1976, p. 162.

152 Text: Henry Vaughan, *Silex Scintillans*, 1650, see no. 151, p. 23. Edition: ed. Alan Rudrum, see no. 151, p. 162.

153 Text: Henry Vaughan, *Silex Scintillans*, 1650, see no. 151, p. 34; Edition: ed. Alan Rudrum, see no. 151, pp. 172–3.

154 Text: Henry Vaughan, *Silex Scintillans*, 1650, see no. 151, pp. 36–7. Edition: ed. Alan Rudrum, see no. 151, pp. 174–5.

155 Text: Henry Vaughan, *Silex Scintillans*, 1650, see no. 151, p. 61. Edition: ed. Alan Rudrum, see no. 151, p. 198.

This poem is a close reworking of George Herbert's 'The Flower' (ed. F. E. Hutchinson, *The Works of George Herbert*, Oxford, 1941, pp. 165–7).

156 Text: William Cartwright, *Comedies*, 1651, see no. 45, sig. **4r–**5r. Edition: ed. Alan Rudrum, *The Works of Thomas Vaughan*, Oxford, 1984, pp. 581–3.

157 Text: Eugenius Philalethes [i.e. Thomas Vaughan], *Anthroposophia Theomagica*, 1650, p. 28. Edition: ed. Alan Rudrum, see no. 156, pp. 70–1.

158 Text: *Strena Vavasoriensis, A New-Years-Gift for the Welsh Itinerants, or a Hue and Cry after Mr. Vavasour Powell*, 1654 [British Library, Thomason E 727 (14)] sig. D4v, p. 24. Reprinted in *The Faithfull Scout*, 27 Jan–3 Feb, 1654 [British Library, Thomason E 223].

159 Text: Anna Trapnel, *The Cry of a Stone or a Relation of Something spoken in Whitehall, by Anna Trapnel, being in the visions of God. Relating to the governors, army, churches, ministry, universities: and the whole nation*, 1654, p. 75.

160 Text: Anna Trapnel, [untitled volume, n.d.] [unique copy, Bodleian Library, Oxford, 5.1.42 Th], p. 257.

161 Text: Anna Trapnel, [untitled volume] see no. 160, p. 941.

162 Text: Elizabeth Major, *Honey on the Rod: Or a comfortable contemplation for one in affliction; with sundry poems on several subjects*, 1656, p. 201.

163 Text: Bodleian Library, MS Eng. Poet. b. 5, pp. 50–1. This volume is the commonplace collection of a Catholic family (the Fairfaxes of Wootton Wawen) dating from the mid-seventeenth century. At the end of this song (p. 51) is written 'finis thus ends the 1 of Anna Alcoxs songs sent from Alveston at Christmas last 1651 written by herselfe.' After a ballad on Easter, pp. 68–9, is written "finis thus ends the 2 song of Anna Alcoxs sent from Alveston the 2 of march 1651.

> This Anna above exprest, as you shall understand
> is a little mayd of six yeares old who writ it with her hand.'

No other author's names are given in the manuscript. It is an unequivocally Catholic collection, compiled in a climate of institutionalized proscription of Catholicism. Perhaps this ascription is given so circumstantially, emphasizing the author's age, because a child was not held to be a legally responsible being until the age of 7.

164 Text: John Collop, *Poesis Rediviva or, Poesie Reviv'd*, 1656, p. 109; Scolar Press facsimile, Menston, 1972.

165 Text: John Collop, *Poesis Rediviva*, 1656, see no. 164, pp. 104–5.

166 Text: British Library, MS Egerton 607, f. 3r. [The manuscript is titled: 'True Coppies of certaine Loose Papers left by the Right honourable Elizabeth Countesse of Bridgewater Collected and Transcribed together here since Her Death Anno Domini 1663'.] Some poems by this author are given in ed. G. Greer, S. Hastings, J. Medoff, and M. Sansone, *Kissing the Rod*, London, 1988, pp. 106–17. She was born Elizabeth Cavendish, became Lady Elizabeth Brackley upon her marriage to John Egerton, Viscount Brackley, and later became Countess of Bridgewater on his elevation to that earldom.

167 Text: Sir Henry Wotton, *Reliquiae Wottonianae*, [second and enlarged edition] 1654, see no. 119, p. 493. Edition: ed. Logan Pearsall Smith, *The Life and Works of Sir Henry Wotton*, Oxford, 1907, pp. 170–1.

168 Text: Richard Corbet: *Certain Elegant Poems*, 1647, pp. 21–2. Edition: ed. J. A. W. Bennett and H. R. Trevor-Roper, *The Poems of Richard Corbett*, Oxford, 1955, p. 88.

169 Text: Aurelian Townshend, *Albion's Triumph personated in a Maske at Court*, 1632, pp. 20–1. Edition: ed. Cedric C. Brown, see no. 81, pp. 88–9. Also in Steven Orgel and Roy Strong, *Inigo Jones: The Theatre of the Stuart Court*, 2 vols., London and Berkeley, 1973, ii. 457–8.

Albion's Triumph is one of the most inturned of the entertainments of the Caroline court. This section, with its vision of the Gods (Neptune, Pluto, Cebele, and Bellona) and the personification of Peace, moving in order like stars about the twin constellation of King and Queen, expresses that alternative reality promulgated by Court iconography which was, by the 1630s, becoming increasingly disjunct from the political realities of Britain.

170 Text: St John's College, Cambridge, MS S. 23, ff. 71v–72v, collated with Bodleian Library, Oxford, MS Rawl. Poet. 209, f. 18v. Edition: ed. Cedric C. Brown, see no. 81, pp. 48–9.

3 a right] arigt *Rawl* 12 which] that 21 one…teares] on…teare 40 ?showe the] shine 42 the] our 52 drame] beame

171 Text: Robert Herrick, *Hesperides*, 1648, see no. 8, pp. 74–6. Edition: ed. L. C. Martin, see no. 8, pp. 67–9.

172 Text: Robert Herrick, *Hesperides*, 1648, see no. 8, pp. 113–15. Edition: ed. L. C. Martin, see no. 8, pp. 101–2.

173 Text: Robert Herrick, *Hesperides*, 1648, see no. 8, p. 317. Edition: ed. L. C. Martin, see no. 8, p. 269.

174 Text: Robert Herrick, *Hesperides*, 1648, see no. 8, p. 368. Edition: ed. L. C. Martin, see no. 8, p. 310.

175 Text: Robert Herrick, *Hesperides*, 1648, see no. 8, p. 121. Edition: ed. L. C. Martin, see no. 8, p. 107.

176 Text: Robert Herrick, *Hesperides*, 1648, see no. 8, p. 214. Edition: ed. L. C. Martin, see no. 8, p. 185.

177 Text: Robert Herrick, *Hesperides*, 1648, see no. 8, p. 125. Edition: ed. L. C. Martin, see no. 8, p. 110.

178 Text: Robert Herrick, *Hesperides*, 1648, see no. 8, pp. 88–90. Edition: ed. L. C. Martin, see no. 8, pp. 80–1.

179 Text: Thomas Carew, *Poems*, 1640, see no. 16, pp. 45–7. Edition: ed. Rhodes Dunlap, see no. 16, pp. 27–9.

180 Text: Thomas Carew, *Poems*, 1640, see no. 16, pp. 126–30. Edition: ed. Rhodes Dunlap, see no. 16, pp. 74–7.

181 Text: Thomas Carew, *Poems*, 1640, see no. 16, [second title-page] *A Masque at Whitehall in the Banquetting house, on Shrove-Tuesday-night, the 18. of February, 1633.*, pp. 252–5. Edition: ed. Rhodes Dunlap, see no. 16, pp. 179–80.

27 Eridanus] Etidanus *1640*

182 Text: James Shirley, *Poems &c*, 1646, see no. 19, pp. 69–70. Edition: ed. Ray Livingstone Armstrong, see no. 19, pp. 16–17.

183 Text: Corpus Christi College, Oxford, MS 325, see no. 91, ff. 59v–60r. Edition: ed. Alastair Fowler, *The New Oxford Book of Seventeenth Century Verse*, Oxford and New York, 1992, p. 351; ed. Bertram Dobell, see no. 87, pp. 20–1.

Westwell is on the border of Oxfordshire and Gloucestershire. This is one of the very first poems about a specific landscape in English and Strode's use of 'Landskipp' in l. 3 should be noted as a very early example of the eighteenth-century phenomenon of reading a natural landscape through the medium of painting.

184 Text: British Library, Add. MS. 27,449 [Knevet's autograph manuscript: 'A Gallery to the Temple, Lyricall Poemes upon Sacred Occasions'], ff. 25v–30r. Edition: ed. Alastair Fowler, *The New Oxford Book of Seventeenth Century Verse*, Oxford and New York, 1992, pp. 359–60; ed. A. M. Charles, *The Shorter Poems of Ralph Knevet*, Columbus, Ohio, 1966, pp. 307–8.

185 Text: Mildmay Fane, Earl of Westmorland, *Otia Sacra, Optima Fides*, 1648, pp. 153–6; Scholars' Facsimiles & Reprints, intro. Donald M. Friedman, Delmar, NY, 1975.

186 Text: William Habington, *Castara*, 1640, see no. 27, pp. 97–8. Edition: ed. Kenneth Allott, see no. 27, pp. 69–70.

187 Text: Thomas Randolph, *Poems with The Muses Looking-Glasse: and Amyntas*, 1638, p. 67. Edition: ed. G. Thorn Drury, *The Poems of Thomas Randolph*, 1929, p. 79.

188 Text: Thomas Randolph, *Poems*, 1638, see no. 187, pp. 68–71. Edition: ed. G. Thorn Drury, see no. 187, pp. 79–82.

189 Text: Thomas Randolph, *Poems*, 1638, see no. 187, pp. 84–5. Edition: ed. G. Thorn Drury, see no. 187, p. 93.

190 Text: Thomas Randolph, *Poems*, 1638, see no. 187, pp. 113–14. Edition: ed. G. Thorn Drury, see no. 187, pp. 117–18.

191 Text: William Davenant, *Madagascar; with other Poems*, 1638, pp. 35–6. Edition: ed. A. M. Gibbs, see no. 29, p. 28.

192 Text: William Davenant, *Madagascar*, 1638, see no. 191, pp. 66–7. Edition: ed. A. M. Gibbs, see no. 29, p. 43.

193 Text: William Davenant, *Madagascar*, 1638, see no. 191, pp. 74–6. Edition: ed. A. M. Gibbs, see no. 29, p. 47.

194 Text: William Davenant, *Madagascar*, 1638, see no. 191, pp. 136–7. Edition: ed. A.M. Gibbs, see no. 29, p. 74.

195 Text: William Davenant, *Works*, 1673, [internal title page] *Poems*, 1672, see no. 29, p. 305. Edition: ed. A. M. Gibbs, see no. 29, p. 150.

John Fletcher's *The Faithful Shepherdess* was written for the Queen's Revels before 1610. This play, in rhymed verse, appears to have been one of the most popular and influential dramas of the early seventeenth century. Sir Richard Fanshawe translated it into Latin (thus claiming for it a European status) as *La Fida Pastora* in 1658.

196 Text: *Tixall Poetry*, 1813, see no. 30, p. 57.

These poems are described by Clifford as having been collected if not written by the Hon. Herbert Aston, son of Walter Aston and Gertrude Sadler, brother of Gertrude Aston (see nos. 30, 31, 133, 134). Herbert Aston attended his father when he was sent as ambassador to Madrid in 1623, at the time of the abortive match between the future Charles I and the Spanish Infanta. His literary contacts would seem to have included Endymion Porter and Sir Richard Fanshawe. The commonplace collection from which Clifford is apparently printing here is dated 1658.

197 Text: *Tixall Poetry*, 1813, see no. 30, p. 64.

198 Text: *Tixall Poetry*, 1813, see no. 30, p. 60.

199 Text: *Tixall Poetry*, 1813, see no. 30, pp. 104–5. Assigned by Clifford to Gertrude Aston, see no. 31.

200 Text: Edmund Waller, *Poems*, 1664, see no. 32, pp. 89–90. Edition: ed. G. Thorn Drury, see no. 32, i. 94.

201 Text: Edmund Waller, *Poems*, 1664, see no. 32, pp. 133–5. Edition: ed. G. Thorn Drury, see no. 32, i. 82.

202 Text: Edmund Waller, *Poems*, 1664, see no. 32, pp. 144–5. Edition: ed. G. Thorn Drury, see no. 32, i. 114–15.

203 Text: Edmund Waller, *Poems*, 1664, see no. 32, pp. 58–71. Edition: ed. G. Thorn Drury, see no. 32, i. 66–74.

204 Text: Edmund Waller, *Poems*, 1664, see no. 32, pp. 30–3. Edition: ed. G. Thorn Drury, see no. 32, i. 44–5.

205 Text: Sir Richard Fanshawe, *Il Pastor Fido*, 1648, see no. 36, pp. 225–9. Collated with British Library, Add. MS 15,228, ff. 32r–34v; Bodleian Library, MS Firth c. 1, pp. 82–6. Edition: ed. Peter Davidson, *The Poems and Translations of Sir Richard Fanshawe,* Oxford, 1997, pp. 55–9.

Historical background is needed for the contrast which Fanshawe makes between the peaceful state of Britain, and the turmoil of Europe. On 20 June 1632, Charles I had repeated a Proclamation of his father's, commanding the gentry to reside on their estates in the country. He issued this Proclamation twice: 9 September 1630 and 20 June 1632. The wars in Europe to which Fanshawe refers are these: the war against the Spaniards had resumed in the Netherlands with the expiry of the Treaty of the Hague; in France on 11 November 1630, Marie de Medici had failed to overthrow Richelieu; the Thirty Years War was at its height—Gustavus Adolphus began his last campaign in Germany in July 1630. The opposing Imperial General, Tilly, had taken Bohemia after the defeat of the Elector Frederick, brother-in-law of Charles I, at the battle of the White Hill in November 1620, since when Protestant forces had been attempting to recover his lost kingdom.

23 furred] furied *1648*] furred *both MSS*

29–32] Who 'gainst the *Persian* now unsheathes
His crooked Cemetar sharp-sett;
And *Mahomet* dire furie breathes
'gainst Mahomet. *Firth c. 1*

206 Text: Bodleian Library, MS Firth c 1, see no. 205, p. 74. Edition: ed. Peter Davidson, see no. 205, p. 46.

Translated from Luis de Gongora, 'En el muerte de Giomar de sa Muger de Juan Fernandez de Espinossa', *Obras Poeticas*, New York, 1921, p. 332.

207 Text: John Milton, *Poems*, 1645, see no. 101, [internal title-page] *Joannis Miltoni Londinensis Poemata*, 1645, pp. 25–30; revised version in *Poems, &c. upon Several Occasions*, 1673. Edition: ed. John Carey and Alastair Fowler, see no. 101, pp. 80–8.

30 quotannis *1645*] perennis *1673* [correction of a false quantity pointed out by Salmasius]

208 Text: Sir John Suckling, *Fragmenta Aurea*, 1646, see no. 38, pp. 26–7. Edition: ed. Thomas Clayton, see no. 38, pp. 30–2.

A final stanza, not present in the printed edition, is supplied by Bodleian Library, Oxford, MS Rawl. Poet. 199, p. 95:

Troth in her face I could descry,
No danger, no divinity.
But since the pillars were so good
On which the lovely fountain stood,
Being once come so near, I think
I should have ventur'd hard to drink.
What ever fool like me had been
If I'd not done as well as seen?
There to be lost why should I doubt,
Where fools with ease go in and out?

209 Text: William Cartwright, *Comedies*, 1651, see no. 45, pp. 220–1. Edition: ed. G. Blakemore Evans, see no. 45, pp. 473–4.

210 Text: William Cartwright, *Comedies*, 1651, see no. 45, pp.247–8. Edition: ed. G. Blakemore Evans, see no. 45, pp. 495–6.

211 Text: the James Marshall and Marie-Louise Osborn Collection, Beinecke Library, Yale University, MS fb 217 ['Ten Books of Epigrams; the Curiosities whereof, for Conception, stile, instruction and other mixtures of show and substance, being no lesse fruitfull, then pleasing to the diligent peruser, are intituled Apollo, and the Muses'], p. 34.

212 Text: Bodleian Library, MS Rawl. Poet. 147, see no. 136, pp. 45–6.

213 Text: Bodleian Library, MS Rawl. Poet. 147, see no. 53, pp. 98–100; *Westminster-Drollery. Or, A Choice Collection of the Newest Songs and Poems Both at Court and Theatres*, 1671 [*The Second Part being a compleat Collection of all the Newest and Choicest Songs and*

Poems at Court and both the Theaters, 1672], pp. 64–9. Edition: ed. Norman Ault, *Seventeenth Century Lyrics from the Original Texts*, 1928, pp. 246–9. This poem is unattributed in any early-modern source. It has been attributed to one Walter Wasse on the strength of a record in *A Collection of the State Papers of John Thurloe, Esq*, 7 vols., 1742, iv. 717–18. In the course of the examination of Nathaniel Brooks of Cornhill, London, stationer on 19 April, 1656, Brooks said 'that of one Walter Wasse he received...the hunting of the gods and several others therein contained.' Anthony Wood's *Athenae Oxonienses* (iv. 460) records papers being sold to Wasse, who would appear to have been a dealer or collector, rather than an author. The evidence for Briggs's authorship is slender. The provenance of MS Rawl. Poet. 147 (see no. 53) would make him a possible candidate; the poem is, however, unattributed in this manuscript which contains a number of poems attributed to him. Stylistic resemblance to no. 53 is perhaps the strongest evidence. Since the poem can be attributed with confidence to Briggs's and Paman's circle, the manuscript text is taken as copy-text.

214 Text: John Cleveland, *The Character of A London-Diurnall*, 1647, see no. 50, pp. 7–8. Edition: ed. Brian Morris and Eleanor Withington, see no. 50, pp. 43–5.

This poem is written to the tune of a ballad of 1634 'Blew cap for me' relating to Charles I's visit to Scotland in the previous year, a ballad which later became a royalist song in the Civil War. The point is that a 'Square-cap' (mortar-board-wearing university graduate) is more attractive than a man of any other profession.

215 Text: Sir John Denham, *Poems and Translations*, 1668, see no. 54, pp. 1–2. Edition: ed. Brendan O Hehir, *Expans'd Hieroglyphicks: A Critical Edition of Sir John Denham's Coopers Hill*, Berkeley and Los Angeles, 1969, pp. 139–62. The textual history of the poem is complex, and for the full history, and for variant readings between the states, the reader is referred to *Expans'd Hieroglyphicks*. In brief, the earliest version of the poem was published at London in 1642 (O Hehir's 'A Text') and was reprinted in 1643, 1650, and 1653. A revised edition (the 'B Text'), claiming to be 'obtained from the Author's owne papers', appeared in 1655; it was, in fact, in the main taken from the same setting of type as 1653. A unique 'Corrected Impression' of 1653 is at Yale. The 1655 edition, with the addition of four new lines, formed the basis for the text which appeared in Denham's *Poems and Translations* in 1668. The copy of the 1668 text in the James Marshall and Marie-Louise Osborn Collection, Beinecke Library, Yale University (see no. 54) has an autograph addition between ll. 188 and 189. Whether the result of the revision of the 1655 text, or a first accurate representation of a text corrupted in 1655, the 1668 text has an undeniable authorial authority.

188+ Rome only conquerd halfe the world, but trade
One commonwealth of that and her hath made
And though the sunn his beame extends to all
Yet to his neighbour sheds most liberall
Least God and Nature partiall should appeare
Commerse makes everything grow everywhere *1668, Osborn Copy*

216 Text: Rev. James Maclagan, The Maclagan Collection of Gaelic MSS, latter half eighteenth century, Glasgow University Library, p. 120. [Orally composed in 1646.] Edition and translation: J. Carmichael Watson, *Gaelic Songs of Mary MacLeod*, Scottish Gaelic Texts Society, Edinburgh, 1965, pp. 14–21.

217 Text: Abraham Cowley, *Poems*, 1656, [*Miscellanies*] see no.59, p. 38. Edition: ed. John Sparrow, see no. 59, p. 58.

218 Text: Alexander Brome, *Songs*, 1661, see no. 110, p. 19. Edition: ed. Roman R. Dubinski, see no. 110, i. 83–4.

219 Text: Margaret Cavendish, Duchess of Newcastle, *Poems, and fancies: written by the Right Honourable, the Lady Margaret Countesse of Newcastle*, 1653, sig. [unsigned gathering between 'A' and 'B'] 4r; Scolar Press facsimile, Menston, 1972. The Cambridge University Library copy of the 1653 edition [CUL, P.3.19] which has been used here, is a presentation copy, inscribed on the inside front board, 'Illustrissima D[omi]na. Margareta Novo-Castrensis Marchionissa Elegantissimum hunc ingenii sui foetum Almae Matris Cantabrigiae gremio fovendum tradidit. Anno Dni. 1655.' [The most noble Lady Margaret, Duchess of Newcastle, gives this most elegant offspring of her wit into the lap of beloved Mother Cambridge for cherishing, in the year of the Lord 1655]

220 Text: Margaret Cavendish, Duchess of Newcastle, *Poems*, 1653, see no. 219, sig. [unsigned gathering between 'A' and 'B'] 4v.

221 Text: Matthew Stevenson, *Occasion's Off-spring or Poems upon Severall Occasions*, 1645 ['54'], p. 102. This song was written for the 'Florists' Feast' at Norwich: for further information, see Ruth E. Duthie, 'English Florist's Societies and Feasts in the Seventeenth and first half of the Eighteenth Centuries', *Garden History*, 10:1, (Spring 1982), pp. 17–35.

222 Text: Matthew Stevenson, *Occasion's Off-spring*, 1645, see no. 221, pp. 66–8.

223 Text: Single Leaf, *A Contemplation on Bassets down-Hill by the most Sacred adorer of the Muses Mrs. A.K.* [?1658] [Bodleian Library, shelf-mark Wood 416 (11)]. A contemporary hand expands the initials with 'Anne Kemp' and glosses the title with 'near Meysay Hampton or Down-Ampney in Glocestershire'.

224 Text: Thomas Stanley, *Poems*, 1651, see no. 73, pp. 167–74. Edition: ed. Galbraith Miller Crump, see no. 73, pp. 156–73. This is a free translation of Theophile de Viau's *La Maison de Sylvie* (*Œuvres Complètes*, ed. M. Alleaume, Paris, 1856, ii. 193 ff.). The French original extends to over a thousand lines describing the duchesse de Montmorency's retreat near Chantilly, ranging over various moods and aspects of the place. Stanley has considerably concentrated his original, as well as rendering the tone more unified. This poem is worthy of our attention as representative of a strong minor genre in early-modern poetry throughout Europe: the half-allegorized and meticulous description of a house and its setting. Of many examples, one of the most influential (upon Marvell among others) and least known is Constantijn Huygens's meditation on his house and garden of *Hofwijk*, published in his *Korenbloemen*, The Hague, 1658.

225 Text: Charles Cotton, *Poems*, 1689, see no. 76, pp. 114–16. Not in Derby MS.

226 Text: Charles Cotton, *Poems*, 1689, see no.76, pp. 133–9. Not in Derby MS.

227 Text: Katherine Philips, *Poems*, 1667, see no. 77, pp. 103–4. Edition: ed. Patrick Thomas, see no. 77, pp. 173–5.

228 Text: *Rump: or an exact collection of the Choycest Poems and Songs relating to the Late Times*, 1662, ii. 94–5. Also in *A Royal Arbor of Loyal Poesie* [1663], see no. 144, p. 26, where the poem is dated '1 Jan 1659'. Also issued as a broadside in 1659 'A Letany for the New-year, with a Description of the New State' (see no. 248). Information on many of the songs in this collection can be found in H. F. Brooks, 'Rump Songs', *Proceedings and Papers of the Oxford Bibliographical Society*, 5, part 4 (1939), pp. 281–304. Text is from *Rump*, with variants from *Royall Arbor*.

Title] *A letany delivered*, Jan. 1. 1659. *to a Friend as a New-Years Gift* 2 you well protected] protection to you 3–4] *wanting in RA* 6 such] those 7*Faces*] features 8] From Reformation, such as pull'd down *Pauls;* 9 *Linsywoolsy Lords*] *Church-land purchasers* 10 *Apron*] Weaving 11–12] *reversed in LA* 13 destroy] betray 17 when] where 18 such] those 22+ *LA inserts 27–8* 23] From zeal that wants both Piety and Knowledge, 24 *red students* now] hot Disputants 25–6] From Coblers which ascend to Council Tables, | From dens of thieves, from Churches turn'd to Stables; 27–8 *inserted at 22+* 29 which may] like to 30 The *Poet*] We humbly

229 Text: Richard Corbet: *Poëtica stromata or a collection of sundry peices in poetry: drawne by the known and approved hand of R. C.* [continental publication?] 1648, see no. 168, pp. 71–5; later text [much expanded with fifteen extra verses by another hand] in *The Triumphs of the Prince D'Amour*, 1660; good early text in Cambridge University Library, MS Add. 4138, ff.14r–16r. Edition: ed. J. A. W. Bennett and H. R. Trevor-Roper, see no. 168, pp. 56–8.

Internal evidence would seem to date the poem to about 1621. The existence of the 1660 version, with its extra verses added by an unskilled imitator, is a testimony to the vitality of this poem throughout the period covered by this anthology. This, in a sense, is the kind of poem which influences, rather than reflects, events. The amused caricature of the 1620s becomes the propaganda, the dehumanizing 'othering', of the 1630s and 1640s. By 1660 it becomes a retrospective exultation over the defeated, again, an amused, divisive caricature.

Richard Greenham was a Puritan divine, Fellow of Pembroke College, Cambridge. His collected *Works* were published in 1599, and reprinted in 1601, 1605, 1612.

William Perkins was also a Cambridge Puritan, and his *Golden Chaine or the description of Theologies* was often reprinted in the years 1608–35. It includes a 'Table declaring the order of the causes of Salvation and Damnation' indicating the individual's progress by diagrams of black, zigzag lines.

230 Text: Edward Herbert, Lord Herbert of Cherbury, *Occasional Verses of Edward Lord Herbert, Baron of Cherbery*, 1665, pp. 85–6. Scolar Press facsimile, Menston, 1969. Edition: ed. G. C. Moore Smith, *The Poems English and Latin of Edward Lord Herbert of Cherbury*, Oxford, 1923, pp. 85–6.

The British Library copy of the 1665 edition misprints the title as 'October 14. 1664'.

231 Text: William Drummond, *The Works of William Drummond of Hawthornden*, Edinburgh, 1711, [internal title-page *Poems Never before Printed*] p. 49. Edition: ed. L. E. Kastner, *The Poetical Works of William Drummond of Hawthornden*, 2 vols., Manchester, 1913, ii. 206. The blank in l. 18 is deliberate, and has stood as such since the poem was first printed from manuscript in 1711; the editor of the 1913 STS edition of Drummond suggests 'some disrespectful epithet for a Prince whose own chief minister had succumbed and who could not save even his own regalia'.

The poem is dated by the taking of Dalkeith Palace, Sunday 2 March, 1639, by the Covenanters. It was surrendered by Traquair, the King's chief Minister in Scotland, and the Scots regalia fell thus into the Covenanters' hands. Drummond can be conjectured reluctantly to have taken the covenant in late March or early April 1639.

Drummond speaks this bitter poem in the persona of the sole surviving moderate in Scotland asking various social groups why they are rebelling, finding their answers illogical, and eventually falling victim to the catch-all accusation that he had failed to subscribe to the Presbyterian National Covenant of 1638 'to defend the Protestant religion and to resist all contrary errors and corruptions'.

232 Text: Richard Brome, *A Joviall Crew: or The Merry Beggars. Presented in a Comedie at The Cock-Pit in Drury-Lane, in the yeer 1641*, 1652, sig. a2r. Edition: ed. A. Haaker, *A Jovial Crew* (Regents Renaissance Drama Series), 1968, p. 14.

Richard Brome's *A Joviall Crew or The Merry Beggars* was the last new play to be performed before the parliament closed the theatres in 1641. The crucial line of this ingeniously disingenuous Prologue is the 'near as he could' of l. 16: the play text does not concern itself with the romance material of escapist fiction, but with '*Fortune-tellers*, Damsels, and their *Squires*' in the context of an uncomfortably real evocation of the England of 1641, which uses the images of Beggary and social marginalization to express the civil disintegration which Brome perceived to be the likely outcome of the Civil Wars. The tone of this Prologue is much grimmer than it appears at a first reading.

Brome's dedicatory letter to Thomas Stanley in the quarto of 1652 stresses the extent to which he was writing a play in abnormal circumstances: 'All the arguments I can use to induce you to take notice of this thing of nothing is that it had the luck to tumble last of all in the epidemical ruin of the scene, and now limps hither with a wooden leg to beg an alms at your hands.'

233 Text: *Rump*, 1662, see no. 228, i. 32–4; Thomas Jordan, *A Royal Arbor*, [1663], see no. 144, p. 78, under the variant title 'The Players Petition to the Long Parliament after being long silenc'd, that they might play again. 1642.'

This satire is ostensibly the petition of the actors from the public theatres which had been closed because of the war, asking Parliament's leave to resume playing. In fact, this is a rhetorical stratagem (Parliament would not have entertained any such petition) to provide an opportunity not only to criticize parliamentary censorship, but also to accuse Parliament of being a stage-regime, a parody government which will not last.

234 Text: Robert Herrick, *Hesperides*, 1648, see no. 8, p. 31. Edition: ed. L. C. Martin, see no. 8, p. 30.

235 Text: Robert Herrick, *Hesperides*, 1648, see no. 8, pp. 184–5. Edition: ed. L. C. Martin, see no. 8, pp. 159–60.

This is a troubling poem: while it is perfectly possible that it could be no more than a conventionally melancholy pastoral, the level of emotion invested by the speakers seems disproportionate to the context. The names of the speakers, however, provide a clue: they are all from the political pastoral play by Guarini, *Il Pastor Fido*, first performed in 1589. In the translation which Sir Richard Fanshawe published in 1647, the play is explicitly politicized: 'our Author (exposing to *ordinary view* an Enterlude of Shepherds, their loves, and other little concernments...) presents through the *perspective* of the *Chorus*, another and more suitable object to his *Royall Spectators*. He shews to *them* the image of a *gasping State* (once the most flourishing in the world): *A wild Boar (the sword)* depopulating the *Country : the Pestilence* unpeopling the *Towns*'. *Il Pastor Fido, The faithfull Shepherd*, 1647, A4r. Herrick's imitation of, and intervention in, Guarini's text, becomes explicitly royalist, explicitly political. Mirtillo speaks for Charles I; the absent Amaryllis merges with the absent Henrietta Maria.

236 Text: Robert Herrick, *Hesperides*, 1648, see no. 8, pp. 263–4. Edition: ed. L. C. Martin, see no. 8, pp. 224–5.

237 Text: Robert Herrick, *Hesperides*, 1648, see no. 8, p. 24. Edition: ed. L. C. Martin, see no. 8, p. 25.

238 Text: Robert Herrick, *Hesperides*, 1648, see no. 8, p. 251. Edition: ed. L. C. Martin, see no. 8, p. 214.

239 Text: British Library, Add. MS 32,497, see no. 15, f. 54r–v. Edition: ed. Douglas Grant, see no. 15, pp. 75–6.

240 Text: Francis Quarles, *The Shepheardes Oracle: delivered in an Eglogue*, 1644, pp. 11–12. This poem was immensely popular all through the civil war period and survives in a vast number of manuscript copies. It was probably composed in 1641, and was reprinted many times, significantly, in *Rump*, 1662, see no. 228, i. 14–16. The attribution to Quarles is confirmed by the evidence of Bodleian Library MS Don. c. 57, f. 27v.

241 Text: James Shirley, *Poems &c*, 1646, see no. 19, p. 62. Edition: ed. Ray Livingstone Armstrong, see no. 19, p. 15.

242 Text: *Rump*, 1662, see no. 228, i. 86–7. There is also a text in British Library MS Harl. 6918, f. 95.

This poem, royalist wishful thinking put into the mouth of a personified City of London, laments the divided state of the kingdom in the early 1640s, when the court had removed to Oxford, thus leaving the predominantly parliamentarian City and the parliament itself in a kind of constitutional limbo, at least from a royalist perspective.

Echo poems, claiming a kind of intrinsic truth for the fragmentary replies of the echo, are frequent in the seventeenth century. One of the best known is in Act V of John Webster's *The Duchess of Malfi* (played before 1614, published 1623).

243 Text: S.N.[M.], *The loyal garland, containing choice songs and sonnets of our late unhappy revolutions*, 4th edn, 167[?3], sig. A3r–v. Editions: William Chappell, *Old English Popular Music*, 1893, pp. 210–13 [with a listing of texts]; ed. Alastair Fowler, *The New Oxford Book of Seventeenth Century Verse*, Oxford and New York, 1992, no. 465, pp. 373–4; ed. David Norbrook and H. R. Woudhuysen, *The Penguin Book of Renaissance Verse 1509–1659*, 1992, no. 43, pp. 163–5 [comprehensive listing of texts pp. 772–3]. This was a popular ballad which clearly circulated in a variety of versions from the probable time of its composition in c.1643 untill the Restoration. It had an afterlife with its appropriation as a Jacobite song in the late seventeenth and early eighteenth centuries. There are two pre–Restoration texts in single-sheet broadside ballads: British Library, Roxburghe Ballads; British Library, 1876.f.1(3). Both have the refrain 'When the King comes homes home in Peace again'. There is a post-Restoration version in the Euing Collection, Glasgow University Library, dating from 1660–1, under the title *Englands great prognosticator*, with the refrain 'Now the King injoyes his own again'. The text given here is from about the time of the Restoration, as witnessed by the glossing of the 'peaceful Dove' of l. 43 as General Monck.

Chappell, *Popular Music*, 1893, p. 212, quotes, in support of Parker's authorship from *The Gossip's Feast; or, Moral Tales*, 1647: 'By my faith Martin Parker never got a fairer brat: no, not when he penn'd that sweet ballad, *When the King injoyes his own again*.'

244 Text: Gilbert Burnet, *The Memoires of the Lives and Actions of James and William, Dukes of Hamilton and Castleherald*, 1677, pp. 381–3. Edition: ed. W. Chappell and J. Woodfall Ebsworth, *The Roxburghe Ballads*, 9 vols., 1869–97, vii, Hertford, 1893, pp. 619–20. The question of poems attributed to Charles I is unlikely ever to be fully resolved. This poem is the only one which makes a serious attempt to claim his authorship, with Burnet offering provenance and circumstantial evidence. 'I shall therefore insert a Copy of verses written by his Majesty in his Captivity, which a very worthy gentleman, who had the honour of waiting on him then, and was much trusted by him, Copied out from the original, who avoucheth it to be a true copy.' With hindsight, the consonance of the imagery of these verses with so much of the hagiographic propaganda which appeared after the execution of Charles in 1649, particularly with the *Eikon Basilike*, serves strongly to undermine his claims for authorship. The case here is the same as with the poems attributed to the Marquis of Montrose: the possibility of authorship is slender at best, but the existence and ascription of the poems reveals a consensus as to what the King ought to have written, according to the schemes of both propaganda and iconography current amongst his supporters.

245 Text: *A Choice Collection*, 1706–11, see no. 46, iii. 117–20. Edition: ed. Harriet Harvey Wood, see no. 46, I. iii. 117–20. These verses are certainly not by Charles. They are, on the other hand, a specimen of the survival of the aureate style of Scottish verse of the sixteenth century into the seventeenth, and provide a remarkable instance of the revival of a poetic high style in a literary culture which had fragmented and lost direction, and had ceased to develop in Scots/English since the departure of the Court in 1603, concentrating all developmental poetic energies into Latin poetry, mostly published and distributed in the Low Countries.

246 Text: Pamphlet, *His Majesties Complaint. Occasioned by his late sufferings, and a not right understanding between him and his parliament*, 1647. British Library, Thomason E 393, no. 38, pp. 1–4 (sig. A2r–A3v). This poem is an appropriation of George Herbert's 'The Sacrifice', a poem spoken in the persona of Christ in His Passion. This poem explicitly, and no. 247 implicitly, puts the suffering Charles in parallel with the suffering Christ. This parallel becomes unmistakable, if this poem is read together with Herbert's original (ed. F. E. Hutchinson, *The Works of George Herbert*, Oxford, 1941 [reprint 1978], pp. 26–34).

247 Text: *King Charles his speech* [Broadside (fragment): John Rylands University Library of Manchester, II, 54]. Edition: ed. H. E. Rollins, *Cavalier and Puritan: Ballads and Broadsides Illustrating the Period of the Great Rebellion 1640–1660*, New York, 1923, pp. 233–5. The ballad of which this is a propagandist variant would appear to be in origin a devotional ballad on the Passion of Christ. An earlier political use, equally daring, is recorded, dating from 1603: 'A lamentable Ditty composed upon the Death of Robert Lord Devereux late Earle of Essex'. It is also dittied to the tune of 'Welladay' and begins

Sweet England's pride is gone
Welladay, welladay

(ed. William Chappell, *The Roxburghe Ballads*, 1871, pp. 563–70).

This is a propaganda poem working with some skill on two levels: emphasizing the status of Charles I as a martyr, and refuting, with the apparent authority of his (essentially invented) dying words the commonest charges laid against him.

248 Text: *Rump*, 1662, see no. 228, ii. 95–6; a broadside of 1659 contained 'A Letany for the New-Year, with a Description of the New State'. Jordan's 'Letany' (no. 228) is found in *A Royal Arbor of Loyal Poesie* [1663], see no. 144, but without this companion poem. On balance, Jordan's authorship seems likely.

249 Text: Mildmay Fane, Earl of Westmorland, *Otia Sacra*, 1648, see no. 185, p. 127.

250 Text: *A Collection of Loyal Songs written against the Rump Parliament between the Years 1639 and 1661*, 1731, i. 223–5; also in *The loyal garland*, 1686, see no. 243, and in *Rump*, 1662, see no. 228, i. 333–5.

This (royalist) propaganda poem, apparently of the later 1650s, employs one of the commonest tropes against the parliament and protectorate, that the rule of law had been replaced by government by military dictatorship. As with the majority of the anti-parliamentarian poems (see no. 240 onwards) another central insinuation is that the parliament's intention is to abolish all social distinctions and set up the outsiders of society in positions of influence and power.

251 Text: Sir William Davenant, *Works*, 1673, [internal title-page] *Poems*, 1672, see no. 29, p. 288. Edition: ed. A. M. Gibbs, see no. 29, p. 125, poem dates 1623–4. The subject, Elizabeth Sheldon, was wife of Christopher Villiers (?1593–1630), Earl of Anglesey, younger brother of the Duke of Buckingham. When he was created Earl in 1623, he was granted lands and forests at Pewsham, Chippenham forest, Wiltshire. His policy of disafforestation was highly unpopular.

252 Text: Sir William Davenant, *Works*, 1673, see no. 29, [internal title-page] *The siege of Rhodes: The First and Second Part*, 1672, p. 9. Edition: ed. A. M. Gibbs, see no. 29, p. 247.

The siege of Rhodes, staged by Davenant in London in 1656, was a hybrid work, designed to circumvent the parliamentary ban on the acting of stage-plays. A moral spectacle, represented in tableaux and music, it can be seen, on one hand, as a possible adaptation of masque techniques into something like proto-opera. On the other hand, the rather static nature of the piece, and its formal, distanced dramaturgy, would appear to have much in common with the form of early-modern art which, on the whole, gave the least offence to ultra-Protestants: the moral emblem.

253 Text: *Tixall Poetry*, 1813, see no. 30, p. 54. Collected by Herbert Aston, 1658. The essential conceit of this poem is similar to that of no. 268.

254 Text: Edmund Waller, *Poems, &c*, 1664, see no. 32, p. 158. Edition: ed. G. Thorn Drury, see no. 32, i. 112.

255 Text: Bodleian Library, MS Firth. c. 1., see no. 205, p. 82. Edition: ed. Peter Davidson, see no. 205, p. 49.

This poem, from its placing in the MS, would appear to be a translation from the Spanish, but its source remains unidentified.

256 Text: Sir Richard Fanshawe, *Selected Parts of Horace Prince of Lyricks*, 1652 [unique surviving copy of the second and corrected state of the edition, Beinecke Library, Gnbh a 652f.(2)], pp. 59–60. Edition: ed. Peter Davidson, see no. 205, pp. 205–6. The absence of this translation from either the Bodleian or British Library manuscripts, see no. 205, would suggest that it was translated between 1645 and 1651. This translation had a particular meaning for the family of its royalist author, as a personal poem of consolation in adversity. Ann, Lady Fanshawe, quotes it in her *Memoirs* immediately following her account of Fanshawe's death (ed. John Loftis, *The Memoirs of Ann, Lady Fanshawe*, Oxford, 1979, pp. 184–5).

257 Text: Sir Richard Fanshawe, *Il Pastor Fido*, 1648, see no. 36, p. 254 [facing Fanshawe's Latin translation]. This text ascribed the poem to the same Thomas Cary who wrote no. 36. While it is clear that this poem enjoyed a considerable circulation in the 1640s (perhaps because of its application to the departure of Henrietta Maria for the Continent on 23 February 1642 to raise revenue for the royalist war effort) its authorship remains doubtful. Fanshawe ascribes it to Thomas Cary 'of his Majesties Bed-Chamber'; H. Lawes's *Ayres and Dialogues*, 1653, i. 10, to 'Mr Thomas Cary, son of the Earl of Monmouth'. Manuscript attributions are variable, including Sir Kenelm Digby (Bodleian Library, MS Eng. Poet. c. 53, f. 9v) and W. Murray (Bodleian Library, MS Rawl. Poet. 116, f. 47v). However, it appears to be a Scots poem of the sixteenth century, with an attribution to William Fowler (1560–1612), uncle of William Drummond of Hawthornden. The attribution to Fowler is discussed by M. M. Gray, *Scottish Poetry from Barbour to James I*, 1935, pp. xxi–xxii. As it now exists, the poem is substantially revised from Fowler's version; a text of which is given on pp. 351–2 of Gray's anthology. Again, as with no. 89, it is possible that there has been a deliberate recasting of an earlier text. Due to the recent researches of Victoria Burke, it is possible to give for comparison a Scots-spelling text, also circulating in the 1640s. This text, from the 'Lady Margaret Wemyss Manuscript', see no. 48, (Edinburgh, National Library of Scotland, Sutherland Papers, dep. 314/23) is found at f. 72v rev. (refoliated by Matthew

Spring as f. 2 in his article, 'The Lady Margaret Wemyss Manuscript', *Journal of the Lute Society*, 27 (1987), pp. 5–29). I am again indebted to Victoria Burke for bringing this text to my attention.

Fare weill fair saint may not the saes nor winds
Suell lyk the heart and eyes yow leawe behind
Bot calm and gentell lyk the looks yow beare
Smill in your face and whisper in your eare
Lett no bold billow ofer to arys
That it may neiuer look wpon your eyes
Lest winds and waus enamured of your forme
May throng and crud themselus into a storme
Bot if it bee your fate waste seas to love
of my becalmed breast learne houe to mowe
Mowe then bot in a ge[n]tell lovers pace
No wrinkels nor no furries in your face
And yow ferce windes sei that you tell your teall
In such a breath as may fill her saill
That whillest yow boeth doe court your seurall wayss
Yow may her safly to her port conuaye
And loos her in a nobell uay of w[oo]ing
Whills both contribut to your oun wndoing

258 Text: Trinity College, Cambridge, MS R. 3. 4, f. 47r. Edition: ed. John Carey and Alastair Fowler, see no. 101, pp. 326–7. Not printed in Milton's lifetime. First printed, in a corrupt text, in Edward Phillip's edition of Milton's *Letters of State*, 1694.

5–6] And fought God's Battels, and his Work pursu'd *1694*

259 Text: John Milton, *Poems*, 1645, see no. 101, pp. 49–50. Edition: ed. John Carey and Alastair Fowler, see no. 101, p. 285. In the Trinity MS, see no. 258, the original title 'On his door when the City expected an assault' has been corrected to 'When the assault was intended to the City' and dated, in Milton's hand, '1642'.

3] If ever deed of honour did thee *Trinity MS*

260 Text: Gerrard Winstanley, *A Mite cast into the common treasury* [British Library, Thomason copy received 18 Dec. 1649], pp. 6–8. Edition: ed. George H. Sabine, *The Works of Gerrard Winstanley*, Ithaca, NY, 1941, pp. 659–61.

261 Text: Worcester College, Oxford, MS Clarke 18, ff. 32r–33v. Edition: ed. C. H. Firth, *Clarke Papers: Selections from the Papers of William Clarke*, Camden Society, 4 vols., 1891–1901, ii. 221–4; ed. David Norbrook and H. R. Woudhuysen, *The Penguin Book of Renaissance Verse*, 1992, no. 211, pp. 464–6.

The poem is unattributed in the Worcester College MS, a manuscript which contains several writings by Winstanley. In 1649, the probable date of the poem, Winstanley, Henry Bickerstaffe, and Thomas Star cultivated common land, paying no rent, at St George's Hill, Walton, Surrey. Their stock was attacked with clubs and they were prosecuted.

262 Text: Gerrard Winstanley, *The Law of Freedom*, 1652, p. 29. Edition: ed. George H. Sabine, see no. 260, p. 533.

263 Text: William Cartwright, *Comedies*, 1651, see no. 45, pp. 279–81. Edition: ed. G. Blakemore Evans, see no. 45, pp. 526–8.

264 Text: Broadsheet; Bodleian Library, Wood 416, no. 120. The British Library copy [Brit. Lib. MS 669, f. 11] is dated in manuscript 'November 6 1647'. Edition: ed. G. Blakemore Evans, see no. 45, pp. 560–3. Humphrey Moseley, the printer of the 1651 edition of Cartwright, refers in it to the broadsheet publication: 'And (take it on his word who never *subscribed* to a Lye) there's nothing kept from you but only one short Paper of Verses; what that is, and why it is not here, we need not tell you; for it has been twice already Printed, though above our Power to bring it with its fellows' [unsigned preliminary pages].

265 Text: James Marshall and Marie-Louise Osborn Collection, Beinecke Library, Yale University, MS fb 217, see no. 211, p. 35.

266 Text: Bodleian Library, MS Fairfax 40 ['The Recreations of my Solitude'], p. 600.

For a biography of Fairfax, his resistance to the execution of the King, and his patronage of Andrew Marvell, see Appendix 2.

267 Text: *Loyal Songs*, 1731, see no. 250, i. 27; also in *Rump*, 1662, see no. 228, i. 30.

Title COMPLAINT] Short and Sweet *Rump*

268 Text: *A Choice Collection*, 1706–11, see no. 46, iii. 107–8. Edition: ed. Harriet Harvey Wood, see no. 46, pp. 107–8.

This poem circulated widely in the latter half of the seventeenth century. The earliest text is a broadsheet entitled *Montrose to his Mistress* in the Roxburghe Ballads in the British Library; there is an undated broadsheet in the National Library of Scotland (Ry.III.a.10.34) entitled 'I'le never love thee more, To be sung with its pleasant new Tune', which may represent simply a variant of the original to which Montrose contrafacted his verses. There is a manuscript copy of Montrose's poem dating from the years of the interregnum in British Library MS Harleian 3889. The second part of 'My deare and only Love', printed in 1711, pp. 108–12, is omitted as spurious, as constituting the early seventeenth–century ballad to whose tune Montrose dittied his poem. Lines 13–16 gain a particular resonance if we know that Montrose's personal motto and book motto was 'Si totius illabitur orbis' ['Even if the whole world should fall to ruin']. This inscription is found on Montrose's Bible in the Innerpefferay Library, near Crieff, Perthshire. [This library itself is a shy institution, not easily found: the OS reference, for the convenience of future scholars, is NN 8616.] There seem to be no copies of Montrose's books with verse inscriptions in this library, contrary to persistent academic legend. There are possibly some such flyleaves in the Laing Collection in the Edinburgh University Library, but they are currently untraced and will probably remain inaccessible.

Variants for this poem are given from the Roxburghe broadsheet (*M*) and from MS Harleian 3889 (*H*).

2 This Noble] That noble *M*; That little *H* 4 But] Than *M* 5 have] get *H* 7 And hold] I'll call *M*; And make *H* 7 a Synod] a senate *H* 9 Like] As *M* will] must *H* 10 I will reign] ever rule *H* 11 shall] did *M* evermore disdain] ever scorne to daigne *H* 14 are] be *H* [stanzas 3 and 4 are in inverted order in *H*] 17 But] For *H* 18 always] ever *H* 20 to] must *H* 21 But 'gainst my Battery] Against my batt'ries *H* 22] Thou strivest thy power to soare *H* 25 Or] For *H* 26 Where I should] When I shall *H* 27 do] shall *H* 28 dares] dare *H* 30 And goes] Or rulest *H* 31 at thy] thee to *H* 33 constant then] faithful still *H* 34 faithful of] constant to *H* 35 glorious by...Pen] famous with...Quill *H* 36 famous by] glorious with *H* 38 heard] knowen *H* 40] And ever love the more. *H*

269 Text: Bodleian Library, MS Rawl. Poet. 84, ff. 80v–81v. The manuscript appears to date from the early 1660s (there is a poem on the 'Returne of K. Charles 2' on f. 10 and a poem dated 1663 on f. 123v). Edition: [as Montrose's] ed. Sir James Fergusson, *The Green Garden*, London and Edinburgh, 1946, pp. 172–4. Fergusson claims to take his text from an eighteenth-century broadsheet, *Verses composed by James Marquis of Montrose*, which remains untraced. In James Fraser's *Chronicles of the Frasers* (written 1669–90), ed. William MacKay, Edinburgh, 1905, p. 364, it is attributed to George Wishart, Montrose's chaplain, who would, given the content, certainly seem a more likely author than the Presbyterian Montrose.

Lines 1–6 use an extended metaphor drawn from (Real) Tennis: the essential point is the powerlessness of the individual. Thrown at the wall (for service in an indoor court); emotionally up and down (struck by the two rackets). A full stop has to be understood at the end of l. 4. The metaphor appears to shift at this point: humanity becomes the players failing to place the ball at the centre point of the court. Tennis is often moralized and allegorized in the emblem literature of the sixteenth and seventeenth centuries.

270 Text: *A Choice Collection*, 1706–11, see no. 46, iii. 113–14. Edition: ed. Harriet Harvey Wood, see no. 46, I. iii. 113–14.

271 Text: *The Poems of John Cleveland, with additions never before printed*, 1653, p. 88; Scolar Press facsimile, Menston, 1971. This poem had an understandably wide circulation, being printed in *Reliquiae Sacrae Carolinae*, 1650, p. 355, and in a broadsheet of c.1660, British Library, Thomason E 1874 (2). There are numerous manuscript copies, amongst them Bodleian Library MS Add. B. 83, f. 13; MS Rawl. C. 986, f. 15, and MS Rawl. D. 108, f. 109, all of which ascribe the poem to Montrose. There is a musical setting in *Songs for one, two and three voices, composed by Henry Bowman, Philomusicus*, Oxford, 1679. Copy-text here is Cleveland's *Poems*, 1653, variants from *A Choice Collection*, 1706–11, see no. 46, iii. 116 [*W*] and from Edinburgh, NLS, MS Adv. 33.2.7, f. 102r [*E*]

Title] *Epitaph on King* Charles I. *W*; One K. Charles the I *E* 2 and] to *W, E* 3 to] in *W, E* 4 should Deluge once] would once deluge W

4–7 As should deludge it ones againe
Bot since thy fait far more requyres
Briarius handes, then Argus eyes
Ill toune thy obsequies to trumpets sounds *E*

7 sing thy Obsequies, with] tune Thy Elegies to *W* 8 with] in *W, E* [9–10 not in *W, E*]

272 Text: National Library of Scotland, Adv. MS 19.3.8., f. 49v.

The distinct Scots in which this poem survives gives some indication of the variety of language in which Montrose would most probably have written, and serves as a reminder how distant most available texts of his works are from authorial originals.

273 Text: *A Choice Collection*, 1706–11, see no. 46, iii. 115. Edition: ed. Harriet Harvey Wood, see no 46, I. iii. 115.

274 Text: *A Choice Collection*, 1706–11, see no. 46, iii. 116. Edition: ed. Harriet Harvey Wood, see no. 46, I. iii. 116.

This poem seems to have been called into being by propagandist need for a final statement from Montrose. In fact, in his captivity before his execution on 21 May 1650, he was closely guarded, and would have had no opportunity to compose these lines, which seem to survive from an earlier execution ballad.

275 Text: Harvard College Library, MS Eng. 1264, f. 41v, ed. Brian Morris and Eleanor Withington, see no. 50, p. 66. Although this poem was clearly widely circulated in the seventeenth century, and although it has been much quoted subsequently, there has always been an element of uncertainty about its authorship. It was printed as Cleveland's in the first edition of his *The Character of a London-Diurnall, with severall select Poems by the same Author*, 1647. In the 'optima et novissima Editio' of 1647, see no. 50, a section-heading on p. 41 divides works claimed unequivocally as Cleveland's from 'Additionall Poems by uncertain Authors'. This epitaph appears on pp. 43–4. The poem is claimed for Cleveland by two contemporary MSS collections: British Library, MS Harl. 4931, and Bodleian Library, MS Don. c. 6. There appear to be at least fourteen contemporary MSS in which the poem is unattributed.

The first really convincing questioning of Cleveland's authorship comes in an unsubmitted Oxford M.Phil. dissertation by Ms Anne Sinnett. She demonstrates that the poem was claimed for Paman in 1667 in the manuscript now at Harvard (used here as copy-text), a mauscript which bears every indication of having been compiled in memory of Paman by a scribe who had known him well. The title-page of the manuscript would certainly support such an assumption: 'Some few of those Golden Remains which the Reverend, Deepe, Calme, and most Orthodox and Pious Divine Dr. Clement Paman, Chaplaine to the Late E. of Strafford, And Deane of Elphin in Ireland, Left behind him...Written Anno Domini 1667.' The earlier poems of Paman's included in the 'Golden Remaines' MS appear to have been copied from MS Rawl. Poet. 147, on the verso of the flyleaf of which is a listing of Paman's poems in the order in which they appear in the 'Golden Remaines'. This would suggest co-operation in the compilation of the 'Golden Remaines' by those who had preserved Paman's earlier poems and would add to the impression of a carefully compiled memorial volume, one which would be unlikely to claim a celebrated poem for a comparatively obscure poet, unless sure of its authorship.

There is a little more negative evidence: *Clievelandi Vindiciae*, 1677, does not include the 'Epitaph'. Neither of the major modern editions of Cleveland (Berdan, 1903; Morris and Withington, see no. 50, 1967) consider it more than 'possible' that the poem is Cleveland's. The claim on the title-page of the 'Golden Remaines' that Paman had been chaplain to Strafford, again slightly strengthens Paman's claim. The poem does not appear in MS Rawl. Poet. 147, but MS Rawl. Poet. 62, also compiled by Henry Some, see no. 53, contains (f. 14r) Paman's longer Latin epitaph on Strafford, the closing lines of which bear a strong resemblance to the English 'Epitaph' and convince the present editor to accept Ms Sinnett's attribution of the poem to Paman:

> Illa effervescit huius cruentatus vena
> Cuius nobis heu! Superstitibus propitiator Cruor.

(The bloodstained one pours forth blood from that vein of his: but whose blood, alas, can redeem us who survive?)

276 Text: Bodleian Library, MS Rawl. Poet. 62, ff. 10r–11v. This manuscript is in the hand of Henry Some, the compiler of MS Rawl. Poet. 147, see nos 53, 105.

277 Text: Thomas Jordan, *Divinity and Morality in Robes of Poetry* [n.d.], see no. 144, sig. SS7v–8v.

278 Text: Thomas Jordan, *A Royal Arbor* [1663], see no. 144, [internal heading 'SONGS'] pp. 5–6.

279 Text: Thomas Jordan, *A Royal Arbor* [1663], see no. 144, [internal heading 'The Cheaters Cheated. *A Representation in four parts to be sung*, Nim, Filcher, Wat *and* Moll, *made for the Sheriffs of* London.'] pp. 40–1.

280 Text: Thomas Jordan, *A Royal Arbor* [1663], see no. 144, pp. 7–9.

281 Text: *Rump*, 1662, see no. 228, i. 57–8.

282 Text: Sir John Denham, *Poems and Translations*, 1668, see no. 54, pp. 78–9. Edition: ed. Theodore Howard Banks, Jr., see no. 54, p. 179.

283 Text: British Library, MS Harley 3511, ff. 8r–9r; contemporary manuscript copies in Bodleian Library: MS Add. B. 106, f. 45, MS Don. c. 57, f. 34, MS Rawl. Poet. 142, f. 146. Contemporary printed copies: *The Rump*, 1662; *Parnassus Biceps*, 1656, where the poem is titled 'The Liberty and Requiem of an Imprisoned Royalist'.

For a discussion of this poem and its provenance, see *Notes and Queries*, 26 March 1904, p. 250.

284 Text: Martin Lluelyn, *Men-Miracles with other Poemes*, 1646, see no. 145, pp. 145–6.

285 Text: *Miscellany Poems by Buckingham, Milton, Prior and others*, 1692, p. 26. Edition: ed. John Sparrow, see no. 59, p. 492. The story of Charles I picking this ill-omened passage of Dido's curse on Aeneas from *Aeneid*, IV (615–20) in the Bodleian Library during the siege of Oxford is told in Aubrey, *Brief Lives* (ed. Oliver Lawson Dick, 1949, [reprint] Penguin, Harmondsworth, 1962, p. 169). The practice of seeking illumination of the future by picking a passage at random from the *Aeneid* was a survival of medieval beliefs concerning Virgil as magician and prophet which persisted into the early-modern period.

286 Text: Abraham Cowley, *Poems*, 1656, see no. 59, pp. 4–5.

287 Text: Hertford County Record Office, Panshanger MS D/EP/F.48, ff 10r–19r. Edition: ed. Allan Pritchard, *The Civil War*, Toronto, 1973, pp. 90–106. Pritchard's edition gives a full and illuminating textual history of this poem which was never printed in Cowley's lifetime, and only printed thereafter in an imperfect and partial copy of Book I. Cowley composed the three books of *The Civil War*, a poem which he neither completed nor published, in the royalist stronghold of Oxford, beginning in the summer of 1643. The first intention of the poem was triumphalist: when it was begun the royalists appeared to be firmly in the ascendant (see Appendix 4). After the battle of Newbury in September 1643, their fortunes waned. Cowley appears to have abandoned the poem the following winter. This central book deals with the events of July to September 1643 (see Appendix 4); the change in its course from celebratory narrative to the epic conclave in Hell suggests that Cowley was altering the mode of his poem as news reached him of further royalist defeats. He made no attempt to publish the abandoned poem, even after the Restoration.

The published fragment appeared in 1679 as *A Poem on the Late Civil war. By Mr. Abraham Cowley*: this text of part of Book I appears to have been printed from a manuscript deriving from an early and unrevised state of Cowley's original, but without any of the authorial revisions incorporated in the Hertford County Record Office MS. There are two other manuscripts of similar status: British Library Add. MS 36,913 and Bodleian Library MS Douce 357.

The Hertford County Record Office manuscripts were discovered by Allan Pritchard in the 1960s, and his text of the poem is derived from Panshanger MS D/EP/F.48. This manuscript is in three hands: two scribal hands, the second of which Pritchard conjectures to be an early version of Cowley's own hand, and a revising and correcting hand which is Cowley's beyond doubt. Book II is written throughout in the second scribal hand with corrections and deletions in Cowley's autograph. (The second of these manuscripts, MS.D/EP/F.36, is a copy deriving from the first, made by Sarah Cowper after 1670, and possessing no independent authority.)

Book II presents few textual problems, apart from the earlier part of l. 138, which is deleted in MS D/EP/F.48, and is blank in MS D/EP/F.36.

288 Text: *Rump*, 1662, see no. 228, i. 328–9. A popular and widely distributed song, texts are also found in *An Antidote against Melancholy*, 1661, p. 53; Durfey's *Pills to Purge Melancholy*,1719–20, vi. 182 (with music); *Loyal Songs*, 1731, see no. 250, i. 217–19.

289 Text: Richard Lovelace, *Lucasta*, 1649, see no. 65, p. 3. Edition: ed. C. H. Wilkinson, see no. 65, p. 18.

290 Text: Richard Lovelace, *Lucasta*, 1649, see no. 65, pp. 97–8. Edition: ed. C. H. Wilkinson, see no. 65, pp. 78–9.

291 Text: Richard Lovelace, *Lucasta*, 1649, see no. 65, pp. 49–52. Edition: ed. C. H. Wilkinson, see no. 65, pp. 48–51.

292 Text: Richard Lovelace, *Lucasta*, 1649, see no. 65, pp.142–4. Edition: ed. C. H. Wilkinson, see no. 65, pp. 105–6.

293 Text: Richard Lovelace, *Lucasta, Posthume Poems*, 1659, see no. 67, pp. 13–14. Edition: ed. C. H. Wilkinson, see no. 65, pp. 134–5.

This may appear at first only obliquely to be a war poem, but when it is read particularly in conjunction with no. 295, the uneasy applications of Lovelace's beast-fables begin to emerge.

294 Text: Richard Lovelace, *Lucasta*, 1649, see no. 65, p. 45. Edition: ed. C. H. Wilkinson, see no. 65, p. 46.

295 Text: Richard Lovelace, *Lucasta, Posthume Poems*, 1659, see no. 67, pp. 21–25. Edition: ed. C.H. Wilkinson, see no. 65, pp. 141–5.

296 Text: Richard Lovelace, *Lucasta*, 1649, see no. 65, pp. 34–6. Edition: ed. C. H. Wilkinson, see no. 65, pp. 38–40.

This poem of consolation in adversity owes much to Horace, *Odes*, I. 9: the opposition of friendship and the hearth (those aspects of life under the control of the individual) to the (uncontrollable) winter outside reappears as a trope of royalist resistance throughout the Interregnum.

297 Text: Morgan Llwyd, *Gweithiau Morgan Llwyd o Wynedd*, ed. Thomas E. Ellis, Bangor and London, 1899, p. 18.

298 Text: Morgan Llwyd, *Gweithiau Morgan Llwyd o Wynedd*, 1899, see no. 297, pp. 30–1.

299 Text: Morgan Llwyd, *Gweithiau Morgan Llwyd o Wynedd*, 1899, see no. 297, pp. 1–6.

300 Text: Alexander Brome, *Songs*, 1661, see no. 110, pp. 33–4. Edition: ed. Roman R. Dubinski, see no. 110, i. 94–5.

301 Text: Alexander Brome, *Songs*, 1661, see no. 110, pp. '43', '46'. [The pagination of the 1661 text is somewhat disordered: these incorrectly numbered pages are sig. D7r–v.] Edition: ed. Roman R. Dubinski, see no. 110, i. 117–18.

302 Text: Alexander Brome, *Songs*, 1661, see no. 110, pp. 102–3. Edition: ed. Roman R. Dubinski, see no. 110, i. 165–6.

303 Text: Alexander Brome, *Songs*, 1661, see no. 110, pp. '47', '46', sig. D8r–v. Edition: ed. Roman R. Dubinski, see no. 110, i. 118–19.

304 Text: Alexander Brome, *Songs*, 1661, see no. 110, n.p. [sig. d1v–2r]. Edition: ed. Roman R. Dubinski, see no. 110, i. 95–6.

305 Text: Alexander Brome, *Songs*, 1661, see no. 110, pp. 91–4. Edition: ed. Roman R. Dubinski, see no. 110, i. 156–8.

306 Text: *Rump*, 1662, see no. 228, i. 195–7. This poem appeared in Cleveland's *Poems by John Cleavland With Additions never before Printed*, 1659, pp. 96–8, although the author would appear to be R. Fletcher. The poem was printed as his in his *Ex Otio Negotium*, 1656, p. 136. It also appears in *Loyal Songs*, 1731, see no. 250, i. 124–6.

307 Text: Marchamont Nedham, *A short history of the English Rebellion. Compiled in verse, by Marchamont Nedham; And formerly extant, in his Weekly Mercurius Pragmaticus*, 1660, pp. 10–11.

308 Text: Marchamont Nedham, *A short history of the English Rebellion*, 1660, see no. 307, pp. 12–13.

309 Text: Marchamont Nedham, *A short history of the English Rebellion*, 1660, see no. 307, p. 21.

310 Text: Marchamont Nedham, *A short history of the English Rebellion*, 1660, see no. 307, p. 33.

311 Text: Andrew Marvell, *Miscellaneous Poems. By Andrew Marvell, Esq;*, 1681, pp. 20–2; Scolar Press facsimile, Menston, 1969. Edition: ed. Elizabeth Story Donno, *Andrew Marvell: The Complete Poems*, Harmondsworth, 1972, pp. 42–3. Marvell's *Miscellaneous Poems* were published posthumously in 1681: there is comparatively little record of their circulation in the mid-century, although their influence might be detected in, for example, nos. 79 and 205 in this collection. For an account of cancel states of the 1681 text, see no. 313, below.

312 Text: Andrew Marvell, *Miscellaneous Poems*, 1681, see no. 311, pp. 14–17. Edition: ed. Elizabeth Story Donno, see no. 311, pp. 67–70.

313 Text: Andrew Marvell, *Miscellaneous Poems*, 1681, see no. 311, pp. 115–18. Edition: ed. Elizabeth Story Donno, see no. 311, pp. 55–8; ed. David Norbrook and H. R. Woudhuysen, *The Penguin Book of Renaissance Verse*, 1992, pp. 166–9 (no. 45) and textual commentary, p. 773.

In all but two surviving copies of the 1681 edition of Marvell's *Poems*, the pages containing this, and two other poems on Cromwell, are cancelled. These copies are in the Huntington Library, San Marino, California and the British Library. A copy in the Bodleian Library (MS Eng. Poet. d. 49) contains MS corrections and additions to the volume. In these MS additions, this poem is divided into four-line stanzas (thus emphasizing its relation to Sir Richard Fanshawe's translation of Horace, *Odes*, IV. 4). These variants from the printed 1681 text are identified as 1681MS:

Title Horatian] *1681MS* Horation *1681* 15 thorough] *1681MS* through *1681* 35 Kingdome] *1681* Kingdoms *1681MS* 85 *Commons*] commons *1681MS* Common *1681* 100 crown] crowns *1681MS*

314 Text: *Rump*, 1662, see no. 228, i. 335–6. Texts also found in *Merry Drollery*, 1661, ii. 72; *Loyal Songs*, 1731, see no. 250, i. 225–6; British Library MS Harl. 3991, f. 10.

315 Text: *Rump*, 1662, see no. 228, i. 289–90. Texts also found in *Wit and Drollery*, 1661, p. 150; *Loyal Songs*, 1731, see no. 250, i. 1–2.

316 Text: Henry Vaughan, *Olor Iscanus*, 1651, p. 27. Edition: ed. Alan Rudrum, see no. 151, pp. 94–5. Thomas Lewis, Rector of Llanfigan, was expelled from his living by the Brecon Sequestration Committee. This poem of friendship in adversity draws heavily on Horace, *Odes*, I. 9. Compare no. 296.

317 Text: Margaret Cavendish, *Natures pictures drawn by fancies pencil to the life*, 1656, pp. 88–9. The copy used here is a presentation copy in the Cambridge University Library (CUL Sel. 3. 57.) with inscription on the inside front board: 'Illustrissima Do[mi]na. Margareta Novo-Castrensis Marchionissa Elegantissimum hunc ingenii sui foetum Almae Matris Cantabrigiae gremio fovendum tradidit Anno. Dni. 1656'. [The most noble Lady Margaret, Duchess of Newcastle, gives this most elegant offspring of her wit into the lap of beloved Mother Cambridge for cherishing, in the year of the Lord 1656.]

318 Text: Margaret Cavendish, *Natures pictures*, 1656, see no. 317, pp. 89–90.

319 Text: *Loyal Songs*, 1731, see no. 250, ii. 279–85, or *Rump*, 1662, see no. 228, ii. 183–8 [the last page misprinted as 189], or *Roxburghe Ballads*, vii. 665.

320 Text: *Rump*, 1662, see no. 228, ii. 162–5. Also in *Loyal Songs*, 1731, see no. 250, ii. 253–6.

321 Text: The Maclagan Collection of Gaelic MSS, see no. 216, p. 225. [Orally composed in 1647.] Editions: ed. Rev. Angus J. Macdonald and Rev. Archibald MacDonald, *The MacDonald Collection of Gaelic Poetry*, Inverness, 1911, p. 57; ed. Annie MacKenzie, *Orain Iain Luim*, Edinburgh, 1964, p. 28. Translation: revised Meg Bateman and Jane Stevenson. The language of this poem is Scottish Gaelic, using a stress metre with end-rhyme and *aicill* (a system of rhyming from the end of one line to the beginning or middle of the next).

322 Text: A. and D. Stewart, *Cochruinneacha Taoghta de Shaothair nam Bard Gaelach*, Edinburgh, 1804, p. 416. [Orally composed in 1651.] Editions: ed. Rev. A. Maclean Sinclair, *Orain le Iain Lom*, Antigonish, 1895, p. 20; ed. Annie MacKenzie, *Orain Iain Luim*, Edinburgh, 1964, p. 56; this edition and translation: Colm O Baoill and Meg Bateman, *Gàir nan Clàrsach*, Edinburgh, 1994, p. 130. The language of this poem is Scottish Gaelic, using a syllabic metre (three lines of seven syllables, accent on the penultimate syllable, with one of six, accent on the last). It also has end-rhyme, and the final stress of each verse rhymes throughout the poem.

323 Text: The MS of Dr Maclean of Grulin, compiled in Mull, mid-eighteenth century, Public Archives, Halifax, Nova Scotia, p. 107. [Orally composed in 1645.] Editions: ed. Patrick Turner, *Comhchruinneacha do Dh'orain Taghta Ghaidhealach*, Edinburgh, 1813, p. 49; ed. Rev. A. Maclean Sinclair, *The Gaelic Bards from 1411 to 1714*, Charlottetown, 1890, p. 68; also ed. Rev. A. Maclean Sinclair, *Orain le Iain Lom*, Antigonish, 1895, p. 6; ed. W. J. Watson, *Bàrdachd Ghàidhlig*, Stirling, 1932, p. 213; ed. Annie MacKenzie, *Orain Iain Luim*, Edinburgh, 1964, p. 20; this edition and translation: Colm O Baoill and Meg Bateman, *Gàir nan Clàrsach*, Edinburgh, 1994, p. 106. The language is Scottish Gaelic, using a stressed metre with end-rhyme.

324 Text: ed. J. L. Campbell, *Songs Remembered in Exile*, Aberdeen, 1900, p. 245. Editions: ed. A. MacLean Sinclair, *Mac Talla nan Tur*, Sydney, Cape Bretton, 1901; ed. C. MacPharlain, *Binneas nam Bàrd,* Stirling, 1908, p. 32; this edition and translation revised Meg Bateman and Jane Stevenson. The language is Scottish Gaelic, using a stressed metre. Each line is to be sung twice, between a refrain of meaningless vocables. The sparse emotional tone of the song is characteristic of the unlearned tradition of Gaelic poetry, which was largely the work of women.

325 Text: ed. Seán Ó Tuama and Thomas Kinsella, *An Duanaire*, see no. 23, pp. 104–9.

326 Text: Thomas Stanley, *Psalterium Carolianum the devotions of his Sacred Majesty in his solitudes and sufferings, rendered in verse*, 1657, sig. H2r–v. Edition: ed. Galbraith Miller Crump, see no. 73, pp. 299–300.

327 Text: Donnchadh Mac Rath, Fernaig MS, see no. 24, f. 25a–b. Editions: Calum MacPhàrlainn, *Lamh-Sgriobhainn Mhìc Ràth*, Dundee, 1923, p. 118. The language is Scottish Gaelic, and the metre is based on a Classical syllabic metre with six syllables to a line, and accent on the penultimate syllable.

328 Text: Donnchadh Mac Rath, Fernaig MS, see no. 24, ff. 25b–26a. Editions: ed. Calum MacPhàrlainn, *Lamh-Sgriobhainn Mhìc Ràth*, Dundee, 1923, p. 123; this edition and translation: Meg Bateman. The language is Scottish Gaelic, and the metre is loosely based on a Classical heptasyllabic metre (with accent on the last syllable) called *rannaigheacht mhór*, in use from the eighth century to the mid-seventeenth century.

329 Text: *The Ladies Lamentation*, 1651 [Broadside: British Library, C.20.f.14(32)]. Edition: ed. H. E. Rollins, see no. 247, pp. 316–19. The tune, *Highlander's March*, appears in *The Dancing Master*, 1665, [internal heading] *The Tunes of the French Dances*, p. 41.

330 Text: Charles Cotton, *Poems on Several Occasions*,1689, see no. 76, pp. 439–40. Collated with Derby Central Library, fmss. 8470, see no. 76, pp. 145–6.

331 Text: Charles Cotton, *Poems on Several Occasions*,1689, see no.76, pp. 446–8. Collated with Derby Central Library fmss. 8470, see no. 76, pp. 149–50.

6 *Cromwel*] —— *MS* 18 sprightly] Sprightfull *MS* 21 the cure of] the of *MS* 40 King] —— *MS*

332 Text: Charles Cotton, *Poems on Several Occasions*,1689, see no. 76, pp. 361–2. Collated with Derby Central Library, fmss. 8470, see no. 76, pp. 27–8.

Title Montross.] Montrosse. *MS*

333 Text: Katherine Philips, *Poems*, 1667, see no. 77, pp. 1–2. Edition: ed. Patrick Thomas, see no. 77, pp. 69–70. Thomas can find no trace of the libel by Vavasour Powell (see no. 158) to which the poem alludes, but points out that Powell was a colleague of James Philips, Orinda's parliamentarian husband, as a Commissioner for the 'Act for the better Propagation and Preaching of the Gospel in Wales'.

334 Text: Thomas Shipman, *Carolina: or, Loyal Poems*, 1683, p. 31; Scholars' Facsimiles & Reprints, Delmar NY 1980.

335 Text: ed. Seán Ó Tuama and Thomas Kinsella, *An Duanaire*, 1981, see no. 23, p. 195.

336 Text: Edmund Waller, *To the King, upon his Majesties Happy Return*, 1660. Pamphlet in Bodleian Library, Oxford: Gough London 2 (8). Edition: ed. G. Thorn Drury, see no. 32, ii. 35–9.

337 Text: Rachel Jevon, *Exultationis Carmen to the Kings most excellent majesty upon his most Desired Return. By Rachel Jevon, Presented with her own Hand, Aug. 16th.*, 1660. Pamphlet in Bodleian Library, Oxford: Gough London 2 (6). The pamphlet also contains a highly accomplished Latin version of the same poem, also the work of Rachel Jevon.

338 Text: ed. W. J. Gruffydd, *Y flodeugerdd gymraeg*, Cardiff, 1946, p. 97; reproducing text from *Eos Ceiriog*, 1823.

339 Text: John Ogilby, *The Relation of His Majesties Entertainment Passing through the City of London, To His Coronation: with a description of the Triumphal Arches, And Solemnity*, 1661, pp. 7–8. Pamphlet in Bodleian Library, Oxford: Gough London 2 (2).

340 Text: Rev. Donald McNicol, Colin Campbell Collection, Edinburgh University Library, MS C, p. 44; ed. Rev. James Maclagan, see no. 216, p. 106. [Orally composed in 1660.] Editions: Patrick Turner, see no. 323, p. 56; Rev. A. MacLean Sinclair, see. no. 322, p. 25; this edition: ed. Annie MacKenzie, see no. 321, p. 76. Translation revised Meg Bateman. The language of this poem is Scottish Gaelic, using a strophic metre. Each verse consists of three phrases united by end-rhyme, with a half-phrase whose final rhyme unites the whole poem.

341 Text: Katherine Philips, *Poems*, 1667, see no. 77, pp. 3–5. Edition: ed. Patrick Thomas, see no. 77, pp. 71–3.

342 Text: George Wither, *Speculum Speculatium: or, a considering-glass; being an inspection into the present and late sad Condition of these nations*, 1660, pp. 15–17. Against l. 15, of the copy used here is drawn a pointing hand; in the margin against ll. 99–100 is written 'meant by take[ing] of the kings head'. This copy, with *adversaria* in a contemporary hand, is in the possession of Dr Nigel Smith, Oxford. This poem is not given in ed. Frank Sidgwick, *The Poetry of George Wither*, 1902.

APPENDIX 1
INDEX OF CLASSICAL AND BIBLICAL NAMES

Abigail Old Testament. Devoted wife of Nabal who saved him from King David, who admired her courage and beauty, and later married her himself (1 Samuel 25: 39). (127)

Absalom Old Testament. David's beloved son Absalom rebelled against him. He had remarkably long, thick hair, and died when his hair became entangled in the branches of an oak as he rode, and his mule went out from under him, leaving him hanging helplessly. Joab, a lieutenant of King David, then killed him with three spears (2 Samuel 18). (287)

Achilles Greek myth. The greatest of the warriors on the Greek side at the Trojan War, he was the son of Peleus and Thetis (qv). Thetis attempted to make him invulnerable by plunging him in the Styx (qv), a river of the Underworld, but his heel, which she was holding, escaped contact with the water, and so became his vulnerable spot. He was eventually wounded in the heel by Paris, and died of it. (287)

Acteon Greek myth. Actaeon was a young huntsman who spied on the goddess Diana bathing, was turned into a stag, and so pursued and killed by his own hounds (see Ichnobates and Melampus). (224)

Adam Old Testament. The first man, father of all mankind, created by God to live in innocence in the garden of Eden; expelled with his wife Eve after disobeying God: tempted herself by the Serpent, Eve persuaded Adam to eat the fruit of the Tree of the Knowledge of Good and Evil (trad. an apple), they become ashamed of their nakedness and covered themselves with fig leaves (the 'Breeches Bible' translates this as making themselves breeches of fig leaves); after this Fall, Adam is forced to work the land to survive, and his wife is punished with the pains of childbirth (Genesis). (146, 306, 310)

Aegyptian Queene see Cleopatra

Aeneas The hero of Virgil's *Aeneid.* He was a Trojan prince, the son of Venus and Anchises. When Troy was destroyed, he managed to save his father, his son Ascanius, and his household gods, though he lost his wife Creusa as they left the city. Leaving Troy with a fleet of ships, he was kindly received by Dido, Queen of Carthage, who fell in love with him. After extensive adventures, he reached Italy, and established himself, after a series of battles with the inhabitants, on the banks of the Tiber. He is thus the founder of the Roman people. Virgil often attaches the epithet *pius*, 'faithful', to him. (203)

Aeolian Hunter see Orion

Aeolian Maid The ancient Greek poetess, Sappho of Lesbos, flourishing in the fifth century BC (Lesbos is one of the Aeolian isles, named for Aeolus, god of the winds). (256)

Aeolian Tugge/ Aeolian Breath The blast of winter winds. (222)

Aeolus Classical: god who was guardian of winds and storms. Has an important role in the *Aeneid*, Book 1. (213, 337)

Aetna Mount Etna: Sicilian volcano whose eruptions were said to be the anger of the giant Briaraeus, buried beneath. Etna is high enough to be snowy, and the close juxtaposition of (volcanic) fire and snow struck the Latin poet Claudian, whose passage on Etna is imitated by seventeenth-century writers. (*De raptu Proserpinae*, I. 165–70). (287, 296)

Ahaz Old Testament. King of Judah whose idolatry and desecration of holy altars caused God to bring low his kingdom (2 Kings; 2 Chronicles). His sundial was used by the prophet Isaiah to show a miracle to his heir (2 Kings 20: 11). (130)

Ajax Classical. One of the bravest Greek warriors at Troy, famed for his violence and short temper. He was later visited by madness, and murdered his family; there is a famous play on this theme by Sophocles. (311)

Albanact Like Brutus (qv), part of the mythical history of Britain: the founder of Scotland. He was the third son of Brutus. See Geoffrey of Monmouth, *Historia Regum Britanniae*, part 2. (215)

Albion Personification of Britain. It has a widely accepted false etymology from Latin *albus*, 'white', thought to describe the chalk cliffs of the south coast of England where the Romans first landed. Actually, the island was known as *Albion* (which is a name in Greek form) at least two centuries earlier, and the name is based on the Celtic word *albiu*, which appears to mean 'the earth' or 'the land'. (62, 121, 287, 337)

Alcaeus A famous Greek lyric poet, native of Lesbos; contemporary and suitor of Sappho (fifth century BC). (256)

Alcides see Hercules (213, 245)

Alecto see Erynnis

Alexander Greek historical character. Alexander the Great was born in 355 BC, heir to Macedonia. He was the pupil of Aristotle and the military genius of his era. His conquests stretched through Egypt, Persia, Syria, and India. He died in Babylon, aged 32, allegedly sighing for more worlds to conquer. (268, 335, 336)

Alexis/Alexus Generic pastoral name, derived from Virgil's second *Eclogue*. (69, 109)

Alpheus Classical. The god of this river (modern Greek Alpheo) fell in love with the nymph Arethusa, a follower of Diana. He pursued her till she was changed into a fountain, which can be found near Syracuse on Sicily. Since then their waters are said to mingle under the sea. (62)

Althea Invented name, from the Greek for 'truth'. (290)

Amarillis Classical. The original Amaryllis is a rural character in Virgil's *Eclogues* 1, 2, and 8; from whence this becomes a typical name for a pastoral heroine. (235)

Amber Often (as in no. 215) for ambergris, a waxy, natural product found in lumps on the seashore, and a very important ingredient in perfumery. It is a by-product of sperm-whales' digestions.

Ambrosia Classical. The food of the gods in Olympus, sweeter than honey, which preserved their immortality. (170)

Amintas see Amyntas

Amphialus Pseudo-classical. Son of the wicked Cecropia, in Sir Philip Sidney's poem *Arcadia*: Cecropia carried off the lovers Pyrocles, Philoclea, and Philoclea's sister Pamela, and made assiduous attempts to persuade one or other sister to marry Amphialus. (39)

Amyntas Classical. A shepherd in Virgil's second *Eclogue*. (213)

APPENDIX 1

Anacreon A celebrated Greek lyric poet, equally famed for drunken debauchery. (111, 256, 331)

Angel In the Bible and Christian tradition, God's messengers to mankind and guardians of souls (*anggelos* is the Greek word for a messenger). In heaven, the many different ranks of angels sing eternal praises to God: the seven principal orders are angels, archangels, cherubim, seraphim, thrones, dominions, and powers. In Revelation (qv) angels take an active part in the events of the Apocalypse and its interpretation to St John. (29, 45, 81, 93, 107, 137, 138, 139, 140, 141, 149, 153, 164, 287, 290, 337)

Angell In no. 170, the angel with the flaming sword is the one that drove Adam and Eve out of Paradise and barred the way back, often identified with the Archangel Michael (qv) (Genesis 3: 24). (148)

Anti-Christ The Book of Revelation prophesies the end of the world in an Apocalypse when the Anti-Christ arises to do battle with the Risen Christ for the souls of mankind. Thought originally to be an allegory of the Emperor Nero, a notorious persecutor of the early Christians (see Nero, Revelation, Whore of Babylon). (229, 240)

Antinetta The poet's invention. (74)

Antipodes A Greek word, meaning 'reverse-footed'. Some writers use it to mean inhabitants of a southern continent (who are, from a position north of the Equator, walking upside-down), but more naïve authors of the Middle Ages and Renaissance, following Servius's commentary on Virgil's *Georgics*, I. 235, thought Virgil was speaking of people who actually stood on their heads. (214)

Apollo Greek god of music, prophecy, and the sun (also called Phoebus). Son of Jove and Latona; twin brother of Diana. They were born on Delos, so 'Delian' is one of his epithets. His priestess at Delphi gave important oracles (qv). The Muses (qv) living on Parnassus nearby were his agents in inspiring the different arts. His amorous pursuit of the nymph Daphne resulted in her being turned into a laurel tree to escape his attentions: the laurel (bay) remains sacred to him, the Muses, poets, and poetry under his patronage. (60, 105, 149, 150, 185, 195, 203, 207, 213, 223)

Apollo's Bouncing Girl A Muse (qv). (214)

Appelles Properly Apelles: a famous painter of the time of Alexander the Great, noted for an ability to imitate nature so perfectly that even animals could be fooled by it. (223)

Arabia The Yemen area, in the extreme south of Arabia, known to the Romans as *Arabia Felix*, 'Fortunate Arabia'. It was the Romans' main source of spices and perfumes such as myrrh and frankincense. This is why the Phoenix (qv), which built its funeral pyre of precious spices, is associated with Arabia. (76, 178, 207)

Arabian Bird see Phoenix

Araphil Invented pastoral name, 'lover of the altar'. (186)

Ararat Old Testament. Mountain in Armenia where Noah's ark came safely to rest after the Flood, guided there by the dove who brought back an olive branch from the first dry land (Genesis 8). (243)

Arcadia An ancient Greek kingdom, mountainous and richly wooded; the home of the god Pan and shepherds with the gift of poetry. The name is used for any idyllic country retreat where poets could commune with nature and find inspiration. Also the title of Sir Philip Sidney's influential prose romance, published in 1590.

Archimedes Greek historical character (287–212 BC), a mathematician and theoretical engineer. Among his discoveries was the principle of leverage, on which he observed 'give me a place to stand, and I will move the earth'. (336)

Argus Classical. The hundred-eyed guardian of Io (qv). When he was killed by Mercury, Juno set his eyes in her peacocks' tails. (271)

Arion Greek myth. A poet and musician of Lesbos, who became wealthy. Travelling home from Italy, he was thrown overboard by the sailors, who wanted his money, but allowed him to sing a song as his last request. A dolphin, which had been charmed by his voice, rescued him, and carried him to land. (341)

Ark/Arke Old Testament (1). The boat built by Noah on God's orders so that he and his virtuous family and pairs of all living things could escape the Flood sent to wipe out evil on earth (Genesis 6–8). (120) (2) The Ark of the Covenant: the holy object of the Israelite nation, which contained the Scriptures. David danced before it 'with all his might' (2 Samuel 6: 14). (126)

Assumption Christian. Of the Virgin Mary, mother of Jesus: the belief that instead of dying she was taken body and soul to heaven to be crowned its Queen. Taught by the Church from the fifth century, although not formally adopted as Catholic doctrine until 1950. (140)

Astraea Ovid, *Metamorphoses*, I. 150 *et seq*. The goddess of Justice who left the earth after the Golden Age (qv; a classical Greek and Latin concept equivalent to the Christian idea of the Garden of Eden). Until she returns, she resides in the heavens as the constellation Virgo. (213, 337)

Arthur Legendary King of Britain. If he had any historical existence, which is doubtful, he flourished in the fifth century. His story is developed by a twelfth-century Norman writer, Geoffrey of Monmouth, in his *Historia Regum Britanniae*. According to Geoffrey, Arthur was the illegitimate son of Utherpendragon and Ygerna, chosen King of Britain at the age of 15. He was an almost invincible military commander, successful in fighting off the Saxons, and all the rulers of Britain submitted to him. He was mortally wounded by his son Mordred and carried off to the Isle of Avalon, from whence he will return some day. As his story was developed in the Middle Ages, he acquired a Round Table, and a group of noble knights, whose principal task was a search for the Holy Grail. (215, 228)

Athanasius Byzantine historical character (AD 296–373). He was bishop of Alexandria in the reign of Constantine, and steadfastly opposed the Arian heresy, which denies the equal status of God the Father and God the Son, and was repeatedly driven into exile and hiding on this account. The statement of orthodox Christian belief known as the Athanasian Creed is associated with him. (341)

Atlas Classical. The Titan who carried the heavens on his shoulders. One of the labours of Hercules (qv) was to take a turn at this and give Atlas a break. (215)

Aufid Classical. A river in Apulia in Southern Italy, noted for the swiftness and violence of its current. (256)

Augustus Roman historical character. The name taken by Octavius Caesar on becoming first Emperor of Rome in 32 BC after the death of Mark Antony. (205)

Aurora Roman goddess of the dawn. One of the more promiscuous goddesses, though not lost to shame: she frequently blushes at the memory of her indiscretions. Her lovers included the god Mars, and the mortals Orion (qv), Cephalus (qv), Clitus, Astraeus, and Tithonus (qv). (113, 171, 207, 213, 224)

Baasha's Head see Jacobs Stemme

Babel for Babylon. (342)

Babell Towre Old Testament. The arrogant attempt by Nimrod to build a tower as high as heaven at Babel is frustrated by God, who causes the builders to start speaking different languages and abandon the work in confusion (Genesis 11). (253)

Babels Whore/Babylon see Whore of Babylon

Bacchus Latin myth. He was the god of wine and drinkers. Worshipped in ecstatic celebrations (his followers are called bacchantes, or maenads), and often shown crowned with grapes. He was a son of Jove by Semele (qv), and called Dionysus by the Greeks. Liber is another of his names. (111, 178, 188, 203, 213, 218, 222, 288, 296)

Baccus see Bacchus

Basiliskes Classical. Fabulous monsters, half-serpent, half-cockerel, so ugly their stare could kill. (93)

Bayes Classical. Laurel wreaths worn in honour of victory, particularly in an artistic competition, or artistic tribute to Apollo. (39, 49, 111, 123, 150, 178, 208, 227, 268, 313)

Beast of Revelation: see Whore of Babylon

Belisarius Character from Roman history. A great military commander during the reign of the Byzantine Emperor Justinian (AD 527–65); legend has it that he was accused of conspiracy and treason, his eyes were put out, and he was imprisoned for a year. He thus becomes an example of a man who seems to be Fortune's favourite, but ends his life in tragic misfortune.

Bellona Roman goddess of war, close kin or wife of Mars. (169, 203, 213, 215, 249)

Bel-Zebub Biblical. One of the principal demons, his name means 'Lord of Flies'. He is named as prince, or chief, of the devils in the Gospels (Matthew 12: 24, Mark 3: 22, Luke 11: 15). (287)

Bethanen Old Testament. Modern Ainitha (Hebrew *Beth-annath*, 'house of Anat'), identified with Anaitis or Anahit, the Persian mother-goddess. Site of a pagan temple where idolatry and temple prostitution were an abomination to the Israelites. (269)

Bethel Old Testament (Hebrew *Beth-el*, 'house of God'). The chief sanctuary of the Israelite tribes, where solemn sacrifices were made to Jehovah. Cavalier metaphor for the King, on the grounds that he was divinely appointed and anointed, like the stone set up there. (269)

Betis Baetis: the Latin name for a river in Southern Spain, now the Guadalquivir. (206)

Bird of Paradise see Phoenix (170)

Bootes The Greek for 'ploughman', or 'wagoner': the name of a constellation situated at the tail of the group known as the Plough (or the Great Bear), containing the bright star Arcturus. (207)

Boreas The North Wind. (269, 283)

Briarius Classical giant with 50 heads and 100 hands. He was imprisoned under Etna for waging war against the gods. (271, 287)

Brontes Greek myth. He was one of the three one-eyed Cyclops who were among the original children of Mother Earth, and like his brothers, a master smith. The name means 'thunder'. Pyracmon is presumably intended to be a similar personage: the name means 'point of flame'. (287)

Brute Brutus, son of Silvius, was a legendary ancestor of the Britons, invented, as far as anyone knows, by the twelfth-century Geoffrey of Monmouth (*History of the Kings of Britain*, parts 1 and 2). When the English, as an imperial power, began to feel the need to graft themselves onto the stock of Roman history, they enthusiastically adopted Geoffrey's story, which is recycled in Book 2, Canto 10 of Spenser's *Faerie Queene*. Brutus was imagined as a great-grandson of Aeneas who, after various adventures, is told by a goddess that he will found a second Troy in an island in the West, and does so, becoming the founder of London, which he calls Trinovantum, 'New Troy'. (215)

Caean Of the island Ceos, one of the Cyclades; with reference to the Greek poet Simonides, who was born there. (256)

Caesar (1) Caesar was the name used by the second-in-command of the later Roman emperors, and thereafter by other rulers (both the Russian *czar* and the German *kaiser* are derived from this name). The name is used as an epithet for any general, ruler, or occasionally tyrant. (288, 313, 337, 341) (2) In particular, Julius Caesar, the conqueror of Britain. (215, 335)

Calais see Horace (11).

Calvarie New Testament, Calvary: the hill where Christ was crucified. (148)

Calves at Bethel In 1 Kings 12: 28, King Jeroboam made two calves of gold as substitute gods for the Israelites, and set one of them up at Bethel ('God's House') and the other at Dan. (149)

Cantacles Canticles: Old Testament book also known as the Song of Solomon or Song of Songs.

Capitol One of the seven hills of Rome; the temple of Jove was there, where the most important sacrifices were made and where all triumphal processions culminated.

Carthage Long-standing rival of Rome (the capital is on the site of modern Tunis); see Hannibal. (203)

Castalia see Muses

Castara A name of the poet's invention, based on Latin *casta*, 'chaste'. (27, 28, 186)

Cataline/Catiline The Catiline of Ben Jonson's tragedy: a Roman noble who, first wasting his inheritance with debauched living, conspired to overthrow the government of Rome in 63 BC. (233, 287)

Cato A respected Roman censor, famed for his piety, temperance, and outspoken honesty. In youth he fought against Hannibal, later was outspoken against the decadence and luxury of the Empire; author of *De re rustica*, a widely read book on gardening, including advice on growing figs. (203, 293)

Catullus Roman lyric poet (84–54 BC), famous for his stormy affair with an upper-class lady he refers to by the name of Lesbia. (178)

Caucasus A mountain-range, running across the neck of land between the Caspian and the Black Seas. Prometheus (qv) was chained to a rock in the Caucasus with a vulture pecking at his liver, until Hercules (qv) pleaded with Jove to release him. (213)

Cebele see Cybele

Ced Ceadda, or Chad, was the first bishop of Lichfield, and died in 672. His brother, also a saint, was Cedda, later Ced, and Cowley seems to have confused the two names. Both brothers were renowned for holy simplicity, and canonized shortly after death. Chad is the patron of Lichfield. (287)

Celia Abbreviation of Cecilia, popularized by Shakespeare in *As You Like It* and Jonson in *Volpone*. (18, 212)

Centaure Classical monsters, half-man, half-horse. Most famous for their great battle with Hercules, resulting from a drunken orgy when they attacked the Lapith women under the hero's protection (this battle is represented on one of the friezes on the Parthenon). (213)

Cephalus Classical. Loving and loyal husband of Procris. He preferred his wife to the goddess Aurora (qv), who abducted but failed to seduce him. (224)

Cerberus Classical. The formidable three-headed dog who guarded the entrance to the Underworld. Hercules (qv) successfully subdued and bound him, and dragged him to Mycenae as one of his labours. (245)

Ceres Classical. Goddess of corn, harvest, and bread; mother of Proserpine (qv). (58, 207, 213, 222, 223, 296)

Ceres Gold Corn. (223)

Cesar see Caesar

Ceybele see Cybele

Chanaan Old Testament. Canaan: the promised land of the Israelites. (229)

Chaos The formless void before the creation of earth, in both Christian and classical usage. (2, 302)

Charlemain The name Charlemagne (*Carolus magnus*: 'the great Charles') is normally given to the Charles (742–814) who was King of the Franks and Emperor of the West. In retrospect, he was seen as an outstanding monarch, and he and his paladins became legendary heroes, particularly in medieval French literature. The name was adopted for other kings called Charles. (337)

Charles his Wain Charles's Wain (Wagon) is an English name for the constellation also called the Plough, or the Great Bear, which contains the Pole Star. (243, 269, 291, 337)

Cherubs/Cherubin Christian. An order of angels (qv). (101, 139, 147, 156)

Children (of Israel) The Jewish people as described in the Old Testament: by extension, the persecuted faithful. (299)

Chiron Classical. A centaur (qv), famed for his learning in music and medicine; tutor to Achilles, among others, and killed in the battle between the Lapiths and Centaurs. He was made immortal as the constellation Sagittarius. (213)

Chloe Originally a title of Ceres (qv) (the Greek word *chloe* means 'verdant', or 'the first young shoots of Spring'), and as such a suitable name for a very young heroine. See also Horace. (11, 44)

Chloris Another name for Flora (qv), from a Greek word meaning 'green', and a typical choice of name for a pastoral heroine. (44, 69, 91, 254, 330)

Cicero Marcus Tullius Cicero, a Latin orator, 106–43 BC, whose writings represent the classical standard of Latin prose. He was consul at the time of Catiline (qv), and wrote a famous series of speeches against him, warning Rome of the danger he represented. Later, he was put to death by the future emperor Augustus. He thus stands for responsible Republicanism. (287)

Cimeris The country of the Cimmerii, who were imagined to prefer living in the depressing gloom of dark caves to life in daylight and sunshine. (213, 292)

Cimmerian see above

Clarastella The poet's invention, from the Latin *clara,* 'clear', and *stella,* 'star'. (58)

Cleopatra Queen of Egypt most famous for her love affairs and last marriage to Mark Antony (qv), which led to war with Rome. After their defeat at the Battle of Actium, both committed suicide. A legendary beauty, she represents the classic *femme fatale.* (32, 53, 173)

Cloris see Chloris (44, 91)

Corinna (1) A celebrated poetess and rival of Pindar, as talented as beautiful. (2) The mistress of the poet Ovid. On both these counts, an ideal alias for a poet's romantic addressee. (171)

Corydon Standard name for a fictional shepherd in the pastoral works of Virgil, Theocritus and their Cavalier followers. In Virgil's second *Eclogue*, he is crossed in love. (213)

Craesus Greek myth. Croesus, King of Lydia in the sixth century BC was fabled to be the richest man in the world. (111).

Creusa Trojan princess, first wife of Aeneas. At the fall of Troy they were separated in the confusion and he sought her desperately until her ghost appeared to him and explained her fate (*Aeneid*, Book 2). (203)

Cupid God of love; son of Venus and Mars (qv). Most often seen as a mischievous winged boy shooting arrows to enflame his victims with passion ('Cupid's darts'). He is often blindfold, or depicted sightless to illustrate the blindness of passion. (4, 12, 20, 34, 45, 49, 52, 53, 76, 82, 180, 190, 203, 205, 213, 224, 300, 311, 329)

Cybele The Great Mother; a goddess of Asiatic origin, adopted into the Roman pantheon. She was iconographically distinguished as a dignified, matronly figure wearing a crown decorated with turrets and battlements. She was served by eunuch priests. Sometimes identified with Ceres (qv). (169, 207, 215)

Cyclops Greek myth. Three one-eyed giants, who were among the earliest humanoid offspring of Mother Earth, called Brontes (qv), Steropes, and Arges. They were killed by Apollo, and their ghosts live in the volcano Etna (see Aetna). Their descendants, who included Polyphemus, were a wild race of giant shepherds, encountered by Odysseus in Homer's *Odyssey*. (287)

Cydonian Bow Cydonia was an ancient town on the north coast of Crete; see Teucer. (256)

Cynthia A title of the goddess Diana (qv). (3, 78, 207)

Cypress An evergreen tree sacred to Pluto (qv) and used at Roman funerals. Cyparissus was a lovely youth changed to a cyprus and greatly mourned by Apollo. (Ovid, *Metamorphoses*, X. 121–42). (92, 150, 170, 209, 332)

Cytherea/Cytherean A title of the goddess Venus (qv). (213)

Daemons Classical. It was believed that the gods set a *daemon* or *genius* to watch over every individual and give good (or bad) advice throughout life.

Danaë Princess seduced by Zeus in the form of a shower of gold, a myth which permitted much play on women's susceptibility to gifts. (91)

Daphne The daughter of Peneus. A nymph pursued by Apollo and saved from rape by being turned into a laurel tree. Remorseful, the god made the tree sacred to himself and wore a wreath of laurel leaves in her honour. (60, 185, 207).

Daulian Minstrell A nightingale; see Philomel. (236)

David Old Testament King of Israel. As a boy, slayer of the giant Goliath and later the composer of the Psalms. He made his son Solomon king after him, and the people said, 'God make the name of Solomon better than thy name, and make his throne greater than thy throne', so he was thus a great king succeeded by a still greater one (1 Kings 1: 47). (132, 337)

David's Proud Sonne see Absalom

Deiphob Greek myth. Deiphobus was a prince of Troy and husband to Helen after the death of his brother Paris. Killed by her original Greek husband Menelaus with her connivance. (256)

Delphian Oracle see Oracle

Diana Classical. Apollo's twin sister, known as Artemis to the Greeks; virgin goddess of hunting, chastity, the moon, and, rather surprisingly, childbirth. (3, 78, 195, 207, 213, 224, 312)

Diomed Greek myth. Diomedes was one of the most distinguished of the Greek warriors fighting in the Trojan War. His career was considerably extended by later writers such as Chaucer, who told the story of Troilus and Cressida: Diomed(es) was the Greek lover who supplanted Troilus in Cressida's affections. (256)

Doeg Old Testament. A servant of Saul who sacrilegiously massacred the city of priests on the king's orders (1 Samuel 22). Typifying the oppressors of true religion. (269)

Dorcas New Testament. A woman famed for her good works and almsgiving. So much mourned at her death that St Peter (qv) raised her from the dead (Acts of the Apostles 9). (127)

Dorique Doric: a dialect of Greek (with rustic overtones). (188)

Doris Greek myth. A sea goddess, mother of the Nereids (qv).

Dove (1) Classical, a bird sacred to Venus. (2) Old Testament, one which brought the olive branch back to Noah's ark (qv): a symbol of peace. (3) New Testament, in the Gospels, Christ sees the Holy Spirit descending from heaven like a dove at his baptism.

Drowsie Swain see Endymion

Druina An invented name signifying 'nymph of the oak-tree' (from Greek *drus*, 'oak'). (337)

Dryad Classical: a forest nymph. (207)

Duina For Diuma, roving bishop of Mercia, Lindsey, and the Middle Angles in the 650s. He was thus Chad's predecessor as bishop of the Mercians, though Chad is the first to be associated firmly with Lichfield, and the cathedral's official record thus starts with Chad's consecration in 664 (Bede, *Historia Ecclesiastica Gentis Anglorum*, III. 24, IV. 3). (287)

Easter Christian celebration of the Resurrection of Christ. (123)

Echo An indiscreet attendant on Juno, who punished her gossiping by removing most of her power of speech: she could only answer questions put to her. She pined away with unrequited love of the vain Narcissus; although turned to stone, her voice lingers on. (213, 235, 240)

Eden Earthly paradise; the garden God created for Adam and Eve, from which they were banished for disobedience (Genesis 3). (147)

Egyptian Queen see Cleopatra (32)

Electra Tragic heroine, daughter of Agamemnon and Clytemnestra, who assisted her brother Orestes in murdering their mother; more probably chosen by the poet because of its aesthetic significance: Greek *elektron*, 'amber'. (8).

Electra's Poet Euripides (480–406 BC), a great Athenian tragedian. *Electra* is one of his most notable plays. (259)

Elijah Old Testament. A prophet of God, flourishing in the reign of the Hebrew king Ahab. Notable events in his life include his being miraculously fed by ravens at the brook Cherith, his raising the son of a widow at Zarephath from the dead, confuting the prophets of the pagan god Baal, and being finally carried up to heaven in a chariot of fire (1 Kings 17 and following). (149)

Elisha Old Testament. Also a prophet, and a junior contemporary of Elijah (qv), who bequeathed him his mantle as a sign that he was to be his successor. He performed a number of miracles, including healing the leprosy of Naaman (qv) (2 Kings 3 and following). (149)

Elisium/Elizium/Elyzium Or the Elysian Fields: in Greek and Roman myth, it was a garden, or island, where the souls of the good and heroic were sent after death. An idyllic and restful haven, where it is forever springtime. (39, 79, 95, 115, 185, 189, 223, 312, 337).

Emathian Conqueror Alexander (Emathia is a district of Macedonia). (59)

Endymion A beautiful shepherd. He was lying asleep in a cave on Mount Lamus when Diana saw him, and became chastely infatuated by his charms. He sleeps eternally, without ever appearing a day older, and she visits him to admire his beauty. (3, 115, 192, 224)

Enoch Old Testament patriarch, prophet, and father of Methuselah. The Book of Genesis has no mention of his death, but states that he 'walked with God and he was not; for God took him' (Genesis 5: 24). (139)

Epicedium Funeral song. (295)

Epicure Follower of the Greek philosopher Epicurus, who taught that human happiness consisted in pleasure, stressing the delights of doing good. He was popularly misunderstood to be preaching the importance of sensuality. Hence, a libertine. (62)

Eridanus Classical. Mythical and poetic name for the river Po in Italy: also the name of a constellation. (181, 215, 226)

Erynnis The three Furies, Tisiphone, Megara, and Alecto: ancient goddesses who avenged the victims of primal crimes like matricide. Also known as the Eumenides (the Kindly Ones) to flatter and placate them. (205, 244, 287)

Esther Old Testament. The formidable and short-tempered Ahasuerus dismissed his wife Vashti for paying him insufficient respect, and he made his choice of a second wife from among the virgins of his kingdom, who were brought before him. Esther, a beautiful Jewish girl, was chosen (see the Book of Esther). (336)

Eumorphe The author's invention, from the Greek for 'beautiful shape'. (105)

Euridice Greek myth. Beloved wife of Orpheus the musician (qv). Dying of a snakebite, she was nearly rescued by him from Hades after his playing softened the heart of the god of the dead, and won him permission to take her back, but he turned to see if she was following him, just as they reached the world above, and she was lost to him for ever. (92, 106)

Eurus Latin. The East Wind.

Euterpe Greek. Muse (qv) of music, especially of the flute and other wind instruments. (185)

Faunus Roman myth. Legendary king of Italy. Deified as a being half-man, half-goat, giver of oracles. Fauns (generalized) are Roman equivalents of the Greek satyrs. (207, 213, 215, 224)

Favonius The West Wind of the Romans. (224)

Ferryman (in Hell) Classical. Charon rowed the dead across Styx, the river of forgetfulness which led to Hades. (139)

Festus New Testament. The judge before whom St Paul appears (Acts of the Apostles 25–6). (229)

Fidelia A pseudo-classical name meaning 'faithful'. (278)

Flora Roman goddess of flowers and gardens; wife of Zephyrus. (58, 171, 213, 221, 223).

Fortune Roman myth. Fortuna, the goddess of plenty, pleasures, and blessings but also their opposites. In classical times she bore a cornucopia; in medieval times more often seen with her turning wheel bestowing arbitrary and transient gifts on mankind. (329)

Furies see Erynnis

Galen Roman historical character. Claudius Galenus, scholar, great physician, and friend of the Emperor Marcus Aurelius, d. AD 193: author of the theory of the humours. (97).

Gathite Old Testament. Goliath, the giant champion of Gath, killed by the future Israelite king David when still a shepherd boy with a slingshot.

Genius Classical. A spirit or daemon presiding over each man's birth and life; classical version of a guardian angel. (7, 287)

Glaucus Greek myth. Friend and companion of Sarpedon at the Trojan War (qv); famous for swapping his golden armour for the iron armour of Diomedes; killed by Ajax the Greek. (282)

Gloriana Pseudo-classical epithet originally coined by Edmund Spenser in *The Faerie Queene* for Elizabeth I; subsequently transferred to Queen Henrietta Maria. (201)

Gods Great Mother see Cybele

Gog and Magog Represent the nations of the earth that are deceived by Satan (Revelation 20: 7–9). (298)

Golden Age Described in Ovid, *Metamorphoses,* I. 150 and following. The classical equivalent of the Garden of Eden, the earth before the Fall: the rule of Saturn (qv) on earth, when the gods lived in sympathy with humanity, when the earth was fruitful without cultivation, and when all humans lived in peace and amity. The idea that Astrea (qv) left the earth when the Golden Age ended, was much used by writers of the mid-seventeenth century. Apart from Ovid, the classical text most used by early-modern writers was Virgil, *Eclogue,* IV, which prophesies the coming of a divine child and the return of the age of gold. This poem has a long tradition of appropriation by Christian writers. (207, 337, 308)

Golgotha The Hebrew form of Calvary (qv). (126)

Good Friday Christian. The day of the Crucifixion and its annual observance; the most solemn day of fasting and penance in the Christian calender. (136)

Gordian Knot Classical myth. Gordius was a peasant who became King of Phrygia when an oracle advised the people to crown the first man they met approaching the temple of Jove in a wagon. Gordius was the lucky man, and subsequently dedicated the wagon to Jove. The knot which fastened the yoke to the pole was unfathomably intricate, and there was a story that whoever untied it would become Emperor of Asia. Many tried and failed, but Alexander (qv) simply cut the knot in half with his sword (and proceeded to conquer Asia). (336)

Gorgon (like) Greek myth. The Gorgons were three monstrous sisters with snakes for hair and scaly bodies. All who looked at them were turned to stone. (93)

Gosple The four Gospels in the New Testament: the authors are Saints Matthew, Mark, Luke, and John. (276)

Graces Greek myth. The three daughters of Jove and Eurynome, attendants upon Venus; young, beautiful, and scantily draped, if not nude. They are always pictured elegantly posed and holding hands; sometimes their feet are winged. (264)

Gyges Ring Greek myth. A brass ring that made the wearer invisible, by which means Gyges killed the King of Lydia, then married its queen and usurped the crown. (10)

Halcyon Greek myth. A woman who drowned herself with grief at her husband's death in a shipwreck; they were both turned to kingfishers, who supposedly bring calm seas and fine weather when they nest. (57, 205)

Hannah Old Testament. Mother of the prophet Samuel; a patient and God-fearing matriarch (1 Samuel). (127)

Hannibal Character from Roman history. Carthaginian general who fought against Rome, most famous for crossing the Alps to Italy with an army of elephants. (313)

Hector Greek myth. Oldest son of King Priam and captain of the Trojan army; treacherously slain by Achilles and dragged around the besieged city at his horse's heels. (111, 256, 279, 287)

Helen Greek myth. Spartan queen, daughter of Leda (qv) and Jove, whose abduction by Trojan prince Paris led to the ten-year siege of Troy by the massed Greek armies determined to win her back. Her semi-divine beauty was thought by some to be a worthwhile cause for war; her morals were more debatable. (32, 256)

Helicon A mountain in Boeotia sacred to the Muses (qv), the source of the Hippocrene spring (qv). (215, 245)

Hellen see Helen

Hercules Greek myth. One of the many sons of Jove, by a mortal woman, Alcmene (after whom he is also called Alcides, 'son of Alcmene'). He was uniquely strong, and carried a club. He was driven mad by Juno, and murdered children in a fit of insanity. He undertook his twelve labours (which ridded the world of a number of dangerous pests) in expiation of this involuntary crime, and was thus a benefactor to mankind. (213, 245, 272)

Hermes Greek; the messenger of the gods, and also entrusted with conducting souls down to the Underworld. He is associated with trickery and thieving. The Romans identified him with their god Mercury. He carried a herald's staff (*caduceus*), wreathed with two serpents (qv). (34, 213)

Hero Greek myth. A priestess of Venus and secret lover of Leander, who nightly swam the Hellespont to visit her. Drowned herself with grief when he sank *en route* one stormy night. (115)

Herod New Testament. Jewish king under Roman rule at the time of the birth of Christ. Ordered the massacre of the Innocents when he learned of the birth of a greater king than himself from the three Magi. (244)

Hesper Classical. Hesperus, the father of the Hesperides (see next); also the name given to the planet Venus seen in the glow of sunset. Lucifer is the name given to the same planet seen just before dawn. (287, 296)

Hesperian Garden Where the nymphs, the Hesperides, were entrusted to guard the golden apples which were Juno's wedding gift to Jove. Also guarded by a dragon which never slept, the garden was idyllically fruitful and safe from all intruders but Hercules, one of whose labours was to steal the apples. (203)

Hester see Esther

Hilas see Hylas

Hills on Hills Greek myth. The Titans heaped the mountain Ossa on top of the mountain Pelion in order to scale the heights of heaven during their unsuccessful revolt against the Olympian gods. (287)

Hippocrene Greek. A spring on Mount Helicon (qv), sacred to the Muses (qv). It first arose when the ground was struck by the winged horse Pegasus with his hoof (the name means 'Horse-Spring'). (213)

Homer The blind Greek poet, author of the *Iliad* and *Odyssey*, possibly flourishing in the eighth century BC. His legend is that he lived an obscure and poverty-stricken life, and hence his birth went unnoticed (he died on Ios, of vexation at his inability to solve a riddle posed by some fisher-boys), but, in later years, seven Greek cities all asserted that he had been born a citizen of theirs. (178, 212, 215, 256)

Horace Roman poet. His work was admired on his arrival in Rome by Virgil, who recommended him to Augustus for patronage. More self-indulgent than ambitious, his *Odes* reflect his elegance, good humour, and Epicureanism (qv). Lydia and Chloe are names by which he refers to two of his ex-mistresses, *Odes*, III. 9. Ilia and Calais the son of Ornytes are mentioned in the same poem. (11, 59)

Hours Latin *Horae*; the three nurses of Venus and constant companions of the Graces (qv). They are goddesses of eternal springtime, patronesses of fine weather and fecundity. (264)

Hydra Greek myth. Many-headed monster, associated with Lerna, near the city of Argos: when one head was chopped off, several more grew in its place. It was killed by Hercules as one of his labours, who took its deadly blood as poison for his arrows. (339)

Hyems The personification of winter as a gnarled and frost-bitten old man (Latin *hiems*, 'winter'). (222)

Hylas A beautiful young prince, kidnapped by the infatuated Hercules and taken on board the *Argo* on the quest for the Golden Fleece. He drowned accidentally *en route* (or was abducted by envious water-nymphs). His name is often used in elegies for drowned friends. (209)

Hymen/Hymenaeus God of marriage. 'Io, Hymenaeus' is a ritual cry which was used by participants in a Roman marriage-procession, while a bride was being brought to her new home. (15, 169, 207, 213)

Hymettus A mountain in Greece, famous for its honey and its marble. (207)

Iason For Aeson, the father of Jason. According to one version of the myth, Jason's mistress the sorceress Medea drained the blood from Aeson's decrepit body, substituting a magic elixir, and restored him to youthful vigour. (283)

Ichnobates Classical. The name of one of Actaeon's hounds (Ovid, *Metamorphoses,* III. 207). (213)

Idean Opis Opis was one of Diana's nymphs, a mountain-spirit dwelling on Mount Ida, near Troy (from *Aeneid* XI. 836). (207)

Ilia see Horace. (11)

Io Greek myth. A priestess of Juno but much desired by Jove, who turned her into a heifer to disguise his intentions. Not fooled, Juno vengefully had her guarded by Argus (qv) and later chased through Europe by a vicious stinging insect. The Bosporus ('cattle-crossing') is supposed to be her passage over into Asia. She found refuge in Egypt, where she may have been worshipped as Isis, who is sometimes represented as horned like a cow.

Ixion Greek myth. A treacherous and ungrateful king who attempted to seduce Juno: Jove, who was not deceived, shaped a cloud into a false Juno, then surprised him in the act of adultery with this substitute. He was finally punished by being tied for ever to a fiery wheel in Hades (8)

Jacobs Stemme Old Testament. The line of Jacob (the Patriarch) and Jesse (father of King David) was the line of the Kings of Israel. Under the leadership of Jeroboam, Northern Israel revolted against Rehoboam of the house of Jesse, and became a separate monarchy with a new royal family. Then Baasha, King of Israel, deposed his predecessor, a son of

Jeroboam, and murdered all remaining members of Jeroboam's line. Zimri (qv) then murdered all the family of Baasha. This is therefore a tale of events going from bad to worse after an initial revolt against legitimate monarchy (1 Kings 12 and 15-16). (287)

Jael Old Testament. Her heroic murder of an enemy of the Israelites has made Jael a famous example of resourcefulness and cunning in a good cause. When the Canaanite Sisera sought refuge in her tent, she soothed him with a glass of milk till he slept, then calmly rammed a tent-peg through his head. This fulfilled a saying of the prophet Deborah (Judges 4). (127)

Jerico Old Testament. The city of Jericho was besieged by the Israelites under Joshua. The Israelite priests processed round the city blowing trumpets, and the walls fell of their own accord (Joshua 6). (336)

Joab Old Testament. Slayer of Absalom (qv), son of King David (2 Samuel 18: 14). (287)

Job Old Testament. His patience, despite great sufferings, is proverbial; knowing himself to be innocent and God-fearing, he rejects the opinion that his miseries are a divine punishment and remains faithful to God, although his prayers to be relieved are not answered (Book of Job). (244)

Jonah Old Testament. The prophet, who survived being thrown overboard by sailors anxious to placate a pagan sea-god in a storm (which he slept through: Jonah 1:5), was swallowed by a great fish and eventually cast up from its belly to preach in Nineveh. (139, 287)

Jordan River running through Israel, from Galilee to the Dead Sea. The Hebrews crossed it to reach their Promised Land. Christ was baptized in its waters. It symbolizes purity and the goal of spiritual blessedness. (165)

Jove Classical. King and father of the Olympian gods (the Zeus of the Greeks). He defeated and superseded his father Cronus (Greek) or Saturn (Roman), won the whole world, and shared it with his brothers, giving the sea to Neptune and the Underworld to Pluto. The oak and eagle were sacred to him and he is often depicted with thunderbolts in hand poised to express his wrath by sending storms upon mankind. (46, 53, 91, 181, 205, 207, 213, 214, 215, 222)

Jubily Jubile (modern jubilee); the original Old Testament use defines a solemn celebration every fiftieth year, marked by the blowing of trumpets and the proclamation of liberty throughout all the land (Leviticus 25: 8 *et seq.*). (101)

Judah One of the twelve Tribes of Israel, named after one of the sons of Jacob; after the reign of King Solomon, Judah (with Benjamin) became a separate kingdom. Lion of Judah is a title of the royal house of David. (170, 341)

Judah's Court The court of King Solomon. (341)

Judas New Testament. Judas Iscariot; disciple of Jesus and the one who betrayed him to the Jewish priests. He hanged himself in remorse. (327)

Juno The Latin name for the queen of the Olympian gods, sister and wife of Jove; goddess of power, empire, riches, marriage, and childbirth. She was particularly jealous of Jove's many affairs and children by mortal women, persecuted them severely when she could, and is particularly the patroness of respectable wives and matrons. Notable attributes include her peacock-drawn chariot and her attendant Iris, the Rainbow. (8, 53, 98, 207, 213)

Jupiter Another name for Jove. (213)

King of Egypt Old Testament. The Pharaoh who was persuaded by a series of plagues to let Moses take the Hebrew slaves out of Egypt to the Promised Land. (322)

Knute Cnut the Great, otherwise Canute, King of both England and Denmark in the eleventh century (1016–35). Perhaps surprisingly for a Viking ruler who maintained two wives simultaneously, one in England and one in Denmark, he was noted as a lawgiver and a Christian monarch, as well as for his military prowess. (215)

Lambe Christian. Jesus Christ as the Lamb of God, the perfect Sacrifice (an image which derives in part from the Book of Revelation 14–19). (141)

Laurel see Bayes

Leander see Hero (115)

Leda Seduced by Jove in the shape of a swan, the eggs she laid hatched into two sets of twins: Castor and Pollux, divine sons, and Clytemnestra and Helen (later, of Troy), mortal daughters. (222)

Ledaean Stars The constellation of the Heavenly Twins, Castor and Pollux. (150)

Leper Like either Naaman of the Old Testament (qv) or a leper cured by Christ (Luke 5: 12–14). (165)

Lesbian Lute The Greek island of Lesbos was famed for its poets and musicians, who included Sappho (qv) and Alcaeus (qv). (185)

Lethe Classical. One of the rivers of the Underworld: drinking its waters brought complete forgetfulness of the newly dead soul's life on earth. (178, 223)

Leviathan A monstrous animal of the Old Testament, also used as a name for the Devil. Appropriately mentioned in a poem about fishing: God inquires of Job, 'Canst thou draw out leviathan with an hook?' (Job 41: 1). (225) An apocalyptic dragon, to be slain at the last day (Isaiah 27: 1). (139)

Liber Pater 'Father Liber', a title of Bacchus (qv). (213)

Lollio Marcus Lollius, a Roman consul of the Augustan era. Horace addressed two Epistles to him. (256)

Love see Cupid (12, 20, 45, 76, 99, 169, 300, 311)

Lucan Talented Roman poet (AD 39–65), first patronized, then persecuted by Nero (for having beaten him in a poetry contest). His chief work is the *Pharsalia*, a heroic poem on the civil war between Julius Caesar and Pompey. Joined a conspiracy to dethrone the emperor and committed suicide on its discovery, aged only 26. (180)

Lucifer Biblical. He was created an angel, but fell to hell because of his pride; identified as the Devil, Satan, and the serpent in the Garden of Eden (Old Testament, Genesis; New Testament, the Gospels, Revelation). (287)

Lucina Roman goddess, daughter of Jove and Juno (or Latona); patroness of childbirth and women in labour. Alternatively, a title for Diana (qv), as in no. 213.

Lycian People of Lycia, a country on the south coast of Asia Minor. Sarpedon led the Lycian contingent to Troy. (282)

Lydia see Horace

Macedonian see Alexander

Magdalene see Mary Magdalene (165)

Magellanick Fishes Fishes from the Pacific Ocean. Magellan was one of the early mariners in this region, and the Straits of Magellan are near the extreme tip of South America, linking the Pacific and Atlantic oceans. (287)

Maia Mother of Mercury by Jove; as one of the Pleiades (stars), the brightest of the Seven Sisters. (213)

Maria Christian. Latin form of Hebrew Miriam: (the Virgin) Mary: see Mary, Assumption

Marius see Sulla

Mark (Saint) Christian. Author of the Gospel bearing his name; his emblem is a lion. (152)

Marke Antonye Roman history. Marcus Antonius, the friend of Julius Caesar, spoke his funeral oration after his assassination; with Octavius Caesar (Augustus, qv) and Lepidus formed the triumvirate to share the Empire between them, Antony taking the eastern provinces. Fought the murderers of Caesar at the battle of Philippi with Octavius; his liaison with Cleopatra (qv) led him to divorce Octavius' sister Octavia, which provoked the enmity between them ending in the battle of Actium and Antony's death. (53)

Mars God of war; son of Jove and Juno; lover of Venus; patron of soldiers, gladiators, huntsmen, and the city of Rome. (98, 201, 213, 215, 300)

Martha St. Martha, friend of Jesus and sister of Lazarus and Mary Magdalene (qv). Because of her conscientious busyness in Luke 10: 38–41 she typifies the lifestyle of an 'active' Christian. (127)

Martial A Roman poet (AD 40–104); initially the panegyrist of the emperors and rewarded by Domitian with a tribuneship. He satirized the emperor after his death, exposing his many vices, and subsequently went into retirement. His 14 books of epigrams combine poetic genius of style with vicious wit and scandalous observation. (55, 150)

Mary The Blessed Virgin; Our Lady; Mother of Christ: see also Assumption. (140, 149, 325)

Mary Magdalene Identified by Roman Catholic tradition as the Mary of several Gospel references: the sister of Martha (qv) and by contrast with her the ideal 'contemplative' Christian (Luke 10: 39–42); the woman from whom Jesus cast out seven devils (Luke 8); who anointed him with fragrant oil (John 12); witnessed the Crucifixion (Mark 15); found the empty tomb (Mark 16); and was the first to meet the risen Christ (Matthew 28, John 20). (127, 165)

Matthew (Saint) Apostle and author of the Gospel bearing his name; his emblem is a human figure. (154)

Medorus Invented name. (74)

Melampus 'Black-foot': the name of one of Actaeon's (qv) dogs, in Ovid, *Metamorphoses*, III. 206. (213)

Mene Tekel Old Testament. The doom-laden writing on the wall which disturbed the impious feast of pagan King Belshazzar after the defeat of the Israelites, interpreted by the prophet Daniel. Book of Daniel 5: 25: 'And this is the writing that was written, MENE, MENE, TEKEL, UPHARSIN. This is the interpretation of the thing: MENE; God hath numbered thy kingdom and finished it. TEKEL; Thou art weighed in the balances, and art found wanting. PERES; Thy kingdom is divided, and given to the Medes and Persians.' The king was murdered later that night. (269)

Mercury The Roman Hermes, son of Jove and Maia; messenger of the gods; patron of travellers, merchants, shepherds, orators, and all criminals. He invented the lyre which he gave to Apollo in exchange for the caduceus, the winged wand which is his chief symbol. (213)

Mermydons Greek myth. The Myrmidons were the followers of Achilles (qv). (314)

Metamorphosis Miraculous shape-changing by the gods of themselves, each other, or mortals. (213)

Michael (Saint) Christian. The Archangel, protector of all Christians and special patron of soldiers, from the description in Revelation of his captaining the heavenly host against the devil. (325)

Minerva Roman myth. Goddess of wisdom, reason, and the constructive arts; she was born fully armed from the head of her father Jove and remained a virgin. As Greek Athena, patroness of Athens. The olive was sacred to her as with it, the emblem of peace, she triumphed over Neptune and his war-horses in a contest to show what was of most use to mankind. Minerva's shield, the *aegis*, was protected with a Gorgon mask, or, according to some authorities, actually made out of the Gorgon's skin. (170, 213)

Mirrhe see Myrrh

Mirtillo Mirtillo, in love with Amaryllis, is the hero of Guarini's *Il Pastor Fido*, a work which was extremely popular in the seventeenth century. Mirtillo suggests the myrtle (qv), sacred to Venus, so is a suitable name for a sighing lover. Fidelity was a salient characteristic of the Marquess of Montrose, so its associations in the work of Guarini make it appropriate to him also. (235, 332)

Momus Classical. God of mirth and ridicule, driven out of Olympus for satirizing the other gods. (213)

Montano A perfectly suitable pastoral name for a hill shepherd ('Man of the Mountains'); could also derive from the Latin poet Montanus. (235)

Moses Jewish patriarch who liberated the Israelite slaves after bringing down plagues on Egypt to demand their release from Pharoah (qv); received the Ten Commandments from God and eventually led the Israelites to the Promised Land (Exodus). (287, 326)

Mulciber A surname of Vulcan, god of smiths and metal. (213)

Muse/Muses Classical. Nine goddesses who under Apollo (qv) are patronesses of the arts. Their names were Clio (history), Euterpe (music), Thalia (comedy), Melpomene (tragedy), Terpsichore (dance), Erato (love-poetry), Polyhymnia (sacred poetry), Urania (astronomy), and Calliope (epic poetry). The palm and laurel trees are sacred to them, as are the waters of Hippocrene (qv), and the mountains of Pindus, Helicon, and Parnassus (qv), where they live. (126, 149, 150, 185, 188, 199, 203, 207, 213, 215, 223, 245, 256, 263, 313, 336, 337)

Muses Hill see Parnassus (170)

Myrrh Myrrh is a fragrant and expensive gum-resin used in perfumes and incense. Always recalls the gift of the Magi (Wise Men) to the Infant Jesus and Virgin Mary in Matthew 2: 11. (151)

Myrtle A favourite flowering plant of both Greeks and Romans, with small white sweet-scented flowers. Myrtles and roses were twined together to make crowns worn during formal dinners, or exchanged as gifts between lovers, and myrtle hence has associations with quiet pleasures. The myrtle was sacred to Venus (qv). (39, 227)

Naiad One of many minor goddesses of rivers, springs, wells, and fountains; seen as beautiful maidens bathing in the waters and guarding them. (223)

Na'man Old Testament. Naaman was a brave Syrian captain struck with leprosy; he travelled to Israel and was cured by the prophet Elisha (qv) who told him to bathe seven times in the Jordan (qv). The miracle persuaded him to believe in the God of the Jews (2 Kings 5). Luke 4 records that when Christ preached in the synagogue at Nazareth, on prophecy and its accomplishment in his own person, the story of Na'man was one of the histories which he cited. (165)

Narcissus Classical. An exquisitely beautiful youth who fell in love with his own reflection in a pool, became obsessed with it, and killed himself in despair. His blood turned into the flower that takes his name (see Echo). (213, 215)

Nectar The drink of the gods in Olympus (see Ambrosia). (213, 218)

Nephews In no. 213, the field of Diana's nephews is an extensive one. Apollo had children by Pthia (Dorus), the muse Thalia (the Corybantes), Coronis (Asclepius), Aria (Miletus), and Cyrene (Aristaeus).

Neptune God of the seas, brother of Jove, ruler of all lesser water deities and spirits; generally pictured in a sea-shell chariot drawn by dolphins or sea-horses, and brandishing the trident which raises sea storms, floods, and earthquakes. (57, 69, 74, 139, 169, 203, 213, 218, 222, 337)

Nereides Sea nymphs; the fifty daughters of Nereus and Doris (qqv) and attendants on Neptune; worshipped by sailors and coastal dwellers, on seashores, in grottoes and caves. (224)

Nereus Son of Oceanus; father of the Nereides (qv). (283)

Nero Roman emperor, Claudius Domitius Caesar, whose reign over the Empire declined into tyranny and debauchery. It is said that Rome was burned on his orders to inspire a poem on the burning of Troy, and that he composed and sang to his lyre as he watched the city destroyed by fire (see Anti-Christ). (276)

Night (Nox) Classical. Night was personified as a goddess, the mother of the Fates, and feared even by Jove. *Nox* is her Latin name. (12, 26, 62)

Nimphs see Nymphs

Niobe Greek myth. Her boasting of her superiority as a mother to even Latona, mother of Apollo and Diana, brought about a savage retribution. Apollo slaughtered her seven sons, Diana six of her seven daughters. Her sudden and terrible grief caused Niobe to turn to stone, but even then she did not stop weeping for them. (52, 110)

Nymphs Classical. Junior nature deities, always seen as young and beautiful virgins, often semi-nude. There are nymphs of both land and water, presiding over every hill, dale, forest and tree, river and grotto. (99, 143, 215, 226, 337)

Ocean Greek myth. Oldest of sea gods, son (and brother) of Uranus and Terra; father of Nereus (qv).

Olympicall Rector Jove (qv), ruler of Olympus. (213)

Olympus A mountain in Thessaly, believed to be the home of the Olympian gods. (207)

Oracle There were several oracles in the classical world. Delphi at the foot of Parnassus was the site of Apollo's most famous temple, where his priestess would give enigmatic and ecstatic prophecies to pilgrims seeking advice. The oracles ceased in the first century AD, explained by Plutarch, a priest of Delphi, in his *Why Oracles Are Silent*: Christian writers naturally interpreted this as related to the birth of Christ. See Sybil (149, 249)

Oread Classical. A mountain nymph. (207)

Originall Sin The sin of Adam (qv) and Eve: the primal act of disobedience, eating an apple from the Tree of Knowledge after the express prohibition of God. This one sin contaminated all mankind. (276, 287)

Orion Greek myth. Orion was an extremely handsome hunter and the son of Poseidon. One of the goddess Aurora's many lovers, he also boasted that he would rid the earth of all wild beasts, and went hunting with the goddess Diana, or Artemis (immune to manly charms). There are several versions of his end: one is that Diana accidentally shot him, another that he was killed by a scorpion, sent by Apollo who was suspicious of his association with his sister. His image was then set among the stars as the constellation Orion. Orion is normally associated with Boeotia, not Aeolia. (207)

Ornithes see Horace (11)

Orpheus Greek myth. Son of Apollo and Calliope, the Muse (qv) of eloquence and heroic poetry; as a mortal, a prince of Thrace; such a musical genius that his songs calmed savage beasts and stopped rivers flowing. Mountains moved and trees bent down to hear his playing. Husband of Eurydice (qv) whose death so grieved him that he tried, and failed, to lead her back from the Underworld. (60, 92, 224)

Ovid Roman poet, 43 BC– AD 18. His full name was Publius Ovidius Naso, the last part of which means 'nose'. His works include *Amores*, *Heroides*, *Ars Amatoria*, and *Metamorphoses*. He was exiled to Tomi near the mouth of the Danube by Augustus, on the grounds of his frivolity, obscenity, and corrupting effect on the youth of Rome. (178)

Pales Roman tutelary deity of shepherds and cattle. (235)

Pallas A title of Athene or Minerva (qv). (139)

Palurus The author's pseudo-classical invention. (74)

Pan Classical. Son of Hermes and god of the countryside, of shepherds, huntsmen, and fertility; his top half was man (with horns), the lower half goat; also known to the Romans as Faunus the chief of satyrs. The pipes of Pan were his invention; his presence (in mischief or anger) caused men and animals to panic. Maenalus was a range of mountains in Arcadia, sacred to Pan. (149, 195, 207, 213, 235)

Pandora Greek myth (from Hesiod's *Theogony*, eighth century BC). The first mortal woman made, on Jove's orders, to be wife to Prometheus, and punishment for stealing fire from heaven for mankind. All the gods gave her gifts but her intended husband was too wise to be tricked into marriage and she wed his brother instead. When Pandora opened her gift from Jove, it was found to contain all the evils that have ever hurt mankind: she was too slow to prevent them escaping into the world, but closed the lid in time to keep hope secure: Jove's compensation for his spiteful trick. (213)

Pans Death Plutarch, a priest at Delphi in the first century AD, says that a sailor in a ship bound for Italy heard a voice crying 'Great Pan is dead!' as he passed the island of Paxi. Christian writers assumed that this happened at the time of the birth of Christ (as Milton does in 'On the Morning of Christ's Nativity', stanza 20). (149)

Paris Greek myth. Paris was a son of Priam, King of Troy, who successfully seduced Helen (qv) and brought her back to the city. This was the event which led to the Trojan war and the destruction of Troy. (287)

Parnassus Classical. Mountain near Delphi with a double peak, sacred to Apollo, the Muses, and Bacchus (qqv). Symbolizes the ideal home of poetry and source of all artistic inspiration. (170, 207, 215, 337)

Pasipheme An error for Polyphem(us), a Cyclops (one-eyed giant) blinded by Odysseus. When he was left blind, after Odysseus and his sailors had made their successful escape, he raged and ranted, and offended the neighbouring Cyclopes (*Odyssey*, Book 9). (336)

Patrick (Saint) A Briton of good family, flourishing in the fifth century AD, who received a divine injunction to become the apostle of Ireland, where he had spent many years as a slave. He is the patron saint of Ireland. (250, 325)

Paul (Saint) New Testament. The Pharisee and Roman citizen Saul was originally a keen persecutor of the early Christians, but was converted by a revelation on the road to Damascus, changed his name to Paul, and became a zealous Apostle, especially to the Gentiles. His many Epistles became the foundation of Christian theology and his teaching provides absolute definitions of the authority of the Church. He was imprisoned by the Imperial authorities and sent to Rome for trial, on which occasion he was caught in a severe storm, 'and neither sun nor stars in many days appeared', and suffered shipwreck. (Acts of the Apostles 27). (276, 307)

Peace A personification rather than a classical goddess. As an emblematic figure, she is shown bearing an olive-branch, and/or as a dove. (169, 205, 236)

Pegasus Greek myth. Winged horse ridden by Perseus when he rescued the princess Andromache from the sea-monster; by Bellerophon when he destroyed the monster Chimera. After that Bellerophon tried to fly to heaven on his back but was thrown off to his death; Pegasus continued to Olympus where Jove set him amongst the stars. On earth a favourite of the Muses, he made his home on Helicon with them. (213, 286, 295)

Peleus Greek myth. Determined wooer and husband of Thetis (qv). (264)

Pelops Greek myth. Murdered by his father Tantalus and served to the gods as dinner, Pelops was brought back to life by Jove. Only Ceres, preoccupied, had eaten any of him, so he was restored with a magical ivory shoulder to replace the missing portion. (8)

Peneus see Daphne

Pernassus see Parnassus

Peter (Saint) Simon Peter the fisherman was the first Apostle called by Jesus (Matthew 4: 18–19), walked on water to him (Matthew 14: 29, no. 139), denied him (Luke 15), repented, and became the first leader of the early Church. Martyred in Rome, on the Vatican hill, he was the first Pope. His emblems are the Keys of Heaven, entrusted to him by Christ (Matthew 16: 19). (139)

Pharaoh King of Egypt, who figures more than once in the Old Testament, particularly the Pharaohs who ruled during the time of Joseph and Moses: the former welcomed the refugee Israelites during a time of famine, the latter was reluctant to release their descendants from slavery but was temporarily persuaded by spectacular plagues (Genesis, Exodus). (287, 325)

Phebe see Phoebe

Phenix Riddle The enigma of the phoenix, immortal bird, was that it renewed itself in fire and rose from the ashes of its own funeral pyre. (58)

Phillis Greek myth. The mythical Phyllis was a beautiful princess who killed herself when deserted by her lover; even the trees wept over her grave and miraculously blossomed when he returned too late. Thus, a pastoral name symbolizing devotion and fidelity. (50, 213)

Philoclea From the Greek 'lover of glory': daughter of Basilius and lover of Pyrocles in Sir Philip Sidney's prose romance, the *Arcadia.* (39)

Philomel Greek myth, a name for the nightingale. Procne and Philomela were sisters, daughters of Pandion. Procne married Tereus, King of Daulis, who fell in love with his wife's young sister. He concealed his wife, and reported her death to Pandion, who gave him Philomela as his second wife. He cut out Procne's tongue so she could not expose him, and put her among the household slaves but she wove the story into a robe and thus informed her sister. They took the dreadful revenge of killing and cooking up his son but before Tereus could eat him, all three were turned into birds (Procne became a swallow, and Tereus a hoopoe). Philomel regained a more beautiful voice than before as compensation from the gods. (167, 188, 207, 217, 223, 224, 236)

Phoebe/Phebe A name given to the goddess Diana (qv) as the moon. (19, 185)

Phoebus/Phaebus A name given to the god Apollo (qv) as the sun. (105, 150, 195, 203, 207, 213, 224, 331 337)

Phoenix The phoenix, an immortal bird, and the only one of its kind, renewed itself in fire and rose from the ashes of its own funeral pyre. (88, 170, 185, 212, 221, 295)

Phrygian Melody Phrygia was a country famous for its music; and the invention of the pipe of reeds is attributed to its natives (see Pan). Phrygian music had associations with wildness and sensuality. (188)

Pigmalion Pygmalion: a sculptor who so exactly carved a statue of an ideal woman that he fell in love with her. Venus answered his prayers and turned the marble into a real woman (called Galatea), whom he married. (52)

Pindar/Pindarus Celebrated lyric poet of Thebes, author of a series of odes on Greek athletic heroes (c.522–442 BC). When Alexander razed Thebes, he left Pindar's house standing as a mark of respect forhis genius. (256, 259)

Pious Trojan see Aeneas (203)

Pirocles Pyrocles: son of the King of Macedon and lover of Philoclea (qv) in Sir Philip Sidney's prose romance *Arcadia.* (39)

Pithon Python: a monstrous serpent sent by Juno to persecute Latona, but killed by Apollo in Delphi, whose ancient name was Pytho (qqv). (170)

Pleiades Stars also called the Seven Sisters; the daughters of Atlas (qv, see also Maia). (269)

Pluto God of Hades, the Underworld, also of riches (as in 'plutocracy'). His kingdom sometimes takes his name and is imagined at the centre of the earth. He is called Taenarian after Taenarus, a promontory in Sparta, which has near it a cave which was thought to be the entrance to the Underworld (e.g. Virgil, *Georgics*, IV. 467, refers to the *Taenariae fauces*: 'the Taenarian jaws of hell'). (169, 207)

Po see Eridanus

Pomona Roman nymph, patroness of gardens; cultivation generally and fruit-trees in particular. (188)

Pontius Pilate The Roman procurator (governor) of Judaea who authorized the Crucifixion of Christ, saying and demonstrating that he washed his hands of the matter. Identified with unjust judges and regicides through history. (143, 244)

Pontus Pontus is the Greek and Roman name for the Black Sea, and also a poetic word for the sea generally. (337)

Prometheus Greek myth, first told in Hesiod's *Theogony* (eighth century BC). Prometheus was a Titan, who made mankind out of clay. When Jove denied them fire, he stole fire from heaven for them, and taught them many useful arts. Jove then sent him and his brother Epimetheus Pandora (qv) as his revenge. He also had Prometheus chained to a rock on Mt Caucasus, where a vulture came each day to peck at his liver, which was restored during the night. He was rescued from this torture by Hercules (qv) as one of his labours. (204)

Propertius Roman poet, 50–16 BC, author of elegies mostly to do with his unhappy relationship with a lady he calls Cynthia. (178)

Prophet (Samuel) Judge of Israel; anointed Saul its king, then when he sinned, rebuked him, and chose and anointed King David as his substitute (1 Samuel). (158)

Prophet's Cloud God fulfilled his promise to the prophet Elijah (qv) by sending rain in answer to his prayer. The storm clouds were seen arriving from the distance, at first seeming no bigger than a man's hand but growing to tremendous size (1 Kings 18). (264)

Proserpina/Proserpine Daughter of Ceres abducted by Pluto and held in the Underworld (Greek Persephone). During her absence her mother allowed bitter cold to cover the earth. Now Proserpina divides her time above and below the earth; summer when she is with her mother, winter with her husband in the darkness of Hades. She is known as 'Sicanian' because she was carried off from Enna, in Sicily, where she had been gathering flowers. (207, 213)

Protean The sea god Proteus had prophetic gifts from Neptune but is most famous for his shape-changing ability, which he would employ to avoid seekers after oracles. (305)

Psyche A nymph, wife of Cupid (qv).

Pyracmon see Brontes

Pyrrha A beautiful Roman prostitute ('Fiery'), long admired by the poet Horace (qv). (59)

Pythagoras The most famous of Greek mathematicians, and also a religious leader, who believed in reincarnation and the transmigration of souls from one type of body to another. His followers are known as Pythagoreans, and observed strict food taboos on account of their beliefs: they wished to avoid eating any previously human creatures. (139)

Queen of Love see Venus (57)

Rebecca Old Testament. Wife of Isaac, chosen as his bride because of her modesty and hospitality; mother of the twins Esau and Jacob (Genesis 24). (127)

Redd Dragon see Whore of Babylon

Revelation Last book of the Bible, the prophecies of St John of the Apocalypse (end of the world and Last Judgement). Much interpreted by Protestants to the detriment of the Catholic Church; and by anticlericals and Puritan activists against the Anglican episcopacy and Anglo-Catholic divines (see Anti-Christ, Seal, Whore of Babylon). (229)

Salamander A mythical animal, believed to live in fire. (52, 283)

Sarpedon After failing to take the kingdom of Crete from his brother Minos, he first founded a city in Caria on the nearby mainland then ended up in Troy (qv) fighting for Priam against the Greeks; attended loyally by his friend Glaucus (qv); fought heroically and made great slaughter of the enemy but was finally killed by Patroclus. Apollo ordered his funeral to be held in Lycia. Said to be a son of Jove. (282)

Satan Biblical. Hebrew 'adversary'. See also Lucifer. (320, 339)

Saturn Classical. Father of the gods, ruler of the earth during the Golden Age (qv).

Satyrs Greek myth. Rural demi-gods; half-men, half-animal, often shown with animals' ears and horses' tails but attendants on Bacchus (qv); they were much given to orgies and drunken rioting. Their sexual partners are the nymphs, always represented as fully human in shape. (185, 207, 215)

Saul see Paul (Saint)

Seals In the Book of Revelation, chapters 5–8, St John describes his vision of 'the book sealed with seven seals' and its opening by Christ the Lamb of God. (159)

Seamless Coat Discarded by Christ at his Crucifixion and diced for by Roman soldiers at the foot of the Cross (John 19: 23). (151)

Sejanus A Roman historical character. Captain of the Praetorian Guard and favourite of Tiberius; his attempt to seize power in Rome during the Emperor's retirement in Capri came close to success but the coup was prevented and he was strangled in prison. The subject of Ben Jonson's most successful Roman tragedy. (233)

Semele Greek myth. She was the mother of Bacchus (qv). Jove seduced her in mortal form, but, at her insistence, appeared to her in his divine shape, and she was killed outright by his glory. (336)

Seraphim/Seraphins/Seraphick Christian. An order of angels (qv). (101, 115, 119, 141, 223, 244, 277, 337)

Serpent Old Testament. Identified with the Devil, who tempted Eve to disobey God in the Garden of Eden, leading to Man's banishment from earthly paradise. As punishment, he was turned into a snake. (148)

Seven Deadly Sins Christian. The seven 'mortal' sins likely to lead to damnation: pride, envy, lust, anger, covetousness, gluttony, and sloth.

Seven-Hilled City Rome; see Revelation, Whore of Babylon.

Sheba Old Testament. Sheba son of Bichri was a rebellious Benjamite who blew his trumpet and anounced that his people had no part in the kingdom of David (2 Samuel 20: 1). (287)

Sheba's Queen Old Testament. The Queen of Sheba paid a state visit to the court of King Solomon at Jerusalem, bringing a magnificent retinue, because she had heard of his wisdom and glory (1 Kings 10). (341)

Shimei Old Testament. He cursed King David, and threw stones at him (2 Samuel 16: 6–7).

Sicanian Fountain Classical; i.e. Sicilian, see Alpheus.

Sicanian Goddess see Proserpina

Silenus Classical. The nurse, attendant, and tutor of the god Bacchus; as a drunk he is seen crowned with flowers, red-faced, and riding on a donkey, but as a philosopher, speaking words of wisdom no matter how much he has drunk. (213)

Silvanus see Sylvanus.

Silvio Like Silvanus, a name derived from Latin *silva*, forest or woodland. A character of the name in Virgil's *Aeneid*, VIII. 5. (235, 312)

Sirens Classical. Sea-nymphs with such enthralling voices that anyone who heard their song was trapped till he died, without noticing, of hunger and thirst. Used for any enticing or rapacious female, or for sublime musical genius. They first appear in Homer's *Odyssey*, Book 12. (101)

Smectymnius see Appendix 2

Sodom Old Testament. One of the Cities of the Plains, its inhabitants were so wicked that God decided to destroy it (Genesis 19). (279)

Sol The Sun (Latin) (87)

Somnus Latin. The god of sleep, guarded in his unending slumbers by a host of dreams: his waking agent, bringing sleep to mortals, is his son, Morpheus. (213)

Sons of Adam (1) Cain and Abel. (2) More generally, all mankind. (306)

Sophonisba Historical character of the Roman period. Carthaginian princess first married to Scyphax the Numidian, but captured in war by the Romans' African ally Masinissa, who first married her then commanded her to commit suicide to please (or defy) the Romans. The serenity with which she drank poison has been attributed equally to her courage and her grief for her lost love. (39)

Sors Virgiliana An attempt to foretell the future by opening a volume of Virgil (qv) at random and interpreting the first passage glanced at. The Diary of Dr Edward Lake (entry for 29 January 1677–8) recalls an instance of Charles I attempting such an experiment and being dismayed by happening on Dido's curse on Aeneas. (285)

Stagyrite A name for Aristotle, born at Stagira. (156)

Stella The name which Sir Philip Sidney gave to Penelope Devereux in his sonnets, and Edmund Waller gave to Lady Dorothy Sidney. (212)

Stesichore Stesichorus, a Greek lyric poet of the late seventh century BC from Sicily. (256)

Stoicks Stoics: a school of Greek philosophers, followers of the philosopher Zeno, named after the market-place (Greek *stoa*) where they met. He stressed the importance of transcending human passions; so stoics are those who by courage master, or by apathy ignore, their feelings and emotions. (283)

Stone see Niobe (134)

Stygian Associated with the Styx, one of the rivers of the classical Underworld.

Sueno Swein Forkbeard, one of the great Viking kings holding power in England and Denmark, and father of Cnut (qv), was acknowledged King of England from 1013 to 1014. (287)

Sylla Roman historical character. Gaius Marius (155–86 BC) and Lucius Cornelius Sulla (138–78 BC) were deadly political enemies in the days of the Roman republic. When Marius became consul, he massacred the followers of Sulla, and when Sulla subsequently became dictator, he carried out savage reprisals against the followers of Marius. (287)

Suns Bright Sister see Diana

Susanna A virtuous woman falsely accused of adultery by wicked elders whose carnal advances she had rejected. Her innocence was proved by the prophet Daniel (Apocryphal part of the Book of Daniel). (127)

Sybil(s) Prophetesses of mythological and classical times inspired by Apollo, they traditionally wrote their prophecies on leaves; one Sibyl came to King Tarquin in Rome and offered to sell him her nine books of wisdom at great cost. He was tempted but refused, consequently she burnt three volumes and offered him six and finally three, still at the original price. The surviving books (the *Sibylline Oracles*) were bought and became one of ancient Rome's greatest and most solemn treasures, finally lost in a fire which destroyed their temple on the Capitol. (139)

Sylvanus Roman: a deity presiding over woods, and all places planted with trees. Identified with Faunus (qv), or thought to be his brother; half-man, half-goat, and patron of shepherds and gardens. Also a typical pastoral name (associated with Latin *silva*, 'a wood').(207, 215)

Sylvia Female equivalent of Silvio or Silvanus (qqv) and popular pastoral name from Latin *silva*, 'a wood'. (223)

Syrens see Sirens.

Tabernacle Old Testament. The portable shrine of the Israelites during their wanderings, finally brought to rest in Shiloh; a tent divided into an altar section for sacrifices and worship, and the innermost Holy of Holies where the Ark of the Covenant (containing the tablets of the Commandments given by God to Moses) was preserved (Joshua 18). During the Feast of Tabernacles, the Israelite people made little booths from green branches (Leviticus, 23: 40–3). (171)

Tagus The Tagus (now the Tajo) is a river in Lusitania, Roman Portugal, celebrated for its golden sands. (206, 226)

Talus From Edmund Spenser, *The Faerie Queene* (first published 1589–96). He was the henchman of Astraea (qv): when she left the world, she left Talus behind her to execute her judgements (V. 1,12): he carries an iron flail for dispatching criminals, and represents the power of government. (203)

Tartarus The Roman concept equivalent to Hell, where certain notorious malefactors like Ixion (qv) were tormented. (207)

Tartesside Lympha/Tartessian Waters Tartessus was a very ancient maritime town in Spain, now El Rocadillo, very near Gibraltar. To the Mediterranean civilizations of Greece and Rome, the Straits of Gibraltar represented the westernmost point of the known world.

From this perspective, the sun appears to sink in the West, into the Atlantic (Milton's *Hesperiis aquis*). (207)

Tellus A Latin name for the Earth, as Mother Goddess. (207, 337)

Tempe The Vale of Tempe, in Greece, a valley in Thessaly with Mount Olympus to the north and Mount Ossa to the south. A famous beauty-spot, celebrated by many poets, including Horace (qv), *Odes,* III. 1. (185)

Tempus Time: a personification rather than a god, often depicted carrying a scythe. (169, 207, 221)

Tereus see Philomel

Tethys According to Greek myth, a Titaness, later a personification, rather than goddess, of the sea. (139, 207, 222)

Teucer Greek hero, half-brother of Ajax (qv); like him a valiant warrior at Troy. He was the best archer among the Greeks. (256)

Thetis Greek myth. Nereid (qv) wooed by both Neptune and Jove, finally married Peleus (a mortal) after a prolonged and exhausting courtship: the Fates had prophesied that her son would be far more powerful than his father, which made her less attractive to the gods. She became the mother of Achilles. (139, 222, and 287: for Tethys (qv), 213, 264)

Thirsis Thyrsis is a shepherd in Virgil's seventh *Eclogue*. (213)

Thorn A single thorn from the crown of thorns forced onto Christ's head in mockery by Roman soldiers before the Crucifixion, and worn until his death. (126)

Thracian Verse Songs of Orpheus (qv), a Thracian.

Thyrse Greek: the thyrsis was a wand, wreathed in ivy and topped with pine-cones, which was carried by maenads and other followers of Bacchus. (178)

Tibullus Roman poet, 60–19 BC, author of two books of elegies. (178)

Time see Tempus

Titan The giant sons of Uranus (qv), or specifically his firstborn. Some poets use the name for Saturn; Virgil and Ovid apply the name to the sun. (171)

Tithonus Greek myth. A beautiful Trojan prince, son of Laomedon. Aurora, goddess of the dawn (qv), fell in love with him, and granted him immortality at his own request: neither of them thought to ask for eternal youth, so he dragged out an endless old age until the goddess resolved the problem she had created by turning him into a grasshopper. (207)

Tree Christian. Often the Cross of the Crucifixion and/or the Tree of Life in Genesis 2: 9. As the fall of man was linked to the tree of the knowledge of good and evil in the Garden of Eden, the Redemption is seen as its mirror image. In Christian legend, even the wood of the Cross was taken from the original tree whose stolen fruit caused man's banishment from earthly paradise. (126, 147, 148)

Tricongius The Lombards were a Germanic people who held power in early medieval Italy, but this is not a Germanic name. It appears to be an invention meaning 'three [wine] measures', the second part deriving perhaps from Latin *congero*, 'heap up, accumulate' (288)

Trinity Christian. The Father, Son, and Holy Spirit, three Persons, but one God. (233)

Triptolemus Greek myth. A semi-divine hero worshipped at Eleusis. Ceres (qv) was hospitably received by his father when she was searching for her daughter, and rewarded him by teaching Triptolemus the art of agriculture, and giving him a winged chariot in which he travelled the world, passing on this knowledge to mankind. (287)

Tritons Classical. Sea gods, sons of Neptune, depicted as half-man, half-dolphin, often blowing a shell-trumpet. (114, 224)

Trojans Classical. The people of Troy, a city with a long and splendid pedigree in myth before the events of its siege and fall narrated in the *Iliad* of Homer (qv). The immediate cause of the long Trojan Wars was the abduction by Paris of the Spartan (Greek) Queen Helen (qv). (256, 287, 335)

Troy see Trojans

Troyeborne Eagle Greek myth. Jove's cupbearer in Olympus was the beautiful Trojan prince Ganymede, stolen from earth by an eagle, therefore most often depicted riding one. (213)

Troyes Fatall Seed The descendants of the Trojan hero Brutus (qv), an early and mythical King of Britain. (287)

Trumpe Biblical. Seven angels with trumpets announce seven stages of the Apocalypse (Revelation 8: 2–10: 7). (276) .

Tyrian Dewes Drops of blood, from the classical use of purple dye obtained from the murex (a shellfish related to the whelk), which was produced at Tyre, on the coast of Lebanon. (238)

Tyrrean Sufferings i.e. the cruelty of Tereus (see Philomel).

Tytirus A shepherd in Virgil's first *Eclogue*, a poem which is an indirect eulogy of the Emperor Augustus. (205)

Venus Latin name for the goddess of love and beauty (the Greek Aphrodite); patroness of all pleasures, lovers, and prostitutes. Cronus (father of Jove, or Zeus) castrated his father, Saturn, or Uranus, and threw his genitals into the sea, where they spontaneously generated Aphrodite, who rose naked from the foam of the sea, and rode on a scallop-shell (as in Botticelli's famous painting) first to Cythera, then to Paphos, where she made her principal residence. 'Paphian' and 'Cytherean' are therefore adjectives which are used of her. She became the wife of Vulcan and lover of Mars (qv), and the mother of Cupid (by Mars). Doves and sparrows are birds sacred to Venus, and the myrtle is her sacred plant. (51, 52, 53, 57, 180, 201, 207, 213, 214, 215, 218, 300)

Vesta Roman goddess of the hearth. (207)

Vestall Flames The virgin priestesses of the goddess Vesta in Rome were vowed to keep an eternal fire burning at the sacred hearth of her temple. The fire was first lit from the pure beams of the sun and the Romans identified the prosperity of their city and republic (later empire) with its (and their) integrity. (196)

Virgil 70–19 BC. Favourite poet of the Emperor Augustus; author of the *Aeneid*, the *Georgics*, and the *Eclogues*. (178, 180, 205)

Voices Daughter see Echo

Vulcan Classical. The smith of the gods, the Greek Hephaistus, he was club-footed and misshapen, but a miraculous craftsman, who, among other creations, was responsible for forging thunderbolts for Jove. He was the mis-matched husband of Venus. (213, 287)

Whitsontide Whit Sunday or Pentecost; Christian celebration of the descent of the Holy Spirit to the Apostles (Acts of the Apostles). (123)

Whore of Babel/Babilon In his vision of the Apocalypse, an angel showed St John a woman arrayed in purple and scarlet, bejewelled and drinking from a golden cup; she rides a scarlet beast with seven heads and ten horns; upon her forehead is written MYSTERY, BABYLON THE GREAT, THE MOTHER OF HARLOTS AND ABOMINATIONS OF THE EARTH (Revelation 17–18). In detail, her nature, the beast's, and the manner of their destruction make plain an allegory of the destruction of decadent pagan Rome. The beast is often described as a dragon to represent the Devil in serpent guise. Protestant propagandists reinterpreted the passage as a prophecy of the downfall of Catholic Rome and its adherents. (229, 240, 308)

Worthyes Nine The 'Nine Worthies' were the nine greatest heroes of history: Hector of Troy, Alexander the Great, and Julius Caesar from the ancient world, Joshua, David, and Judas Maccabaeus from the Old Testament, and King Arthur, Charlemagne, and Geoffroi de Boullion (who was a hero of the Crusades) from the Christian era. (318)

Xanthus River god and actual river on the Lycian Plain (qv) in Asia Minor. (282)

Zephire/Zephyr/Zephirus The West Wind of the Greeks; husband of Flora. (68, 207, 223)

Zimri Old Testament. A servant of Elah son of Baasha (qv), King of Israel, who murdered his master and the whole of the family of Baasha, became briefly king, but, surrounded by his enemies, went into his palace and burned himself in it (1 Kings 16). (287)

APPENDIX 2
INDEX OF CONTEMPORARY NAMES

Alasdair mac Colla Chiotaich Alasdair mac Colla (MacDonald) (c.1610–47). Younger son of Colla Ciotach (Colkitto) of Iona, and Colonsay, a famous MacDonald warrior. He took service under Raghnall, second Earl of Antrim, after his father Colla Ciotach had been captured and imprisoned by the Earl of Argyll, and was sent to Scotland by him at the head of a chiefly MacDonald army in 1644 to fight for the King, and against the Earl of Argyll. He joined forces with Montrose, and fought under him for a year of astounding victories all over central and eastern Scotland. He and his MacDonalds separated from Montrose in the autumn of 1645 in order to pursue their vendetta against the Campbells, which enabled the Covenanting forces to defeat Montrose at Philiphaugh. Alasdair continued to ravage in Scotland until 1647, when Argyll finally managed to chase him back to Ireland. He was killed later that year fighting for the Catholic confederacy at Cnoc na nOs in Munster.

Anglesey, Countess of Elizabeth Sheldon, wife of Christopher Villiers, younger brother of the Duke of Buckingham. In 1623 Villiers was created Earl of Anglesey and also granted the remaining forests and lands at Chippenham Forest, or Pewsam, where the disafforestation, completed the following year, was extremely unpopular with local farmers. (191, 251)

Argyll Gilleasbaig Caoch, or Archibald Campbell, Lord Lorne and eighth Earl of Argyll (1607–61). He was leader of the powerful and predatory Clan Campbell, and a leading Presbyterian nobleman. He and his clan were hated by Gaelic-speaking Catholics. His main power-base was in Argyll, effectively a buffer state between the Highlands and the Lowlands, from whence the Campbells gradually extended their hegemony over their Highland neighbours. He emerged as a leader of the anti-Royalist forces in Scotland, though he was noted for his personal cowardice, particularly evident at Inverlochy, where he escaped by boat, leaving his clansmen to be cut to pieces by Alasdair mac Colla and Montrose. He was executed by Charles II shortly after the Restoration. (323, 324, 340)

Atkins, Alderman Sir Edward Atkins (1587–1669), baron of the exchequer from 1645. He was defence counsel for Prynne at his Star Chamber trial for libelling the Queen in his *Histriomastix*. Atkins served the Commonwealth and Cromwell, but was knighted at the Restoration, which suggests that both sides regarded him as a man of honour (320)

B— Robert Greville, Lord Brooke. (282)

Bellarmine Roberto Francesco Romolo Bellarmine (1542–1621), an Italian cardinal, and a powerful controversialist in defence of Catholic orthodoxy against Protestant theologians. (306)

Black Prince, The (1330–76) Son of Edward III; great English leader against the French in the Hundred Years' War. So called both for his ferocity as a general, and for his black campaign armour. Father of Richard II. (215)

Booker John Booker (1603–67), astrologer. His first published work was *Telescopium Uranum* in 1631. His great fame was founded on predicting the deaths of Gustavus Adolphus and the Elector Palatine. He was appointed licenser of mathematical books, and published a successful rhymed *Dutch Fortune Teller* in 1650. (243)

Bourchier Sir John Bourchier (d. 1660), regicide. A Yorkshire landowner who first came to prominence disputing enclosures with Strafford, for which he was fined and imprisoned. Bourchier was elected to the Long Parliament as MP for Ripon, and in 1651–2 was a member of the council of state. He surrendered himself at the Restoration, but died before his case was decided. (287)

Bradshaw, John (1602–59), regicide. He trained as a lawyer, and was elected judge of the sheriff's court in London. He was a partner with Prynne in the prosecution of the Irish rebels in 1641, and was defence counsel for Lilburne's successful appeal to the Lords against a charge of sedition. He became lord president of the commission to try the King. (see Appendix 4 for trial) Having been specifically exempted from any future pardon by Charles II as early as 1654, he was attainted at the Restoration despite being already dead and buried in Westminster Abbey (319)

Brahe, Tycho (1546–1601) A Danish nobleman and internationally famous astronomer. He built a great observatory on the Danish island of Hven, known as the Uraniborg, for Frederick II of Denmark. (185)

Brereton Sir William Brereton (1604–61). Parliamentary commander. MP for Cheshire in both the Short and Long Parliaments, Brereton put himself at the head of the parliamentarian movement in Cheshire at the outbreak of war, becoming commander-in-chief of forces there and in adjacent counties. His military successes include the defeat of Sir Thomas Aston at Nantwich where he lifted the siege together with Fairfax; the defeat of Prince Rupert at Tarvin; the capture of Liverpool and Shrewsbury; the complete victory over the royalists under Sir William Vaughan at Denbigh; and the capture of Lichfield. (287)

Brookes Robert Greville, Lord Brooke (1608–43) was a consistent opponent of both royal and episcopal power, and Pym's strongest supporter in the House of Lords. He died in action with the parliamentary army in 1643. Having seized Lichfield from the royalists and led his troops in a desperate assault on the royalists' last stronghold in the cathedral itself, he was killed there by a stray shot during an interval in the fighting. (233)

Buckingham, Duke of George Villiers, first Duke (1592–1628), favourite and minister of James I, and subsequently of his son Charles I. His extraordinary influence over both kings was resented by many, and he was ultimately assassinated by the Puritan John Felton (qv) (241)

Carlisle, Lady Lucy Percy (1599–1660), daughter of the ninth Earl of Northumberland, married Lord Hay of Sawley in 1617 much against her father's wishes. As the Countess of Carlisle, she became a notable beauty and wit at the court of Charles I. She became the Queen's confidante and the subject of many flattering poems by various authors. (208)

Cartwright, Mr William see Appendix 3. (156)

Cary Lucius Cary, Viscount Falkland (1610–43). He was an MP in the Long Parliament, where he opposed Strafford, but supported the Anglican Church in its episcopal form. He was the centre of a literary and philosophical coterie centred at Great Tew in Oxfordshire. He was Secretary of State to Charles I from 1642, fought for the King, and was killed at Newbury in September 1643. He is said to have despaired of the state of England, and to have deliberately courted his death in battle. (286)

Charles I, King of England. Charles Stuart (1600–49), King of Great Britain and Ireland, the second son of James VI and I and Anne of Denmark. He was first brought to England in

1604, and brought up by Lady Cary, after many others had declined the responsibility on account of his physical frailty. In 1612, his older brother's death made him heir apparent and he was created Prince of Wales in 1616. From 1618, his closest and most influential friend was his father's favourite, Buckingham.

Initial plans for Charles to marry a French princess were shelved in favour of a Spanish alliance which led to several years of ultimately futile negotiation and dissimulation. The marriage treaty was ultimately dropped when the restitution of the Palatinate became a necessary condition: Charles finally married Henrietta Maria (qv), in 1625, shortly after his accession. The implications of this Catholic marriage and the Commons' distrust of Buckingham fuelled the first political crises of his reign. Future collisions between the King and his parliaments combined religious and financial disputes with constitutional controversy.

His extortion of ship-money and other forms of taxation further alienated his subjects: successive confrontations led to civil unrest and open conflict. The Civil War was ultimately precipitated by the King's unsuccessful attempt personally to arrest the Five Members (q.v.) in January 1642: the King raised his standard and declared war on 22 August. See Appendix 4. (169, 205, 211, 215, 231, 233, 237, 238, 242, 243, 244, 245, 246, 247, 264, 266, 271, 283, 287, 326, 327, 333)

Charles II, King of England Charles Stuart (1630–85), oldest son of Charles I and Henrietta Maria. As Prince of Wales he had his own household from about 1638, supervised by the Duke of Newcastle (qv), and in 1640, took his seat in the House of Lords. After the outbreak of war, the Queen attempted and failed to negotiate a marriage for him with both the Dutch and Portuguese royal houses. After the breakdown of the Uxbridge negotiations (see Appendix 4) the King sent Prince Charles into the West Country for safety: as the royal cause became more desperate, he withdrew further: into Cornwall (August 1645) the Scilly Isles (March 1646) and Jersey (April) before finally joining his mother in Paris. Charles II was proclaimed King, first in Scotland, days after his father's death, and later, less wholeheartedly, across Ireland, England and the Channel Isles. He negotiated with the Scottish commissioners for their support, committing himself and the whole nation to the terms of the Covenant shortly before hearing of the defeat of Montrose (qv). Further stringent terms were agreed on his arrival in Scotland, preceding his coronation at Scone in January 1651.

The King's anticlimactic march south into England and defeat at Worcester in September left him embittered, but his escape from the battle and subsequent flight became the stuff of Cavalier legend: so much so that, after the Restoration, the King dictated a true version of events to Pepys in order to refute, amongst others, the 1660 best-seller *Boscobel* by Thomas Blount. (278, 328, 329, 336, 337, 338, 340, 341)

Cromwell, Oliver (1599–1658). Politician, general and Lord Protector of the Commonwealth from 1653 till his death. Born in Huntingdon, he attended the Puritanical Sidney Sussex College, Cambridge, 1616–17. He was first elected member for Huntingdon in 1628. By 1640, Cromwell was very active in Parliament, particularly in the defence of commoners against enclosures and against the episcopate. On the outbreak of war he joined Essex's army, and rapidly rose to a position of command. The extremists of his party grew to distrust him as he worked towards the arbitration of a tenable structure for the future government of the country. Negotiations with the King discredited Cromwell with hardliners, though the eventual trial and execution of the King seemed to Cromwell the just conclusion of an otherwise unstoppable tyranny. He assumed the title of Lord Protector in

1653. Parliament formally voted to offer him the crown in 1657, which he refused, though contemporary satirists wasted no time in doubting his unbounded personal ambition. He died in 1658 and was briefly succeeded by his son Richard. (254, 258, 341, 331)

Devereux, Robert see Essex

Digby Lord George Digby (1612–77), son of the Earl of Bristol and subsequently the second earl; a great favourite and friend of Charles I from the start of his reign. (287)

Donne, John Celebrated poet and preacher of the previous generation(1571/2–1631). Originally a Catholic and trained as a lawyer, Donne sailed twice with Essex in the 1590s, took Anglican orders in 1615, and became Dean of St Paul's in 1621, often preaching before Charles I. His poetry (both sacred and profane) and sermons were influential, and he was much admired by other important writers such as Jonson and Carew. (170)

Earl (Duke) of Newcastle see Appendix 3

Edward III (1312–77) King whose claim to the French crown started the Hundred Years' War. (215)

Elizabeth, Queen of Bohemia Elizabeth Stuart (1596–1662), sister of Charles I and eldest daughter of James VI and I and of Anne of Denmark. She married Frederick V, Elector Palatine and later King of Bohemia, a key Protestant figure in central Europe. She was the mother of Frederick's nominal successor to the lost throne of Bohemia, Charles Louis; and of Frederick Henry, Prince Rupert of the Rhine (qv), Prince Maurice (qv), and Princess Sophia (mother of George I). Frederick V was deprived of his kingdom of Bohemia by a coalition of Catholic monarchs in 1620, and much of Charles I's foreign policy was directed into various attempts to restore his sister's family to their lost possessions. (167)

Elizabeth I, Queen of England Elizabeth Tudor, born 1533, reigned 1558–1603. The daughter of Henry VIII and Anne Boleyn. She restored the Protestant Anglican Church of her brother Edward VI after the intervening Catholic reign of her sister Mary; presided over the defeat of the Spanish Armada, English expansion in the New World; and authorized the twenty-years' imprisonment and eventual execution of Mary, Queen of Scots. She was succeeded, however, by Mary's Protestant son James VI and I, who became the first Stuart monarch of both kingdoms. Elizabeth is also remembered as a patron of the arts, especially vernacular literature and drama, and as a spectacular propagandist of the cult of the monarchy, especially as Gloriana, the Virgin Queen. Her reign was viewed by many parliamentarians of the mid-seventeenth century as a Protestant golden age. (264)

Essex (1591–1646). Robert Devereux, Earl of Essex, military commander for the Parliament, formerly Chamberlain of the King's Household to Charles I. A simple man, he was persuaded that he had been wronged by the King and the court, and consequently changed his allegiance. (276, 281)

Fairfax (Ferfax), see Appendix 3. (253)

Falkland, Lord see Cary (286)

Fane, Francis Earl of Westmorland, see Appendix 3 (80)

Felton, John Protestant fanatic who assassinated the Duke of Buckingham in 1628. (253)

Finch, Sir John (1584–1660). Speaker of the House of Commons and Lord Keeper, who incurred much hatred by pronouncing the King's exaction of ship money to be legal. His support for royal prerogatives was unwavering. He was impeached by the Long Parliament, and went into exile in Holland in 1640. He was one of the commissioners for the trial of the regicides. (280)

Fines (Fiennes) see Saye and Sele (287)

Five Members 4 January 1642, Charles I attempted to curb his increasingly hostile Parliament by appearing in person in the House of Commons to arrest the five Members of Parliament (Pym, Hampden, Holles, Haslerig, and Strode) and the Peer (Lord Kimbolton) who were most hostile to him. Forewarned, they were absent, and the incident gave Pym an opportunity to issue propaganda which escalated hostility against the King. (281)

Gell Sir John Gell (1593–1671), parliamentarian commander. Chiefly remembered from the incident after the battle of Hopton Heath when, together with Sir William Brereton, he witheld the Earl of Northampton's body in an unsuccessful and ugly attempt to bargain with it for the return of artillery held by the royalists. The Earl's son refused to negotiate. (287)

Gough William Gough, (d. c.1680) Officer in the New Model Army. He sat on the High Court of Justice which tried and condemned the King in 1649, and was one of the signatories of the death-warrant. He fought at Dunbar and Worcester, and fled to America at the Restoration, where he died. (320)

Graham see Montrose, Appendix 3.

Gustavus Adolphus (1594–1632). King of Sweden from 1611, known as 'The Lion of the North'. In 1630 he invaded Germany in a celebrated campaign, but subsequently died in battle. (170, 205)

Hammond John Hammond, a Presbyterian ballad-maker and author of *The new bloody almanack for this ensuing yeare* in 1644. (243)

Haslerigg Sir Arthur Haslerig(g) (1601–61) was a statesman and staunch Puritan, said to have been 'brought up by Mr Pym after his father's death'. He was a bitter opponent of Laud, active in the bill of attainder against Strafford, the proposer of the Militia Bill of December 1641 and was one of the Five Members (qv). He was a bold soldier in the war and an independent in Parliament. In December 1647, Fairfax appointed him Governor of Newcastle. Haslerigg refused to act as one of the King's judges but spoke approvingly of his execution in 1649. He was prominent in public affairs throughout the Commonwealth and freely accused of abusing his position for personal gain. Monck's intervention saved his life at the Restoration but he was still in the Tower when he died. (319, 320)

Hastings Henry Hastings (1609?–67), a distinguished royalist commander, second son of the fifth Earl of Huntingdon. He was a zealous and popular figure, nicknamed 'Rob-carrier' for the frequency of his attacks on parliamentarian couriers. In 1643 the King gave him the title Baron Loughborough as a reward for his services. After the battle of Naseby, Hastings surrendered Leicester to Fairfax and went into exile abroad. He joined Charles II in Holland and was active in all manner of plots in aid of the royalist cause. (287)

Henrietta Maria (1609–69). Wife of Charles I and mother of Charles II and James II, among others. She was a Catholic princess of France, daughter of Henri IV and sister of Louis XIII. She and Charles married (by proxy) in 1625, but relations between the royal pair remained notably cold until the assassination of Buckingham: thereafter, they were devoted to one another, and became the parents of a numerous family. She was a woman of considerable courage and a patron of the arts, though her indifferent, sometimes provocative, flouting of English Protestant sensibilities did nothing to conciliate Charles's enemies. In 1642, she raised men, weapons and money in Europe for the King's cause, returning to England with them in 1643. In 1644, she again went to France to plead for further assistance and remained there until the Restoration. (81, 169, 191, 193, 215, 238, 245, 246, 264, 278)

Henry VIII King of England, reigned 1509–47. Initiator of the break with the Papacy and 'single supreme head of the church of England'. Father of Elizabeth I by Anne Boleyn, the second of his six wives. The title *fidei defensor* was conferred on him by Pope Leo X in 1521. (215)

Hervey, William A friend and Cambridge contemporary of Abraham Cowley, who died young. (150)

Hewson (Cobbling Colonell, Cobbling Lord) Colonel John Hewson (d. 1662), formerly a shoemaker based in Westminster, served in the parliamentary army from the outbreak of war. He was knighted by Cromwell in 1657 and called to his 'house of lords' (*Mercurius Politicus*, 3–10 December 1657) When ordered to suppress a riot by London apprentices petitioning for a free Parliament in 1659, he was blamed for the several deaths and many injuries that ensued. A public outcry followed, with many lampoons and caricatures satirizing his 'cobbling' origins. He was pardoned by Parliament, fled abroad at the Restoration and died in Amsterdam. (250, 319, 320)

Holinshed Raphael Holinshed (d. c.1580). Author of *Chronicles of England, Scotlande, and Irelande* licensed for publication in 1578, which was an immediate and lasting success, much read in the seventeenth century. (64)

Hotham Sir John Hotham (d. 1645). Son of the sheriff of Yorkshire, he served as a soldier on the Continent, was knighted in 1617, and made baronet in 1621-2. In 1639 it was proposed to take the government of Hull, which he held as Strafford's deputy, from him. The insult immediately drove him to support the opposition, holding Hull for Parliament against the King's personal demands for entrance in 1642. In the ensuing controversy, Hotham's actions were supported by Parliament. Despite quarrels with Fairfax he remained a staunch supporter of Parliament till 1643. Caught in negotiation with the enemy, he was tried and, after two reprieves, finally executed: 'a rough and rude man, of great covetousness, of great pride, and of great ambition'. (280)

Hoyle, Thomas (d. 1650) A Rump MP who committed suicide on the first anniversary of the death of Charles I, although he had been directly involved neither in his trial nor execution. (319)

Ireton Colonel Henry Ireton (1611–51), regicide. A parliamentary Commissary General, who married Cromwell's daughter Bridget in 1646. He became Cromwell's Deputy in Ireland and died there in 1651. His body was exhumed from Westminster Abbey at the Restoration and was one of the four hanged posthumously at Tyburn. (319, 320)

Isaack see Pennington (233, 281)

Jack see Pym, John (319)

James, Duke Prince James Stuart (1633–1701), Duke of York; the second son of Charles I and Henrietta Maria. He succeeded his brother as James II in 1685. (338)

Kimbolton (K——) Edward Montague, Lord Kimbolton and Viscount Mandeville (1602–71), from 1642, Earl of Manchester. He was amongst those in the House of Lords most hostile to the King and was one of the few peers to remain with Parliament in 1642. As resistance to the King turned into actual war, he was given a parliamentarian commission and fought at Marston Moor. He became a more and more reluctant and lethargic commander, and opposed the impeachment of the King. He retired from public life when the commonwealth became inevitable. (281, 287)

King, of Sweden see Gustavus Adolphus

Knox, John (?1505–72). Leader of the Protestant reformation in sixteenth-century Scotland. (265)

Lambert John Lambert (1619–83). A soldier under Fairfax at the start of the Civil War, he displayed exceptional ability and courage. In 1647 he was the spokesman for discontented army officers to the parliamentary commissioners, was a notable public figure during Cromwell's Protectorate, being particularly conspicuous for his involvement in the constitutional innovations of the 1650s. He was gaoled for life at the Restoration (320)

Lawes, Henry Musician (1596–1662). Composer for Carew's *Coelum Britannicum* performed at Whitehall and possibly also Shirley's *Triumph of Peace*, both 1633–4. He was probably the initiator of the masque *Comus*, since his name, not Milton's, was on the first published edition in 1634. His collection of settings for the Psalms was dedicated to the King in 1637 and his work is frequently anthologized in Playford's books of airs. Not to be confused with his brother William (1602–45), also a composer and Royalist, who was killed at the siege of Chester. (77, 117)

Lenthall William Lenthall (1591–1662). Speaker of the House of Commons and MP for Woodstock in both the Short and Long Parliaments. When Charles attempted to arrest the Five Members in 1642, Lenthall declared that, as Speaker, he was only the mouthpiece of the House of Commons, without personal responsibilities. He voted against negotiations with Charles I in 1647. He was a supporter of limited monarchy rather than a republican and supported the offer of the crown to Cromwell in 1650. (281)

Sir John Lenthall Son of William Lenthall. (320)

Lilley William Lilly (1602–81). He became an astrologer in 1632, and was notorious for his participation in an attempt to divine for buried treasure in Westminster Abbey. He had many pupils, and practised with great success. He published his first almanac *Merlinus Anglicus Junior* in 1644, which was followed by many pamphlets of prophecy. In 1645, following an attack by a rival astrologer, the royalist George Wharton, he became a vigorous parliamentarian. In 1647 he was summoned along with Booker (qv), to Fairfax, and dissuaded from practising astrology unless he could be sure such practices were pleasing to God. In 1648, he secretly supplied the King means for escape from Carisbrook Castle while still ostensibly serving the Parliament. (315, 320)

Livesey, Sir Michael (1611–63). A fanatical Independent and member of the County Committee for Kent, later a regicide. He was an ineffectual soldier for Parliament and was censured for being cowardly and overbearing. Several articles of complaint were made against him, but his social influence prevailed. In April 1645 he actively encouraged his men to mutiny rather than join forces with Fairfax. Elected MP for Queensborough in 1645, he was declared unfit to sit, but subsequently appointed a commissioner to try the King. At the Restoration he escaped to the Low Countries. He may have been denounced as a regicide and murdered by Dutch royalist sympathizers, as only rumours exist of his subsequent return to England. (280)

Lunsford Sir Thomas Lunsford (1610?–53?) Violent and impetuous from an early age, he was imprisoned on a charge of murderous assault on a kinsman, escaped from Newgate, fled abroad, and was exiled; served in the French army, returned, and was pardoned, joining the King's army against the Scots. Colonel Lunsford was the King's highly controversial appointment as lieutenant of the Tower in December 1641. Extreme protests against his 'ruined and desperate character' caused his removal soon afterwards, but he was knighted in compensation. Imprisoned after the battle of Naseby, he was later heard of in Amsterdam, and later still, emigrated to Virginia with his family, having given up the Stuart cause as lost. (287)

Machivile Niccolò Machiavelli (1469–1527), Florentine statesman and author of political treatises which include *The Art of War* and *The Prince*. His name became an archetype of villainy from Elizabethan times, due to popular simplifications of his analyses of ruthless political expediency, and sometimes a general name for a plotter and schemer. (64, 111)

Marten, Henry (Harry Martin) (1602–80). A regicide and noted libertine. His zeal for republicanism was stimulated by a public insult from the King, who called him 'an ugly rascal' and 'a whore master', and had him turned out of Hyde Park. He became an influential republican MP and a prime mover in the trial of Charles I. The fact that he was imprisoned and not executed at the Restoration reflects the absence of known vindictive behaviour on his part during the Interregnum. (319, 320)

Mary, Princess (1631–60). Daughter of Charles I and Henrietta Maria, Princess Royal. She was married to William II of Orange at the age of 10 after the King failed to negotiate an alliance with the Spanish heir. She was celebrated for her grace, beauty and courtly accomplishments but was not well educated. When the Queen left England, Mary accompanied her to Holland and was fully installed as Princess of Orange. She continued to support her father's cause, welcoming her exiled brothers to the Dutch court in 1658, and she maintained warm relations with her aunt the Queen of Bohemia, also chiefly resident in the Low Countries. In 1650, the Prince of Orange failed in his attempt to seize Amsterdam and establish his absolute power; he died the same year leaving Mary pregnant with a son, subsequently William III of Orange, husband of Mary II and joint King of England in his own right. (264)

Matchavil see Machivile

Maurice Prince Maurice of Nassau (1620–52), fourth son of the Elector Palatine and Elizabeth, sister of Charles I. Sent, with his older brother Prince Rupert, to learn soldiering in the army of the Prince of Orange. From 1642 to 1646 the brothers fought zealously for the King in England. He died at sea in the West Indies. (287)

Mildmay, Sir Henry (1593–1664). He was master of the king's jewel house, brought up as a courtier, spy and flatterer. In 1641 he changed sides, ultimately becoming an MP in the Rump Parliament. His defection was regarded as an important coup by the Parliament despite his notorious reputation. He is thought to have embezzled from the Royal Collection. At the Restoration, he was ordered to give an account of the crown jewels, and was captured as he attempted to flee abroad. He was confined to the Tower, and later sentenced to transportation to Tangiers, though he died *en route*. (319)

Monck, Lord George Monck, first Duke of Albemarle (1608–70). A career soldier, who learned his trade fighting for the Dutch. He was offered a command in Ireland in 1642, where he distinguished himself. He fought briefly for Charles I in England, was captured, and spent two years in the Tower. The parliamentarians offered him a commission to return to Ireland, which he accepted. Thereafter he fought loyally for Parliament, and was appointed General-in-Chief in 1648. He was subsequently left as parliamentarian commander in Scotland, and was instrumental in the restoration of Charles II. (338, 320)

Montrose (Montross, Montrois) James Graham, Marquis of Montrose, see Appendix 3 (321, 322, 332)

Mounson, Lord William (Munson) Judge at the trial of Charles I. (319,320)

Newcastle, Earl of William Cavendish, see Appendix 3 (272)

Pennington, Isaac (1587–1660). An ardent Puritan; MP for London in both the Long and Short Parliaments. In 1640 he presented a petition to the Commons against the innovations of Archbishop Laud. On the outbreak of war, his influence in the city of London was invaluable to the Parliament. He became Lord Mayor of London in 1642, on the removal by Parliament of the royalist Sir Richard Gurney. As lieutenant of the Tower, he conducted Laud to the scaffold that same year. He was a member of the commission to try the King, but declined to sign the warrant for his execution. He was knighted in 1649, and became a close friend of the poet Milton. At the Restoration he was convicted of treason and died in prison. (233, 281)

Peter, Hugh (1598–1660). An Independent divine, minister at Salem, Massachusetts, until the outbreak of war. In England, he was a chaplain in the parliamentary armies from 1642. He was chaplain to the Council of State from 1650, and attended Cromwell at Worcester. He was executed at the Restoration. (320)

Philip, Queen Philippa of Hainault, consort of Edward III of England (215)

Powell, Vavasour (1617–70). A Fifth Monarchist. That is, he came to believe in the imminent return of Jesus to reign in glory and therefore in the extreme transience and unimportance of earthly power. These religious extremists combined with discontented army factions to create a politically explosive element in Cromwell's England, undermining the security of the state. See also Appendix 3. (333)

Pride, Col. Thomas Soldier (d.1658). Lieutenant in the New Model Army, distinguishing himself at Naseby. When the army and Parliament quarrelled, Pride was one of the commanders most actively insistent on the rights of the soldiers to redress their grievances. He gave his name to 'Pride's Purge' in December 1648: under orders from Fairfax, Pride set a guard around the House of Commons, forcibly prevented around ninety MPs from gaining access, and arrested around forty others. This was to prevent an intended agreement with the King being passed. When Prynne demanded to know on what authority Pride was acting, he simply pointed to his armed troops. He was subsequently a commissioner for the King's trial. (320)

Pym, John (also **Pymme**) (1584–1643). He began his career as a clerk in the Office of the Exchequer, became an MP in 1614 and came to prominence in the Short Parliament (see Appendix 4) He appeared at the opening of the Long Parliament as an opponent of the Laudian Church and one of the chief movers against the Earl of Strafford. After his evasion of the attempted arrest of the Five Members in 1642 (qv) he guided the Parliament into the most extreme courses against the King. He died in 1643. (233, 253, 287)

Robinson, Luke. A Yorkshire radical MP 'most fierce against the King'. (319)

Rupert Prince Rupert of the Rhine (1619–82), third son of Elizabeth of Bohemia (qv) and Frederick V, Elector Palatine. He received a military training on the Continent and came to England in 1636. As a professional soldier and the King's nephew, he became a leading royalist commander, though not a wholly successful one, partly because his high-handedness alienated potential supporters. He accompanied Prince Charles to Holland in 1648, and subsequently took command of the royalist navy and harried the parliamentarian fleet in the West Indies. He returned to England after the Restoration. (287)

St John, Oliver (1598–1673). A lawyer, MP in the Long Parliament and intimate of John Hampden. He led the attack on ship-money and, as Solicitor-General, drew up the impeachment of Strafford. He sided with the army from 1647 and became Chief Justice of the Common Pleas. He took no part in the trial of the King, but was excluded at the Restoration from holding any public office (276, 319). His son, also Oliver St John (d. 1642), was killed at Edgehill. (276)

Salloway Major Richard Salway, a republican London merchant, prominent in the early 1650s, although opposed to Cromwell's Protectorate. He was a close friend and associate of Henry Vane and may be assumed to have shared his quasi-mystical religious position. Vane was the author of *The Retired Man's Meditations*, 1655. (320)

Say and Seal William Fiennes, Viscount Saye and Sele (1582–1662).A nobleman of extreme Puritan views, stern opponent of the ecclesiastical hierarchy, and hostile to any act of the King's which infringed strictest precedent and the bounds of custom. (281, 287)

Scot, Mr. Thomas Scot (or Scott), (d.1660) Regicide. MP for Aylesbury in the Long Parliament 1645. One of the commissioners for the trial of Charles I. He was elected a member of each of the three councils of state during the Commonwealth. In July 1649, he was appointed head of intelligence both at home and abroad. He was a vehement supporter of the republic, and opposed Cromwell's dissolution of Parliament and subsequent Protectorate. At the Restoration he escaped to Flanders, but was persuaded to surrender. He was tried and executed for treason. (320)

Sidney, Sir Philip (1554–86), celebrated Elizabethan author influencing the development of sonnet writing, prose fiction and prosody in the English language, although his books appeared in print only posthumously (the celebrated pastoral, *Arcadia*, 1590, *Astrophel and Stella*, 1591, *Defense of Poesy*, 1598). His death on active service at Zutphen was glamorised in many contemporary elegies, and he passed into early modern legend as a Protestant champion of the Elizabethan golden age. (49)

Skippon, General Philip (d.1660). General of Infantry in the Army, and Commander of the City Trained Bands. He assisted Pride's Purge by withdrawing his men, but never took his place at the King's trial. He was also the author of three works of religious devotion (1643/4/5) addressed to his fellow soldiers. (319)

Smectymnius Properly, Smectymnuus: the pen-name of a group of five Presbyterian divines whose initials were added together to form a collective pseudonym for their pamphlet attack on episcopacy. They were supported by Milton, who wrote a defence of them in 1641. (319)

Spenser (also **Spencer**) Edmund Spenser (1552?–99), author of *The Faerie Queene* and other influential poems. (204, 249)

Stow John Stow (1525?–1605). Chronicler and antiquary. (64)

Strafford, Earl of Thomas Wentworth, Earl of Strafford (1593–1641). The most influential adviser of Charles I and his President of the Council of the North and then Lord Deputy in Ireland. He was impeached by the Parliament, accused of being prepared to support the arbitrary government which he had advised, by bringing in an Irish army to support the King. He was tried, condemned by an act of attainder in 1641, and executed in the same year. Charles I gave a fatal exhibition of weakness by consenting to his execution under pressure from Parliament and from the London mob. (275, 280, 281, 307)

T., John John Thurlow, or Thurloe (1616–68). A protégé of Oliver St John, known as Cromwell's master-spy. He was secretary to the Council of State under the Commonwealth. (319)

Tanfield, Sir Lawrence (d. 1625). Judge and MP for New Woodstock (Oxfordshire) from 1584 and throughout the reign of Elizabeth. In 1607 he was made chief baron of the exchequer, retaining the office till his death. (1)

Tasso Torquato Tasso (1544–95). Italian poet. He spent many years in the service of the d'Este Dukes of Ferrara, but increasingly obtrusive mental illness caused him first to be imprisoned and then banished from the city. He spent the later years of his life wandering from court to court and died at Rome. His chief work was the epic, *Gerusalemme Liberata* (1580), which influenced Spenser's *Faerie Queene* and other English works. (180)

Saint Teresa of Avila (1515–82). A formidable Spanish saint of the Counter-Reformation. After the childhood attempt to convert the Moors recorded by Crashaw, she became a nun of the Carmelite order and the successful foundress of the strictly observant 'Discalced Carmelites'. She was both a contemplative and a figure with a European reputation. Her works include spiritual treatises, amongst them *The Way of Perfection*, as well as visionary writings. Her works were available in early-modern England (in editions printed at Antwerp in the Spanish Netherlands) and they appear to have been much read and admired in Laudian circles in 1630s Cambridge, which numbered Crashaw and Beaumont amongst their members. (141)

Titchbourne, Col. Robert (Tichburn) A linen-draper of London who took part in the trial of Charles I. (319, 320)

Tychobrahe see Brahe, Tycho

Van Dyck Sir Anthony Van Dyck (1599–1641), Dutch-born court painter to Charles I and the chief creator of his public image. (204)

Vane, Sir Henry (The Vanes, Harry Vane). The elder Sir Henry (1589–1655) was Secretary of State and Charles I's ambassador on a number of confidential missions abroad. He was instrumental in the ruin of Strafford (qv) and thereafter sided with the parliamentarians. The younger Sir Henry, his son (1613–62), was a convinced Puritan, briefly governor of Massachusetts and leader of the army's party in the House of Commons, executed by Charles II for his involvement in the regicide. (287, 319, 320)

Venne, Captain John . A London MP of pronouncedly radical views, signatory to the death warrant of Charles I. (281)

Waller Sir William Waller (1597?–1668). Parliamentarian general; distant cousin of the poet Waller. (287)

Walton, Izaak (1593–1683) A London ironmonger, close friend of John Donne, Sir Henry Wotton, several bishops, and the King. Biographer of Donne, Wotton and Richard Hooker. Most famous as author of *The Compleat Angler* (1653). (225, 226)

Warwick, Earl of Robert Rich, Earl of Warwick (1587–1658), friend of Pym and Hampden. A Puritan peer, who was an early opponent of ship money, the most important early patron of Oliver Cromwell, and subsequently admiral of the parliamentary navy. (203, 281, 287)

APPENDIX 3
BIOGRAPHICAL NOTES ON AUTHORS

Anna **Alcox** Almost nothing is known of Anna Alcox. She was the child of a Catholic family, living in the 1650s at Alveston, near Bristol. She was born in about 1645, and composed her two surviving poems when still a child. (163)

Philip **Ayres** Born in 1638, and educated at Westminster School and St John's College, Oxford. In the 1660s he accompanied Sir Richard Fanshawe's embassy to Spain. In later life, he was a friend of Dryden's, but composed all his surviving work very much in the style of the mid-century. His *Lyric Poems* were published in 1687, his *Emblemata Amatoria* in 1683. He died in 1712. (78)

Joseph **Beaumont** Joseph Beaumont was born at Hadleigh in Suffolk in 1616. He entered Peterhouse, Cambridge, in 1631, proceeding to his MA in 1638. He was a friend of Richard Crashaw (qv). He was ejected for his royalist sympathies in 1644. At the Restoration he was appointed a chaplain to Charles II and in 1663 he became Master of Peterhouse. He died in November 1699 and was buried in Peterhouse chapel. (147, 148)

Samson **Briggs** Samson Briggs was born at Epsom in Surrey, and educated at Eton, entering King's College in Cambridge in October 1630. He became a Fellow of King's in 1633. He was 'slaine in the King's Armie at the siege of Gloucester 1644' and 'his aged father, Rector of Fulmere, in Buckinghamshire, with extreme grief for the death of his son became distracted'. Only two of his poems were published in his lifetime, neither under his name. (53, 105, 213)

Alexander **Brome** Alexander Brome was born in 1620, and became an attorney in the Lord Mayor's Court or the Court of the King's Bench. He was a convinced royalist in the Civil Wars. He wrote and edited plays, and compiled a variorum edition of translations of Horace in 1666. He is one of the very few poets of the mid-century who wrote in anything like the 'Cavalier' style imagined by the nineteenth century. (110, 111, 218, 300, 301, 303, 304, 305)

Richard **Brome** Richard Brome, no relation to Alexander, was born about 1590, and was for a time a servant to Ben Jonson, and as a playwright, echoes his dramatic style and satirical interests. *A Joviall Crew*, which was acted on the eve of civil war in 1641, is both an uncomfortable allegory of an England sliding into chaos and a humorous romance, showing an escapist nostalgia for an England populated by generous and adventurous aristocrats and carefree roving gypsies. Other plays satirize contemporary society and especially the rapacious behaviour of the court. Brome was a thriving and popular playwright whose career was cut off by the closing of the theatres; he died c.1653. (232)

Thomas **Carew** Thomas Carew was born in Kent in 1594–5, and educated at Merton College, Oxford, and the Middle Temple and held thereafter various diplomatic posts until in 1630 he received a court appointment as Sewer in Ordinary to the King. He wrote the masque *Coelum Britannicum* in 1634. He was with Charles's expedition against Scotland in the first Bishops' War. He died in March 1640. (16, 17, 18, 88, 89, 126, 179, 180, 181)

William **Cartwright** William Cartwright was born in 1611 in Northway, Gloucestershire, and educated at Christ Church, Oxford, taking his MA in 1635. His play *The Royal Slave* was performed before Charles I and Henrietta Maria in 1636, a repeat performance being ordered at Hampton Court. He took orders in 1638. His oratory was much commended, and he preached the victory sermon after the battle of Edgehill in 1642. During the siege of Oxford he was active in the garrison, dying in 1643 of a 'fatall, choice Feaver' raging through the besieged town. (45, 209, 210, 263, 264)

Thomas **Cary** Courtier, Gentleman of his Majesty's Bedchamber, member of the circle of Fanshawe. (36, 257)

Elizabeth **Cavendish** Countess of Bridgewater (1626–1663), daughter of William Cavendish, first Duke of Newcastle (qv) by his first wife, Elizabeth Bassett. At the age of 15, she married John Edgerton, Viscount Brackley (1622–86), later the second Earl of Bridgewater. (166)

Margaret **Cavendish** Duchess of Newcastle. Called 'Mad Madge' and publicly mocked and ridiculed for her literary efforts, Margaret Cavendish, Duchess of Newcastle (1624–74), launched on a literary career with the express purpose of achieving both knowledge and fame. Born Margaret Lucas, daughter of the Earl of Colchester, she became maid of honour to Henrietta Maria, whom she accompanied into exile in Paris in 1644. There she met her future husband William Cavendish (qv), then Marquis of Newcastle, who was her senior by at least thirty years. At the Restoration, after a fifteen-year stay on the Continent, they returned to England to settle on their estate and spend the rest of their lives writing and publishing. (219, 220, 317, 318)

William **Cavendish** Duke of Newcastle. He was born in 1592, and educated at St John's College, Cambridge. He then travelled abroad. In the earlier part of the Civil War he lent vast sums of money to Charles I and fought for the king. After the royalist defeat at Marston Moor in 1644 he went to France where he married Margaret Lucas, a maid of honour to the exiled Henrietta Maria. After the Restoration he passed much time with his wife in retirement at Welbeck in Nottinghamshire, both writing copiously. He died in 1676. (15, 239)

Laurence **Clarkson** (1615–70). He was born at Preston in Lancashire, brought up amongst Lancashire Puritans, and served as a soldier in the New Model Army for some time. He turned itinerant preacher, and was successively a Baptist, and a Seeker. He moved politically to the extreme left, publishing a near-Leveller pamphlet in 1647. His chief activity as Ranter led for a time to that sect being sometimes referred to as 'Claxtonites' ('Clarksonites'). He was arrested in 1650, but soon released. By 1659, after a period as an astrologer, and a magician, he had been converted to much milder forms of Protestantism, and renounced his former extreme beliefs. (146)

John **Cleveland** John Cleveland was born in Loughborough in 1613, the eldest son of a country clergyman. He entered Christ's College, Cambridge, in 1627, taking his MA in 1635. He was a Fellow of St John's College from 1634. He was a strong royalist and left Cambridge for the more sympathetic atmosphere of Oxford in 1643. By 1645, Cleveland had been appointed Judge Advocate for Newark, and surrendered to the Scots army at the fall of that town. For the following ten years his movements are obscure, but he seems to have been active in the publication of various royalist pamphlets. In 1655 he was for a time imprisoned at Yarmouth. He died, perhaps at Grays Inn in London, in 1658. (50, 51, 52, 214)

John **Collop** Very little is known of the life of John Collop. He is thought to have been born c.1625, possibly attended Pembroke College, Cambridge, and practised as a doctor of medicine in London. He seems to have been alive in 1676. In addition to one volume of verse he published the peaceable treatise *Medici Catholicon* in 1656. (164, 165)

Richard **Corbet** Richard Corbet was born in 1582 at Ewell in Surrey and educated at Broadgates Hall (Pembroke College) and Christ Church, Oxford, taking his MA in 1605. He remained in Oxford, becoming Junior Proctor in 1612. His high-church views, and the favour of the Duke of Buckingham promoted a career of rapid ecclesiastical advancement: he was Dean of Christ Church in 1620, Bishop of Oxford in 1628, and Bishop of Norwich in 1632. He died in 1635. (168, 229)

Charles **Cotton** Charles Cotton the younger was born in 1630, the son of the Derbyshire gentleman who is the addressee of Lovelace's 'The Grasse-hopper' (296). He travelled widely while still young, gaining a comprehensive knowledge of French, and Italian literature. He spent most of his life in literary, and country pursuits, although he served in the army in Ireland in 1670. He was a close friend of Izaak Walton, and wrote a second part to *The Compleat Angler*. His poems were not published until after his death in 1687. (76, 116, 225, 226, 330, 331, 332)

Abraham **Cowley** Abraham Cowley was born in London in 1618, and educated at Westminster School, and Trinity College, Cambridge, where he held a fellowship until ejected by Parliament, whereupon he went to Oxford. He held office in the court of Charles I, and was employed abroad. He was a royalist spy in London during the Interregnum. His output was large, his first work, *Poetical Blossoms,* being published when he was only 15. He died in 1667. (59, 60, 61, 62, 63, 64, 149, 150, 217, 285, 286, 287)

Richard **Crashaw** Richard Crashaw was born about 1613 and educated at Pembroke College, Cambridge. He became a Fellow of Peterhouse, until his ejection by the parliamentary visitors for refusing to take the 'Solemn League and Covenant'. It is worth noting that his most baroque devotional poems were written while he was still a Laudian Anglican. After the loss of his fellowship he travelled in France and Italy, becoming a Catholic and ending his life as a sub-canon of the church of Our Lady of Loretto. (49, 140, 141, 142, 143)

Sir William **Davenant** William Davenant was born in Oxford in 1606, son of a vintner. According to Aubrey, rumours current in the London of the 1660s suggested that he was either the godson or illegitimate son of Shakespeare. It is possible that he briefly attended Lincoln College, Oxford. Thereafter he was a page to the Duchess of Richmond and passed in 1624 into the service of Lord Brooke. In 1633 he returned to a career as a poet, and dramatist, producing, amongst other works, the last and saddest of the Caroline masques, *Salmacida Spoila*. He was a staunch royalist in the Civil War, serving under the Duke of Newcastle (qv) in the North, and being imprisoned for his part in the First Army Plot of 1641. He travelled much and was captured, and imprisoned in 1650, sentenced, and yet mysteriously released on bail in 1652. He evaded Parliament's restrictions on the theatre by producing *The Siege of Rhodes*, a 'dramatic entertainment' with music in 1656. After the Restoration he was manager of the Duke of York's theatre until his death in 1668. (29, 94, 95, 96, 97, 191, 192, 193, 194, 195, 251, 252)

Sir John **Denham** John Denham was born in Dublin in 1615, the son of the chief baron of the Exchequer in Ireland. He was educated at Trinity College, Oxford, and Lincoln's Inn. He lived an extravagant life, having come into his inheritance at an early age. His first literary success was *The Sophy*, which appeared in 1640. At the outbreak of the Civil War he was made Governor of Farnham Castle for the King, but failed to hold it. At Oxford, during the siege, his poem *Cooper's Hill* (an anticipation of the Augustan topographical poem) was published. In 1647 he assisted the escape of the younger children of Charles I. He passed the Interregnum abroad, and under the protection of the Earl of Pembroke at Wilton. At the Restoration he was made Surveyor of the King's Works, preceding Sir Christopher Wren. His later years were marked by fits of madness and he died in 1669. (54, 55, 215, 282)

William **Drummond** Born at Hawthornden near Edinburgh in 1585, the nephew of William Fowler (qv), he was educated at Edinburgh University, and travelled abroad. He wrote in many genres: hymns, elegies, satires, political pamphlets, and a history of Scotland, first published after his death. Drummond was a royalist, and episcopalian; a friend of Michael Drayton, John Donne, and Ben Jonson. He died in 1649. (231)

Katherine, Lady **Dyer** There is little record of the life of Lady Dyer: she was the daughter of Thomas D'Oyley of Marton in Oxfordshire, and wife of Sir William Dyer 'of the Antient Family of the Dyers in Somerset' who died in 1621. She died in 1654. (22, 127)

Thomas, Lord **Fairfax** (1612–71). General who led the parliamentarians to victory at Naseby. He opposed the execution of the King, refused Parliament's order to march north and attack Scotland (before the coronation of Charles II there), and retired to the country. He was related to the Earl of Westmorland (see below). Andrew Marvell was tutor to his daughter. (266)

Mildmay **Fane** Earl of Westmorland. Mildmay Fane was born in 1602, and educated at Emmanuel College, Cambridge. He was MP for Peterborough in the Short Parliament of 1620–1, and knighted at the coronation of Charles I. At the outbreak of the Civil War he was imprisoned in the Tower as a royalist, being released on parole the following year. He was fined and his estates were sequestered. In 1644 he took the Solemn League and Covenant and was set at liberty. At the Restoration he was made joint Lord Lieutenant of Northamptonshire. He received a secret service payment in 1662. He died in 1666. (185, 249)

Sir Richard **Fanshawe** Richard Fanshawe was born at Ware Park in Hertfordshire in 1608, the younger son of an unusually cultivated civil servant. He was educated at Jesus College, Cambridge, and thereafter studied the law unenthusiastically until the death of his mother set him free to travel. He passed some time in Spain, attached to the Embassy in Madrid. At the outbreak of the Civil War he went to the King, and remained with the court through the siege of Oxford, following Prince Charles into the west country, and exile. During the war he travelled extensively, returning eventually to England, and being put under house arrest. At the Restoration he was ambassador to both Portugal, and Spain, dying in Madrid in 1666. A linguist of unusual ability, he translated the *Pastor Fido* of Guarini, Camoens's *Lusiads*, much lyric poetry by Gongora and his contemporaries, and the greater part of the works of Horace. (100, 205, 206, 255, 256)

Piaras **Feiritéar** Born c.1600, a chieftain of Norman descent ruling in the Dingle peninsula, Co. Kerry. His poetry was esteemed both by his own people and the new Elizabethan colonists and he remains a much quoted folk-hero in the Gaeltacht. In the rising of 1641, Feiritéar was wounded in an attack on Tralee Castle: he was hanged in Killarney in 1653. (23)

Owen **Felltham** Felltham was born around 1602, the son of Thomas Felltham of Mutford in Suffolk. The first edition of *Resolves* was published when Felltham was 18. Little is known of his life, except that he was chaplain or secretary to the Earl of Drummond at Great Billing in Northamptonshire. His best-known work was a prose tract describing and attacking the country and inhabitants of Holland. He died in 1668. (25, 26)

William **Fowler** (1560–1612). Scottish author of the original version of *Farewell fair saint*, see **Cary**.

Sidney **Godolphin** Sidney Godolphin was born in January 1611 at Godolphin near Helston in Cornwall, and proceeded to Exeter College, Oxford, in 1624, leaving without a degree in 1627. He became MP for Helston in 1628 and at this time was attached to the Court, accompanying the Earl of Leicester in his embassy to Denmark. He remained MP for Helston in the Long Parliament, until the King ordered those in opposition to withdraw. In the earlier part of the Civil War he was with the King's army in the West. He was killed in a skirmish at Chagford in February 1643. (42, 43, 44, 102)

James **Graham** Marquis of Montrose. Montrose was born in 1612, son of John, fourth Earl of Montrose. He succeeded to his title young and was educated at St Andrews and on the Continent. He supported the Covenanting, anti-royalist party in the first Bishops' War, but was imprisoned afterwards, chiefly through the contrivance of the Earl of Argyll who feared him for his moderation. After the raising of the King's standard in 1642, Montrose made an approach to Henrietta Maria's court at York, but did not receive his commission as Captain-General in Scotland until 1644, whereupon he led an astonishing campaign in the wildest parts of Scotland through the worst of the winter culminating in the victory of Alford in July 1646. He went on to take the Lowlands for the King. Defeated for lack of support at the battle of Philiphaugh, he withdrew into the Highlands, obeyed the command to disband his army, and went into exile. He returned to Scotland in 1650, to lead a forlorn hope for Charles II, who was already negotiating with Argyll. He was betrayed by Mc Leod of Ardvreck and was hanged by the Covenanters at the Market Cross of Edinburgh on 21 May 1650. (46, 47, 48, 268, 269, 270, 271, 272, 273, 274)

William **Habington** William Habington was born in 1605 in Worcestershire of a Roman Catholic family and educated in France with a view to entering the priesthood. He returned to England in 1626 and studied privately for some time with his father. He married Lucy Herbert, daughter of Lord Powis, the 'Castara' of his poems. Due to the disabilities imposed on Recusants and to his own quiet nature, he passed much of his life in retirement. He wrote historical works and a play, *The Queene of Arragon* (1640). He died in 1654. (27, 28, 132, 186)

John **Hall** John Hall was born in Durham in 1627, and educated at Durham School and St John's College, Cambridge. At the age of 19 he published a collection of essays, *Horae Vacivae*, which was received with enthusiasm in Europe as well as Britain. He remained at Cambridge until 1647 when he moved to Gray's Inn, feeling that he had received inadequate recognition from his university. In 1649 he published a tract on university reform. Thereafter he became an apologist, and pamphleteer for Cromwell, from whom he received a pension of £100 per year. It was the opinion of Thomas Hobbes that he was a potentially great man ruined by debauchery and intemperance. He died in 1656. (74, 75)

Henry **Harington** Harington, possibly of Witham in Lincolnshire, was born in1619. He matriculated at St Mary Hall, Oxford, 1635, was a student of Gray's Inn in 1640, and a Fellow of All Souls from 1640. He would appear to have been deprived of his fellowship during the Interregnum, and to have had it renewed in 1660. Attributed author of no. 37.

Robert **Heath** Robert Heath was born probably between 1615, and 1620, the son of Sir Robert Heath of London. He was educated at Corpus Christi College, Cambridge, and the Inner Temple. He was a barrister by 1652 and was the auditor in the Court of Wards. The date of his death is unknown. (56, 57, 58)

Edward **Herbert** Lord Herbert of Cherbury. Edward Herbert was born at Eyton on Severn in 1583, brother of the better known poet George Herbert. He was educated at University College, Oxford. Until 1622 he was engaged in travel, and in various military and diplomatic appointments. He was created Baron of Castle Island in the Irish Peerage in 1624, and Lord Herbert of Cherbury in 1629. In 1639 he was summoned to the King's Standard at York and then to the council of Peers. He tried to steer a middle course in the parliament of 1642 and was imprisoned in the Tower. He withdrew to Montgomery Castle and tried to remain neutral. To save his library, he admitted a parliamentary garrison to the castle in September 1644, and was disowned by the royalists. Now dependent on Parliament, he made a last trip to Paris before his death in 1644. (230)

Robert **Herrick** He was born in 1591, the son of a London goldsmith, and was educated at St John's College, and Trinity Hall, Cambridge. He took orders, and was presented to the living of Dean Prior in Devon, from which he was ejected by Parliament in 1647. He passed the Interregnum in London, returning to Dean Prior at the Restoration, and remaining there until his death in 1674. (8, 9, 10, 11, 85, 86, 120, 121, 122, 123, 171, 172, 173, 174, 175, 176, 177, 178, 234, 235, 236, 237, 238)

Rachel **Jevon** Rachel Jevon emerges out of provincial obscurity in 1660 as the author of two parallel Restoration Odes, one in English and one in Latin. She was the daughter of a Worcestershire clergyman, Daniel Jevon, and his wife Elizabeth. She was christened in 1627 in Broom in that county. Her family were possibly connected with a gentry family of Jevons in Staffordshire. In 1662 she petitioned Charles II for a place in the service of the Queen. The petition stresses the royalism and loyalty of her clergyman father, and his attempt to foster royalist allegiance through the years of Interregnum. (337)

Thomas **Jordan** Thomas Jordan was born in London in about 1612, and was a player at the Red Bull theatre in Clerkenwell. At the suppression of the theatres in 1642, he contrived to make a living on the fringes of the literary world by writing dedications and pamphlets. At the Restoration he was for a time an actor before becoming a very successful poet to the Corporation of London. He died in 1685. (144, 277, 278, 279, 280)

Anne **Kemp** Gentlewoman, fl. 1650s. On the internal evidence of her one surviving poem, she lived in Gloucestershire. (223)

Henry **King** Henry King, divine, was born in 1591, and educated at Westminster School, and Christ Church, Oxford. He held many distinguished posts in the Church before his elevation to the see of Chichester in 1642. He was deprived of his bishopric from 1643 until the Restoration, whereafter he held it until his death in 1669. He had many eminent literary friends, amongst them John Donne and Ben Jonson. (12, 13, 14, 124, 125)

Ralph **Knevet** Ralph Knevet, clergyman, was born in 1601 at Hardwick in Norfolk, a distant connection of the famous Norfolk family of Paston. He attended Peterhouse, Cambridge, but left without taking a degree. Thereafter he was possibly a tutor or chaplain in the household of the Pastons at Oxnead. Knevet accompanied William Paston on extensive travels in Italy between 1637 and 1639. He worked at a sequence of devotional poems, *A Gallery to the Temple* during the Interregnum. He was first Rector of Oxnead, then of Lyng, and died c.1671–2. Amongst his works are a pastoral play *Rhodon and Iris*, written for the Norwich Florist's Feast in 1631, an interesting *Supplement to the Faery Queene*, and the devotional poems of *A Gallery to the Temple*. (184)

Sir Francis **Kynaston** Francis Kynaston was born in 1587 at Otley in Shropshire, and educated at Oriel College, Oxford, and Trinity College, Cambridge, where he took an MA in 1609. He also studied at Lincoln's Inn. He was MP for Shropshire in the 1621 Parliament. On the accession of Charles I, Kynaston became an Esquire of the Body. He founded an academy called the Musaeum Minervae in his house in Bedford Square, Covent Garden, to instruct young gentlemen in arts and languages as a preparation for foreign travel and translated Chaucer's *Troilus and Criseyde* into Latin, thinking to preserve a work which he valued in an imperishable language. He died in 1642. (2, 3)

Sir Roger **L'Estrange** Roger L'Estrange was born in 1616, of a distinguished Norfolk family. He was an active royalist pamphleteer during the Civil War, was imprisoned, and forced subsequently to flee the country. After the Restoration he was appointed Licenser of the Press, and continued many journalistic activities. He fled the country again at the time of the Popish Plot and was imprisoned again at the Revolution. He made many translations from various languages in the course of his life, and died in 1704. (283)

Martin **Lluelyn** Martin Lluelyn, poet and physician, Principal of St Mary's Hall, Oxford, was born in the parish of St Bartholomew, Smithfield, London in 1616. He was educated at Westminster, and Corpus Christi College, Oxford, taking his MA in 1643. At the outbreak of the Civil War, he enlisted in the King's Army, being ejected from Oxford by the parliamentary visitors in 1648. He became a member of the College of Physicians in 1654. After the Restoration, he became Physician to Charles II, dying in Buckinghamshire in 1682. (145, 284)

Morgan **Llwyd** Born in Cynhafal, Maentwrog, Merioneth, in 1619. Served with the parliamentary forces during the first, and second Civil Wars. He was the author of *Llyfr y Tri Aderyn* ('The Book of the Three Birds') in 1653: a work written in the form of a conversation between the Eagle (representing the government and administration), the Raven (institutional religion, episcopacy), and the Dove (Puritanism, which was Morgan Llwyd's own standpoint). He showed a critical interest in Quakerism and consulted George Fox through intermediaries on matters of creed. Llwyd resented Cromwell's adoption of the title Lord Protector, and his name was included on the protest document known as *A Word for God*, but he denied any part in the document. He died in 1659. (297, 298, 299)

Richard **Lovelace** Richard Lovelace was born in 1618 into a wealthy Kentish family. He was educated at Charterhouse, and Gloucester Hall (Worcester College) Oxford. A courtier of Charles I, he was imprisoned by Parliament in 1642 for presenting the Kentish Petition, which sought to limit the use of the Militia. In 1646–7 he served in the army of the King of France and was imprisoned again at his return to England. The events of his life until his death in 1658 are obscure: the despair, and poverty of his last years are reflected in the edgy and bitter tone of his second volume *Lucasta, Posthume Poems* (1659). (65, 66, 67, 68, 69, 70, 106, 107, 289, 290, 291, 292, 293, 294, 295, 296)

Iain Lom **Macdonald** Born around 1624. He is known by his nickname 'Lom', meaning 'bald' or 'cutting'. He belonged to the ruling family of the MacDonalds of Keppoch, and looked on various national events as occasions for praise of his own clan and dispraise of the rival Campbells. He lived till at least 1707, when he wrote a bitter poem on the union with England, but it is likely that he died soon after. (321, 322, 323, 340)

Murdo **MacKenzie** of Achilty. Murdo MacKenzie, fifth chief of Achilty in Contin, died about 1689. He is known by his patronymic Murchadh Mor mac mhic Mhurrchaidh 'Great Murdo, son of the son of Murdo'. In religion and politics he was a royalist and episcopalian. His poems are unusual in the Gaelic world in that they were written down as early as 1688. (327, 328)

Mary **McLeod** Màiri nighean Alasdair Ruaidh ('daughter of Alasdair') may have been born in Rodel, Harris, around 1615, and died c.1705: there are many stories about her, but few of them are substantiable. She was a semi-professional poet of clan MacLeod, and may have been a nurse in the household of the MacLeod chieftain at Dunvegan, or associated with another MacLeod household, at Berneray. (216)

Cathal **Mac Mhuirich** Very little is known of his life: he was one of the last, and greatest of the Mac Mhuirich family of professional poets, known to have been composing before 1618, and after 1650. He composed poetry for Clanranald, and MacDonald of Sleat. (129)

Alasdair **Mac Mhurchaidh** (d. c.1642) The fourth MacKenzie of Achilty, known by his patronymic Alasdair Mac Mhurchaidh. He was the father of Murdo MacKenzie, and both father,and son seem to have functioned as factors to Lord Seaforth in Lewis. (24)

Elizabeth **Major** fl. 1650s. Little is known of the life of this Elizabeth Major, an index of the extent to which the lives of early-modern women go undocumented, unless they are of the high rank, or become involved in a case at law. Elizabeth Major appears, at the time when she was writing, to have been a parishioner of St Magnus, London Bridge. It is possible that she came from the Hampshire family whose daughter Dorothy married Richard Cromwell in 1649. The household of a 'John Maior' is recorded as living near Blackfriars in *The Visitation of London*, 1634. She could equally possibly have been a daughter of this family. (162)

Andrew **Marvell** Andrew Marvell was born in 1621 at Winestead in Holderness in Yorkshire and educated at Hull Grammar School and Trinity College, Cambridge. At the outbreak of the Civil War he sold the small estate which he had inherited from his father, and travelled in Europe. On his return to England he wrote verses in commendation of Lovelace's *Lucasta* (1648). During the Interregnum he lived for some time in the household of General Fairfax in Yorkshire. In 1653 he moved to London and failed to be appointed as Latin Secretary to the Council of State. In 1659 he was elected MP for Hull, a position which he held for twenty years. After the Restoration he continued as an MP and continued to travel. The many satirical writings of the later part of his life move steadily to a position of opposition to the royal and ecclesiastical establishment. He died in 1678. (311, 312, 313)

John **Milton** Born in London in 1608, the son of a scrivener. Educated at St Paul's School and Christ's College, Cambridge. He began writing poetry, in both English, and Latin, while still at university. Milton retired to Horton, Bucks., between the years 1632 and 1638, writing the poems *L'Allegro*, *Penseroso*, and *Lycidas*. He also wrote the masque *Comus* which was produced at Ludlow Castle in 1634. He travelled in Europe throughout 1638–9 and returned to support the Puritan cause in many prose essays, and political tracts. He became Latin Secretary to Cromwell in 1649. He became completely blind by 1652, continuing to dictate his poetry to the women in his household. At the Restoration Milton was prosecuted for his political activities but escaped with nominal imprisonment and, retiring from public life published *Paradise Lost* in 1667, its sequel *Paradise Regained*, and the verse drama *Samson Agonistes* in 1671. Milton died in 1674. (101, 207, 258, 259)

Huw **Morys** (1622–1709). Born in Hafodgynfor, Llangollen, Denbighshire. He avoided censure during the Commonwealth period by resorting to the fifteenth-century beast-fable technique of giving characters in his work the name of animals. His style reveals him as an antiquarian, a conscious imitator of fifteenth-century classicist *cywyddau*. He also wrote popular verses to be sung to well-known tunes, of which *Yr Arglwydd Mwnc* is an example. (338)

Marchamont **Nedham** Nedham came from Burford in Oxfordshire, and attended All Souls College, Oxford. His sympathies were republican, and he became a London journalist, the author/editor of a series of journals: a royalist newsbook, *Mercurius Pragmaticus*, then when times changed, *Mercurius Politicus*, the principal newspaper of the Commonwealth, a lively, and witty vehicle of parliamentarian propaganda on which Milton also worked from 1651. Notoriously disloyal, he survived into the days of the Protectorate, and continued to issue a government journal, though a considerably less witty one. (307, 308, 309, 310)

Henry **Noel** Henry Noel was the son of Lord Viscount Cambden. He was born at Brooke Castle in Rutland in 1615 and died a prisoner in parliamentary quarters in 1643. (87)

Sir John **Ogilby** John Ogilby (1600–76) was a royalist author, and printer. He translated Virgil, Homer, and Aesop, and was principally famous as a topographer, author and editor of the 'Road Books of England, and Wales'. He wrote the City of London's coronation entry for Charles II, subsequently publishing an account of the coronation. (339)

Fear Dorcha Ó **Mealláin** Only one poem survives by Ó Mealláin and very little is known about his life: he may have been a priest and was probably a native of County Down. (325)

Clement **Paman** Clement Paman was born in 1612 on his father's estate at Chevington in Suffolk, and educated at Lavenham and Bury schools and at Sidney Sussex College, Cambridge, where he took his MA in 1635. He appears to have been chaplain to the first Earl of Strafford in which capacity he spent some time in Ireland, at least from 1637 to 1640. After various appointments in England (from 1650–60 he was private chaplain to the Earl of Northampton and later to Sir Henry North at Bansfield) he rose to the position of Dean of Elphin (now Sligo) in 1661. He died in 1664. (136, 137, 138, 139, 212, 275, 276)

Martin **Parker** Very little is known of the life of Martin Parker, a prolific writer of ballads: passing references in the popular literature of the time suggest that he was a Londoner, possibly a tavern-keeper. A satirical elegy on Parker is dated 1656. (243)

Thomas **Philipott** Thomas Philipott was born about 1620, son of John Philipot, Somerset Herald. In 1633 he became a fellow-commoner of Clare Hall, Cambridge, taking his MA in 1635. He incorporated his degree at Oxford in 1640. He appears to have lived a quiet and prosperous life near Greenwich. In his will he left money for fellowships, and almshouses. He died and was buried at Greenwich in 1682. (71, 72)

Katherine **Philips** Born Katherine Fowler in 1631, the daughter of a prosperous merchant with Puritan sympathies. At the age of 8 she was sent to school in Hackney,and there met Mary Aubrey, the 'Rosania' of her poems. On her widowed mother's remarriage to a Welsh baronet in 1639, Katherine was taken to Pembrokeshire. At 16 she was married to James Philips, a kinsman of her stepfather, and thirty-eight years her senior. Throughout the Interregnum, Katherine Philips, whose personal sympathies were royalist, lived quietly in Wales, writing and bearing two children. Henry Vaughan (qv) took notice of her writing in 1651. She was a translator (of Horace and Corneille) as well as a lyric poet in her own right. At the Restoration James Philips lost much property, his seat in parliament, and narrowly escaped prosecution as a regicide, but Katherine's loyal writings, and contacts at court protected their fortunes. Her original poems and translations were published together in 1667, three years after her early death from smallpox. (77, 117, 227, 333, 341)

John **Polwhele** John Polwhele, clergyman, was born at St Erme in Cornwall in 1586, and was educated at Exeter College, Oxford. He was a Fellow of Exeter from 1608–22 and then vicar of Whitchurch in Devon from 1622 until his death in 1648. His poems have never been published. They are of uneven quality, but include a translation of the verse part of Boethius' *De Consolatione* which appears to have been revised to express a passionate concern for the events of the Civil War:

> The Ostro-Gothes doe tread uppon
> Most sacred necks to mounte the throne.
> Patricians in exile hide
> At home true patriots have died
> For treason. (82)

Vavasour **Powell** (1617–70) A Welsh nonconformist He studied at Oxford without taking a degree, and was never ordained, but became a passionate itinerant evangelist. He was first arrested for his preaching in 1640. Left Wales for London at the outbreak of civil war (August 1642) and preached in, and around the capital until 1646 before returning to his native land. Powell is said to have been the first nonconformist to have been prosecuted at the Restoration on no more evidence than his preaching. (158)

Francis **Quarles** Francis Quarles was born in 1592, and was educated at Christ's College, Cambridge, and Lincoln's Inn. He held various appointments in Church and State. In the Civil War he wrote a tract in defence of Charles I, which led Parliament to confiscate his property and destroy his manuscripts. He never recovered from these misfortunes, dying in 1644. His mild and devout religious poems remained popular into the eighteenth and nineteenth centuries. (240)

Thomas **Randolph** Thomas Randolph was born in Northamptonshire in 1605, and from an early age he showed unusual literary ability. He was educated at Westminster School and Trinity College, Cambridge, of which college he was a Fellow from 1629. He received recognition both for his verses, and his plays, and was considered to be perhaps the most promising poet of his generation. He was a friend of Ben Jonson, and associated with many of the poets in his circle. He died in 1635. (187, 188, 189, 190)

Henry **Reinolds** (Reynolds) fl. 1628–32. Associate of Michael Drayton, who addressed a verse epistle to him. Translator, notably of Ovid, allegorizer, and poetic theorist. (12)

Daniel **Scargill** Clergyman, fl. 1680. (79)

Thomas **Shipman** Thomas Shipman was born in 1632, son of William Shipman of Scarrington in Nottinghamshire. He was educated at St John's College, Cambridge. 'In that miserable storm the Civil War it was his good Fortune to retire from a total Ruine; and that quiet recess gave the opportunity of these Papers his poems.' He was buried at Scarrington in October 1680. (334)

James **Shirley** James Shirley was born in 1596 and educated at both Oxford, and Cambridge. After being ordained, he became a Roman Catholic and spent some years teaching until the success of his first comedy in 1625 took him to London. He worked as a professional dramatist, producing numerous plays and masques before the closure of the theatres in 1642. He took part in the Civil War, fighting under his patron the Duke of Newcastle (qv) and accompanying him into exile in France. On his return to England he became a schoolmaster again and wrote books on education. He died in 1666, a casualty of the Great Fire of London. (19, 20, 21, ?89, 182, 241)

Thomas **Stanley** Thomas Stanley was born at Cumberlow Green in Hertfordshire in 1625 into a wealthy family. He was educated at Pembroke College, Cambridge, taking his MA in 1642. At the outbreak of the Civil War he left Britain, and travelled on the Continent. He returned after 1646 and lived in the Middle Temple, where he was both a patron of poets and a member of a discreet royalist society, 'The Order of the Black Ribbon'—gentlemen who wore a black twist about their arms to express their sympathy with the King. After the King's execution Stanley went into retirement at Cumberlow Green. He devoted himself to classical scholarship after the publication of his poems in 1651. After the Restoration he became a Fellow of the Royal Society and died in London in 1678. (73, 224, 326)

Matthew **Stevenson** Matthew Stevenson was probably of Yorkshire origin, and passed most of his life in Norfolk. He appears to have been a minor member of a group of royalist poets including Cowley. He was active between 1625 and 1685. (221, 222)

William **Strode** William Strode, orator, and clergyman, was born in Devon c.1600–1. He was educated at Christ Church, Oxford, taking his MA in 1624. He took holy orders, and gained some celebrity as a preacher. In 1629 he was made Public Orator in the University, and was chaplain to Richard Corbett (qv), the bishop of Oxford. His play *The Floating Island* was performed before Charles I and Henrietta Maria in 1636. He wrote some royalist propaganda in the Civil War and died in March 1645. He was buried in Christ Church. (90, 91, 92, 93, 130, 131, 183)

Charles **Stuart** King Charles I, see Appendix 2. (attributed, 244, 245, 246, 247)

Sir John **Suckling** Suckling was born in 1609 into an old Norfolk family and was educated at Trinity College, Cambridge. He inherited his fortune young and travelled in France, and Italy, serving for a time in the army of Gustavus Adolphus. On his return to England in 1632 he lived an extravagant life at court, producing his play *Aglaura* with great magnificence in 1637. In 1639 he equipped a troop of horse for Charles I's expedition against the Scots. He was later accused of being involved in a royalist plot, and fled to France where he is thought to have committed suicide in 1642. (38, 39, 40, 41, 208)

Lady **Tanfield** Elizabeth, Lady Tanfield (?1565–1628), was the daughter of Giles Symondes of Claye, Norfolk, and wife of Sir Lawrence Tanfield (qv, Appendix 2). As allegations of fraud, and corruption proliferated against him, common rumour openly suggested that Lady Tanfield was equally ready to take bribes to influence her husband's legal judgements. Her husband's tenants at Great Tew, Oxfordshire complained of her that 'she saith that we are more worthy to be ground to powder than to have any favour showed to us, and that she will play the very devil among us'. The couple's sole heiress, also Elizabeth, married Sir Henry Cary, Viscount Falkland, and was the mother of Lucius Cary (qv, Appendix 2). (1)

Poets of the **Tixall** Circle Tixall in Staffordshire, situated near the confluence of Sow and Trent, was the seat of the Aston family, and something of a provincial literary centre. Drayton enjoyed the patronage of Walter, first Lord Aston, who had been twice ambassador to Spain: in 1619, and in 1635–8. The Astons and their children had some acquaintance with Fanshawe and Waller, and at the least access to unpublished texts by Crashaw, Sandys, and Davenant. In 1813, Arthur Clifford, descendant of the Astons through the female line, published a generous selection of Aston poetry from the seventeenth century under the title of *Tixall Poetry*. The people who wrote and collected the poems contained therein consisted of five distinct families and their friends: Fowler of St Thomas, Aston of Tixall, Aston of Bellamore, Persall of Canwell, all in Staffordshire, and Thimelby of Irnham in Lincolnshire. The principal authors appear to have been children of the first Lord Aston: Herbert Aston of Bellamore, his sister Gertrude Aston, wife of Henry Thimelby, and his sister Constantia, later Fowler. (30, 31, 133, 134, 196, 197, 198, 199, 253)

Aurelian **Townshend** Aurelian Townshend lived in London, a shadowy life on the fringes of the court. He was born not later than 1583, and was sent to Paris and Venice in his early manhood under the patronage of Sir Robert Cecil, possibly as a spy. He returned in 1605, travelling abroad again in 1608. He may have held minor court employment thereafter through the patronage of Sir Robert Cecil, Earl of Salisbury. In 1622 he appears to be living in the parish of St Giles, Cripplegate, he wrote the court masque *Albion's Triumph* in collaboration with Inigo Jones in 1632, and he was admitted to Gray's Inn in 1633. He is lost to sight after 1643, and may have left England. He was dead by 1652. (81, 169, 170)

Anna **Trapnel** Anna Trapnel was born c.1620, the daughter of a shipwright. Following her mother's death in 1642, she became subject to religious raptures, and began to utter prophecies.

She was aligned with the Fifth Monarchists, a group of religious extremists who expected the imminent return of Christ to rule the world in glory (the 'Fifth Monarchy'). She was seized by inspiration in Whitehall in 1654 while a Fifth Monarchist leader, Vavasour Powell (qv), was undergoing questioning: her utterances were taken down verbatim, and published as *The Cry of a Stone*, probably because her utterances, which criticized Cromwell for undue moderation, could be put to political use by his enemies. She died some time after 1660. (159, 160, 161)

Sir Thomas **Urquhart** Sir Thomas Urquhart was born in 1611 on his father's estates at Cromarty in the north of Scotland. He was educated at Aberdeen University, and fought against the Covenanters in the opening skirmishes of the Civil War. He was knighted at London in 1641. He followed Charles II to defeat at Worcester, and was subsequently imprisoned. He went into exile in the Netherlands and is thought to have died at Middelburg in 1660. Apart from his hitherto unpublished *Apollo, and the Muses* (two epigrams from which are included in this book) his chief works are fantastical mathematical and philological treatises, and his translation of the first three books of Rabelais, published in 1653 and 1693. (211, 265)

Henry **Vaughan** Henry Vaughan, poet and physician, was born in Brecknockshire in 1621/2 and educated at Jesus College, Oxford. He started to practise medicine in 1645, and died in 1695. (151, 152, 153, 154, 155, 316)

Thomas **Vaughan** Thomas Vaughan was the twin brother of Henry Vaughan. He took orders and was installed as Rector at Llansanffraid (St Bridget) by 1645. Both brothers took part in the Civil War on behalf of the royalist forces in the defence of Chester in September 1645. He was ejected from his living in 1650, moved to London, and worked on the alchemical treatises for which he is best known. He died in 1666. (156, 157)

Edmund **Waller** Edmund Waller was born in 1606 in Hertfordshire, and educated at Eton and King's College, Cambridge. He became an MP, but was expelled in 1643 for his part in a plot to gain control of London for Charles I and thus end the Civil War. He was imprisoned, fined, and banished. He lived in Paris until he was pardoned in 1651; he gained the favour of Cromwell and wrote poems in his praise. He disowned these at the Restoration, when he became MP for Hastings, which he represented until his death in 1687. He was very highly esteemed in his lifetime, and indeed did much to prepare the way for the Augustan style which was to predominate from the late seventeenth century. (32, 33, 34, 35, 99, 200, 201, 202, 203, 204, 254, 336)

Gerrard **Winstanley** Gerrard Winstanley was born in 1609, and became a cloth merchant and Freeman of the City of London. When the Civil War ruined his business, he devoted his energies to writing mystical theology, and was moved by his religious beliefs to become a political activist, becoming the leader of the Digger movement in 1649–50. Winstanley called for a kind of primitive, Protestant communism to succeed the monarchy, and set a practical example by leading a group of poor men to St George's Hill in Walton where, claiming communal ownership of the area, they dug and planted the waste land. The colony they tried to found there was destroyed by order of the Council of the Army. In his last work, *The Law of Freedom*, Winstanley petitioned Cromwell for a new style of government similar to the Leveller ideal, based on religious toleration, manhood suffrage, and regular elections. The date of his death is unknown. (135, 260, 261, 262)

George **Wither** (1588–1667). Born in Hampshire and entered Magdalen College, Oxford, but failed to acquire a degree. In 1606, Wither entered one of the Inns of Chancery. In 1611, his first publication, 'Abuses Stript and Whipt' offended the authorities. His patroness, whose intervention seems to have saved him on this occasion, was Princess Elizabeth: his dedication to her of his translation of the Psalms (1632) makes his gratitude clear. The subsequent reprint of 'Abuses' in 1613 went through at least five editions, but landed him in prison. Whilst there he wrote pastorals to support himself. Imprisonment ruined him financially and he lived in retirement during 1636–9, then became a soldier for the King against the Covenanters. His best religious poetry dates from this period. Upon the outbreak of Civil War, he sold up his estate to raise a troop of horse for Parliament. In 1642/3 Parliament ordered him two thousand pounds in recompense for a royalist raid on his home. Sir John Denham is said to have saved his life after his capture by royalists, he 'desired his majesty not to hang him, for that whilst G.W. lived he [Denham] should not be the worst poet in England'. He was imprisoned at the Restoration and his last years seem to have been lived in poverty, and discontent. (342)

Sir Henry **Wotton** (1568–1639). Educated at Winchester and Oxford, he entered the Middle Temple, from which time dates a close friendship with John Donne. In 1595 Wotton became secretary to the Earl of Essex, acting as his agent in collecting foreign intelligence. He subsequently became ambassador to the court of Venice and was employed on various diplomatic missions abroad between 1604 and 1624. Wotton was the author of short prose biographies and architectural writings as well as poetry: his own biography was written by Izaak Walton in 1670. (119, 167)

Lady Mary **Wroth** Lady Mary Wroth (1587–c.1652) was the daughter of Sir Robert Sidney, Earl of Leicester, niece of Sir Philip Sidney. She was brought up at Penshurst and in the Netherlands, when her father succeeded his brother as Governor of Flushing. She married at an early age Sir Robert Wroth with whom, although they appear to have had little in common, she remained on friendly terms. In 1614 he died and, having entertained King James too lavishly, left his widow in debt for the rest of her life. Lady Wroth lost favour with Queen Anne, and retired to Penshurst during 1618–20, where she composed a long prose romance in imitation of Sidney's *Arcadia. The Countess of Montgomeries Urania* appeared in 1621 and offers satirical descriptions of court intrigues in the quest for royal favour. It is the first full-length work of prose fiction written by an English-speaking woman. A sequel was written but never published. Appended to the *Urania* is an elaborate sonnet sequence called *Pamphilia to Amphilanthus* from which the poems anthologized here are taken. She also wrote a pastoral entertainment, *Love's Victory*, edited and published privately in 1988. (4, 5, 6, 7, 83, 84)

APPENDIX 4
CHRONOLOGY 1625–1660

1625 Charles I acceded, aged 25, and married the Catholic Henrietta Maria of France. Conflict between Charles and his ministers began almost immediately, since Parliament was hostile to the continental projects suggested to Charles by George Villiers, Duke of Buckingham (1592–1628), now Charles's favourite, and formerly his father's. Following Buckingham's advice, he engaged in war with Spain (Catholic) and an alliance with Holland and Denmark (Protestant): both decisions had a religious dimension, and also involved family loyalties: the husband of his sister Elizabeth ('the Winter Queen', no. 167) had lost his Palatinate to Spain in 1621. Charles's desire to play a significant role in European politics made him anxious to assure himself of adequate financial resources.

1626 Charles's Second Parliament impeached Buckingham, declared the taxes of tonnage and poundage (a form of Customs tax, which represented a substantial portion of the King's revenue) illegal, and was dissolved by the King. Charles then tried to assure himself of income by other means, and resumed non-parliamentary levies.

1627 Both parliament and country resisted Charles's attempts to raise money by levying forced loans to the Crown. Two high-church clergymen, Sibthorpe and Manwaring, preached 'Apostolic Obedience' to the King's wishes, which helped to confirm Puritan opposition to the established church, as opposition to apostolic authority was identified with opposition to unpopular taxes. George Abbot, Archbishop of Canterbury, was sequestered for refusing to license Sibthorpe's sermon for the press. Expedition to the Ile de Rhé: an abortive gesture towards an attack on France.

1628 Third Parliament. The Petition of Right (which gave the judiciary ultimate power even over Parliament) became law. The King's pressing need for money was met to some extent by subsidies voted him by Parliament. William Laud (1573–1645), who enjoyed the King's favour, and promoted an extremely unpopular policy of the imposition of religious uniformity, became bishop of London, while Archbishop Abbot was restored to favour. The Duke of Buckingham was assassinated (no. 241), leaving Charles without a mentor. His relations with his Queen had been cold and distant up to this point, but the royal couple suddenly began to show a mutual devotion which continued without interruption for the rest of their lives. A second expedition to La Rochelle, where the Huguenot (Protestant) subjects of the French King, Louis XIII, continued to endure a prolonged siege, was a total failure. Aiding the Huguenots was a matter of personal honour to Charles, who had guaranteed an earlier treaty subsequently broken by the French king, and had been strongly supported by Buckingham, who had led the first expedition. Thomas Wentworth (1593–1641), later the Earl of Strafford, became President of the Council of the North (the King's deputy north of the Humber).

1629 Parliament passed resolutions against Popery and the high-church doctrine of Arminianism, voicing a widely felt suspicion that the King, now devoted to his Catholic wife, was gradually transforming the Church of England into an imitation of the Church of Rome. It also renewed opposition to tonnage and poundage, and to the King's claim that he had the right to levy duties without the consent of Parliament. It was again dissolved by the King. Some leading parliamentarians were imprisoned. The King went ahead with exacting the impositions he required. Bishop Laud rallied to his royal master with his attempts to control the press and to place restrictions on religious lecturers. Peace was made with France.

1630 Birth of the future Charles II. Peace was made with Spain, further fuelling English fears that Charles was siding with Europe's Catholic monarchs. Charles's creditors became increasingly pressing, and so he revived an obsolete but technically legal source of revenue: all subjects who owned estates worth more than £40 a year were summoned to receive knighthoods and pay for the privilege. Knighthood fines and impositions were levied (no. 205). Bishop Laud became Chancellor of Oxford, where he proceeded to enforce religious conformity. Large-scale Puritan emigration to Massachusetts began, including John Winthrop and other religious dissidents. Plague broke out in London, and an extraordinary drought brought disastrous harvests and presaged widespread famine.

1631 A commission for poor relief was set up, and measures to control the price of corn were instituted. Charles was considering intervention in the conflict between Spain and the Protestant kings of northern Europe. His policies were dictated largely by his desire to restore his sister Elizabeth to her throne in Bohemia, and thus vacillated between supporting Spain and the Protestant King of Sweden, Gustavus Adolphus, who later rejected his offers. Birth of Princess Mary (mother of William II). John Donne died.

1632 Futile and contradictory negotiations with Holland, Spain, and France continued. Gustavus Adolphus and the Elector Palatine both died, leaving Elizabeth struggling to regain the Palatinate on behalf of her eldest son. Meanwhile Charles continued to struggle with poverty and debt, though the settlement of Anthony Van Dyck in England inaugurated a period of introverted splendour in the arts at court which gives a wholly different impression. Life at court became increasingly enclosed and sophisticated. Henrietta Maria gave offence to many Protestant Londoners by supporting the theatre, dancing in public, and acting in masques and plays. William Prynne (1600–69), a Puritan pamphleteer, published *Histriomastix: A Scourge of Stage Players*, and was sentenced to lose his ears in the pillory. George Herbert died.

1633 Birth of the future James VII and II. Laud became Archbishop of Canterbury: Lady Eleanor Davies published a book of prophecies against him, declaring him to be the Beast in the Book of Revelation, and was imprisoned. Charles was formally crowned as King of Scotland in Edinburgh, in an atmosphere of mutual religious, and political mistrust. The *Declaration of Sports*, which allowed the English people to play games and otherwise entertain themselves on Sundays, was reissued by Charles: this was obnoxious to the Puritans, strict observers of the Sabbath. Wentworth began his administration as Lord Deputy of Ireland, which, although efficient, and in many ways beneficial, was high-handed and aimed at improving the prosperity not of the Irish people but of the English exchequer. His policies were directed towards the raising of revenue, and alienated both recent Protestant settlers, and the old Catholic élite. He supported the plantation of Scots and English settlers in various parts of the country.

1634 Laud enforced religious conformity throughout the realm. New canons were forced upon the Protestant Church in Ireland. Witch-trials were held in Lancashire. The King began negotiating secretly with Spain for a naval alliance against the Dutch, the principal maritime competitors against the English. He thus wished to raise the cash for equipping a fleet without summoning Parliament to vote him a subsidy, which would make his intentions public. Reviving a medieval statute requiring all port towns to man and equip ships for the defence of the realm, he instituted a new and very unpopular tax, ship money. The City of London raised a petition in protest, which was ignored. Charles also attempted to raise money by revoking the boundaries of English forests which had been fixed for three hundred years (forests belonged directly to the Crown), and claiming the much greater territory which had been under Forest Law in the thirteenth century as his rightful property. This would place seventeen towns and their inhabitants under the direct dominance of the King, with no protection from law or Parliament.

1635 The second writ of ship money was issued: this time the tax was extended to inland counties and approved by the judges. The first signs of serious resistance to the tax appeared. Charles alienated many merchants by his distribution of trade monopolies. This caused widespread public indignation, especially since many of the monopolists were known to be Catholics. Diplomatic relations were entered into with the Papacy, encouraged by the Queen, and the conditions for the reunification of the English Church with Rome discussed with a Papal envoy, Gregorio Panzani. Charles made further efforts to secure the position of his sister and nephew by negotiating with Spain for the return of the Palatinate. Another daughter (Elizabeth) was born to Charles I, and Henrietta Maria. Wentworth's government in Ireland began to seem increasingly arbitrary to his subjects, especially when he set aside the representations of native Irish lords and claimed that the whole of Ireland belonged entirely to the King.

1636 The judges affirmed the King's superiority to the law, and a third writ of ship money was issued. Charles became increasingly anxious to claim and enforce English sovereignty over the North Sea and Channel, against the rights assumed by the Dutch and other maritime nations. The King and Archbishop Laud visited Oxford with great ceremony, and Laudian statutes were promulgated for the University, alienating many of its members.

1637 The judges reaffirmed the King's right to levy ship money at discretion, and the future parliamentary leader John Hampden was brought to trial for resisting this. The verdict went narrowly against him. Further attempts were made to tighten control of the press. The Scots fiercely resisted the imposition of the new Anglican service books and canons. Ben Jonson died.

1638 There was general resentment in England over the King's continued exactions, and over Laud's policy of religious conformity, which permitted no freedom of worship to the country's many dissenters. In Scotland the reaction against Laud's episcopalian church was even stronger. The National Covenant, binding its signatories to defend their (Presbyterian) religion to the death, was signed widely and enthusiastically (no. 231). The Marquess of Montrose was one of the first signatories.

1639 Charles mounted an invasion of Scotland known as the first Bishops' War in an attempt to discipline the Scots. After some successes on both sides (Montrose distinguishing himself as one of the ablest generals among the Covenanters) it ended with the Pacification of Berwick. When it became increasingly clear that Charles was unlikely to honour the concessions he had made in the Treaty, trouble began anew (no. 231). Wentworth returned from Ireland to support and advise the King. Birth of Prince Henry.

1640 The first parliamentary elections for twelve years were held. Charles asked the new parliament for massive financial support to renew his campaign against the Scots. John Pym and John Hampden led the Commons in defending their right to resist royal exactions. The parliament was promptly dissolved (15 May) thus becoming known as the Short Parliament, while the King turned to non- parliamentary ways of raising money. The second Bishops' War was initiated, against the wishes of the Commons, and ended in English defeat, the loss of Newcastle upon Tyne to the Covenanters, and in the Treaty of Ripon (26 October). A new parliament was convened (3 November), known as the Long Parliament. One of its first actions was to impeach Wentworth (now Earl of Strafford) for treason, on a variety of heads which amounted to encouraging, and facilitating the arbitrary government of his royal master. The parliament also imprisoned Archbishop Laud. Charles was forced to consent to a bill which laid down that the parliament could not be dissolved except by its own consent. This done, it went on to ban ship money and other non- parliamentary taxes, and to make Laud's canons, which had imposed a forced unity on the English Church, illegal (no. 251). The London Root and Branch petition for the abolition of bishops in the English Church was introduced by Puritan parliamentarians.

1641 The Princess Royal, aged 10, married William of Orange, thus creating ties of mutual obligation between England and the Netherlands. The Earl of Strafford was executed on 12 May. Charles had promised him protection, but the level of the public demonstrations against him eventually persuaded the King to sign his death-warrant (no. 275). Parliament continued to pass sweeping reforms (no. 228). The King went to Scotland in August to negotiate with his rebellious subjects. Once Charles had made concessions to Presbyterianism, Montrose, among others, resumed his loyalty to him. The Scottish army withdrew from England. A widespread and successful rebellion broke out in Ireland (23 October), causing Charles to cut short his stay in Edinburgh. The army became a visible force in the political life of the country. Returning to London, the King was confronted by the Grand Remonstrance (1 December), a summary of the woes of England since the 1620s, setting forth all Charles's misdemeanours and implying that the country would be better governed by Parliament, which was steered through the Commons by their leader John Pym, and passed by a narrow majority. The theatres were closed, and remained closed until the Restoration (nos. 232, 233) Suckling, Hobbes, and many other writers left the country, some temporarily, some for longer periods of exile.

1642 The King reacted to the Grand Remonstrance by impeaching five members of the Commons (including Pym and Hampden) for High Treason, but failed in his attempt to arrest them by force on 4 January (no. 281). He was forced to leave London on 10 January. When he attempted to enter Hull on 23 April, the governor refused to admit him (no. 280). War became inevitable, and the King's standard was set up at Nottingham on 22 August and his headquarters for the next four years established at Oxford following the indecisive Royalist victory at Edgehill on 23 October (no. 276). Many writers and intellectuals were drawn into the war (Falkland, Denham, Fanshawe, Cleveland, Davenant, Cowley, Wither); Lovelace was imprisoned; Marvell travelled abroad.

1643 The war continued, with several royalist victories, before Oliver Cromwell, operating in the eastern counties, gained the first parliamentary victory at Winceby on 11 October (nos. 299, 331). The Westminster Assembly of Divines proposed Presbyterian church government for England (nos. 240, 306, 309). By taking the Solemn League and Covenant on 25 September, both the Assembly and Parliament undertook to impose this on England in return for Scottish military aid against the King.

1644 The Scots army having entered England on 19 January, Parliament set up the Committee of Both Kingdoms, to maintain communications with its field commanders, and won its first decisive victory at Marston Moor (no. 230). In Cornwall its army, under Essex, was forced to surrender; and in Scotland, the former Covenanter James Graham, Marquis of Montrose, leading a mainly Highland force, won the first of many victories at Tippermuir. On 14 July, after the birth of her youngest child, the Queen left England for France (no. 257). Waller was imprisoned.

1645 Archbishop Laud was executed on 10 January and the Prayer Book abolished. The New Model Army Ordinance (17 February), creating a single field army under a unified command,

and the Self-Denying Ordinance (3 April), making it impossible for a member of either House of Parliament (except Cromwell, and a few others) to hold any military command, paved the way for a series of parliamentary victories, including that at Naseby on 14 June, under the new Captain-General, Sir Thomas Fairfax (nos. 237, 303, 304). Even Montrose passed from victory at Kilsyth to defeat at Philiphaugh, and the King's attempts to obtain Irish and foreign troops met with little success (nos. 277, 284).

1646 The King's military cause, virtually hopeless since Naseby, was lost with his flight to the Scots army at Newark on 5 May and the subsequent surrender of Oxford on 13 July (no. 301). The Newcastle Propositions of 14 July (inevitably more stringent than those put forward at Oxford in 1642–3, and at Uxbridge in 1645) were put to the King, who considered them for nearly a year. The Prince of Wales went to Jersey, on his way to exile in France. Episcopacy was abolished on 9 October.

1647 The Scots army withdrew from England, handing the King over to the Parliamentarians (30 January), from whom he was later taken by an army detachment, the army having further emerged as a powerful political force in its own right, with its own Heads of Proposals (23 July) for the settlement of the country. On 11 November, the King, having treated both with Parliament and with the army, escaped from Hampton Court to the Isle of Wight, rejected the fuller set of demands known as the Four Bills, and entered into a secret 'Engagement' with the Scots on 26 December. Herrick was ejected from his church, and living.

1648 Parliament resolved (3 January) that in future 'No Addresses' should be made to the King; but after the escape to France of James, Duke of York, and the failure of the royalist cause in the five-months-long second Civil War (culminating in Cromwell's defeating the Scots army under the 'Engager' Hamilton at Preston) negotiations began again at Newport, Isle of Wight (nos. 307, 308, 327). The prospect of a treaty was nullified by the action of the army in having Colonel Thomas Pride and his men 'purge' the House of Commons (first elected eight years before) of some three-fifths of its members on 6 December, leaving a majority of those prepared to support the trial of the King before a specially constituted 'High Court of Justice' on capital charges of treason and levying war against his people (no. 319).

1649 The trial began on 20 January. Charles I was found guilty as charged and executed on 30 January (nos. 244–47, 271). Charles II was provisionally proclaimed in Scotland on 5 February. England was declared a free Commonwealth on 19 May (no. 248), kingship and the House of Lords were abolished (17 and 19 March), and the sale of Crown lands began. Gerrard Winstanley's Diggers came together and settled in Surrey, to the horror of the inhabitants. In Ireland, a powerful coalition between Irish Catholics, Protestants, and royalists came together at the beginning of that year, intending to take over the whole country, and then attack England in the name of Charles II (no. 321). Parliament was left holding only Dublin and Londonderry. Cromwell landed in Ireland on a mission of reconquest, and sacked Drogheda and Wexford (11 September, 11 October) in an attempt to terrify the rest of Ireland into submission. His campaign was brutally effective, and left the island under English control. Richard Crashaw died at Loretto (no. 149).

1650 Montrose landed in Scotland to lead a forlorn hope for Charles II, but was defeated and executed on 21 May (nos. 274, 322, 332). The emergence of extremist religious groups, including those sometimes identified as 'Ranters' (no. 146), inspired moral panic among less extreme Protestants. Cromwell left Ireland (no. 313), succeeded Fairfax as Lord-General, and invaded Scotland. He achieved one outstanding victory at Dunbar (3 September), and went on to exploit divisions among the royalists to great effect. Davenant was imprisoned for two years.

APPENDIX 4

1651 Charles II, having reluctantly taken the Covenant, was crowned in Scotland on 1 January, even though Cromwell held the relatively rich and prosperous south of the country. Moving south with a mixed Royalist, and Covenanting army, he was followed by Cromwell and defeated at Worcester on 3 September, whence he escaped in disguise to France (no. 311, 328, 329). Cromwell continued south, leaving George Monck to keep up parliamentarian pressure on Scotland. The Rump Parliament resolved not to extend its existence beyond November 1654.

1652 At home, the parliament passed acts of 'Pardon and Oblivion', and of settlement with Ireland, and offered the Scots an incorporating union. Abroad, it involved the Commonwealth in an expensive and indecisive naval war with the United Provinces of the northern Netherlands, indirectly caused by the Dutch–Spanish peace treaty of 1648, which allowed the Dutch merchant fleets free access to all trading spheres (the East Indies, the Mediterranean, the West Indies), and cut into English interests. The Friends, or Quakers, began to organise collectively and to mobilize themselves for evangelisation.

1653 Cromwell, losing patience with the parliament, dissolved it by force; it was succeeded by an assembly chiefly composed of those nominated by army leaders, known as the nominated or Little Parliament (or simply as 'the Barebones', after one of its members). This lasted for only five months and was succeeded immediately by the adoption of a new constitution, 'The Instrument of Government', based on a tripartite structure of Lord Protector, Council of State, and Parliament, each limiting the others' powers, and the installation of Cromwell as Lord Protector (no. 314). The war with the Dutch turned in England's favour. Irish resistance continued, and Piaras Feiritéar (no. 23) was publicly hanged in Killarney.

1654 The war with the Dutch ended in a treaty in England's favour; but a war (not formally declared until October 1655) was begun against Spain in the Caribbean, and this 'Western Design' with its extension into European waters dragged expensively on until after the Restoration. The first Protectorate parliament, lasting less than five months, added not a single act to the Statute Book. In Ireland, all Catholics east of the Shannon were evicted that winter and driven into Connacht, and Clare: hundreds died on the road (no. 325). Cowley returned to England after three years abroad.

1655 Various plans, and plots, both royalist and republican, were directed against Cromwell and the government without success. To counter these attempts at subversion, the country was divided into some twelve districts, each under the rule of a Major-General, and this efficient but unpopular system lasted for a little over a year. Cromwell, after representations from the small colony of Jews in London (Jews had officially been expelled from England in the thirteenth century), offered them some assurances concerning their status. In Scotland, power was transferred from General Monck to a new Council for Scotland, a move towards the return of local power to the Scots themselves. In the Caribbean, the navy succeeded in taking Jamaica. Cleveland and Cowley were both imprisoned.

1656 Within three months of the announcement of elections in June, the second Protectorate parliament met, losing almost a quarter of its members immediately through disqualification (later overturned by the Humble Petition), and doing very little business for some months, even though the government was eager to have extra taxes voted for the Spanish war in which Admiral Blake had begun to achieve naval successes.

1657 After the defeat in parliament of the military party's 'decimation' tax (to legalise the financing of a select militia) interest centred on the 'Remonstrance' later revised as the 'Humble Petition, and Advice' with a further 'Additional Petition.' This offered Cromwell the crown, which he declined, and set out a new and more parliamentary constitution, with a restored

Second House, which he accepted. He was installed for a second time as Lord Protector (no. 314). Admiral Blake died; an alliance was entered into with France, which was also at war with Spain. Anna Trapnel prophesied in Whitehall: a symptom of the disunity of the religious radicals, and of the feeling amongst the most extreme that their cause had been betrayed (nos. 159–61).

1658 A new session of parliament was called, after six months' adjournment, presumably in the hope of raising more money; but Cromwell, fearing an opposition alliance between radical political elements, and disgruntled army officers, dissolved it after only two weeks. After a summer which saw Anglo–French victories in the war (including the occupation of Dunkirk), the execution of the last three royalists, and the death of Cromwell's favourite daughter, Cromwell himself fell ill and died on 3 September, his son Richard being proclaimed Lord Protector in his place (no. 334).

1659 The parliament was called (again to provide money) by Richard Cromwell, and his council was dissolved, under threat of military action, after only three months, during which time mistrust grew between Richard Cromwell, and the army leaders. Thereafter the generals restored the Rump Parliament (from 1653), and Richard resigned and retired to the country, the Protectorate being replaced by a restored Commonwealth. Friction began again between Parliament, and the army, which dissolved the Rump after some five months, leaving the country with no legal civil government. This provided a decisive spur to General George Monck, commander-in-chief in Scotland, who, by the time the Rump reassembled in late December (with support from the fleet and the Irish army) for its final sitting, was at Coldstream with his remodelled army, ready to cross into England.

1660 Entering England on 1 January, and London a month later, Monck obliged the sitting members of the Rump to readmit those excluded since Pride's Purge (no. 338). A new Council of State was elected with a monarchist majority; Monck became Captain-General of all the land forces of the Commonwealth, and co-Admiral of the Fleet with Edward Montague; and acts were passed for a new parliament, and new elections, which were held in April, the Long Parliament having at last reached its end in mid-March. On 4 April the text of Charles II's Declaration of Breda (putting the onus of the settlement on to the new parliament) became known;, and the Convention Parliament, opening at the end of the month, voted, on 5 May, that the government of the country should be vested in King, Lords, and Commons, and on 11 May that Parliament should send a representative to the King, who entered London on 29 May amid widespread rejoicing (nos.138, 336–342). George Wither was arrested. The theatres reopened, Davenant being granted a patent as licensee of one of the theatres royal.

APPENDIX 5
NEW POEMS FROM MANUSCRIPT

FRANCES (DOROTHY) FEILDING

1 one the morening the king was taken ill my dreame of him

in a deep sleep
a sene of darknes did my soule a fryght:
I saw mee thout a man home I beefore had seene
throune cross a chair pale and coold as if hee dead had beene
one of his arms held up a surgion by
to Lett him bloud in this Extreamity
in great distraction I crying said,
hoe is itt hould him up a Lass I am afraid
that he can never Bleed, for sure that arm is dead
with my still asking hoe hee was mee thought the Roome did ring
in this confution I heard one say, oh god itt is the king.

1 Title one: on 2 *a fryght*: affright 3 *home*: whom 4 *throune*: thrown 6 Draining a pint or two of blood from the arm was considered restorative 8 *hoe*: how; *a Lass*: alas 10 *hoe*: how

LADY HESTER PULTER

2 On those two unparalleld friends, S^{r}: G: Lisle and S^{r}: C: Lucas, who were shott to death at Colechester

Is Lisle and Lucas slaine? Oh say not soe
Who could kill love and valour at a blow?
Just as Minerva's darling clos'd his eyes
Love kissing wept and on his bosome dies
Ah me what horrid Hidra had the hart
Them in theire Deaths thus to unite and part
Mars on the Areopagie once was tried
His vallour sav'd him or he else had died
His Judg and Jurie were the best of Gods
These worst of Men, ô me what ods
Had Joves three sons of everlasting fame
Borne of a mortall and Celestiall flame
Had they bin here this busines to deside
Then these two Noble Gallants had not died
Or had Astreus (lover of the Moon
Of whose bright womb her brighter babe was born)
Had he bin here hee would have tooke delight

To save theire lives that for his child did fight
Then had theire Judges bin the Gods eternall
Or upright Men, nay or the powers infernall
This unambiguous busines to deside
Then this unparaleld friendship had not died
But Jewes, Turks, Atheists Independents all
That Cursed Rabble, made these gallants fall
How could they doe it were they not Amazed
When as the cruell Parcae sat and Gazed
On theire perfections as Lachis drew the thred
What wont you part a sunder then shee sed
They striving in theire lives to imbrace each other
Shee twirl'd and twisted both of them together
Then Clotho at theire constant love did wonder
And in meere pitty pul'd them not asunder
Shee being it seems the Tendrest hearted Lass
Goe Noble Soules shee said and let them pass
But Atropos inrag'd begun to chide
Saying these trew loves knots should be untied
But seeing theire Lives she could not stay to untwist
Let those sit Idling here (she said) that list
How can wee give account unto those powers
That us imploy, in trifeling out our houres
Then scolding at her sisters for theire sloth
Shee with her fatal Cizers snipt them both
Shee then cryed out, alas but hurring fate
Forced her poore Girle, her pitty came too late
Licaon Tantall tender to this brood
Who fed on Hostagis and Infants blood
Why are they now more cruell then at first
Theyr Drunk with Christian blood yet still they thirst
Doth that ould Vulture and his preying brood
Think to grow young with sucking spritely blood
Oh let them next suck Nessus's poys'und gore
Like mad Alcides let them Rave and Rore
And as they have bin three kingdooms sore annoyers
Let them like him at last be selfe destroyers
Had these undaunted loving Heros died
In former times they had bin Deified
Then theire Renown and love had spread as far
As those two famous Thunderbolts of War
Effigies, Piramids, Collums, Collosses,
Had bin erect to memorise our losses
But wee are now denied, our Just desires
Trew gratefull love in this our age expires
Yet som sad Swan I know there will be found
That for this onely Action will be Cround

That shall beare lovely Lisle, and Lucas name
Unto the Temple of Eternall fame
When that black Armie after theire short Dreame
Shall floating bee on Stix his Sable Streame
They by the Angrey billowes shall be tost
Till in oblivioun s Horrid womb ther'e lost
If he that fired Diana's Phane for fame
Lost both his expectation and his name
If covetous Cambices who presum'd
To rob the Gods till sand his mein consum'd
Or that Fierce Gaule who Delphus ment to plunder
Till firey Phebus routed him with Thunder
If these live now in Honour then noe doubt
Fame shall attend this Sacrilegi'us rout
Who have our Truths defenders over powerd
And Temples, Alters, Victims, all devourd,
But these victorious soules live now above
And gloriously goe on in endles love
Whilst theire faire frames which here did close their lives
Shall live in fame till they in Glory rise.

2 1 *Lisle and Lucas*: Sir George Lisle (d. 1648) and Sir Charles Lucas (1613–1648) (brother of the celebrated Margaret Lucas, later Cavendish, Duchess of Newcastle) royalist commanders in the First and Second Civil Wars; both were in arms with the royalist insurgents that occupied Colchester from 14 June 1648 until the city fell to Fairfax on 27 August. Lucas and Lisle were shot to death on Fairfax's orders for breaking their parole, the occasion of much royalist recrimination 3 *Minerva's darling*: more probably Sir Charles Lucas 5 *Hidra*: many-headed ravening monster slain by Hercules 7 *Mars on the Areopagie*: It was on the 'hill of Ares' (Mars) near Athens that the god answered for his adultery with Aphrodite (Venus) 11 *Joves three sones*: perhaps the sons of Zeus and Europa, Rhadamanthus, Minos and Sarpedon, since two out of three were famous judges, or perhaps Hercules, son of Alcmena, Dionysus, son of Semele, and a third. 23 *Independents*: sectaries and militant parliamentarians 26 *Parcae*: the three Fates, Lachesis, Clotho, and Atropos 42 *Cizers*: scissors 43 *hurring*: hurrying 45 *Licaon Tantall*: by comparison with Tantalus, who butchered his own son and made a feast of him for the gods 51 *Nessus's*: the centaur Nessus had venomous blood: a shirt dipped in it was given to Hercules (Alcides) by his wife Iole, who believed it to be a love-charm, and he died in agony 58 *Thunderbolts of War*: Castor and Pollux 64 *Cround*: Crond MS 68 *Stix*: one of the rivers of the underworld 72 *he*: the great temple of Diana at Ephesus, one of the wonders of the ancient world, was destroyed by Herostratus, who hoped this vandalism would make his name immortal 73 *Cambices*: Cambyses of Persia, his story is told by Herodotus 75 *Fierce Gaule*: Brennus, who raided Delphi in 279 BC and was repelled by a miraculous snowstorm sent by Apollo, which was commemorated by the festival of Soteria

3 [Upon the Death of my deare and lovely Daughter J[ane] P[ulter]]

Tell mee noe more her haire was lovly brown
Nor that it did in Curious curles hang down
Or that it did her Snowey Shoulders shrowed
Like Shineing Cinthia in a Sable Clowd
Tell mee noe more of her black Diamond eyes
Whose cheerful looke made all my sorrowes fly,
Like Glittring Phebus Influence and light
After a Northern Winters halfe years Night
Tell mee noe more her cheeks exceld the Rose

Though Lilly leaves did sweetly interpose
Like Ruddy Aurora riseing from her bed
Her snowey hand shadeing her Orient he'd
Tell mee noe more, of her white even Nose
Nor that her Ruby lips when they disclose
Did soe revive this drooping heart of mine
Like Golden Aples on a silver shrine
Tell mee noe more, her brests were heaps of Snow
White, as the swans, where Cristall Thams doth flow
Chast as Diana was her virgin Brest
Her noble Mind can never bee exprest
This but the casket was of her rich soule
Which now doth shine above the highest pole
Tell mee noe more of her perfection
Because it doth increase my heart's dejection
Nor tell mee that shee past her happy dayes
In singing heavenly and the Muses layes
Nor like the swans on Cristall Poe
Shee sung her Dirges ere shee hence did goe
Nor never more tell my sad soule of Mirth
With her I lost most of my Joyes on earth
Nor can I ever raise my drooping spirit
Untill with her those Joyes I can inherit
Those Glories which our finite thoughts transcend
Where wee shall prayses sing world without end
To him that made both her and mee of Earth
And gave us spiritts of Celstiall Birth
Tell mee noe more of her Unblemished fame
Which doth Immortalize her virgin Name
Like fragrant odours Aromatick Fumes
Which all succeeding Ages still perfumes
Nor why I mourn for her aske mee noe more
For all my life I shall her loss deplore
Till infinite power her dust and mine shall raise
To sing in Heaven his everlasting praise.

3 4 Cinthia: the moon 12 he'd: head 28 Poe: the river Po in northern Italy, associated with the poet Virgil

4 On the Kings most exelent magisty, K. Charles the first

Victorious Palm, triumphing Lawrell Boughs
Encircles round illustrious Caesars Browes
Whose valour fills with wonder future story
Whilst vertue Crowns him with immortall Glory
Let bright Minerva's Olive Tree still Grow
To shade his Throne, whence truth and Peace may flow
Down to our Humble Orbs; O let him live
Still to receive from Heaven, to us to give.

And let his lovly, Loyall, Royall Queen
To all succeeding Ages still be seen
A most unparrild pattern of true Love
Begun on earth ending in Heaven above
O let them in their shineing spheares bee fixt
And never with Prodigious Meteors mixt
But by the Primum Mobile turn'd round
Lasting as Delia's let their race bee found
And when those Glittring Globes are all Dissolv'd
Let them in endles Glory bee involvd
Till when let Grace and blessing from above
Descend on them and all that doe them love.

4 15 Primum Mobile: the first motion, the axle of the imagined spheres of the renaissance heaven.

5 The invocation of the Elements the longest Night in the Year 1655

Have Patience my afflicted Soul
Thou shalt not long in Darknes Rowl.
I will the Elements implore,
Then shall I Need to beg noe More,
To come unto my last best feast;
The Lymped Lady'es my first guest, *Water*

Cool cristall Water take thy part,
First that which Circles my sad Heart
Or if my Tears will satisfie,
To tears Il'e quickly Rarifie;
Number them not, count sand or star
You'l sooner number them by farr,
Oh that they had bin shed for sin
Then they in heaven had botled bin;
Why were they shed; O ask not why,
If I repeat my woes, I dye
A dubble death, O ask noe more,
Let mee alone, my loss deplore.
Fair Nymph thoust oft Quencht thirst in mee
Retaliate and drink up mee
Seaven lovly Buds thou hast drawn dry,
Oh spare the Rest, or elce I dye
A treble Death, O heare mee speake
Let not my heart soe often breake
But Let Death strike mee once for all,
A little blow will make mee Fall.
Thou didst a whole World once involve
Then let mee into thee dissolve.

Sweet Ayr Refresher of Mankind, *Ayr*
Let mee at last thy Favour Find
Doe but exhaust a little vapour,
Thoul't quickly blow out my life's tapour,
Twill bee my last request of thee
Thou'rt free to all, bee soe to mee,
I oft have made thee such a feast
That all the Odours, of the east
Could not with their sweet Breath compare
Blossoms soe Lovly Young and Rare,
The Woodbine, ere Aurora doth arise;
The July Flower before the shadow Flyes,
The dewey Vi'let ore the halfe blown Rose
Ah say noe More my grief or'e Flowes
I into teares am Rarified,
And thou thy part will bee denied
Ah take this sigh then for thy part,
For such another breaks my Heart.

Most Noble and illustrious Fier *Fier*
Whom (though I knew not) I admire
If such an Ellement there bee
My strange petition is to thee
Oh hearken to my last desire
And help my sad soul to expire
Contract thy vigour hold thy heat
Then will my heart forget to beat
And trepidate within my Breast
O then how sweet will bee my rest
What a sweet slumber shall I take
When my sad Dreams doe me forsake
And cease my aflicted soul t'afright
Welcome Oh welcome that blest Night
Then doe but my short Breath exhale
My structure straight to dust will fall
Welcome Oh Welcome that blest Night
Which ushers in Eternall Light
For what is Death but Cold and Night
Life beeing onely Heat and light
Then all my Heat to thee Il'e give
And though I Die in thee I Live

Dear dust from thee I drew my Birth *Dust, or Earth*
Then come, and 'tis but Earth to Earth
My lovly Children thou hast taken
Shall their sad Mother bee forsaken
Aye mee thou took'st them young and faire

And leav'st mee here with Hoarie Haire
They lovly faire with snowey skin
Did too soone thy favour win
But I involved with sin and sorrow
Sadly expect thee Night and Morrow.
I ask noe Piramide nor stately Tomb
Doe but involve mee in thy spacious Womb
To beg this once dear Mother give mee leave
Oh Let thy Bowels yern and mee receive.

Pardon mee my dearest Love
That I place my thoughts above
What's subsolary is yours
And soe shall Bee while Life indures
Onely my aspiring mind
Noe felicity can find
In this Dirty Dunghill earth
My soul remembers still her Birth
Shee being a sparkle of that Light
Which ne're shall set in Death or night
Nothing here is worth her Love
Her *summum bonum* is above
But this Body shortly must
Melt and moulder into Dust
This due debt cant bee denied
The Elliments must mee Divide.
Thus like Trators quarter'd out
Are old Adams Rebell rout
Then shall my infranchis'd spirit
Those eternall Joyes inherit
Which from mee shall never part
With these thoughts I cheer my heart
Then pardon thy poor Turtle Dove
That hath plac'd her thoughts above
Where is endles Joy and Love.

5 last best feast: the poet's anticipated death 16 rarifie: alchemical term meaning to be transformed or purified into liquid or vapour 21 buds: the dead children, who are also the "blossoms" of l.38 27 involve: cover (with water as at the time of the Biblical flood) 33 lifes]lif's MS 81 the address to earth as a mother and the image of the grave as the womb of earth are the reiteration of a mediaeval devotional commonplace 83 *et seq* would appear to be addressed to the poet's husband: the turtle-dove is a common emblem of married fidelity 90 et seq. these lines follow the summarised Platonism of Boethius's *Consolations of Philosophy*, a text which was much in the minds of mid-seventeenth century poets. Both Fanshawe and Polwhele made translations. 94 *summum bonum*: true good, here in the sense of the happiness of the blessed in heaven. 99 quarter'd: the bodies of executed traitors were dismembered and the quarters publicly displayed. Here Pulter compares the decomposition of the body into the four elements to this dismemberment.

LUCY HUTCHINSON

6 Another on the Sun Shine

Heavens glorious Eie, which all the world surveyes,
This morning through my window shot his rayes
Where with his hatefull and unwellcome beames
He guilt the Surface of aflictions Streames;
In anger at their bold intrusion I
Did yet into a darker Covert fly:
But They like impudent Suters brisk and rude
Me even to my thickest Shade persude,
Whome when I saw that I could no where shun
I thus began to chide th'immodest Sun.
'How, Gawdy Masker, darst thou looke on me
Whose Sable Coverings thy reproaches be?
Thou to our murtherers thy taper bearst,
Th'oppressive race of men thou warmst and Chearst,
The blood which thou hast Seene pollutes thy light
And renders it more hatefull than the Night.
All good men loath thee growne a common bawd
The Brave that Leadst Impieties abroad,
Who Smiling doest on lust and rapine shine
Nor Shrinkst thy head in at disgorgd wine,
Which Sinners durst not let the see before.
Now thy conniving lookes they dred no more,
Becas thou makst their pleasant gardins growe
And Chearishest the fruitefull seeds they sowe
In feilds, which unto them descended not,
By Violence briberry and oppression gott.
Thou sawst the league of God himselfe dissolvd
Which a whole Nation in one curse Involvd,
Thou Sawst a thankelesse people slaughtring those
Whose noble blood redeemd them from their foes,
Thy staind beames into the Prison came
But lost their boasts, outshind with vertues flame.
Thou sawst the Innocent to exile Led,
And for all this veildest not thy radiant head,
But comst as a gay courtier to deride
Reuines we would in Silent shadows hide.
Since then thou wilt thurst into this darke roome,
By thyne owne light read thy most certeine doom,
Darkenesse shall shortly quench thy impure light
And thou Shalt Sett in Everlasting Night.
Those whome thou flattriest shall se thee expire,
And have no light but their one funerall fire;

Theire shall they in a dreadfull wild amaze
At once see all their glorious Idolls blaze.
Thy Sister, the pale Empris of the Night,
Shall never more reflect thy borrowd light,
Into black blood shall her darke body turne
While that polluted spheres about yow burne,
And the Elementall heaven like melting lead
Drops downe Upon the impious rebells head.
Then Shall our King his Shining host display
At whose approach our mists shall fly away
And wee Illuminated by his Sight
No more shall neede Thy everquenched Light.'

7 *Suters*: Probably intended to evoke the legendarily chaste Penelope besieged by her suitors in the Odyssey 11 *Masker*: performer in a masque. Although several godly households themselves staged masques, the primary association of the genre was with the increasingly extravagant and distant court of Charles and Henrietta Maria 19 *rapine*: rampine MS 21 *no[t]*: no MS; *The*: thee 22 *Becas*: because 35 *Reuines*: Ruines 36 *thurst*: thrust from 39 cf. Thomas Campion (1567–1620) imitation of Catullus, *Carmina* v, 'My sweetest Lesbia': 'But, soone as once set is our little light/Then must we sleepe one ever-during night' 41 *one*: own 48 *melting lead*: molten lead was a useful *ad hoc* weapon of defence in sieges 51 King: Christ

Notes on the Authors

FRANCES (DOROTHY) FEILDING, née LANE, later JAMES (?1650–1709) Frances Feilding, whose given name was Dorothy, was the daughter of Francis Lane of Glendon by Rothwell, Northamptonshire and fourth and last wife of Basil Feilding, second Earl of Denbigh, the Civil War hero. At the time of her marriage, she was considerably younger than her husband. After his death in 1675 she married Sir John James. Though not the only person of her name to be listed in late-seventeenth-century and early-eighteenth-century Feilding genealogies, she is probably the signatory of a versified compliment to Christabella Rogers, which survives in the Berkshire Record Office (Barrett & Belson papers, D/EBT Z34). She was most probably the compiler of a MS now at Yale (Beinecke Library, Osborn MS B 226), a collection of original poems, copied poems, prayers, recipes and remedies, written by a female member of the Feilding family in the late seventeenth century, and containing several powerful confessional poems reacting to the author's widowhood. This MS is of particular interest, since most of the 'private' verse which women allow to survive casts the writers in a more or less edifying light, this, by contrast, contains a variety of verse reflecting a range of emotions including depression, selfpity and rage. Frances Feilding's friend and correspondent Christabella Rogers was the author of substantial quantities of verse: one of her poems survives in the British Library's Losely microfilms (M 437, no. 125), 'A songe made by Mrs Christabell Rogers', beginning 'Cupid away for I defy', addressed to 'my much honourd Cosen Al. ffennell'.

HESTER PULTER, née LEE (1596–1678) Lady Hester Pulter was the daughter of James Lee or Ley, first Earl of Marlborough, by his first wife Mary, daughter of John Pettie of

Stoke Talmage, Oxon, one of eleven children. Though Marlborough rose to be Lord Treasurer, he is a figure of little political significance, whose reputation never recovered from the fact that he was Buckingham's appointee. She married Arthur Pulter, who enjoyed a modestly successful public life, culminating in his appointment as Lord Lieutenant of Hertfordshire. On the outbreak of civil was, he retired into the country, and spent his time building a house on his estate at Broadfield. Despite his firmly maintained neutrality, it is clear that his wife was a vehemently committed royalist. Her work is preserved in a single manuscript, which appears to be a scribal fair copy with her own corrections, containing some 120 poems together with a romance (*The Unfortunate Florinda*), written between 1646 and 1665, entitled 'Hedassa's chaste fancies' (Hedassa being another name for the Biblical Esther). It encompasses a considerable variety of genres, satires, love-poetry, elegies, emblems, allegories, and also includes a romance in two parts, the second of which is incomplete, called *The unfortunate Florinda*.

She was the mother of fifteen children, all but one of whom she outlived; and by her own account, tended to write poetry during her confinements (which, according to the childbirth practice of the seventeenth century, left her mewed up in her room for prolonged periods of time). The absence of any mention of her husband in her poetry, together with their political divergence, may suggest a lack of sympathy between them. Despite her considerable skill, she appears to have had no connection with any other known poets, and her writing is not mentioned by anyone else; a far more unusual state of affairs with women poets of her time than is generally believed. However, she was apparently reading the works of other contemporaries, most notably the poet Andrew Marvell, whose work she appears to have accessed in manuscript before its publication.

LUCY HUTCHINSON, née APSLEY (1620–AFTER 1662) She was born in the Tower of London, the daughter of the Lieutenant of the Tower, Sir Allan Apsley, and his third wife Lucy, daughter of Sir John St John of Lidiard Tregoze in Wiltshire, where a prodigious collection of early-modern family monuments still survive. She was a precocious child: according to her own account of her life, she could read by the age of four, and by the time she was seven, she had eight tutors in languages, music, dancing, writing, and needlework. She also learned Latin, at the express wish of her father.

Her husband, Colonel John Hutchinson, came of an ancient Nottinghamshire family, a skilled fencer, viol-player and marksman, a graduate of Peterhouse, Cambridge, and a late convert to Calvinism. Her introduction to Colonel John Hutchinson was a romantic one: he came across a sonnet of hers, admired it, and sought her out. Though she was unlucky enough to catch smallpox before her marriage, which took place in 1638, Hutchinson's love for her was undaunted by the damage to her looks. Both husband and wife were sympathetic to the political programme of the Levellers. Hutchinson was a regicide, one of the signatories in January 1649 of the death warrant of the 'man of blood', Charles Stuart, and a member of the English Republic's Council of State. After Cromwell's dissolution of the Long Parliament in 1653, he retired to his country seat at Owthorpe, where he harboured an implacable hostility towards Cromwell, whom they both regarded as having been corrupted by power. After the Restoration, Hutchinson escaped execution for regicide, but died in September 1664 at Sandown Castle, on the coast of Kent, of a fever caused by the damp conditions. After her husband's death, Lucy Hutchinson lived partly on the equity in property which she still owned, partly on the assistance of relatives and patrons.

In the later 1660s she wrote an account of her husband and their life together, *Memoirs of the Life of Colonel Hutchinson*: transcribed (in part) out of a diary and intended only for her children: this is the most brilliant of all the Civil War memoirs. It remained unpublished until 1806, and was, until very recently, all that she was remembered by. However, very recently, a number of her poems have been discovered at Nottingham (one of which is printed here), and edited by David Norbrook. Although Nottingham was a little remote from the court and London, Lucy Hutchinson was by no means isolated from the wider literary world. She also wrote a scornful reply to Edmund Waller's panegyric on Cromwell: there is a copy endorsed by the Earl of Clarendon in the British Library (Add MS 17018, ff. 214–217v). Sir John Denham's translation of Virgil's *Aeneid*, II–VI, his earliest known poetic composition (c. 1636), survives only in a verse miscellany compiled by her (Nottinghamshire Record Office, HU/3, pp. 5–135, which also contains part of Sidney Godolphin's translation of the same text). Her translation of Lucretius's *De Rerum Natura* survives (now edited by Hugh de Quehen, Ann Arbor: University of Michigan Press, 1997), while another classical translation, of part of Vergil's *Aeneid*, which was in the possession of the vicar of Tisbury in Wiltshire in the late nineteenth century, seems to have been lost. Professor Norbrook has also discovered that a long and ambitious religious epic on *Genesis* (previously attributed to her Royalist brother, Sir Allen Apsley), called *Order and Disorder; or the world made and undone*, 1679) is her work, making her one of the most important poets, man or woman, of the mid-seventeenth-century.

Notes on the Text

1 New Haven, Connecticut, Yale University, Beinecke Library, The James Marshall and Marie-Louise Osborn Collection, MS b.226, p. 9

2 University of Leeds, Brotherton Library, MS Lt.q.32 , ['Poems Breathed forth by the Nobel Hadasas'], pp. 22–25.

3 University of Leeds, Brotherton library, MS Lt.q. 32 pp. 30–32. The title is found on p. 28, this poem is headed 'On the same' 26 Muses: Museses MS Celestiall: Celetiall MS

4 University of Leeds, Brotherton Library, MS Lt.q.32, pp. 83–[84] the general resemblance of the celestial imagery of the poem to Thomas Carew's disastrously laudatory court masque *Coelum Britannicum* (1634) is an index of the extent to which Pulter was a full participant in the metropolitan literary discourses of her time. 5 Pallas sacred] bright Minerva's [as alternative in] MS.

5 University of Leeds, Brotherton Library, MS Lt.q.32, pp. 114–120 This remarkable poem of personal grief on the deaths of children, draws on ideas from early-modern medicine concerning the balancing of the four elements within the human body, asking each element in turn either to withdraw or to predominate, so that the poet may die of the consequent imbalance. Like Donne, in his great *Nocturnall*, Pulter locates her poem on the darkest day of the year; unlike Donne her poem is essentially a prayer that she should be extinguished with the year and never revive on earth but live rather in the eternal spring of heaven.

6 Nottingham, Nottinghamshire Record Office, DD/HU2 (a MS not in Hutchinson's hand) pp. ix–xi. This poem deliberately inverts the expected Royalist vocabulary of Restoration verse. As the bitter utterance of a convinced Republican, the Stuarts are rebels, there is no king but Christ and therefore Charles II is an usurper. The recollections of John Donne's 'The Sunne Rising' are as deliberate as they are ironic.

INDEX OF AUTHORS

INDEX OF TITLE AND FIRST LINES

In this index, first lines are given in roman type throughout, titles are given in italic throughout. Poems are indexed by poem number rather than page number.

INDEX OF TITLES AND FIRST LINES

INDEX OF TITLES AND FIRST LINES

INDEX OF TITLES AND FIRST LINES

INDEX OF TITLES AND FIRST LINES